# Internet Technology and Web Design

STRICTLY AS PER NEW DOEACC SYLLABUS

A2–R4

Dr. R. K. Jain

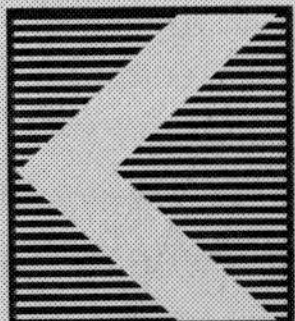

**KHANNA BOOK PUBLISHING CO. (P) LTD.**

Publisher of Engineering and Computer Books

4C/4344, Ansari Road, Darya Ganj, New Delhi-110002

**Phone** : 011-23244447-48 **Mobile:** +91-9910909320

**E-mail** : contact@khannabooks.com

**Website :** www.khannabooks.com

Dear Readers,

To prevent the piracy, this book is secured with HIGH SECURITY HOLOGRAM on the front title cover. In case you don't find the hologram on the front cover title, please write us to at contact@khannabooks.com or whatsapp us at +91-99109 09320 and avail special gift voucher for yourself.

Specimen of Hologram on front Cover title:

Moreover, there is a SPECIAL DISCOUNT COUPON for you with EVERY HOLOGRAM.

How to avail this SPECIAL DISCOUNT:

Step 1: Scratch the hologram
Step 2: Under the scratch area, your "coupon code" is available
Step 3: Logon to www.khannabooks.com
Step 4: Use your "coupon code" in the shopping cart and get your copy at a special discount
Step 5: Enjoy your reading!

Thanks,
Khanna Publishing House

**Price: ₹450.00**

**Internet Technology and Web Design**
*by* **R.K. Jain**


**ISBN:** 978-93-80016-62-7

**Edition:** 2015
**Reprint:** 2023, 2025


To view complete list of books, please scan the QR Code:

*Published by:*
**Khanna Book Publishing Co. (P) Ltd.**
*CIN: U22110DL1998PTC095547*

*Visit us at:* www.khannabooks.com
*Write us at:* contact@khannabooks.com

Printed in Bharat.

# Preface

The new syllabus of DOE's various levels of courses, popularly called O-level, A-level, B-level and C-level is out. Keeping in mind the various developments taking place around the world in the field of computers, these syllabus include most of them. While keeping in mind the level of students studying the various levels, the degree of difficulties of the syllabus have been very well designed. I hope that after the new syllabus the courses would be as popular as they were before.

There had been a long struggle between Training Institutes and Government Organizations, since these organizations would not recognize the degree/diploma given by them. Students passing out from these institutions were not given jobs based upon the said diplomas/degrees. Ultimately, the Government formed a society under the Department of Electronics, called DOEACC, who conducts tests and gives grades to the students irrespective of the institutes where they have studied. It is also possible to give the test without having any proper institutional studies. This is more or less on the terms of SAT and GRE conducted by USA. The only difference is that this is not online. There are fixed dates for the exams.

The course for this has been designed for students to appear in the exams at various levels. These levels are O-level, A-level, B-level, C-level. The most popular among these is the O-level, since it is the entry level. Once you have cleared the O-level, you are eligible for a government job. Each course has been divided into various modules. Various books are available for various modules. This book is also made for you to prepare for the O-level course.

This book has been written totally in accordance with the syllabus provided. Each chapter has been embedded with the screen shots for you to know what to expect on the screen, while running the application. Each chapter contains examples which can be attempted to supplement the reading. At the end of the chapter, there is a thorough revision of the text read. Not to mention of the questions provided in the beginning, both in the form of objective and subjective. The book also contains Sample papers which are based on the samples provided by DOEACC society. These would help you in preparing for the exams.

**R. K. Jain**

# SYLLABUS

# A2-R4: INTERNET TECHNOLOGY AND WEB DESIGN

The aim of this course is to provide you the conceptual and technological and technological developments in the field of Internet and Web Designing with the emphasis on comprehensive knowledge of Internet, it applications and the TCP/IP protocols widely deployed to provide Internet connective worldwide. The World Wide Web with its widespread usefulness has become an integral part of the Internet. Therefore, this course also puts emphasis on basic concepts of web design.

At the end of the course the students will be able to:

- Review the current topics in Web & Internet Technologies.
- Describe the basic conceptsfor network implementation.
- Learn the basic working scheme of the Internet and World Wide Web.
- Understand the fundamental tools and technologies for web design.
- Comprehend the technologies for Hypertext Mark-up Language (HTML).
- Specially design rules in constructing web pages and sites.
- Effectively deal with programming issues relating to VB Script, JavaScript, Java, ASP, Front Page and Flash.
- Figure out the various security hazards on the Internet and need of security measures.

## Outline of Course

| *S.No.* | *Topic* | *Minimum No. of Hours* |
|---|---|---|
| 1. | Introduction to Internet | 02 |
| 2. | TCP/IP | 03 |
| 3. | Internet Connectivity | 03 |
| 4. | Internet Network | 04 |
| 5. | Services on Internet (Definition and Functions) | 04 |
| 6. | Electronic Mail | 07 |
| 7. | Current Trends on Internet | 03 |
| 8. | Web Publishing and Browsing | 10 |
| 9. | HTML Programming Basics | 12 |
| 10. | Interactivity Tools | 08 |
| 11. | Internet Security Management Concepts, Information and Copyright Issues | 04 |

| | | |
|---|---|---|
| **Lectures** | = | 60 |
| **Practicals /Tutorials** | = | 60 |
| **Total** | = | 120 |

## Detailed Syllabus

**1. Introduction to Internet** **02 Hrs.**

Internet, Growth of Internet, Ownersof the Internet, Anatomy of Internet, ARPANET and Internet history of the World Wide Web, Basic Internet Terminology, Net etiquette, Internet Applications — Commerce on the Internet, Government on the Internet, Impact of Internet on Society — Crime on/through the Internet.

**2. TCP/IP — Internet Technology and Protocol** **03 Hrs.**

Packet switching technology, Internet Protocols: TCP/IP, Router, Internet Addressing Scheme: Machine Addressing (IP address), E-mail Addresses, Resources Addresses.

**3. Internet Connectivity** **03 hrs.**

Connectivity types: level one, level two and level three connectivity, Setting up a connection: hardware requirement, selection of a modem, software requirement, modem configuration, Internet accounts by ISP: Telephone len options, Protocol options, Service options, Telephone line options — Dialup connections through the telephone system, dedicated connections through the telephone system, ISDN, Protocol options — Shell, SLIP, PPP, Service options — E-mail, WWW, News Firewall, etc.

**4. Internet Network** **04 Hrs.**

Network definition, Common terminolgies: LAN, WAN, Host, Workstation, bandwidth, Interoperability, Network administrator, network security, Network Components: Server, Clients, Communication Media, Types of network: Peer to Peer, Clients Server, Addressing in Internet: DNS, Domain Name and their organization, understandingthe Internet Protocol Address. Network topologies: Bust, star and ring, Ethernet, FDDI, ATM and Intranet.

**5. Services on Internet (Definition and Functions)** **04 Hrs.**

E-mail, WWW, Telnet, FTP, IRC and Search Engine.

**6. Electronic Mail** **07 Hrs.**

E-mail Networks and Servers, E-mail protocols — SMTP, POP3, IMAP4, MIME6, Structure of an E-mail — E-mail Address, E-mail Header, Body and Attachments, E-mail Clients: Netscape mail clients, Outlook Express, Web bases E-mail. E-mail encryption — Address Book, Signature Files.

**7. Current Trends on Internet** **03 Hrs.**

Languages, Internet Phone, Internet Video, collaborative computing, e-commerce.

**8. Web Publishing and Browsing** **10 Hrs.**

Overview, SGML, Web hosting, HTML, CGL, Documents Interchange Standards, Components of Web Publishing, Document management, Web Page Design, Consideration and Principles, Search and Meta Search Engines, WWW, Browser, HTTP, Publishing Tools.

**9. HTML Programming Basics** **12 Hrs.**

HTML page strucutre, HTML Text, HTML links, HTML document tables, HTML Frames, HTML Images, Multimedia.

**10. Interactivity Tools** **08 Hrs.**

ASP, VB Script, Java Script, JAVA, Front Page and Flash.

**11. Internet Security Management Concepts, Information Privacy and Copyright Issues** **04 Hrs.**

Overview of Internet Security, Firewall, Internet Security, Management Concepts and Information Privacy and Copyright Issues, Basics of Asymmetric Cryptosystems.

# Contents

# Introduction to Internet 1

## 1.1 Internet

Before you understand what Internet is, you must understand what networking is. It is a method of connecting two or more computers, either by means of connecting them or through wireless. Now come to Internet. It is the network consisting of millions of machines. Millions of machines are networked together to share the data and information. Data you require may be scattered across the globe updated and kept consistent by the owner of the data and you can retrieve it when needed via Internet.

Now with the onward march of technology it is possible to keep the program that work with the data along with the data that it works on and call upon both when needed a sort of 'just in time' software that you call upon when you needed and discard when no longer required.

You no longer need to locally store and maintain the data and programmes. Internet is not just one network. It is co-ordinated union of networks. Computer users on the Internet anywhere in the world, very much like a telephone user can communicate with user anywhere in the world. So internet is also called Internet works. Internet is also the common language of different or computers dissimilar in hardware and software to communicate with each other, via a standard protocols (protocols is a set of rules and regulations for computers to communicate via networks).

Sitting on a PC at home one can trip round the globe in minutes, one can get any kind of information one needs. Internet is a large source of enjoyable, important and up to data information, which can be accessed and shared by millions of users across the world. Every information on the internet is there because some person or group of people, somewhere in the world, had an idea, developed it and then most important, made it available to the entire world using Internet. It has become a major part of business.

One can use Internet for many different purposes like as discussed below:

1. Sending and receiving E-mails (it is an instantaneous way of sending and receiving messages, called electronic mail) round the world at minimal price.
2. Finding information on any topic or can be used as educational tool. One can find information on infinite number of topics ranging from how to make a cake to how to write a program for a computer. To visit a bookstore on the Internet this all can be done on the Internet sitting at home PC.
3. One can participate in discussions on wide range of topics from recreational activities to scientific researches via a utility called Usenet news group.
4. It is also used to send data inform of files from one computer to other with the facility called FTP (File Transfer Protocol). There are sites offering information on paid basis but on the other hand there are many sites, which provide information free of cost. There are called anonymous FTP sites. The biggest advantage of FTP is one don't have to wait for days to receive some information after ordering with FTP files will be one in minutes after ordering.
5. One can use it for research purpose. With every major university connected to Internet one can be sure to find information that help in research projects.

6. It is also a form of education. Using Internet is great learning experience. One will learn things from the content one is reading and will also be more proficient at navigating computer tools, forming searches for information. Writing and typing skills also improves.
7. One can enjoy reading jokes, stories, articles, play games with other users s on Internet join with chess matches and one can enjoy Internet relay chat to talk to different people round the world.
8. On can login on to other network via as if one is a member of that network this is done through utility called Telnet. This is only possible if one get permission to log on to that network.
9. To search some topics on the Internet one can use gopher.
10. Archive is a search utility that search on the Internet based on file names or partial file names.
11. One can make profits on the Internet. Internet can be an effective medium for business communications. Services such as gopher and World Wide Web (WWW) are the best ways to distribute information about your product or service. E-mail is a great medium to communicate with contacts and customers in business.
12. To find a particular world on the Internet in text documents one can use the utility WIAS (Wide Area Information System).
13. One can have a live talk with persons all round the world and can held meetings as if sitting just by there side by video conferencing of multimedia conferencing.

## 1.2 Growth of Internet and APRANet

In 60s a project was undertaken by the U.S. Defense Advanced Research Projects Agency (DARPA). It was in fact looking for some technology that could enable it to maintain its strategic military-based communication worldwide in case of a nuclear attack. This can be said as the main conception of the Internet.

Later, these developments led to the establishment of the Advanced Research Projects Agency Net (ARPANet). The main interest of this was looking for a technology that could link computers in various locations by using a new technology called Packet Switching Technology. This new technology enabled several users to simultaneously share a single communication line. It also allowed the creation of nets that could automatically route data around downed circuits or computers. This technology was then used by National Science Foundation to create to its own net, and called it NSDnet. It met with a large of success though its main users were universities and schools for information available over it.

Since the users were mostly scientists and researchers, the demand went on increasing endlessly, NSF found itself unable to cope with it. As a result, a decision was taken to open the Net for use by private organizations as well. This allowed anyone with a modem and a computer to access the Net. The beginning was made. Thus, NSFnet became the backbone of communication service for the Internet and continues to do so even now. At present, NSFNet comprises a set of highspeed data connections that join the major network all over the world.

This lead to several users using the net for information and then came the phase when its potential for doing business was exploited and companies started marketing services and information over the net. Today in fact, anybody with a computer and modem with dedicated phone line can access Internet with the help of some service provided by local Internet Service Providers.

The net quickly grew to spread to entire country. From this point onwards the journey can be traced by years:

1972 The first E-mail program was created and The Advanced Research Projects Agency (ARPA) was renamed The Defense Advanced Research Projects Agency TCP/IP, it was developed by a group headed by Bob Kahn from DARPA and Vinton Cerf from Stanford. This new protocol was to allow diverse computer networks to interconnect and communicate with each other.

1974 The term Internet was used for the first time.

1976 Dr. Robert M. Metcalfe develops Ethernet, which allowed coaxial cable to move data extremely fast. This was a crucial component to the development of LANs.

1979 In 1979 USENET (the decentralized news group network) was created by Steve Bellovin (a graduate student at University of North Carolina) and programmer Tom Truscott and Jim Ellis. It was based on UUCP. The Creation of BITNET, by IBM, "Because its Time network", introduced the "store and forward" network. It was used for email.

1980 Additional networks especially LANs were connected to the ARPANET. As the scale increased finding hosts addresses became increasingly expensive so DNS (Domain Naming System) was created by University of Wisconsim to organize machines into domains and map names onto IP (Internet Protocol) addresses. This allowed packets to be directed to a domain name, which would be translated by the server database into the corresponding IP number. This made it much easier for people to access other servers, because they no longer had to remember numbers.

1981 National Science Foundation created backbone called CSNET 56 Kpbs network for institutions without access to ARPANET. Vinton Cerf proposed a plan for an inter-network connection between CSNET and the ARPANET.

1983 Internet Activities Board (IAB) was created. On January 1st, every machine connected to ARPANET had to use TCP/IP. TCP/IP became the core Internet protocol and replaced NCP entirely.

1984 In 1984 The ARPANET was divided into two networks: MILNET and ARPANET. MILNET was to serve the needs of the military and ARPANET to support the advanced research component, Department of Defense continued to support both networks. New circuits would be T1 lines, 1.5 Mbps which is twenty-five times faster than the old 56 Kpbs lines. IBM wold provide advanced routers and Merit would manage the network. New network was to be called NSFNET (National Science Foundation Network), and old lines were to remain called CSNET. So network broke into two parts, Millnet for military sciences and smaller Arpanet for managing non military sites.

1986 The Internet Engineering Task Force to IETF was created to serve as a forum for technical coordination by contractors for DARPA working on ARPANET, US Defense Data Network (DDN), and the Internet core gateway system.

1987 BITNET and CSNET merged to form the Corporation for Research and Educational Networking (CREN), another work of the National Science Foundation.

1988 Soon after the completion of the T1 NSFNET backbone, traffic increased so quickly that plans immediately began on upgrading the network again. Merit and its partners formed a not for profit corporation called ANS, Advanced Network Systems, which was to conduct research into high-speed networking. It soon came up with the concept of the T3, a 45 Mbps line. NSF quickly adopted the new network and by the end of 1991 all of its sites were connected by this new backbone.

1990 In 1990 while the T3 lines were being constructed, the Department of Defense disbanded the ARPANET and it was replaced by the NSFNET backbone. The original 50kbps line of ARPANET were taken out of service. Tim Berners-Lee and CERN in Geneva implement a hypertext system to provide efficient information access to the members of the international high-energy physics community.

1991 CSNET (which consisted of 56kbps lines) was discontinued having fulfilled its important early role in the provision of academic networking service. A key feature of CREN is that its operational costs are fully met through dues paid by its member organizations. The NSF established a new network, named NREN, the National Research and Education Network. The purpose of this network is to conduct high speed networking research. It was not to be used as a commercial network, nor was it to be used to send a lot of the data that the Internet now transfers.

1992 Internet Society is chartered. The site http://www.worldbank.org/ comes on-line World-Wide Web released by CERN.

1993 InterNIC created by NSF to provide specific Internet services: directory and database services (by AT&T), registration services (by Network Solutions Inc.), and information services (by General Atomics/CERFnet). Merc Andreessen and NCSA and the University of Illinois develops a graphical user interface to the WWW, called "Mosaic for X".

1994 No major changes were made to the physical network. The most significant thing that happened was the growth. Many new networks were added to the NSF backbone. Hundreds of thousands of new hosts were added to the INTERNET during this time period. ATM (Asynchronous transmission Mode, 145 Mbps) backbone is installed on NSFNET.

1995 The National Science Foundation announced that as of April 30, 1995 Foundation contracted with four companies that would be providers of access to the NSF backbone (Merit). These companies would then sell connections to groups, organization, and companies. $50 annual fee is imposed on domains, excluding .edu and .gov domains which are still funded by the National Science Foundation.

1996 Internet phones catch the attention of US telecommunication companies who ask the US Congress to ban the technology (which has been around for years). Malaysian Prime Minister Mahathir Mohamad, PLO Leader Yasser Arafat, and Phillipine President Fidel Ramos meet for ten minutes in an online interactive chat session on 7 January. The controversial US Communication Decency Act (CDA) becomes law in the US in order to prohibit distribution of indecent materials over the Net. A few months later a three-judge panel imposes an injunction against its enforcement. Supreme Court unanimously rules most of it unconstitutional in 1997.

## 1.3 Owners of the Internet

Internet is dependent on the existing infrastructure developed by telephone and other telecommunication companies, for transmission. Internet Service Providers (ISP) lease data circuits from the telephone networks, and have dedicated computers at the end points or nodes. They rely on the distributed intelligence of networking equipment known as routers, thus bypassing the telephone company's expensive switching computers, while using their telephone lines. It can also be said that the networks on the Internet use a router to communicate with other networks. The router on a network accepts packets addressed to it and passes them as addressed to other networks. Each computer system with a direct connection to the Internet has to have the necessary hardware and software to allow it to work with these packets of information.

All the contents of the Intenet are held by computers known as the servers, which are owned by organizations or companies who want to distribute the information. Most of the Internet services operate according to a scheme called client and server. Most of you are familiar with networking, know these words. Server is the main computer, which controls all the other computers known as clients and nodes. When a request is made to these servers for information, they bundle the required information in small packets with the address as to where it is to be sent, and send them down to the nearest connection to the Internet. The packets are read by the router and then are sent down in the same general direction as the address. A packet is delivered to the right address, where it is put together again with other packets to make up the original information.

## 1.4 Anatomy of Internet

All computers and other equipments are given network are basically connected to each other with the help of cables. The messages travel across the network with the help of networking protocols. The protocols used over the Internet provide addresses for the computers attached to the physical network. In this way, different types of networks communicate with each other using the same protocol. To interpret the information being transmitted it is essential that theon the right software and hardware be in place.

The commonly used protocols are:

**Internet Protocols (IP)**

**Transmission Control Protocol (TCP)**

Together they are called as TCP/IP protocol. It offers a simple naming and addressing scheme, whereby resources on the Internet can be easily located.

## 1.5 Internet history of the Wold Wide Web

A global hypertext system that uses the Internet as its transport mechanism is called World Wide Web. In a hypertext system, you navigate by clicking hyperlinks, which display another document (which also contains hyperlinks). What makes the Web such an exciting and useful medium is that the next document you see could be housed on a computer next door-or halfway around the world. The Web makes the Internet easy to use.

Created in 1989 at the European Laboratory for Particle Physics (CERN), a research institute in Switzerland, the Web relies upon the HyperTExt Transport Protocol (HTTP), an Internet standard the specifies how an application can locate and acquire resources (such as document, sound or graphic) stored on another computer on the Internet. HTTP provides transparent, easy-to-use access to Web documents, FTP (File transfer Protocol) file archives, Gopher menus, and even UseNet newsgroups, users of Web navigation software, called Web browsers, simply click on an underlined word or phrase, and HTTP takes care of locating and downloading the desired documents. Most Web documents are created using the HyperText markup language (HTML), a markup language that is easy to learn and will soon be supplanted by automated tools. Incorporating hypermedia (graphics, sound, animations, and video), the Web has become the ideal medium for publishing information on the Internet.

A key 1995 agreement on security protocols ensures that Web will quickly become an important commercial medium, in which consumers can browse on-line catalog and place orders without worrying about anyone intercepting the supplied credit card information.

## 1.6 Basic Internet Terminology

Before you start using (browsing/surfing) the Web, it is necessary for you to understand the following terms and their meanings specially in connection with the Internet:

**Home page:** It is the first page that you would see on the Website. Also known as the Welcome page. It is from here that you would start the navigation of various other pages of the site.

Hypertext and Hyperlinks Information on the Web is made available in the form of Hypertext. It is a method of presenting information wherein some portion is highlighted. When this highlighted portion is selected, it displays more information on the topic/s that you choose. The highlighted items selected by you are technically called Hyperlinks. In fact, they allow you to navigate from one Web document to another on the same computer or on a different computers in your own city, country or anywhere else in the world.

**Internet Information Server:** It is a group of Internet servers including the additional capabilities of Windows NT and Windows 2000.

**Internet Protocol:** It is responsible for the addressing and sending data from one computer to another computer.

**Internet Service Provider:** It is one gateway to the Internet. As mentioned earlier, you need this service to connect to Internet from your computer.

**Multimedia:** At the heart of the Web is the ability to display multimedia information, such as images, audio, video, animation, and other multimedia data types.

**Transmission Control Protocol:** It uses a set of rules to exchange messages with other Internet points at the information packet level.

**Web Browser:** It is a software application that resides on your PC and can display text, images, and multimedia data found on different Web pages. It allows you to specify a Web page, navigate using links, and bookmark your favourite Web pages, The commonly used Web browsers are Internet Explorer and Netscape Navigator.

**Web Server:** A Web server refers to a location (computer) on the Internet that contains information in the form of Web pages. Technically speaking, a Web Server means a computer on the Internet having the capability to run software. A page stored on a Web server can be accessed by Web users. It may also be mentioned here that Internet Service Providers (ISPs) normally offer space on their Web servers on which their registered users can publish their Web pages free of charge.

**Web Site:** A Web site comprises of a collection of Web pages that may be maintained and updated by an organization like a Government or University department, a business house, a research institution etc. even a single individual can also create and maintain his/her own Web site to promote certain ideas. The information on a Web site is stored in the form of a series of files that may be stored on one or more computers. Do remember that the material on a Web site is stored in Hypertext.

**Web Page:** A Web page refers to a document on the Web. Web pages can be used to display written text, show pictures, play music/sound effects and run video. Do also remember that you need to use Hyper Text Markup Language (HTML) to create Web pages.

## 1.7 Net etiquette

Since in Internet you are not facing the other party, this does not mean that you can take the liberty of saying whatever you want to. There are set rules and manners defined by the users of the net, which are called Net Etiquettes. You have to abide by them while using the Net or even while sending e-mail through the net. For example, never use capital letters while sending the mail, it is taken as bad mannered mail. On the other hand never send e-mail to a party unknown to you. Though the marketing people would not agree with me but you should not indulge in sending e-mail in bulk. This is called spam mail and most of time contains the virus.

## 1.8 Internet Applications

To understand how the information is transferred through the Internet, we will have to study more about the Internet technology. After all it is very strange that it allows you share information not in the form of written words but also allows you to have the information in the vocal form.

Remember what I had said earlier, about Packet Switching. This packet switching technology is still used to transfer the data. Digital data made up of a series of 0s (OFFs) and 1s (ONs) are grouped in unique sequences. Each sequences of 0s (OFFs) and 1s (ONs) have a particular meaning, which is translated by the computers to enable you to view the matter on your computer's screen. To understand it more clearly, do remember that computers do not understand languages in the manner in which we speak and write. Instead, they understand languages based on electrical impulses that go 'ON' and 'OFF'. Speaking scientifically, such a system is called the Binary System in which specific combinations of 'ON' and 'OFF".

Thus, a message, sent by you through the Internet, first gets converted (translated) by your computer in to a digital format, made up of a series of ONs (1s) and OFFs (0s) that are grouped in specific and unique sequences. Each sequence of 1s and 0s has a particular meaning. At the final receiving point, these sequences are reconverted (re-translated) by your friend's computer so that your friend can read your message on his computer's screen.

It is not that the Internet is used only for sending and receiving information. It has its commercial aspect too. Internet today offers a number of standardized services to all its users. In fact, it is like a multipurpose tool to communicate with one another, collect information and enhance your knowledge about the subjects that you like, conduct research, play games, invest in shares or just look around (usually called browsing) in search of recipes or even jokes or the latest technological developments. The description that follows will acquaint you with some of the well-known ways in which Internet is used worldwide. Some of the famous usages of Internet are:

### 1.8.1 Information Retrieval

One of the most commonly used services on the Net comprises retrieval of information about various topics that interest you. This retrieval (getting) of information is made possible through the World Wide Web (popularly called WWW or W3).

### 1.8.2 Internet and e-mail

The Internet facility used to the maximum is e-mail. It involves writing messages on a computer and transmitting them to another computer so that the addressee can read them, thus saving paper, time, energy and cost. In fact, it can be said that e-mail is the essence of all communications on the Internet. Practically, everyone with Internet access does have an e-mail account.

### 1.8.3 Newsgroups (Usenet)

The Internet provides you a major avenue to communicate with large groups. Popularly, referred to as 'Newsgroups', this service is technically called Usenet and comprises a distributed bulletin board system. The information (news) shared by Usenet groups can be 'unmoderated' (unedited) or 'moderated' (edited.).

### 1.8.4 Accessing People

Internet would help you in locating your long lost friend, who was probably lost in school or college. That person must have an e-mail account. Rest is easy. For this purpose, you can visit a commonly used site such as whowhere (use your search engine to locate it by typing http://whowhere.lycos.com). Now, to find the e-Mail address, type the name of the person in the name field. Thereafter, type the e-mail server domain name (like hotmail.com) in the domain field. Once you click the Go Get It button, the result will be displayed on your computer's screen. You will also find that the on-screen display serves as a link, wherefrom, you can get the person's e-mail address.

### 1.8.5 Telnet

It is a text-based Internet service that connects you to a remote host (server). Using a special protocol known as the Network Terminal Protocol, it enables you to log onto another computer on the Internet and use its resources as if they existed on your own machine. To use this service, you need to provide your valid login and user password.

### 1.8.6 Chat

Everybody likes to chat. Even if it on the Internet. You can in fact chat with totally unknown people. Technically known as Internet Relay Chat (IRC), it is multi-user and multi-channel chatting net that allows users to communicate in real time. Remember! Chatting through IRC is in the written form, i.e., while communicating with some one, you type your message and the receiver responds (types back) with his/her comments. In short, it is form of instant talking, almost like a telephone conversation but in a written form. Residing on many systems on the Net, it is a software, which provides access to a series of interactive services. By availing these services, one can chat or play on-line games with people on the Internet.

### 1.8.7 FTP (File Transfer Protocol)

It connotes an Internet service that transfers files from one computer to another. It is a common procedure to download and upload files over the Internet. With FTP you can login to another Internet site and transfer (meaning send or receive) files. FTP works on the client/server principle. A client program enables the user to interact with a server in order to access information and services on the server computer.

### 1.8.8 Anonymous FTP

Some sites have public file archives that you can access by using FTP with the account name 'anonymous' and your e-Mail address as the password. This type of access is called anonymous FTP.

### 1.8.9 e-commerce

e-commerce means doing business online. It refers to any manner of conducting business on line by an individual/organization. As part of e-commerce, large organizations also send data from the Internet to conduct research and plan their marketing strategies globally. With credit cards becoming more popular along with computerized banking services, payment for services through Internet is becoming very easy.

### 1.8.10 Employment Generation

Job placement agencies and employers have started to increasingly use the Internet as a source of recruitment by advertising on the Net to fill up vacancies. Side by side, people seeking job or better employment opportunities also sue the Internet.

### 1.8.11 Medicare

Doctors now increasingly use the Internet to know the latest treatment techniques to benefit their patients. Hospitals sometimes use video conferencing to provide on-line guidance for conducting complicated operations.

### 1.8.12 Shopping Online

Some department stores offer their products, both new and old to Internet users to payment, which is usually made in advance through a credit card. While in the case of software, developers often post the software they have written – a process similar to posting a message. You can also download and use these programs free of cost and give a feedback to the programmer about its usefulness.

### 1.8.13 Entertainment

Internet now gives you unlimited opportunities to watch latest films, TV programs and listen to music. You can download your favorite movies and music from different sources.

### 1.8.14 World Wide Web (WWW)

The World Wide Web is a collection of million of files stored in thousand of computers (called Web server) all over world. Using WWW a user can download files, listen to sounds, view video files and jump to other documents on or Net sites by using hypertext links.

### 1.8.15 Educational Opportunities

Suppose you wish to study in America after passing the Senior Secondary examination. Just surf the Web and you will find that almost every university in the U.S. maintains a web site. Each of these sites provides extensive information, ranging from courses available to credit prices, course fees, etc., details of programs leading to various degrees and career planning services

Lastly I can say that with the help of computer and Internet, you can see the World on your desktop only. And that too anytime of the day.

## 1.9 Commerce on the Internet

Innovations in information and communications technologies have created a digital revolution that is changing the way the world works, learns, communicates and transacts business. This revolution is helping to foster economic growth and social development across the globe.

Businesses are using the tools of electronic commerce to increase productivity, access global markets, reduce the time required to develop new products and forge closer relationships with their customers. Some observers estimate that by 2003 global e-commerce could well exceed $1.8 trillion. The Internet and other technologies also are helping as tackle some of our toughest social challenges.

They are helping us educate our children, protect our health and make government more efficient, responsive, particularly and transparent. Ultimately, the Internet and other technologies are helping us to renew our most cherished values: raising standards of living, literacy and learning while widening the circle of democracy and empowering the individual. Unfortunately, not all countries or communities are participating fully in these dramatic developments.

We must work together to realize the potential of the Digital Revolution for all our citizens. Together, we have the chance to create "digital opportunities" worldwide: to improve access to information and communications technology in underserved regions and communities; to bring 21st century learning to all corners of the world; to bring the latest medical insights to areas where there are barely enough doctors today to strengthen democracy and freedom; and to create networks that allow every business no mater how small to market and sell products directly to the entire world.

This vision is not necessarily self-fullfilling, however. Governments must adopt appropriate policies if they wish to foster the growth of the Internet. Perhaps the single most important contribution they can make is to establish conditions that unleash the dynamism, technology and capital of the private sector.

This means letting the private sector lead in the development of the Internet, avoiding unnecessary regulations, and adopting minimal government regulation only where necessary to protect the public interest. It means encouraging private investment, competition, open access, flexible regulatory frameworks and universal service.

### 1.9.1 General Business Terminology:

B2B — Business to Business – marketing, advertising, communications, sales and other activities perpetrated between businesses.

B2C — Business to Consumer – marketing, advertising, communications, sales and other activities inflicted by a business or consumers.

PC — Political Correct – as in recommending a Windows NT server to management at a Fortune 500 company who's CEO has just returned from an all expense paid trip to Microsoft's Redmond campus or recommending a Linux server to management at a small ISP. The opinion or action that will upset "the powers that be" least.

PHB — Pointly Haired Boss – the utterly clueless boss who presides over Dilbert and his coworkers in the cartoon strip of that time. Any boss who's only significant skill is in climbing the corporate management ladder. The PHB is too incompetent to realize he is incompetent – in short, the represents the nearly all mid and high level management in corporate America. Note that being too incompetent to realize one is incompetent is not limited to PHBs, but can also be found in technical circles – or in any other field of endeavor.

Proprietary — Property of a particular company which has effective control. Said of software, protocols, hardware etc.,

Open — Said of "standards" that are published and available to everyone (sometimes for a fee). Ideally said of publicly controlled standard but much abused by marketing departments who refer to proprietary protocols as "open" if at least a small part of the specification is available to public view. The term "Open Systems" generally refers to Unix and the communications protocols surrounding it.

| | |
|---|---|
| POS | Point Of Sale – Refers to computer equipment and software specialized for retail point of sale particularly cash drawers, pole displays, receipt printers, bar – code scanners and software that supports them. |
| CRM | Customer Relationship Management – Major business buzzword for year 2000. |
| ERP | Enterprise Resource Planning – Major business buzzword of the 1990s, displaced by new buzzword CRM. |
| MRP | Material Requirement Planning – Major business buzzword of the 1980s, displaced by new buzzword ERP. |

## 1.10 Governance on the Internet

Every network is connected to the Internet is responsible for its own part. However, there are 3 main organizations which are supposed to guide and coordinate the working of Internet are:

### 1.10.1 Internet Engineering Task Force (IETF)

It develops and maintains the Internet's communication protocols, which are the methods by which computers on the Internet are connected.

### 1.10.2 Internet Research Task Force (IRTF)

It looks into long term research problem, many of which are at times critical to the Internet.

### 1.10.3 Internet Architecture Board (IAB)

This oversees the IETF and IRTF and ratifies any major change to the Internet that comes from the IETF.

## 1.11 Impact of Internet on Society

The most important thing which Internet has done is that it has brought people of World very close to each other. The communication has become so good that whereas it used to take 15 days for a letter to come from USA, it now takes 15 seconds to send an e-mail to anywhere in the World. This has done a very significant difference to the approach of people towards computers too. Whereas it as thought to be a learning tool only, now it has become a necessary tool for each home.

## 1.12 Crime on/through the Internet

Most of the crimes on the Internet are related to breaking codes of various information available on the net. You can crack password of somebody's credit card and encash money. The other is of spreading virus. Even spreading of wrong and inflamatory information too.

### 1.12.1 What is Cyber Crime?

When Internet was developed, the founding fathers of Internet hardly had any inclination that Internet could also be misused for criminal activities. Today, there are many disturbing things happening in cyberspace. Cyber Crime refers to all the activities done with criminal intent in cyberspace. These could be either the criminal activity in the conventional sense or could be activities, newly evolved with the growth of the new medium. Because of the anonymous nature of the Internet, it is possible to engage into a variety of criminal activities with impunity and people with intelligence, have been grossly misusing this aspect of the Internet to perpetuate criminal activities in cyberspace. The field of Cyber Crime is just emerging and new forms of criminal activities in cyberspace are coming to the forefront with the passing of each new day.

### 1.12.2 Exhaustive definition of Cyber Crime?

There can be no one exhaustive definition about Cyber Crime. However, any activities, which basically offend human sensibilities, can also be included in its ambit. Child Pornography on the Internet constitutes one serious Cyber Crime. Similarly, online pedophiles, using Internet to induce minor children into sex, are as much Cyber criminals as any others.

### 1.12.3 Various categories of Cyber Crimes

Cyber Crimes can be basically divided into 3 major categories being Cyber Crimes against persons, property and Government.

### 1.12.4 Cyber Crimes against Persons

Cyber Crimes committed against persons include various crimes like transmission of child pornography, harassment of anyone with the use of a computer such as e-mail, and cyber-stalking.

The trafficking, distribution, posting, and dissemination of obscene material including pornography, indecent exposure, and child pornography, constitutes one of the most important Cyber Crimes known today. The potential harm of such a crime to humanity can hardly be overstated. This is one Cyber Crime, which threatens to undermine the growth of the younger generation as also leave irreparable scars and injury on the younger generation, if not controlled.

### 1.12.5 Is Cyber Harassment also a Cyber Crime?

Cyber Harassment is a distinct Cyber Crime. Various kinds of harassment can and does occur in cyberspace, or through the use of cyberspace. Harassment can be sexual, racial, religious, or other. Persons perpetuating such harassment are also guilty of Cyber Crimes.

Cyber Harassment as a crime also brings us to another related area of violation of privacy of netizens. Violation of privacy of online citizens is a Cyber Crime of a grave nature. No one likes any other person invading the precious and extremely touchy area of his or her own privacy, which the medium of Internet grants to the netizen.

### 1.12.6 Cyber Crimes against property

The second category of Cyber Crimes is that of Cyber Crimes against all forms of property. These crimes include unauthorized computer trespassing through cyberspace, computer vandalism, transmission of harmful programs, and unauthorized possession of computerized information.

### 1.12.7 Is Hacking Cyber Crime?

Hacking and cracking are amongst the gravest Cyber Crimes known till date. It is a dreadful feeling to know that a stranger has broken into your computer systems without your knowledge and consent and has tampered with precious confidential date and information. Coupled with this, the actuality is that no computer system in the world is hacking proof. It is unanimously agreed that any and every system in the world can be hacked.

The recent denial of service attacks seen over the popular commercial sites like E-bay, Yahoo, Amazon and others are a new category of Cyber Crimes, which are slowly emerging as being extremely dangerous. Using one's own programming abilities as also various programmes with malicious intent to gain unauthorized access to a computer or network are very serious crimes. Similarly, the creation and dissemination of harmful computer programs are virii, which do irreparable damage to computer systems is another kind of Cyber Crime. Software piracy is also another distinct kind of Cyber Crime, which is perpetuated by many people online who distribute illegal and unauthorized pirated copies of software.

### 1.12.8 Cyber Crime against Government

The third category of Cyber Crimes relates to Cyber Crimes against Government. Cyber Terrorism is one distinct kind of crime in this category. The growth of Internet has shown that individuals and groups to threaten the international governments as also to terrorize the citizens of a country are using the medium of Cyber Space. This crime manifests into terrorism when an individual "cracks" into a government or military maintained web site.

### 1.12.9 Comprehensive law on Cyber Crime

Development has to take place in terms of putting into place the relevant legal mechanism for controlling and preventing Cyber Crime. As of now, there is absolutely no comprehensive law on Cyber Crime anywhere in the world. This is reason that the investigating agencies like FBI are finding the Cyberspace to be an extremely difficult terrain. These various Cyber Crimes fall into that Grey area of Internet law, which is neither fully nor partially covered by the existing laws and that too in some countries.

## Let us Revise

1. Internet is network of networks.
2. Nobody controls Internet.
3. NSFnet is the backbone of communication service for the Internet.
4. Intranet is a private network within a company or an organization.
5. A message, sent by through Internet, first gets converted by your computer into a digital format, made up of a series of ONs (1s) and OFFs (0s).
6. For connecting to Internet, you need a computer system with a software like Microsoft Internet Explorer or Netscape Navigator loaded into it; A telephone line. A modem (modular-demodulator); a connection provided by Internet Service Provider (ISP).
7. Home page is the first page that you would see on the Website.
8. Information on the Web is made available in the form of Hypertext.
9. The highlighted items selected by you are technically called Hyperlinks.
10. Internet Information Server is a group of Internet servers including the additional capabilities of Windows NT and Windows 2000.
11. Internet Protocol is responsible for the addressing and sending data from one computer to another computer.
12. Internet Service Provider is one gateway to the Internet.
13. At the heart of the Web is the ability to display multimedia information, such as images, audio, video, animation, and other multimedia data types.
14. Transmission Control Protocol uses a set of rules to exchange messages with other Internet points at the information packet level.
15. Web Browser is a software application that resides on your PC and can display text, images, and multimedia data found on different Web pages.
16. A Web server refers to a location (computer) on the Internet that contains information in the form of Web pages.
17. A Web site comprises of a collection of Web pages.
18. A Web page refers to a document on the Web.
19. Internet can be used for various purposes.

## Multiple Choice Questions

1. Internet is network of :

   (a) Networks (b) Humans (c) Workers

2. Initially Internet was used for:
   (a) Medicine (b) Military Intelligence (c) Communications
3. What is not needed for running Internet:
   (a) Modem (b) Telephone Line (c) Printer
4. Using Internet you can chat with other users :
   (a) Yes (b) No
5. A browser allows you to search and log :
   (a) web sites (b) hard disk (c) modem
6. Which of the following, domain name does not have?
   (a) Country (b) Computer Id (c) Serial number
7. The browser is which is available free:
   (a) Internet Explorer (b) Netscape Navigator (c) Lynx
8. Which of the following is not a search engine:
   (a) Yahoo! (b) Internet Explorer (c) Lycos
9. Web server is a :
   (a) Hardware (b) Software (c) Both

## True/False Questions

1. Nobody controls Internet.
2. Internet can be used for various purposes.
3. TCP/IP defines the way the data is accessed on the Internet.
4. Point to Point Protocol incorporates superior data negotiation, compression, and error corrections.
5. A URL does not describe the location and a method of accessing a resource on the Internet.
6. Web allows you to skip from one page to another using hyperlink.
7. With Web you cannot get information from the user too.
8. Most popular Web browser is Microsoft Internet Explorer.
9. HTTP is used as the communication protocol to transport hypertext documents over the Internet.

## Match Columns

Match the matter in Column A with the matter in Column B.

| Column A | Column B |
|---|---|
| A. URL | 1. Device to convert computer signals to telephone signals |
| B. Internet Explorer | 2. The first and main page of web site |
| C. Browser | 3. Network of Networks |
| D. Home Page | 4. Uniform Resource Locator |
| E. Modem | 5. A software to see and use various web sites |
| F. Internet | 6. Popular Internet Browser |

## Fill in the Blanks with Appropriate Words

| | | |
|---|---|---|
| a. Internet Service Provider | b. Hypertext | c. Intranet |
| d. Web | e. Home page | f. network of networks |
| g. Internet | h. Web pages | i. Internet Protocol |

1. Internet is ____________________.
2. _________ is a private network within a company or an organization.
3. __________ is the first page that you would see on the Website.
4. Information on the Web is made available in the form of ____________.
5. ___________ is responsible for the addressing and sending data from one computer to another computer.
6. __________________ is one gateway to the Internet.
7. A Web site comprises of a collection of _________.
8. A Web page refers to a document on the ______.
9. ________ can be used for various purposes.

## Descriptive Type Questions

1. What is Internet?
2. How was Internet developed?
3. What all you need for running Internet?
4. What do you understand by the Governance on the Internet?
5. How the crime on the net can be prevented?
6. Write short notes on the following:

| | |
|---|---|
| Information Retrieval | Internet and e-mail |
| Newsgroups (Usenet) | Accessing People |
| Telnet | Chat |
| FTP (File Transfer Protocol) | Anonymous FTP |
| e-commerce | Employment Generation |
| Medicare | Shopping Online |
| Entertainment | World Wide Web (WWW) |
| Educational Opportunities on the Net | |

## Answers to Objective Type Questions

### *Multiple Choice Questions*

| | | | |
|---|---|---|---|
| 1. a | 2. b | 3. c | 4. a |
| 5. a | 6. b | 7. a | 8. b |
| 9. a | | | |

### *True False Questions*

| | | | |
|---|---|---|---|
| 1. T | 2. T | 3. T | 4. T |
| 5. F | 6. T | 7. F | 8. T |
| 9. T | | | |

### *Matching Columns*

| | | | |
|---|---|---|---|
| A. 4 | B. 6 | C. 5 | D. 2 |
| E. 1 | F. 3 | | |

### *Fill in the Blanks*

| | | | |
|---|---|---|---|
| 1. f | 2. c | 3. e | 4. b |
| 5. i | 6. a | 7. h | 8. d |
| 9. h | 10. g | | |

# TCP/IP - Internet Technology and Protocol 2

## 2.1 Packet Switching Technology

Packet switching is a digital network communications method that groups all transmitted data – irrespective of content, type, or structure – into suitably-sized blocks, called packets. Packet switching features delivery of variable-bit-rate data streams (sequences of packets) over a shared network. When traversing network adapters, switches, routers and other network nodes, packets are buffered and queued, resulting in variable delay and throughput depending on the traffic load in the network.

Packet switching contrasts with another principal networking paradigm, circuit switching, a method which sets up a limited number of dedicated connections of constant bit rate and constant delay between nodes for exclusive use during the communication session. In case of traffic fees, for example in cellular communication, circuit switching is characterized by a fee per time unit of connection time, even when no data is transferred, while packet switching is characterized by a fee per unit of information.

Two major packet switching modes exist; **connectionless packet switching**, also known as **datagram switching**, and **connection-oriented packet switching**, also known as **virtual circuit switching**. In the first case each packet includes complete addressing or routing information. The packets are routed individually, sometimes resulting in different paths and out-of-order delivery. In the second case a connection is defined and preallocated in each involved node before any packet is transferred. The packets includes a connection identifier rather than address information, and are delivered in order. See below.

Packet mode communication may be utilized with or without intermediate forwarding nodes (packet switches). In all packet mode communication, network resources are managed by statistical multiplexing or dynamic bandwidth allocation in which a communication channel is effectively divided into an arbitrary number of logical variable-bit-rate channels or data streams. Each logical stream consists of a sequence of packets, which normally are forwarded by the multiplexers and intermediate network nodes asynchronously using first-in, first-out buffering. Alternatively, the packets may be forwarded according to some scheduling discipline for fair queuing or for differentiated or guaranteed quality of service, such as pipeline forwarding or time-driven priority (TDP). Any buffering introduces varying latency and throughput in transmission. In case of a shared physical medium, the packets may be delivered according to some packet-mode multiple access scheme.

Packet switching is used to optimize the use of the channel capacity available in digital telecommunication networks such as computer networks, to minimize the transmission latency (i.e. the time it takes for data to pass across the network), and to increase robustness of communication.

The most well-known use of packet switching is the Internet and local area networks. The Internet is implemented by the Internet Protocol Suite using a variety of Link Layer technologies. For example, Ethernet and Frame Relay are common. Newer mobile phone technologies (e.g., GPRS, I-mode) also use packet switching.

X.25 is a notable use of packet switching in that, despite being based on packet switching methods, it provided virtual circuits to the user. These virtual circuits carry variable-length packets. In 1978, X.25 was used to provide the first international and commercial packet switching network, the International Packet Switched Service (IPSS). Asynchronous Transfer Mode (ATM) also is a virtual circuit technology, which uses fixed-length cell relay connection oriented packet switching.

Datagram packet switching is also called connectionless networking because no connections are established. Technologies such as Multiprotocol Label Switching (MPLS) and the Resource Reservation Protocol (RSVP) create virtual circuits on top of datagram networks. Virtual circuits are especially useful in building robust failover mechanisms and allocating bandwidth for delay-sensitive applications.

MPLS and its predecessors, as well as ATM, have been called "fast packet" technologies. MPLS, indeed, has been called "ATM without cells". Modern routers, however, do not require these technologies to be able to forward variable-length packets at multigigabit speeds across the network.

## 2.2 Internet Protocols

The Internet Protocol (IP) is a protocol used for communicating data across a packet-switched internetwork using the Internet Protocol Suite, also referred to as TCP/IP.

IP is the primary protocol in the Internet Layer of the Internet Protocol Suite and has the task of delivering distinguished protocol datagrams (packets) from the source host to the destination host solely based on their addresses. For this purpose the Internet Protocol defines addressing methods and structures for datagram encapsulation. The first major version of addressing structure, now referred to as Internet Protocol Version 4 (IPv4) is still the dominant protocol of the Internet, although the successor, Internet Protocol Version 6 (IPv6) is being deployed actively worldwide.

## 2.3 TCP/IP

The Internet Protocol Suite (commonly known as TCP/IP) is the set of communications protocols used for the Internet and other similar networks. It is named from two of the most important protocols in it: the **Transmission Control Protocol** (TCP) and the **Internet Protocol** (IP), which were the first two networking protocols defined in this standard. Today's IP networking represents a synthesis of several developments that began to evolve in the 1960s and 1970s, namely the Internet and LANs (Local Area Networks), which emerged in the mid- to late-1980s, together with the advent of the World Wide Web in the early 1990s.

The Internet Protocol Suite, like many protocol suites, may be viewed as a set of layers. Each layer solves a set of problems involving the transmission of data, and provides a well-defined service to the upper layer protocols based on using services from some lower layers. Upper layers are logically closer to the user and deal with more abstract data, relying on lower layer protocols to translate data into forms that can eventually be physically transmitted.

The TCP/IP model consists of four layers (RFC 1122). From lowest to highest, these are the **Link Layer**, the **Internet Layer**, the **Transport Layer**, and the **Application Layer**.

TCP/IP stack operating on two hosts connected via two routers and the corresponding layers used at each hop

Encapsulation of application data descending through the protocol stack.

The functional groups of protocols and methods are the Application Layer, the Transport Layer, the Internet Layer, and the Link Layer (RFC 1122). It should be noted that this model was not intended to be a rigid reference model into which new protocols have to fit in order to be accepted as a standard.

The following table provides some examples of the protocols grouped in their respective layers.

| | |
|---|---|
| **Application** | DNS, TFTP, TLS/SSL, FTP, Gopher, HTTP, IMAP, IRC, NNTP, POP3, SIP, SMTP, SMPP, SNMP, SSH, Telnet, Echo, RTP, PNRP, rlogin, ENRP |

| | |
|---|---|
| | Routing protocols like BGP and RIP which run over TCP/UDP, may also be considered part of the Internet Layer. |
| **Transport** | TCP, UDP, DCCP, SCTP, IL, RUDP, RSVP |
| **Internet** | IP (IPv4, IPv6), ICMP, IGMP, and ICMPv6 |
| | OSPF for IPv4 was initially considered IP layer protocol since it runs per IP-subnet, but has been placed on the Link since RFC 2740. |
| **Link** | ARP, RARP, OSPF (IPv4/IPv6), IS-IS, NDP |

## 2.4 Router

A router, is an electronic device that is used to forward data between computer networks.

More technically, a router is a networking device whose software and hardware are usually tailored to the tasks of routing and forwarding information. Routers connect two or more logical subnets, which do not necessarily map one-to-one to the physical interfaces of the router. The term "layer 3 switching" is often used interchangeably with routing, but switch is a general term without a rigorous technical definition. In marketing usage, a switch is generally optimized for Ethernet LAN interfaces and may not have other physical interface types. In comparison, the network hub (predecessor of the "switch" or "switching hub") does not do any routing, instead every packet it receives on one network line gets forwarded to all the other network lines.

Routers operate in two different planes:

**Control plane**, in which the router learns the outgoing interface that is most appropriate for forwarding specific packets to specific destinations,

**Forwarding plane**, which is responsible for the actual process of sending a packet received on a logical interface to an outbound logical interface

Routers may provide connectivity inside enterprises, between enterprises and the Internet, and inside Internet Service Providers (ISPs). The largest routers (for example the Cisco CRS-1 or Juniper T1600) interconnect ISPs, are used inside ISPs, or may be used in very large enterprise networks. The smallest routers provide connectivity for small and home offices.

### 2.4.1 Routers for Internet connectivity and Internal use

Routers intended for ISP and major enterprise connectivity will almost invariably exchange routing information with the Border Gateway Protocol (BGP). RFC 4098 defines several types of BGP-speaking routers:

**Edge Router**: Placed at the edge of an ISP network, it speaks external BGP (EBGP) to a BGP speaker in another provider or large enterprise Autonomous System(AS).

**Subscriber Edge Router**: Located at the edge of the subscriber's network, it speaks EBGP to its provider's AS(s). It belongs to an end user (enterprise) organization.

**Inter-provider Border Router**: Interconnecting ISPs, this is a BGP speaking router that maintains BGP sessions with other BGP speaking routers in other providers' ASes.

**Core router**: A router that resides within the middle or backbone of the LAN network rather than at its periphery.

**Within an ISP**: Internal to the provider's AS, such a router speaks internal BGP (IBGP) to that provider's edge routers, other intra-provider core routers, or the provider's inter-provider border routers.

**"Internet backbone**:" The Internet does not have a clearly identifiable backbone, as did its predecessors. See default-free zone (DFZ). Nevertheless, it is the major ISPs' routers that make up what many would consider the core. These ISPs operate all four types of the BGP-speaking routers described here. In ISP usage, a "core" router is internal to an ISP, and used to interconnect its edge and border routers. Core routers may also have specialized functions in virtual private networks based on a combination of BGP and Multi-Protocol Label Switching (MPLS).

## 2.5 Internet Addressing Scheme

Unlike in most other network protocols like IP, the address is not attached to an interface but to the whole physical node. Also a node can only possess one single address which identifies it throughout the whole network.

The addressing scheme is mapped to the logical Network Topology. The human readable notation is <Z.C.N> where Z stands for Zone, C for Cluster and N for Node. Internally the address is represented as a 32-bit integer. Here, the 8 most significant bits identify the Zone, the next 12 ones the Cluster and the 12 least significant bits the individual Node.

## 2.6 Machine Addressing (IP Address)

An Internet Protocol (IP) address is a numerical label that is assigned to devices participating in a computer network that uses the Internet Protocol for communication between its nodes. An IP address serves two principal functions: host or network interface identification and location addressing. Its role has been characterized as follows: "A name indicates what we seek. An address indicates where it is. A route indicates how to get there."

The designers of TCP/IP defined an IP address as a 32-bit number and this system, known as Internet Protocol Version 4 or IPv4, is still in use today. However, due to the enormous growth of the Internet and the resulting depletion of available addresses, a new addressing system (IPv6), using 128 bits for the address, was developed in 1995 and last standardized by RFC 2460 in 1998. Although IP addresses are stored as binary numbers, they are usually displayed in human-readable notations, such as 208.77.188.166 (for IPv4), and 2001:db8:0:1234:0:567:1:1 (for IPv6).

The Internet Protocol also routes data packets between networks; IP addresses specify the locations of the source and destination nodes in the topology of the routing system. For this purpose, some of the bits in an IP address are used to designate a subnetwork. The number of these bits is indicated in CIDR notation, appended to the IP address; e.g., 208.77.188.166/24.

As the development of private networks raised the threat of IPv4 address exhaustion, RFC 1918 set aside a group of private address spaces that may be used by anyone on private networks. They are often used with network address translators to connect to the global public Internet.

The **Internet Assigned Numbers Authority** (IANA), which manages the IP address space allocations globally, cooperates with five Regional Internet Registries (RIRs) to allocate IP address blocks to Local Internet Registries (Internet service providers) and other entities.

## 2.7 E-mail Addresses

An e-mail address identifies an email box to which e-mail messages may be delivered. An e-mail address on the modern Internet looks like, for example, jsmith@example.com and is usually read as "jsmith at example dot com". Many earlier e-mail systems used different address formats.

Most e-mail on the Internet uses the Simple Mail Transfer Protocol (SMTP), which is defined in the Internet standards RFC 5321 and RFC 5322.

E-mail addresses, such as jsmith@example.com, have two parts. The part before the @ sign is the local-part of the address, often the username of the recipient (jsmith), and the part after the @ sign is the domain which is a domain name to which the e-mail message will be sent (example.com). The domain is looked up in the Domain Name System to find the mail transfer agent or Mail eXchangers (MXs) accepting e-mail for that address.

The domain may have semantic meaning for any mail-system handling the address; the meaning is well defined, and any changes in meaning involve changing every mail server in existence. The local-part, by contrast, is supposed to be opaque to every mail system except the system which is authoritative for the domain. This is what makes e-mail a federated system.

When a host receives an e-mail, it will be delivered to an e-mail mailbox. Some hosts allow more than one e-mail address to be sent to the same mailbox via an e-mail alias or even allow a catch-all address where the local-part can be undefined and e-mail would be delivered to a configured and existing e-mail address.

Often, the domain of an e-mail address is that of an e-mail service provider. The domain can also be the domain name of the organization that the recipient represents, or of the recipient's personal site.

Addresses found in the header fields of e-mail should not be considered authoritative, because SMTP has no generally-required mechanisms for authentication. Forged e-mail addresses are often seen in spam, phishing, and many other Internet-based scams; this has led to several initiatives which aim to make such forgeries easier to spot.

To indicate whom the message is intended for, a user can use the "display name" of the recipient followed by the address specification surrounded by angled brackets, for example: John Smith <john.smith@example.com>.

Earlier forms of e-mail addresses included the somewhat verbose notation required by X.400, and the UUCP "bang path" notation, in which the address was given in the form of a sequence of computers through which the message should be relayed. This was widely used for several years, but was superseded by the generally more convenient SMTP form.

## 2.8 Resource Addresses

A URL describes the location and a method of accessing a resource on the Internet. For example, the URL http://www.adobe.com may lead you to the home page of the company called Adobe Corporation, makers of various publishing software like Pake Maker, etc. Each URL is unique. It identifies a particular point on the Internet. It consists of a string that supplies the Internet address of a resource on the WWW along with the protocol by which the resource is accessed. The most common URL type is 'http' which gives the Internet address of a World Wide Web page. Some other URL types are 'gopher' which gives the Internet address of a Gopher directory, and 'ftp' which gives the address of a FTP resource. All Web sites have URLs. One could say a URL is what a telephone number is to a telephone or a street address is to a house.

### 2.8.1 Structure of a URL

The following is an outline of the most common form of a URL. For example,

http://www.wikipedia.org.1234/path/subdir/file.htm

where.

| | |
|---|---|
| http | service |
| address.edu | host |
| 1234 | port |
| subdir/file.htm | file and resource details. |

## Let us Revise

1. Packet switching features delivery of variable-bit-rate data streams (sequences of packets) over a shared network.
2. Packet switching is used to optimize the use of the channel capacity available in digital telecommunication networks such as computer networks, to minimize the transmission latency (i.e. the time it takes for data to pass across the network), and to increase robustness of communication.
3. The Internet Protocol (IP) is a protocol used for communicating data across a packet-switched internetwork using the Internet Protocol Suite, also referred to as TCP/IP.
4. The TCP/IP model consists of four layers (RFC 1122). From lowest to highest, these are the Link Layer, the Internet Layer, the Transport Layer, and the Application Layer.
5. A router, is an electronic device that is used to forward data between computer networks.
6. Routers intended for ISP and major enterprise connectivity will almost invariably exchange routing information with the Border Gateway Protocol (BGP).
7. Unlike in most other network protocols like IP, the address is not attached to an interface but to the whole physical node.
8. The Internet Assigned Numbers Authority (IANA), which manages the IP address space allocations globally, cooperates with five Regional Internet Registries (RIRs) to allocate IP address blocks to Local Internet Registries (Internet service providers) and other entities.
9. An e-mail address identifies an e-mail box to which e-mail messages may be delivered.
10. A URL describes the location and a method of accessing a resource on the Internet.

## Multiple Choice Questions

1. URL stands for:
   (a) Uniform Resource Locator
   (b) Uniform Resource Location
   (c) Uniform Research Locator
2. TCP/IP stands for:
   (a) Transmission Control Product/Internet Protocol
   (b) Transmission Control Protocol/Internet Protocol
   (c) Transmission Control Protocol/Internet Product
3. BGP is:
   (a) Border Gate Protocol
   (b) Border Giveaway Protocol
   (c) Border Gateway Protocol
4. IANA is :
   (a) Internet Acting Numbers Authority
   (b) Internet Assigned Numbers Authority
   (c) Internet Assigned Numbers Author
5. RIR is :
   (a) Regional Internet Registries

(b) Regional Internet Registry

(c) Regional Internal Registries

## True/False Questions

1. The Internet Protocol (IP) is a protocol used for communicating data across a packet-switched internetwork using the Internet Protocol Suite, also referred to as TCP/IP.
2. A router, is not used to forward data between computer networks.
3. Routers intended for ISP and major enterprise connectivity will almost invariably exchange routing information with the Border Gateway Protocol (BGP).
4. Unlike in most other network protocols like IP, the address is not attached to an interface but to the whole physical node.
5. An e-mail address does not identify an e-mail box to which e-mail messages may be delivered.

## Match Columns

Match the matter in Column A with the matter in Column B.

| Column A | Column B |
|---|---|
| A. URL | 1. Internet Protocol |
| B. TCP | 2. Internet Assigned Numbers Authority |
| C. IP | 3. Border Gateway Protocol |
| D. BGP | 4. Uniform Resource Locator |
| E. IANA | 5. Regional Internet Registries |
| F. RIR | 6. Transmission Control Protocol |

## Fill in the Blanks with Appropriate Words

a. router b. Border Gateway Protocol (BGP)
c. physical node d. e-mail address e. Internet Protocol
f. URL g. Shared Network

1. Packet switching features delivery of variable-bit-rate data streams (sequences of packets) over ________.
2. The ____________ is a protocol used for communicating data across a packet-switched internetwork using the Internet Protocol Suite, also referred to as TCP/IP.
3. A ________, is an electronic device that is used to forward data between computer networks.
4. Routers intended for ISP and major enterprise connectivity will almost invariably exchange routing information with the __________________.
5. Unlike in most other network protocols like IP, the address is not attached to an interface but to the whole ______________.
6. An ______________ identifies an e-mail box to which e-mail messages may be delivered.
7. A _______ describes the location and a method of accessing a resource on the Internet.

## Descriptive Type Questions

1. What is Packet Switching Technology?
2. Describe the various Internet Protocols
3. Describe the working of TCP/IP.
4. What is a router?
5. Describe Internet Addressing Scheme.
6. What is Machine Addressing?
7. Describe E-mail addresses.
8. What are resource Addresses?

## Answers to Objective Type Questions

### *Multiple Choice Questions*

| | | | |
|---|---|---|---|
| 1. a | 2. b | 3. c | 4. b |
| 5. a | | | |

### *True False Questions*

| | | | |
|---|---|---|---|
| 1. T | 2. F | 3. T | 4. T |
| 5. F | | | |

### *Matching Columns*

| | | | |
|---|---|---|---|
| A. 4 | B. 6 | C. 1 | D. 3 |
| E. 2 | F. 5 | | |

### *Fill in the Blanks*

| | | | |
|---|---|---|---|
| 1. g | 2. e | 3. a | 4. b |
| 5. c | 6. d | 7. f | |

# Internet Connectivity 3

## 3.1 Connectivity Types

There are many ways of connecting to the Internet. Some of them are easy and some of them are difficult. They also vary from cheap to expensive ones. Large companies choose dedicated Internet access or LAN dial-up. Smaller organizations are happy with PC dial-up access and terminal emulation, which provides E-mail and other services through a service provider's computer.

There are serveral ways of connecting your computer to the Internet. Some of the options are given below:

#### *3.1.0.1 Dumb terminal*

The specific meaning of the term dumb terminal can vary depending on the context in which it is used.

In the context of traditional computer terminals that communicate over a serial RS-232 connection, dumb terminals are those that can interpret a limited number of control codes (CR, LF, etc.) but do not have the ability to process special escape sequences that perform functions such as clearing a line, clearing the screen, or controlling cursor position. In this context dumb terminals are sometimes dubbed glass teletypes, for they essentially have the same limited functionality as does a mechanical teletype. This type of dumb terminal is still supported on modern Unix-like systems by setting the environment variable TERM to dumb. Smart or intelligent terminals are those that also have the ability to process escape sequences, in particular the VT52, VT100 or ANSI escape sequences.

In the broader context that includes all forms of keyboard/screen computer communication devices, including personal computers, diskless workstations, network computers, thin clients, and X Terminals, the term dumb terminal is sometimes used to refer to any type of traditional computer terminal that communicates serially over a RS-232 connection that does not locally process data or execute user programs.

The term dumb terminal sometimes also refers to public computer terminals that are limited to monochrome text-only capabilities, or to terminals that transmit each character as it is typed rather than waiting until it is polled by a host computer.

#### *3.1.0.2 Terminal emulation*

A terminal emulator, terminal application, term, or tty for short, is a program that emulates a "dumb" video terminal within some other display architecture. Though typically synonymous with a command line shell or text terminal, the term terminal covers all remote terminals, including graphical interfaces. A terminal emulator inside a graphical user interface is often called a terminal window.

A terminal window allows the user access to a text terminal and all its applications such as command line interfaces (CLI) and text user interface applications. These may be running either on the same machine or on a different one via telnet, ssh, or dial-up. On Unix-like operating systems it is common to have one or more terminal windows connected to the local machine.

Terminals usually support a set of escape sequences for controlling color, cursor position, etc. Examples include the family of terminal control sequence standards known as ECMA-48, ANSI X3.64 or ISO/IEC 6429.

Early adopters of computer technology, such as banks, insurance companies, and governments, still make frequent use of terminal emulators. They typically have decades old applications running on mainframe computers. The old "dumb" video terminals used to access the mainframe are long since obsolete; however, applications on the mainframe are still in use. Quite often, terminal emulators are the only way a user can access applications running on these older machines.

#### *3.1.0.3 Direct connection*

LANs or large computers such as mainframes can be directly connected to the Internet. When a LAN is connected to the Internet, all the computers on the network can have full access to the Net. This kind of access is common inside corporations.

#### *3.1.0.4 SLIP (Serial Line Internet Protocol)*

The Serial Line Internet Protocol (SLIP) is a mostly obsolete encapsulation of the Internet Protocol designed to work over serial ports and modem connections. It is documented in RFC 1055. On personal computers, SLIP has been largely replaced by the Point-to-Point Protocol (PPP), which is better engineered, has more features and does not require its IP address configuration to be set before it is established. On microcontrollers, however, SLIP is still the preferred way of encapsulating IP packets due to its very small overhead.

#### *3.1.0.5 PPP (Point to Point Protocol)*

PPP is used over many types of physical networks including serial cable, phone line, trunk line, cellular telephone, specialized radio links, and fiber optic links such as SONET. Most Internet service providers (ISPs) use PPP for customer dial-up access to the Internet. Two encapsulated forms of PPP, Point-to-Point Protocol over Ethernet (PPPoE) and Point-to-Point Protocol over ATM (PPPoA), are used by Internet Service Providers (ISPs) to connect Digital Subscriber Line (DSL) Internet service.

#### *3.1.0.6 ISDN Line*

Integrated Services Digital Network (ISDN) is a set of communications standards for simultaneous digital transmission of voice, video, data, and other network services over the traditional circuits of the public switched telephone network.

Prior to ISDN, the phone system was viewed as a way to transport voice, with some special services available for data. The key feature of ISDN is that it integrates speech and data on the same lines, adding features that were not available in the classic telephone system. There are several kinds of access interfaces to ISDN defined as Basic Rate Interface (BRI), Primary Rate Interface (PRI) and Broadband ISDN (B-ISDN).

#### *3.1.0.7 Cable modem*

A cable modem is a type of network bridge and modem that provides bi-directional data communication via radio frequency channels on a cable television (CATV) infrastructure. Cable modems are primarily used to deliver broadband Internet access in the form of cable Internet, taking advantage of the high bandwidth of a cable television network. They are commonly deployed in Australia, Europe, and North and South America. In the USA alone there were 22.5 million cable modem users during the first quarter of 2005, up from 17.4 million in the first quarter of 2004

#### *3.1.0.8 Network Computer*

Network Computer (often abbreviated NC) is a trademark of Oracle Corporation that was used, from approximately 1996 to 2000, to market a range of diskless desktop computer devices. The devices were designed and manufactured by an alliance, which included Sun Microsystems, IBM, and others. The devices were designed with minimum specifications, based on the Network Computer Reference Profile. The brand was also employed as a marketing term to try to popularize this design of computer within enterprise and among consumers. The term, today, is also used somewhat interchangeably to describe a diskless desktop computer or a thin client.

The NC brand was mainly intended to denote and forecast a range of desktop computers from various suppliers that, by virtue of their diskless design and use of inexpensive components and software, were cheaper and easier to manage than standard fat client desktops. However, due to the commoditization of standard desktop components, and due to the increasing availability and popularity of various software options for using full desktops as diskless nodes, thin clients, and hybrid clients, the Network Computer brand never achieved the popularity hoped for by Oracle and was eventually mothballed.

#### *3.1.0.9 WebTV*

MSN TV (formerly WebTV) is the name of both a thin client which uses a television for display (rather than a computer monitor), and the online service that supports it.

The product and service was developed by WebTV Networks, Inc., a company purchased by Microsoft Corporation and absorbed into MSN (the Microsoft Network). While most thin clients developed in the mid-1990s were positioned as diskless workstations for corporate intranets, WebTV was positioned as a consumer device for web access.

The WebTV product is an adapter that allows a television set to be connected to the internet, primarily for web browsing and e-mail. The setup includes a web browser, cord or wireless (i.e. bluetooth or IRDA) keyboard and connection to the Internet (i.e. using modem, ADSL, cable, Power line communication).

While WebTV does not allow as much functionality as a computer-based browser, it is a low-cost alternative to a traditional computer connection to the Internet.

#### *3.1.0.10 Online services*

An online service provider can for example be an internet service provider, email provider, news provider (press), entertainment provider (music, movies), search, e-shopping site (online stores), e-finance or e-banking site, e-health site, e-government site, Wikipedia, Usenet (commonly accessed through Google Groups).In its original more limited definition it referred only to a commercial computer communication service in which paid members could dial via a computer modem the service's private computer network and access various services and information resources such a bulletin boards, downloadable files and programs, news articles, chat rooms, and electronic mail services. The term "online service" was also used in references to these dial-up services. The traditional dial-up online service differed from the modern Internet service provider in that they provided a large degree of content that was only accessible by those who subscribed to the online service, while ISP mostly serves to provide access to the internet and generally provides little if any exclusive content of its own. In the U.S., the Online Copyright Infringement Liability Limitation Act (OCILLA) portion of the U.S. Digital Millennium Copyright Act has expanded the legal definition of online service in two different ways for different portions of the law. It states in section 512(k):

(A) As used in subsection (a), the term "service provider" means an entity offering the transmission, routing, or providing of connections for digital online communications, between or among points specified by a user, of material of the user's choosing, without modification to the content of the material as sent or received.

(B) As used in this section, other than subsection (a), the term "service provider" means a provider of online services or network access, or the operator of facilities therefor, and includes an entity described in subparagraph (A).

### 3.1.1 Level 1 connectivity

Level 1 access through a gateway. Level 1 services are limited to what gateway supports. For example, department's or university's computer network.

### 3.1.2 Level 2 connectivity

Level 2 access via modem to host connected to network.

- Services are limited to what the connected to host ($H_2$) provides.
- Everything is accomplished through $H_2$.
- File transfers from Internet to $H_1$, requires two downloads:
  a) Internet to $H_2$.
  b) H2 to $H_1$.
- Level 2 connectivity is the most common of Internet access.

### 3.1.3 Level 3 connectivity

Some local companies provide Serial Line Interface Protocol (SLIP) or Point to Point Protocol (PPP) internet access.

#### *3.1.3.1 Serial Line Internet Protocol (SLIP)*

A commonly used abbreviation for the type of dialup Internet access that integrates your computer with the Internet. It is an older serial line protocol that does not support automatic negotiation of network configurations. It has been since replaced by Point to Point Protocol (PPP), mentioned next.

#### *3.1.3.2 Point to Point Protocol (PPP)*

One of the two standards for directly connecting computers to the Internet via dialup telephone connections. Unlike SLIP, PPP incorporates superior data negotiation, compression, and error corrections. However, these features add overhead to data transmission, and are unnecessary when both the sending and receiving modems offer hardware error correction and on-the-fly data compression.

A typical dial-up session using PPP is completely automated and requires no real-time user input. It has four stages:

- **Link establishment**: PPP user Link Control Protocol (LCP) to establish and maintain a PPP link over a serial transmission line. LCP frames are sent over the data link to test its integrity and establish the link.
- **User authentication**: PPP uses one of several authentication protocols.
- **Call back**: PPP call back control user Call Back Control Protocol (CBCP) if it is configured.
- **Configuration**: Network Connection Protocol (NCP) are used to establish network connections, perform compression and encryption, lease IP addresses using Dynamic Host Configuration Protocol (DHCP) and so on. NCP frames are sent over the link to establish a network connection between the PPP server and the remote PPP client.

## 3.2 Setting up a Connection

The Internet Connectivity Wizard can be accessed through Start/Accessories/Communications/Internet Connection Wizard. This has in all 10 screens, which come on screen one by one and ask you for information to be provided by you. Once done you will have the internet connection. They are self-explanatory, so no explanation is required. The screens are shown on the next pages.

## 3.3 Hardware requirements

To connect to Internet, you need to have the followings:

1. A computer system with a software like Microsoft Internet Explorer or Netscape Navigator loaded into it.
2. A telephone line. It will be better to have a dedicated telephone line, i.e., a line exclusively for your Internet connection only. It is because, with the passage of time, you may fine that you are spending most of your time on the Net. This will prevent others from using your telephone or calling you, as

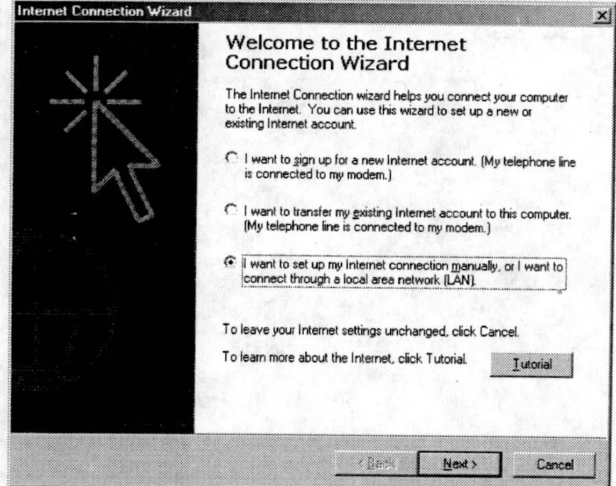

Internet Connection Wizard
Welcome to the Internet Connection Wizard
The Internet Connection wizard helps you connect your computer to the Internet. You can use this wizard to set up a new or existing Internet account.
I want to sign up for a new Internet account. (My telephone line is connected to my modem.)
I want to transfer my existing Internet account to this computer. (My telephone line is connected to my modem.)
I want to set up my Internet connection manually, or I want to connect through a local area network (LAN).
To leave your Internet settings unchanged, click Cancel.
To learn more about the Internet, click Tutorial.
Tutorial
< Back
Next >
Cancel


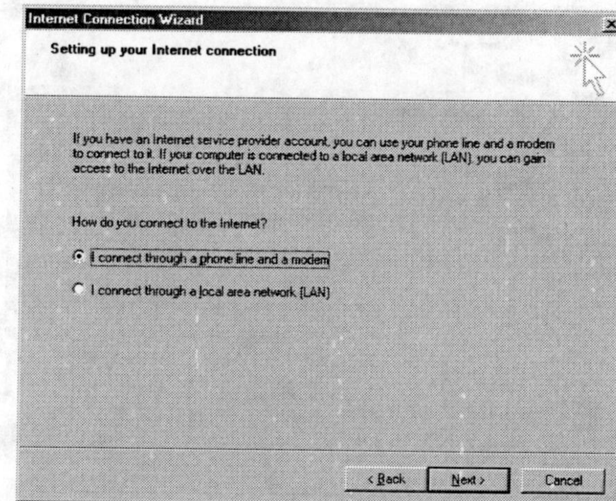

Internet Connection Wizard
Setting up your Internet connection
If you have an Internet service provider account, you can use your phone line and a modem to connect to it. If your computer is connected to a local area network (LAN), you can gain access to the Internet over the LAN.
How do you connect to the Internet?
I connect through a phone line and a modem
I connect through a local area network (LAN)
< Back
Next >
Cancel


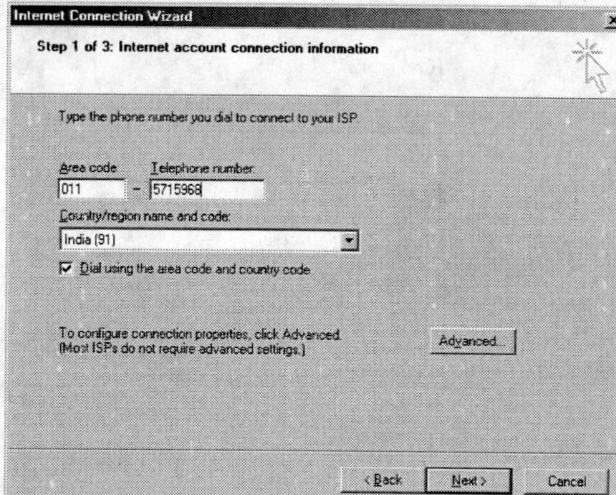

Internet Connection Wizard
Step 1 of 3: Internet account connection information
Type the phone number you dial to connect to your ISP.
Area code:
Telephone number:
011
5715968
Country/region name and code:
India (91)
Dial using the area code and country code
To configure connection properties, click Advanced. (Most ISPs do not require advanced settings.)
Advanced...
< Back
Next >
Cancel


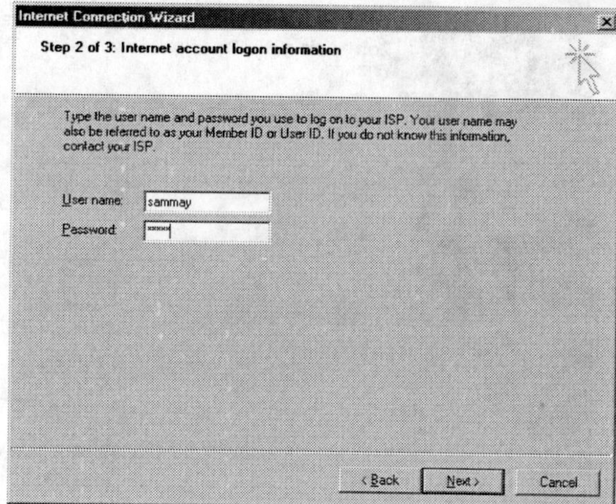

Internet Connection Wizard
Step 2 of 3: Internet account logon information
Type the user name and password you use to log on to your ISP. Your user name may also be referred to as your Member ID or User ID. If you do not know this information, contact your ISP.
User name:
sammay
Password:
< Back
Next >
Cancel


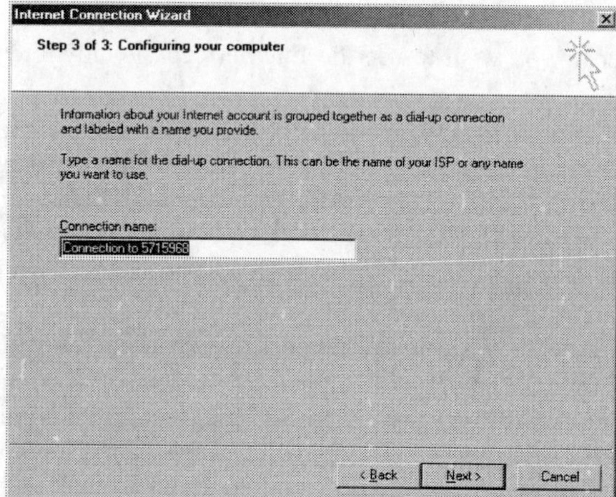

Internet Connection Wizard
Step 3 of 3: Configuring your computer
Information about your Internet account is grouped together as a dial-up connection and labeled with a name you provide.
Type a name for the dial-up connection. This can be the name of your ISP or any name you want to use.
Connection name:
Connection to 5715968
< Back
Next >
Cancel


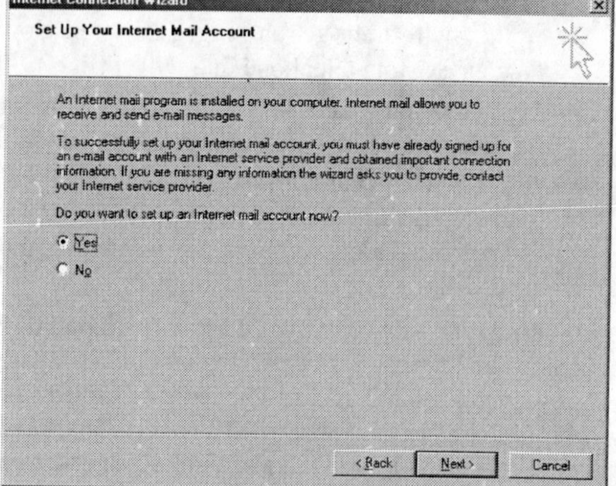

Internet Connection Wizard
Set Up Your Internet Mail Account
An Internet mail program is installed on your computer. Internet mail allows you to receive and send e-mail messages.
To successfully set up your Internet mail account, you must have already signed up for an e-mail account with an Internet service provider and obtained important connection information. If you are missing any information the wizard asks you to provide, contact your Internet service provider.
Do you want to set up an Internet mail account now?
Yes
No
< Back
Next >
Cancel

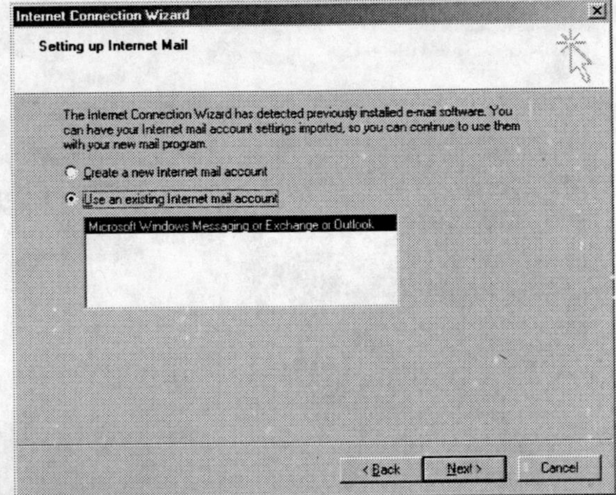


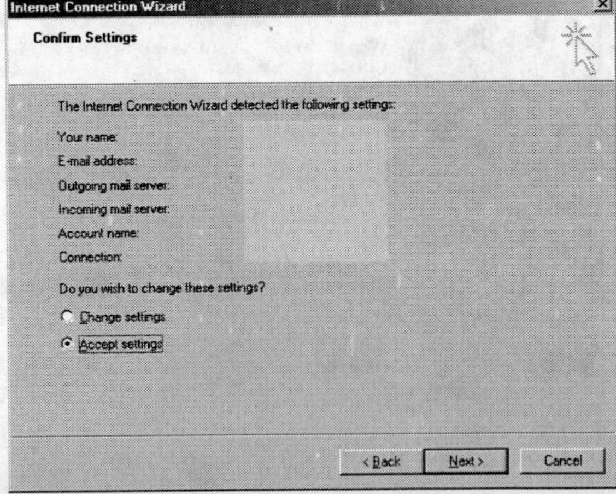


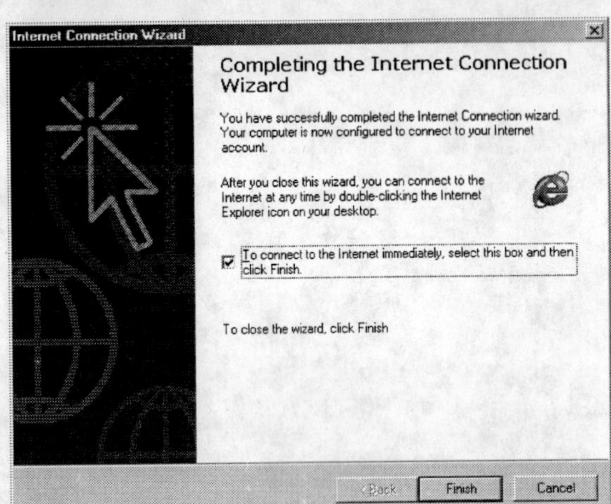


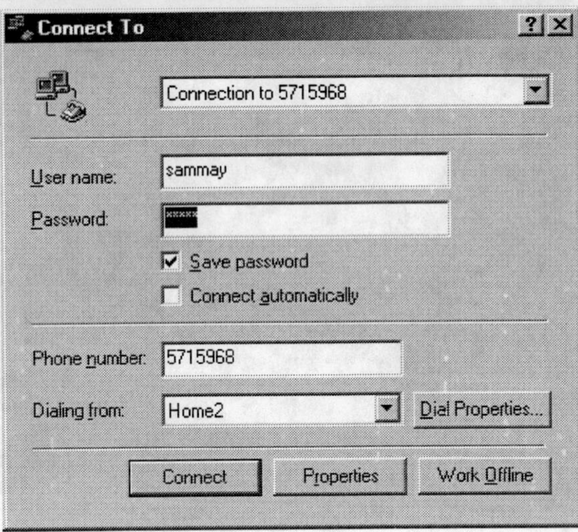


they will often get an 'engaged' tone. However, if you wish to use the Internet occasionally, then your existing telephone line will suffice.

3. A modem (modular-demodulator) is a electronic device that converts digital data from computers into signals. These signals can then be transmitted over a normal telephone line. At the receiving end, another modem converts the signals back into digital data understood by computers. Modems can be internal, i.e., inserted in a slot on your computer's motherboard or external, i.e., fitted externally. Irrespective of whether your modem is internal or external, you will need a jack to connect your telephone line to your computer.
4. As mentioned earlier, there are companies who provide you with the services of providing you with the Internet Services. They are called Internet Service Provider (ISP). You have to open an account with ISP to have the connection. An ISP is a company that gives you access to the Internet for a fee. Presently, a number of ISPs are available in India. These include VSNL (Videsh Sanchar Nigam Limited); Satyam Online; Mantra Online; Tata Nova; etc. Each one of these allow you to open an account with them and they would give an e-mail address too.

## 3.4 Selection of a Modem

A modem (modulator-demodulator) is a device that modulates an analog carrier signal to encode digital information, and also demodulates such a carrier signal to decode the transmitted information. The goal is to produce a signal that can be transmitted easily and decoded to reproduce the original digital data. Modems can be used over any means of transmitting analog signals, from driven diodes to radio.

The most familiar example is a voiceband modem that turns the digital 1s and 0s of a personal computer into sounds that can be transmitted over the telephone lines of plain old telephone services (POTS), and once received on the other side, converts those 1s and 0s back into a form used by a USB, Ethernet, serial, or network connection.

Modems are generally classified by the amount of data they can send in a given time, normally measured in bits per second (bit/s, or bps). They can also be classified by Baud, the number of times the modem changes its signal state per second. For example, the ITU V.21 standard used audio frequency-shift keying, aka tones, to carry 300 bit/s using 300 baud, whereas the original ITU V.22 standard allowed 1,200 bit/s with 600 baud using phase-shift keying.

Faster modems are used by Internet users every day, notably cable modems and ADSL modems. In telecommunications, wide-band radio modems transmit repeating frames of data at very high data rates over microwave radio links. Narrow-band radio modem is used for low data rate up to 19.2k mainly for private radio networks. Some microwave modems transmit more than a hundred million bits per second. Optical modems transmit data over optical fibers. Most intercontinental data links now use optical modems transmitting over undersea optical fibers. Optical modems routinely have data rates in excess of a billion (1x109) bits per second. One kilobit per second (kbit/s, kb/s, or kbps) as used in this article means 1,000 bits per second and not 1,024 bits per second. For example, a 56k modem can transfer data at up to 56,000 bit/s (7 kB/s) over the phone line.

In the summer of 1960, the name Data-Phone was introduced to replace the earlier term digital subset. The 202 Data-Phone was a half-duplex asynchronous service that was marketed extensively in late 1960. In 1962, the 201A and 201B Data-Phones were introduced. They were synchronous modems using two-bit-per-baud phase-shift keying (PSK). The 201A operated half-duplex at 2,000 bit/s over normal phone lines, while the 201B provided full duplex 2,400 bit/s service on four-wire leased lines, the send and receive channels running on their own set of two wires each.

The famous Bell 103A dataset standard was also introduced by Bell Labs in 1962. It provided full-duplex service at 300 baud over normal phone lines. Frequency-shift keying was used with the call originator transmitting at 1,070 or 1,270 Hz and the answering modem transmitting at 2,025 or 2,225 Hz. The readily available 103A2 gave an important boost to the use of remote low-speed terminals such as the KSR33, the ASR33, and the IBM 2741. AT&T reduced modem costs by introducing the originate-only 113D and the answer-only 113B/C modems.

The modem is a device which allows you to connect your computer to any other computer, anywhere else in the world using a telephone line. This allows you to communicate with the connected person, transfer data, copy software/programs from the connected computer, sent and received mail using e-mail, etc.

Currently, the modem can also be used to sent and receive fax, for this you use modem as fax device. Also you can use modem to connect to the Internet. There are two main types of modems: Internal and External Modems. When the computer is switched on and is ready to transmit data, it sends a Data Terminal Ready (DTR) signal to the modem. When the modem is ready to receive data or instruction from the computer, it sends a Data Set Ready (DSR) signal to the computer. Both these signals must be present before the next step can happen. Next, the computer sends a command to the modem to go "Off Hook", *i.e.*, to open communication with the phone line. Next, the computer issues a command to modem to dial a phone number.

## 3.5 Software requirement

If you are using Windows 2000 or XP system software, appropriate 16 bit TCP/IP stack software will be required. Most of these have an auto-instal program, which, during installation will ask for two IP addresses for the DNS services, one primary and one secondary. If you are also installing e-mail software such as Eudora, then one more IP address, for a SMTP server, needs to be entered.

For a TCP/IP account, in addition to the browser and e-mail applications, you may need software for other applications, like Telnet and FTP. Internet software such as **Chameleon** and **Internet in a Box**, usually, have many of these applications bundled in. Application software packages for networking employ a desing called client/server architecture, where the software sitting on the PC. i.e., your software packages, are optimized for ease-of-use and may be referred to as the **Client**.

## 3.6 Modem configuration

There are two ways by which the modem can be installed. One of them is Automatically and the other is Manually.

### *3.6.0.1 Automatically*

After connecting the modem when you switch on the computer system, Windows 95/98 should automatically detect the modem and ask for the modem driver software. If the auto detection does not work then:

1. Click on the Start/Setting/Controls Panel.
2. In the control panel window double click on Add New Hardware icon.
3. In the next Add New Hardware Wizard screen, to automatically detect new hardware click on Next>option.
4. In the next screen select Yes for Do you want Windows to search for your new hardware? question and click on Next option.
5. Click on Modem to select it.
6. Click on the Next>option, it will start the auto detection process, which may take some time.
7. Finally next screen will appear with an option to click on Details..... button to see the list of detected hardware.
8. Click on Finish option to install the drivers for the detected hardware.

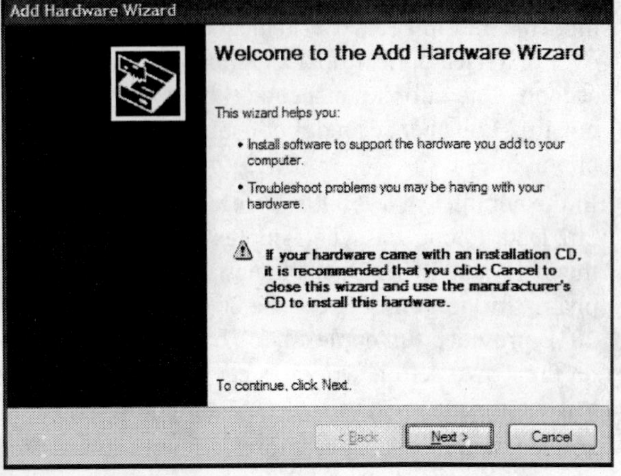


If your modem was not detected during this process then you need to manually install the modem driver software.

### *3.6.0.2 Manually*

For this, follow the above instructions for step 1 & 2 and in the 3rd, in Add New Hardware Wizard screen, do the following:

1. Click on No, I want to select the hardware for a list, to the Do you want Windows to search for your new hardware? question.
2. Click on Next>option.
3. In the next screen a list of hardware appear, from the list click on Modem.
4. Click on Next>option.

5. Next Windows will try to automatically detect the modem.

To manually install the modem driver,

1. Click on Don't detect my modem; I will select it from a list.
2. Click on Next>option. A list of modem manufacturers and their modem models are shown on the next screen. There is also an option called Have Disk ....., if you have received a modem driver disk or CD with your modem then.
3. Click on the Have Disk . . . . option.
4. Place the driver disk/CD into proper drive and in the next Install From Disk screen select the proper drive. You can also click on Browse . . . . option to search for the driver disk/CD.
5. Once the driver is found on disk, click on OK, this will install the modem driver into the computer system. The driver could be on some sub-directory of the driver disk/CD, check the manual that came with the modem.
6. Restart the computer to make the modem active.

Sometimes the driver disk/CD that comes with the modem contains a SETUP.EXE or INSTALL.EXE program. Running this program will automatically install the modem driver to the Windows.

## 3.7 Internet accounts by ISP

An Internet Service Provider (ISP), also sometimes referred to as an Internet access provider (IAP), is a company that offers its customers access to the Internet. The ISP connects to its customers using a data transmission technology appropriate for delivering Internet Protocol datagrams, such as dial-up, DSL, cable modem, wireless or dedicated high-speed interconnects.

ISPs may provide Internet e-mail accounts to users which allow them to communicate with one another by sending and receiving electronic messages through their ISP's servers. (As part of their e-mail service, ISPs usually offer the user an e-mail client software package, developed either internally or through an outside contract arrangement. ISPs may provide other services such as remotely storing data files on behalf of their customers, as well as other services unique to each particular ISP.

### 3.7.1 Telephone line options

See section 3.8 for Telephone Line Options

### 3.7.2 Protocol options

See section 3.9 for Protocol Options.

### 3.7.3 Service options

See section 3.10 for Service Options.

## 3.8 Telephone Line Options

If you are using the telephone system to get onto the Internet your telecommunication connection follows either the normal phone system (POTS) or an ISDN or ADSI, line until it reaches the telephone company's central office. The central office router calls either through its own network of copper fiber optic, or satellite links, or to a long distance carrier's point of presence or POP. The POP is the point at which a local call is handed off to a long distance company. The call is then routed to the central office nearest your Internet Service Provider (ISP).

### 3.8.1 Dialup connections through the telephone system

Dial-up Internet access is a form of Internet access that uses telephone lines. The user's computer or router uses an attached modem connected to a telephone line to dial into an Internet service provider's (ISP) node to establish a modem-to-modem link, which is then used to route Internet Protocol packets between the user's equipment and hosts.

The term was coined during the early days of computer telecommunications when modems were needed to connect dumb terminals or computers running terminal emulator software to mainframes, minicomputers, online services and bulletin board systems via a telephone line.

Dial-up connections to the Internet require no infrastructure other than the telephone network. As telephone access is widely available, dial-up remains useful to travelers. Dial-up is usually the only choice available for rural or remote areas where broadband installations are not prevalent due to low population and demand. Dial-up access may also be an alternative for users on limited budgets as it is offered for free by some ISPs, though broadband is increasingly available at lower prices in many countries due to market competition.

Dial-up requires time to establish a usable telephone connection (several seconds, depending on the location) and perform handshaking for protocol synchronization before data transfers can take place. In locales with telephone connection charges, each connection incurs an incremental cost. If calls are time-metered, the duration of the connection incurs costs. Dial-up access is a transient connection, because either the user or the ISP terminates the connection. Internet service providers will often set a limit on connection durations to prevent hogging of access, and will disconnect the user — requiring reconnection and the costs and delays associated with it. Technically-inclined users often find a way to disable the auto-disconnect program such that they can remain connected for days. This is particularly useful for downloading large files such as videos.

A 2008 Pew Internet and American Life Project study states that only 10 percent of American adults still use dial-up Internet access. Reasons for retaining dial-up access span from lack of infrastructure to high broadband prices.

### 3.8.2 Dedicated connections through the telephone system

Dedicated connections are also called leased lines. Leased lines are direct cables laid to conect your computer to an Internet Service Provider's (ISPs) server. Dedicated links provide high speed connection to user. Modems are not required for the direct lines.

## 3.9 ISDN

Integrated Services Digital Network (ISDN) is a set of communications standards for simultaneous digital transmission of voice, video, data, and other network services over the traditional circuits of the public switched telephone network.

Prior to ISDN, the phone system was viewed as a way to transport voice, with some special services available for data. The key feature of ISDN is that it integrates speech and data on the same lines, adding features that were not available in the classic telephone system. There are several kinds of access interfaces to ISDN defined as Basic Rate Interface (BRI), Primary Rate Interface (PRI) and Broadband ISDN (B-ISDN).

ISDN is a circuit-switched telephone network system, which also provides access to packet switched networks, designed to allow digital transmission of voice and data over ordinary telephone copper wires, resulting in potentially better voice quality than an analog phone can provide. It offers circuit-switched connections (for either voice or data), and packet-switched connections (for data), in increments of 64 kilobit/s. A major market application for ISDN in some countries is Internet access, where ISDN typically provides a maximum of 128 kbit/s in both upstream and downstream directions. ISDN B-channels can be bonded to achieve a greater data rate, typically 3 or 4 BRIs (6 to 8 64 kbit/s channels) are bonded.

ISDN should not be mistaken for its use with a specific protocol, such as Q.931 whereby ISDN is employed as the network, data-link and physical layers in the context of the OSI model. In a broad sense ISDN can be considered a suite of digital services existing on layers 1, 2, and 3 of the OSI model. ISDN is designed to provide access to voice and data services simultaneously.

However, common use has reduced ISDN to be limited to Q.931 and related protocols, which are a set of protocols for establishing and breaking circuit switched connections, and for advanced call features for the user. They were introduced in 1986.

In a videoconference, ISDN provides simultaneous voice, video, and text transmission between individual desktop videoconferencing systems and group (room) videoconferencing systems.

## 3.10 Protocol options

### 3.10.1 Shell

A shell is a piece of software that provides an interface for users to an operating system shell which provides access to the services of a kernel. However, the term is also applied very loosely to applications and may include any software that is "built around" a particular component, such as web browsers and email clients that are "shells" for HTML rendering engines. The name shell originates from shells being an outer layer of interface between the user and the innards of the operating system (the kernel).

Operating system shells generally fall into one of two categories: command-line and graphical. Command-line shells provide a command-line interface (CLI) to the operating system, while graphical shells provide a graphical user interface (GUI). In either category the primary purpose of the shell is to invoke or "launch" another program; however, shells frequently have additional capabilities such as viewing the contents of directories.

The relative merits of CLI- and GUI-based shells are often debated. CLI proponents claim that certain operations can be performed much faster under CLI shells than under GUI shells (such as moving files, for example). However, GUI proponents advocate the comparative usability and simplicity of GUI shells. The best choice is often determined by the way in which a computer will be used. On a server mainly used for data transfers and processing with expert administration, a CLI is likely to be the best choice. On the other hand, a GUI would be more appropriate for a computer to be used for image or video editing and the development of the above data.

In expert systems, a shell is a piece of software that is an "empty" expert system without the knowledge base for any particular application.

### 3.10.2 SLIP

The Serial Line Internet Protocol (SLIP) is a mostly obsolete encapsulation of the Internet Protocol designed to work over serial ports and modem connections. It is documented in RFC 1055. On personal computers, SLIP has been largely replaced by the Point-to-Point Protocol (PPP), which is better engineered, has more features and does not require its IP address configuration to be set before it is established. On microcontrollers, however, SLIP is still the preferred way of encapsulating IP packets due to its very small overhead.

SLIP modifies a standard TCP/IP datagram by appending a special "SLIP END" character to it, which distinguishes datagram boundaries in the byte stream. SLIP requires a serial port configuration of 8 data bits, no parity, and either EIA hardware flow control, or CLOCAL mode (3-wire null-modem) UART operation settings.

SLIP does not provide error detection, being reliant on upper layer protocols for this. Therefore SLIP on its own is not satisfactory over an error-prone dial-up connection. It is however still useful for testing operating systems' response capabilities under load (by looking at flood-ping statistics).

SLIP is also currently used in the BlueCore Serial Protocol for communication between Bluetooth modules and host computers

### 3.10.3 PPP

In networking, the Point-to-Point Protocol, or PPP, is a data link protocol commonly used to establish a direct connection between two networking nodes. It can provide connection authentication, transmission encryption privacy, and compression.

PPP is used over many types of physical networks including serial cable, phone line, trunk line, cellular telephone, specialized radio links, and fiber optic links such as SONET. Most Internet service providers (ISPs) use PPP for customer dial-up access to the Internet. Two encapsulated forms of PPP, Point-to-Point Protocol over Ethernet (PPPoE) and Point-to-Point Protocol over ATM (PPPoA), are used by Internet Service Providers (ISPs) to connect Digital Subscriber Line (DSL) Internet service.

PPP is commonly used as a data link layer protocol for connection over synchronous and asynchronous circuits, where it has largely superseded the older, non-standard Serial Line Internet Protocol (SLIP) and telephone company mandated standards (such as Link Access Protocol, Balanced (LAPB) in the X.25 protocol suite). PPP was designed to work with numerous network layer protocols, including Internet Protocol (IP), Novell's Internetwork Packet Exchange (IPX), NBF and AppleTalk.

PPP is also used over broadband connections. RFC 2516 describes Point-to-Point Protocol over Ethernet (PPPoE), a method for transmitting PPP over Ethernet that is sometimes used with DSL. RFC 2364 describes Point-to-Point Protocol over ATM (PPPoA), a method for transmitting PPP over ATM Adaptation Layer 5 (AAL5), which is also sometimes used with DSL.

## 3.11 Service Options

### 3.11.1 E-mail

Electronic mail, most commonly abbreviated email and e-mail, is a method of exchanging digital messages. E-mail systems are based on a store-and-forward model in which e-mail computer server systems accept, forward, deliver and store messages on behalf of users, who only need to connect to the e-mail infrastructure, typically an e-mail server, with a network-enabled device for the duration of message submission or retrieval. Originally, e-mail was always transmitted directly from one user's device to another's; nowadays this is rarely the case.

An electronic mail message consists of two components, the message header, and the message body, which is the email's content. The message header contains control information, including, minimally, an originator's email address and one or more recipient addresses. Usually additional information is added, such as a subject header field.

Originally a text-only communications medium, email was extended to carry multi-media content attachments, which were standardized in with RFC 2045 through RFC 2049, collectively called, Multipurpose Internet Mail Extensions (MIME).

The foundation for today's global Internet e-mail service was created in the early ARPANET and standards for encoding of messages were proposed as early as 1973 (RFC 561). An e-mail sent in the early 1970s looked very similar to one sent on the Internet today. Conversion from the ARPANET to the Internet in the early 1980s produced the core of the current service.

Network-based email was initially exchanged on the ARPANET in extensions to the File Transfer Protocol (FTP), but is today carried by the Simple Mail Transfer Protocol (SMTP), first published as Internet standard 10 (RFC 821) in 1982. In the process of transporting e-mail messages between systems, SMTP communicates delivery parameters using a message envelope separately from the message (header and body) itself.

### 3.11.2 WWW

The World Wide Web, abbreviated as WWW and commonly known as The Web, is a system of interlinked hypertext documents contained on the Internet. With a web browser, one can view web pages that may contain text, images, videos, and other multimedia and navigate between them by using hyperlinks. Using concepts from earlier hypertext systems, British engineer and computer scientist Sir Tim Berners Lee, now the Director of the World Wide Web Consortium, wrote a proposal in March 1989 for what would eventually become the World Wide Web. He was later joined by Belgian computer scientist Robert Cailliau while both were working at CERN in Geneva, Switzerland. In 1990, they proposed using "HyperText [...] to link and access information of various kinds as a web of nodes in which the user can browse at will", and released that web in December.

"The World-Wide Web (W3) was developed to be a pool of human knowledge, which would allow collaborators in remote sites to share their ideas and all aspects of a common project." If two projects are independently created, rather than have a central figure make the changes, the two bodies of information could form into one cohesive piece of work.

### 3.11.3 News Firewall

A firewall is a part of a computer system or network that is designed to block unauthorized access while permitting authorized communications. It is a device or set of devices configured to permit, deny, encrypt, decrypt, or proxy all (in and out) computer traffic between different security domains based upon a set of rules and other criteria.

Firewalls can be implemented in either hardware or software, or a combination of both. Firewalls are frequently used to prevent unauthorized Internet users from accessing private networks connected to the Internet, especially intranets. All messages entering or leaving the intranet pass through the firewall, which examines each message and blocks those that do not meet the specified security criteria.

There are several types of firewall techniques:

Packet filter: Packet filtering inspects each packet passing through the network and accepts or rejects it based on user-defined rules. Although difficult to configure, it is fairly effective and mostly transparent to its users. It is susceptible to IP spoofing.

Application gateway: Applies security mechanisms to specific applications, such as FTP and Telnet servers. This is very effective, but can impose a performance degradation.

Circuit-level gateway: Applies security mechanisms when a TCP or UDP connection is established. Once the connection has been made, packets can flow between the hosts without further checking.

Proxy server: Intercepts all messages entering and leaving the network. The proxy server effectively hides the true network addresses.

### Let us Revise

1. There are many ways of connecting to the Internet. Some of them are easy and some of them are difficult.
2. In the context of traditional computer terminals that communicate over a serial RS-232 connection, dumb terminals are those that can interpret a limited number of control codes.
3. A terminal emulator, terminal application, term, or tty for short, is a program that emulates a "dumb" video terminal within some other display architecture.
4. LANs or large computers such as mainframes can be directly connected to the Internet.
5. The Serial Line Internet Protocol (SLIP) is a mostly obsolete encapsulation of the Internet Protocol designed to work over serial ports and modem connections.
6. Point to Point (PPP) is used over many types of physical networks including serial cable, phone line, trunk line, cellular telephone, specialized radio links, and fiber optic links such as SONET.
7. Integrated Services Digital Network (ISDN) is a set of communications standards for simultaneous digital transmission of voice, video, data, and other network services over the traditional circuits of the public switched telephone network.

8. A cable modem is a type of network bridge and modem that provides bi-directional data communication via radio frequency channels on a cable television (CATV) infrastructure.
9. MSN TV (formerly WebTV) is the name of both a thin client which uses a television for display (rather than a computer monitor), and the online service that supports it.
10. Level 1 access through a gateway. Level 1 services are limited to what gateway supports.
11. Level 2 access via modem to host connected to network.
12. The Internet Connectivity Wizard can be accessed through Start/Accessories/Communications/Internet Connection Wizard.
13. A modem (modulator-demodulator) is a device that modulates an analog carrier signal to encode digital information, and also demodulates such a carrier signal to decode the transmitted information.
14. For a TCP/IP account, in addition to the browser and e-mail applications, you may need software for other applications, like Telnet and FTP.
15. The ISP connects to its customers using a data transmission technology appropriate for delivering Internet Protocol datagrams, such as dial-up, DSL, cable modem, wireless or dedicated high-speed interconnects.
16. Dial-up Internet access is a form of Internet access that uses telephone lines.
17. A shell is a piece of software that provides an interface for users to an operating system shell which provides access to the services of a kernel.
18. The Serial Line Internet Protocol (SLIP) is a mostly obsolete encapsulation of the Internet Protocol designed to work over serial ports and modem connections.
19. Electronic mail, most commonly abbreviated email and e-mail, is a method of exchanging digital messages.
20. The World Wide Web, abbreviated as WWW and commonly known as The Web, is a system of interlinked hypertext documents contained on the Internet.

## Multiple Choice Questions

1. WWW is :
   **(a) World Wide Web** (b) Word Wide Web (c) World Way Web
2. SLIP is :
   (a) Serial Line Internet Product
   **(b) Serial Line Internet Protocol**
   (c) Serial Live Internet Protocol
3. FTP is :
   (a) File Transfer Produc (b) File To Protocol **(c) File Transfer Protocol**
4. PPP is :
   **(a) Point to Point Protocol** (b) Point to Point Prompt (c) Point to Power Protocol
5. ISDN is :
   (a) Integrated Serial Digital Network
   **(b) Integrated Services Digital Network**
   (c) Integrated Services Direct Network

## True/False Questions

1. A terminal emulator, terminal application, term, or tty for short, is a program that emulates a "dumb" video terminal within some other display architecture.
2. LANs or large computers such as mainframes can be directly connected to the Internet.

3. Point to Point (PPP) is used over many types of physical networks including serial cable, phone line, trunk line, cellular telephone, specialized radio links, and fiber optic links such as SONET.
4. **A cable modem is not a type** of network bridge and modem that provides bi-directional data communication via radio frequency channels on a cable television (CATV) infrastructure.
5. Level 1 access through a gateway. Level 1 services are limited to what gateway supports.
6. Level 2 access via modem to host connected to network.
7. A modem (modulator-demodulator) is a device that modulates an analog carrier signal to encode digital information, and also demodulates such a carrier signal to decode the transmitted information.
8. **Dial-up Internet** access is a form of Internet access that does not use telephone lines.
9. A shell is a piece of software that provides an interface for users to an operating system shell which provides access to the services of a kernel.
10. Electronic mail, most commonly abbreviated email and e-mail, is a method of exchanging digital messages.

## Match Columns

Match the matter in Column A with the matter in Column B.

| Column A | Column B | |
|---|---|---|
| A. Dumb Terminal | 1. Point to Point Protocol | H |
| B. Terminal emulation | 2. World Wide Web | I |
| C. SLIP | 3. Device to watch TV on the net | F |
| D. E-mail | 4. Modulator-Demodulator | G |
| E. ISDN | 5. Method of sending mail through Internet | D |
| F. WebTV | 6. Emulates the Terminal | B |
| G Modem | 7. Terminal with limited controls | A |
| H. PPP | 8. Serial Line Internet Protocol | C |
| I. WWW | 9. Integrated Services Digital Network | E |

## Fill in the Blanks with Appropriate Words

a. Integrated Services Digital Network (ISDN) b. modem c. telephone
d. TCP/IP e. cable modem f. dumb terminals g. Point to Point (PPP)
h. Electronic Mail i. Serial Line Internet Protocol (SLIP)

1. In the context of traditional computer terminals that communicate over a serial RS-232 connection, ________ are those that can interpret a limited number of control codes.
2. The __________________________ is a mostly obsolete encapsulation of the Internet Protocol designed to work over serial ports and modem connections.
3. ______________ is used over many types of physical networks including serial cable, phone line, trunk line, cellular telephone, specialized radio links, and fiber optic links such as SONET.
4. ___________________ is a set of communications standards for simultaneous digital transmission of voice, video, data, and other network services over the traditional circuits of the public switched telephone network.
5. A _____________ is a type of network bridge and modem that provides bi-directional data communication via radio frequency channels on a cable television (CATV) infrastructure.
6. A __________ is a device that modulates an analog carrier signal to encode digital information, and also demodulates such a carrier signal to decode the transmitted information.
7. For a _________ account, in addition to the browser and e-mail applications, you may need software for other applications, like Telnet and FTP.

8. Dial-up Internet access is a form of Internet access that uses ________ lines.
9. ____________, most commonly abbreviated email and e-mail, is a method of exchanging digital messages.

## Descriptive Type Questions

1. Describe the various connectivity types.
2. How would you set up a connection?
3. What are the Hardware requirements?
4. What are the Software requirements?
5. Describe how would you configure Modem.
6. Describe the following terms

| | |
|---|---|
| Dumb Terminal | Terminal emulation |
| SLIP | ISDN |
| WebTV | ISP |
| Shell | PPP |
| E-mail | WWW |
| Firewall | |

## Answers to Objective Type Questions

### *Multiple Choice Questions*

| | | | |
|---|---|---|---|
| 1. a | 2. b | 3. c | 4. a |
| 5. b | | | |

### *True False Questions*

| | | | |
|---|---|---|---|
| 1. T | 2. T | 3. T | 4. F |
| 5. T | 6. T | 7. T | 8. F |
| 9. T | 10. T | | |

### *Matching Columns*

| | | | |
|---|---|---|---|
| A. 7 | B. 6 | C. 8 | D. 5 |
| E. 9 | F. 3 | G. 4 | H. 1 |
| I. 2 | | | |

### *Fill in the Blanks*

| | | | |
|---|---|---|---|
| 1. f | 2. i | 3. g | 4. a |
| 5. e | 6. b | 7. d | 8. c |
| 9. h | | | |

# Internet Network 4

## 4.1 Network definition

It is not that the Personal Computers are for personal use only. They can be used for sharing of information too with others having similar type of equipments. Logically it sometimes is fisible to have a number of PCs then having a bigger computer which can give the same thoughput as the number of PCs. But, overall it becomes a expensive proposition and sometimes is not fisible, specially for individuals and small businesses or small companies.

Another problem arises for those who are physically placed at a distance. They would need to send messages and receive messages, or use the same data at, or share program at, many different locations. One answer to this problem is to keep separate data files at each location, but this approach is very costly and potentially a dangerous solution. It is very expensive to maintain these redundant files of data and difficult to ensure the continuing accuracy of data at any one location. The solution of both, the need for more power and the ability to receive, send messages and share data, are found in data communication technology.

## 4.2 Common terminologies

### 4.2.1 LAN

A network covering a small geographic area, like a home, office, or building. Current LANs are most likely to be based on Ethernet technology. The defining characteristics of LANs, in contrast to WANs (wide area networks), include their much higher data transfer rates, smaller geographic range, and lack of a need for leased telecommunication lines.

A local area network (LAN) is two or more computers directly linked within a small well-defined area such as a room, building, or group of closely placed buildings. A LAN may be made up of only microcomputers or any combination of microcomputers and large systems.

A LAN usually consists of the following:

1. Two or more computers
2. Peripheral devices such as printers and hard-disk drives
3. Software to control the operation of the computers or other devices connected to the LAN
4. Special cables, usually coaxial or fibre optic, to connect the computers and other devices
5. A plug-in board to handle the data transmissions.

Some computers require that all the computers be of a certain brand, while others allow a variety of brands to be connected. The number of computers in a LAN varies from smaller LANs that typically connect 2 to 25 computers, to large LANs that can connect as many as 10,000 computers.

The length of the cable connecting a computer to a LAN also varies depending on the LAN. Most LANs allow cables of about 1,000 feet, but some allow cables of several miles to be used. The data transfer speeds range from several thousand bits per second to around 10 million bits per second.

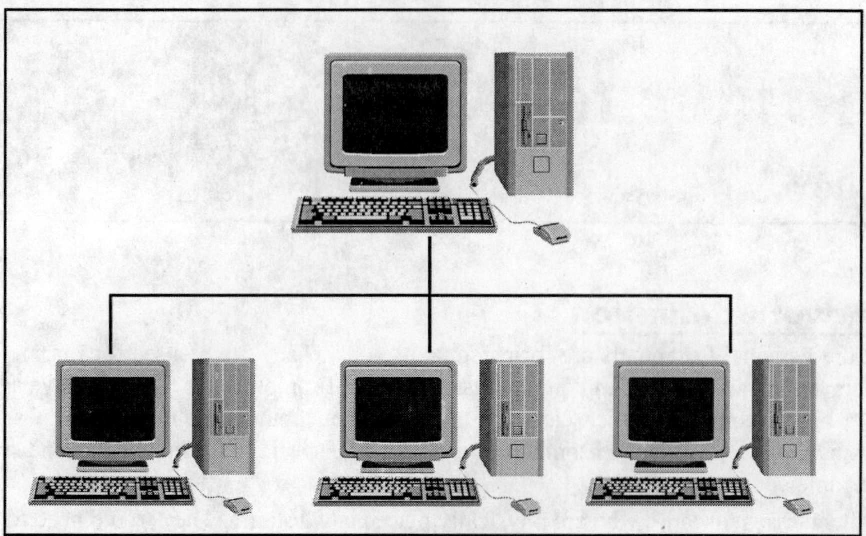

Some programs allow the user of more than one operating system; others allow only one. On some LANs file access is limited to one user at a time; on others, more than one user can access a file simultaneously.

#### *4.2.1.1 Hardware for LAN*

The following are the major hardware components/devices for establishing LAN:

1. Transmission Channel
2. Network Interface Unit or NIU
3. Servers
4. Workstations.

#### *4.2.1.2 Server and Workstations*

One of the major benefits of implementation of LAN is sharing expensive resources such as storage devices, printers, etc. This is achieved through providing servers on the LAN. It is dedicated computer that controls one or more resources. This contains both hardware and software interface for LAN. Three major categories of services used in LANs are:

1. File Server
2. Printer Server
3. Modem Server.

In networking, file server is used to share storage for files. Besides providing storage space for files in a LAN environment, it is used for taking periodical backup, and also to provide gateway to other servers with and between LANs. Similarly printer server is used to handle printing works of all workstations connected in the network. In LAN environment also modem is required to get connected to other network or simply to use a telephone. A modem server is used to share this expensive resource by all connected workstations in a network ring.

#### *4.2.1.3 Software for LAN*

LAN operating system is required to operate on the LAN system. It has basically two aspects:

1. Server Software
2. Workstation Software.

LAN operating system facilitates :

1. Sharing of expensive resources, e.g., printer, storage space, etc.
2. Security for data
3. Connection to other network.

There are various types of LAN operating system. Some popular LAN operating systems are :

— Novel Netware
— Ethernet
— Corvus
— ArcNet
— LAN Server
— Omni Net
— PC Net
— IBM PC LAN
— Etherlink Plus, etc.

#### *4.2.1.4 Features of Local Area Networks*

- Typically connects computer in a single building or campus.
- Developed in 1970s.
- Medium : optical fibres, coaxial cables, twisted pair, wireless.
- Low latency (except in high traffic periods).
- High speed networks (0.2 to 100 Mb/sec).
- Speeds adequate for most distributed systems
- Problems : Multi media based applications
- Typically buses or rings.
- Ethernet, Token Ring.

#### *4.2.1.5 Advantages of Local Area Networks*

- It allows sharing of expensive resources.
- High speed data transfer.
- More applications can be used.
- Increases productivity.

#### *4.2.1.6 Disadvantages of Local Area Networks*

- High cost.
- Required high memory.
- More manpower and resources needed to maintain.
- User loses control.
- Difficult to keep confidential.
- Data loss due to high memory requirements

### 4.2.2 WAN

A WAN is a data communications network that covers a relatively broad geographic area and that often uses transmission facilities provided by common carriers, such as telephone companies. WAN technologies generally function at the lower three layers of the OSI reference model: the physical layer, the data link layer, and the network layer. A wide area network is two or more computers that are geographically dispersed, linked by communication facilities such as telephone system or microwave relays. This type of network is usually limited to use by large corporations and government agencies because of the high cost involved in building and maintaining them. The main difference between a WAN and LAN is under the complete control of the owner, whereas the WAN needs the involvement of another authority like telecom department. LANs are successful and capable of handling very high data transfer rates at low cost because of the small area covered. Besides LANs have a lower error rate than WANs.

#### *4.2.2.1 Hardware Requirements for WAN*

There are mainly 4 hardware devices which are required to establish linkage between geographically separated computers. These are:

1. Bridges
2. Routers
3. Gateways
4. X.25 Standard Interface.

These are explained below.

**Bridges:** These are used to connect two LANs that use the identical protocols over a wide area. The bridge acts as an address filter which picks up packets from one LAN that are intended for a destination on another LAN and passes these packets on the network. The amount of processing required at the bridge is minimal because all the devices use the same protocols. In case the distance between two LANs is very large then the user is required to employ two identical bridges at either end of the communication link.

**Routers:** It is a special type of device that can be used to connect networks that may not be similar. Such type of devices provide connectivity between two LANs and two WANs over large geographical distances. These devices operate at the Network Layer of the OSI model. These devices participate in a routing protocol to access the network topology, and on the basis of this information routers compute the best route from a sender to the receiver.

**Gateways:** These are used to connect two dissimilar LANs. The terms Gateways and Routers are used interchangeably, though there is discriminating difference between the two. A router operates at the network layer whereas a gateway operates on the application layer of the OSI model. A gateway is required to convert data packets from one protocol format to another before forwarding it, as it connects two dissimilar networks.

**X.25 Standard Interface:** X.25 is a protocol for interfacing to a Public Packet Switched Network. It is not a protocol used for implementing a network. Two systems that support X.25 can't necessarily be connected back-to-back. They can only be connected through a DCE in a Public Packet Switched. International Telegraph and Telephone Consultative Committee (ITTCC) developed X.25 as the standard interface between the Data Terminal Equipment (DTE) and Data Circuit Terminating Equipment (DCTE). This recommendation has been widely accepted as the industry standard for public packet switched networks.

#### *4.2.2.2 Types of Wide Area Networks*

There are mainly two types of WAN:

**Public Networks:** These are those networks which are installed and run by the telecommunication authorities and are made available to any organization or individual who go for their subscription.

**Private Networks:** The basic technique used in all forms of private WAN is to use private circuits to link the locations to be served by the network. Between these fixed points the owner of the network has complete freedom to use the circuits in any way they want. They can use the circuits to carry large quantities of data or for high speed transmissions. Private wide area networks can be built using whatever standard technology is available.

#### 4.2.2.3 *Features of Wide Area Networks*

- Developed in 1960s.
- Generally covers large distances (states, countries, continents).
- Medium : communication circuits connected by routers.
- Routers forwards packets from one to another following a route from the sender to the receiver. Store-and-Forward
- Hosts are typically connected (or close to) the routers.
- Typical latencies : 100ms - 500ms.
- Problems with delays if using satellites.
- Typical speed : 20 - 2000 Kbits/s.
- Not (yet) suitable for distributed computing.
- New standards are changing the landscape.

### 4.2.3 Metropolitan Area Network or MAN

It is a larger network that usually spans several buildings in the same city or town. The IUB network is an example of a MAN.

#### 4.2.3.1 *Features of Metropolitan Area Networks*

- Generally covers towns and cities (50 kms)
- Developed in 1980s.
- Medium : optical fibres, cables.
- Data rates adequate for distributed computing applications.
- A typical standard is DQDB (Distributed Queue Dual Bus).
- Typical latencies : < 1 msec.
- Message routing is fast.

### 4.2.4 Personal Area Network (PAN)

PAN is used for communication among the personal devices (intrapersonal communication), or for connecting to a higher level network and Internet. The reach of a PAN is typically a few meters.

A personal area network (PAN) is used for communication among computer devices. For example,

- Telephones
- Personal digital assistants.

Personal area networks may be wired with computer buses such as USB and FireWire. A wireless personal area network (WPAN) can also be made possible with network technologies such as IrDA and Bluetooth.

### 4.2.5 Campus Area Network (CAN)

A network that connects two or more LANs but that is limited to a specific (possibly private) geographical area such as a college campus, industrial complex, or a military base. A CAN, may be considered a type of MAN (metropolitan area network), but is generally limited to an area that is smaller than a typical MAN.

## 4.3 Node

In networking, a device, such as a client computer, a server, or a shared printer, that is connected to the network and is capable of communicating with other network devices. 3. In tree structures, a location on the tree that can have links to one or more nodes below it. Some authors make a distinction between node and element, with an element being a given data type and a node comprising one or more elements as well as any supporting data structures

## 4.4 Host

A unique identification for a computer system on a TCP/IP network such as the Internet. The address is usually in the format of four numbers (between 1 and 254) separated by periods or dots (hence the slang term "dotted quak"). Each machine on the TCP/IP network must have its own address (such as 128.127.126.125), but a machine may also have a verbose alias such as anvahb. snabpub.com).

## 4.5 Workstation

High-performance, signal user microcomputer or minicomputer that has been specialized for graphics, CAD, CAE or scientific application. In a LAN, a personal computer that serves a signal user in contrast with a file server that serves all users in the network. Any terminal or personal computer.

## 4.6 Bandwidth

The measure of the amount of information (voice, data, video) that a particular communication medium can carry. It is expressed in cycles per second (Hertz), the bandwidth being the difference between the lower and highest frequencies transmitted. Bandwidth is also often stated in bits or bytes per second.

## 4.7 Interoperability

Referring to components of computer systems that are able to function in different environments. For example, Microsoft's NT operating system is interoperable on Intel, DEC Alpha, and other CPUs. Another example is the SCSI standard for disk drives and other peripheral devices that allows them to interoperate with different operating systems. With software, interoperability occurs when programs are able to share data and resources. Microsoft Word, for example, is able to read files created by Microsoft Excel.

## 4.8 Network Administrator

It is a person who manages the maintenance and use of network. Network management refers to the maintenance and administration of large-scale computer networks and telecommunication networks at the top level.

Network management is the execution of the set of functions required for controlling, planning, allocating, deploying, coordinating and monitoring the resources of a network. It includes performing following functions:

- Initial network planning
- Frequency allocation, predetermined traffic routing to support load balancing.
- Cryptographic key distribution authorization.
- Configuration management
- Fault management
- Security management
- Performance management
- Bandwidth management
- Accounting management

A large number of protocols exist to support network and network device management. Common protocols include:

- SNMP
- CMIP
- WBEM
- Common Information Model

- Transaction Language 1
- Java Management Extensions - JMX

## 4.9 Network Security

Computer or network security has been violated when unauthorized access by any party occurs. So it becomes your duty as the Network Administrator to work on the security to guard against any such incidence taking place.

### 4.9.1 Need of Network Security

Computer security is required because most organizations can be damaged by hostile software or intruders. There may be several forms of damage which are obviously interrelated. These include:

- Damage or destruction of computer systems.
- Damage or destruction of internal data.
- Loss of sensitive information to hostile parties.
- Use of sensitive information to steal items of monitary value.
- Use of sensitive information against the organization's customers which may result in legal action by customers against the organization and loss of customers.
- Damage to the reputation of an organization.
- Monitary damage due to loss of sensitive information, destruction of data, hostile use of sensitive data, or damage to the organization's reputation.

The methods used to accomplish these unscrupulous objectives are many and varied depending on the circumstances. This guide will help administrators understand some of these methods and explain some countermeasures.

### 4.9.2 Security Issues

Computer security can be very complex and may be very confusing to many people. It can even be a controversial subject. Network administrators like to believe that their network is secure and those who break into networks may like to believe that they can break into any network.

There are many fallacies that network administrators may fall victim to. These fallacies may allow administrators to wrongfully believe that their network is more secure than it really is. This guide will attempt to clarify many issues related to security by doing the following:

- Help you determine what you are protecting.
- Break computer security into categories.
- Explain security terms and methods.
- Point out some common fallacies that may allow administrators to be overconfident.
- Categorize many common attacks against networks and computers.
- Explain some attack methods.
- Describe tools that can be used to help make a network more secure.

### 4.9.3 Security Interdependence

There are many different aspects to computer and network security as you will read in this book. These different areas of computer security are interdependent on each other in order for a network to be secure. If one or more areas of computer security are ignored, then the entire security integrity of the organization's network may be compromised. A clear example of this is in the area of computer virus or worm protection.

Computer virus protection programs can only filter known viruses or worms. There are viruses or worms that are not yet recognized as virus programs immediately after their release. Some of these vulnerabilities are operating system and application program errors. When security patches are created for software, they should be quickly applied. In this way the vulnerability to viruses is minimized but not eliminated. There are other steps which may further reduce this vulnerability, but it can never be completely eliminated.

### 4.9.4 Security Limitations and Applications

If you are reading this document and are thinking that you can get all the information required to make your network completely secure, then you are sadly mistaken. In many ways, computer security is almost a statistical game.

You can reduce but not eliminate the chance that you may be penetrated by an intruder or virus. This is mainly for one reason.

This is why even those who consider themselves hackers will say that the number one computer security threat is the lack of quality in the applications and operating systems. At this point, I could talk about the various corporate entities that write software and why software lacks the quality that many of us believe that it should possess, but that subject is not only way beyond the scope of this document, but also way beyond the scope of this project.

Additionally the users on your network are potentially a greater security risk than any programs. Obviously removing all vulnerabilities is impossible and will not secure your network against user errors. I have even considered the possibility that an operating system without a network interface can be completely secure, but even this cannot be guaranteed. Unknown viruses or trojan programs can creep in with applications on CDs or floppies. This has been known to happen. Although an attacker may not be able to get data from the system, they can damage or destroy data.

### 4.9.5 Layered Security

The fact that complete security is impossible is the reason security experts recommend "layered security". The idea is to have multiple ways of preventing an intrusion to decrease the chance that intrusions will be successful. For example, you should have virus protection on your client computers. To help layer this security you should also filter viruses at your email server.

Another good defense layer would also include educating your users about viruses, how they spread, and how to avoid them.

### 4.9.6 Hackers

There are many documents that attempt to define the term hacker. I believe that the term hacker is a connotative term. This means that it is more defined by people's beliefs rather than by a dictionary.

Others believe that hackers are those that perform unauthorized break-ins to computer systems. The media and many sources have caused many uninformed people to believe that a hacker is a threat to computer and network security while this is not the case. A hacker is no more likely to break the law than anyone else. It would be wise to use the more accurate descriptive term, "intruder" to describe those who intrude into networks or systems without authorization.

### 4.9.7 Physical Security

This book will not talk about physical computer security beyond this paragraph. Your organization should be aware how physically secure every aspect of its network is because if an intruder gets physical access, they can get your data.

Be sure that your organization properly secures locations and consider the following:

- **Servers** - Contain your data and information about how to access that data.
- **Workstations** - May contain some sensitive data and can be used to attack other computers.

- **Routers, switches, bridges, hubs** and any other network equipment may be used as an access point to your network.
- **Network wiring and media** and where they pass through may be used to access your network or place a wireless access point to your network.
- **External media** which may be used between organizational sites or to other sites the organization does business with.
- **Locations of staff** who may have information that a hostile party can use.
- **Some employees** may take data home or may take laptops home or use laptops on the internet from home then bring them to work. Any information on these laptops should be considered to be at risk and these laptops should be secure according to proper policy when connected externally on the network (more on this later).

### 4.9.8 Some Technical Terms

This paragaph describes some commonly used computer security terms.

- **Protocol** - Well defined specification allowing computer communication.
- **Confidentiality** - Information is available only to people with rightful access.
- **Integrity** - Information can only be changed by authorized personnel. Integrity - The receiver of the message should be able to tell that the message was not modified. Requires key exchange.
- **Availability** - Information is available to only those who need it.
- **Verification - nonrepudiation** - There is proof that the sender sent the message.
- **Authentification** - The receiver of the message should be able to be sure of the origin of the message. Requires a digital signature (One way hash, public key algorithm, and symmetric algorithm) or a public key algorithm.
- **Spyware** - A computer program whose purpose is to spy on your internet activities usually for marketing purposes and usually done by a shady corporate entity.
- **Malware** - A computer program with some evil intent. It may on the surface have a good or useful intent, but may be a trojan (with a hidden purpose) which can be used to gain unauthorized access to your computer.

## 4.10 Network Components

All networks are made up of basic hardware building blocks to interconnect network nodes, such as Network Interface Cards (NICs), Bridges, Hubs, Switches, and Routers. In addition, some method of connecting these building blocks is required, usually in the form of galvanic cable (most commonly Category 5 cable). Less common are microwave links (as in IEEE 802.11) or optical cable ("optical fiber").

### 4.10.1 Network Interface Cards

A **network card, network adapter** or **NIC** (network interface card) is a piece of computer hardware designed to allow computers to communicate over a **computer network**. It provides physical access to a networking medium and provides a low-level addressing system through the use of MAC addresses. It allows users to connect to each other either by using cables or wirelessly.

### 4.10.2 Bridges

A **network bridge** connects multiple network segments at the data link layer (layer 2) of the OSI model. Bridges are similar to repeaters or network hubs, devices that connect network segments at the physical layer, however, a bridge works by using bridging where traffic from one network is managed rather than simply rebroadcast to adjacent network segments.

### 4.10.3 Hubs

A hub is a piece of hardware which provides the connectivity of a segment of a network by directing traffic through the network. It does this in a rudimentary way, it simply copies the data to all of the Nodes connected to the hub. Hubs are commonly used to connect segments of a LAN. A hub contains multiple ports. When a packet arrives at one port, it is copied to the other ports so that all segments of the LAN can see all packets.

### 4.10.4 Switches

Switches are the device of networking that directs traffic to the correct node by filtering and forwarding packets between Nodes. Switches operate at the data link layer (layer 2) and sometimes the network layer (layer 3) of the OSI Reference Model and therefore, support any packet protocol. LANs that use switches to join segments are called switched LANs or, in the case of Ethernet networks, switched Ethernet LANs. In a circuit-switched data network, a switch is used to create a virtual circuit between the pairs of endpoints. This means that it creates a path to the destination node from the source node.

### 4.10.5 Routers

Routers are the networking device that forwards data packets along networks by using headers and forwarding tables to determine the best path to forward the packets. Routers also provide interconnectivity between like and unlike devices on the network. This is accomplished by examining the Header of a data packet. They use protocols such as ICMP to communicate with each other and configure the best route between any two hosts. A router is connected to at least two networks, commonly two LANs or WANs or a LAN and its ISP's network.

## 4.11 Servers

Server (also called a server application) is "an application program that accepts connections in order to service requests by sending back responses." (RFC 2616 (Hypertext Transfer Protocol — HTTP/1.1)) A server application can run on the same computer as the client application using it, or they can connect through a computer network. Examples include file server, database server, backup server, print server, mail server, web server, FTP server, application server, VPN server, DHCP server, DNS server, WINS server, logon server, security server, domain controller, backup domain controller, proxy server, firewall, etc.

A server operating system is intended, enabled, or better able to run server applications. The differences between the server version and the "workstation" version of an operating system vary. Sometimes (as in the case of Windows 2000 and Windows 2000 Server), the primary difference is the removal of arbitrary license-dependent limits on the number of network file share connections accepted. Some server editions include additional server applications bundled with the operating system. Some server applications (e.g. Microsoft IIS) impose arbitrary limits on the number of HTTP connections they will accept, depending on whether they are running under a server operating system or not.

A computer that is designated for only one server application is often named for that application. For example, when Apache HTTP Server (software) is a company's web server, the computer running it is also called the web server. Server applications can be divided among server computers over an extreme range, depending upon the workload. Under light loading, every server application can run concurrently on a single computer. Under heavy loading, multiple server computers may be required for each application. Under medium loading, it is common to use one server computer per server application, in order to limit the amount of damage caused by failure of any single server computer or security breach of any single server application. Any server computer can also be used as a workstation, but it is avoided in practice, again to contain risk.

Server or server computer is also a designation for computer models intended for use running server applications, often under heavy workloads, unattended, for extended time. While any "workstation" computer can run server operating systems and server applications, a server computer usually has special features intended to make it more suitable. Distinctions often include faster processor and memory, more RAM, larger hard drives, higher reliability, redundant power supplies, redundant hard drives (RAID), compact size and shape, modular design (e.g., blade servers often used in server farms), rack or cabinet mountability, serial console redirection, etc.

The name server or server appliance also applies to network-connected computer appliances or "appliance hardware" that provides specific services onto the network. Though the appliance is a server computer, loaded with a server operating system and a server application, the user need not configure any of it. It is a black box that does a specific job. The simplest servers are most often sold as appliances, for example switches, routers, gateways, print servers, net modems.

### 4.11.1 Server Hardware

Although servers can be built from commodity computer components—particularly for low-load and/or non-critical applications—dedicated, high-load, mission-critical servers use specialized hardware that is optimized for the needs of servers.

For example, servers may incorporate "industrial-strength" mechanical components such as disk drives and fans that provide very high reliability and performance at a correspondingly high price. Aesthetic considerations are ignored, since most servers operate in unattended computer rooms and are only visited for maintenance or repair purposes. Although servers usually require large amounts of disk space, smaller disk drives may still be used in a trade-off of capacity vs. reliability.

CPU speeds are far less critical for many servers than they are for many desktops. Not only are typical server tasks likely to be delayed more by I/O requests than processor requirements, but the lack of any graphical user interface (GUI) in many servers frees up very large amounts of processing power for other tasks, making the overall processor power requirement lower. If a great deal of processing power is required in a server, there is a tendency to add more CPUs rather than increase the speed of a single CPU, again for reasons of reliability and redundancy.

Because servers must operate continuously and reliably, noisy but efficient and trustworthy fans may be used for ventilation instead of inexpensive and quiet fans; and in some cases, centralized air-conditioning may be used to keep servers cool, instead of or in addition to fans. Special uninterruptible power supplies may be used to ensure that the servers continue to run in the event of a power failure.

Typical servers include heavy-duty network connections in order to allow them to handle the large amounts of traffic that they typically receive and generate as they receive and reply to client requests.

The major difference between servers and desktop computers is not in the hardware but in the software. Servers often run operating systems that are designed specifically for use in servers. They also run special applications that are designed specifically to carry out server tasks.

Servers have a unique property where the more powerful and complex the system, the longer it takes for the hardware to turn on and begin loading the operating system. Servers often do extensive pre-boot memory testing and verification, along with starting up remote management services. The hard drive controllers then start up banks of drives in sequence so as not to overload the power supply with the sudden surge of everything turning on at once, then followed by RAID system prechecks for correct operation of redundancy. It is not uncommon for all these preboot hardware checks to take several minutes, but then for the machine to run continuously for months at a time.

### 4.11.2 Server Operating Systems

The Microsoft Windows operating system is predominant among desktop computers, but in the world of servers, the most popular operating systems—such as FreeBSD, Solaris, and GNU/Linux—are derived from or similar to the UNIX operating system. UNIX was originally a minicomputer operating system, and as servers gradually replaced traditional minicomputers, UNIX was a logical and efficient choice of operating system for the servers.

Server-oriented operating systems tend to have certain features in common that make them more suitable for the server environment, such as the absence of a GUI (or an optional GUI); the ability to be reconfigured (in both hardware and software) to at least some extent without stopping the system; advanced backup facilities to permit online backups of critical data at regular and frequent intervals; facilities to enable the movement of data between different volumes or devices in such a way that is transparent to the end user; flexible and advanced networking capabilities; features (such as daemons in UNIX or services in Windows) that make unattended execution of programs more reliable; tight system security, with advanced user, resource, data, and memory protection, and so on.

Because the requirements of servers are, in some cases, almost diametrically opposed to those of desktop computers, it is extremely difficult to design an operating system that handles both environments well; thus, operating systems that are well suited to the desktop may not be ideal for servers and vice versa. Nevertheless, certain versions of Windows are also used on a minority of servers as are recent versions of the popular Mac OS X (which is Unix-based, and gives users complete access to the Unix operating system) family of desktop operating systems and even some proprietary mainframe operating systems (such as z/OS); but the dominant operating systems among servers continues to be UNIX versions or clones. Even in the case of GNU/Linux, a popular UNIX-like operating system frequently used on servers, configurations that are ideal for servers may be unsatisfactory for desktop use, and configurations that perform well on the desktop may leave much to be desired on servers.

The rise of the microprocessor-based server was facilitated by the development of several versions of the Unix operating system to run on the Intel x86 microprocessor architecture, including Solaris, GNU/Linux and FreeBSD. The Microsoft Windows family of operating systems also runs on Intel hardware, and versions beginning with Windows NT have incorporated features making them suitable for use on servers.

Whilst the role of server and desktop operating systems remains distinct, improvements in both hardware performance and reliability and operating system reliability have blurred the distinction between these two classes of system, which at one point remained largely separate in terms of code base, hardware and vendor providers. Today, many desktop and server operating systems share the same code base, and differ chiefly in terms of configuration. Furthermore, the rationalisation of many corporate applications towards web-based and middleware platforms has lessened the demand for specialist application servers.

### 4.11.3 Servers on the Internet

Almost the entire structure of the Internet is based upon a client-server model. Many millions of servers are connected to the Internet and run continuously throughout the world.

Among the many services provided by Internet servers are: the Web; the Domain Name System; electronic mail; file transfer; instant messaging; streaming audio and video, online gaming, and countless others. Virtually every action taken by an ordinary Internet user requires one or more interactions with one or more servers.

There are also technologies that operate on an inter-server level.

### 4.11.4 Servers in Daily Life

Remember that any computer or device serving out applications or services can technically be called a server. In an office or enterprise environment, the network server is easy to identify. However, if you are reading this, you probably have a server in your home. Your DSL/Cable router is a server as it provides your computer with application services such as assigning an IP address via Dynamic Host Configuration Protocol, DHCP), and Network Address Translation (NAT) services which is the firewall that protects your computer from the internet.

Your iTunes software on your computer acts as your music server for your iPod. When you share your printer or a folder on your computer, your computer suddenly becomes a server. It is these instances, often, that can cause security problems in homes. Your wireless access point, if not secured properly, can also serve out your network connection to your neighbour who then can see the folder you shared out to your wife's computer with all the financial information she needs to do your taxes. Hence why securing home networks has become so important.

## 4.12 Client Server

An arrangement used on LANs (local area networks) that makes use of distributed intelligence to treat both the server and the individual workstations as intelligent, programmable devices, thus exploiting the full computing power of each. This is done by splitting the processing of an application between two distinct components: a "front-end" client and a "back-end" server. The client component is a complete, stand-alone personal computer (not a "dumb" terminal), and it offers the user its full range of power and features for running applications. The server component can be a personal computer, a minicomputer, or a mainframe that provides the traditional strengths offered by minicomputers and mainframes in a time-sharing environment: data management, information sharing between clients, and sophisticated network administration and security features. The client and server machines work together to accomplish the processing of the application being used. Not only does this increase the processing power available over older architectures but it also uses that power more efficiently. The client portion of the application is typically optimized for user interaction, whereas the server portion provides the centralized, multiuser functionality.

## 4.13 Communication Media

It is actually the media through which data is transmitted from one place to another. There are 3 types of communication channels.

### 4.13.1 Wire Cable

These are the most popular and widely used channels to transmit data from one location to another. This is so because it is cheaper and easier to use. Wire cable includes telegraph lines, telephone lines and coaxial cables. An advantage of wire cable is that the technology used to transmit data over wire cables is standardized, thus reducing the compatibility problems.

A disadvantage of wire cable is that it is subject to electrical interference making it less reliable than other types of communication channels. Another disadvantage is that wire cable must transmit data in analog form. Therefore, digital data must be converted to an analog signal before they reach the wire cable. This conversion not only needs special hardware, i.e., modem but also slows down the transmission of digital data.

Various items used are:

#### *4.13.1.1 Telephone Lines*

Telephone lines may be used to transmit computer data using the modems. The lines themselves may be either leased or switched.

#### *4.13.1.2 Leased Lines*

A leased line is a telephone line that is leased for the express purpose of maintaining a communication channel between two computers. The line is not shared with any other users and is available at all times for data communication between the computers. A leased line is similar to a telephone connection that is always open. Both computers are always listening for a signal to start the communication. Leased lines are used in computer networks where computers or terminals in the network must be in constant contact with one another. For example, leased lines are used in a network employing point-of-sale terminals, as the terminals must be in constant contact with the main computer. Leased lines are often conditioned to limit the level of noise on the line. Conditioned leased lines are usually necessary to carry on high speed data communication. Security requirements often require that leased lines be shielded from outside interference and unauthorized snooping.

#### *4.13.1.3 Switched Lines*

A switched line can be used for either voice or data communication and is switched from user to user, as requirements dictate. When switched lines are used, one computer must establish contact with the other by dialing a telephone number. After the transmission has been completed, the connection between the computers is broken, just as if a telephone receiver were hung up.

#### *4.13.1.4 Twisted Pair Cable*

Twisted pair [YP] is a common scheme for using copper wire as telecommunication cable. Because copper is such a good conductor of electrons, copper wires do not constrain electromagnetic signals well. When two copper wires conduct electric signals in close proximity, a certain amount of electromagnetic interference occurs. This type of interference is called cross-talk. In addition, because of the electromagnetic range used, TP transmits and receives unwanted signals from other sources. Twisting the copper wires reduces cross-talk and signal emissions. Each intertwined strand conducts a current whose emitted waves are cancelled out by the other wire's emissions. Twisted pairs are formed by two insulated 22 to 26 gauge copper wires that are twisted about each other. When one or more twisted pairs are combined within a common jacket, they form a twisted pair cable.

The two types of TP cables are:

**Unshielded Twisted Pair Cable**

This type of cable is composed of a set of twisted pairs with a simple plastic encasement. You may be familiar with UTP because it is commonly used in telephone systems. It is widely available and has been largely standardized. The Electrical Industries Association (EIA) popularized a category labeling scheme for five different qualities of twisted pair cable.

Category 3 and Category 5 UTP are commonly used in computer networking. While Category 3 is suitable for most contemporary computer networks, Category 5 included some enhancements, such as more twists per foot and a higher grade insulator, to improve the transmission media performance. Category 5 installations also require compatible equipment and more exacting installation techniques. Due to its voice telecommunication heritage, computer network UTP is often installed in the same manner as most telephone installations. A user device contains a port which accommodates a modular RJ-45 (4-pair) or RJ-11 (2-pair) telephone connector. The cost of UTP is extremely low compared to other transmission media. It continues to be mass produced for telecommunications and has become a popular computer network medium.

Some network integrators use existing spare wires from telephone cables to significantly reduce the already low implementation costs. However, this practice is not recommended if the existing UTP cable is lower than Category 3, if the cable drops exceed 100 meters, or if significant crosstalk is already present between the voice wires. UTP installation equipment is also inexpensive, easy to use and widely available.

Installation techniques are so simple that the cable can be adequately installed with very little training. Because voice telecommunication connection techniques have been optimized for easy moves, adds and changes, UTP is easily managed and reconfigured. Using current and emerging techniques, UTP may support data transfer rates from 1 to 100 Mbps at distances up to 100 m. Ten Mbps is the most common transmission rate in use today. All copper wire suffers from rapid attenuation when used as a communication medium. UTP is no exception.

Current technology restricts the effective range of UTP to hundreds of meters.

The copper cable used in UTP is very susceptible to EMI. Although the twists greatly reduce crosstalk, a certain amount of interference exists between pairs of wires.

Also, signals on the pairs are easily influenced by outside emitters of electromagnetic waves. External devices can also be used to intercept signals that are emitted from the pairs, breaching the security of a network.

**Shielded Twisted Pair Cable**

Though most of the cable is unshielded, but some forms of Shielded Twisted Pair (STP) is also used at some places. STP is insulated cable which included bundled pairs wrapped in a foil shielding. Various transmission media specifications from Apple Computer and IBM use STP cable. STP is more difficult to install than UTP. Like coaxial cable, an electric ground, created by special connectors and installation techniques, must be provided for the shield. However, STP is more difficult to install than coaxial cable. If you use standardized and pre-configured cables, it makes installation simple. Bulk STP is moderately expensive. It currently costs more than UTP but is less expensive than thick coaxial or fiber optic cable. With the reduction of outside interference, STP can use higher frequencies and more bandwidth-efficient signaling techniques.

It is capable of greater transmission speeds, up to 500 Mbps at 100 m, but has not been widely implemented at data rates higher than 155 Mbps. The most common transmission rate is 16 Mbps. The biggest difference between UTP and STP is the reduction of interference and EMI emissions provided by STP's shielding. However, STP still suffers from relatively low immunity from interference. STP suffers from attenuation at a rate similar to UTP. Current technology also restricts the effective range of STP to hundreds of meters.

#### *4.13.1.5 Coaxial Cables*

This type of cable come in protective cover which shields the cable from physical dangers as well as from electromagnetic interference. Within the cover, the various cables are shielded from interference with one another. Coaxial cables are used in communication networks that require many simultaneous communication links. Each coaxial cable can provide more than 5000 links. The initial installation of coaxial cable is relatively simple. However, current installation techniques usually use a single strand of cable, which may become difficult to manage and reconfigure.

Local drops may be connected to the base cable to make device connections easier. Using current technologies, coax supports data transfer rates between twisted pair and fiber optic cable, although the typical data rate in use today is 10 Mbps. Much greater data rates are available. However, these higher rates are only infrequently used in computer networking. It is important to note that coaxial cable's bandwidth potential increases with the diameter of the inner conductor.

The cost of coaxial cable increases with the diameter and composition of the conductor. The cost of thin coaxial cable is relatively low (less than STP or Category 5 UTP). Thick coaxial cable is moderately expensive (more than STP or Category 5 UTP). Both are more expansive than Category 3 UTP (all comparisons are made in reference to bulk cable with no connectors).

As a copper wire media, coaxial cable suffers from high attenuation, but at a much lower rate than either variety of twisted pair. Using current LAN technology, the effective range of coaxial cable is in the low thousands of meters. While copper wire generally is a poor resistor to EMI, the shielding provided by coaxial cable greatly reduces its effects.

There are two types of coaxial cables: baseband and broadband.

A baseband coaxial cable transmits a single signal at a time at very high speed, while a broadband coaxial cable can transmit many simultaneous signals using different frequencies. A baseband cable transmits a single stream of digital data at a very high communication rate (millions of bits per second) but must be amplified every 1000 feet or so. It is mainly used for local area networks. A baseband coaxial cable can carry only an analog signal, so it must be used in conjunction with a modem. It is more complex to use in a network.

#### *4.13.1.6 Fiber Optics*

They are very reliable communication channels and they transmit data in digital form. They use light impulses that travel through clear flexible tubing (tiny threads of glass or plastic). A single glass fiber is thinner than the size of a human hair and it can transmit all the characters in dozens of books of the same size of this one across the country in a single second. It would take about 21 hours to send the same information over a copper telephone line. Since thousands of these fibers can be fit in the same amount of space required for one wire cable, the future cost of broad band transmission capability should be within the reach of small organizations and individuals.

Fiber optics can transmit data at very high speed with no errors. Unlike wire cables, fiber optic cables are not subject to electrical interference. They do, however, require repeaters to read and boost the signal strength because light pulses will lose signal strength over long distances. Optical fibers support extremely high bandwidths because they are limited by the high-frequency photon properties of light rather than by lower frequency properties of electrical systems.

Current technologies allow data rates from 100 Mbps to over 2 Gbps, at distances from 2 to 25 km. The data rate of a given fiber optic system is dependent upon the fiber composition (glass or plastic), the mode and the wavelength of the light transmitted. The most common LAN installations include glass multi-mode fiber and 850 nm wavelength LEDs. This configuration can sustain a transmission rate of 100 Mbps at distances of approximately 20 km. Historically, bulk fiber and connectors have been relatively expensive compared to copper wire, but these costs are falling rapidly.

However, the extreme cost of installation far outpaces the cost of materials. The nature of fiber optic cable poses installation problems. Every fiber junction, splice, or connection must be made with extreme care to ensure that the light path is unobstructed. Installers must be careful not to excessively stretch or bend the fiber. Fiber optic cables have extremely low attenuation rates. The amount of attenuation varies depending upon the operating wavelength, but effective ranges are usually measured in kilometers. Therefore, fiber optic cable attenuates much less than any copper wire transmission medium. Due to the use of the light spectrum, fiber optic cables do not leak signals and are immune to electromagnetic interference and eavesdropping. Also, the light spectrum does not require electrical grounds, so fiber optic cables do not suffer from potential shifts to the electrical ground not do they produce sparks. These characteristics make fiber ideal for hazardous, high voltage, or eavesdropping sensitive environments.

#### *4.13.1.7 Microwave*

This is also a type of analog communication channel. Microwave signals are transmitted through the atmosphere rather than through wire cables, similar to the way radio and television signals are transmitted. Microwave signals must be transmitted in a straight line, they do not bend around corners or around the curve of the earth. Transmitter stations redirect and boost the signals. The data may be beamed to a communications satellite that acts as a reflector by accepting signals from one point on earth and returning the same signals to some other point on earth.

The satellite appears from the earth to be stationary target for the microwave signals because its precisely positioned 22,300 miles above the equator with an orbit speed that matches the earth's rotation. Dozens of satellites are now in orbit to handle international and domestic data, voice and video communications.

Compared to wire cable, microwave has a much lower error rate, making it more reliable. Also, because there are no physical links between the sending and receiving systems communication links can be made over large distance and rough terrains. The only disadvantage is the high cost of ground stations and satellites to support a microwave network.

### 4.13.2 Bandwidth Channels

The bandwidth, or grade, of a communication channel determines the rate or speed that data can be transmitted over a channel. The term **bandwidth** is often shortened to **band**.

There are 3 bands for communication channels.

#### 4.13.2.1 Narrow-band

The narrow-band channel is used where data volume is relatively low and which transmits data at a rate between 40 to 100 bits per second (bps). Telegraph lines are an example of narrow-band channels and their transmission rate is slow.

#### 4.13.2.2 Voice-band

The voice-band channels are able to speed up the transmission rate between 110 to 9600 bits per second. Telephone lines are an example of voice-band channels. In many cases, a terminal operator at a remote location uses the regular dial-up telephone switching network, calls a number at the control processor location and enters the data. For large volumes of data, it is cheaper for an organization to acquire its own dedicated or leased line which can be used for both voice and data transmissions.

#### 4.13.2.3 Broad-band

The broad-band channels are used where data volumes are large and which transmit data at rate upto several megabits per second. Microwaves, coaxial cables, fiber optics and communications satellites are examples of broad-band channels.

### 4.13.3 Data Transmission

The 2 forms of data transmission are discussed below.

#### 4.13.3.1 Analog Data Transmission

Here the transmission of data is in a continuous wave form. The telephone system, for instance, is designed for analog data transmission.

Waves are measured using one or more of the following 3 characteristics.

**Amplitude**

You can consider the amplitude of a wave as the signal strength compared to some reference value (measured in volts). Analog signals are based upon amplitude, or strength, shifts which vary constantly from positive to negative values. Amplitude is commonly expressed in volts when measuring electrical potential, amps when measuring electrical current, watts when measuring electrical power, and decibels when measuring the ratio between the power of two signals.

**Frequency**

The frequency of a wave is the time it takes for a wave to complete one cycle. In other words, if a signal takes one second to make a transition from high amplitude to low and back to high, the frequency of the wave is one second. Frequency is typically measured in hertz[Hz], or cycles per second.

**Phase**

The phase of a signal refers to the relative state of the wave when timing began. Two signals cross at a slightly different time. Signal phase is measured in degrees. As with digital signals, analog signals can be modulated on encoded to represent binary data.

**Current State**

The most common analog current state strategies use different signal amplitudes or frequencies to represent data. These are two type of analog signal encoding schemes:

**Amplitude-shift keying (ASK)**

Amplitude-shift keying encodes binary data by varying the signal's amplitude between two or more levels. For example, a binary 0 might be one volt and a binary 1 might be three volts.

**Frequency-shift keying (FSK)**

Frequency-shift keying encodes binary data by varying the signal's frequency between two or more values. For example, a binary 0 would be one frequency or group of frequencies and a binary 1 would be some other frequency or group of frequencies. Network devices, using current state analog signaling, periodically measure the signal's amplitude, frequency, or both simultaneously.

**State Transition**

Transitions from one analog phase to another can also encode data on an analog signal. This method of analog signaling is called Phase-Shift Keying (PSK). This encodes binary data by varying the phase of the signal to indicate a value. For example, a 180 degree phase shift could represent 1 and no shift could indicate 0. Network devices periodically measure the analog signal to determine if a phase change has occurred.

#### *4.13.3.2 Digital Data Transmission*

It is the transmission of data using distinct **ON** and **OFF** electrical states. Computer circuitry represents data as a pattern of **ON** or **OFF** electrical states. These two states are represented by a 1 or **ON** and 0 for **OFF**. Digital data communication is faster and more efficient than analog. All the data communication between the computers is in digital form as the computers understand and work only in digital forms.

However, telephone system, an analog data transmission system, is used for a great percentage of data communication because it is the largest and the most widely used communication system in the world. The modem, sometimes referred as interface element, is used to bridge the gap between digital and analog data transmission, or to allow the digital data to be transmitted/received over from the telephone lines.

## 4.14 Types of Network

Network connection devices connect the various segments of network media that make up a network or internetwork. A segment is one section of network transmission media that is assigned a specific network address; it provides servers and clients on the network with access to network resources.

A network interface board attaches a device, such as a computer, to a transmission medium. Network interface cards (NICs) are circuit boards that provide the means to change a computer's electric signals to those used by the transmission medium.

### 4.14.1 Hubs

A hub is a wiring concentrator for a LAN or WAN that provides a central attachment point for network cabling. Coaxial cable doesn't use hubs.

An active hub can regenerate or amplify a signal, it connects multiple media segments, extends cable length and thereby increases transmission length.

### 4.14.2 Switches - Data Link - Switching hubs (Switches)

These are intelligent hubs which contain circuitry that very quickly routes signals between ports on the hub. This method reduced bandwidth waste because only the device which needs to receive the packet does receive rather than the entire network segment.

Switch filters traffic through MAC addresses. A switch receives a transmission and retransmits it using only that port through which the intended receiver can be reached.

### 4.14.3 Repeater - Physical

Regenerates signals for retransmission. Moves packets from one physical media to another. Will pass broadcast storms. Cannot connect different network topologies or access methods.

Repeaters work in the Physical layer of the OSI model to provide fast signal regeneration. In digital computer networks, repeaters aren't simply amplifiers; repeaters deal with attenuation by receiving and evaluating the data then immediately re-transmitting a clean copy of the signal on to the next segment of the network cable.

### 4.14.4 Bridge - Data Link (MAC Sublayer)

Bridges are used to segment networks. They forward packets based on address of destination node. Uses

RAM to build a routing table based on hardware addresses. Will connect dissimilar network topologies. Will forward all protocols. Regenerates the signal at the packet level.

Bridges are used to segment networks. They forward packets based on address of destination node. Uses RAM to build a routing table based on hardware addresses. Some bridge types are capable of connecting dissimilar network topologies. Will forward all protocols. A hub is a single point where media segments can connect.

#### *4.14.4.1 Remote Bridge - Data Link (MAC Sublayer)*

Same as bridge, but used for telephone communications. Uses STA (Spanning Tree Algorithm).

### 4.14.5 Router - Network

Routes packets across multiple networks. Uses RAM to build a routing table based on network addresses (i.e. TCP address). Shares status and routing information to other routers to provide better traffic management and bypass slow connections. Will not pass broadcast traffic. Are slower than bridges due to complex functions. Strips off Data Link Layer source and destination addresses and then recreates them for packets. Routers can accommodate multiple active paths between LAN segments. Will not pass unroutable protocols.

Routers, operating in the Network layer, use network address information to move data through the best path to its destination. To connect different networks, routers must be aware of network addresses. Because routers can determine network addresses, they can be "intelligent" about routing data through a complex internetwork involving multiple networks.

### 4.14.6 Multiplexers

Multiplexers (mux) enable several devices to simultaneously share a high-bandwidth line.

Half-duplexing - each device in the configuration can send and receive information, but only one at a time; while sending the device cannot receive, very much like walkie-talkies.

Full-duplexing - each device in the configuration can send and receive simultaneously. The best example of this is the telephone.

### 4.14.7 Router - Data Link and Network

Will act as a router for specified protocols and as a bridge for other specified protocols. Brouters are a hybrid of routers and bridges. Brouters function like routers, relaying data transmissions between networks, but when they encounter a data unit that uses a protocol with which they are unfamiliar, they work like a bridge and forward the data to the next segment by using a physical address. Because of this ability, you can use brouters for networks on which there is mixed-protocol traffic and for networks that use protocols that do not support routing.

### 4.14.8 Channel Service Unit/Digital Service Unit (CSU/DSU)

The units are designed to shield network users from electric voltages as well as electrical interference. They also ready data for transmission by adhering to any network rules.

Both units are parts of a data communications equipment (DCE) device and are collectively referred to as a CSU/DSU. A CSU/DSU operates like a modem; however, it is a digital-to-digital device rather than digital-to-analog. It readies digital signals and guarantees that they have sufficient strength and the proper format to be transmitted over digital WAN links.

**Gateway** - Transport, Session, Presentation and Application. Used for communications between different NOS's. Takes the packet, strips off the old protocol and repackages it for the receiving network. A gateway basically grants a workstation a direct connection to the host computer and acts as a messenger between the two systems. Gateways operate between the OSI Transport layer through the Application Layer.

**Transmission Media Adapter** - - Adapter used to connect dissimilar NIC and cable connections (i.e. RJ-45 to

RS-232 adapter).

**MAUs - (Multistation Access Unit)** An access device used to connect the main cabling structure to devices in use on a Token Ring network. This device adds fault tolerance to the network so that a single failure doesn't stop the whole network.

### 4.14.9 Broadband and Baseband

**Baseband** transmissions use the entire medium's capacity for a single channel over digital signaling. Since only one signal at a time can occupy a channel, the use of a MUX will allow multiple devices to send multiple signals using a single transmission medium. Provide excellent throughput because the digital signal occupies the entire channel.

**Broadband** transmissions share the medium's bandwidth over multiple analog channels unidirectionally. This is performed using different frequencies and a process known as FDM (frequency division multiplexing). Since these transmissions work very well over long distances, WAN communications take advantage of this technology.

### 4.14.10 NICs

A **network card, network adapter** or **NIC** (network interface card) is a piece of computer hardware designed to allow computers to communicate over a computer network. It is both an OSI layer 1 (physical layer) and layer 2 (data link layer) device, as it provides physical access to a networking medium and provides a low-level addressing system through the use of MAC addresses. It allows users to connect to each other either by using cables or wirelessly.

Although other network technologies exist, Ethernet has achieved near-ubiquity since the mid-1990s. Every Ethernet network card has a unique 48-bit serial number called a MAC address, which is stored in ROM carried on the card. Every computer on an Ethernet network must have a card with a unique MAC address. This is accomplished by the Institute of Electrical and Electronics Engineers (IEEE), which is responsible for assigning unique MAC addresses to the vendors of network interface controllers.

Whereas network cards used to be expansion cards that plug into a computer bus, the low cost and ubiquity of the Ethernet standard means that most newer computers have a network interface built into the motherboard. These motherboards either have Ethernet capabilities integrated into the motherboard chipset, or implemented via a low cost dedicated Ethernet chip, connected through the PCI (or the newer PCI express bus). A separate network card is not required unless multiple interfaces are needed or some other type of network is used. Newer motherboards may even have dual network (Ethernet) interfaces built-in.

The card implements the electronic circuitry required to communicate using a specific physical layer and data link layer standard such as Ethernet or token ring. This provides a base for a full network protocol stack, allowing communication among small groups of computers on the same LAN and large-scale network communications through routable protocols, such as IP. There are four techniques used to transfer data, the NIC may use one or more of these techniques.

- Polling is where the microprocessor examines the status of the peripheral under program control.
- Programmed I/O is where the microprocessor alerts the designated peripheral by applying its address to the system's address bus.
- Interrupt-driven I/O is where the peripheral alerts the microprocessor that it's ready to transfer data.
- DMA is where the intelligent peripheral assumes control of the system bus to access memory directly. This removes load from the CPU but requires a separate processor on the card.

A network card typically has a twisted pair, BNC, or AUI socket where the network cable is connected, and a few LEDs to inform the user of whether the network is active, and whether or not there is data being transmitted on it. The Network Cards are typically available in 10/100/1000 Mbit/s(Mbit/s). This means they can support a transfer rate of 10 or 100 or 1000 Megabits per second.

### 4.14.11 Notable manufacturers

3Com
AEI Intelligent Technologies
AMD
ASIX Electronics
Belkin
Broadcom
Cisco
Digital Equipment Corporation (DEC)
Intel
Marvell Technology Group
National Semiconductor
Netgear
Novell
Realtek
VIA Networking.

### 4.14.12 Hubs

An **Ethernet hub** or **concentrator** is a device for connecting multiple twisted pair or fiber optic Ethernet devices together, making them act as a single segment. Hubs work at the physical layer (layer 1) of the OSI model. The device is thus a form of multiport repeater. Ethernet hubs are also responsible for forwarding a jam signal to all ports if it detects a collision.

Hubs also often come with a BNC and/or AUI connector to allow connection to legacy 10BASE2 or 10BASE5 network segments. The availability of low-priced Ethernet switches has largely rendered hubs obsolete but they are still seen in older installations and more specialist applications.

### 4.14.13 Technical information

A hubbed Ethernet network behaves like a shared-medium, that is, only one device can successfully transmit at a time and each host remains responsible for collision detection and retransmission. With 10BASE-T and 100BASE-T links (which generally account for most or all of the ports on a hub) there are separate pairs for transmit and receive but they are used in half duplex mode in which they still effectively behave like shared medium links. An Ethernet hub, or repeater, is a fairly unsophisticated broadcast device. Hubs do not manage any of the traffic that comes through them, and any packet entering any port is broadcast out on every other port (every port other than the port of entry). Since every packet is being sent out through every other port, packet collisions result—which greatly impedes the smooth flow of traffic.

The need for hosts to be able to detect collisions limits the number of hubs and the total size of the network. For 10 Mbit/s networks, up to 5 segments (4 hubs) are allowed between any two end stations. For 100 Mbit/s networks, the limit is reduced to 3 segments (2 hubs) between any two end stations, and even that is only allowed if the hubs are of the low delay variety.

Some hubs have special (and generally manufacturer specific) stack ports allowing them to be combined in a way that allows more hubs than simple chaining through Ethernet cables, but even so a large Fast Ethernet network is likely to require switches to avoid the chaining limits of hubs.

Most hubs detect typical problems, such as excessive collisions on individual ports, and *partition* the port, disconnecting it from the shared medium. Thus, hub-based Ethernet is generally more robust than coaxial cable-based Ethernet, where a misbehaving device can disable the entire segment. Even if not partitioned automatically, a hub makes troubleshooting easier because status lights can indicate the possible problem source or, as a last resort, devices can be disconnected from a hub one at a time much more easily than a coaxial cable. They also remove the need to troubleshoot faults on a huge cable with multiple taps.

### 4.14.14 Dual speed hubs

In the early days of Fast Ethernet, Fast Ethernet switches were relatively expensive devices. However, hubs suffered from the problem that as simple repeaters they could only support a single speed. Whilst normal PCs with expansion slots could be easily upgraded to Fast Ethernet with a new network card, computers with less common expansion mechanisms, or no expansion bus at all, and other equipment, such as printers, could be expensive or impossible to upgrade.

Therefore, a compromise between a hub and a switch appeared known as a dual speed hub. These split the network into two segments, each acting like a hubbed network at its respective speed with a two-port switch between them. Therefore, they allowed mixing of the two speeds without the cost of a Fast Ethernet switch.

### 4.14.15 Usefulness

Historically, the main reason for purchasing hubs rather than switches was price. This has largely been eliminated by reductions in the price of switches, but hubs can still be useful in special circumstances:

- A protocol analyzer connected to a switch does not always receive all the desired packets since the switch separates the ports into different segments. Connecting the protocol analyzer to a hub allows it to see all the traffic on the segment. (Expensive switches can be configured to allow one port to listen in on traffic on another port. However, these cost much more than a hub.)
- Some computer clusters require each member computer to receive all of the traffic going to the cluster. A hub will do this naturally; using a switch requires implementing special tricks.
- When a switch is accessible for end users to make connections, for example, in a conference room, an inexperienced or careless user (or saboteur) can bring down the network by connecting two ports together, causing a loop. This can be prevented by using a hub, where a loop will break other users on the hub, but not the rest of the network. (It can also be prevented by buying switches that can detect and deal with loops, for example by implementing the Spanning Tree Protocol.)
- A cheap hub with a 10BASE2 port is probably the cheapest and easiest way to connect devices that only support 10BASE2 to a modern network (cheap switches don't tend to come with 10BASE2 ports). The same goes for linking in an old thicknet network segment using an AUI port on a hub (individual devices that were intended for thicknet can be linked to modern Ethernet by using an AUI-10BASE-T transceiver).

### 4.14.16 Repeaters

A **repeater** is an electronic device that receives a weak or low-level signal and retransmits it at a higher level or higher power, so that the signal can cover longer distances without degradation.

Use of the term has continued in telephony and data communications.In telecommunication, the term **repeater** has the following standardized meanings:

1. An analog device that amplifies an input signal regardless of its nature (analog or digital).
2. A digital device that amplifies, reshapes, retimes, or performs a combination of any of these functions on a digital input signal for retransmission.

Because repeaters work with the actual physical signal, and do not attempt to interpret the data being transmitted, they operate on the Physical layer, the first layer of the OSI model.

Repeaters are often used in trans-continental and trans-oceanic cables, because the attenuation (signal loss) over such distances would be completely unacceptable without them. Repeaters are used in both copper-wire cables carrying electrical signals, and in fibre optics carrying light.

Repeaters are used in radio communication services. Radio repeaters often transmit and receive on different frequencies. A special subgroup of those repeaters is those used in amateur radio.

When providing a point-to-point telecom link using radio beyond line of sight, one uses repeaters in a microwave radio relay. A reflector, often on a mountain top, that relays such signals around an obstacle, is called a **passive repeater.**

In optical communications the term **repeater** is used to describe a piece of equipment that receives an optical signal, converts that signal into an electrical one, regenerates it, and then retransmits an optical signal. Since such a device converts the optical signal into an electrical one, and then back to an optical signal, they are often known as Optical-Electrical-Optical (OEO) repeaters.

Before the invention of electronic amplifiers, mechanically coupled carbon microphones were used as amplifiers in telephone repeaters. The invention of the audion tube made transcontinental telephony practical. In the 1930s vacuum tube repeaters using hybrid coils became common place, allowing the use of thinner wires.

In the 1950s negative impedance gain devices were more popular, and a transistorized version called the E6 repeater was the final major type used in the Bell System before the low cost of digital transmission made all voice band repeaters obsolete.

## 4.15 Peer to Peer Networks

In *peer-to-peer networks*, the connected computers have no centralized authority. From an authority viewpoint, all of these computers are equal. In other words, they are peers. If a user of one computer wants access to a resource on another computer, the security check for access rights is the responsibility of the computer holding the resource.

Each computer in a peer-to-peer network can be both a client that requests resources and a server that provides resources. This is a great arrangement, provided the following conditions are met:

- Each user is responsible for local backup.
- Security considerations are minimal.
- A limited number of computers are involved.

Networks that run Windows 95/98 as their network operating system or networks using Windows NT in a workgroup are considered peer-to-peer networks. Peer-to-peer networks present some challenges. For example, backing up company data becomes an iffy proposition. Also, it can be difficult to remember where you stored a file. Finally, because security is not centralized, users and passwords must be maintained separately on each machine, Passwords may be different for the same users on different machines.

## 4.16 Clients Server

In contrast to a peer-to-peer network, a *client/server network* uses a network operating system designed to manage the entire network from a centralized point, which is the server. Clients make requests of the server, and the server responds with the information or access to a resource.

Client/server networks have some definite advantages over peer-to-peer networks. For one thing, the network is much more organized. It is easier to find files and resources because they are stored on the server. Also, client/server networks generally have much tighter security.

Finally, client/server networks have better performance and can scale almost infinitely. It is not uncommon to see client/server networks with tens of thousands of workstations. Note that the server now holds the database of user accounts, passwords, and access rights.

### 4.16.1 Peer-to-Peer vs. Client/Server Architecture

The purpose of networking is to share resources. How this is accomplished depends on the architecture of the network operating system software. The two most common network types are peer-to-peer and client/server.

If you were to look at an illustration of a group of computers in a LAN, it would be impossible to determine if the network was a peer-to-peer or a client/server environment. Even a videotape of this same LAN during a typical workday would reveal few clues as to whether it is peer-to-peer or client/server. Yet, the differences are huge. Since you can't see the differences, you might guess correctly that they are not physical but logical.

## 4.17 Addressing in Internet

As Internet is a network of networks. It basically consists of network nodes like computers. All these devices are interconnected to communicate with each other. Each device in a network must have a unique address to be identified. This address makes this device unique on that network and any other computer or device can communicate with it by using this specific address. There are two major types of addressing schemes that are used in the internet environment:

1. IP addressing
2. DNS addressing

In the IP addressing scheme IP stands for internet protocols. IP is a number or value that is used to uniquely identify a computer on the internet. It is a 32-bit value and this number/value can be divided into four different sections. All these sections are separated by a period. As each section is of 8 bits thus, it can represent a value in the range of 0 to 255. Each section is known as an octet. Each time a computer is connected to the internet, it is assigned a specific IP address dynamically by the ISP. The DNS stands for domain name system. Unlike the IP addressing scheme in this addressing scheme, DNS address text is used instead of numbers. It is easier to remember than IP address.

## 4.18 DNS

A program that runs on an Internet-connected computer system called a DNS server and provides an automatic translation between domain names (such as watt.seas.virginia.edu) and IP addresses (128.143.7.186). The purpose of this translation process called resolution is to enable Internet users to continue using a familiar name (such as www.yahoo.com) even though the service's IP address may change.

In the system of domain names used to identify individual Internet computers, a single word or abbreviation that makes up part of a computer's unique name (such as watt.seas.virginia.edu). Reading from left to right, the parts of a domain name go from specific to general; for example, "watt" is a specific computer, one of several RS-6000 minicomputers in service at the School of Engineering and Applied Science (seas) at the University of Virginia (Virginia). At the end of the series of domain names is the top level domain (here, edu), which includes hundreds of colleges and universities throughout the U.S.

## 4.19 Domain Name and their Organization

The domain name defines the registered hosts according to their generic behaviour. Each node in the tree defines a domain, which is an index to the domain name space database. The first level in the generic domain section allows seven possible three-character labels. These labels describe the organization types as listed in the following table:

| Label | Description |
|---|---|
| art | Cultural organizations |
| com | Communication organization |

| | |
|---|---|
| edu | Educational organization |
| firm | Business or firms |
| gov | Government organization |
| info | Information Service Providers |
| int | International organizations |
| mil | Military organizations |
| net | Network support organizations |
| nom | Personal nomenclatures |
| org | Nonprofit organizations |
| rec | Recreation/entertainmet organization |
| store | Business offering goods to purchase |
| web | Web-related organizations |

## 4.20 Understanding the Internet Protocol Address

### 4.20.1 Country Domains

The country domain section follows the same format as the generic domains but uses two-character country abbreviations (e.g., "us" for United States) in place of the three-character organizational abbreviations at the first level. Second level labels can be organizational, or they can be more specific, national destinations. The United States, for example, uses state abbreviationss as a subdivision of "us" (e.g., ca.us.)

### 4.20.2 Inverse Domains

The inverse domain is used to map an address to a name. This may happen, for example, when a server has received a request from a client to do a task. Whereas the server has a file that contains a list of authorized clients, the server lists only the IP address of the client (extracted from the received IP packet). To determine if the client is on the authorized list, it can send a query to the DNS server and ask for a mapping of address to name.

## 4.21 Network Topologies

There are ways in which you can connect the various computers for networking. This physical arrangement is called Topology. Topology determines the complexity of connecting computers and therefore the cost of network cable installation. They also determine the strategy for physically expanding the network, in future. Different types of topologies are:

### 4.21.1 Bus

In this case all the server/nodes share a common bus of connecting cables. Every computer can communicate directly with every other computer or device in the network. Each node is given an address. To access a particular, a user just needs to know its address. This topology is frequently used with local area networks. Going through a hierarchy of nodes is not necessary.

***Advantages of the Bus Network***

1. **Short cable length and simple wiring layout:** Because there is a single common data path connecting all nodes, the bus topology allows a very short cable length to be used. This decreases the installation cost and also leads to a simple, easy to maintain, wiring layout.
2. **Resilient architecture:** The bus architecture has an inherent simplicity that makes it very reliable from a hardware point of view. There is a single cable through which all data passes and to which all nodes are connected.

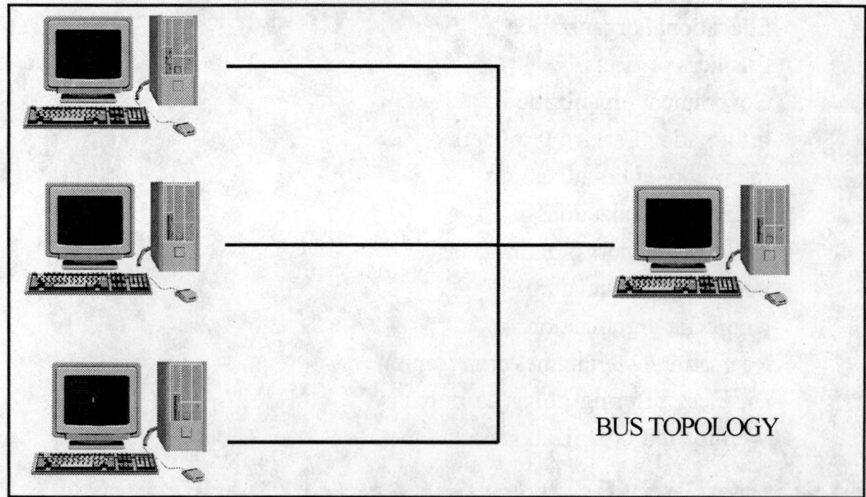


3. **East to extend:** Additional nodes can be connected to an existing bus network at any point along its length. More extensive additions can be achieved by adding extra segments connected by a type of signal amplifier known as a repeater.

***Disadvantages of the Bus Network***

1. **Fault diagnosis is difficult:** Although the simplicity of the bus topology means that there is very little that can go wrong, fault detention is not a simple matter. In most LANs based on a bus, control of the network is not centralized in any particular node. This means that detection of a fault may be performed from many points in the network.
2. **Fault isolation is difficult:** In the star topology, a defective node can easily be isolated from the network by removing its connection at the center. If a node is faulty on a bus, it must be rectified at the point where the node is connected to the network. Once the fault has been located the node can simply be removed. In the case where the fault is the network medium itself, an entire segment of the bus must be disconnected.
3. **Repeater configuration:** When a bus-type network has its backbone extended using repeaters, reconfiguration may be necessary. This may involve tailoring cable lengths, adjusting terminators, etc.
4. **Nodes must be intelligent:** Each node on the network is directly connected to the central bus. This means that some way of deciding who can use the network at any given time must be performed in each node. It tends to increase the cost of the nodes irrespective of whether this is performed in hardware of software

### 4.21.2 Star

In this case all the computers and the main server form a star like shape. All the computers are connected to a single main host. All communication first goes through the centralized computer allowing it to control the operation, work load, and resource allocation of the other computers in the network.

For example, a bank with branch offices would typically use a star network to control and coordinate those branches. The advantage is relative simplicity, but a problem exists with the single-point vulnerability of the network. If the central computer breaks down, none of the other computers can communicate with each other.

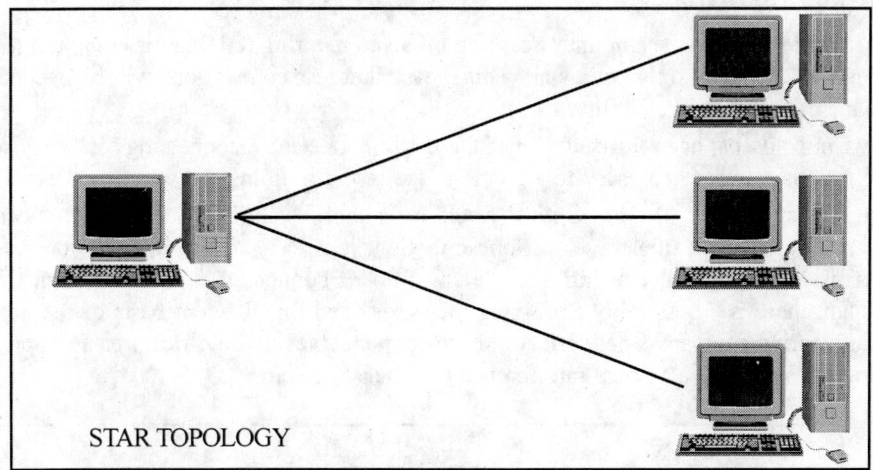


*Advantages of the Star Network*

1. **Ease of service:** The star topology has a number of concentration points, i.e. at the central node or at intermediate wiring closets. These provide easy access for service of reconfiguration of the network.
2. **One device per connection:** Connection points in any network are inherently prone to failure. In the star topology, failure of a single connection typically involves disconnecting one node from an otherwise fully functional network.
3. **Centralized control/ problem diagnosis:** The fact that the central node is connected directly to every other node in the network means that faults are easily detected and isolated. It is a simple matter to disconnect failing nodes from the system.
4. **Simple access protocols:** Any given connection is a star network involves only the central node and one peripheral node. In this situation, contention for who has control of the medium for transmission purposes is easily solved. Thus in a star network, access protocols are very simple.

*Disadvantages of the Star Network*

1. **Long cable length:** Because each node is directly connected to the center, the star topology necessitates a large quantity of cable. While the cost of the cable is often small, congestion in cable ducts and maintenance and installation problems can increase costs considerably.
2. **Difficult to expand:** The addition of a new node to a star network involves a connection all the way to the central node. Expansion is usually catered for by providing large numbers of redundant cables during the initial wiring. However, problems can arise if a longer cable length is needed or an unanticipated concentration of nodes is required.
3. **Central node dependency:** If the central node in a star network fails, the entire network is rendered inoperable. This introduces heavy reliability and redundancy constraints on this node.

### 4.21.3 Ring

As the name suggests all the server/nodes are joined together to form a ring. There is no central server in this case. A ring may be unidirectional or bi-directional. A unidirectional ring moves data in one direction only; a bi-directional ring moves data in both directions, but only one direction at a time. In a unidirectional ring, if one computer breaks down, special software is required to keep the network functional. When one node malfunction in a bi-directional ring, a message can usually be sent in the opposite direction still allowing the node to communicate with all the other active nodes in the network.

*Advantages of the Ring Network*

1. **Short cable length:** the amount of cabling involved in a ring topology is comparable to that of a bus and is small relative to that of a star. This means that less connections will be needed, which will in turn increase network reliability.
2. **No wiring closet space required:** Since there is only one cable connecting each node to its immediate neighbours, it is not necessary to allocate space in the building for wiring closets.
3. **Suitable for optical fibers:** Optical fibers offer the possibility of very high speed transmission. Because traffic on a ring travels in one direction, it is easy to use optical fibers as a medium of transmission. Also, since a ring is made up of nodes connected by short segments of transmission medium, there is a possibility of mixing the types used for different parts of the network. Thus, a manufacturing company's network could use copper cables in the office area and optical fibers in the factory areas, where electrical interference may be a problem.

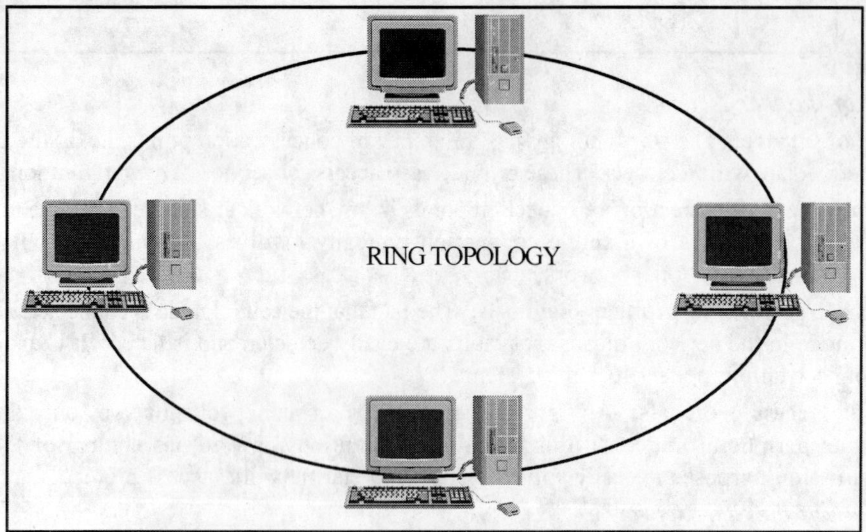


*Disadvantages of the Ring Network*

1. **Node failure causes network failure:** the transmission of data on a ring goes through every connected node on the ring before returning to the sender. If one node fails to pass data through itself, the entire network has failed and no traffic can flow until the defective node has been removed from the ring.
2. **Difficult to diagnose faults:** The fact that failure of one node will affect all other has serious implications for fault diagnosis. It may be necessary to examine a series of adjacent nodes to determine the faulty one. This operation may also require diagnostic facilities to be built into each node.
3. **Network reconfiguration is difficult:** The all or nothing nature of the ring topology can cause problems when one decides to extend or modify the geographical scope of the network. It is not possible to shut down a small section of the ring while keeping the majority of it working normally.
4. **Topology affects the access protocol:** Each node on a ring has a responsibility to pass on data that it receives. This means that the access protocol must take this into account. Before a node can transmit its own data, it must ensure that the medium is available for use.

### 4.21.4 Mesh Topology

A network topology featuring a direct path between two nodes. The backbone of this topology looks like this, where most major cities have a direct connection to most major cities.

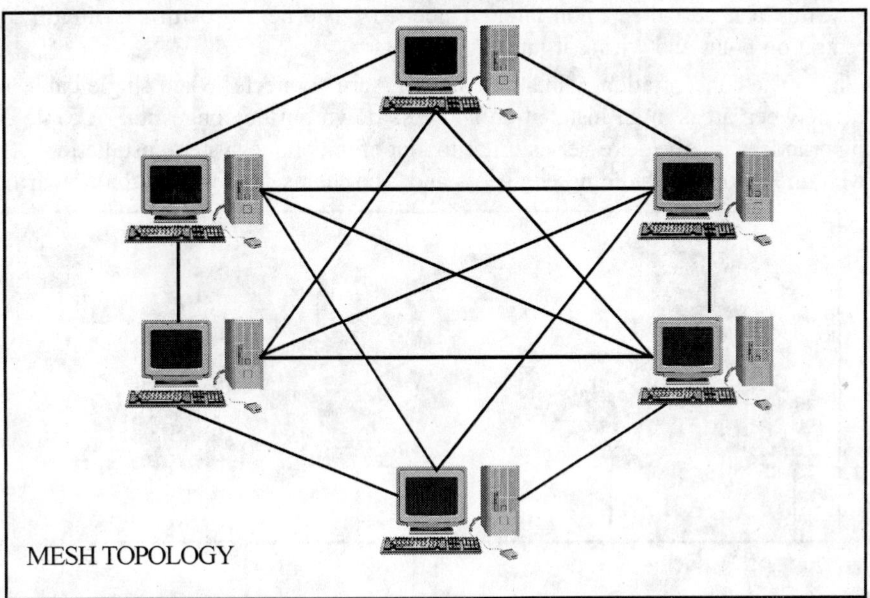


***Advantages and Disadvantages of the Mesh Network***

1. **Units affected by media failure:** Mesh topologies resist media failure better than other topologies. Implementations that include more than two devices will always have multiple paths to send signals from one device to another. If one path fails, the transmission signals can be routed around the failed link. Theoretically, no units are affected by media failure. However, if all paths normally use the maximum capacity of each link, some performance degradation will occur are signals are routed around a failed link.
2. **Ease of installation:** Mesh networks are relatively difficult to install because each device must be linked directly to all other devices. As the number of devices increases, the difficulty of installation increases geometrically.
3. **Ease of troubleshooting:** Mesh topologies are easy to troubleshoot because each medium link is independent of all others. You can easily identify faults and can isolate the affected link.
4. **Ease of reconfiguration:** Mesh topologies are difficult to reconfigure for the same reasons that they are difficult to install.

### 4.21.5 Hybrid Topology

A combination of two or more network topologies. The resultant is a hybrid network. Although the backbone is mostly a mesh network, each local loop is a star network with the central office at each hub.

***Advantages of the Hybrid Network***

1. **Fault diagnoses and isolation:** The presence of concentration points in the network greatly eases fault diagnosis. If a fault is detected on the network, the initial problems to find out which concentration point in the ring is to blame. The fact that this ring is quite small in relation to the total size of the network makes this problem more manageable. The offending concentration point can be

isolated easily, leaving the network in a fully functional state while further fault diagnosis is carried out.

2. **Ease of expansion:** The modular construction of a star-ring network means that new sections may be easily added. When designing the network originally, each concentration can have extra, unused lobes which can be called upon later, if needed. The next growth step involved adding a new concentration point and wiring it into the ring.
3. **Cabling:** The concentration points in a star-ring are connected via a single cable. This simplifies wiring between areas in an installation and cuts down on the congestion of cable ducts. Also, the wiring practices involved are very similar to that of telephone system installation. These techniques are well understood by building engineers and lend themselves well to the prewiring of buildings.

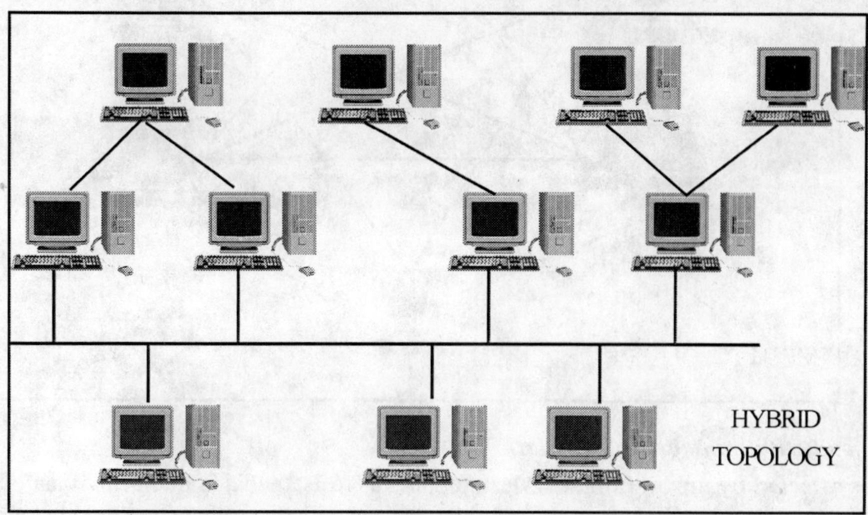


*Disadvantages of the Hybrid Network*

1. **Intelligent concentration points required:** Depending on the implementation used, the concentration points may need to have built in intelligence/processing ability. This will be necessary if it is to assist in network fault diagnosis, node isolation or conversion from one form of transmission medium to another.
2. **Cabling:** The intercloset cabling in a star ring is critical to its operation. This may mean that redundant cabling in the form of one or more back up rings may be necessary to meet reliability requirements. The largest section of the network (i.e. between the concentration points and the nodes) is laid out in a star. This means that a considerable amount of cable may be required.

### 4.21.6 Tree Topology

From a purely topological viewpoint, this network resembles a interconnection of star networks. Individual peripheral nodes must transmit to and receive from one other node only, toward a central node. An advantage of a tree structure is that functional groupings can be created.

For example, one branch could contain all the general ledger terminals, another branch all the accounts receivable terminals, and so on. If one branch stops functioning, the other branches in a tree network are not affected. However, data movement through this network can be slow.

*Advantages of the Tree Network*

1. **Easy to extend:** Because the tree is of its very nature, divided into subunits, it is easier to add new nodes or branches to it.

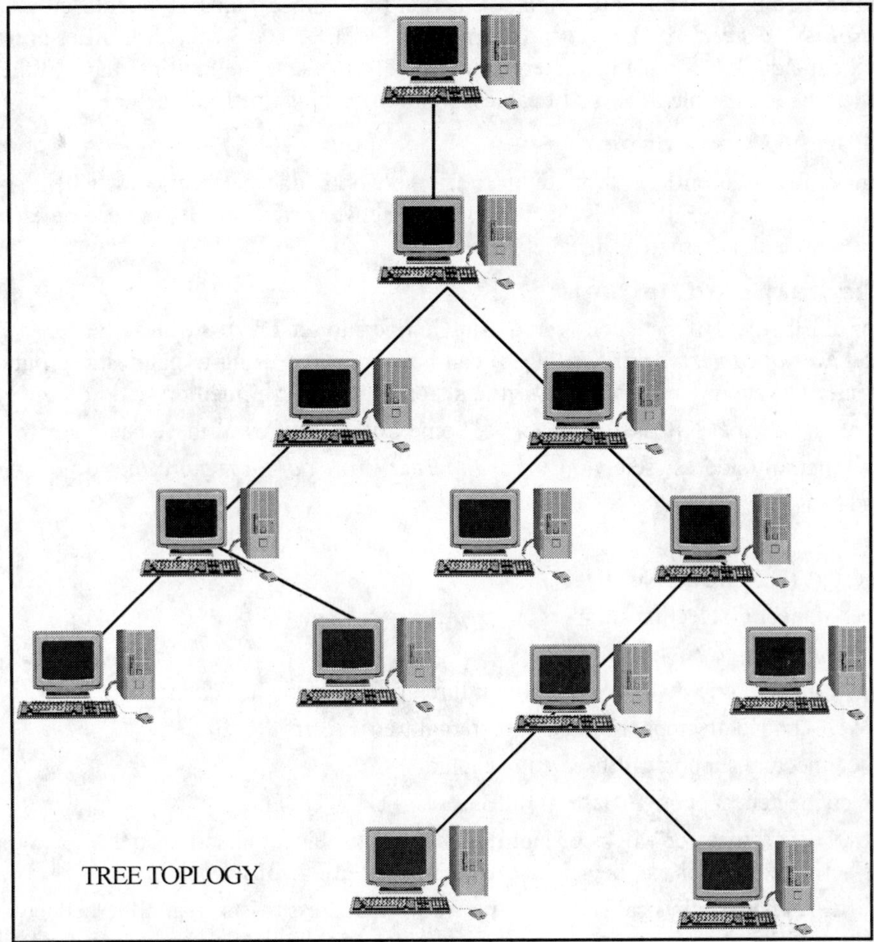


2. **Fault isolation:** It is possible to disconnect whole branches of the network from the main structure. This makes it easier to isolate a defective node.

***Disadvantages of the Tree Network***

1. **Dependant on the root:** If the "headend" device fails to operate, the entire network is rendered inoperable. In this respect, the tree suffers from the same reliability problems as the star.

## 4.22 Ethernet

*Ethernet* was originally developed by DIX - the Digital Corporation, the Intel Corporation, and the Xerox Corporation in the early 1970s. Ethernet is known as a *spanning tree topology* because the networks expand by branching in tree structures that do not allow redundant paths between nodes. Ethernet uses the *CSMA/CD* (Carrier Sense Multiple Access with Collision Detection) media contention access method and supports a maximum throughput of 10 or 100 Mbps. The original Ethernet and later *IEEE 802.3 protocols* are similar but not usually interchangeable.

The origins of Ethernet are commemorated in the initials *DIX*, which is a 15-pin connector used to interface Ethernet components (also called the *AUI* - Attachment Unit Interface). The acronym "DIX" is derived from the combination of leading letters of the founding Ethernet vendors — Digital, Intel, and Xerox.

The term Ethernet commonly refers to original Ethernet (now most frequently identified as *Ethernet II*) as well as the *IEEE 802.3 standards*. However, Ethernet and the IEEE 802.3 standards differ in ways significant enough to make standards incompatible in terms of packet formats. At the Physical Layer, Ethernet and IEEE 802.3 are generally compatible in terms of cables, connectors, and electronic devices.

### 4.22.1 RG 58 A/U Coax cable

Ethernet is generally used on light to medium traffic networks, and performs best when a network's data traffic is sent in short bursts. Ethernet is the most popular network standard. It has become especially popular in many university and government installations.

### 4.22.2 Ethernet Board Settings

Most versions of Ethernet NICs are configured using jumpers to set *addresses* and *interrupts*. Certain models of newer type *Network Interface Cards* (NICs) can be configured using a diagnostic program that allows changing of interrupt and memory address settings stored in a special memory chip on the NIC.

An example of an Ethernet NIC is shown above. Some of the features of these cards are:

- Shared memory address selection *(most Ethernet cards do not require the use of shared memory)*
- I/O address
- Interrupt
- Connectors (DIX/AUI, BNC, RJ-45)
- Active connector selection jumpers
- Socket for a remote boot PROM.

Ethernet cards can have one, two, or possibly all three of the following *connectors*:

- DIX/AUI connectors support 10Base5 external transceivers
- BNC connectors support 10Base2 coax cabling
- RJ-45 connectors support 10Base-T/100Base-TX (UTP) cabling.

In many cases, DIP switches or blocks of jumpers are used to select the active connector. With some cards, however, the active connector can be selected with configuration software.

A limitation of 1,024 nodes (physical addresses) per network address exists on an Ethernet network. Addresses are assigned by IEEE to the vendor for the first three bytes of a six-byte address. The vendor is responsible for assigning the rest of the address and ensuring unique IDs. These unique addresses are called *Burned-In Addresses* (BIA).

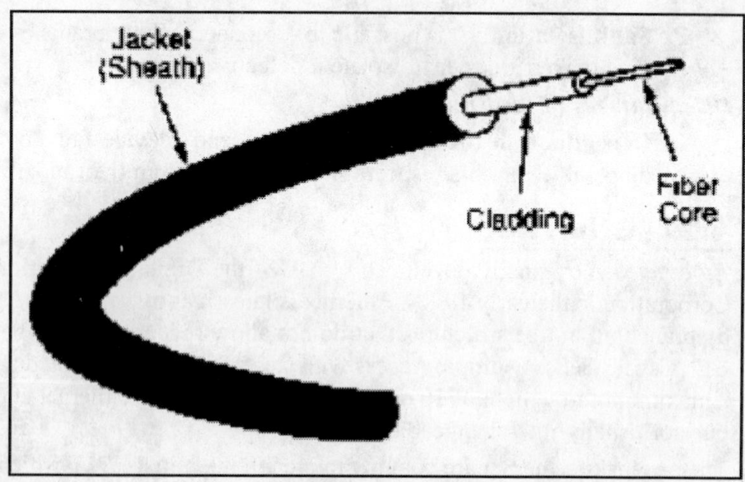


As with the Token Ring cards, the card's manufacturer *"burns in"* a unique node address into a ROM on each NIC. Unless you override the *burned-in address* (using what are called Locally administered Addresses - LAA), address conflicts should not occur on an Ethernet. Vendors sometimes label their cards with the node address. If the address is not visible, use the diagnostic disk supplied by the vendor.

### 4.22.3 Ethernet Cabling

A variety of cables can be used to implement Ethernet networks. Traditionally, Ethernets have been cabled with *coax cables* of several different types (similar to RG 8 for 10Base5 and RG 58 A/U for 10Base2). *Fiber optic cables* (FOIRL) Fiber Optic Inter-Repeater Link; are now frequently employed to extend the geographic range of Ethernets.

The contemporary interest in using *twisted pair wiring* (UTP) has resulted in a new scheme for cabling using unshielded twisted pair. The 10Base-T cabling standard, which uses UTP in a star topology, is described later.

Ethernet remains closely associated with coaxial cable, however. Two types of coaxial cable still used in small and large environments are *thin net* (also known as cheapernet) and *thick net*. The Ethernet networks have different limitations based on thinnet and thicknet cable specifications. The best way to remember the requirements is to use the following rule of thumb for each cable type.

### 4.22.4 Typical Ethernet Coax Cable Specifications

- RG-58 A/U, stranded conductor, CL2, 95%+ copper braided shield, PVC jacket, nominal 50 ohm impedance, 29.5 nominal capacitance/ft.
- RG-58 A/U, stranded conductor, CL2P, 95%+ copper braided shield, Plenum jacket, nominal 50 ohm impedance, 27.0 nominal capacitance/ft.
- RG-58/U, solid conductor, CL2, 90%+ copper braided shield, PVC jacket, nominal 50 ohm impedance. 26.0 nominal capacitance/ft.
- Thick Ethernet Yellow Trunk Cable, solid conductor, CL2, double foil and braided shield, PVC jacket, nominal 50 ohm impedance, 26.0 nominal capacitance /ft.

### 4.22.5 The 5-4-3 Rule

*The 5-4-3 rule* states that between any two nodes in the Ethernet network can be:

- Up to (5) five segments in a series
- Up to (4) four concentrators or repeaters
- Up to (3) three populated segments (coax only).

### 4.22.6 10Base2 (ThinNet)

The 10Base2, *thinnet* topology generally uses the *on-board transceiver* of the network interface card to translate the signals to and from the rest of the network. Thin net cabling uses RG-58 A/U coaxial type cable, 50 Ohm terminators, and BNC T-connectors that directly attach to the connector on the NIC. A *grounded terminator* must be used on only one end of the network segment. The components of a *thin net network* are shown below.

Several additional rules must be adhered to in 10Base2 thinnet Ethernet environments, including the following:

- The minimum cable distance between workstations must be 1.5 feet or .5 meters.
- Pig tails, also known as drop cables, from BNC T-connectors should *not* be used to connect to the BNC connector on the NIC. The BNC T-connector on the coax must be connected directly to the NIC.
- You may not go beyond the maximum network segment limitation of 607 feet or 185 meters (not the 200 meters commonly stated).
- The entire network cabling scheme cannot exceed 3,035 feet or 925 meters.
- The maximum number of nodes per network segment is 30 (this includes workstations and repeaters).

The *IEEE 802.3 standard* for thinnet is 10Base2. This standard describes a 10 Mbps baseband network with a maximum segment length of approximately 200 meters (the actual limit, as stated above is 185 meters).

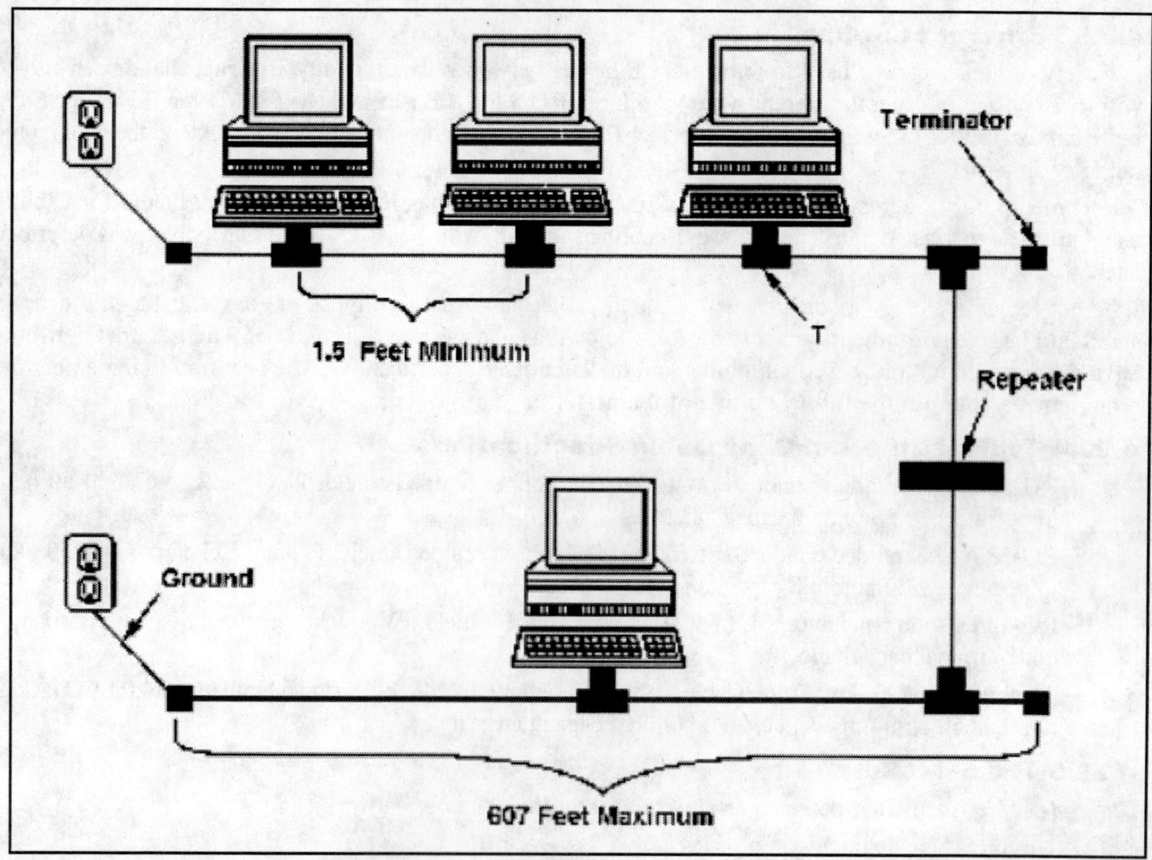


### 4.22.7 10BASE5 (ThickNet)

The 10Base5, *thicknet* topology uses an *external transceiver* to attach to the network interface card. The NIC attaches to the external transceiver by an *AUI cable* to the *DIX connector* on the card. Some external transceivers clamp to the thick net cable with metal points that resemble a vampire's teeth *(vampire tap)*, others connect with standard *BNC* or *N-series barrel connectors.* As with thin net, each network segment must be terminated at both ends with one end using a grounded terminator. The components of a *thicknet network* are shown in the figure next.

Several additional guidelines along with the 5-4-3 rule must be followed in 10Base5 thicknet Ethernet networks:

- The minimum cable distance between transceivers is eight feet or 2.5 meters.
- You may not go beyond the maximum network segment length of 1,640 feet or 500 meters.
- The entire network cabling scheme cannot exceed 8,200 feet or 2,500 meters.
- One end of the terminated network segment must be grounded.
- The maximum number of nodes per network segment is 100. (This includes all repeaters.)

The *IEEE 802.3 standard* that describes thicknet is 10Base5. This standard describes a 10 Mbps baseband network that can have segments up to 500 meters long.

The 10Base5 cabling scheme and components are shown next.

### 4.22.8 10Base-T/100Base-TX (Twisted Pair Ethernet)

The trend in wiring Ethernet networks is to use unshielded twisted pair (UTP) cable. UTP cable has a lower

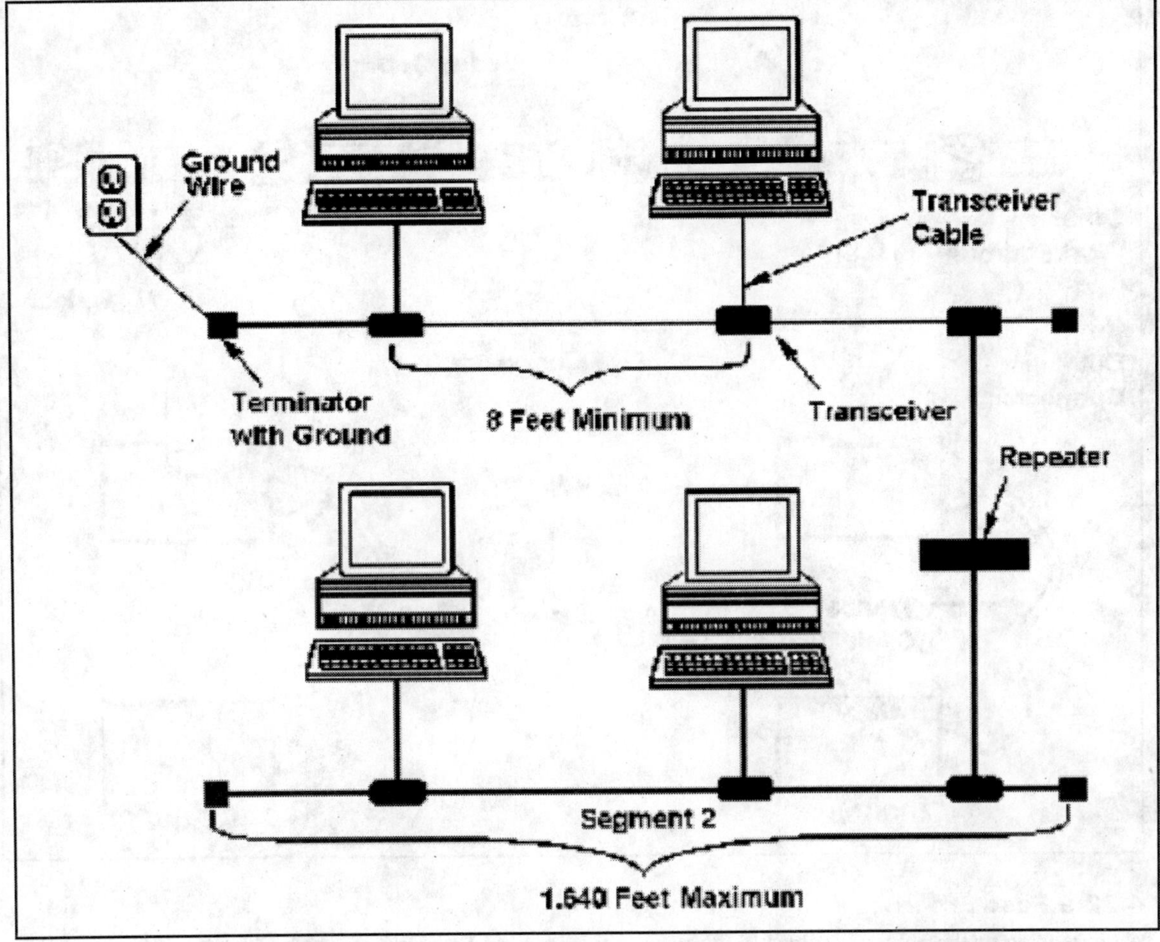


cost than coax. Another significant advantage is that UTP is smaller than coax, which relieves congestion of wiring conduits. *UTP Ethernet* is wired in a star-shaped design and is referred to in the technical world as 10BaseT. The cable uses *RJ-45 connectors*, and the network interface card can have RJ-45 jacks built into the back of the cards. External transceivers attached to a DIX connector can also be used to connect standard Ethernet cards into a twisted pair topology.

The figure next shows 10Base-T Ethernet cabled using twisted pair and a concentrator.

Networks with star wiring topologies can be significantly easier to trouble shoot and repair than bus wired networks. With a star network, a problem node can be isolated from the rest of the network by simply disconnecting the cable and directly connecting it to the cable hub. If the hub is considered "intelligent", management software developed for that hub type can disconnect the suspect port.

The additional rules for a 10Base-T network are as follows:

- The maximum number of network segments is 1,024.
- The maximum unshielded cable segment length is 328 feet or 100 meters.

10Base-T requires that the UTP cable system be compliant with a minimum rating of Category 3. RJ-45 connectors wired with two pairs (4 wires) on pins 1,2,3, & 6 are used with 10Base-T. Level IV is cable certified to operate at 10Base-T required throughput.

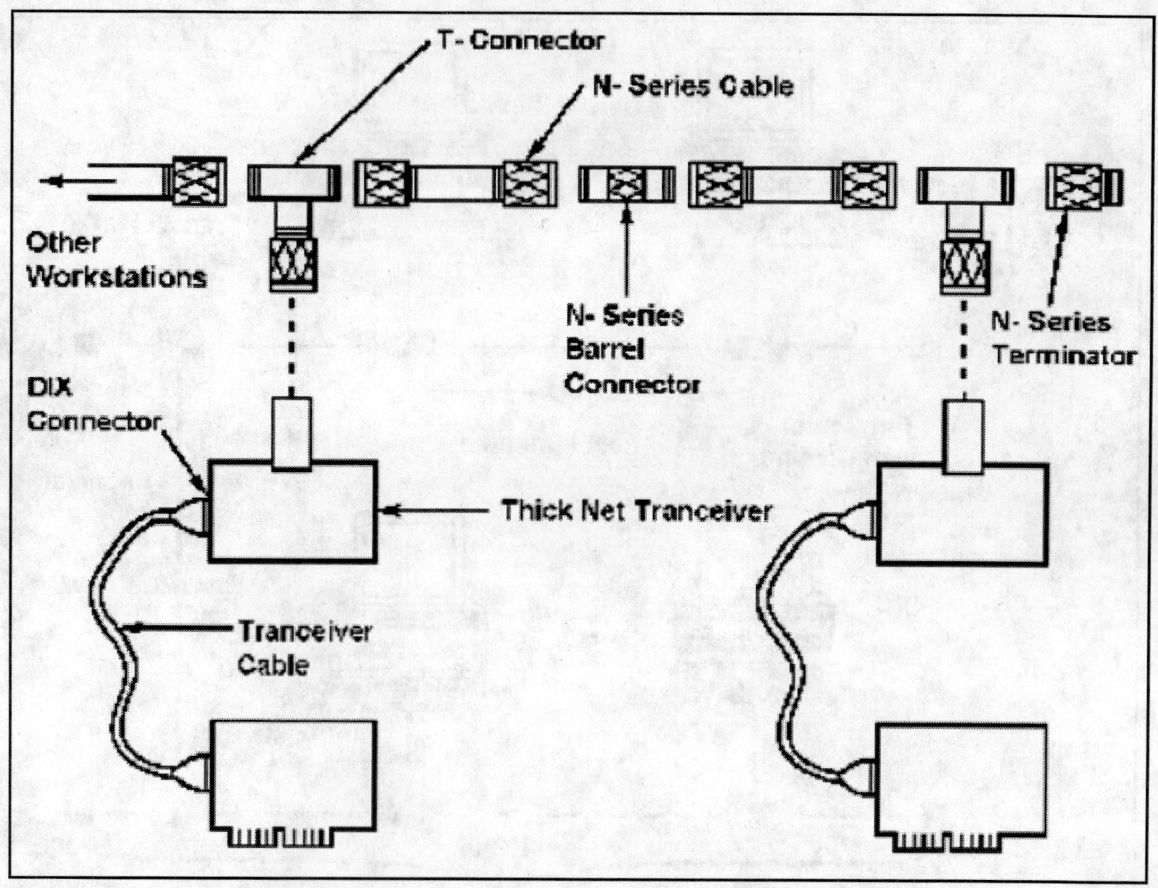


### 4.22.9 Fast Ethernet

An extension of the popular 10Base-T Ethernet standard, **Fast Ethernet** transports data at 100 Mbps. With rules defined by the **IEEE 802.3u** standard, Fast Ethernet leverages the familiar Ethernet technology and retains the CSMA/CD protocol of 10 Mbps Ethernet. Three types of Fast Ethernet are available: **100Base-TX**, which runs over Category 5 UTP; **100Base-T4** which runs over existing Category 3 UTP; and **100Base-FX**, which operates over multimode fiber optic cabling.

EIA/TIA T568B Colour Codes & Pin-out for the 10Base-T & 100Base-TX
RJ-45 connector

| **1** | **2** | **3** | **4** | **5** | **6** | **7** | **8** |
|---|---|---|---|---|---|---|---|
| **TD+** | **TD-** | **RD+** | **N/C** | **N/C** | **RD-** | **N/C** | **N/C** |

Pins 1 & 2 - Pair #1 Transmit Data

Pins 3 & 6 - Pair #2 Receive Data

Pins 4, 5, 7, & 8 - Not Connected

As specified for 10Base-T (CAT3 minimum) & 100Base-TX (CAT5 minimum), cables should be 100 Ohm unshielded or shielded twisted pair (UTP or STP) wire of AWG gauge 24, 26, or 28. Maximum length is 100 meters. IBM Type-1 cable and other 150 Ohm STP cables are not suitable.

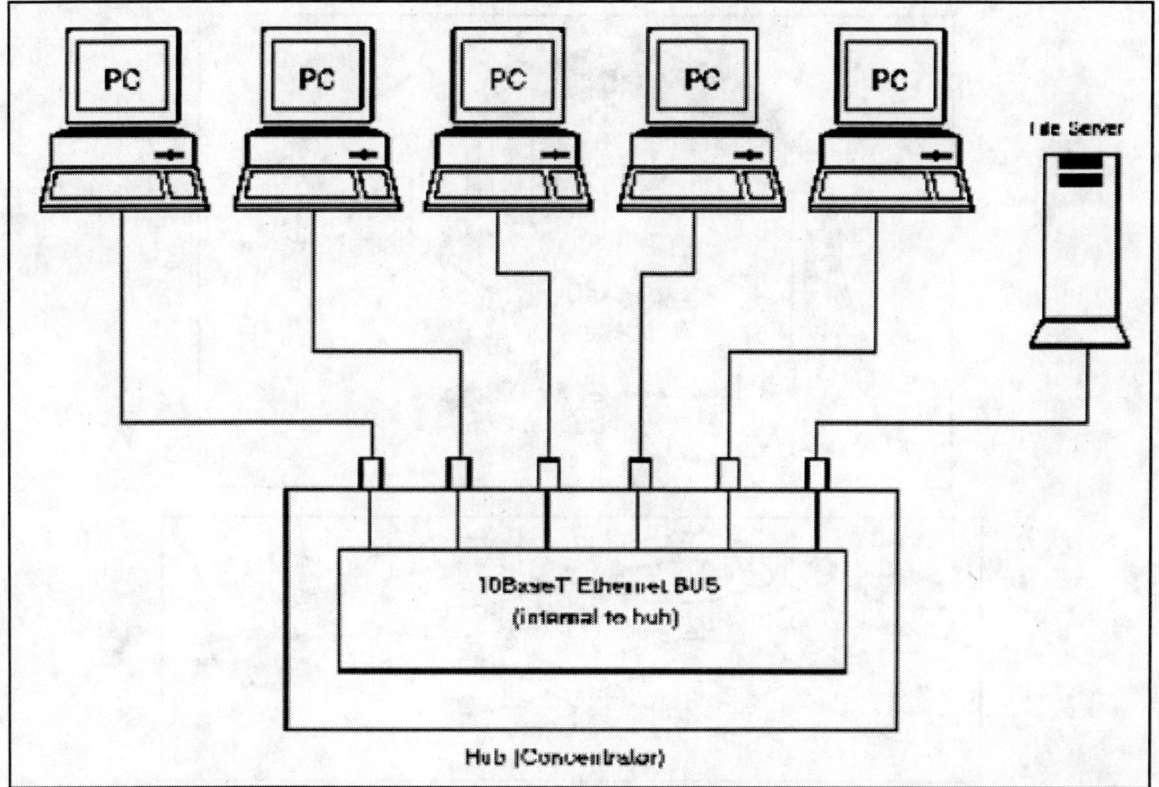


### 4.22.10 Categories for UTP Cable

*Category 3* - The characteristics are specified up to 16 MHz. They are typically used for voice and data transmission rates up to and including 10 Mbps, e.g. IEEE 802.5 4-Mbps UTP (Token Ring) and IEEE 802.3 10Base-T (Ethernet).

*Category 4* - The characteristics are specified up to 20MHz. They are typically used for voice and data transmission rates up to and including 16 MHz, e.g. IEEE 802.5 16-Mbps UTP (Token Ring).

*Category 5* - The characteristics are specified up to 100 MHz. They are typically used for voice and data transmissions up to and including 100 Mbps e.g. the 100Base-TX Fast Ethernet, 100 Mbps Fast ARCnet, and others.

### 4.22.11 Ethernet Trouble Shooting

Look for the following things when trouble shooting Ethernets:

- With 10Base-T & 100Base-TX, make sure that the cable used has the correct number of twists to meet the data grade specifications.
- Electrical interference can be caused by tying the network cable together with monitor and power cords. Outside interference also can be caused by fluorescent lights, electric motors, and other electrical devices.
- Make sure that connectors are pinned properly and crimped tightly.
- Check the cable lengths to make sure that distance specifications are not exceeded.
- If excess shielding on coax cable is exposed, it may be grounding out the connector.

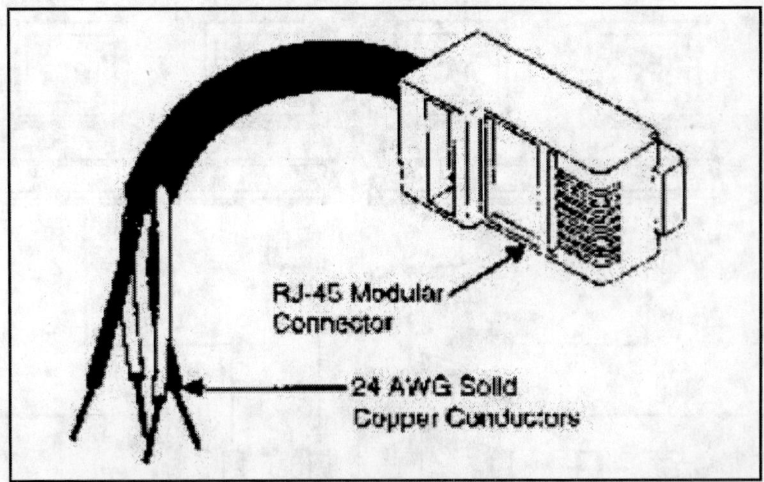


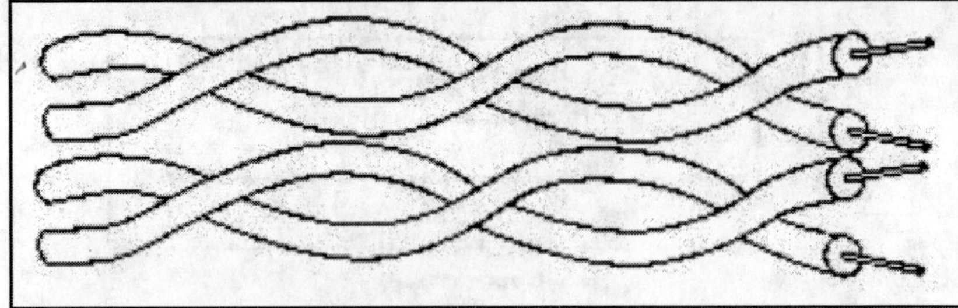

- Make sure that coax cables are not coiled tightly together.
- Check the grade of the cable being used. For thinnet, RG-58 A/U is required. Thick net cable must meet Ethernet specifications.
- If using a linear bus setup, make sure that the topology rules are followed.
- Check for missing terminator or terminators with improper impedance ratings.
- Make sure that all the component cables in a segment are connected together. A user who moves his workstation and removes the T-connector incorrectly can cause a broken segment.

10Base2, thinnet and 10Base5, thick net cable can be combined to extend the distance of an Ethernet network topology (spanning tree topology). The following formula can be used to define the maximum amount of thinnet cable that can be used in one network segment combination:

Maximum length of thinnet that can be used =

1,640 feet (length of new networksegment to be added)

A linear bus topology is economical to wire because it is not necessary to have a separate cable run for each workstation. However, some local problems on a linear bus have the capability of bringing the entire network down.

If a break is in the cable or a streaming (beaconing) NIC is in the channel, the entire network can go down. Streaming is more frequently referred to as a broadcast storm. This occurs when a network card fails, and the transmitter floods the cable with traffic, just like a faucet that is stuck open. At this point, the network becomes unusable.

## 4.23 FDDI

Acronym for Fiber Distributed Data Interface. A standard developed by the American National Standards Institute (ANSI) for high-speed fiber-optic LANs (local area networks). FDDI provides specifications for transmission rates of 100 megabits (100 million bits) per second on networks based on the token ring standard. It is another ring-based network, and unlike Token Ring, it is implemented without hubs, although you can use devices called concentrates to perform a similar function. FDDI uses fiber-optic cable to implement very fast, reliable networks.

The FDDI cabling consists of two fiber rings, one transmitting clockwise and the other transmitting counterclockwise. If either one breaks, the other can be used as a backup. If both breakup at the same point, due to a fire or other accident in the cable duct, the two rings can be joined into a single ring approximately twice as long. Each station contains relays that can be used to join the two rings or bypass the station in the event of station problems. Wire centers can also be used, as in IEEE 802.5 protocol.

## 4.24 ATM

It is the newest type of topology. Unlike others, it can carry both voice and data over network wire or fiber. ATM transmits all packets as 53-byte cells, that have a variety of identifiers on them to determine such things as Quality of Service.

On a ATM network, every station is always transmitting. However, most of the cells transmitted are empty cells that can be discarded at the switch. When a cell that is not empty, enters the switch, the addresses are read to determine where the cell will go next. The cell is then send out in the next available slot, according to the type of cell it is.

ATM has emerged as one of the technologies for integrating LANs and WANs. ATM can support any traffic type in separate or mixed streams, delay-sensitive traffic, and non-delay-sensitive tranffics. ATM can also scale from low to high speeds. It has been adopted by all the industry's equipment vendors, from LAN to private branch exchange (PBX). With ATM, network designers can integrate LANs and WANs to support emerging applications with economy in the enterprise.

## 4.25 Intranet

A private network based on Internet protocols such as TCP/IP but designed for information management within a company or organization. Its uses include such services as document distribution, software distribution, access to databases, and training. An intranet is so called because it looks like a World Wide Web site and is based on the same technologies, yet is strictly internal to the organization and is not connected to the Internet proper. Some intranets also offer access to the Internet, but such connections are directed through a firewall that protects the internal network from the external Web.

### Let us Revise

1. When more than two computers are connected to each other and sharing information, resources and remote systems then this is called Networking.
2. PAN is used for communication among the personal devices (intrapersonal communication), or for connecting to a higher level network and Internet. The reach of a PAN is typically a few meters.
3. A network covering a small geographic area, like a home, office, or building is called Local Area Network.
4. WAN technologies generally function at the lower three layers of the OSI reference model: the physical layer, the data link layer, and the network layer.
5. If connected to the Internet, the intranet or extranet is normally protected from being accessed from the Internet without proper authorization

6. All networks are made up of basic hardware building blocks to interconnect network nodes, such as Network Interface Cards (NICs), Bridges, Hubs, Switches, and Routers.
7. A network card, network adapter or NIC (network interface card) is a piece of computer hardware designed to allow computers to communicate over a computer network.
8. A network bridge connects multiple network segments at the data link layer (layer 2) of the OSI model.
9. A hub is a piece of hardware which provides the connectivity of a segment of a network by directing traffic through the network.
10. Switches are the device of networking that directs traffic to the correct node by filtering and forwarding packets between Nodes.
11. Routers are the networking device that forwards data packets along networks by using headers and forwarding tables to determine the best path to forward the packets.
12. Closely related to the concept of a model is that of an architecture.
13. A MAN (metropolitan area network) is a larger network that usually spans several buildings in the same city or town.
14. A WAN (wide area network), in comparison to a MAN, is not restricted to a geographical location, although it might be confined within the bounds of a state or country.
15. The length of the cable connecting a computer to a LAN also varies depending on the LAN.
16. One of the major benefits of implementation of LAN is sharing expensive resources such as storage devices, printers, etc.
17. Three major catègories of services used in LANs are: File Server; Printer Server and Modem Server.
18. Some popular LAN operating systems are : Novel Netware; Ethernet; Corvus; ArcNet LAN; Server Omni Net; PC Net; IBM PC LAN and Etherlink Plus, etc.
19. Features of LAN are: Typically connects computer in a single building or campus; Developed in 1970s; Medium : optical fibres, coaxial cables, twisted pair, wireless; Low latency (except in high traffic periods); High speed networks (0.2 to 100 Mb/sec); Speeds adequate for most distributed systems; Problems : Multi media based applications; Typically buses or rings and Ethernet, Token Ring.
20. Routers is a special type of device that can be used to connect networks that may not be similar.
21. Features of Wide Area Networks are: Developed in 1960s; Generally covers large distances (states, countries, continents); Medium : communication circuits connected by routers; Routers forwards packets from one to another following a route from the sender to the receiver. Store-and-Forward; Hosts are typically connected (or close to) the routers; Typical latencies : 100ms - 500ms; Problems with delays if using satellites; Typical speed : 20 - 2000 Kbits/s; Not (yet) suitable for distributed computing; and New standards are changing the landscape.
22. Features of MAN are: Generally covers towns and cities (50 kms); Developed in 1980s; Medium: optical fibres, cables; Data rates adequate for distributed computing applications; A typical standard is DQDB (Distributed Queue Dual Bus); Typical latencies : $< 1$ msec and Message routing is fast.
23. All network communications (including LAN and WAN communications) can be categorized as half-duplex or full-duplex.
24. The term host is most commonly used when discussing TCP/IP related services and functions.
25. The purpose of networking is to share resources.
26. In peer-to-peer networks, the connected computers have no centralized authority.
27. Network topology is the study of the arrangement or mapping of the elements (links, nodes, etc.) of a network, especially the physical (real) and logical (virtual) interconnections between nodes.
28. In Bus topology all the server/nodes share a common bus of connecting cables.
29. In Star topology all the computers and the main server form a star like shape.
30. In Ring topology all the server/nodes are joined together to form a ring.
31. In Tree topology all the server/nodes are joined together to form a tree.

## Multiple Choice Questions

1. LAN is :
   (a) Local Area Network (b) Local Around Network (c) Love Area Network.
2. WAN is :
   (a) Windows Area Network (b) Wide Area Network (c) Well Area Network.
3. MAN is :
   (a) My Area Network (b) Metro Area Network (c) Metropolitan Area Network.
4. CAN is :
   (a) Campus Area Nework (b) Clear Area Network (c) Clean Area Network.
5. PAN is :
   (a) Power Area Network (b) Personal Area Network (c) Pop Area Network.

## True/False Questions

1. A network covering a small geographic area, like a home, office, or building is called Local Area Network.
2. If connected to the Internet, the intranet or extranet is not protected from being accessed from the Internet without proper authorization.
3. A network bridge connects multiple network segments at the data link layer (layer 2) of the OSI model.
4. Routers are the networking device that forwards data packets along networks by using headers and forwarding tables to determine the best path to forward the packets.
5. Closely related to the concept of a model is that of an architecture.
6. The length of the cable connecting a computer to a LAN also varies depending on the LAN.
7. Three major categories of services used in LANs are: File Server; Printer Server and Modem Server.
8. Routers is a special type of device that can be used to connect networks that have to be similar.
9. The term host is most commonly used when discussing TCP/IP related services and functions.
10. The purpose of networking is to share resources.
11. In peer-to-peer networks, the connected computers have no centralized authority.
12. In Bus topology all the server/nodes share a common bus of connecting cables.
13. In Ring topology all the server/nodes are joined together to form a ring.

## Match Columns

Match the matter in Column A with the matter in Column B.

| Column A | Column B |
|---|---|
| A. LAN | 1. Personal Area Network |
| B. WAN | 2. Client Computer |
| C. MAN | 3. Wiring Connector |
| D. CAN | 4. Local Computer |
| E. PAN | 5. Stores and Sends Information |
| F. Node | 6. Local Area Network |
| G Host | 7. Arrangement of Networking |
| H. HUB | 8. Wide Area Network |
| I. Router | 9. Campus Area Network |
| J. Topology | 10. Metropolitan Area Network |

## Fill in the Blanks with Appropriate Words

a. Routers b. Local Area Network c. three

d. WAN (wide area network) e. PAN f. MAN (metropolitan area network)

1. A ____________ is a larger network that usually spans several buildings in the same city or town.
2. A ____________, in comparison to a MAN, is not restricted to a geographical location, although it might be confined within the bounds of a state or country.
3. __________ is used for communication among the personal devices (intrapersonal communication), or for connecting to a higher level network and Internet. The reach of a PAN is typically a few meters.
4. A network covering a small geographic area, like a home, office, or building is called ____________.
5. WAN technologies generally function at the lower ____________ layers of the OSI reference model: the physical layer, the data link layer, and the network layer.
6. _______ is a special type of device that can be used to connect networks that may not be similar.

## Descriptive Type Questions

1. What is a computer network?
2. Define the various types of networks.
3. Which are the various hardware components required for networking?
4. Describe the various models of network computing.
5. What is Local Area Networks?
6. Describe Wide Area Networks.
7. Describe the various network services.
8. What is Peer-to-peer network?
9. What is Client/Server network?
10. Write a short note on the following:

    Bus Topology
    Star Topology
    Ring Topology
    Mesh Topology
    Tree Topology
    Hybrid Topology.

## Answers to Objective Type Questions

### *Multiple Choice Questions*

| | | | |
|---|---|---|---|
| 1. a | 2. b | 3. c | 4. a |
| 5. b. | | | |

### *True False Questions*

| | | | |
|---|---|---|---|
| 1. T | 2. F | 3. T | 4. T |
| 5. T | 6. T | 7. T | 8. F |
| 9. T | 10. T | 11. T | 12. T |
| 13. T. | | | |

### *Matching Columns*

| | | | |
|---|---|---|---|
| A. 6 | B. 8 | C. 10 | D. 9 |
| E. 1 | F. 2 | G. 4 | H. 3 |
| I. 5 | J. 7 | | |

### *Fill in the Blanks*

| | | | |
|---|---|---|---|
| 1. f | 2. d | 3. e | 4. b |
| 5. c | 6. a | | |

# Services on Internet 5

## 5.1 E-mail

Since the facility of e-Mail provided by Internet, people have more or less stopped using the post. It has been in fact, named as Snail mail, or the mail which moves at the snail speed. Whereas electronic mail is fast and moves over from one computer to another electronically at an amazing speed. Most of the Internet users are very happy with this facility. In fact, you can send not only the text, but pictures and graphics too.

Most of the offices are sending their mail through computers. No more fussy papers or carbons. In fact, no need to file them too. All is stored in computers and can be accessed whenever needed. All you need is to open an e-mail account and start mailing your letters even if you do not have a computer. You can send the mail using your account number from any Cyber cafe too.

So to work with e-mail you must have an account of your own. For this, as already mentioned in the earlier chapter, each popular search engine allows you to open an e-mail account. Here, in our case, I am using the account opening process of Hotmail.com.

### 5.1.1 Opening of e-mail account

The following are the popular sites which allow you to open an e-mail account:

| | |
|---|---|
| Yahoo | http://www.mail.yahoo.com |
| Hotmail | http://www.hotmail.com |
| Rediff | http://www.deiff.com |
| Mailcity | http://www.mailcity.com |

Besides these most of your ISPs would allow you to open an account. Please remember that these e-mail services are all free and the sites do not charge any amount for using the same.

The following dialog boxes would show you how to create your own e-mail account with hotmail.

### 5.1.2 e-mail organization

With reference to the e-mail program named Outlook Express, the messages in the software can be roughly organized in the following folders:

| | |
|---|---|
| Inbox | For all incoming messages |
| Outbox | For all messages queued for sending |
| Sent Items | For all messages previously sent |
| Deleted items | For all messages marked for deletion |
| Drafts | For all messages which are pending completion |

All these can be seen in the figure on the next page.

Before we start reading and sending the e-mails, we must understand few e-mail terms which are quite useful in reading and sending messages.

#### *5.1.2.1 Using Abbreviations*

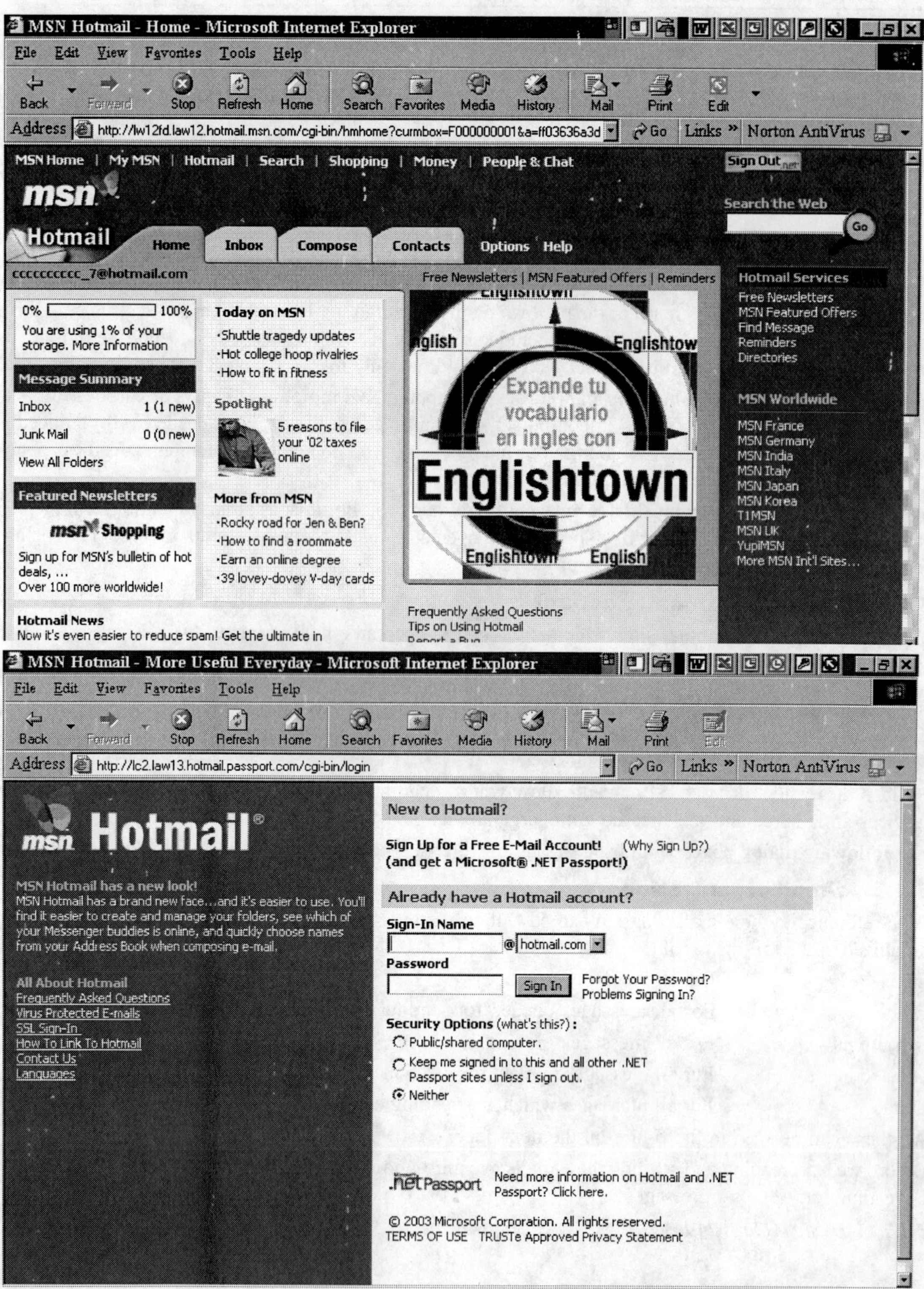
MSN Hotmail - Home - Microsoft Internet Explorer
File Edit View Favorites Tools Help
Back Forward Stop Refresh Home Search Favorites Media History Mail Print Edit
Address http://lw12fd.law12.hotmail.msn.com/cgi-bin/hmhome?curmbox=F000000001&a=ff03636a3d
Go Links Norton AntiVirus
MSN Home | My MSN | Hotmail | Search | Shopping | Money | People & Chat
Sign Out
msn
Hotmail
Home Inbox Compose Contacts Options Help
Search the Web
Go
ccccccccc_7@hotmail.com
Free Newsletters | MSN Featured Offers | Reminders
0% 100%
You are using 1% of your storage. More Information
Message Summary
Inbox 1 (1 new)
Junk Mail 0 (0 new)
View All Folders
Featured Newsletters
msn Shopping
Sign up for MSN's bulletin of hot deals, ...
Over 100 more worldwide!
Today on MSN
·Shuttle tragedy updates
·Hot college hoop rivalries
·How to fit in fitness
Spotlight
5 reasons to file your '02 taxes online
More from MSN
·Rocky road for Jen & Ben?
·How to find a roommate
·Earn an online degree
·39 lovey-dovey V-day cards
Expande tu vocabulario en ingles con
Englishtown
Hotmail Services
Free Newsletters
MSN Featured Offers
Find Message
Reminders
Directories
MSN Worldwide
MSN France
MSN Germany
MSN India
MSN Italy
MSN Japan
MSN Korea
T1MSN
MSN UK
YupiMSN
More MSN Int'l Sites...
Hotmail News
Now it's even easier to reduce spam! Get the ultimate in
Frequently Asked Questions
Tips on Using Hotmail
MSN Hotmail - More Useful Everyday - Microsoft Internet Explorer
File Edit View Favorites Tools Help
Back Forward Stop Refresh Home Search Favorites Media History Mail Print Edit
Address http://lc2.law13.hotmail.passport.com/cgi-bin/login
Go Links Norton AntiVirus
msn Hotmail®
MSN Hotmail has a new look!
MSN Hotmail has a brand new face....and it's easier to use. You'll find it easier to create and manage your folders, see which of your Messenger buddies is online, and quickly choose names from your Address Book when composing e-mail.
All About Hotmail
Frequently Asked Questions
Virus Protected E-mails
SSL Sign-In
How To Link To Hotmail
Contact Us
Languages
New to Hotmail?
Sign Up for a Free E-Mail Account! (Why Sign Up?)
(and get a Microsoft® .NET Passport!)
Already have a Hotmail account?
Sign-In Name
@ hotmail.com
Password
Sign In
Forgot Your Password?
Problems Signing In?
Security Options (what's this?):
Public/shared computer.
Keep me signed in to this and all other .NET Passport sites unless I sign out.
Neither
.net Passport
Need more information on Hotmail and .NET Passport? Click here.
© 2003 Microsoft Corporation. All rights reserved.
TERMS OF USE TRUSTe Approved Privacy Statement

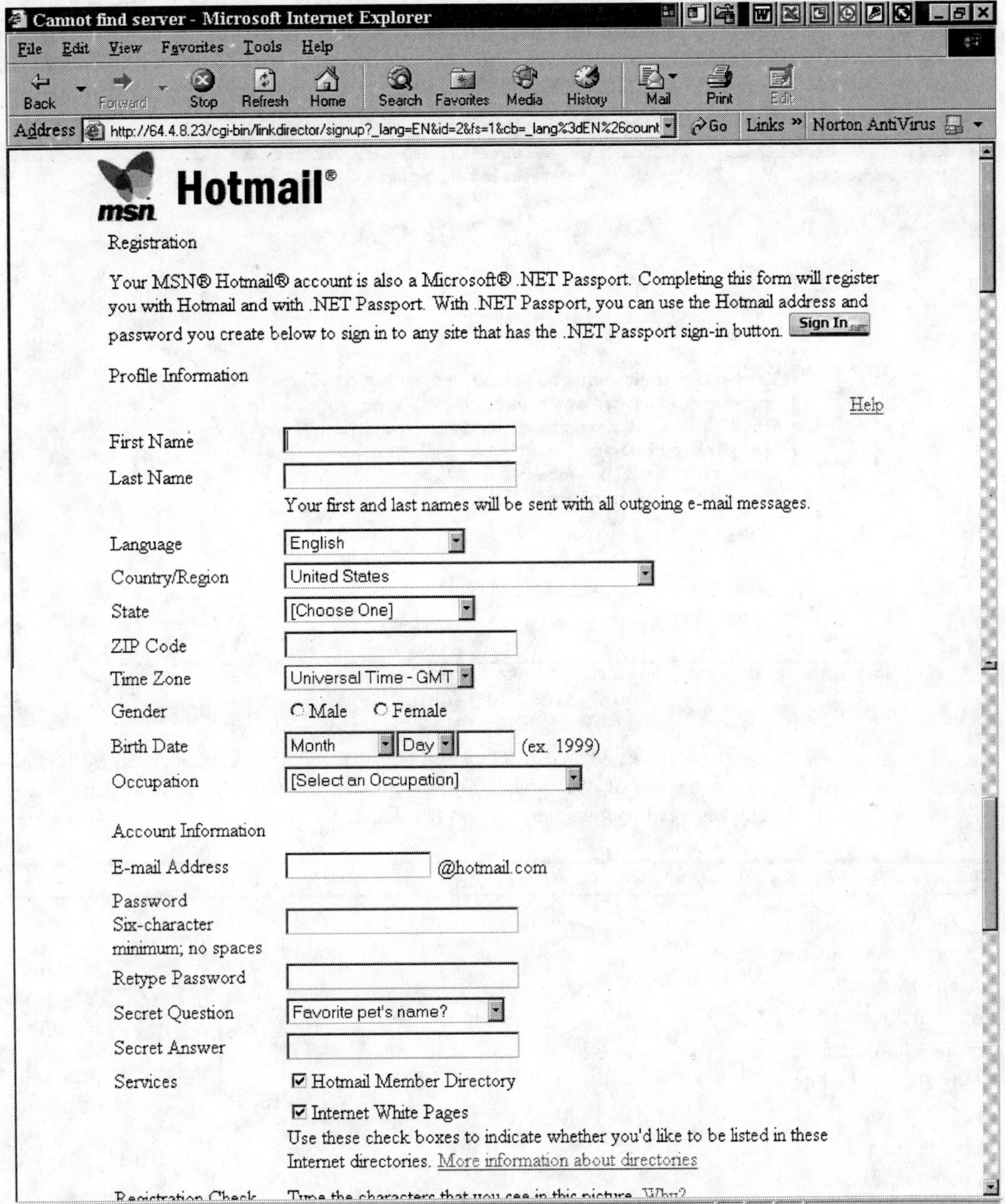

Cannot find server - Microsoft Internet Explorer

File Edit View Favorites Tools Help

Back Forward Stop Refresh Home Search Favorites Media History Mail Print Edit

Address http://64.4.8.23/cgi-bin/linkdirector/signup?_lang=EN&id=2&fs=1&cb=_lang%3dEN%26count Go Links » Norton AntiVirus

msn Hotmail®

Registration

Your MSN® Hotmail® account is also a Microsoft® .NET Passport. Completing this form will register you with Hotmail and with .NET Passport. With .NET Passport, you can use the Hotmail address and password you create below to sign in to any site that has the .NET Passport sign-in button. Sign In

Profile Information

Help

First Name

Last Name

Your first and last names will be sent with all outgoing e-mail messages.

Language: English

Country/Region: United States

State: [Choose One]

ZIP Code

Time Zone: Universal Time - GMT

Gender: Male Female

Birth Date: Month Day (ex. 1999)

Occupation: [Select an Occupation]

Account Information

E-mail Address @hotmail.com

Password Six-character minimum; no spaces

Retype Password

Secret Question: Favorite pet's name?

Secret Answer

Services: Hotmail Member Directory

Internet White Pages

Use these check boxes to indicate whether you'd like to be listed in these Internet directories. More information about directories

Registration Check Type the characters that you see in this picture. Why?

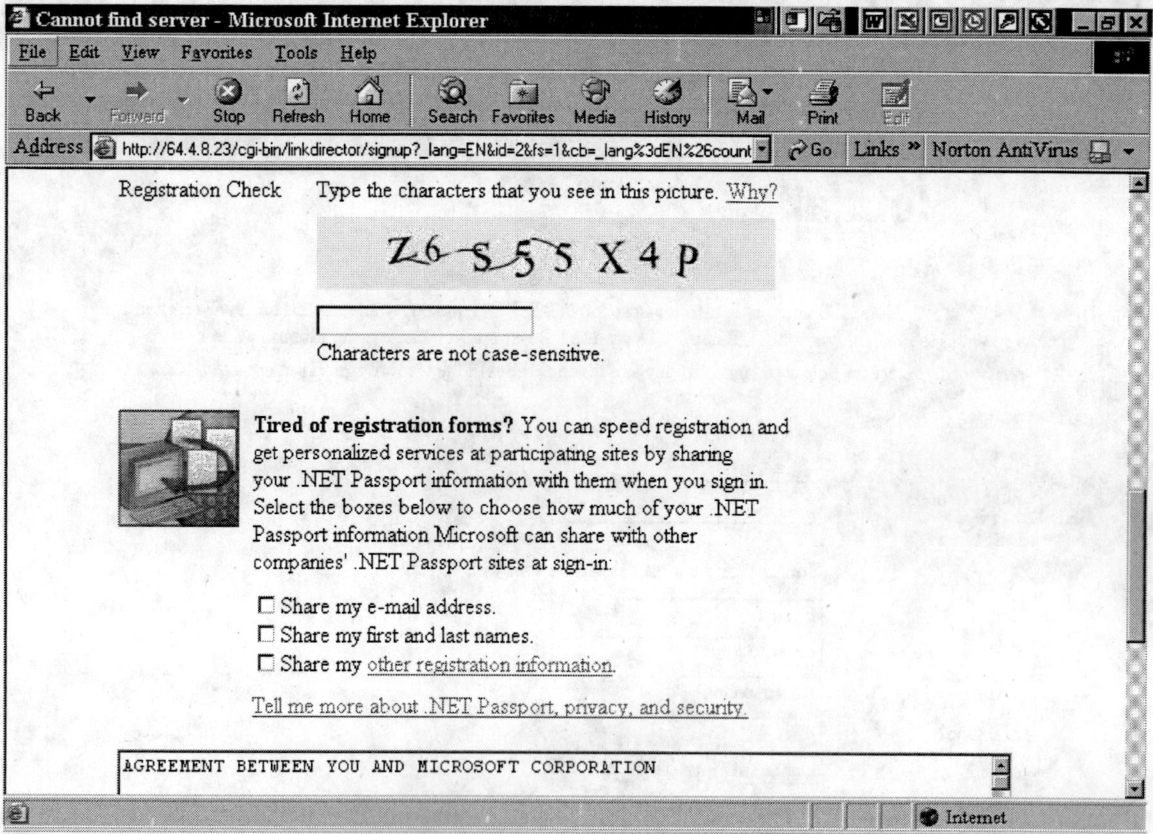


An abbreviation would save both time and space. It is important that the abbreviations used by you are understood equally well by the receiver of your e-Mail. So I give here a list of abbrevations which have by now become the universally accepted abbrevations around the world.

| ***Full Word/Term/Phrase*** | ***Abbreviation*** |
|---|---|
| By The Way | BTW |
| Frequently Asked Questions | FAQ |
| Friend of a friend | FOAF |
| For what it is worth | FWTW |
| For Your Information | FYI |
| In My Humble Opinion | IMHO |
| In My Opinion | IMO |
| In my opinion | IMO |
| In other words | IOW |
| In Regard To | IRT |
| Later | LR |
| Laughing out loud | LOL |
| Member of the appropriate sex | MOTAS |

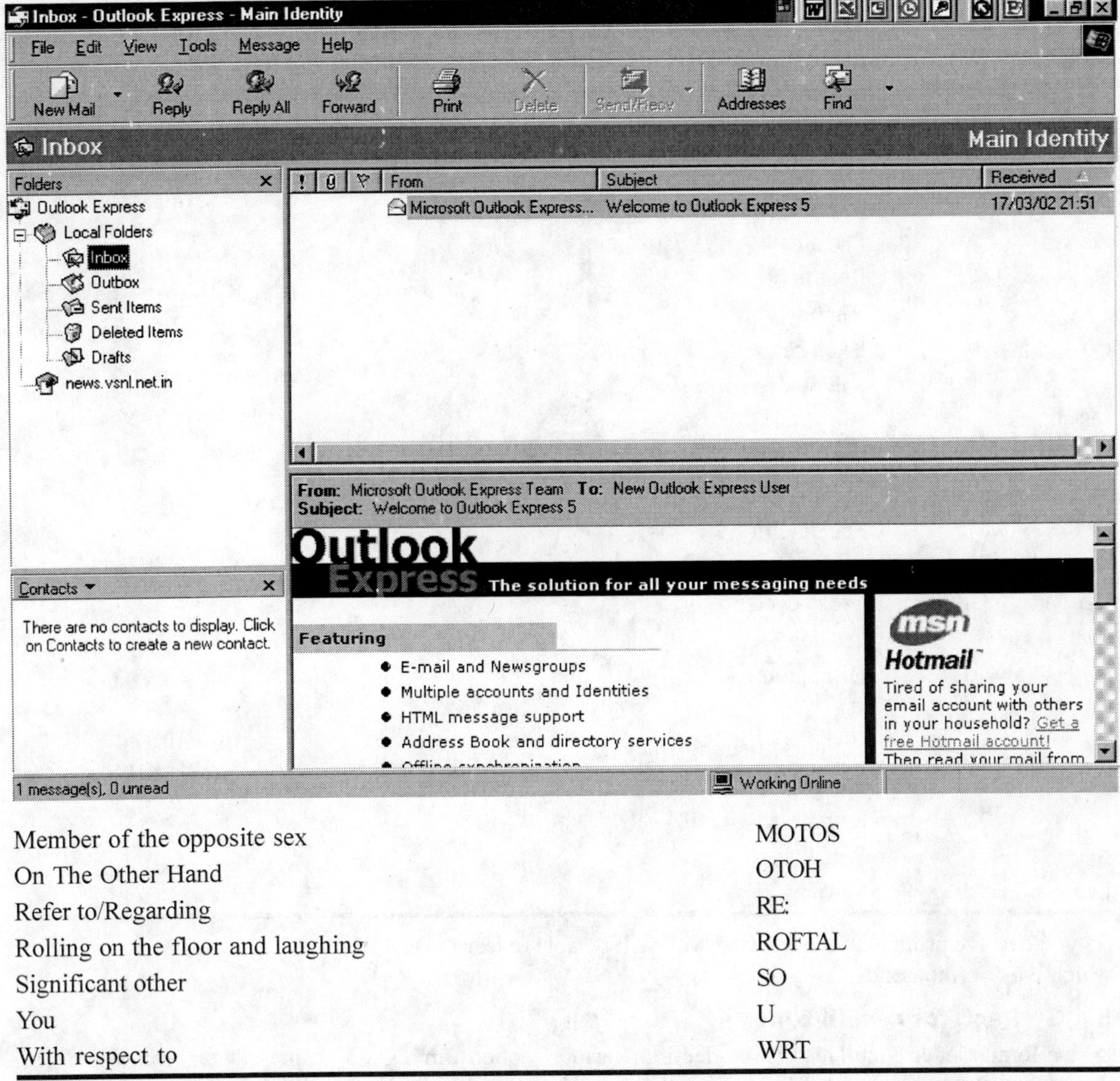


| | |
|---|---|
| Member of the opposite sex | MOTOS |
| On The Other Hand | OTOH |
| Refer to/Regarding | RE: |
| Rolling on the floor and laughing | ROFTAL |
| Significant other | SO |
| You | U |
| With respect to | WRT |

### *5.1.2.2 Using Smilies*

There are lots of ways that you can convey your messages across. Not, only in terms of abbrevations but in terms of small similies too. These are also like abbrevations are finding their way into most of the computers around the world. A smiley is a sequence of characters on your computer's keyboard. For example, the colon represents the eyes, the dash represents the nose and the right parenthesis represents the mouth.

Given below a list of the most common smileys.

| *Emotions* | *Meaning* |
|---|---|
| 8:-) | Little girl |
| X-( | Mad |

| | |
|---|---|
| &-L | Makes me cry |
| :-(*) | Makes me sick |
| :-S | Makes no sense |
| :-{ | Moustache |
| :-# | My lips are seaed |
| 8-O | Omigod! |
| :^) | Personality |
| :-C | Real unhappy |
| :-)^< | Big boy |
| (:-) | Big face |
| :-D | Said with a smile |
| :-)8< | Big girl |
| :-@ | Screening |
| :-V | Shouting |
| :-(< | Standing firm |
| :-0 | Talkative |
| H-) | Cross-eyed |
| :-@! | Cursing |
| :-E | Disappointed |
| (:-( | Very unhappy |
| :-6 | Eating something spicy |
| ]-I | Wearing sunglasses |
| :") | Embrassed |
| '-) | Winking |
| L-O | Yawning |

As you become proficient in e-Mailing, you will be able to learn many more of these fascinating emoticons, which exist in thousands.

### 5.1.3 Parts of e-mail text

Like a formal letter e-mail also is divided into various sections. In a good business letter, you would have, date, the name and address of the person to whom the letter is addressed, salutation, text matter, sender's name, etc. Most of these you would find here too but with some difference. Lets see what an e-mail is supposed to have.

#### *5.1.3.1 Headers*

It is very important that your header must be loud and clear for it can be seen and read from a distance too.

#### *5.1.3.2 To*

The To: field contains the e-mail address of the person to whom you are sending the e-mail. If you are sending e-mail to someone in your own domain, you do not need to include @ domain.

#### *5.1.3.3 From*

In most of the cases, you would not be typing this, since it would be taken from the system. It in fact includes your e-mail address.

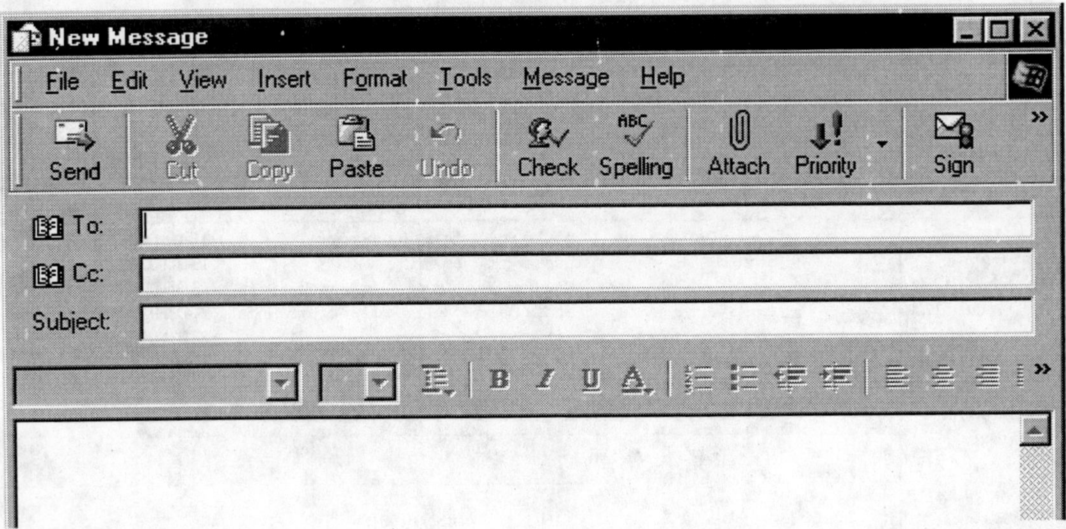


***5.1.3.4 Subject***

The Subject: field should contain a very short description (20-30 characters) of what your message is about. This field can also be called Subject of the Message: or simply message. It is not compulsary to have a subject.

***5.1.3.5 Cc***

You can send the copy of the same e-mail to another person. For this you have to mention the e-mail address of the second receipt. The software would take care that the same message is sent to the second recepient too.

***5.1.3.6 Bcc***

It is the short form of Blind Carbon Copy, which gives you a way of copying and transmitting an e-Mail message to another person, without the first person (the main addressee), knowing about it.

***5.1.3.7 Attachments***

Using this option you can attach a file created in other software along with this e-mail. In most of the cases while applying for a job, the letter is typed in the e-mail text and the bio-data which is mostly in some word processing mode, attached to it.

***5.1.3.8 Date***

Date and time are usually taken from the system. You need not type it.

***5.1.3.9 Body***

The body of an e-Mail message is simply the text that you want to send to the other person.

## 5.1.4 Working with Messages

The first thing that you would do on opening the software would be receive the messages. For this you will have to click on Send/Receive button.

You can also set Outlook to automatically check for messages at regular intervals, or you can have Outlook check for message whenever you want.

1. Click the Send/Receive button on the Standard toolbar, as shown below.
2. The Intenet connection will be made depending upon the type of connection you have. Its progress will be shown to you in the dialog box in the lower right corner of the window.

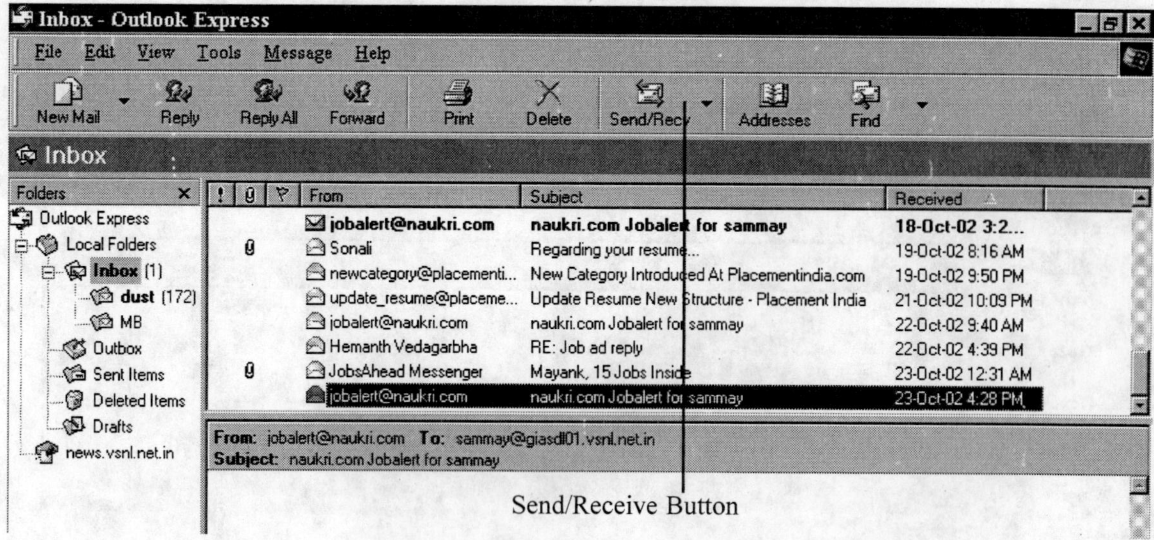


3. When messages arrive, Outlook asks you whether you want to start reading them. Click Yes in the Microsoft Outlook dialog box to starting reading messages, or click No to read them later.

### 5.1.5 Reading a Message

Once the messages have been received in the Inbox, they will be appended to the other ones, i.e., in the last. The last few messages are always new. There are various type of messages which are there in the mailbox. The messages in the Inbox can have the following symbols attached to them.

- Unread message
- High importance message
- Low importance message
- Message that has been read
- Message with attachment
- Message that has been forwarded
- Message that has been replied to
- Meeting for which response is requested
- Follow-up flag

All these have a symbol attached to them.

#### *5.1.5.1 Reading the Message*

1. Double-click a message in the Inbox list.

   Or

   Select the message to open and press Ctrl + O

   Or

   Select the message to open and from the File menu, choose Open. Then choose Selected Items from the submenu.

Each message opens in a separate window.

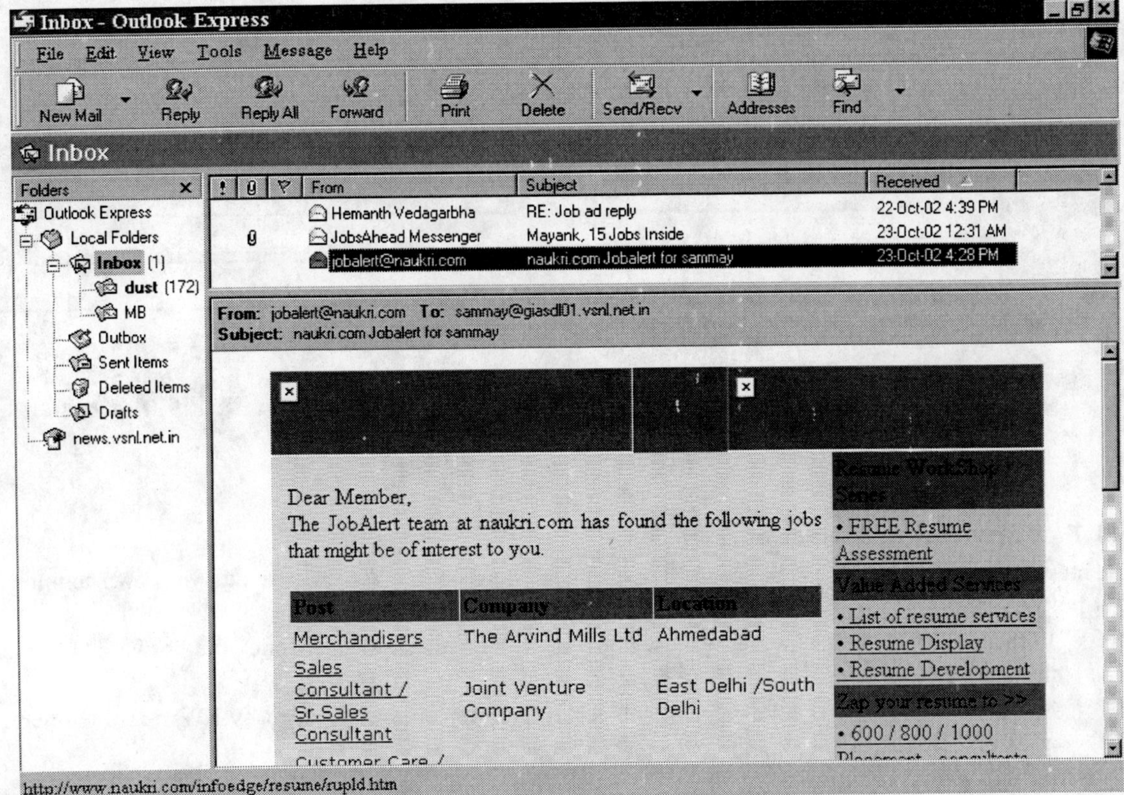


### 5.1.6 Replying to a Message

Once read, a message can either be replied or trashed.

#### *5.1.6.1 To reply to a message:*

1. With a message selected in the Inbox window or with the message open, click the Reply button on the Standard toolbar. The reply has the sender in the To box and the original subject in the Subject box preceded by RE.
2. In the text area, type your reply. The reply appears above the original message.

#### *5.1.6.2 Replying in a Phased Manner*

You can reply in phases. You can type half a reply now, save it and then complete it later. In this case, since the reply is half baked, it is stored in drafts folder.

For this do the following:

1. Click Save on the Standard toolbar.

   Or

   From the File menu, choose Save.
2. Close the window.
3. Outlook places the reply in the Drafts folder. You can open it there to continue working on it.
4. To reply to all of them, click the Reply to All button on the Standard toolbar.
5. You can still edit a message that is waiting in the Outbox. Just double-click the message, make your changes, and then click Send again.

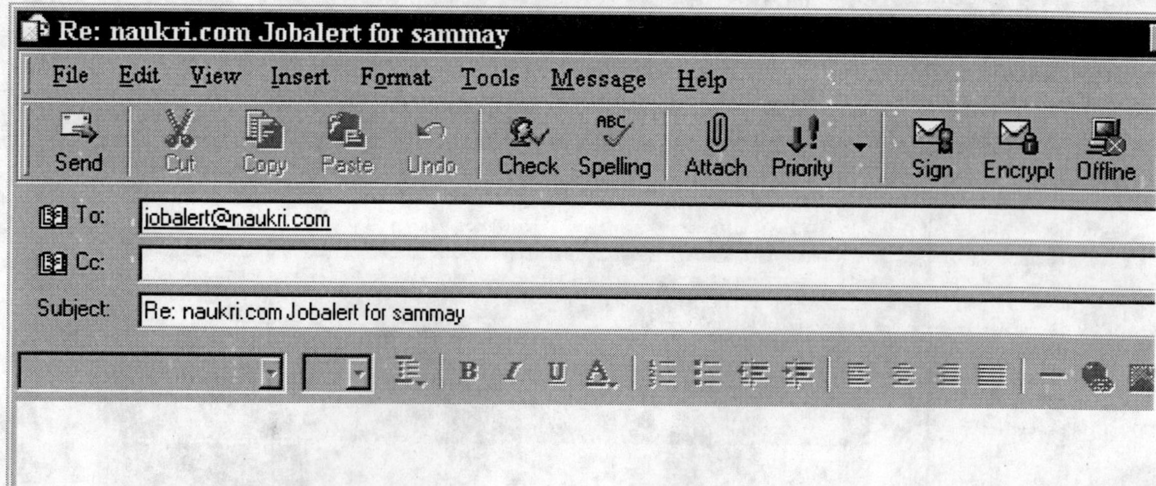


### 5.1.7 Forwarding a Message

The message received from A can be sent to B by using Forward option. You can also add your own comments to it before sending it.

1. With a message selected in the Inbox window or with the message open, click the Forward button on the Standard toolbar.

   The new message shows the original subject in the Subject box preceded by FW, as shown here.
2. Type the recipient's e-mail address in the To box.

   Or

   To select an address from the Address Book, click the To button, select one or more names in the Select Names dialog box, click the To button in the dialog box, and click Ok.
3. Type comments which you want to add in the space above the message.
4. Click Send on the Standard toolbar to move the message to the Outlook folder.
5. If a message has files attached, the files are forwarded as well.

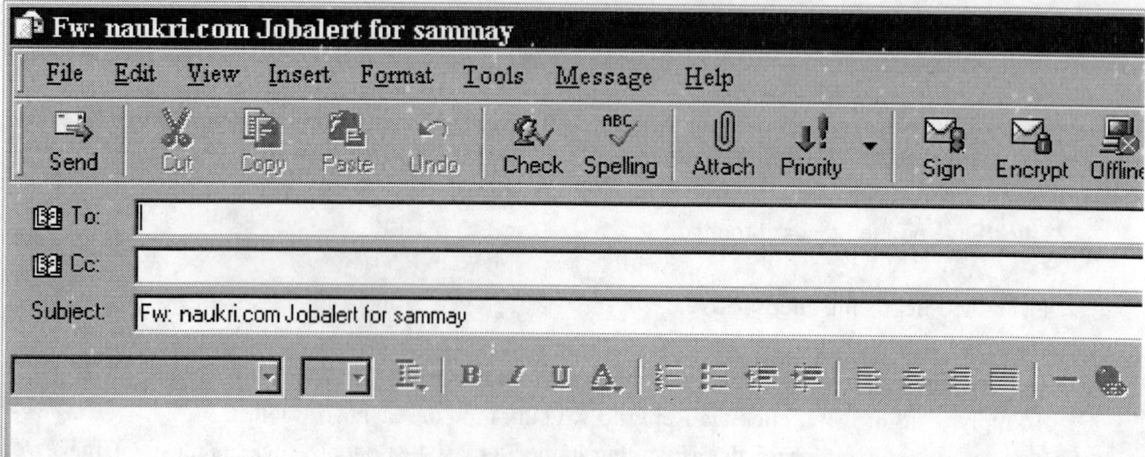

### 5.1.8 Deleting a Message

If you do not require any message, you can delete it or others too.

1. Click the Delete button on the toolbar in the message window.

   Or

   Press Ctrl + D

The message is moved to the Deleted Items folder.

## 5.2 WWW

A global hypertext system that uses the Internet as its transport mechanism is called World Wide Web. In a hypertext system, you navigate by clicking hyperlinks, which display another document (which also contains hyperlinks). What makes the Web such an exciting and useful medium is that the next document you see could be housed on a computer next door-or halfway around the world. The Web makes the Internet easy to use.

Created in 1989 at the European Laboratory for Particle Physics (CERN), a research institute in Switzerland, the Web relies upon the HyperTExt Transport Protocol (HTTP), an Internet standard the specifies how an application can locate and acquire resources (such as document, sound or graphic) stored on another computer on the Internet. HTTP provides transparent, easy-to-use access to Web documents, FTP (File transfer Protocol) file archives, Gopher menus, and even UseNet newsgroups, users of Web navigation software, called Web browsers, simply click on an underlined word or phrase, and HTTP takes care of locating and downloading the desired documents. Most Web documents are created using the HyperText markup language (HTML), a markup language that is easy to learn and will soon be supplanted by automated tools. Incorporating hypermedia (graphics, sound, animations, and video), the Web has become the ideal medium for publishing information on the Internet.

A key 1995 agreement on security protocols ensures that Web will quickly become an important commercial medium, in which consumers can browse on-line catalog and place orders without worrying about anyone intercepting the supplied credit card information.

### 5.2.1 Basic Features

Before we go any further in WWW we must learn more about the basics of it. We had earlier learned what Home page, Web page, Hypertext Hyperlinks, etc., mean. Now we will learn what all comes into play when a web page is opened. The following information is not sequential.

1. Information System
2. Graphical Navigation
3. Platform
4. Distribution
5. Accessing Information
6. Interactiveness

Let us read about them in details.

#### *5.2.1.1 Information System*

As we all know that Internet is full of information. It is upto you to explore it. This information is available in the form of a book. As you can jump from one page to another, the Web also allows you to skip from one page to another using the Hyperlink. Once this information is there on the screen, you can copy, move or transfer it to your hard disk for later reading.

#### *5.2.1.2 Graphical Navigation*

The best part of Web is that it can display both text and graphic with equal ease. What's more there are sites which have sound and video too. So much so that they can be called truly multimedia applications.

#### *5.2.1.3 Platform*

The World Wide Web is not limited to any one kind of machine, or developed by any one company. The Web is entirely cross-platform. It can be displayed on any computer hardware using any operating system.

#### *5.2.1.4 Distribution*

When you run the Internet and access any site, everything works in RAM. There is no hard disk space involved. The information is totally distributive and can be distributed anywhere even to the hard disk, only if the need be.

#### *5.2.1.5 Dynamic*

A web site goes through various changes at various instances. So everytime you load the site, you get the latest site on your screen. You need not go to buy any new software or hardware for that purpose. The web site developer would probably not come and tell you when the site is updated. So while getting the data from the site make sure that you are getting the latest data.

#### *5.2.1.6 Accessing Information*

As mentioned earlier, Internet is full of information. You can get the information from the net using any of the method, maybe FTP, Usenet, Telnet or even e-mail. Although the most popular way of getting the information is by using the software called browsers and the famous ones are Microsoft Internet Explorer and Netscape Navigator. Web browsers can also read files from other Internet services and you can create links to information on those systems just as you would create links to information on Web pages.

#### *5.2.1.7 Interactiveness*

This means that web sites are not just one way information. There are sites which ask for information from you, the users too. This information is mostly taken in the form of Forms. This way the web site developers not only get the information but also are able to access and compile the information in any form.

### 5.2.2 Web Browsers

A software program that is used to view Web pages is called a Browser. Browser help you to connect to Web sites. You can surf the Web, view Web sites and/or download files and programs. A Web browser works by using a protocol called Hypertext Transfer Protocol (HTTP) to request a specially encoded text document from the Web server.

Browsers are so designed that they can run on many kinds of computers and operating systems (also called platforms). Some of the popular browsers are – Microsoft Internet Explorer, Netscape Navigator, Mosaic, Lynx, etc. Amongst these, two browsers are very widely used, namely Netscape's Navigator and Microsoft's Internet Explorer.

### 5.2.3 Popular Web Browsers

To begin with, there was only one browser, named Mosaic, in use and it was available free of cost. It was written by Marc Andreesen, who later started a new venture for making a new browser called Netscape. With the passage of time, Microsoft incorporated in its browser Internet Explorer many of the features for which Netscape used to be preferred by the users. Others are:

#### *5.2.3.1 Lynx*

It is the text only browser and works on Unix platform. It was developed by University of Kansas. It requires the emulation of terminal VT-100. Designing pages that work equally well in Lynx and in graphical browsers is one of the more interesting challenges of Web page design.

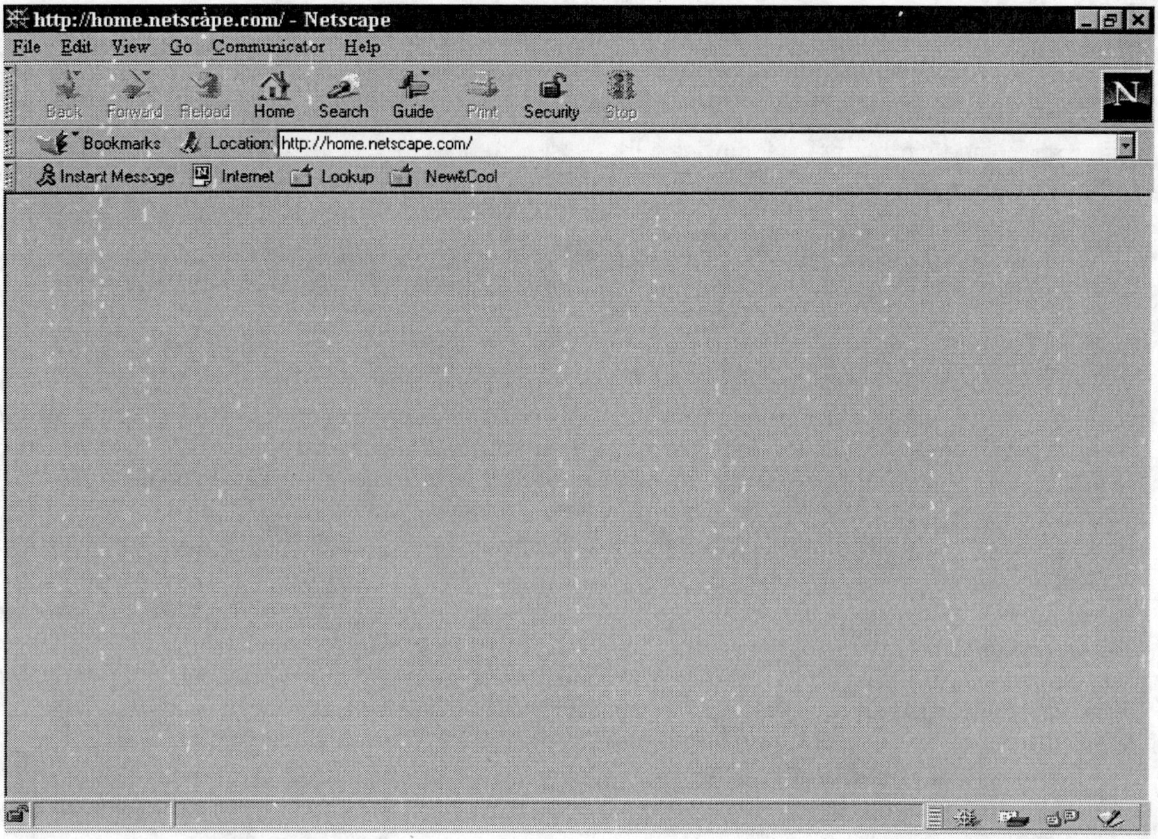

### *5.2.3.2 Netscape Navigator*

It is available for Windows, Macintosh Operating System and Unix too. It supports features like integrated news and mail reader, etc.

### *5.2.3.3 Microsoft Internet Explorer*

No doubt the most popular one. It also runs on most of the operating systems. What's more it is usually free with Windows operating system.

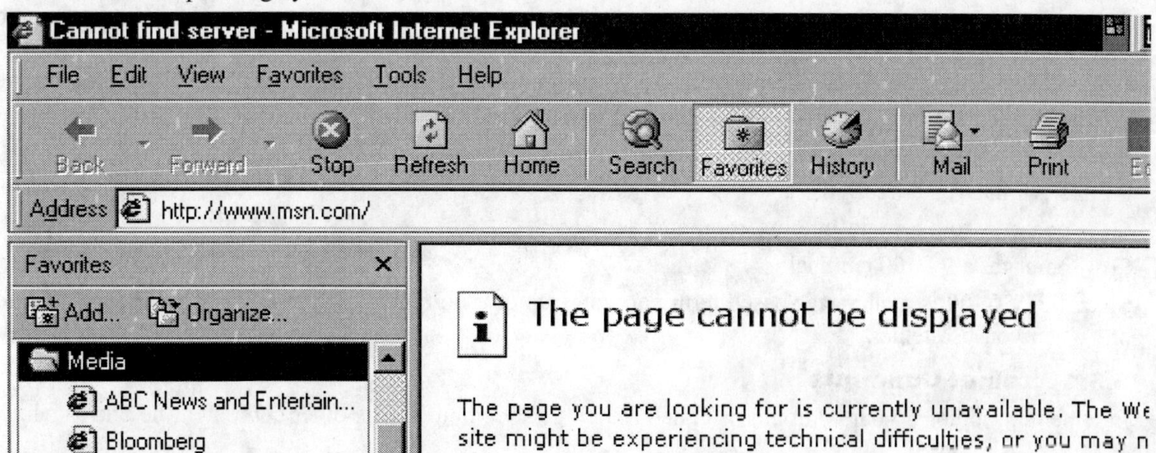

### 5.2.4 Web Servers

To upload a web site a host computer and server software is needed. This manages the communications protocols and the related software required to create a Web site on the Internet. The host machine usually uses Unix. There are different types of servers available.

A web server mostly performs the following jobs:

1. The server software includes configuration files and utilities to secure and manage the Web site in a variety of ways.
2. It passes requests to run CGI (Common Gateway Interface) scripts to the CGI applications. These scripts run external mini-programs, such as a database lookup or interactive forms processing.

## 5.3 Telnet

TELNET is the Internet service that allows you to log in to a remote Internet computer. To utilize this service, you run a telnet client program on your computer. This program uses the Internet to connect to the remote computer. Once the connection is made, your telnet client acts as an intermediary between you and the other computer. Everything you type on your keyboard passed on to the other computer. Everything the other computer displays is sent to your computer, where it appears on your screen. As a result, your keyboard and screen seem to be connected directly to the remote computer. Telnet is actually the oldest of the various Internet services.

Though it may not matter at this stage but let me go though the development of Telnet or the historical background of it. The Internet is the descendent of the Arpanet, a network created in the late 1960s by the U.S. Department of Defense. At that time, there were no personal computers. There were only large, expensive mainframe computers and smaller, expensive "minicomputers". To work a computer interactively, you used a terminal, a device with a screen, a keyboard, some electronics and not much more.

The first service provided on the Arpanet was "Remote login", that is, Telnet. This service, which was a remarkable achievement, allowed researches to work on remote computes from a distance. To do so, they used the Arpanet to connect their terminal to a computer that was part of the Arpanet.

Once the connection was made, a researcher could log in, by typing a user name and password, and use the keyboard and screen on his terminal, just as if it were connected directly to the remote computer. In those days, terminals could only display characters—letters, numbers, punctuation and so on—there were no graphics or windows or pictures. However, compared together methods of using a computer (such as punch cards) terminals were extremely convenient. For this reason, when the Unix operating system was developed, it was designed to work with terminals. And, within a few years, Unix became an important part of the Arpanet. Although Unix was designed to work with many types of terminals, one specific terminal became a de facto standard. This was the VT-100 terminal, manufactured by the Digital Equipment Corporation(DEC). The VT-100 standard became so accepted that, whenever someone wrote a program which needed to provide the functionality of a terminal, he would design the program to act like a VT-100.

In technical terms, we would way that the program would "emulate" a VT-100.

So this is what Telnet really is: a service that

- ❑ connects to a remote Internet computer and
- ❑ emulates a VT-100 terminal.

Since the VT-100 is a character-based terminal, you cannot use graphics (pictures, icons, windows and so on) when you use telnet.

### 5.3.1 Telnet Concepts

In telnet terminology, your computer is called the LOCAL computer. The other computer, the one to which your telnet client connects, is called the REMOTE computer. We use these terms no matter how far away the other computer actually is: whether it is across the world or in the same room. On the Internet, we sometime refer to Internet computers as “hosts”. Using this terminology, we can say the job of your Telnet client is to connect your local computer to a remote Internet host. In general, there are two ways to use Telnet. First, you can connect to any computer on the Internet for which you have a shell account. When you do, you will see the standard login: and Password: prompts. You can now log in and use the computer in the usual manner. Second, there are many public resources which you can access via Telnet. Some of these do not require a password. As soon as your Telnet client makes the connection, you can start working with the remote computer. For example, a number of public library catalogs are set up in this manner. Other public services (such as MUDs) do require passwords. The first time you connect to one of these systems, you will be asked to choose a user name and password. From then on, you would log in using whatever name and password you have chosen.

### 5.3.2 Using Telnet Client

To use Telnet, you turn a Telnet client program. This program connects you to a remote Internet host and then emulates a VT-100 terminal. If you across the Internet using a shell account your telnet client will be the Unix telnet program. Otherwise, you use telnet by running a client program on your own computer. If you have a PC, you will run a Windows client. If you have a Macintosh, you will run a Macintosh client program. Windows 95 comes with its own telnet clients. You can use the built-in client or you can find another one. Telnet clients for PCs are readily available on the Net. With Windows 95, you can start the telnet program in the regular manner (by double-clicking on an icon or by putting it in your Start menu), or you can go to a DOS prompt and enter the telnet command. Regardless of how you start the program, it works the same.

Using a telnet client is easy. All you have to do is start the program, and tell it the name of the remote host to which you want to connect. Once the connection to the host is established, you will see whatever message that computer displays as part of the starting procedure. If you connect a Unix computer which experts you to log in, it will start by displayed the line:

```
Login:
```

Type the appropriate user name and press ENTER. You will then see the line:

```
Password:
```

Type the password and press ENTER. You will now be logged in. Once your Telnet client starts, there is generally nothing special to do. Just log into to the remote computer and start work. However, there are certain facets of the telnet program you can control by using the pull-down menus. Each program operates differently, so be sure to read the help information for your particular program.

### 5.3.3 Working with Telnet

To start Telnet, enter the name of the command followed by the address of the remote host to which you want to connect. For example, say that you want to connect to a computer named **nim**, whose full address is **nim.ucsb.edu**. Enter the following:

```
telnet nim.ucsb.edu
```

If you are connecting to a computer on your local network, you can usually get by with just the name of the computer, instead of the full address. For example:

```
telnet nim
```

When the telnet program starts, it will initiate a connection to the remote host that you specified. As telnet is waiting for a response, you will see;

```
Trying...
```

or a similar message. Once the connection is made, which might take a few moments if the host is far away, you will see a message like the following:

```
Connected to nim.ucsb.edu.
Escape character is '^]'.
```

If, for some reason, telnet is unable to make the connection, you will see a message telling you that the host is unknown. For example, say that you want to connect to the remote host nippet.com. However, you mistakenly enter:

```
telnet nippet.com
```

You will see:

```
nippet.com: unknown host
telnet?
```

At this point you can either specify another host name or quit the program. Another problem that may arise is that your local network may, for some reason, not be able to make connections to certain parts of the Internet. One reason is that a particular host may be off-limits for security reasons. Another reason is that some locations just do not have a way to connect to other locations. In that case you will get a message similar to:

```
Host is unreachable
```

If this happens to you, double-click that you are entering your telnet command correctly. You can also ask your system manager if there is some trick that you don't understand about making such a connection. However, if the remote host is really unreachable from where you are, there is not much you can do about it. Once telnet makes a connection, you will be interacting with the remote host. At this point, most hosts display some type of informative message, usually identifying the computer. If you are expected to log in, you will see the standard prompt. For example if you have connected to a remote Unix computer, you will see:

```
Login:
```

You can now log in in the regular manner:

Type your userid and press RETURN. You will then see.

```
Password:
```

Now enter your password and press RETURN again. When you type your password, it will not be displayed. This prevents someone else from finding out your password by watching you log in. When you are finished working with the remote computer, all you need to do is log out in the regular manner. The connection will break and telnet will stop automatically.

### 5.3.4 A Second Way to Start telnet

The second way to start telnet without specifying a host. Simply enter:

```
telnet
```

the program will start by will not make a connection. You will see:

```
telnet>
```

this is the telnet prompt. It means that the program has started and is waiting for you to enter a command. To make a connection to a remote host, type open, followed by the address of the host. For example:

```
open nim.ucsb.edu
```

the connection will be made just as if you had specified it when you entered the telnet command. If you need to specify a port number, simply type it after the computer name. Be sure to leave a space before the number. For example:

```
open nighemare.winternet.com 1701
```

Earlier a telnet command had been given with a bad address. In the example, the remote host was named nipper.com, but we mistakenly entered:

```
telnet nippest.com
```

What happens in such a case is that telnet tries to make the connection. When it can't it gives up and display its prompt, waiting for you to enter a command. In this case, you would see:

```
Nippest.com: unknown host
telnet>
```

You can now enter an open command with the correct address;

```
Open nipper.com
```

If this address doesn't work, you can try another one. If you decide to give up, enter:

```
Quit
```

This will stop the telnet program.

### 5.3.5 The Escape Character: CTRL+]

As you interact with a remote host, there is a way to put your work on hold and enter commands directly to telnet. For example, you are having problems with the remote host, you can pause your work session, return to telnet and enter the Quit command. To do so, you press the special key combination CTRL+]. That is, you hold down the CTRL key and press ] (the right square bracket). When you press this key combination, it sends a signal to telnet to pause the remote connection and display the prompt:

```
telnet>
```

You can now enter any telnet command that you want. With some commands, telnet will automatically resume the connection after carrying out the command. Otherwise, you can resume the connection at any time by pressing RETURN at the telnet> prompt. The technical term for a key like CTRL is an ESCAPE CHARACTER. Many programs allows you to use an escape character to request a special service or to indicate that what follows is to be interpreted differently. In the world of Unix, there is a convention that CTRL keys are often indicated by using the ^ (carat) character. For example CTRL-C would be written as ^C. Now we can make sense out of the message at appears whenever telnet makes a remote connection:

```
Escape character is '^]'
```

You are being reminded that the telnet escape character is CTRL. It is possible to change this to another character but there is usually no reason to do so.

### 5.3.6 Using Telnet Commands

Any time you are the at the telnet> prompt, there are a number of different commands that you can use. Now, I will go over the most important ones. Before I do, I will remind you that if instead of entering a command you just press RETURN, telnet will resume the remote connection. To display a summary of the various telnet commands, you can enter the ? character:

```
?
```

Here is a typical summary:

| *Command* | *Description* |
|---:|---|
| close | close current connection |
| display | display operating parameters |
| mode | try to enter line-by-line or character-at-a-time mode |

| | |
|---|---|
| open | connect to a site |
| quit | exit telnet |
| send | transmit special characters |
| set | set operating parameters |
| status | print status information |
| toggle | toggle operating parameters |
| z | suspend telnet |
| ? | print help information |

Out of all these commands, the most important ones are **?**, **open**, **close**, **quit** and **z**.

#### *5.3.6.1 Open*

The open command tells telnet to make a connection to a remote computer. Enter open followed by the address of the computer: For example:

```
Open nim.ucsb.edu
```

This will leave the telnet> prompt and connect you to the remote computer.

#### *5.3.6.2 Close*

The close command terminates a remote connection without stopping the telnet program. Here is how this might come in handy. Let's say you are working with a remote host and something goes wrong. For some reason, the host seems to be ignoring your commands. No mater what you type, nothing happens and you can't even log out. One solution is to press CTRL, wait for the telnet> prompt and then enter the Close command. You can now re-establish a connection to the same host. You can, of course, also connect to a different host.

#### *5.3.6.3 Quit*

The quit command stops telnet. If a remote connection is active, telnet will terminate it.

#### *5.3.6.4 Other commands*

All the other commands are less important and you will probably never need to use them. For the most part, they control various technical aspects of the communication session that you can almost always ignore. If you want to display a summary of the send, set or toggle commands, enter the command followed by a ? character. For example:

```
Send ?
```

#### *5.3.6.5 Job Control*

Unix systems support a facility, called JOB CONTROL, that allows you to pause a program, work with another program and then return to the first one. At the telnet prompt, you can enter the **z** command. This tells telnet to pause itself and return you to the shell (the program that reads and process your commands.). This allows you to enter regular commands on your local computer in the middle of a remote session. The z command will only work if your shell supports job control.

## 5.4 FTP

FTP is the short name for File Transfer Protocol. FTP is the Internet service that allows you to transfer files from one computer to another. Like all Internet services, ftp uses a client/server system. You run a client program on your computer which connects to a server program on a remote compute. You tell your client what to do and it carries out your orders by sending commands to the server.

When you copy a file from a remote computer to your own computer, we say that you are DOWNLOADING the file. When you copy a file from your computer to the remote one, you are UPLOADING the file. In ftp terminology, your computer is called the LOCAL HOST. The other computer is called the REMOTE HOST. Thus, we can say that ftp allows you to upload and download files to and from a remote host. Sometimes we use the word "ftp" as a verb.

### 5.4.1 Anonymous Ftp

The ftp service lets you transfer files from one Internet computer to another. However, there is one basic restriction: you cannot access a computer unless you can log into it. In other words, you cannot copy fields to or from a remote computer unless you have a user name and a password. ANONYMOUS FTP is a facility that lets you connect to certain remote hosts and download files without having to be registered as a user. To do so, you log in using a special user name: **anonymous**. With this user name you do not need a regular password. Instead, you type your mail address.

For example, say your mail address is laxmi@nim.com. When you connect to an anonymous ftp server, you would log in as anonymous and use a password of laxmi@nim.com. The beauty of this system as it allows anyone on the Internet to lot in to a remote host and download public files without having an account on that system. It is important to understand that the anonymous user name will only work with computers that have been set up to act as anonymous ftp servers: that is, with those computers that are set up as repositories of publicly-available files. Moreover, the anonymous user name is only for ftp access. You cannot, for example, use a telnet connection and expect to log in as anonymous.

As you might imagine, allowing people all over the Internet to access your computer is not something you do frivolously. There are a number of security considerations which must be addressed. Anonymous ftp hosts are set up to be secure so that outsiders cannot cause trouble, even inadvertently. For example the system manager can control exactly which files on the computer are available for anonymous ftp access. The rest of the files are off limits and cannot be accessed except by people with valid user accounts.

As an extra security measure, many anonymous ftp hosts will not allow you to upload files. In other words, you can copy all the files you want from the remote host to your computer, but you cannot copy files from the remote host to your computer, but you cannot copy files from your computer to the host. Some anonymous ftp hosts to allow anyone.to upload files, which will then be upload the files to a special, designated directory which is not accessible for files, he or she will move them to one of the public download areas. In this way, remote users are protected against people who might upload troublesome files, such as programs with viruses.

#### *5.4.1.1 The importance of Anonymous Ftp*

At first, anonymous ftp sounds useful but not really all that special. Okay, so anyone on the Internet can access files on an anonymous ftp host. What's the big deal?

The big deal is that the public anonymous ftp achieves are so vast as to be well beyond human understanding. The internet has thousands of anonymous ftp hosts offering all kinds of files for free. Virtually every type of information and every type of many organizations have generously donated disk space and computing facilities to make these files available. Nobody gets paid for proving and anonymous ftp service, but countless people set up and maintain anonymous ftp hosts as a public service available to anyone. Until you start to use anonymous ftp this may not sound like much. Anonymous ftp is one of the most significant inventions in the history of mankind. This can be credited to for three important reasons.

*First,* anonymous ftp allows you to download virtually any type of information. Until you are an experienced Internet user it is difficult to appreciate how important this is, but, put simply, anonymous ftp provides access to the largest library of information ever accumulated. Moreover, it is an ever-growing library that never closes, covers every conceivable topic and best of all, is free. *Second,* anonymous ftp is the principal way in which software is distributed on the Internet. Indeed, the reason the Internet can exist at all is that we all use standardized programs. Most of these programs are distributed via anonymous ftp and hence, are available to anyone who wants to use the Internet or to set up an internet host.

For example, in order to provide access to the Usenet discussion groups. Your Internet service provider must have installed the Usenet software on their computer. Where does the system manager acquire his software? Anonymous ftp. Here is another example. In order to use the Internet with a PC, you need client programs to run on your computer. Where do you get such clients? You could buy them or get them for free from your Internet service provider, but many people download their clients for free by using anonymous ftp. This is especially important when a new version of a client is released. You can download it the same day from one of the anonymous ftp sites. Indeed, if you were to write a new Internet exposure for your product would be to make it available to the public via anonymous ftp (and this is exactly what people do).

The *final reason* anonymous ftp is so important is it is used to achieve and disseminate the technical information that defines the Internet itself. It is called REQUEST FOR COMMET or RFC. Each RFC is given a number and is made freely available to anyone who wants to read it. In this manner, the technical information that supports the Internet is distributed around the world in an organized, reliable manner. Programmers and engineers who must design products to work with the Internet protocols can ensures that everyone is using the same specifications and that all Internet programs are designed to follow the same set of standards. Thus, without anonymous ftp, there would be no modern-day Internet.

### 5.4.2 Using a Browser For Anonymous Ftp

There are two different types of ftp clients. First, there are programs that can serve as ftp clients, but which were really designed for some other primary purpose. For example, web browsers are designed to serve as web clients, but can also act as ftp clients. Alternatively, there are programs designed specially to be ftp clients and nothing else.

If you spend most of your time using the Web and your anonymous ftp needs are small, a browser will work just fine. However, if you use anonymous ftp a lot, you will be better off with an actual ftp client program. There are two ways to access an anonymous ftp resources using a browser. From time to time, you will encounter an ftp resources as a link on a web page. When you click on that link, your browser will automatically contact the ftp site, log in as anonymous, send your mailing address as a password and request the file. Depending on how your browser has been configured. You may have to specify where you want to put the file before the actual data transfer takes place.

For example, say you are reading a web page having to do with stupid things and you encounter a link that says the Stupid FAQ. When you move your mouse pointer to this link, you see the following URL:

```
ftp://ftp.sunet.se/pub/usenet/news.answers/stupidity/FAQ
```

This URL points to a particular anonymous ftp resources on the computer named ftp.sunset.se in a directory named /pub/usenet/news.answers/stupidity. Within that directory is the information in question, stored in a file named FAQ.

When you click on this link, your browser will act like an ftp client and contact the specified computer in order to download the file on your behalf. It will all the be automatic. As an alternative to finding an anonymous ftp resource on a web page, all browsers have a way for you to enter a URL directly. This means you can jump directly to an ftp site by just entering the appropriate URL. Here is an example that shows how this works.

Let's say you read about a file containing cheese recipes. The file is available via anonymous ftp from the computer named ftp.spies.com On that computer, in a directly named /Library/Article/Food the recipes are contained in a file named cheese.rcp. To construct the appropriate URL, use the following format:

```
ftp://computer/pathname
```

(The pathname is the directory + file name.) in this case, the URL to use would be:

```
ftp://ftp.spies.com/Library/Article/Food/cheese.rcp
```

Just tell your browser that you wish to enter a URL and type this URL. The browser will connect to the remote ftp host and download the recipe file for you.

### 5.4.3 Using an Ftp Client for Anonymous Ftp

An ftp client is a program designed for one purpose: to use the ftp service to copy files from one Internet computer to another. It is possible to access anonymous ftp resources with a browser, but an ftp client will provide more features and afford more control over the process. Now, I describe how to use an ftp client for anonymous ftp. Here I refer to files and directories, which are explained in the next section. For now, if you are not familiar with how directories are used, you only need to understand three things:

1. On a Windows computer, directories are called "folders".
2. Directories are used to organize files.
3. Directories can contain either files or other directories, or both.

If you access the Internet via PPP or a direct network connection, you will use a graphical ftp client that runs on your own computer. If you access the Internet via a shell account, you will use a text-based ftp client that runs on the host computer.

The most common text-based client is called ftp and runs under Unix.

If you access the Internet via PPP or a direct network connection, you will use a graphical ftp client that runs on your own computers. If you access the Internet via a shell account, you will use a text-based ftp client that runs on the host computer. The most common text based client is called ftp and runs under Unix. All graphical clients work more or less the same way. Typically, your window will be divided into two sections, one on the right and one on the left. The directory names are in the top part; the file names are in the bottom part. On the left, you can see similar information about the local computer.

All ftp clients have their own nuances, of course, but the general process of accessing an anonymous ftp resource generally involves the following steps:

1. Establish a connection to the remote host. To establish a connection, you will have to specify the name of the remote computer. You may also have to enter a user name and password. Use a user name of anonymous and your mail address for a password. Some ftp programs let you select "anonymous ftp" as an option, in which case you will not need to specify a user name and password: the program will know what to use. Once the connection is established, your ftp client will request a listing of the contents of the top level directory. When it arrives, the information will be displayed on the right with the directory names on top and the file names on the bottom.
2. Navigate to the directory on the remote host that contains the file you want. To navigate on the remote computer, you select directory names from the list on the right, one name after another, until you get to where you want. Each time you select a directory name you will have to wait for your ftp client to request a listing of the new directory from the remote computer. When this listing arrives, it will be displayed, directories on top, files on the bottom. Eventually, you will reach the directory that contains the file you want. At that point, you should see the name of your file in the list.
3. Set the options you want for the transfer. There are various options you can set to specify what type of file transfer you want. In particular, you can use either an "ASCII" transfer for text files, or a "binary" transfer for binary files. (If you are downloading software, be sure to use "binary".) Your program may also have special options or settings pertaining to your type of computer.
4. Select the file to be transferred. With most ftp programs, you highlight the name of the file you want by clicking on it with your mouse.
5. Navigate to the directory on the local host (your computer) to which you want to download the file. Check the left side of the window to see the current directory on your own computer. This is the

directory into which your ftp client will copy the file. If this is not where you want to copy the file, navigate to the directory you want.

6. Initiate the file transfer. With some programs, you initiate the downloading – copying of the file from the remote computer to your computer – by clicking on a button that has a left arrow. The idea is you are copying a file from the right (remote computer) to the left (local computer). With other programs, you may have to click on a "transfer" button or something similar.

   Basically, that is all there is to downloading a file via anonymous ftp. You ftp client will have its own special features, but the general idea is the same with all ftp programs.

There are two features that are especially useful in your ftp program. The *first* feature is a **view** function. This allows you to select a file and then view it without actually copying it to your local directory the file is copied to your computer, but it is not stored permanently. Indeed your ftp client stores the data in a temporary file and then calls upon an editor program to display the file for you. This feature is handy when you want to take a quick look at a file but you don't want to keep a copy of it (such as a README file).

The *second* feature to look for in your ftp client is the capability of storing various configurations. This allows you to save the names of your favorite anonymous ftp sites, so you can connect to them easily whenever you want. Indeed, most client programs include configurations for well-known, useful anonymous ftp sites. For example, if your program has a list of configurations, you will probably see well-known software archives for Windows and DOS systems, as such sites are useful to just about everyone.

### 5.4.4 Files

Once you start using anonymous ftp, you will find you need to know something about files and directories. Since most of the anonymous ftp hosts are Unix computers, you will need to know something about the Unix file system. Within Unix, the definition of a file is a highly generalized one. A file is considered to be any source of input or any target of output. For our purposes, this definition is too technical so let us be a bit more informal: a FILE is a collection of data. Files can hold any type of information that can be stored on a computer: programs, documents, pictures, sounds and so on. Files are kept on some type of storage device: a hard disk, a floppy disk, a CD or a tape. When you use anonymous ftp, you are almost always accessing files stored on a hard disk.

Every file has a name. Whenever you want to do something with a file, you must refer to it by its name. For example, if you want to download a file using anonymous ftp, you must be able to tell your ftp client the name of the file your want. Unix file names can consist of letters, numbers and certain punctuation characters. Here, for example are two typical Unix file names: rfc1325.txt and rfc-index.txt. Unix distinguishes between uppercase (capital) letters and lowercase (small) letters. For this reason, you must be careful to use the exact letters when you type a file Unix, the letters R and r are completely different, so rfc325.txt and Rfc1325.txt are two completely different names. For the most part, Unix file names consist of all lowercase letters. However, there will be times when you encounter a file name that has uppercase letters. When you do, be sure to type the name exactly.

#### *5.4.4.1 Directories*

Within Unix, files are organized into collections called DIRECTORIES. When you connect to an anonymous ftp site, you will fine a number of directories. In order to download a file, you must be able to specify the exact name of the directory in which the file lies, as well as the name of the file itself. Around the Net, various computers act as Usenet archive sites by making copies of the FAQs available via anonymous ftp. For example, all of these sites will have the file folklore-faq. One well-known Usenet archive is the computer rtfm.mit.edy. On this computer, the file folklore-faq is kept in the directory named /pub/usenet/news.answers.

How can we make sense of that name? To do so, all we need to understand how Unix organizes directories. Being able to collect files into directories is important. However, many Unix systems have thousands of files and merely collecting them into directories is not enough: we need more levels of organization. The solution is to collect the directories themselves into other directories, to form a hierarchy. For example, on the rtfm.mit.edu computer, all the public directories are kept in a directory named pub. Within pub, all the directories containing Usenet information are kept in a directory named usenet. Within the usenet directory, there are files and directories are kept in a directory named usenet. Within the usenet directory, there are files and directories that contain information relating to the various discussion groups.

Now, it happens that there is a special group named news.answers whose purpose is to act as a repository for all the FAQs that are posted to the various other groups. Thus, on the rtfm.mit.edu host, the usenet directory contains a directory named news.answers which is used to hold all the FAQs. That is why the file named folklore-faq is found within the directory named /pub/usenet/news.answers. When a directory contains another directory, the first directory is called the PARENT DIRECTORY and the second directory is called a SUBDIRECTORY. In our example, usenet is a subdirectory of pub, while pub is the parent directory of usenet. Similarly, news.answers is a subdirectory of usenet, while usenet is the parent directory of news.answers.

Each Unix computer has one main directory which is the overall parent for all the subdirectories and files on the system. This main directory is called the ROOT DIRECTORY. Within the root directory are subdirectories; within these subdirectories are other subdirectories; and so on. If you were to draw a diagram of such a system, it would look like a tree with branches and sub-branches growing from one main trunk: hence the name, "root directory" for the main trunk. When we write the fullname of a subdirectory, we start at the root directory and show each directory we must pass through in order to reach the ultimate branch. In our example, we start at the root directory, pass through the pub subdirectory, the usenet subdirectory and finally, we read the news.answers subdirectory. To write this down, we use the following two rules.

First, we use a single / (slash) character to indicate the root directory; we do not actually spell the name, hence, the name /pub/usenet/news.answers. Literally, it means, "Start from the root directory, then go to the pub subdirectory, then go to the usenet subdirectory and finally, go to the news.answers subdirectory." Where you are connected to a Unix computer you can think of yourself as sitting somewhere in the directory tree. Whichever directory you are in is called your CURRENT DIRECTORY or WORKING DIRECTORY. By using the appropriate commands, you can move from one directory to another. Each time you move, your current directory changes.

For convenience, we often describe the location of a file by tacking its name onto find the urban folklore FAQ list, all you have to do is tell him to ftp to rtfm.mit.edu is the same as saying. "The file is folkore-faq and it is found in the directory named news.answers, which is in the directory named usenet, which is in the directory named pub, which is in the root directory."

#### *5.4.4.2 Path*

A description like this – in which the names are separated by / character – is called A PATHNAME or a PATH. Thus, in order to ftp a file, anywhere on the Internet all you need to know is (1) the name of an anonymous ftp host that has the file and (2) the pathname of that file. If you take a look at a catalog of Internet resources, you will see that ftp resources are described in just this way. As a convenience, there are two special names used as abbreviations within the Unix file system. First, the name .(a single period) refer to the current directory. The name ..(two periods) refers to the parent of the current directory. When you talk about these abbreviations, the . character is referred to as "dot". For example, say you are connected to the rtfm., mit.edu computer and your current directory is /pub/usenet. The . (dot) directory is /pub/usenet. The .. (dot-dot) directory is /pub.

You won't use these abbreviations a lot, but you should know what they mean when you see them. In particular, you should know that selecting the item named .. from a list of directories will move you one level higher in the tree. For example, if your current directory is /pub/usenet and you select the ..directory, you will move to /pub.

### 5.4.5 Starting the ftp Program

To download or upload files from a remote host, you use the ftp program. This program acts as a client and connects to the ftp server on a remote host. Once the connection is made, you will be asked to specify a userid and password. You can then enter whatever ftp commands you want. To start ftp, enter the name of the command followed by the address of the remote host to which you want to connect. For example, say you want to download files from the computer named rtfm.mit.edu.

Enter the command:

```
ftp rtfm.mit.edu
```

When the ftp program starts, it will initiate connection to the remote host you specified. Once the connection is made – which might take a few moments if the host is far away – you will see a message like the following:

```
Connected to BLOOM-PICAYUNE.MIT.EDU.
220 rtfm ftpd (wu-2.4(26)); bugs to ftp-bugs@rtfm.mit.edu
Name (rtfm.mit.edu:harley):
```

The first line of this message shows us that we have made the connection. Notice that the name of the computer we have connected to is really bloom-picayune.mit.edu. This is because the name rtfm.mit.edu is actually alias for bloom-picayune.mit.edu.

Such aliasing is fairly common in the world of anonymous ftp because it allows us to use easily remembered names. It also gives system managers the flexibility to change computers whenever they want without confusing people. For example, if it should become necessary for the rtfm system manager to use a different computer for anonymous ftp, he does not have to inform everybody of the change. All he has to do is ensure that the address rtfm.mit.edu is aliased to the new computer.

It is especially common to see names that begin with ftp. For example, the Electronic Frontier Foundation has an anonymous ftp host named ftp.eff.org. (The EFF is a public-service organization dedicated to "the pursuit of policies and activities that will advance freedom and openness in computer-based communications". As part of its work, the EFF maintains an anonymous ftp host that contains a wealth of interesting information, including electronic magazines.) The public name of the EFF's anonymous ftp host is ftp.eff.org. However, when you ftp to this address, you will see that it is actually aliased to another computer. Now, to return to our example, the second line we say was:

```
220 rtfm ftpd (wu-2.4(26)); bugs to ftp-bugs@rtr.mit.edu
```

This tells us the name of the ftp server and the version of the ftp software being used and were to send mail if you find a bug.

Finally, let us look at the last line of the message:

```
Name (ftrm.mit.edu:harley):
```

This is a request from our ftp client program, asking as what userid we want to use to log into the computer named rtfm.mit.edu. As it happens, we are currently logged into the local host as harley. The ftp program knows this and suggests that we may want to use the same userid on the remote system. That is why you see the name harley in parentheses. If you press RETURN, the ftp program will use this userid as a default and send it to the remote host. However, in this case (and most of the time), you will want to log in as anonymous. Simply type this name and press RETURN:

```
anonymous
```

you now see:

```
331 Guest login ok, send e-mail address as password.
password:
```

The ftp server has approved the userid anonymous. You are now being asked to enter your mail address as a password. Out of courtesy, it is a good idea to honor this request.

Indeed, some ftp servers will not let you log in if your password does not look like a valid address. Once you have entered an approved userid and password, you will see a message like the following:

```
230 Guest login ok, access restriction apply.
ftp?
```

This means that you are officially logged in and can use the anonymous ftp facility.

The second line, ftp> is a prompt form your ftp client program. Whenever you see this prompt, you can enter one of the ftp commands. I just want to mention two commands here, rest of them will be taken up later.

1. To display a list of all the ftp commands, enter the ? command.
2. To end the ftp session, use the quit command.

The last point I want to cover is what to expect if your ftp client is unable to connect to the remove host. There are three ways in which this might happen, first, the ftp service may be temporarily unavailable. In such cases, you will see:

```
ftp: connect: Connection refused
```

Second, the network connection to the remote host may be inoperative. This might be a problem with the network to which the host is connected, or it might be that the host computer itself is not working. In such cases, you will see a message like:

```
ftp: connect: Host is unreachable
```

The best thing to do is try again later.

Finally, there may be a problem with the address you specified. For example, say that you want to download files from rtfm.mit.edu, but you accidentally enter the wrong address:

```
ftp rtff.mit.edu
```

You will see a message like the following:

```
rtff.mit.edu: unknown host
ftp>
```

At his point, you can enter the name of another host. Otherwise, you can use the quit command to stop the program.

#### *5.4.5.1 Second Way to Start the ftp Program*

The first way is to enter the ftp command along with the address of the remote host. For example:

```
ftp rtfm.mit.edu
```

the second way is to start ftp without specifying a host. Simply enter:

```
ftp
```

The program will start, but will not make a connection. Instead, you will see:

```
ftp>
```

This is the ftp prompt. It means that the program is waiting for you to enter a command. To connect to a remote host, type open, followed by the address of the host. For example:

```
open rtfm.mit.edu
```

The connection will made just as if you had specified the address when you entered the ftp command.

Earlier, I gave you an example in which an ftp command had a bad address. In the example, the remote host was named rtfm.mit.edy but we mistakenly entered:

```
ftp rtff.mit.edy
```

What happens in such a case is that the ftp program tries to make the connection. When it can't, it gives up and displays its prompt, waiting for you to enter a command. In this case, you would see:

```
Rtff.mit.edu: unknown host
ftp>
```

you can now enter:

```
open rtfm.mit.edu
```

If this address doesn't work, you can try another one. If one decide to give up, enter:

```
Quit
```

This will stop the ftp program.

#### *5.4.5.2 Ftp Commands*

Once you have entered the ftp command and established a connection with a remote host, you will see the prompt:

```
ftp>
```

At this point, you can enter an ftp command (of which there are many). The ftp client program will send whatever command you enter to the ftp server, which will carry out your request. The idea is to enter one command after another until you have achieved your goal (say, to download a file). Then enter the quit command to terminate the ftp session. At any time, you can display a list of all the ftp commands by entering ? or help (either will do). Do not worry is your ftp client does not have all these commands. It will have the most important ones. If you want to see a one-line summary of a particular command, enter ? (or help) followed by the name of the command. For example, if you enter:

```
? quit
```

you will see:

```
quit terminate ftp session and exit
```

notice how many commands there are in figure. The number of commands you see will vary, depending on what version of the ftp software you are using. You might wonder, do you have to learn all these commands? The answer is no. For formal anonymous ftp session, all you need to know few basic commands. I will discuss these commands now.

### 5.4.6 The Basic ftp Commands

We can divide the ftp commands into several groups. First, there are the basic commands. I have already discussed quit? And help (which is the same as ?). The other basic command is ! (exclamation mark). This command is used to send a regular Unix command to your local computer. Simply type the command after the ! character and then press RETURN. The ftp program will put itself on hold and send the command to your Unix shell to be executed. Once the command is finished the ftp program will again control and redisplay its prompt.

Here is an example. We what to use the Unix date command to display the time and date on your local system. At the ftp? Prompt, we enter !date. After the date command display its output, we are returned to an ftp> prompt:

```
ftp> !date
Wed Aug 28 17:42 PDT 1995
ftp>
```

If you would like to enter more than one Unix command, you can use the ! character by itself:

```
ftp> !
```

The ftp program will put itself on hold and start a new shell. You can now enter as many Unix commands as you want. When you are finished, terminate the shell and the ftp program will regain control. With most shells, you would press CTRL-D to terminate the shell. If this does not work, try the exit command.

### 5.4.7 Some Common ftp Commands with Description

Here I give the description of some of the commonly used ftp commands.

#### *5.4.7.1 Basic Commands*

| Command | Syntax | Description |
|---|---|---|
| **quit** | *quit* | close connection to remote host, stop ftp program. |
| **?** | *?* | displays a list of all the ftp commands. |
| **?** | *?* command | displays one-line summary of the specified command. |
| **help** | *help* | display a list of all the ftp commands. |
| **help** | *help* command | displays one-line summary of the specified command. |
| **!** | *!* | local: pause ftp and start a shell. |
| **!** | *!* command | local: execute specified shell command. |
| **open** | *open* [host] | establish connection to specified computer |
| **close** | *close* | close the connection to remote host, stay in ftp |
| **user** | *user* [name [password]] | set user name |
| **cd** | *cd* [directory] | remote: change to specified directory |
| **cdup** | *cdup* | remote: change to parent directory |
| **dir** | *dir* [directory [local-file]] | remote: display a long directory listing |
| **lcd** | *lcd* [directory] | local: change directory |
| **ls** | *ls* [directory [local-file]] | remote: display a short directory listing |
| **pwd** | *pwd* | remote: display name of current directory |
| **get** | *get [remote-file [local-file]]* | download one file |
| **mget** | *mget* [remote-file...] | download multiple files |
| **ascii** | *ascii* | (default) set file type to ASCII text file. |

### 5.4.8 The Connection ftp Commands

The next category ftp commands are those that control the connection to the remote host: **open**, **close** and **user**. I have already discussed the open command, which you can use to establish an ftp connection. The close command will terminate an ftp connection without quitting the ftp program. You can use close when you want to close one connection and then open another one.

If you connect to a remote host successfully, but there is something wrong with your user name or password, you may or may not lose your connection. (This depends on the ftp server.) However, if you do not lose the connection, you will not be able to do anything until you specify a valid userid and password. To do so, you can use the user command. Simply enter:

```
user
```

the ftp program will ask you to enter a userid and then a password. If you want, you can specify the information directly:

```
user anonymous harley@fuzzball.ucsd.edu
```

In this case, we are specifying a userid of anonymous and a password of harley@fuzzball.ucsd.edu.

#### *5.4.8.1 The Directory ftp Commands*

The third group of ftp commands are those which move from one directory to another and display the contents of a directory. Whichever directory you are in is called your working directory (or current directory). Once you establish on ftp connection, you have two working directories to keep track of: one of the remote host and one on your local computer.

With most anonymous ftp hosts, you are automatically placed in the root (top-level) directory to start. To move to another directory, use the cd (change directory) command. Type the command name, followed by the name of the directory you want to move to and then press RETURN. For example, if you want to move to the directory named /pub/usenet/news.answers, Enter:

```
cd /pub/usenet/news.answers
```

If you understand the Unix file system, you can move one directory at a time by using separate cd commands. For example:

```
cd pub
cd usenet
cd news.answers
```

At any time, you can display the name of your remote working directory by using the pwd (print working directory) command. For example, if you enter:

```
pwd
```

you will see a message similar to the following one:

```
257 "/pub/usenet/news.answers" is current directory.
```

At times, you may see a directory name that is different from what you expect. For example on the rtfm.mit.edu system, if you move to the directory named /pub/usenet/news.answers and then enter a pwd command, you will actually see:

```
257 "/pub/usenet-by-usenet/news.answers" is current directory.
```

Do not be confused. All that this means is that the system manager has given the second level directory two different names: usenet and usenet-by-group. In such cases, you can use whichever name you want. The name usenet-by-group is more informative, but the name usenet is a lot easier to type.

The working directory on your local computer will be whatever will be whatever directory you happened to be in when you entered the ftp command. When you download files, this is the directory into which they will be placed. If you want your files to be placed into a different directory, you can use the **lcd** (local change directory) command to move to a different directory before you start the downloading. For example:

```
lcd faq-files
```

This command changes your local working directory to faq-files. There is no ftp command to display the name of your local working directory. However, it is possible to do this by using the ! command to send a pwd command to your local computer.

```
!pwd
```

To display the contents of a directory on the remote host you can use two different commands. The ls (list) command will display the names of the files in the directory. Here is some typical output. It shows the names of some of the files in the news.answers directory.

```
esperanto-faq
feminism
finding-addresses
finding-sources
```

```
fleas-ticks
folklore-faq
fonts-faq
```

The dir command will display a longer listing. Along with the file name, you will also see extra information. Here is some typical output.

```
-rw-rw-r        8 root 3   27120   Jun  2  01:24  esperanto-faq
drwxrwxr-x      2 root 3     512   Jun 12  00:07  feminsim
-rw-rw-r--     14 root 3  288890   Jun 12  03:37  finding-addresses
-rw-rw-r--     12 root 3   41939   Jun 16  04:04  finding-sources
-rw-rw-r--     10 root 3   41533   Jun 16  03:30  fleas-ticks
-rw-rw-r--      8 root 3   84701   Jun 15  03:33  folklore-faq
drwxrwxr-x      2 root 3     512   Jun 18  01:46  fonts-faq
```

If you have some experience with the Unix file commands, you will recognize this output as being from the ls – 1 command. Otherwise, don't worry about it. You only need to understand four things. First, the character at the far left tells you if the line describes a directory of a file. A d character indicates a directory while a - (hyphen) character indicates a file. In this example, we have two directories and five files.

At the far right of each line, we see the name of the file or directory. To the left of the name, the time and date show you when the file or directory was updated. Finally, the number to the left of the time and date shows the size of the file in bytes (characters). This number is not meaningful for directories. Thus, we can see that folklore-faq is a file, it was last updated on June 15 at 3:33 AM and is 84,701 characters long. You can ignore the rest of the information. You will find that it is often convenient to download a copy of a long directory listing to a file on your local computer. To do so, simply specify the name of the directory followed by the name of a file. For example:

```
ls /pub/usenet/news.answers ls.list
dir /pub/usenet/news.answers dir.list
```

Each of these commands generates a directory listing of the specified directory. The first command downloads its output to a file on your local computer named ls.list. The second command sends its output to a local file named dir.list (Of course, you can choose whatever names you want.)

When you use this form of the ls and dir commands, you must always specify a directory name and a local file name. If you want to download a listing of the working directory, you can use a directory name of . (a single period character). In Unix a single . Character stands for your working directory. For example:

```
Ls . ls.list
Dir . dir.list
```

### 5.4.9 The File transfer ftp Commands

There are two commands you can use to download files (that is, to copy files form the remote host to your computer). These commands are **get** and **mget**. The get command allows you to download one file at a time. The mget (multiple get) command allows you to download more than one file at a time.

To use get, specify the name of the remote file followed by the name that you want to give the file on your local computer. For example say that you have established an anonymous ftp session with the rtfm.mit.edu computer mentioned earlier. You would like to download the folklore-faq file. You want the file to be name Durban-legends on your computer. First move to the directory that contains the file:

```
cd /pub/usenet/news.answers
```

Now, enter the get Command to download the file:

```
get folklore-faq urban-legends
```

You will see the following message:

```
200 PORT command successful.
150 Opening ASCII mode data connection for folklore-faq (84701 bytes).
```

At this point, the file is being copied to your computer. Once the copy is complete, you will see:

```
226 Transfer complete.
Local: urban-legends remote: folklore-faq
86113 bytes received in 17 seconds (4.9 kbytes/s)
ftp>
```

You can now enter another command. (BY the way, don't worry about the fact that the file is 84,701 bytes long but we received 86,113 bytes. The extra bytes have to do with how certain characters are encoded when you copy a text file.

Rest assured that the actual downloaded file will be exactly the right size.) If you use the get command with only a single file name, the ftp program will use this name for the new file on your local computer. For example, if you enter.

```
get folklore-faq
```

the downloaded file will automatically be named folklore-faq.

If you are using a Unix system, there is a way to send the remote file as input to a Unix command on your local computer, rather than to a local file. Instead of a second file name, you type a | (vertical bar, called the pipe symbol), followed by the name of the command. For example, suppose that you want to read a remote file named README. One way is to downloaded it to a local file, stop or pause the ftp session, read the file, delete the file and then resume the ftp session. Alternatively, you can read the remote file by sending it directly to a paging program (such as more) on your local computer.

```
get README |more
```

Notice that you cannot put a space after the | character (like you can with a regular Unix command). This is because get expects only two words; the remote file name (in this case, README) and the name of the local target (in this case, |more).

The **mget** (multiple get) command is used when you want to download more than one file at the same time. Type the command, followed by the names of the file you want to download. For example:

```
mget finding-addresses finding-sources folklore-faq
```

when you use mget, you cannot specify alternate names, so as the files will be given the same names when they are copied to your local computer.

The mget command will transfer one file at a time. Before transferring a file, mget will display the file name and ask you for confirmation. For example:

```
mget finding-addresses?
```

At this point you can type either y (yes) or n (no) and press RETURN.

You can specify the name of a directory and mget will process each file in the directory. Similarly, if you know how to use the Unix wildcard characters, you can download all the files whose name matches particular pattern. If you do not know about wildcard characters, I will mention briefly that an * (asterisk) character matches zero or more characters and a ? (question mark) character matches any single character. For example, to download all the files in the remote working directory whose names begin with the letters fi, you can use:

```
Mget fi*
```

### 5.4.10 Setting ftp Options

Within the ftp program, there are several commands you can use to control the downloading operation. The ones worth mentioning are **binary**, **ascii**, **hash**, **prompt** and **status.**

A text file (also called an ASCII file) holds ordinary characters: letters, numbers, punctuation and so on. A binary file contains information that is not textual. For example, if you want to download files that contain pictures, you will be dealing with binary files.

By default, the ftp programs assumes that it is working with text files. If you want to download binary files, you should tell the program before you enter the get or mget command. The binary command tells the ftp program that you will be downloading binary files. If you want to switch back, the ascii command indicates that you will be downloading text files. When you use one of these commands, we say that you are setting the REPRESENTATION TYPE.

For example, say that you are about to download some files that contain pictures. Before you do, you enter the command;

```
Binary
```

When you enter this command, you will see the following message:

```
200 Type set to I.
```

The I stands for "image". If you use the binary command and then download a text file. It's only when you are copying binary files that you should be exact. With some remote hosts, a binary file will not be copied properly unless you have set the representation type to binary. The next option is hash. This tells the ftp program to display a # character (sometimes called a hash mark) after each data block is transferred. This allows you to watch the program when you are downloading a large file. The size of a data block depends on the nature of your ftp connection, but you will be told what it is before the downloading starts.

To turn on the hash option, just enter:

```
hash
```

To turn it off, enter the same command again.

The last option to mention is prompt. The ftp client queries you about each file whenever you use mget. If you set the prompt option off, mget will automatically transfer each file without asking your permission. To turn off the prompt option, just enter:

```
prompt
```

To turn it back on, enter the same command again.

Finally, if you want to display the current setting all the options, you can use the status command:

```
Status
```

When you do, you will see many options, most of which you can safely ignore.

## 5.5 IRC

Everybody loves chatting, specially girls. So how can Internet be far behind. It also allows you to chat with other unknown parties. As in the case of browsers, here also there are software which allow you to chat. Well, the popular among them is Yahoo! again. There are others too like, lycos.com, sifty.com, 123india.com, etc. To chat at yahoo.com you have to follow the following procedure:

1. Log on the site yahoo! and then click at Chat button.
2. The Yahoo chat page opens. When you chat for the first time you have to get registered at yahoo.
3. Click at sign up button to register.
4. The terms and conditions page opens, click at I Accept button to accept the conditions.

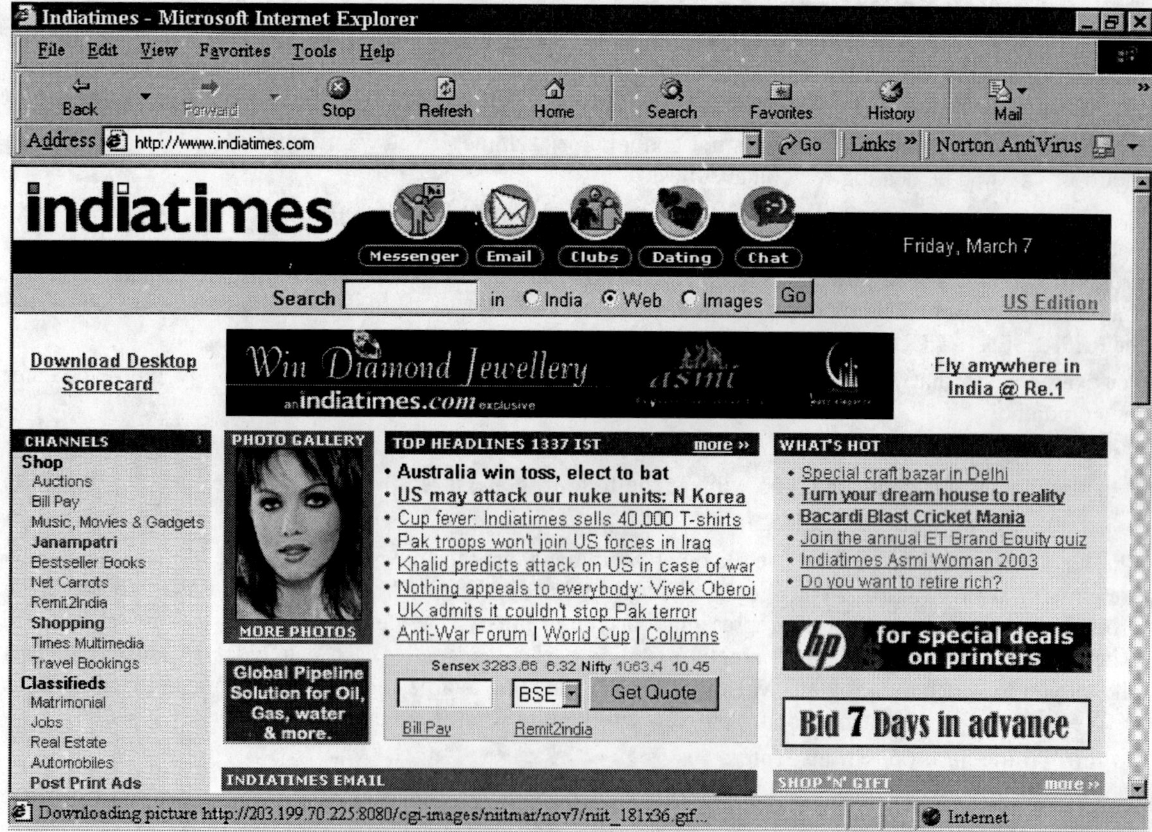


5. Sign on Yahoo!ID page. Fill in the details and click submit button. Once you get your Yahoo!ID, you can sign in and chat.
6. Now it will log you on its chat server and you select the chat room you want to join and you can now chat with other users. Names of other users, who are currently chatting, are displayed in a list box.
7. Type the message you want to submit and click submit button.
8. On some servers, you need to click at Send button to send your message.
9. On most chat sites, you can also change rooms by clicking at Room link. Room basically referes to a group of approachable chat users. One can chat with all other users in the same chat room. To chat with users in other chat rooms, one needs to change the rooms.
10. On chat servers, rooms are defined on the basis of shared interests like parenting, teenagers, ITpeople, society, Life and style, etc.

### 5.5.1 Working of IRC

When you send your message on Internet chat, your message is sent from your server to other servers where people on your channel are logged on. The message gets transferred from server to server. Each server sends you message to the client software of the people connected to the channel at each server. People can read and respond to your message at their computers.

#### *5.5.1.1 Chat Software*

There are various types of software available for chatting. Each one of them serves different purposes.

#### *5.5.1.2 Internet Relay Chat*

For this you need software like mIRC or Ircle.

#### *5.5.1.3 Web-based Chat*

For this you need web browser such as Netscape or Internet Explorer.

#### *5.5.1.4 America Online Program*

For this you need to have ICQ, AOL Instant Messager or other program.

#### *5.5.1.5 Online conferencing*

For this you need to have a conferencing program.

### 5.5.2 Basic Commands of IRC

| *Command* | *Description* |
|---:|---|
| /flush | It discards remaining output for the current command |
| /help | It displays a list of all IRC commands |
| /help command | It displays help information about the specified command |
| /help newuser | It displays information for new users |
| /join channel | It lets you join the specified channel |
| /list | It lists information about all channels |
| /list channel | It lists information about a specific channel |

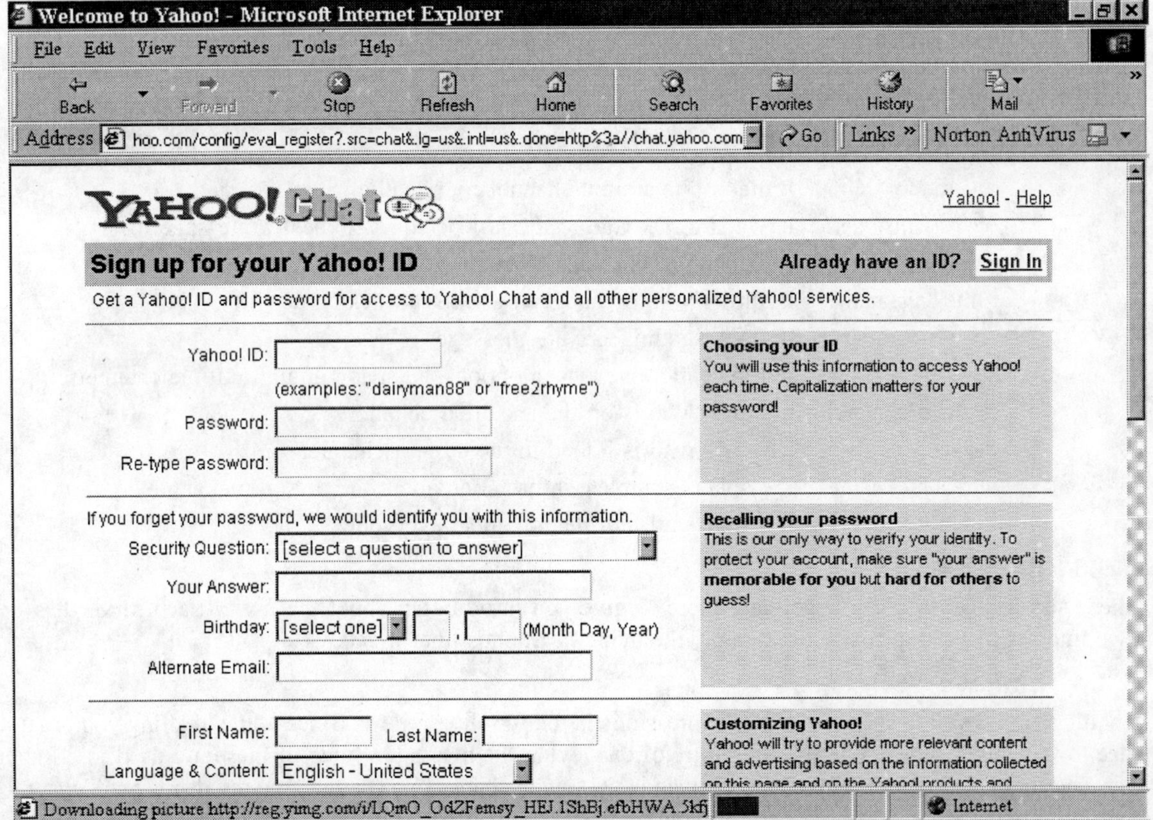

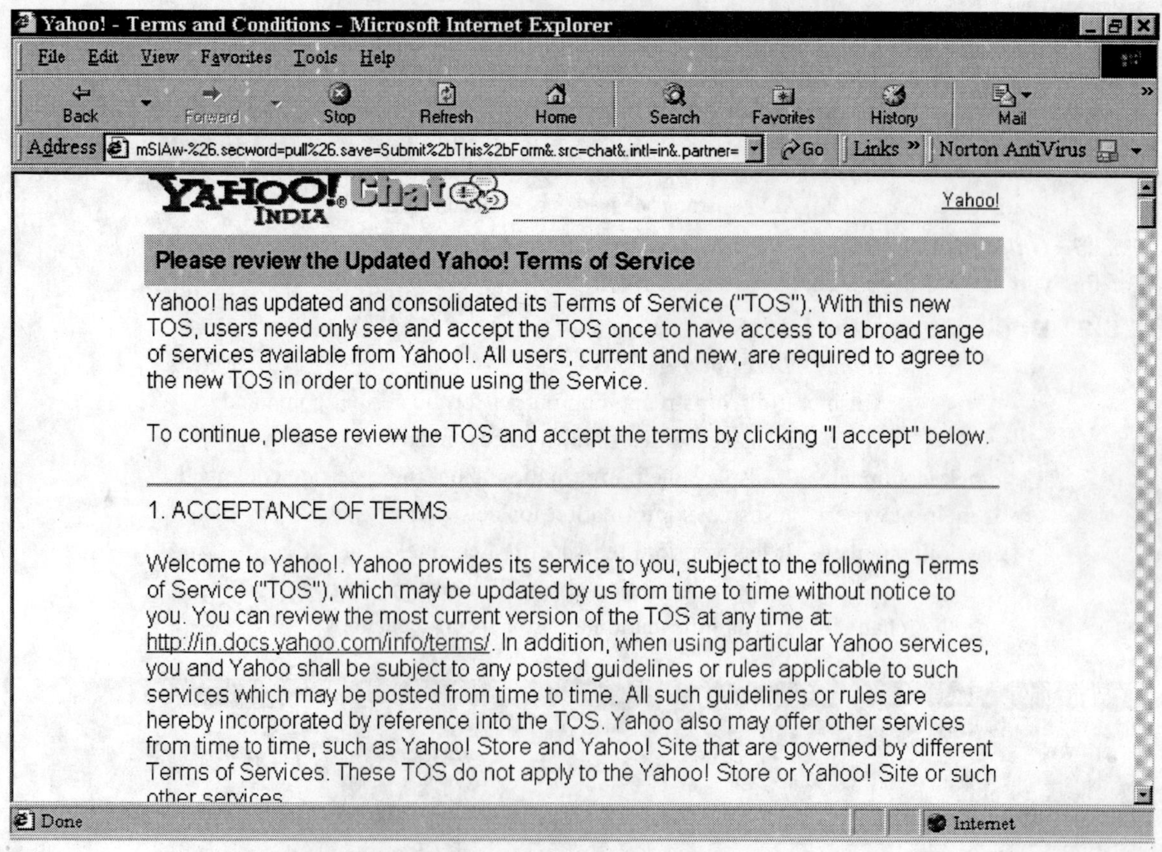

Yahoo! - Terms and Conditions - Microsoft Internet Explorer

**Please review the Updated Yahoo! Terms of Service**

Yahoo! has updated and consolidated its Terms of Service ("TOS"). With this new TOS, users need only see and accept the TOS once to have access to a broad range of services available from Yahoo!. All users, current and new, are required to agree to the new TOS in order to continue using the Service.

To continue, please review the TOS and accept the terms by clicking "I accept" below.

1. ACCEPTANCE OF TERMS

Welcome to Yahoo!. Yahoo provides its service to you, subject to the following Terms of Service ("TOS"), which may be updated by us from time to time without notice to you. You can review the most current version of the TOS at any time at: http://in.docs.yahoo.com/info/terms/. In addition, when using particular Yahoo services, you and Yahoo shall be subject to any posted guidelines or rules applicable to such services which may be posted from time to time. All such guidelines or rules are hereby incorporated by reference into the TOS. Yahoo also may offer other services from time to time, such as Yahoo! Store and Yahoo! Site that are governed by different Terms of Services. These TOS do not apply to the Yahoo! Store or Yahoo! Site or such other services

| | |
|---|---|
| mode * + pi | It makes the current channel completely private |
| /msg.text | It sends a message to the last person who sent a message to you |
| /nick | It displays your own nickname |
| /nick nickname | It allows you to change your current nickname |
| /query | It stops sending private messages |
| /set novice off | It allows more advanced options, such as joining multiple channels |
| /who channel | It shows who is on the specified channel |
| /who * | It shows who is joined to the current channel |
| /who is nickname | It displays complete information about the person nickname |
| /whois* | It displays all information about everyone. |

### 5.5.3 Chat Servers

These servers like Internet servers are there to give you information about the users. Each server has its own number of users. It has a host name, the name of the host that it accesses.

### 5.5.4 Smileys

Chatting allows you to show your face expressions in the form of smileys. Since while chatting you are not face to face, these smileys are the best way of conveying the message. Some of these are used in e-mails too. The complete list of them have been given in the e-mail chapter. You can in fact, divided the smileys into various categories, for example, the following one:

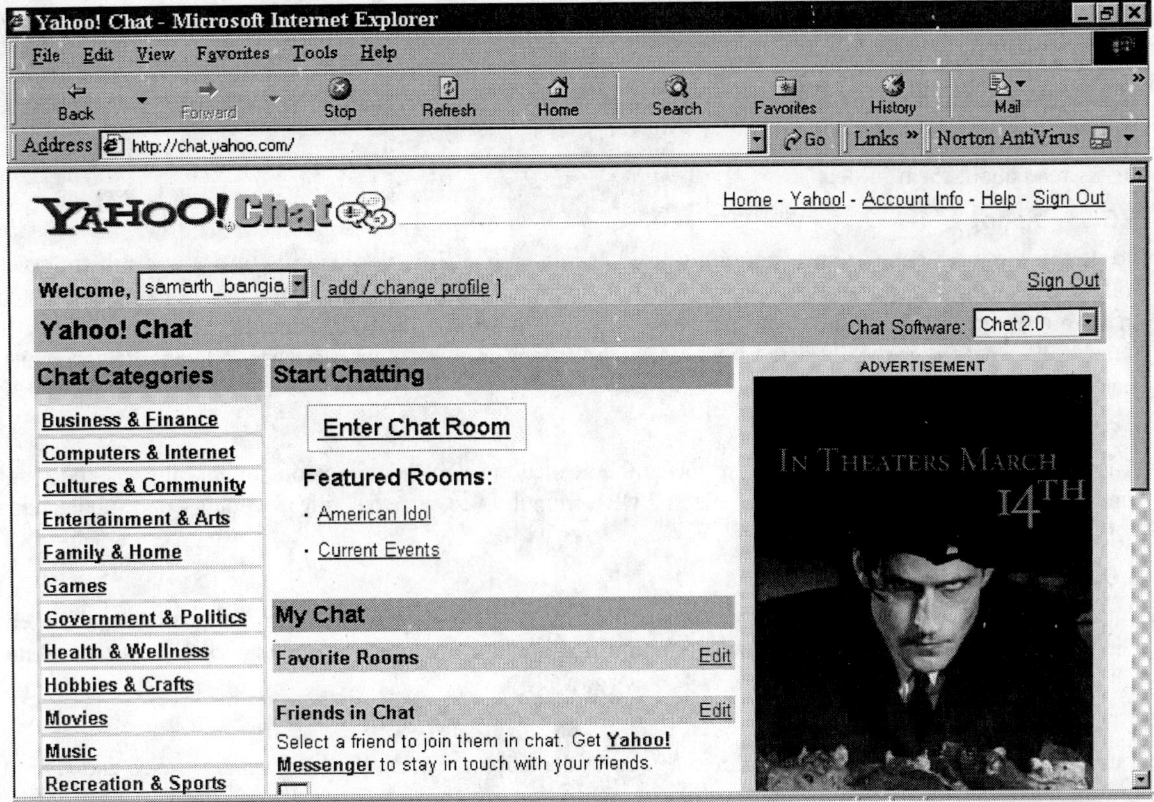


1. Basic Smileys
2. Emotional Smileys
3. Mega Smileys
4. Midget Smileys
5. Usenet Smileys
6. Widely used Smileys

## 5.6 Search Engines

They are programs that locate needed information in a database, but especially an Internet accessible search service that enables you to search for information on the Internet. To use a search engine, you type one or more key words; the result is a list of documents or files that contain one or more of these words in their titles, descriptions, or text. The databases of most Internet search engines contain World Wide Web (WWW) documents; some also contain items found in Gopher menus and File Transfer Protocol (FTP) file archives.

Compiling the database requires an automated search routine called a spider, forms filled out by Web authors, or a search of other databases of Internet documents. The effectiveness of search engine can be measured in terms of Indexing and Term specificity. Since the Internet is a vast collection of information, it is difficult to find specific information you actually need. Therefore, search engines are more than a boom.

### 5.6.1 Search Engine Categories

Some of the popular search engines are:

Yahoo!

Lycos

WebCrawler

Excite

Let us read about them in details.

### 5.6.2 Yahoo!

No doubt, the most popular and commonly used search engine. It is very simple to use and mostly gives you the best results. It indexes Web pages, Usenet and e-mail addresses. The search has 14 categories listed on its homepage. Each of these categories is divided into several subcategories. If the search fails, it is automatically passed on to AltaVista for more search. Yahoo! provides other services too like e-mail accounts, searches to locate people, sites, news, etc.

### 5.6.3 Lycos

This one has a robot to help the software locate the needed in search. For each document indexed, the robot keeps the outgoing links in a queue and selects a URL from it. Lycos indexes, titles, headings, and subheadings of HTML, FTP and Gopher documents.

### 5.6.4 Web Crawler

It has a web robot called Webbot that creates a daily index of keywords from documents all over the Web. The search engine directs the navigation in a modified breadth first mode. It indexes both the title and the full text of HTML document.

### 5.6.5 Excite

It uses a spider and indexer for the full text search of documents. The spider retrieves only Web and Usenet newsgroup documents. It offers services like searches that are case sensitive. It uses the various Boolean operators.

But, this is not the end of the search engines. There are more available on the net, but I have covered here the famous ones.

### 5.6.6 Searching Criterion

So far we have learned about the various search engines. Let us know in brief know how these search engines work. As was mentioned in the case of various search engines above, each one of them uses either the directories, spiders and even the robots for searches. A spider strips away many other markup features so that it simply sees the pure HTML source. Search sites are basically of the following two types:

#### *5.6.6.1 Search Directories*

They contain a list of websites organized hierarchically into categories and sub-categories. These are created manually.

#### *5.6.6.2 Search Engines*

It continuously sends out the so called spiders which start on a homepage of a server and pursue all links stepwise.

When you open a search engine, it asks you what to search. If it is to be case sensitive, make sure that you are using the right case. Click Ok to begin the search and the result is shown in the form of URLs leading to the pages you need.

## Let us Revise

1. e-mail is an important usuage of Internet.
2. All Internet Service Provider allow you to open an e-mail account.
3. In Outlook Express, Inbox is used for incoming messages..
4. Outbox is used for sending messages.
5. Sent items stores all messages previously sent.
6. Deleted items has the messages which are marked for deletion.
7. Drafts has all the half completed messages.
8. To cut down the time of writing a message, lots of abbrevations are used.
9. You can even use similes in your message.
10. Various parts of the e-mail text are: Headers, To, From, Subject, Cc, Bcc, Attachments, Date and Body.
11. Using Send/Receive button on the standard toolbar, you can send and receive mail.
12. Various type of messages are: Unread message, High importance message, Low importance message, Message that has been read, Message with attachment, Message that has been forwarded, Message that has been replied to, Meeting for which response is requested and Follow-up flag.
13. For reading the message you can use Ctrl + O.
14. You can click the RE button for replying to a message.
15. By using FW you can forward a message.
16. You can delete a message by Ctrl+D.
17. A global hypertext system that uses the Internet as its transport mechanism is called World Wide Web.
18. Web allows you to skip from one page to another using hyperlink.
19. Web is independent of the platform.
20. With Web you can get information from the user too.
21. Web browsers allow you to see the web pages.
22. Most popular Web browser is Microsoft Internet Explorer.
23. Web server manages the communications protocols and the related software required to create a Web site on the Internet.
24. HTTP is used as the communication protocol to transport hypertext documents over the Internet.
25. A URL describes the location and a method of accessing a resource on the Internet.
26. Search engines are used to search for different information on the net.
27. Yahoo! is the popular search engine.
28. Search is done using spiders.
29. TELNET is the Internet service that allows you to log in to a remote Internet computer.
30. In telnet terminology, your computer is called the LOCAL computer.
31. To use Telnet, you turn a Telnet client program, which connects you to a remote Internet host and then emulates a VT-100 terminal.
32. To start Telnet, enter the name of the command followed by the address of the remote host to which you want to connect.
33. Any time you are the at the telnet> prompt, there are a number of different commands that you can use.
34. FTP is the short name for File Transfer Protocol.
35. In FTP terminology, your computer is called the LOCAL HOST and the other computer is called the REMOTE HOST.
36. ANONYMOUS FTP is a facility that lets you connect to certain remote hosts and download files without having to be registered as a user.

37. Public anonymous ftp achieves are so vast as to be well beyond human understanding.
38. Each RFC is given a number and is made freely available to anyone who wants to read it.
39. An ftp client is a program designed for one purpose: to use the ftp service to copy files from one Internet computer to another.
40. Since most of the anonymous ftp hosts are Unix computers, you will need to know something about the Unix file system.
41. The main directory in UNIX is called Root directory.
42. Path shows the location of the directory/file.
43. To download or upload files from a remote host, you use the ftp program.
44. ftp> is the promot for giving all the commands.
45. The common ftp commands are open, close and user.
46. Each of the dir commands generates a directory listing of the specified directory.
47. There are two commands you can use to download files (that is, to copy files form the remote host to your computer). These commands are get and mget.
49. Within the ftp program, the commands used to control the downloading operations are: binary, ascii, hash, prompt and status.
50. If you want to display the current setting all the options, you can use the status command.
51. Before you start downloading pictures you must give the Binary command.
52. One way is to downloaded it to a local file, stop or pause the ftp session, read the file, delete the file and then resume the ftp session.
53. With most anonymous ftp hosts, you are automatically placed in the root (top-level) directory to start.
54. Anonymous ftp allows you to download virtually any type of information.
55. The most common ftp commands are:

| | |
|---|---|
| quit | ? |
| help | ! |
| open | close |
| user | cd |
| cdup | dir |
| lcd | ls |
| pwd | get |
| mget | ascii |

56. Internet allows you to chat with unknown users of Internet.
57. Popular software for chatting is Yahoo!
58. Chat servers are used for passing message from one place to another.
59. Each chat server has a name.
60. Smileys are the best way of conveying the message.

## Multiple Choice Questions

1. Commonly used program for e-mail is:
   (a) Outlook Express (b) Internet Explorer (c) Microsoft Windows
2. You half finished messages are stored in:
   (a) Inbox (b) Outbox (c) Drafts
3. For sending and receiving messages you click at:
   (a) Send/Receive button (b) Send button (c) Receive button

4. For replying you use which button :
   (a) REPLY (b) SEND (c) RE
5. For deleting a message you use Ctrl + :
   (a) D (b) Del (c) Esc
6. The browser is which is available free:
   (a) Internet Explorer (b) Netscape Navigator (c) Lynx
7. Which of the following is not a search engine:
   (a) Yahoo! (b) Internet Explorer (c) Lycos
8. A URL is like a :
   (a) Name (b) Vegetable (c) Food
9. Web server is a :
   (a) Hardware (b) Software (c) Both
10. To get information from the users you use :
    (a) Tables (b) Queries (c) Forms
11. Telnet is:
    (a) Telephone which connect to net
    (b) A service for connecting to net
    (c) Network service provider
12. In Telnet, the client computer is called:
    (a) LOCAL (b) NODE (c) REMOTE
13. To start telnet, you type command followed by name of the :
    (a) remote host (b) remote server (c) nothing
14. ftp is the short form of :
    (a) File Transfer Protocol (b) File Transfer Program (c) File Transfer Public
15. Other than your computer, the other computer is called:
    (a) HOST (b) REMOTE HOST (c) OTHER HOST
16. The main directory of UNIX is _____ directory:
    (a) Main (b) New (c) Root
17. Prompt for ftp commands is:
    (a) fpt> (b) f> (c) ft>
18. For downloading files you can use the commands get and :
    (a) use (b) mget (c) down
19. For displaying the current status of the job, you can use the command:
    (a) Status (b) Current (c) Job
20. You cannot chat using Internet.
    (a) Yes (b) No
21. Graphic representations in messages on the Internet are called :
    (a) Icons (b) Smileys (c) Graphs

## True/False Questions

1. In Outlook Express, Inbox is used for outgoing messages..
2. Sent items stores all messages previously sent.
3. Deleted items has the messages which are marked for deletion.

4. To cut down the time of writing a message, lots of abbrevations are used.
5. You cannot use similes in your message.
6. Using Send/Receive button on the standard toolbar, you can send and receive mail.
7. For reading the message you can use Ctrl + O.
8. You can click the RE button for replying to a message.
9. You can delete a message by Ctrl+E.
10. Web allows you to skip from one page to another using hyperlink.
11. Web is independent of the platform.
12. Web browsers allow you to see the web pages.
13. Most popular Web browser is Microsoft Internet Explorer.
14. HTTP is used as the communication protocol to transport hypertext documents over the Internet.
15. A URL describes the location and a method of accessing a resource on the Internet.
16. Yahoo! is the popular search engine.
17. Search is done using snakes.
18. In telnet terminology, your computer is called the LOCAL computer.
19. Any time you are the at the telnet> prompt, there are a number of different commands that you can use.
20. FTP is the short name for File Transfer Protocol.

### Match Columns

Match the matter in Column A with the matter in Column B.

| Column A | Column B |
|---|---|
| A. HTTP | 1. To get information from users |
| B. Yahoo! | 2. Web Browser |
| C. FTP | 3. Place where the incoming messages are kept |
| D. Icons | 4. Graphic representation of emotions |
| E. Forms | 5. Search Engine |
| F. Lynx | 6. Network of Networks |
| G Inbox | 7. Place where the outgoing messages are kept |
| H. Similey | 8. Hyper Text Transfer Protocol |
| I. Outbox | 9. Graphic representation of software |
| J. Internet | 10. File Transfter Protocol |

### Fill in the Blanks with Appropriate Words

| | | | |
|---|---|---|---|
| a. Yahoo! | b. Telnet | c. Local | d. URL |
| e. VT-100 | f. HTTP | g. Search engines | h. spiders |

1. _________ is used as the communication protocol to transport hypertext documents over the Internet.
2. A ___________ describes the location and a method of accessing a resource on the Internet.
3. ___________ are used to search for different information on the net.
4. _________ is a popular search engine.
5. Search is done using _________.
6. _________ is the Internet service that allows you to log in to a remote Internet computer.
7. In telnet terminology, your computer is called the _________ computer.
8. To use Telnet, you turn a Telnet client program, which connects you to a remote Internet host and then emulates a _________ terminal.

## Descriptive Type Questions

1. What is e-mail?
2. How would create your own e-mail account?
3. Which are the different folders in Outlook Express?
4. Which type of messages you have in Outlook Express?
5. Describe the process of replying to a message.
6. How would you forward a message?
7. What is World Wide Web?
8. What are the basic features of World Wide Web?
9. Describe the various popular web browsers.
10. What is the use of a Web server?
11. What is a Search Engine?
12. What is Telnet?
13. What is the concept of Telnet?
14. How would you start Telnet?
15. What is the use of Ctrl+] command?
16. Describe the following commands:
    Open Close
17. What is ftp?
18. What is Anonymous FTP?
19. How can you use browser Anonymouse FTP?
20. What steps would you take for accessing an Anonymous FTP?
21. How are files and directories stored in FTP?
22. What do you understand by Path?
23. How would you start the FTP program?
24. Describe the alternative method of starting FTP.
25. Which are the basic commands of FTP?
26. Which commands are used for connecting to FTP?
27. What are the different options of Directory command?
28. Describe the various setting commands of FTP.
29. What is Chat?
30. Describe the processing of registering for Internet Chat.
31. Describe the various types of smileys.
32. Write short notes on the following:
    Yahoo! Lycos
    WebCrawler Excite
    HyperText Searching Criterion

## Answers to Objective Type Questions

*Multiple Choice Questions*

| | | | |
|---|---|---|---|
| 1. a | 2. c | 3. a | 4. c |
| 5. a | 6. a | 7. b | 8. a |
| 9. c | 10. c | 11. b | 12. c |

| | | | |
|---|---|---|---|
| 13. a | 14. a | 15. b | 16. c |
| 17. a | 18. b | 19. a | 20. b |
| 21. a | | | |

***True False Questions***

| | | | |
|---|---|---|---|
| 1. F | 2. T | 3. T | 4. T |
| 5. F | 6. T | 7. T | 8. T |
| 9. F | 10. T | 11. T | 12. T |
| 13. T | 14. T | 15. T | 16. T |
| 17. F | 18. T | 19. T | 20. T |

***Matching Columns***

| | | | |
|---|---|---|---|
| A. 8 | B. 5 | C. 10 | D. 9 |
| E. 1 | F. 2 | G. 3 | H. 4 |
| I. 7 | J. 6 | | |

***Fill in the Blanks***

| | | | |
|---|---|---|---|
| 1. f | 2. d | 3. g | 4. a |
| 5. h | 6. b | 7. c | 8. e |

# Electronic Mail 6

## 6.1 E-mail Networks and Servers

In the good old golden age, the Post Office was the place where all the incoming and outgoing letters were stored. Similarly in the case of e-mail, we have a place in the hard disk called Post Office. This is where we have Inbox and Outbox which store the incoming and outgoing mail. The method for receiving mail depends upon the sophistication of the system. When multitasking personal computers and workstations are used, mail can be delivered to users while they are working on something else. Otherwise, users have to interrogate their mailboxes (diskspace) in a central system, or file server.

When you send e-mail to someone on the Internet, that message has to travel through a series of networks before it reaches the recipient. Different networks might use different e-mail formats. Gateways perform the job of translating e-mail formats from one network to another, so that the messages can make their way through all the networks of the Internet.

## 6.2 E-mail Protocols

If a user sends a message across a local network to another user running the same message system, the process is relatively simple. But if you want to send a message to a user running a different messaging program, some translation may be necessary. Because of the complexity involved in having many different systems send and receive messages in many different formats, E-mail protocols have become necessary. Any number of vendors may attempt to develop and market their idea of a superior messaging system, using proprietary systems, for sending, receiving, and storing messages. It would be impossible for all vendors to provide support for all other vendor's messaging specification. Instead, vendors have tried to support a limited set of standard specifications, translating messages between their own message system and the accepted standards. There are a few message formats that have evolved into de facto standards and most messaging products include support for them. Some of these protocols are discussed next.

### 6.2.1 SMTP

Simple Mail Transfer Protocol (SMTP) is an Internet standard for electronic mail (e-mail) transmission across Internet Protocol (IP) networks. SMTP was first defined in RFC 821 (STD 15) (1982), and last updated by RFC 5321 (2008) which includes the extended SMTP (ESMTP) additions, and is the protocol in widespread use today. SMTP is specified for outgoing mail transport and uses TCP port 25.

While electronic mail servers and other mail transfer agents use SMTP to send and receive mail messages, user-level client mail applications typically only use SMTP for sending messages to a mail server for relaying. For receiving messages, client applications usually use either the Post Office Protocol (POP) or the Internet Message Access Protocol (IMAP) to access their mail box accounts on a mail server.

Various forms of one-to-one electronic messaging were used in the 1960s. People communicated with one another using systems developed for specific mainframe computers. As more computers were interconnected, especially in the US Government's ARPANET, standards were developed to allow users using different systems to be able to e-mail one another. SMTP grew out of these standards developed during the 1970s.

SMTP can trace its roots to two implementations described in 1971, the Mail Box Protocol, which has been disputed to actually have been implemented, but is discussed in RFC 196 and other RFCs, and the SNDMSG program, which, according to RFC 2235, Ray Tomlinson of BBN "invents" for TENEX computers the sending of mail across the ARPANET. Fewer than 50 hosts were connected to the ARPANET at this time.

Further implementations include FTP Mail and Mail Protocol, both from 1973. The work continued throughout the 1970s, until the ARPANET converted into the modern Internet around 1980. Jon Postel then proposed a Mail Transfer Protocol in 1980 that began to remove the mail's reliance on FTP. SMTP was published as RFC 821 in August 1982, also by Postel.

The SMTP standard was developed around the same time as Usenet, a one-to-many communication network with some similarities.

SMTP became widely used in the early 1980s. At the time, it was a complement to Unix to Unix Copy Program (UUCP) mail, which was better suited to handle e-mail transfers between machines that were intermittently connected. SMTP, on the other hand, works best when both the sending and receiving machines are connected to the network all the time. Both use a store and forward mechanism and are examples of push technology. Though Usenet's newsgroups are still propagated with UUCP between servers, UUCP mail has virtually disappeared along with the "bang paths" it used as message routing headers.

The article about sender rewriting contains technical background info about the early SMTP history and source routing before RFC 1123.

Sendmail was one of the first (if not the first) mail transfer agents to implement SMTP. Some other popular SMTP server programs include Postfix, qmail, Novell GroupWise, Exim, Novell NetMail, Microsoft Exchange Server, Sun Java System Messaging Server.

Message submission (RFC 2476) and SMTP-AUTH (RFC 2554) were introduced in 1998 and 1999, both describing new trends in e-mail delivery. Originally, SMTP servers were typically internal to an organization, receiving mail for the organization from the outside, and relaying messages from the organization to the outside. But as time went on, SMTP servers (Mail transfer agents), in practice, were expanding their roles to become message submission agents for Mail user agents, some of which were now relaying mail from the outside of an organization. (e.g. A company executive wishes to send e-mail while on a trip using the corporate SMTP server.) This issue, a consequence of the rapid expansion and popularity of the World Wide Web, meant that the SMTP protocol had to include specific rules and methods for relaying mail and authenticating users to prevent abuses such as unsolicited e-mail (spam) relaying.

As this protocol started out purely ASCII text-based, it did not deal well with binary files. Standards such as Multipurpose Internet Mail Extensions (MIME) were developed to encode binary files for transfer through SMTP. Mail transfer agents (MTAs) developed after Sendmail also tended to be implemented 8-bit-clean, so that the alternate "just send eight" strategy could be used to transmit arbitrary text data (in any 8-bit ASCII-like character encoding) via SMTP. 8-bit-clean MTAs today tend to support the 8BITMIME extension, permitting binary files to be transmitted almost as easily as plain text.

### 6.2.2 POP3

In computing, the Post Office Protocol (POP) is an application-layer Internet standard protocol used by local e-mail clients to retrieve e-mail from a remote server over a TCP/IP connection. POP and IMAP (Internet Message Access Protocol) are the two most prevalent Internet standard protocols for e-mail retrieval. Virtually all modern e-mail clients and servers support both. The POP protocol has been developed through several versions, with version 3 (POP3) being the current standard.

The design of POP and its procedures supports end-users with temporary Internet connections, such as dial-up access, allowing these users to retrieve e-mail when connected and then to view and manipulate the retrieved messages when offline. Although most clients have an option to leave mail on server, e-mail clients using POP generally connect, retrieve all messages, store them on the user's PC as new messages, delete them from the server, and then disconnect.

In contrast, the newer, more capable Internet Message Access Protocol (IMAP) supports both connected (online) and disconnected (offline) modes of operation. E-mail clients using IMAP generally leave messages on the server until the user explicitly deletes them. This and other aspects of IMAP operation allow multiple clients to access the same mailbox. Many e-mail clients support POP as well as IMAP to retrieve messages; however, fewer Internet Service Providers (ISPs) support IMAP.

Clients with a leave mail on server option generally use the POP3 UIDL (Unique IDentification Listing) command. Most POP3 commands identify specific messages by their ordinal number on the mail server. This creates a problem for a client intending to leave messages on the server, since these message numbers may change from one connection to the server to another. For example if a mailbox contained five messages, and a different client then deletes message #3, the next connecting user will find the last two messages' numbers decremented by one. UIDL provides a mechanism to avoid these numbering issues by assigning a string of characters as a permanent and unique ID for the message. When a POP3-compatible e-mail client connects to the server, it can use the UIDL command to get the current mapping from these message IDs to the ordinal message numbers. The client can then use this mapping to determine which messages it has yet to download. IMAP uses a 32-bit unique identifier (UID) that is assigned to messages in ascending (although not necessarily consecutive) order as they are received. When retrieving new messages, an IMAP client requests the UIDs greater than the highest UID among all previously-retrieved messages, whereas a POP client must fetch the entire UIDL map. For large mailboxes, this can require significant processing.

Irrespective of the mail retrieval protocol, e-mail clients typically use the Message Submission flavor of the Simple Mail Transfer Protocol (SMTP) to send messages. POP3 contains a protocol extension, known as "XTND XMIT", that allows clients to transmit outbound mail. The Qualcomm qpopper and CommuniGate Pro servers and Eudora clients are examples of systems that optionally utilize the XTND XMIT methods of authenticated client-to-server e-mail transmission.

MIME serves as the standard for attachments and non-ASCII text in e-mail. Although neither POP3 nor SMTP require MIME-formatted e-mail, essentially all Internet e-mail comes MIME-formatted, so POP clients must also understand and use MIME. IMAP, by design, assumes MIME-formatted e-mail.

Like many other older Internet protocols, POP originally supported only an unencrypted login mechanism. Although plain text transmission of passwords in POP still commonly occurs, POP3 currently supports several authentication methods to provide varying levels of protection against illegitimate access to a user's e-mail. One such method, APOP, uses the MD5 hash function in an attempt to avoid replay attacks and disclosure of the shared secret. Clients implementing APOP include Mozilla Thunderbird, Opera, Eudora, KMail, Novell Evolution, RimArts' Becky!, Windows Live Mail, PowerMail, and Mutt. POP3 clients can also support SASL authentication methods via the AUTH extension. MIT Project Athena also produced a Kerberized version.

POP uses the Transmission Control Protocol on port number 110. Transmission may be encrypted using Transport Layer Security (TLS) or Secure Sockets Layer (SSL). This is negotiated in the POP3 protocol using the STLS command. Some clients and servers, such as Google Gmail, instead use the deprecated alternate-port method, which uses TCP port 995 (POP3S).

### 6.2.3 IMAP4

The Internet Message Access Protocol (IMAP) is one of the two most prevalent Internet standard protocols for e-mail retrieval, the other being the Post Office Protocol (POP). Virtually all modern e-mail clients and mail servers support both protocols as a means of transferring e-mail messages from a server.

The Internet Message Access Protocol (commonly known as IMAP, and previously called Internet Mail Access Protocol, Interactive Mail Access Protocol (RFC 1064), and Interim Mail Access Protocol) is an

Application Layer Internet protocol that allows an e-mail client to access e-mail on a remote mail server. The current version, IMAP version 4 revision 1 (IMAP4rev1), is defined by RFC 3501.

IMAP supports both on-line and off-line modes of operation. E-mail clients using IMAP generally leave messages on the server until the user explicitly deletes them. This and other characteristics of IMAP operation allow multiple clients to manage the same mailbox. Most e-mail clients support IMAP in addition to POP to retrieve messages; however, fewer Internet service providers (ISPs) support IMAP. IMAP offers access to the mail store. Clients may store local copies of the messages, but these are considered to be a temporary cache.

E-mail messages are sent to an e-mail server that stores messages in the recipient's email box. The user retrieves messages with an e-mail client that uses one of a number of e-mail retrieval protocols. Some clients and servers preferentially use vendor-specific, proprietary protocols, but most support the Internet standard protocols, SMTP for sending e-mail and POP and IMAP for retrieving e-mail, allowing interoperability with other servers and clients. For example, Microsoft's Outlook client uses a proprietary protocol to communicate with an Microsoft Exchange Server server as does IBM's Notes client when communicating with a Domino server, but all of these products also support POP, IMAP, and outgoing SMTP. Support for the Internet standard protocols allows many e-mail clients such as Pegasus Mail or Mozilla Thunderbird to access these servers, and allows the clients to be used with other servers.

#### *6.2.3.1 Original IMAP*

The original Interim Mail Access Protocol was implemented as a Xerox Lisp machine client and a TOPS-20 server.

No copies of the original interim protocol specification or its software exist. Although some of its commands and responses were similar to IMAP2, the interim protocol lacked command/response tagging and thus its syntax was incompatible with all other versions of IMAP.

#### *6.2.3.2 IMAP2*

The interim protocol was quickly replaced by the Interactive Mail Access Protocol (IMAP2), defined in RFC 1064 and later updated by RFC 1176. IMAP2 introduced command/response tagging and was the first publicly distributed version.

#### *6.2.3.3 IMAP2bis*

With the advent of MIME, IMAP2 was extended to support MIME body structures and add mailbox management functionality (create, delete, rename, message upload) that was absent in IMAP2. This experimental revision was called IMAP2bis; its specification was never published in non-draft form. Early versions of Pine were widely distributed with IMAP2bis support (Pine 4.00 and later supports IMAP4rev1).

#### *6.2.3.4 IMAP4*

An IMAP Working Group formed in the IETF in the early 1990s and took over responsibility for the IMAP2bis design. The IMAP WG decided to rename IMAP2bis to IMAP4 to avoid confusion with a competing IMAP3 proposal from another group that never got off the ground. The expansion of the IMAP acronym also changed to the Internet Message Access Protocol.

Some design flaws in the original IMAP4 (defined by RFC 1730) that came out in implementation experience led to its revision and replacement by IMAP4rev1 two years later. There were very few IMAP4 client or server implementations based on RFC 1730 due to its short lifetime.

### 6.2.4 MIME6

Multipurpose Internet Mail Extensions (MIME) is an Internet standard that extends the format of e-mail to support:

- Text in character sets other than ASCII

- Non-text attachments
- Message bodies with multiple parts
- Header information in non-ASCII character sets

MIME's use, however, has grown beyond describing the content of e-mail to describing content type in general, including for the web.

Virtually all human-written Internet e-mail and a fairly large proportion of automated e-mail is transmitted via SMTP in MIME format. Internet e-mail is so closely associated with the SMTP and MIME standards that it is sometimes called SMTP/MIME e-mail.

The content types defined by MIME standards are also of importance outside of e-mail, such as in communication protocols like HTTP for the World Wide Web. HTTP requires that data be transmitted in the context of e-mail-like messages, although the data most often is not actually e-mail.

MIME is specified in six linked RFC memoranda: RFC 2045, RFC 2046, RFC 2047, RFC 4288, RFC 4289 and RFC 2049, which together define the specifications.

MIME is extensible. Its definition includes a method to register new content types and other MIME attribute values.

The goals of the MIME definition included requiring no changes to existent e-mail servers and allowing plain text e-mail to function in both directions with existing clients. These goals were achieved by using additional RFC 822-style headers for all MIME message attributes and by making the MIME headers optional with default values ensuring a non-MIME message is interpreted correctly by a MIME-capable client. A simple MIME text message is therefore likely to be interpreted correctly by a non-MIME client although if it has e-mail headers the non-MIME client won't know how to interpret. Similarly, if the quoted printable transfer encoding is used, the ASCII part of the message will be intelligible to users with non-MIME clients.

## 6.3 Structure of an E-mail

Like a formal letter e-mail also is divided into various sections. In a good business letter, you would have, date, the name and address of the person to whom the letter is addressed, salutation, text matter, sender's name, etc. Most of these you would find here too but with some difference. Lets see what an e-mail is supposed to have.

### 6.3.1 Headers

It is very important that your header must be loud and clear for it can be seen and read from a distance too.

### 6.3.2 To

The To: field contains the e-mail address of the person to whom you are sending the e-mail. If you are sending e-mail to someone in your own domain, you do not need to include @ domain.

### 6.3.3 From

In most of the cases, you would not be typing this, since it would be taken from the system. It in fact includes your e-mail address.

### 6.3.4 Subject

The Subject: field should contain a very short description (20-30 characters) of what your message is about. This field can also be called Subject of the Message: or simply message. It is not compulsary to have a subject.

### 6.3.5 Cc

You can send the copy of the same e-mail to another person. For this you have to mention the e-mail address

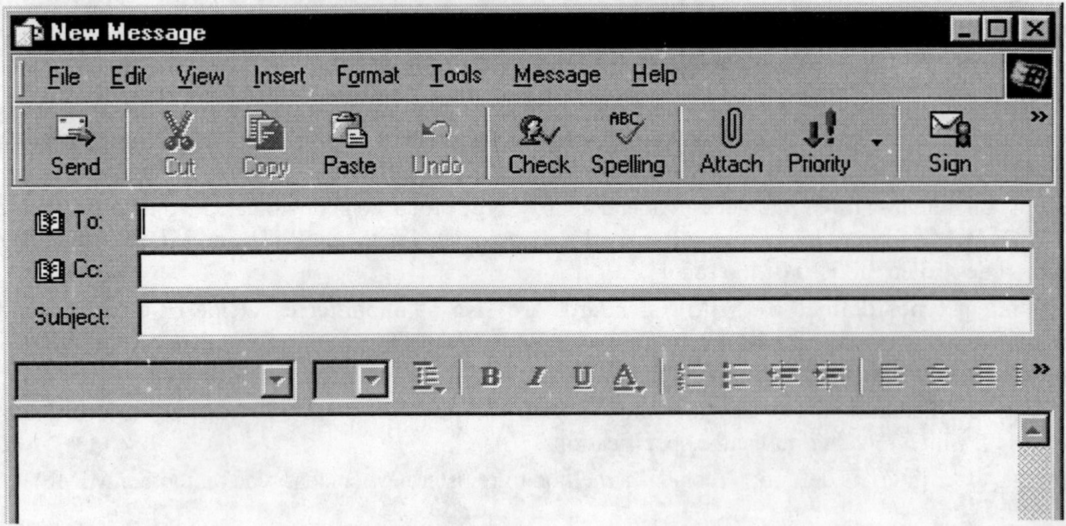


of the second receipt. The software would take care that the same message is sent to the second recepient too.

### 6.3.6 Bcc

It is the short form of Blind Carbon Copy, which gives you a way of copying and transmitting an e-Mail message to another person, without the first person (the main addressee), knowing about it.

### 6.3.7 Attachments

Using this option you can attach a file created in other software along with this e-mail. In most of the cases while applying for a job, the letter is typed in the e-mail text and the bio-data which is mostly in some word processing mode, attached to it.

### 6.3.8 Date

Date and time are usually taken from the system. You need not type it.

### 6.3.9 Body

The body of an e-Mail message is simply the text that you want to send to the other person.

## 6.4 Attachments

You can attach files to your message, and you also attach or include as text the items in your Outlook folders.

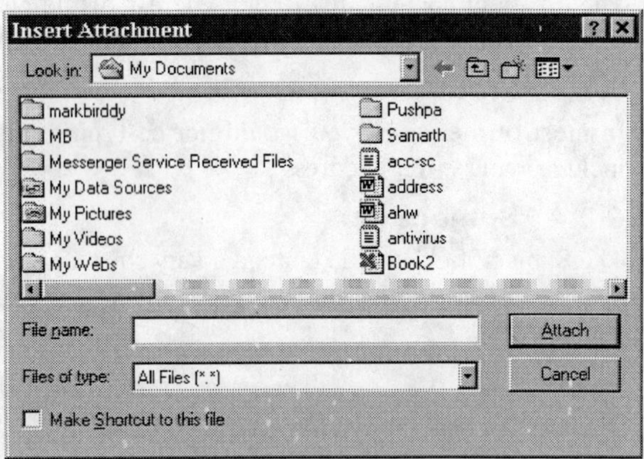


### 6.4.1 Attaching a File

1. From the Insert menu, choose Attachment or Picture whichever the case maybe.

   Or

   Click the Insert File button on the Standard toolbar.
2. In the Insert File dialog box, select the file you want to attach and click Insert.

The file icon appears at the bottom of the message. The recipient can view the attachment by double-clicking its icon.

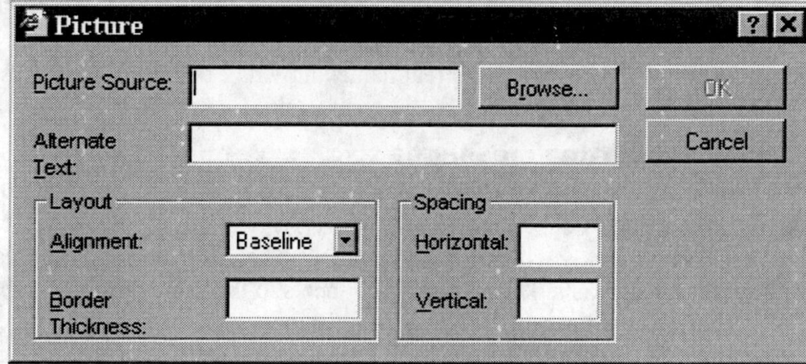


## 6.5 E-mail Clients

An email client, email reader, or more formally mail user agent (MUA), is a computer program used to manage email.

Specifically, the term email client may refer to any agent acting as a client toward an email server, regardless of it being a mail user agent, a relaying server, or a human typing on a terminal. In addition, a web application providing message management, composition, and reception functionality is sometimes considered an email client.

### 6.5.1 Retrieving messages from a mailbox

Like most client programs, an MUA is only active when a user runs it. Messages arrive on the Mail Transfer Agent (MTA) server. Unless the MUA has access to the server's disk, messages are stored on a remote server and the MUA has to request them on behalf of the user.

In the first case, shared disk, a user logs on a server and runs an MUA on that machine. The MUA reads messages from a conventionally formatted storage, typically mbox, within the user's HOME directory. The MTA uses a suitable mail delivery agent (MDA) to add messages to that storage, possibly in concurrence with the MUA. This is the default setting on many Unix systems. Webmail applications running on the relevant server can also benefit from direct disk access to the mail storage.

For personal computing, and whenever messages are stored on a remote system, a mail user agent connects to a remote mailbox to retrieve messages. Access to remote mailboxes comes in two flavors. On the one hand, the Post Office Protocol (POP) allows the client to download messages one at a time and only delete them from the server after they have been successfully saved on local storage. It is possible to leave messages on the server in order to let another client download them. However, there is no provision for flagging a specific message as seen, answered, or forwarded, thus POP is not convenient for users who access the same mail from different machines or clients. On the other hand, the Internet Message Access Protocol (IMAP) allows users to keep messages on the server, flagging them as appropriate. IMAP provides sub-folders. Typically, the Sent, Drafts, and Trash folders are created by default.

Both POP and IMAP clients can be configured to access more mailboxes at the same time, as well as to check each mailbox every given number of minutes. IMAP features an idle extension for real time updates, providing faster notification than polling where long lasting connections are feasible.

Client settings require the server's name or IP address, and the user name and password for each remote incoming mailbox.

### 6.5.2 Formatting messages

Mail user agents usually have built-in the ability to display and edit text. Editing HTML text is a popular feature. Invoking an external editor may be an alternative.

MUAs responsibilities include proper formatting according to RFC 5322 for headers and body, and MIME for non-textual content and attachments. Headers include the destination fields, To, Cc, and Bcc, and the originator fields From which is the message's author(s), Sender in case there are more authors, and Reply-To in case responses should be addressed to a different mailbox. To better assist the user with destination fields, many clients maintain one or more address books and/or are able to connect to an LDAP directory server. For originator fields, clients may support different identities.

Client settings require the user's real name and email address for each user's identity, and possibly a list of LDAP servers.

### 6.5.3 Submitting messages to a server

As a basic function, an MUA is able to introduce new messages in the transport system. Typically, it does so by connecting to either an MSA or an MTA, two variations of the SMTP protocol. The client needs to put a message quickly without worrying about where the message eventually will be delivered: that's why a transport system exists. Thus it always connects to the same preferred server, however, how does that server know that it should accept and relay submissions from that client? There are two ways. The older method recognizes the client's IP address, e.g. because the client is on the same machine and uses internal address 127.0.0.1, or because the client's IP address is controlled by the same internet service provider that provides both internet access and mail services. The newer method, since the SMTP protocol has an authentication extension, is to authenticate. The latter method eases modularity and nomadic computing.

Client settings require the name or IP address of the preferred outgoing mail server, the port number (25 for MTA, 587 for MSA), and the user name and password for the authentication, if any. There is a non-standard port 465 for SSL encrypted SMTP sessions, that many clients and servers support for backward compatibility. Transport Layer Security encryption can be configured for the standard ports, if both the client and the server support it.

## 6.6 Netscape mail Clients

Like Microsoft even Netscape has also got its own mail software called Netscape Messenger. It supports full-featured mail options. It looks like the Microsoft Internet Mail. With the help of Netscape messenger you can receive your e-mail and news very easily and quickly. Netscape messenger has a full feature of sending a mail to more than one person at a time.

### 6.6.1 Steps to send an e-mail using Netscape Messenger

- Click on the Mail icon on the loweer right corner of the Netscape Messenger Window or Choose Windows and then Netscape Mail.
- Netscape asks for your mail password. Type the password in the Password Entry Dialog box and then click OK button.
- Netscape display, the Netscape Mail window. Click on the To Mail toolbar button to display the Messenger Composition window.
- Type the recipient's mail address in the MailTo: text box.
- If you want to send copies of this message to more than one person then type the appropriate addresses in the Cc: text box.
- Type the subject for the message in the Subject: text box.
- Type the body of the message and then click Send button.

## 6.7 Outlook Express

Outlook Express is an e-mail/news client that is included with Internet Explorer versions 4.0 through 6.0. As such, it is also bundled with several versions of Microsoft Windows, from Windows 98 to Windows XP, and is available for Windows 95 and Mac OS 9. In Windows Vista, Outlook Express was superseded by Windows Mail, then again by Windows Live Mail as separate software in Windows 7. Microsoft Entourage, sold as part of Microsoft Office for Macintosh, has replaced the Macintosh version.

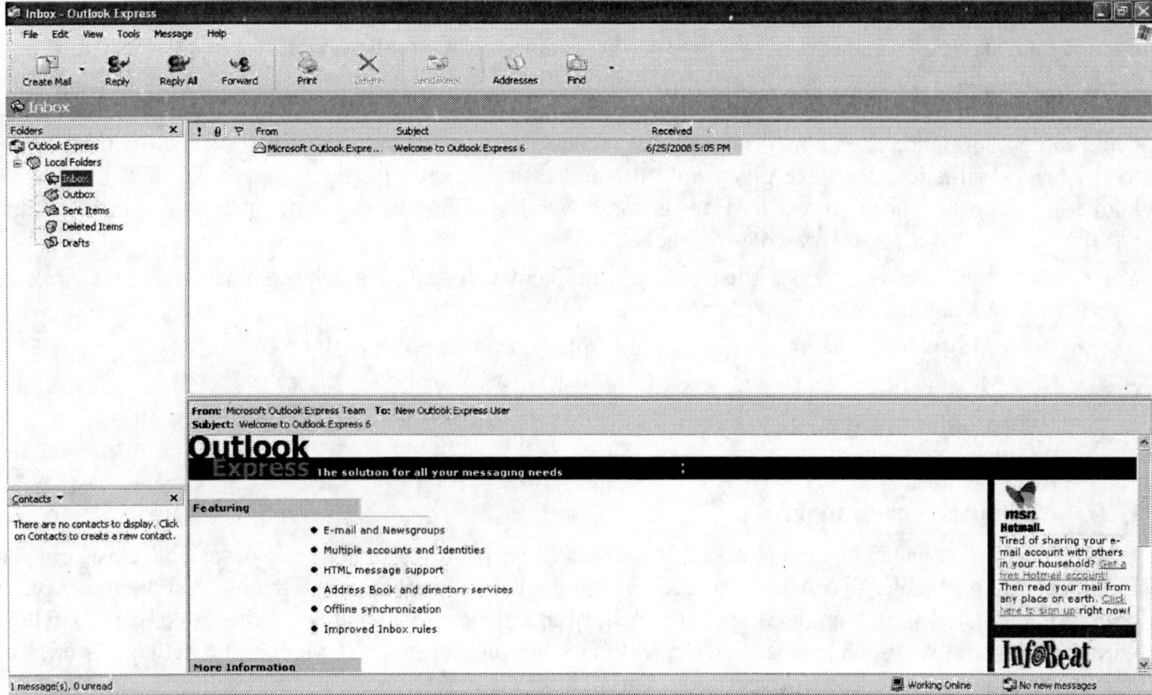


Outlook Express is a different application from Microsoft Office Outlook. The two programs do not share a common codebase, but do share a common architectural philosophy. The similar names lead many people to incorrectly conclude that Outlook Express is a stripped-down version of Microsoft Office Outlook. Outlook Express uses the Windows Address Book to store contact information and integrates tightly with it. On Windows XP, it also integrates with Windows Messenger.

Microsoft Internet Mail and News was a freeware e-mail and news client and ancestor of Outlook Express. Version 1.0 was released in 1996 following the Internet Explorer 3 release. This add-on precedes the Internet Mail profile for Microsoft Exchange 4.0 bundled in Windows 95. Version 2.0 was released at the end of 1996. In 1997 the program was changed and renamed as Outlook Express and bundled with Internet Explorer 4. The executable file for Outlook Express, msimn.exe, is a holdover from the Internet Mail and News era. Internet Mail and News handled only plain text and rich text (RTF) e-mail, lacking HTML e-mail.

At one point, in a later beta version of Outlook Express 5, Outlook Express contained a sophisticated and adaptive spam filtering system; however this feature was removed shortly before launch. It was speculated on various websites and newsgroups at that time, that the feature was not stable enough for the mass market. Nearly two years later, a similar system, using a similar method of adaptive filtering, appeared as a feature of Microsoft Office Outlook.

Internet Explorer 5 required Outlook Express 5 to save Web Archive files.

Outlook Express 6 SP3 is the latest version which is part of Windows XP SP3. Extended support for Windows XP SP3, which covers security hotfixes, will end in 2014.

In October 2005, Microsoft announced that Windows Vista would exclusively include a new application named Windows Mail, based on large parts of Outlook Express source code. Microsoft was also concurrently developing Windows Live Mail Desktop (later renamed to Windows Live Mail), a mail client for its Hotmail service. Windows Live Mail was released in November 2007. In the future, support for Outlook Express and Windows Mail will be discontinued in favor of Windows Live Mail.

## 6.8 Web based E-mail

Each E-mail service - whether it is an online service, commercial e-mail service, has its own way to handle mail. Most of the E-mail services use the Internet as their gateway (describe the path how messages are passed from one service to another service). Internet connects the computers around the world so that people could share information from e-mail service to someone's system, the message will travel across the Internet to reach its destination. We have given only the addressing of the message properly so that the Internet knows where to deliver the message. Here is some web based free E-mail account such as HotMetal and rediffmail.com, that offer web based e-mail access.

You can send mail in several ways while working with Internet. Following are the commands which are related to E-mail button on the Internet Explorer's toolbar.

- **Read Mail:** Opens Outlook Express and display thecontent of your Inbox.
- **New Message:** Create a new Outlook Express Mail Message.
- **Send a Link:** Create a link to attach files with e-mail message.
- **Read News:** Opens Outlook Express News for reading news.

## 6.9 E-mail encryption

With no encryption, much like for postcards, email activity is plainly visible by any occasional eavesdropper. Email encryption enables to safeguard privacy by encrypting the mail sessions, the body of the message, or both. Without it, anyone (examples: the government (warrantless wiretapping, great firewall of China), fellow wireless network users such as at an Internet cafe or other public network, whether the network is open or not) with network access and the right tools can monitor email and obtain login passwords.

Encryption of mail sessions

All relevant email protocols have an option to encrypt the whole session. Remarkably, those options prevent a user's name and password from being sniffed, therefore they are recommended for nomadic users and whenever the internet access provider is not trusted. On sending mail, users can only control encryption at the hop from a client to its configured outgoing mail server. At any further hop, messages may be transmitted with or without encryption, depending solely on the general configuration of the transmitting server and the capabilities of the receiving one.

Encrypted mail sessions deliver messages in their original format, i.e. plain text or encrypted body, on a user's local mailbox and on the destination server's. The latter server is operated by an email hosting service provider, possibly a different entity than the internet access provider currently at hand.

### 6.9.1 Encryption of the message body

There are two models for managing cryptographic keys. S/MIME employs a model based on a trusted certificate authority (CA) that signs users' public keys. OpenPGP employs a somewhat more flexible web of trust mechanism that allows users to sign one another's public keys. OpenPGP is also more flexible in the format of the messages, in that it still supports plain message encryption and signing as they used to work before MIME standardization.

In both cases, only the message body is encrypted. Headers, including originator, recipients, and subject, remain in plain text....

### 6.9.2 Standards

While popular protocols for retrieving mail include POP3 and IMAP4, sending mail is usually done using the SMTP protocol.

Another important standard supported by most email clients is MIME, which is used to send binary file email attachments. Attachments are files that are not part of the email proper, but are sent with the email.

Most email clients use an X-Mailer header to identify the software used to send the message. According to RFC 2076, this is a common but non-standard header.

RFC 4409, Message Submission for Mail, details the role of the Mail submission agent.

RFC 5068, Email Submission Operations: Access and Accountability Requirements, provides a survey of the concepts of MTA, MSA, MDA, and MUA. It mentions that "Access Providers MUST NOT block users from accessing the external Internet using the SUBMISSION port 587" and that "MUAs SHOULD use the SUBMISSION port for message submission."

### 6.9.3 Port numbers

Email servers and client use the following TCP port numbers by default, unless configured for specialized installations:

| *protocol* | *use* | *plain text or encrypt sessions* | *plain text sessions only* | *encrypt sessions only* |
|---|---|---|---|---|
| POP3 | incoming mail | 110 | | 995 |
| IMAP4 | incoming mail | 143 | | 993 |
| SMTP | outgoing mail | 25 | | 465 |
| MSA | outgoing mail | 587 | | |
| HTTP | webmail | | 80 | 443 |

Note that while webmail obeys the earlier HTTP disposition of having separate ports for encrypt and plain text sessions, mail protocols use the STARTTLS technique, thereby allowing encryption to start on an already established TCP connection. RFC 2595 discourages the use of the previously established ports 993 and 995.

## 6.10 Address Book

Windows Address Book is a component of Microsoft Windows that lets users keep a single list of contacts that can be shared by multiple programs. It is most commonly used by Outlook Express. It was introduced with Internet Explorer 3 in 1996 and improved in subsequent versions. The Windows Address Book API can query LDAP servers or read/write data to a local .wab file. In Windows Vista, Windows Address Book was replaced with Windows Contacts.

The Windows Address Book is an application that has a local database and user interface for finding and editing information about people, making it possible to query network directory servers using Lightweight Directory Access Protocol. Other applications can also use the WAB. Microsoft Office Outlook uses its own PST store for email messages. However, it can import contacts from the .WAB format. Microsoft Exchange uses .PAB file for personal address book.

### 6.10.1 Features

- Can store comprehensive contact information in tabs including personal and business information
- Integrates with Outlook Express.
- Programmable API to work with other applications. Applications can also extend functionality such as adding more tabs and fields to store additional custom information, or customizing the toolbar.
- Can store contacts inside contact groups and folders.
- Can selectively send email to contacts only in plain text for additional security.
- Can export and import cards to and from vCard 2.1 and CSV formats. Can also import from LDIF and other formats.
- Search for entries in the contact database, arrange contacts by first name or last name.
- Automatically add contacts from received email.

- Prints contact lists as memo, business card or phone list styles.

## 6.11 Signature File

You can have Outlook add a signature, a special tag line, to each message you send.

### 6.11.1 Creating Default Signature

1. From the Tools menu, choose Options.
2. On the Signature tab of the Options dialog box, click at New.
3. In the Create New Signature dialog box, enter a name for the new signature and click Next.
4. In the Edit Signature dialog box, type the signature that will appear at the end of your message if this signature is selected.
5. You can make this signature as the default signature to appear at all messages sent by you.
6. Click Ok.

### Let us Revise

1. When you send e-mail to someone on the Internet, that message has to travel through a series of networks before it reaches the recipient.
2. There are a few message formats that have evolved into de facto standards and most messaging products include support for them.
3. Simple Mail Transfer Protocol (SMTP) is an Internet standard for electronic mail (e-mail) transmission across Internet Protocol (IP) networks.
4. In computing, the Post Office Protocol (POP) is an application-layer Internet standard protocol used by local e-mail clients to retrieve e-mail from a remote server over a TCP/IP connection.
5. The Internet Message Access Protocol (IMAP) is one of the two most prevalent Internet standard protocols for e-mail retrieval, the other being the Post Office Protocol (POP).
6. Multipurpose Internet Mail Extensions (MIME) is an Internet standard that extends the format of e-mail to support.
7. Like a formal letter e-mail also is divided into various sections. In a good business letter, you would have, date, the name and address of the person to whom the letter is addressed, salutation, text matter, sender's name, etc.
8. You can attach files to your message, and you also attach or include as text the items in your Outlook folders.
9. An email client, email reader, or more formally mail user agent (MUA), is a computer program used to manage email.
10. Like most client programs, an MUA is only active when a user runs it. Messages arrive on the Mail Transfer Agent (MTA) server.
11. Like Microsoft even Netscape has also got its own mail software called Netscape Messenger.
12. Each E-mail service - whether it is an online service, commercial e-mail service, has its own way to handle mail.
13. Windows Address Book is a component of Microsoft Windows that lets users keep a single list of contacts that can be shared by multiple programs.
14. You can have Outlook add a signature, a special tag line, to each message you send.

### Multiple Choice Questions

1. Commonly used program for e-mail is:

   **(a) Outlook Express** (b) Internet Explorer (c) Microsoft Windows

2. You half finished messages are stored in:

   (a) Inbox (b) Outbox **(c) Drafts**

3. MTA is:

   **(a) Mail Transfer Agent** (b) My Transfer Agent (c) Mail Travel Agent

4. MIME is :

   (a) Multipurpose Internet Mail External

   **(b) Multipurpose Internet Mail Extensions**

   (c) Multipurpose Indian Mail Extensions

5. IMAP is :

   (a) Internet Message Access Product

   (b) Indian Message Access Protocol

   **(c) Internet Message Access Protocol**

## True/False Questions

1. There are a few message formats that have evolved into de facto standards and most messaging products include support for them.
2. In computing, the Post Office Protocol (POP) is an application-layer Internet standard protocol used by local e-mail clients to retrieve e-mail from a remote server over a TCP/IP connection.
3. Multipurpose Internet Mail Extensions (MIME) is an Internet standard that extends the format of e-mail to support.
4. **You cannot atta**ch files to your message, and you also attach or include as text the items in your Outlook folders.
5. Like Microsoft even Netscape has also got its own mail software called Netscape Messenger.
6. Each E-mail service - whether it is an online service, commercial e-mail service, has its own way to handle mail.
7. **You cannot have O**utlook add a signature, a special tag line, to each message you send.

## Match Columns

Match the matter in Column A with the matter in Column B.

| Column A | Column B |
|---|---|
| A. SMTP | 1. Internet Message Access Protocol |
| B. POP | 2. Multipurpose Internet Mail Extensions |
| C. IMAP | 3. Carbon copy |
| D. MIME | 4. Blind Carbon Copy |
| E. Bcc | 5. Simple Mail Transfer Protocol |
| F. Cc | 6. Point to Point Protocol |

## Fill in the Blanks with Appropriate Words

a. Multipurpose Internet Mail Extensions (MIME)
b. Internet Message Access Protocol (IMAP)
c. attach
d. mail user agent (MUA)
e. Mail Transfer Agent (MTA)
f. Simple Mail Transfer Protocol (SMTP)
g. Point to Point Protocol

1. ______________________ is an Internet standard for electronic mail (e-mail) transmission across Internet Protocol (IP) networks.

2. In computing, the ________________ is an application-layer Internet standard protocol used by local e-mail clients to retrieve e-mail from a remote server over a TCP/IP connection.
3. The ______________________ is one of the two most prevalent Internet standard protocols for e-mail retrieval, the other being the Post Office Protocol (POP).
4. ________________ is an Internet standard that extends the format of e-mail to support.
5. You can __________ files to your message, and you also attach or include as text the items in your Outlook folders.
6. An email client, email reader, or more formally ____________, is a computer program used to manage email.
7. Like most client programs, an MUA is only active when a user runs it. Messages arrive on the ________________ server.

## Descriptive Type Questions

1. What are E-mail Networks and Servers?
2. Define the various E-mail Protocols.
3. What goes in the sturucture of an e-mail?
4. Describe the process of attaching a file to an e-mail.
5. What do you understand by E-mail clients?
6. Write a short note on Outlook Express.
7. What do you understand by Web based E-mail?
8. How is Email Encryption done?
9. What do you understand by Address Book?
10. How would you attach signatures to the E-mail?

## Answers to Objective Type Questions

### *Multiple Choice Questions*

| | | | |
|---|---|---|---|
| 1. a | 2. c | 3. a | 4. b |
| 5. c | | | |

### *True False Questions*

| | | | |
|---|---|---|---|
| 1. T | 2. T | 3. T | 4. F |
| 5. T | 6. T | 7. F | |

### *Matching Columns*

| | | | |
|---|---|---|---|
| A. 5 | B. 6 | C. 1 | D. 2 |
| E. 4 | F. 3 | | |

### *Fill in the Blanks*

| | | | |
|---|---|---|---|
| 1. f | 2. g | 3. a | 4. b |
| 5. c | 6. d | 7. e | |

# Current Trends on Internet 7

## 7.1 Languages

In the last decade the Internet has become the number one use of the computer. So it is natural that the languages of Internet would also become famous with more and more languages coming up for the same. Here are the few of them.

### 7.1.1 Java

In 1991, while working at Sun Microsystems, James Gosling, Patrick Naughton, Chris Warth, Ed Frank, and Mike Sheridan conceived Java. It took them 18 months to develop the first working version of the software language. This was initially called "Oak" but was renamed "Java" in 1995. Between the initial implementation of Oak in 1992 and the public announcement of Java in 1995, many more people contributed to the design and evolution of the language. Bill Joy, Arthur van Hoff, Jonathan Payne, Frank Yellin, and Tim Lindholm were the key players.

When Java was developed, no body thought of it for a platform like Internet. Instead, the primary motivation was the need for a platform-independent language that could be used to create software to be embedded in various consumer electronic devices, such as microwave ovens and remote controls. As you can probably guess, many different types of CPUs are used as controllers. The trouble with C and C++ (and most other languages) is that they are designed to be compiled for a specific target. Although it is possible to compile a C++ program for just about any type of CPU, to do so requires a full C ++ compiler targeted for that CPU. The problem is that compilers are expensive and time-consuming to create. An easier—and more cost—efficient-solution was needed.

In an attempt to find such a solution, work began on a portable, platform-independent language that could be used to produce code that would run on a variety of CPUs under differing environments. This effort ultimately led to the creation of Java. Around the same time that the details of Java were being worked out, a second, and ultimately more important, factor was emerging that would play a crucial role in the future of Java. This second force was, of course, the World Wide Web. Had the Web not taken shape at about the same time that Java was being implemented, Java might have remained a useful but obscure language for programming consumer electronics.

However, with the emergence of the World Wide Web, Java was propelled to the forefront of computer language design, because the Web, too, demanded portable programs. Most programmers learn early in their careers that portable programs are as elusive as they are desirable. While the quest for a way to create efficient, portable (platform-independent) programs is nearly as old as the discipline of programming itself, it had taken a back seat to other, more pressing problems.

Further, because much of the computer world had divided itself into the three competing camps of Intel, Macintosh and UNIX, most programmers stayed within their fortified boundaries, and the urgent need for portable code was reduced. However, with the advent of the Internet and the Web, the old problem of portability returned with a vengeance. After all, the Internet consists of a diverse, distributed universe populated with many types of computers, operating systems, and CPUs. Even though many types of platforms are attached to the Internet, users would like them all to be able to run the same program.

What was once an irritating but low-priority problem had become a high-profile necessity. During 1993, it became obvious to members of the Java design team that the problems of portability frequently encountered when creating code for embedded controllers are also found when attempting to create code for the Internet. In fact, the same problem that Java was initially designed to solve on a small scale could also be applied to the Internet on a large scale. This realization caused the focus of Java to switch from consumer electronics to Internet programming. So, while the desire for an architecture-neutral programming language provided the initial spark, the Internet ultimately led to Java's large-scale success.

Java, as said before, derives much of its character from C and C++. This is so because, the Java designers knew that using the familiar syntax of C and echoing the object-oriented features of C++ would make their language appealing to the legions of experienced C/C++ programmers. In addition to the surface similarities, Java shares some of the other attributes that helped make C and C++ successful.

*Firsty*, Java was designed, tested, and refined by real, working programmers. It is a language grounded in the needs and experiences of the people who devised it. Thus, Java is also a programmer's language.

*Secondly*, Java is cohesive and logically consistent.

*Thirdly*, except for those constraints imposed by the Internet environment, Java gives you, the programmer, full control. If you program well, your programs reflect it. If you program poorly, your programs reflect that, too.

Putting differently, Java is not a language with training wheels. It is a language for professional programmers. Because of the similarities between Java and C++, it is tempting to think of Java as simply the "Internet version of C++." However, to do so would be a large mistake. Java has significant practical and philosophical differences. While it is true that Java was influenced by C++, it is not an enhanced version of C++. For example, Java is neither upwardly nor downwardly compatible with C++. Of course, the similarities with C++ are significant, and if you are a C++ programmer, then you will feel right at home with Java. One other point: Java was not designed to replace C++. Java was designed to solve a certain set of problems. C++ was designed to solve a different set of problems. Both will coexist for many years to come.

The environmental change that prompted Java was the need for platform-independent programs destined for distribution on the Internet. However, Java also embodies changes in the way that people approach the writing of programs.

Specifically, Java enhances and refines the object-oriented paradigm used by C++. Thus, Java is not a language that exists in isolation. Rather, it is the current instance of an ongoing process begun many years ago. This fact alone is enough to ensure Java a place in computer language history. Java is to Internet programming what C was to systems programming: a revolutionary force that will change the world.

#### ***7.1.1.1 Java as Internet Language?***

As mentioned earlier, Java programming is the key factor of Internet programming. This is so because Internet helped catapult Java to the forefront of programming, and Java, in turn, has had a profound effect on the Internet. The reason for this is quite simple: Java expands the universe of objects that can move about freely in cyberspace. In a network, two very broad categories of objects are transmitted between the server and your personal computer: passive information and dynamic, active programs. For example, when you read your e-mail, you are viewing passive data.

Even when you download a program, the program's code is still only passive data until you execute it. However, a second type of object can be transmitted to your computer: a dynamic, self-executing program. Such a program is an active agent on the client computer, yet is initiated by the server. For example, a program might be provided by the server to display properly the data that the server is sending. As desirable as dynamic, networked programs are, they also present serious problems in the areas of security and portability. Prior to Java, cyberspace was effectively closed to half the entities that now live there. Java addresses those concerns and, by doing so, has opened the door to an exciting new form of program: the applet.

### 7.1.2 ActiveX

ActiveX is a framework for defining reusable software components that perform a particular function or a set of functions in Microsoft Windows in a way that is independent of the programming language used to implement them. A software application can then be composed from one or more of these components in order to provide its functionality. It was introduced in 1996 by Microsoft as a development of its Component Object Model (COM) and Object Linking and Embedding (OLE) technologies and it is commonly used in its Windows operating system, although the technology itself is not tied to it.

Many Microsoft Windows applications — including many of those from Microsoft itself, such as Internet Explorer, Microsoft Office, Microsoft Visual Studio, and Windows Media Player — use ActiveX controls to build their feature-set and also encapsulate their own functionality as ActiveX controls which can then be embedded into other applications. Internet Explorer also allows embedding ActiveX controls onto web pages.

ActiveX controls — small program building blocks — can serve to create distributed applications that work over the Internet through web browsers. Examples include customized applications for gathering data, viewing certain kinds of files, and displaying animation.

One can compare ActiveX controls in some sense to Java applets: programmers designed both of these mechanisms so that web browsers could download and execute them. However, they also differ:

Java applets can run on nearly any platform, while ActiveX components officially operate only with Microsoft's Internet Explorer web browser and the Microsoft Windows operating system. Programmers can grant to ActiveX controls a much higher level of control over Windows than Java applets ever achieve, making them more powerful but also potentially more dangerous.

Malware, such as computer viruses and spyware, can be accidentally installed from malicious websites using ActiveX controls (drive-by downloads). Programmers can write ActiveX controls in any of the following languages/environments:

MFC
ATL
C++
C#
Borland Delphi
Visual Basic

### 7.1.3 JavaScript

Like many other programming languages JavaScript is a programming language, which is mainly used with Web Pages. This language is very useful when providing interactivity to a Web page. There are lots of JavaScript programs available over the net which can be copied and made use by making alterations desired by you. A JavaScript is a program which is included on an HTML page. On the HTML page you enclose the JavaScript program within <SCRIPT> and end it up with </SCRIPT>. When you run it with a browser, it knows that this is a program written under JavaScript it runs it to give you the result instead of just giving the text of the script. The <SCRIPT> tag is most often found within the <HEAD> section of the HTML page, though you can, if you wish, have scripts under the <BODY> section.

#### *7.1.3.1 What you can do with JavaScript*

There are lots of thing which you can do with JavaScript. For example, to enhance your Web page besides making it more interactive. It allows you to have Web pages users feedback by providing buttons on the Web page. You can create forms which the users of the Web page can fill to provide you with the information needed by you. You can even do calculations on these forms using CGI. It also allows you to create new windows, display alert boxes and messages on the Web pages.

#### *7.1.3.2 JAVA and JavaScript*

Let me make it very clear once and for all, JAVA and JavaScript have only name in common and nothing else. They are poles apart. JAVA is basically a programming language which is enhancement of C++ having a distinctive feature of being able to run on various machines and operating systems like Windows NT, Mac OS or even Unix.

#### *7.1.3.3 JavaScript as Object Oriented Language*

An object is some kind of a thing. A computer, a mouse, etc., are all objects. To JavaScript they are all objects it deals with in Web browsers such as windows, forms and elements of the form such as buttons and check boxes.

#### *7.1.3.4 Events*

Events are actions that the user performs while visiting your page. Submitting a form and moving a mouse over an image are two examples of events. JavaScript deals with events with commands called event handlers. There are as many as 12 JavaScript event handlers, as listed below. An action by the user on the page triggers an event handler in your script.

#### *7.1.3.5 Event Handlers*

| ***Event*** | ***What it handles*** |
|---|---|
| onAbort | The user aborted loading the page |
| onBlur | The user left the object |
| onChange | The user changed the object |
| onClick | The user clicked on an object |
| onError | The script encountered an error |
| onFocus | The user made an object active |
| onLoad | The object finished loading |
| onMouseOver | The cursor moved over an object |
| onMouseOut | The cursor moved off an object |
| onSelect | The user selected the contents of an object |
| onSubmit | The user submitted a form |
| onUnload | The user left the window |

## 7.2 Internet Phone

IP telephony is regarded as a service applied by VoIP technology to the whole or a part of the telephone line. IP telephony services also often include videophone/video conferencing services. According to the Telecommunication Business Law, the service category for IP telephony also implies the service provided via Internet, which is not assigned any telephone number.

IP telephony is basically regulated by Ministry of Internal Affairs and Communications (MIC) as a telecommunication service. The operators have to disclose necessary information on its quality, etc., prior to making contracts with customers, and have an obligation to respond to their complaints cordially.

Many Japanese Internet service providers (ISP) are including IP telephony services. An ISP who also provides IP telephony service is known as a "ITSP (Internet Telephony Service Provider)". Recently, the competition among ITSPs has been activated, by option or set sales, in connection with ADSL or FTTH services.

The tariff system normally applied to Japanese IP telephony is described below;

- A call between IP telephony subscribers, limited to the same group, is usually free of charge.

- A call from IP telephony subscribers to a fixed line or PHS is usually a uniformly fixed rate all over the country.
- Between ITSPs, the interconnection is mostly maintained at VoIP level.
- Where the IP telephony is assigned normal telephone number (0AB-J), the condition for its interconnection is considered same as normal telephony.

Where the IP telephony is assigned specific telephone number (050), the condition for its interconnection is described below;

- Interconnection is sometimes charged. (Sometimes, it is free of charge.) In case of free-of-charge, mostly, communication traffic is exchanged via a P2P connection with the same VoIP standard. Otherwise, certain conversions are needed at the point of the VoIP gateway which incurs operating costs.

Since then the MIC has assigned IP telephony telephone numbers on the condition that the service falls into certain required categories of quality.

High-quality IP telephony is assigned a telephone number, normally starting with the digits 050. When VoIP quality is so high that a customer has difficulty telling the difference between it and a normal telephone, and when the provider relates its number with a location and provides the connection with emergency call capabilities, the provider is allowed to assign a normal telephone number, which is a so-called "0AB-J" number.

## 7.3 Internet Video

A telco IPTV service is usually delivered over a complex and investment heavy walled garden network, which is carefully engineered to ensure bandwidth efficient delivery of vast amounts of multicast video traffic. The higher network quality also enables easy delivery of high quality SD or HD TV content to subscribers' homes. This makes IPTV by default the preferred delivery platform for premium content. However, the investment for a telco to build an end-to-end IPTV service can be substantial.

By contrast "Internet TV" generally refers to transport streams sent over IP networks (normally the Internet) from outside the network that connects to the users premises. An Internet TV provider has no control over the final delivery and so broadcasts on a "best effort" basis. Elementary streams over IP networks and proprietary variants as used by websites such as YouTube are now rarely considered to be IPTV services.

Compared to telco IPTV, Internet TV is a quick-to-market and relatively low investment service. Internet TV rides on existing infrastructure including broadband, ADSL, Wi-Fi, cable and satellite which makes it a valuable tool for a wide variety of service providers and content owners looking for new revenue streams. However, due to the fact that IPTV is always delivered over low cost IP STBs, which have limited computing power, the capability for IPTV operators to provide diverse multimedia services is limited. This is where Internet TV has an advantage as it is delivered to a subscriber's (generally) powerful PC.

The relative ease of establishing an Internet TV service seems at first a threat to telco IPTV operators' multimillion dollar investment, but both services do not necessarily compete for the same customers and there are some synergies between the two such as a common technology platform in the form of web-based technologies for content storage and delivery.

Broadcast IPTV has two major architecture forms: free and fee based. As of June 2006, there are over 1,300 free IPTV sources available. This sector is growing rapidly and major television broadcasters worldwide are transmitting their broadcast signal over the Internet. These free IPTV sources require only an Internet connection and an Internet enabled device such as a personal computer, HDTV connected to a computer or even a 3G cell/mobile phone to watch the IPTV content. Various Web portals offer access to these free IPTV sources. Some cite the ad-sponsored availability of TV series such as Lost as indicators that IPTV will become more prevalent.

Because IPTV uses standard networking protocols, it promises lower costs for operators and lower prices for users. Using set-top boxes with broadband Internet connections, video can be streamed to households more efficiently than current coaxial cable. Home networks currently use technology from the Multimedia over Coax Alliance, HomePlug Powerline Alliance or Home Phoneline Networking Alliance to deliver IPTV content to any set-top box in a home, without having to install new Ethernet wires and without relying on technologies like 802.11, which are not optimized for reliable delivery of video streams. ISPs are upgrading their networks to bring higher speeds and to allow multiple High Definition TV channels.

IPTV uses a two-way digital broadcast signal sent through a switched telephone or cable network by way of a broadband connection and a set-top box programmed with software (much like a cable or DSS box) that can handle viewer requests to access to many available media sources.

Local IPTV, as used by businesses for audio visual AV distribution on their company networks is typically based on a mixture of:

- Conventional TV reception equipment and IPTV encoders
- IPTV Gateways that take broadcast MPEG channels and IP wrap them to create multicast streams.

## 7.4 Collaborative Computing

Collaborative computing facilitates the growth of team-based organizations through its ability to allow the geographically distributed teams to develop, edit and utilize a common database. Sometimes called workgroup computing or groupware, collaborative computing provides an opportunity for a group of individuals to share and relay information in such a way accomplishment of duties and attainment of consensus. The essential components of a collaborative computing environment are facilities for processing and disseminating documents and atabases, electronic mail, information-sharing supports through communication and discussion, facilities for mail-authorized and interconnected office automation software and an application development interface. Application of the technology in major companies, including accounting firms, seems to confirm predictions that collaborative computing will recast work patterns.

Collaborative computing environment includes at a minimum the following five classes of functions:

1. Facilities to create, organize, distribute, and route documents and nontransaction-oriented databases, that is, databasees containing information that people access rather than databases of high-speed/volume data, such as a credit card database.
2. Electonic mail.
3. Support for information sharing through communication and discussion, such as real-time bulletin boards and virtual meetings by discussion templates.
4. Facilities for mail-enabled and transparently interconnected office automation software, such as spreadsheets, schedulting programs, and word-processing software, along with graphics packages and telecommunication software. Mail-enabled and transparently interconnected software allows any part of any document constructed in any software package to be mailed with its information content and formatting intact.
5. An application development interface to create applications and to combine and incorporate other computing functions.

## 7.5 E-commerce

E-Commerce is the technology for doing business over the net. It has its roots in computer and commerce. It allows you to do business as you do otherwise too but here the person concerned is not facing you. The whole business is done in writing and without talking and seeing each other, mostly. You type the question and he will answer and vice versa, so the business is done without a chance of saying, "I did not say so", because everything is written here.

Let us first understand by what commerce is.

### 7.5.1 Commerce

According to dictionary commerce is, "It is the exchange or transformation or buying and selling of entities (goods or commodities) on a very large scale involving transportation from one place to another". Commerce deals with buyers (the people who want to purchase items and services with money), sellers (the people who provides items and services to the buyers by taking money from the buyers) and the producer (the people who originate the products and services for the buyers and the sellers).

Let us now understand what E-Commerce or Electronic – Commerce is.

### 7.5.2 E-Commerce

It is nothing but adding electronic to the commerce, i.e., doing business on the net. It can be buying and selling of stocks and bonds, selling a product, buying goods and services for your company's operations or purchasing a fancy dress, or any other such commercial transaction. E-commerce covers the vast of amount of business-to-consumer and business-to-business transactions taking place on the Web (with the help of internet). It is not Just Web Shopping, it is more than the definition. Despite popular belief, there is a lot more to e-commerce than buying goods online. Every day, millions of transactions are conducted via the Web, all of which fall under the E-commerce. E-Commerce is to conduct business by using the IT (Information Technology, i.e., Computer technologies and the electronic communications). In other words it is the buying and selling of items of goods and services on the Web. E-Commerce is the process of doing business electronic. It involves automation of a variety of B2B (Business to Business) and B2C (Business to Consumer) transaction through reliable and secure connections.

The use of electronic transmission medium (tele-communication, internet) to engage in the exchange of business document including buying and selling products and services with physically or digitally from location to another using computer as a component and internet as a media. E-Commerce is a composite of technologies process and business strategies that foster the instant exchange of information within between organization. E-Commerce strengthens relationship with buyers make it easier to attract new customer improves customer responsiveness and open new markets on a global scale.

E-Commerce is the application of various communication technologies to provide the automated exchange of business information with internal and external customer, suppliers and financial institutions. E-Commerce is about setting your business on the Internet, allowing visitors to access your website and go through virtual catalog or your product/services online. When the visitor wants to buy something he/she likes, they merely, add it to their virtual shopping basket, items in the virtual shopping basket can be added or deleted and when you are all set to checkout . You head to the virtual checkout counter, which has your complete total and will ask you for your name, address etc. and method/way of payment (usually credit card). Once all the information is entered the buying and selling procedure is complete and you have to just wait for delivery.

### 7.5.3 The origin of term E-commerce

IBM was the first company who use the term internationally. The 1972, IBM used this term as 'E-business' and the first successful transaction is held between USA and European union in 1973 with the invention of personal computers. The term E-commerce is derived from e-mail means conducting business online with the help of electronic devices like personal computers, phone lines, fax machine, pager, etc. E-Commerce helps conduct traditional commerce through new ways of transferring and processing information, since it is information which is at the heart of any commercial activity.

Information is electronically transferred from computer to computer, in an automated way. E-commerce refers to the paperless exchange of business information using EDI, E-mail, Electronic bulletin Boards, EPT and other network based technologies.

It is not only automates manual processes and paper transactions, but also helps organization move to a fully e-environment and change the way they operate. The most popular areas of business-to-consumer E-commerce include goods sold in the following categories: computer products, consumer products, books and magazines and music and entertainment products. Actually it is thinking small on the WWW (world wide web).

Internet is now-a-days a way of life. You cannot work without it. What started as a simple means of transferring data for government and educational groups has quickly taken on a life of its own. For small business, it is not only a great marketing tool, but also an efficient means of communication and data transfer, as well as an entire sales channel.

World Wide Web provides the perfect backdrop for a small business that is looking to expand its customer base, grow its profits and even increase its product offerings. On the Web, issue like company size and physical location are completely transparent. For this reason, the small business getting involved with e-commerce has a fair chance of succeeding without having to invest in a fancy storefront or additional employees.

Even a one-man-show can make it on the Web. That is why more and more companies are becoming shorter and shorter strength wise. Even people have starting working from what is called Virtual Office, which can even be your car, having a laptop and a phone. And when the going gets tough, there's always outsourcing to help you over the rough spots. Through it all, your customers never need to know that your firm is made up of you and your kitchen table-office.

Present a positive image and deliver the goods and time you'll never have to explain your company's location or employees to anyone. It's Cost Effective. The obvious benefits aside, it's the cost savings that really add up when a company implements an e-commerce strategy. With an investment of as little as Rs.50,000, companies are able to contract professionals to create their e-commerce-enabled sites, which are subsequently hosted by an Internet Service Provider (ISP) for an average of Rs.700 per month. Still others – those who are lucky enough to have tech-savvy workers onboard – are getting the job done for even less.

### 7.5.4 Working of E-commerce

There are several sites which are known as Search Engines. You type the product you want to search and it will give you the name of the sites who are dealing with such product. You then searches those web sites. From there, you decide what you want to purchase and sell. The transaction is done using the online transaction server, where all of the information the gives is encrypted. Once you have placed your order, the information moves through a private gateway to a Processing Network, where the issuing and acquiring banks complete or deny the transaction. This generally takes place in no more than 5 – 7 seconds.

### 7.5.5 E-commerce in India

Gone are the days when India used to be 25 years behind all the developments. These days India is at par with all the new technologies. Almost all major organizations have some presence on the net. The real challenge is to convert this presence into online business. Some companies, notably rediffOnTheNet, SatyamOnline, MantraOnline, have already ventured into this field, and they are working towards giving you foolproof business terms. For example, sitting at home you can enter the web site of your supplier of cellphone connection and giving them your credit card number can buy the extra talk time from them. All this without leaving the desk. This is e-commerce at its best.

## Let us Revise

1. When Java was developed, no body thought of it for a platform like Internet.
2. Java is not a language with training wheels. It is a language for professional programmers.
3. Even when you download a program, the program's code is still only passive data until you execute it.
4. ActiveX is a framework for defining reusable software components that perform a particular function or a set of functions in Microsoft Windows in a way that is independent of the programming language used to implement them.
5. Like many other programming languages JavaScript is a programming language, which is mainly used with Web Pages.
6. IP telephony is regarded as a service applied by VoIP technology to the whole or a part of the telephone line.
7. A telco IPTV service is usually delivered over a complex and investment heavy walled garden network, which is carefully engineered to ensure bandwidth efficient delivery of vast amounts of multicast video traffic.
8. Collaborative computing facilitates the growth of team-based organizations through its ability to allow the geographically distributed teams to develop, edit and utilize a common database.
9. E-Commerce is the technology for doing business over the net. It has its roots in computer and commerce.
10. World Wide Web provides the perfect backdrop for a small business that is looking to expand its customer base, grow its profits and even increase its product offerings.

## Multiple Choice Questions

1. Active X is a :
   (a) Software component (b) Software device (c) Software program
2. Java is a :
   (a) Foreign Language (b) Programming Language (c) Electronic device
3. JavaScript is mainly used with :
   (a) Book Pages (b) Flowers (c) Web Pages
4. IP Telephony works with :
   (a) Telephone lines (b) Railway lines (c) Stored lines
5. E-commerce :
   (a) Doing business on the net (b) Doing business on the net (c) Doing business on the net

## True/False Questions

1. Java is not a language with training wheels. It is a language for professional programmers.
2. Even when you download a program, the program's code is still only passive data until you execute it.
3. Like many other programming languages JavaScript is not a programming language, which is mainly used with Web Pages.
4. IP telephony is not regarded as a service applied by VoIP technology to the whole or a part of the telephone lines.
5. Collaborative computing facilitates the growth of team-based organizations through its ability to allow the geographically distributed teams to develop, edit and utilize a common database.
6. E-Commerce is the technology for doing business over the net. It has its roots in computer and commerce.

## Match Columns

Match the matter in Column A with the matter in Column B.

| Column A | Column B |
|---|---|
| A. Java | 1. Web based programming script |

| | |
|---|---|
| B. E-commerce | 2. Interactive TV |
| C. ActiveX | 3. Used with telephone lines |
| D. JavaScript | 4. Software Component |
| E. IP Telephony | 5. Programming Language |
| F. IPTV | 6. Doing business on the net |

## Fill in the Blanks with Appropriate Words

a. JavaScript    b. IP telephony    c. E-Commerce    d. IPTV
e. Java    f. ActiveX

1. When _________ was developed, no body thought of it for a platform like Internet.
2. _______________ is a framework for defining reusable software components that perform a particular function or a set of functions in Microsoft Windows in a way that is independent of the programming language used to implement them.
3. Like many other programming languages __________ is a programming language, which is mainly used with Web Pages.
4. ____________ is regarded as a service applied by VoIP technology to the whole or a part of the telephone line.
5. A telco __________ service is usually delivered over a complex and investment heavy walled garden network, which is carefully engineered to ensure bandwidth efficient delivery of vast amounts of multicast video traffic.
6. __________ is the technology for doing business over the net. It has its roots in computer and commerce.

## Descriptive Type Questions

1. Describe the working of Java.
2. What is ActiveX?
3. Describe JavaScript?
4. What is Internet Phone?
5. What is Internet Video?
6. What is Collaborativ Computing?
7. Describe E-commerce

## Answers to Objective Type Questions

### *Multiple Choice Questions*

| | | | |
|---|---|---|---|
| 1. a | 2. b | 3. c | 4. a |
| 5. b | | | |

### *True False Questions*

| | | | |
|---|---|---|---|
| 1. T | 2. T | 3. F | 4. F |
| 5. T | 6. T | | |

### *Matching Columns*

| | | | |
|---|---|---|---|
| A. 5 | B. 6 | C. 4 | D. 1 |
| E. 3 | F. 2 | | |

### *Fill in the Blanks*

| | | | |
|---|---|---|---|
| 1. e | 2. f | 3. a | 4. b |
| 5. d | 6. c | | |

# Web Publishing and Browsing

# 8

## 8.1 Overview

A global hypertext system that uses the Internet as its transport mechanism is called World Wide Web. In a hypertext system, you navigate by clicking hyperlinks, which display another document (which also contains hyperlinks). What makes the Web such an exciting and useful medium is that the next document you see could be housed on a computer next door-or halfway around the world. The Web makes the Internet easy to use.

Created in 1989 at the European Laboratory for Particle Physics (CERN), a research institute in Switzerland, the Web relies upon the HyperTExt Transport Protocol (HTTP), an Internet standard the specifies how an application can locate and acquire resources (such as document, sound or graphic) stored on another computer on the Internet. HTTP provides transparent, easy-to-use access to Web documents, FTP (File transfer Protocol) file archives, Gopher menus, and even UseNet newsgroups, users of Web navigation software, called Web browsers, simply click on an underlined word or phrase, and HTTP takes care of locating and downloading the desired documents. Most Web documents are created using the HyperText markup language (HTML), a markup language that is easy to learn and will soon be supplanted by automated tools. Incorporating hypermedia (graphics, sound, animations, and video), the Web has become the ideal medium for publishing information on the Internet.

A key 1995 agreement on security protocols ensures that Web will quickly become an important commercial medium, in which consumers can browse on-line catalog and place orders without worrying about anyone intercepting the supplied credit card information.

## 8.2 Standard Generalized Markup Language (SGML)

It is a high level markup language like HTML. It defines different components of a document and describes formatting and hypertext links. HTML is much simpler than SGML and best suited for transmission over the Internet. SGML is not ideal for transmission across the Internet for many types of computers, users, and browsers applications.

## 8.3 Web hosting

So far we have talked about the user point of view, i.e., how to use the Web sites. Now we will talk about the various aspects of designing and creating the Web site. In this chapter, we talk about the planning and hosting the site and in the next chapter, we talk about creating the matter of the site using HTML. First we should know how to host the site and the various aspects related to it.

### 8.3.1 Costs of Going Online

There are several agencies which allow you to host the site. The cost/fee associated with setting up a Web site and getting it online. First you spend to get your domain name. Your company will also be responsible for whatever fees are involved in creating and designing your Web site. This may mean purchasing Web page creation software. Creating your actual Web site may also require you to hire programmers, graphic artists, writers, photographers, and other professionals-either full-time, part-time, or on a free-lance basis. These costs will vary greatly. You could create a basic Web site in under an hour and by spending little money, using just your own artistic ability and a Web page creation program or service. The professional look of your site will probably be lacking, however. Your level of artistic ability and the time you spend creating your site will impact its overall look.

### 8.3.2 Signing with ISP

To get your site online, it's necessary to sign up with an Internet Service Provider (ISP). You may have the Web server equipment to host your own site in-house, then you do not need ISP. For businesses, this typically means paying a one-time set-up fee plus an ongoing monthly fee to an ISP, which also will vary greatly based on your needs and what services are offered. Some ISPs charge a flat monthly fee as low as about Rs.800 per month, but then charges you for additional services, such as tech support, maintenance, or updating. If your online business will be handling credit card transactions, it will be necessary to use an ISP offering secure transactions. This typically costs more. In some cases, if you use certain e-commerce Web page design software packages, you may need to also hire a second ISP (one that supports your software package) to handle secure financial transactions such as order taking. There may be additional per-transaction fees associated with processing secure transactions, as well.

The ISP/Web-hosting business is extremely competitive, so be sure to shop around for the best rates and the highest level of service/ technical support you can find. Finding a reliable ISP is as easy as:

- Seeking out a reference from someone you know.
- Surfing the Internet, using a search engine and a search phrase, like "ISP" or "Web Hosting."
- Checking the Area Directory.
- Calling the ISP of your area.

Keep in mind that some ISPs are national companies, which means they offer dial-up access through cities nationwide and cater to companies like yours located anywhere in the country. These nationwide service providers tend to offer less personalized service (because they're large), but highly competitive rates. If you decide to affiliate yourself with a national ISP, you also run less of a risk that the ISP you ultimately choose will suddenly go out of business (due to the competitive nature of the business). Choose an ISP that offers the services you need, such as server extensions. Also, make sure you maintain an offsite backup of your site to which you have 24-hour access. Even if the ISP provides a backup, it's an excellent strategy to be able to restore your site at another location should this become necessary. This way the best is the one which is nearer to you and is known to you.

A local ISP is one that caters to companies in a single city or region. These services tend to be a bit more expensive; however, you'll receive much more personalized service. If the ISP /Web-hosting service you choose doesn't offer dial-up Internet access or the ability to maintain your site over the Web, you may be required to dial a long-distance phone number to update or maintain your Web site.

### 8.3.3 Services you need from ISP

Choosing an ISP is a lot like choosing a long-distance phone company. All of the long distance companies, such as AT&T, Sprint, and MCI/ Worldcom, (unfortunately in India there is one only) offer long-distance services of the same basic quality, but each has a different pricing plan, different levels of customer service, and different incentives to get you to sign up with them. Typically, you can also save money by signing up with a little-known long distance phone service. The same general rules that apply to choosing a long distance company apply when choosing an ISP. Most offer the same basic services, but with subtle differences and at different price points. This is why it is important to determine exactly what you need and then shop around for the best rates and services.

Some of the things you should inquire about when investigating a possible ISP /Web-hosting service include the following:

- ❑ Rates — This includes set-up fees, monthly rates, and extra charges.
- ❑ Phone lines — Does the ISP offer nationwide dial-up access or just local or regional access? Does the service support your modem speed? If you're using a 56K modem, it's important your ISP can handle connections at this speed. The 56K connection has become an industry standard; however, if you'll be using an ISDN connection or another type of high-speed Internet connection, the ISP you select may not be compatible.
- ❑ Accounts offered — For Web hosting, you'll probably need a SLIP/PPP account, which are the most common types of dial-up accounts.
- ❑ Storage space — When you sign up with an ISP to host your Web site, you may be limited to a specific amount of file storage space on their server-typically 10MB or 20MB, which should be plenty of space for most sites.
- ❑ Passwords — As the customer of the ISP, can you control select your log-on passwords?
- ❑ Registration services — Does the ISP offer this? If so, make sure your domain name is registered with your company name and you are listed as the owner of the domain name.
- ❑ E-mail — Does an ISP's Web-hosting services include e-mail boxes so you can easily accept e-mail messages from customers, clients, and others? How many e-mail boxes do you receive? Is there an extra fee for e-mail boxes?
- ❑ Special software — Does the ISP offer special software for maintaining your Web site or monitoring traffic to your site? If so, is there an additional cost of this software? Are you able to use your own software?
- ❑ Compatibility — Is the Web site creation software you'll be using compatible with the ISP?
- ❑ Backup services — What type of backup services does the ISP offer? How often does the server go down? When it goes down, how long does it typically take to fix?
- ❑ Secure services — Does the ISP offer secure services such as Netscape Commerce Server for online transactions?
- ❑ Bandwidth — Does the ISP have sufficient bandwidth to accommodate the level of traffic your Web site will be receiving? Or will visitors to your site experience lags?
- ❑ Terms — What are the contract terms you'll be required to sign with the ISP? Is there a minimum length of service (three months? Six? Twelve? Twenty-four?)? What are the penalties if you choose to end your service agreement sooner?
- ❑ Additional services — What additional services does the ISP offer, and at what cost?
- ❑ Extra modem — Does the ISP support modem shotgunning so you can achieve a faster Internet connection? *Shotgunning* refers to the use of two different modems to establish one faster Internet connection.
- ❑ Tracking — Does the ISP offer traffic reports or other information you can use to keep track of who is visiting your site, when they're visiting, which site they linked from, which pages of your site they visited, and so forth?
- ❑ Other Help — Does the ISP offer Web site design and creation services for an extra fee?
- ❑ Data transfer — How much data transfer/traffic comes with the account, and what are the charges for additional data transfer?

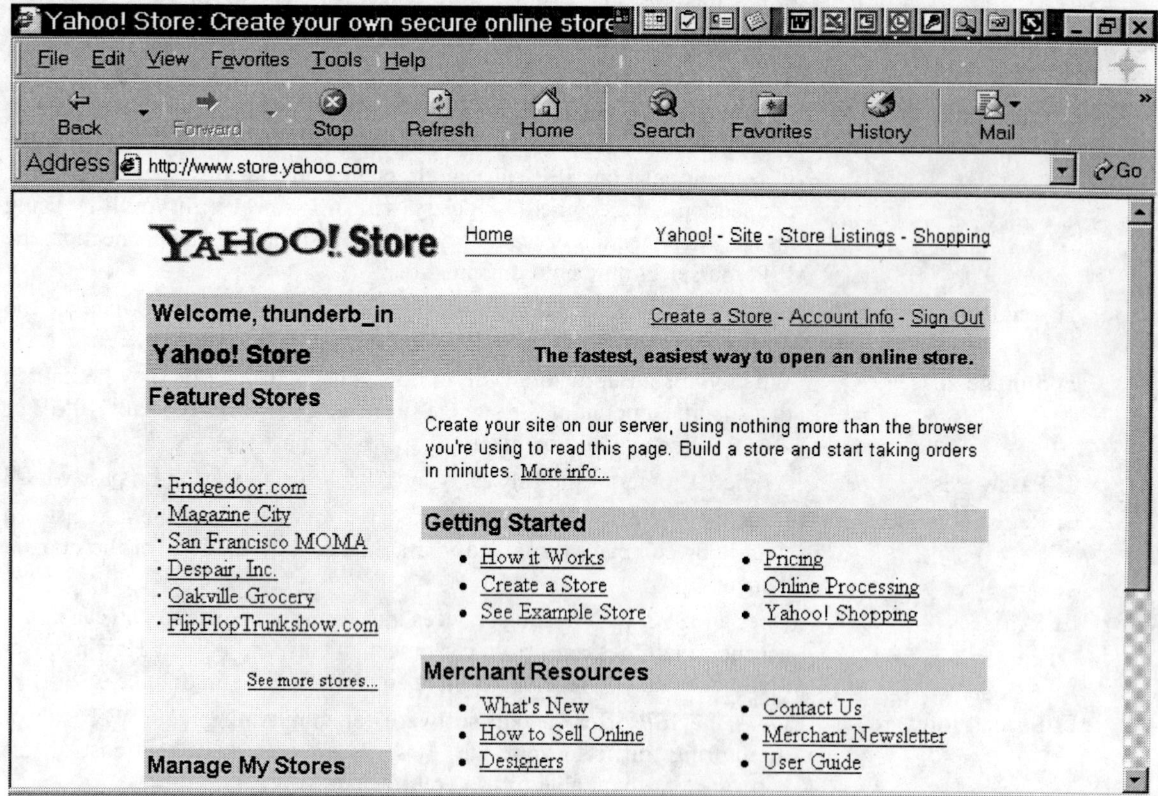


### 8.3.4 Turnkey solutions

Instead of having to invest in Web site creation tools (software), hire an ISP, and figure out the ins and outs of secure Internet connections to handle credit card processing and order transactions, services like Yahoo! Store (store.yahoo.com) offer a one-stop and relatively inexpensive solution. For a monthly fee starting at about $100, Yahoo! Store will help you create a Web site, host your site, and handle all secure transactions. Services like these are also easily expandable as your business grows.

Yahoo! Site (site.yahoo.com/site) is another Web page creation and hosting service. It isn't e-commerce-oriented, but it can be used by businesses looking to create an online presence. The pricing for Yahoo! Site is a flat fee of about $30 per month. This fee includes:

- An easy-to-use site builder.
- As many addresses as you want.
- Hosting on Yahoo!'s servers.
- 25 Megabytes of disk space.
- Unlimited bandwidth (you are entitled to an unlimited number of hits).
- Search engine submission. Yahoo will submit your site to the major search engines.
- Detailed updates daily.

### 8.3.5 Technical Support from ISP

Let's face it-as you get your online business up and running, you're going to have many questions. Being able to get your questions answered quickly, easily, and as accurately as possible will save you time and

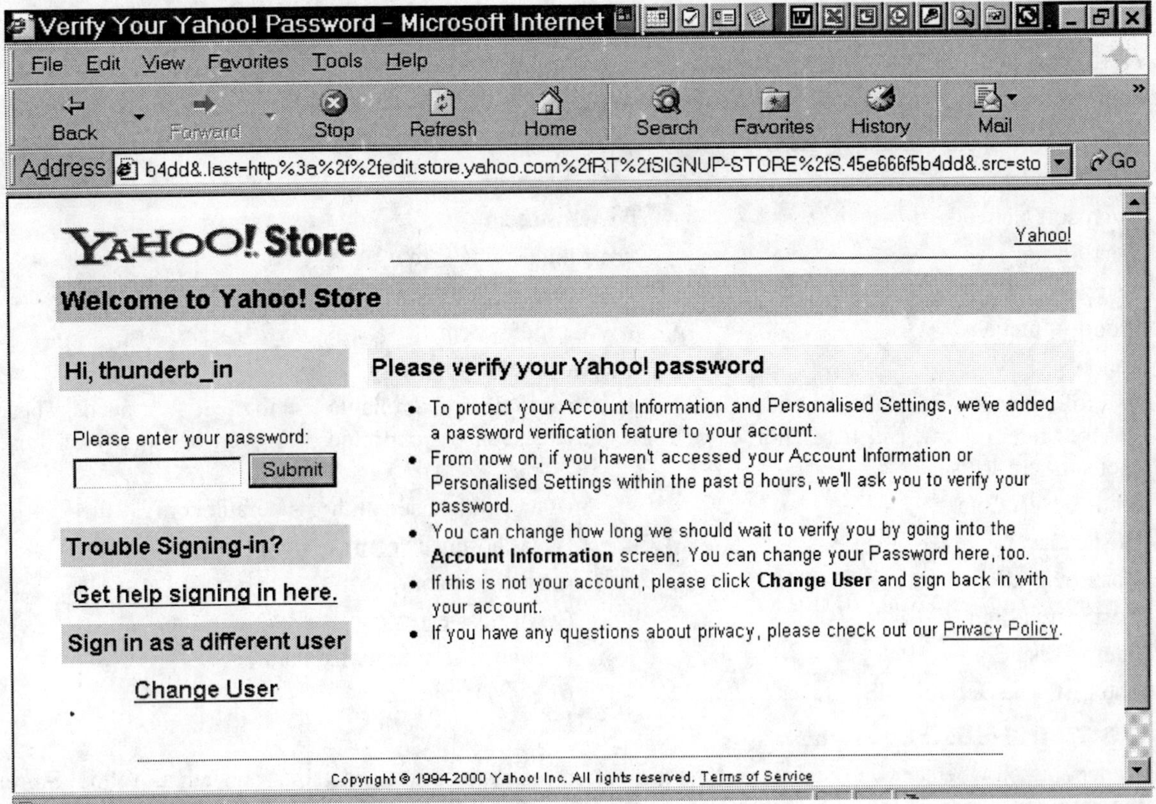


money. How much technical support you'll need will depend on how much you know about creating, publishing, and managing your Web site. As you investigate ISPs, make sure you ask about the availability of technical support. Specifically, you should ask:

- What types of technical support are available?
- During what hours can you speak with a human?
- Does the ISP offer toll-free technical support, or will you rack up large phone bills each time you call and are forced to sit on hold?
- How much does telephone technical support cost?
- Are you limited to how much technical support you're entitled to?
- What other forms of technical support are available (such as online, e-mail, and fax-on-demand)?
- What is the procedure for reporting problems?

There are a variety of Web-hosting companies, in terms of size, services offered, and price. By asking a lot of questions, you should be able to winnow out companies who can't offer you what you need.

### 8.3.6 Finding an ISP

Here's a partial list of the country's largest Web- hosting services, in alphabetical order:

| | |
|---|---|
| America Online | www.aol.com |
| AT&T WorldNet | www.att.net |
| Bell Atlantic Internet Solutions | www.bellatlantic.net |
| CompuServe | www.compuserve.com |

| | |
|---|---|
| EarthLink | www.earthlink.net |
| Galaxy Internet Services | www.gis.net |
| GTE | www.gte.net |
| IBM Internet Connection Services | www.ibm.net |
| MCI/Worldcom | www.internetmci.com |
| Microsoft Network | www.msn.com |
| MindSpring | www.mindspring.com |
| Netcom | www.netcom.com |
| Prodigy Internet | www. prodigy.com |
| Yahoo! | site.yahoo.com |

The following are free online services designed to help people find a reliable ISP to meet their needs. These services rate, review, and list hundreds of ISPs; they're sponsor-supported, however, and many of those sponsors are ISPs.

| | |
|---|---|
| Find-A-Host.Com | (www.findahost.com/hosts/default.com) |
| Host Index | (www.hostindex.com) |
| HostReview.Com | (hostreview.com) |
| HostSearch.Com | (www.hostsearch.com) |
| InternetList. Com | (webhostlist.in ternetlist.com ) |
| The List: The Definitive ISP Buyer's Guide | (thelist.internet.com ) |

### 8.3.7 In-House Equipment

Depending on whether you're using Web page creation software or an online solution such as Yahoo! Store, the core system requirements for creating and maintaining your Web site will be slightly different. If you're planning to host your own Web site, the equipment you'll need will be more extensive and costly. The core system requirements needed to actually create and then manage your Web site will depend in: part on the Web site creation software and graphics development software you'll be using. For a PC-based system, this typically means at least a Pentium 200 computer that's fully multimedia compatible and has a good-sized hard disk (at least five gigabytes).

Choose a system that will be able to handle your applications, but that offers you the ability to upgrade your system as needed. Stay away from PC- based systems that offer "closed architecture." These systems are typically cheaper, but can't be upgraded, so you may wind up having to purchase new equipment sooner than planned. As you shop around for a computer, keep in mind that technology is changing very quickly. Within one year to 18 months, it may be necessary to upgrade your PC with newer and faster technology. Such as a better video card, faster CD-ROM drive, more memory, or a better microprocessor. Within two years, you might need a new PC altogether to keep up with the current technology trends. Before shopping around for a PC system, carefully define your needs. Ask yourself what the computer will be used for. You should also determine, in advance, what primary software applications you plan on running, and what types of accessories and peripherals you'll be connecting to the computer. In addition to creating and managing your actual Web site, you might be using the computer to man- age other aspects of your online business, such as accounting, bookkeeping, order processing, contact management, inventory control, credit card processing, and package shipping processing.

### 8.3.8 Speed

Since you'll definitely need access to the Internet to surf the Web, send and receive e-mail, and maintain your Web site, you want the fastest connection possible. Some options for Internet access include a standard

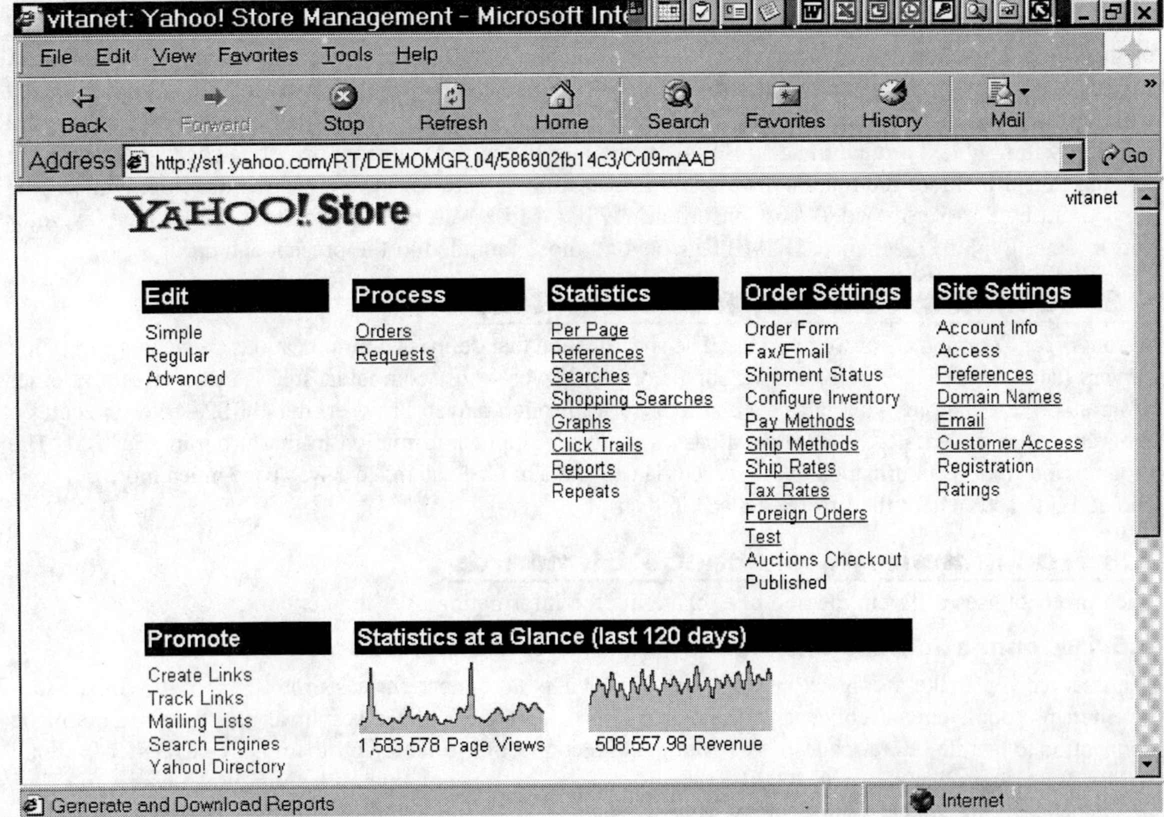


dial-up connection at 28.8K or 56K baud rates. You can also purchase a special type of modem and obtain access (in many cities) to the Internet via an ISDN or TI connection. A growing number of cable TV companies, such as Media One (www.mediaone.net) now also offer access to the Internet at high speeds using a cable modem.

It's also possible to access the net at high speeds using a wireless connection via satellite (this service is available from DirectPC (www.direcpc.com). Many technologies on the horizon will make fast Internet access cheap and readily available. As you're shopping for a computer, you'll need to determine a core system configuration for your computer. To do so, look at the system requirements of the software you plan to use. For example, the minimum system requirements for MultiActive's ecBuilder Pro e-commerce Web site creation and management software (www.multiactive.com) include a Pentium 90 processor (or higher) with 16Mb RAM and at least 50Mb of hard disk space. A CD-ROM drive, VGA monitor, Internet access, and Web browser software (Internet Explorer or Netscape) are also required.

## 8.4 HTML

Acronym for Hypertext Markup Language. The markup language used for documents on the World Wide Web. A tag-based notation language used to format documents that can then be interpreted and rendered by an Internet browser. HTML is an application of SGML (Standard Generalized Markup Language) that uses tags to mark elements, such as text and graphics, in a document to indicate how Web browsers should display these elements to the user and should respond to user actions such as activation of a link by means of a key press or mouse click. HTML 2, defined by the Internet Engineering Task Force (IETF), included features of HTML common to all Web browsers as of 1994 and was the first version of HTML widely used on the World Wide Web. HTML+ was proposed for extending HTML 2 in 1994, but it was never implemented. HTML 3, which also was never standardized or fully implemented by a major browser developer, introduced tables. HTML 3.2 incorporated features widely implemented as of early 1996, including tables, applets, and the ability to flow text around images. HTML 4, the latest specification, supports style sheets and scripting languages and includes internationalization and accessibility features. Future HTML development will be carried out by the World Wide Web Consortium (W3C). Most Web browsers, notably Netscape Navigator and Internet Explorer, recognize HTML tags beyond those included in the present standard.

## 8.5 Common Gateway Interface (CGI)

Acronym for Common Gateway Interface. The specification that defines communications between information servers (such as HTTP servers) and resources on the server's host computer, such as databases and other programs. For example, when a user submits a form through a Web browser, the HTTP server executes a program (often called a CGI script) and passes the user's input information to that program via CGI. The program then returns information to the server via CGI. Use of CGI can make a Web page much more dynamic and add interactivity for the user. See also CGI script,

## 8.6 Documents Interchange Standards

Each protocol uses different method of exchanging the information over the network.

### 8.6.1 Connectionless and Connection – Oriented Protocols

With server you make a connection and with HTTP it is a connection less protocol. With a connection-oriented protocol, clients connect to the server, make a request, get a response and then maintain the connection to handle future requests. An example of a connection-oriented protocol is File Transfer Protocol (FTP). When you connect to an FTP server, the connection remains open after you download a file. The maintenance of this connection consumes system resources. A server with too many open connections quickly gets over loaded. Consequently, many FTP servers are configured to allow only 250 open connections at one time, so only 250 users can access the FTP server at once. The drawback to connectionless protocol is that when the same client requests more data, the connection must be reestablished. To Web users, this means a delay whenever they request more information.

### 8.6.2 Stateless and Stateful Protocols

There are two kinds of protocols for the processed transactions on the Internet. These are stateless and stateful protocols. In a stateless protocol, no information about a transaction is maintained after a protocol, state information is kept even after a transaction has been processed.

Servers using stateful protocols maintain the information about status of the connection, processes running and status of the processes running. Usually, this state information resides in memory and consumes system resources. When a client breaks a connection with a server running a stateful protocol, the state information has to be cleared up and is often logged as well. HTTP is a stateless protocol. Stateless protocols are light because servers using them keep no information about completed transactions and processes. When a client breaks a connection with a server running a stateless protocol, no data has to be cleaned up or logged off. By not tracking state information, there is less overhead on the server, so it can generally handle transactions speedily. With HTTP, you can transfer full-motion video sequences, stereo sound tracks, high-resolution images and any other type of media you can think of. The standard that makes this possible is MIME (Multipurpose Internet Mail Extensions). HTTP uses MIME to identify the type of object using transferred across the Internet.

## 8.7 Components of Web Publishing

The text matter of your product can be best supplied by you. Even to the web site developer it is you who has to provide the information. Since you know your company's products and services and who your target audience is. One advantage of the Web, however, is that things can be changed almost instantaneously; if something is not working or you have some afterthoughts that will improve something about your site, it can be fixed and uploaded quickly and easily.

Some important information which you site should contain:

### 8.7.1 Home page

It is like the content of the book which you are going to read. So be sure that it contains most of the basic information which you want to give. So when someone enters of your company's name in any Uniform Resource Locator (URL) (www.yourcompany.com) into their Net browser, they should be taken directly to your home page.

### 8.7.2 Company information

Before people place an order with your company, they'll probably want to know something about your company—especially if they've never done business with you before. Use this page of your site to tell people about your company's background and boost their confidence in your company's products.

### 8.7.3 Product description

These pages will describe each of your products in detail. In addition to offering detailed descriptions, prices, and ordering information, seriously consider offering a product photo and technical specifications, just as you would if you were creating a mail-order catalog or full-color sales brochure of the product.

### 8.7.4 Promotions

This page conveys news about new or forthcoming products, information about special sales, or other information your visitors might be interested in. Another way to get people excited about your site to hold contests or special promotions, allowing visitors to win prizes.

### 8.7.5 Technical support

Whether customers are shopping in a retail store or online, they will always have questions about the products you are offering, no matter how detailed your descriptions are. In cyberspace, the customer should be able to call a toll-free phone number, send an e-mail message, or send the company a letter via fax or mail. You might consider creating a Frequently Asked Questions (FAQ) page for your site.

### 8.7.6 Customer testimonial

A potential customer will find it very reassuring to read testimonials from other happy customers, specially if they happen to know anyone of them. Of course, if you have a celebrity endorsing your product, this, too, is an extremely powerful marketing tool that goes a long way toward boosting a potential customers's confidence.

### 8.7.7 Online ordering

One of the biggest challenges you will face is designing an order form that is comprehensive, informative, and easy to understand and fill up. Before designing your online order form, determine exactly what information you need to have from the customer. This information might include the customer's name, title, company name, billing and shipping address, phone number, fax number, e-mail address, name of products they want to order, product numbers, quantities, sizes, and other information. Your site must also be able to automatically calculate numbers, such as order sub-totals, sales tax, if any, and shipping charges, if applicable. Finally, your order forms need to spell out exactly what forms of payment you accept, such as cheques (mention here if you are charging extra for cheques), cash, money orders, and credit cards.

### 8.7.8 Response

After someone places an order, he should immediately see an acknowledgment on the screen stating that his order has been received, what his order is and when it is going to be shipped and when should he expect it to arrive. When you visit any departmental store, you see the products carefully displayed in rows and most of the products of similar nature are placed together. It helps the customer to look for the products and their range in the same shelf. Similarly on an e-commerce site, you goal should be build a confidence in the customer with neatly laid out products and their information. Also as the department stores change their displays regularly with new varieties to keep shoppers coming back, the content and even the design of your site should change periodically in order to keep people interested and keep the content fresh.

Graphics should be used only when they are required. Too much of graphics will make your site cumbersome. Only use pictures and graphics that add meaning or value to your site; use fonts, typestyles, and color schemes that are visually appealing and will appear consistent, no matter which browser software someone is using. The fonts and typestyles you choose to convey your text-based information should be readily supported by the most common Web Browser programs.

## 8.8 Document Management

The action of identifying, acquiring, processing, storing, updating and istributing the document is called Document Management. It may includes organization uploading, etc. These are described next.

### 8.8.1 File Organization

Whe organising the files on your site, keep the files in separate folders. That way, the site is easier to update. Have separate folder for images, HTML files, video, sound and CGI scripts. Have obvious folders name too; so put any files relating to the jobs section, in a folder called jobs.

### 8.8.2 Uploading

Uploading means transferring files from your computer to net server. When you are uploading files from your site, do not forget that you need to upload them in the correct file format. HTML and text files should be uploaded in ASCII format, while images, CGI scripts, Flash files, sounds and video should all be uploaded in the Binary format.

### 8.8.3 File Names

When you are naming the files for your site, stick to what is known as 8.3 file names, i.e., 8 characters for file name and 3 characters for extension. Some people may still be looking at your site on older machines. Use the *.htm ending rather than *.html. You would like as many people as possible to see your Website, so do not exclude those who can not see long file names.

### 8.8.4 Backing up

Whateever you do, be sure to backup your files on your Website. Put them on to a Zip disk or CD and then store it away in a safer place. If the worst comes to the worst and you lose everything, at least you have a backup ready to upload the site again.

## 8.9 Web Page Design

There are various steps involved in designing the web site. They are discussed next.

### 8.9.1 Planning Your Web Site

We are living in a world where competition is the key thing. You name a product and there are multiple manufactures of it. So naturally the customer will buy the one which is the best both economic wise and performance wise. There are lots and lots of web sites these days some of which are good, some of which are not so good. Naturally, you would like your web site to be such that it has an attraction such that customer comes back to it more than once.

For this you need to have your web site to have the following:

- ❑ Professional looking
- ❑ Does not take too long to load
- ❑ Has good quality design and layout
- ❑ Good looking graphics
- ❑ Easy to read text
- ❑ Simple to navigate
- ❑ Loaded with information needed by the customer

All this conveys some sort of confidence in the mind of the customer that he is dealing with a professional looking company and will not be cheated out of his money. Also make sure that the customer is not asked to fill up too much information which also puts off the customers. If you'll be taking orders for your products online, you just offer easy-to-understand order forms and make it clear to customers that they'll be participating in secure financial transactions online when visiting your site. This will make them more comfortable using their credit card to place orders.

Your site should answer the most common questions your customers will have, make full use of visuals to show off your products, and display your company's logo, address, e-mail address, and telephone number (preferably a toll-free number). Visitors should be able to contact you directly with questions and comments, or to place their order using an alternate method to online processing.

### 8.9.2 Designing Your Web Site

Once you have made your mind on the site, call some of the Web designers and discuss with your plans. Don't commit yourself to one of them until you have talked to some of them. This helps in gathering the ideas if not the competitive rates. You may decide to give to somebody known to you but it is always better to call upon various professionals in the field, because they can sometimes give good ideas which you can implement in your site.

However, if you want to do it yourself, then there are also a growing number of complete e-commerce turnkey solution available, such as Yahoo! Store (store.yahoo.com). These allow anyone to develop an online store quickly, using just a computer equipped with Internet access and Web browser software. Now the choice is yours whichever way you want to create the site. Make sure that it has the best contents and looks good and readable. Creativity is very important if you want to make your site to stand out among the various sites available on the net, and is unique, enjoyable, and informative.

As you develop your site, it's important to ensure that it is compatible with the major browser software packages (Microsoft Internet Explorer or Netscape Navigator). How your site looks when viewed with one browser may be totally different (in colors displayed and layout) from how it's displayed when viewed with another browser. The graphic resolution your visitor has set will also affect how he sees it. Some of the most common settings for graphic resolutions on PC-based computer are 640 x 480, 800 x 600, 1024 x 768, 1152 x 870, 1280 x 1024, and 1600 x 1200. (Each has 256 colors, high color {16-bit} or true color {24-bit}.

If your online business will be targeting mass market customers on the Web, your best bet is to design your site so it can be easily viewed by the vast majority of Web surfers, without them having to adjust their display resolution or download additional plug-ins for their browser software.

### 8.9.3 Steps For Developing Your Site

Before you start designing your site or putting it together, carefully evaluate and determine the exact purpose of your site. Ask yourself these questions:

- Decide about the information which you are planning to convey to your customers.
- Decide whether this site will supplement your business or will it be a new line of business altogether.
- Decide whether this site will help in the promotion of your current activities and can it become the marketing tool, public relations tool, sales tool, recruiting tool, or it will become an all-purpose electronic commerce site?
- Decide whether it will have the catalog or interactive brochure of all your products.
- Decide what all you are going to show the visitors of your site.
- Decide among above what is your goal of having the site.
- Decide whether you are going to accept the orders on-line and if yes, are you geared for it?
- Decide about the priority of the products/information to be displayed on the site.
- Decide how will the site be laid out and what will be contained in each of the pages? Since most of the sites contain a variety of individual Web pages.

### 8.9.4 Basic Layout of Your Site

You must have seen people sitting in front of a TV with remote in their hand. They would just browse through the channels as if they have nothing else to do. Only a channel which is very interesting probably can stop them and hold them there for some time. It could be a sports channel or FTV. There should be some attraction to hold them. Similar thing is applied to the Web surfers. They are very impatient lot. This is why they are so called because once they are connected to the net, they would never stop at one site but will keep on exploring various sites. When it comes to buying something they do the same thing. Look around at various sites and then make the decision of buying. So what you, as a designer of the site, have to do it to make a site which can hold the surfer. One look at the site and the visitor is compelled to hold on to it. If he does hold on then whatever you want to say would be conveyed, otherwise not.

Graphics and text form the main part of the site. Some graphics are in the form of photographs, while others are logos, line drawings, computer-generated graphics (bullets, arrows, lines), or animated graphics. The use of high-quality images is an absolute must on an e-commerce Web site or a site designed to generate business. As you choose which images will be incorporated into your site, keep in mind the file size of the image as well as the color scheme. For example, the background color of your product shots or the color of your logo should fit well into the overall color scheme of your site. Using colors that clash will detract from the professional appearance of your site.

## 8.10 Consideration and Principles

It is not true that everything is perfect. It applies to the web sites too. You are quite likely to make mistakes too. I can always warn you about the pitfalls which most of the designers who are not successful make:

### 8.10.1 Bad Spelling

If possible take the help of some professional proof reader. Get proofread all of the text in your site. There should be absolutely no editing mistakes. Don't just rely on the spell checker built into your word processor or Web site creation software.

### 8.10.2 Being Pushy

Never force visitors to your site to register or provide personal information about themselves until they are ready to place an order.

### 8.10.3 Big File Size

As said earlier, graphics take longer time to come on the screen. So when choosing images for your site, make sure that the file size of the electronic image isn't too large. Otherwise, it will take too long to load, and many Web surfers have no patience.

### 8.10.4 Choice of Fonts

Some fonts simply don't look good when viewed using Web browser software, using them would disturb the display of your site.

### 8.10.5 Excessive Scroll

As you plan each page on your site, don't make the visitors scroll too much. Keep the information on each page short and to the point. You can also offer buttons that will link to other areas of your site.

### 8.10.6 Frames

Avoid using frames! They can be used so visitors can view several windows worth of information simultaneously. But this often make a site confusing to look at and to navigate.

### 8.10.7 Hidden Navigation Icons

Place your navigation icons for your site near the top of every page, so people don't have to scroll to the bottom of a page to determine where they should go next.

### 8.10.8 Incompatibility

If you are poor in selecting which colour goes with which colour, take the help of some professional in this regard, specially those who are associated with the printing presses. They have very sharp eyes for colours. When choosing colors of backgrounds, text, and even graphic images, maintain continuity throughout your site, paying careful attention to making your site compatible with all of the popular Web browser programs.

### 8.10.9 Overload

Too many Web sites add tons of bells and whistles, such as flashy graphics, audio, animation, video, too many fonts and typestyles, and busy background just to get a visitor's attention. This would overkill the main purpose.

### 8.10.10 Poor Directions

While your goal to get visitors to visit your main home page first and then navigate through your site from there, this doesn't always happen. Some Web search engines will send surfers directly to the page of a site that contains the keyword or search phrase they were looking for.

As a result, they may find themselves visiting a sub-page of your site and not know where they are. To compensate for this, every page of your site should contain your company name and logo, a navigation bar or buttons, and an easy way for the visitors to return to your home page.

### 8.10.11 Poor Quality Photos

If you'll be using photographs on your site, make sure they appear crystal clear and are in focus. They should not be blurb. The viewer should be able to make out visual details of the product.

### 8.10.12 Poor Targeting

Make sure all of the content of your site is directed to your target audience. If you don't understand who your target customers are, that their needs are, and what they're looking for, you have little hope of providing a product that addresses their needs.

### 8.10.13 Shifting Styles

Once you choose a color scheme, background, and font group for your site, stick to it to maintain visual continuity.

### 8.10.14 Too Much Information

Unlike print materials and radio or television advertising, the Web is interactive. Make sure you reshape information from your traditional advertising to take full advantage of these interactive qualities.

## 8.11 Search and Meta Search Engines

They are programs that locate needed information in a database, but especially an Internet accessible search service that enables you to search for information on the Internet. To use a search engine, you type one or more key words; the result is a list of documents or files that contain one or more of these words in their titles, descriptions, or text. The databases of most Internet search engines contain World Wide Web (WWW) documents; some also contain items found in Gopher menus and File Transfer Protocol (FTP) file archives. Compiling the database requires an automated search routine called a spider, forms filled out by Web authors, or a search of other databases of Internet documents. The effectiveness of search engine can be measured in terms of Indexing and Term specificity. Since the Internet is a vast collection of information, it is difficult to find specific information you actually need. Therefore, search engines are more than a boom.

### 8.11.1 Search Engine Categories

Some of the popular search engines are:

### 8.11.2 Yahoo!

No doubt, the most popular and commonly used search engine. It is very simple to use and mostly gives you the best results. It indexes Web pages, Usenet and e-mail addresses. The search has 14 categories listed on its homepage. Each of these categories is divided into several subcategories. If the search fails, it is automatically passed on to AltaVista for more search. Yahoo! provides other services too like e-mail accounts, searches to locate people, sites, news, etc.

### 8.11.3 Lycos

This one has a robot to help the software locate the needed in search. For each document indexed, the robot keeps the outgoing links in a queue and selects a URL from it. Lycos indexes, titles, headings, and subheadings of HTML, FTP and Gopher documents.

### 8.11.4 Web Crawler

It has a web robot called Webbot that creates a daily index of keywords from documents all over the Web. The search engine directs the navigation in a modified breadth first mode. It indexes both the title and the full text of HTML document.

### 8.11.5 Excite

It uses a spider and indexer for the full text search of documents. The spider retrieves only Web and Usenet newsgroup documents. It offers services like searches that are case sensitive. It uses the various Boolean operators.

But, this is not the end of the search engines. There are more available on the net, but I have covered here the famous ones.

### 8.11.6 Searching Criterion

So far we have learned about the various search engines. Let us know in brief know how these search engines work. As was mentioned in the case of various search engines above, each one of them uses either the directories, spiders and even the robots for searches. A spider strips away many other markup features so that it simply sees the pure HTML source. Search sites are basically of the following two types:

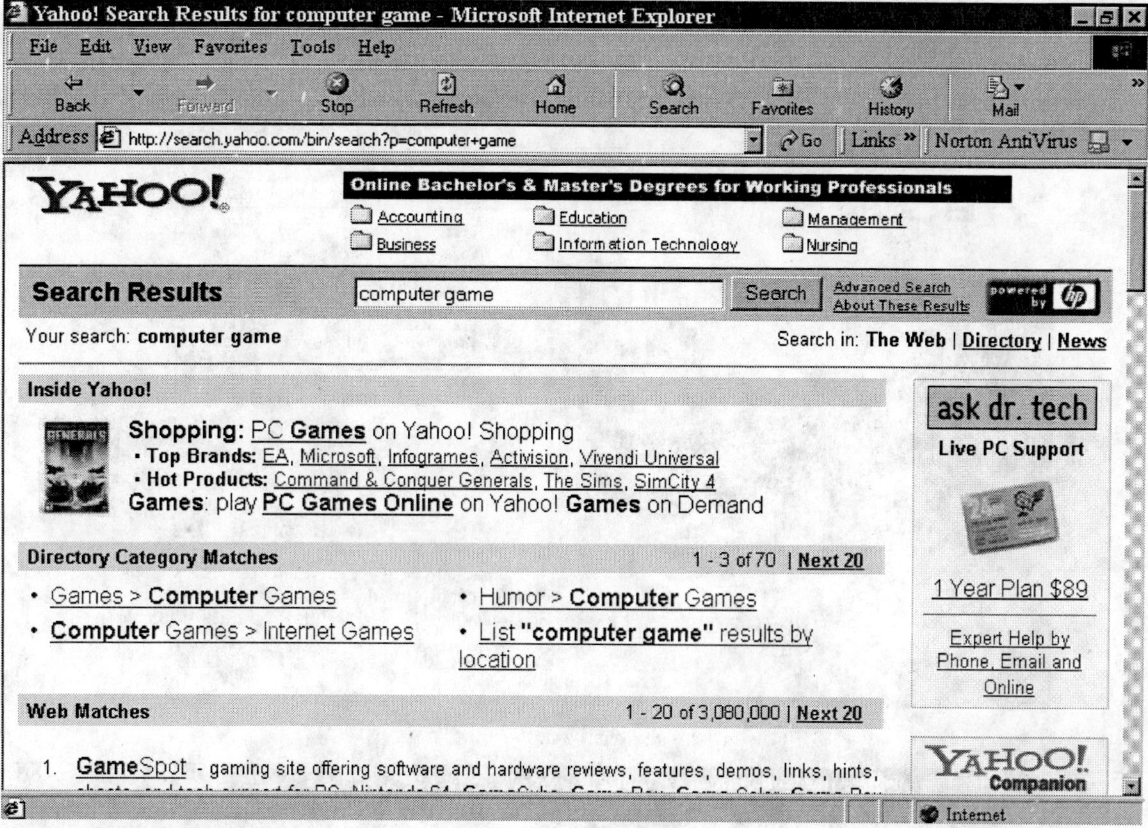


### *8.11.6.1 Search Directories*

They contain a list of websites organized hierarchically into categories and sub-categories. These are created manually.

### *8.11.6.2 Search Engines*

It continuously sends out the so called spiders which start on a homepage of a server and pursue all links stepwise.

When you open a search engine, it asks you what to search. If it is to be case sensitive, make sure that you are using the right case. Click Ok to begin the search and the result is shown in the form of URLs leading to the pages you need.

## 8.11.7 Finding People on the Net

If you want to find out a person's e-mail-id, phone number, street address, you can use the service. To do this, all you have to do is go to one such site and then supply some information (like name, etc.) required to search desired information. The most commonly used site is Yahoo! and on it the utility called People Search. For instance, if you want to search e-mail-id of a person follow these steps:

1. Log onto www.yahoo.com.
2. Now click at People Search link on the home page of Yahoo!
3. You will see the people search page on your screen. Now type the first name and last name of the person whose e-mail-id you want to search.

Discover great singles near you at Yahoo! Personals. You'll love the online dating site where i - Microsoft In...
File Edit View Favorites Tools Help
Back Forward Stop Refresh Home Search Favorites History Mail
Address http://personals.yahoo.com/
Go Links Norton AntiVirus
YAHOO! personals
Welcome Sign In | Yahoo! | Help
Discover great singles near you...
Search ads for FREE
I'm a: Woman Seeking a: Man
Age: to Show photo ads only
Location: Enter City or ZIP/Postal Code
Find My Match
Post a Free Ad
Let the person you're looking for find you! Add voice and video.
Post your Ad Now!
Subscribe
Find someone you like and contact them for less than $25 a month!
Subscribe Now!

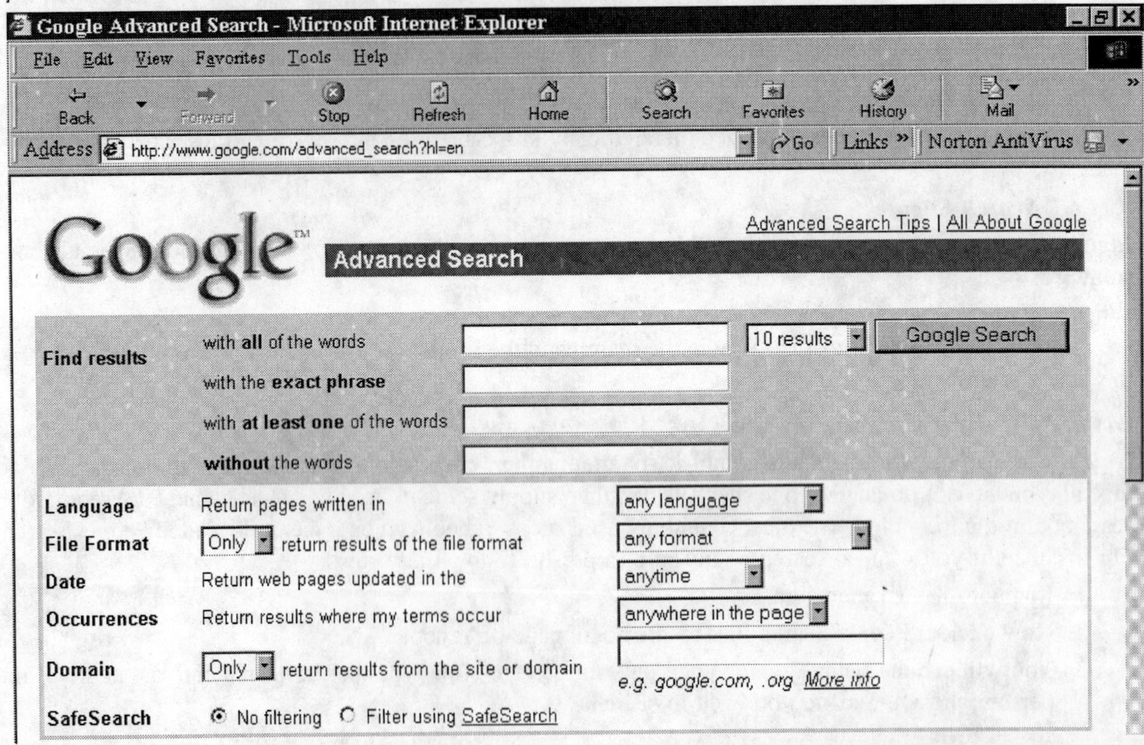
Google Advanced Search - Microsoft Internet Explorer
File Edit View Favorites Tools Help
Back Forward Stop Refresh Home Search Favorites History Mail
Address http://www.google.com/advanced_search?hl=en
Go Links Norton AntiVirus
Google
Advanced Search Tips | All About Google
Advanced Search
Find results
with all of the words
10 results
Google Search
with the exact phrase
with at least one of the words
without the words
Language Return pages written in any language
File Format Only return results of the file format any format
Date Return web pages updated in the anytime
Occurrences Return results where my terms occur anywhere in the page
Domain Only return results from the site or domain
e.g. google.com, .org More info
SafeSearch No filtering Filter using SafeSearch

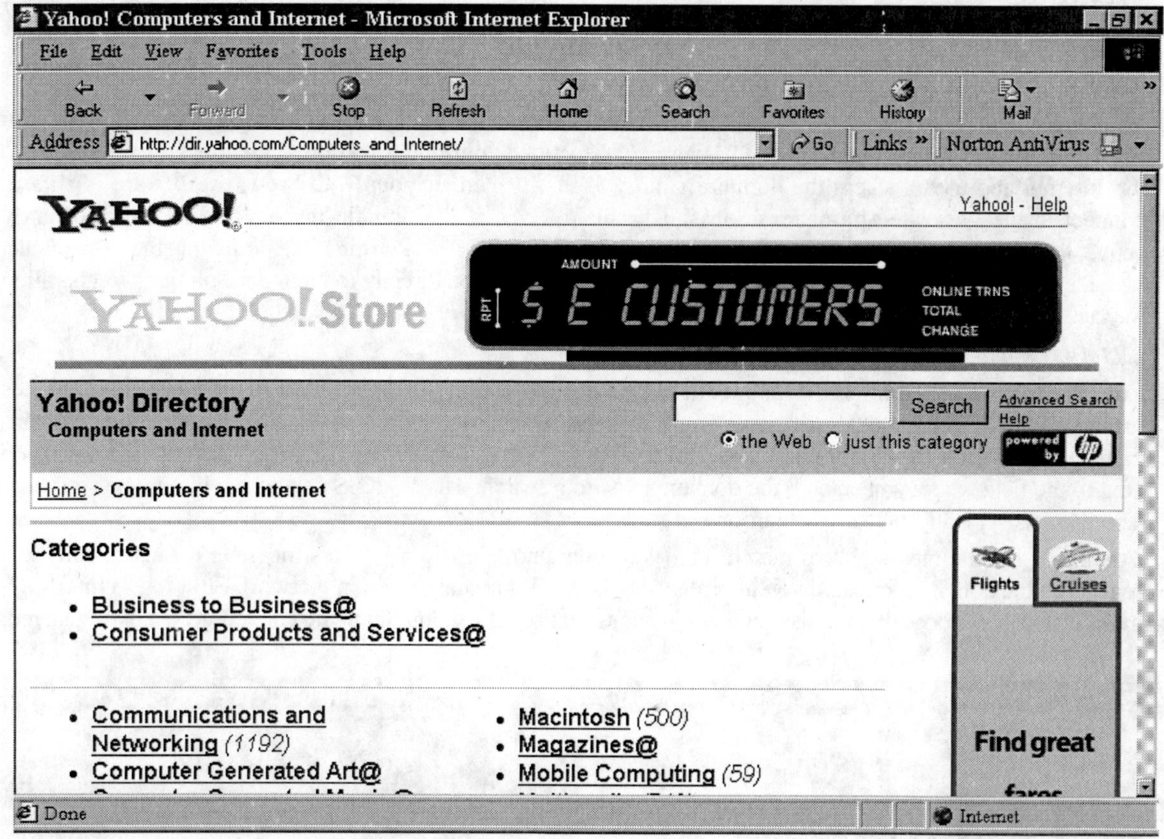


4. Click Search button and the search engine will search for the name given its database and display the results on your screen.

Apart form Yahoo! You may also try following Web sites:

| | |
|---|---|
| www.excite.com | (People Finder, E-mail Lookup and Yellow Pages) |
| www.infoseek.com | (Find Businesses, Find people and Find E-mail) |
| www.lycos.com | (People find and Yellow Pages) |
| www.webcrawler.com | (Reference and Phone Books) |

Some popular online e-mail and phone directories listed below can also be used for searches.

www.bigfoot.com
www.bigyellow.com
www.foreall.com
www.infospace.com
www.whowhere.com
www.worldpages.com

### 8.11.8 Choosing your domain name

There are three basic approaches you can take when deciding upon a domain name your company name. When someone is looking for a specific company's Web site, they instinctively try a Web address that includes the company name. Coming up with the perfect name for your business may take a lot of thought and creativity. As you kick around ideas in your head, seek out the advice of friends, relatives, and other people you respect. Also, consider carefully what you are naming.

### 8.11.9 Checking Availability of the name

You've come up with names that would be absolutely perfect for your business-congratulations! What you need to do now is determine if anyone has already registered your potential domain names. First, connect to the Internet and try to access the domain name you've selected. If your Web browser software is able to connect to the Web site, the name is obviously taken. Even if the domain name you like isn't currently active, that doesn't mean someone else hasn't already registered it. To determine if a domain name is available, visit the InternetNIC Web site (www.internic.net). This will take you directly to Network Solutions Registration Services site.

#### *8.11.10 Looking for Name*

Look for the site called InterNIC as mentioned above and search the database of registered domain names using WHOIS and type the domain name you are interested in researching. You should only enter the "domain-name.com" portion of the domain name, not the "http://www."part. Next, click the "Search" icon, located next to the field where you entered the domain name to research. The WHOIS database will now be searched. The process typically takes less than one minute.

You might see the message "No match for '(your domain name).com.' " This message means nobody has registered the domain name and you are free to register it immediately. From Network Solutions' (InterNIC) main Web page, choose the "Register a domain name" option. If the domain name entered is already registered,

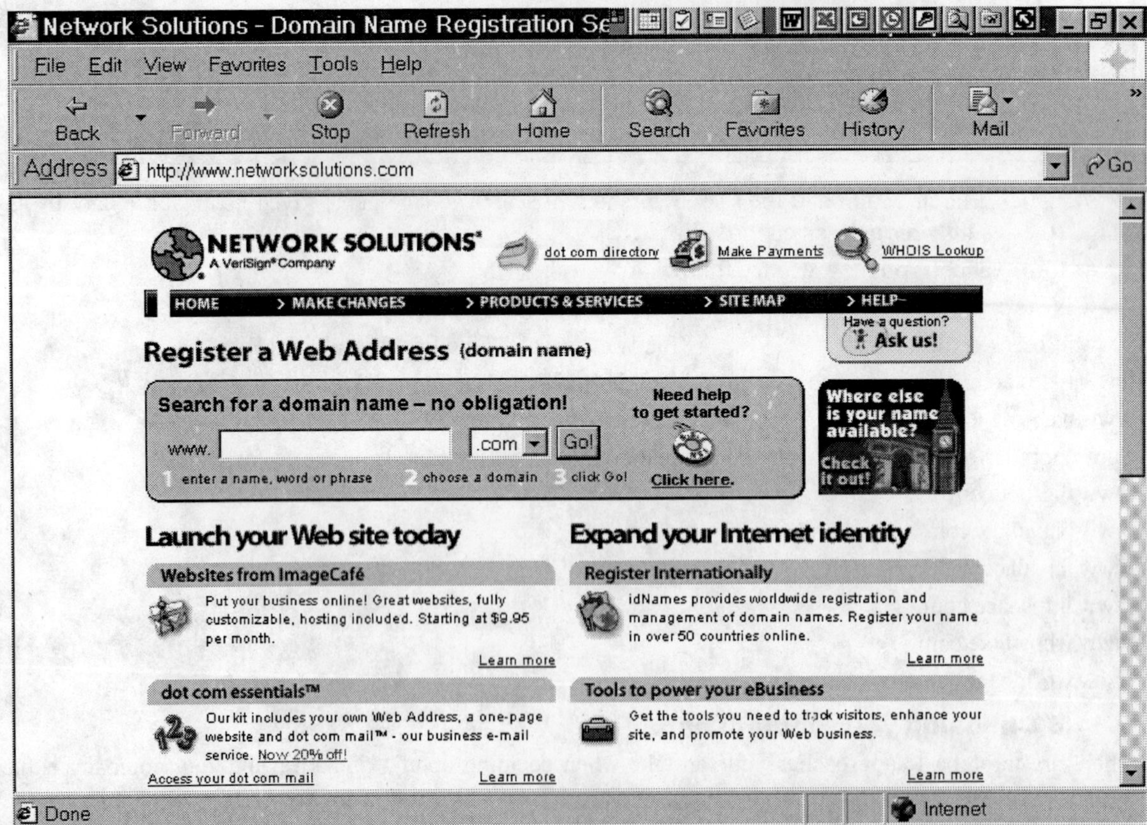

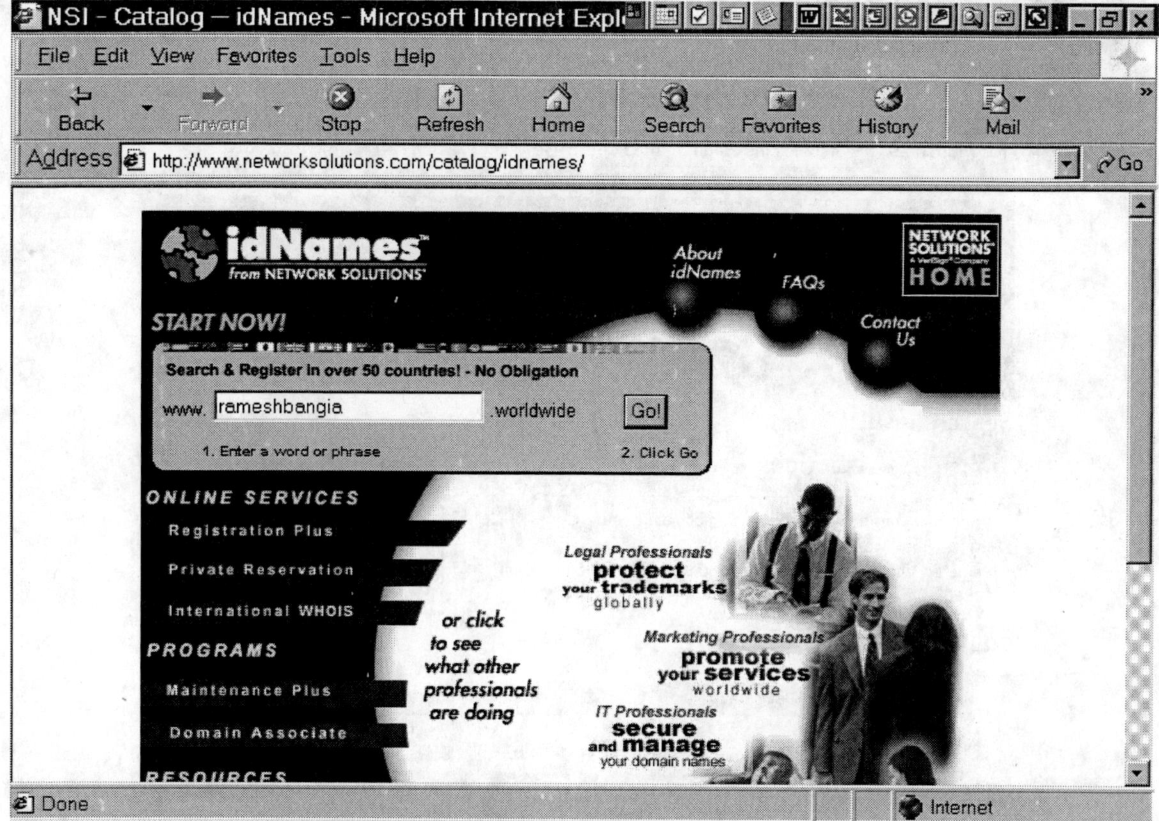


information about the registrant, including the registrant's company name, address, phone number, e-mail address, domain name, administrative contact, billing contact, and domain servers will be listed.

If you received a response from the WHOIS database indicating that the domain name you have entered is in "On Hold", this means that one of the following things, according to Network Solution/InterNIC:

- ❑ Payment for the domain is not current.
- ❑ The domain name is involved in a dispute with a trademark owner.
- ❑ Name server administrative or technical matter is pending.
- ❑ Another administrative or technical matter is pending.

### 8.11.10 Registering with InterNIC

Congratulations! your name is open for use. Now, you have to just register to move further. If the domain name you want is not already taken, registering one wanted by you is a relatively quick and easy process. Contact the Internet Service Provider (ISP) that will be hosting your Web site. From the ISP, obtain their server's IP addresses and host names. You will also be required to provide a valid e-mail address for yourself or your organization. You will need this information to continue with the online domain name registration process.

Click on the "Register a domain name" link found on InterNIC's main Web page. When the domain Name Registration screen appears, you will need to provide the general information that is required, including your e-mail address and the domain name you are attending to register. In the "Your e-mail address" field, type your complete e-mail address. The domain name should be entered as the domain name, followed by the

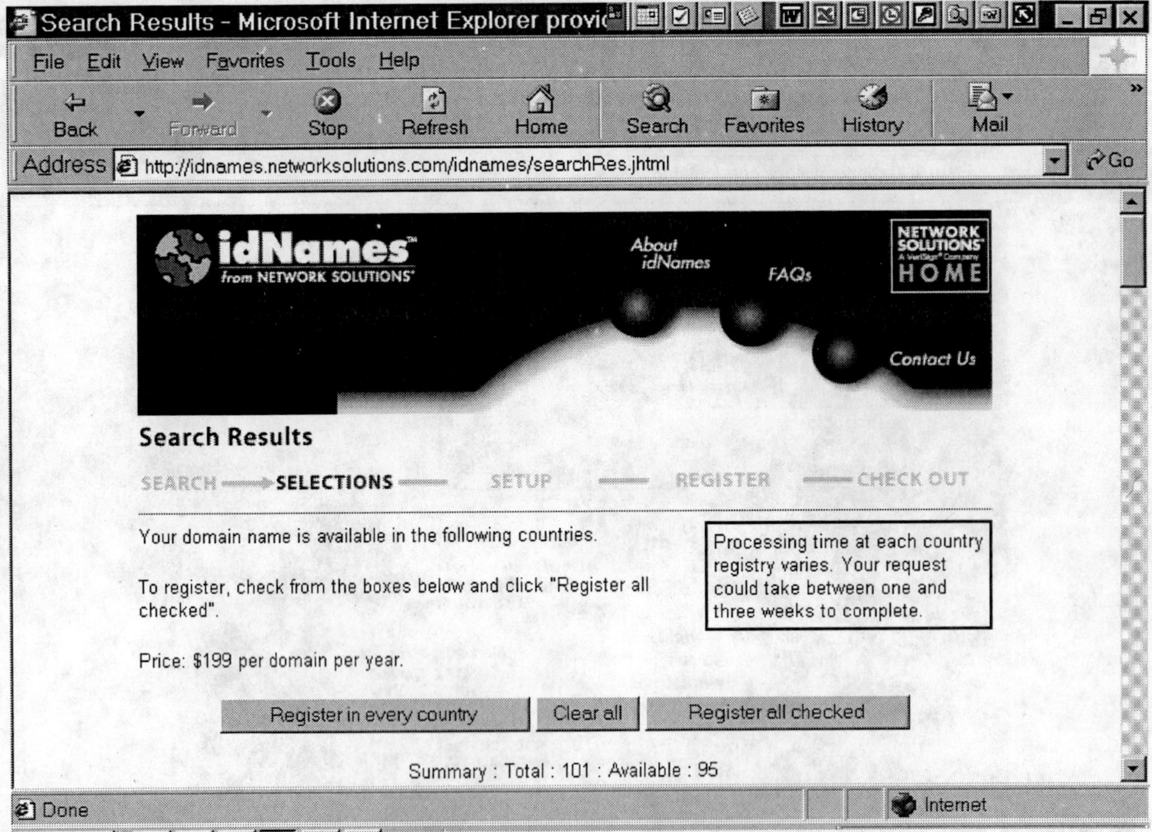


extension. It should not include the "http://www" portion. Finally, on this initial screen, you will be asked to choose one of three options: "New Registration," "Modifying Existing Domain," or "Delete Domain." Since you're registering a new domain name, select "New Registration" option and click the "Process" icon found near the bottom of the screen.

The Second screen in the Domain Name Registration process requests the following information:

#### *8.11.10.1 New Domain Registration for*

Your domain name should appear here. The one which you are trying to register.

#### *8.11.10.2 Organization Name*

Name of the ogranization which owns the domain name.

#### *8.11.10.3 Organization Address*

Complete address of the organization who own the above name.

#### *8.11.10.4 City, State, and Zip*

The required information of the company.

#### *8.11.10.5 Country*

Country of the origin of the company.

#### *8.11.10.6 Technical Contact*

Here you enter your assigned NIC handle, identify the technical contact as the same person as the supplied administrative contact, or the technical contact, choose to enter the contact person's full information.

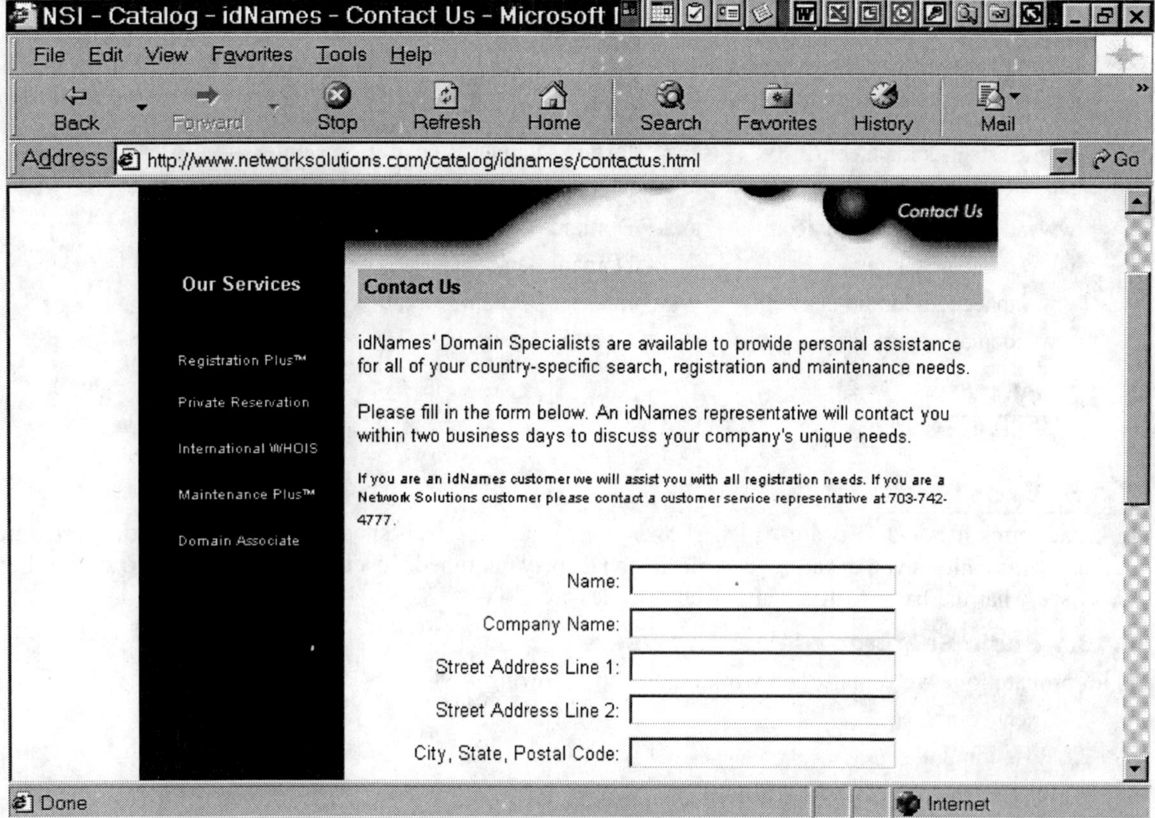


### *8.11.10.7 Billing contact*

Here you can enter your assigned NIC handle, or identify the billing contact as being the same person as the administrative contact or the technical contact. You also have the option of entering the contact person's full information.

Once all the information requested by the Domain Name Registration form has been entered, click the "Submit This Form For Processing" button located at the bottom of the form. Usually within minutes, you'll receive an e-mail message from InterNIC containing the Domain Name Registration Agreement. This is legal document, so read it carefully. If you agree with the terms, you must cut and paste the e-mail message into a new e-mail message and send it back to InterNIC using the address of the site: hostmaster@internic.net.

Once the Domain Name Registration Agreement has been returned, it will be followed by another automatic reply e-mail message from InterNIC. This message will contain a tracking number for your registration. Any correspondence with InterNIC in the future must contain this tracking number in the "Subject" line of your e-mail message. If you don't receive an additional confirmation of your registration within 48 hours, contact the InterNIC Help Desk by calling 001-703-742-4777, or send an e-mail message to hostmaster@internic.net.

## 8.11.11 Costs of Registering Domain Names

The host of registering each new domain name through InterNIC is Rs.3000. This fee covers the initial registration and most updates to the domain name's database record for a period of two years. After the initial two-year period, the annual renewal fee $35 covers one year of maintenance for the domain name record. The annual renewal fee is assessed each year on the anniversary of the initial registration.

Some other companies which are available for registration of domain name:

| | |
|---|---|
| www.worldnic.com | WorldNIC |
| www.doaminnameregistration.com | Direct Line Domain Name Registration.Com |
| www.aplus-domain.com | A+ Domain Name Registration Center |
| www.instant-domain.com | Instant Domain Registration Center |
| name.space.xs2.net | Name.Space |
| www.domainnameregistry.com | Domain Name Registry |
| www.domainbank.net | Domain Bank |
| www.ibnet.com.idb-home.shtml | Internet Domain Bureau |
| www.domainagency.com | Domain Agency |

## 8.12 WWW

Discussed in Chapter 3.

## 8.13 Browsers

In broad terms it is the software which allows you to view the web sites. It is a multi-function software package which allows you to access, download, and display multimedia documents. Before we go any further, let us see what the basic features of a Web browser are.

### 8.13.1 Basic Features of Web Browsers

In all probability a web connection would have the following:

1. Client computer
2. Host computer
3. Internet Service Provider (ISP)
4. Communication network

Let us see what these are:

#### *8.13.1.1 Client Computer*

This is the base computer from where you access the Internet. This computer as expected would have modem, a telephone line attached to it and a software to browser the Internet, such as Internet Explorer or Netscape Navigator.

#### *8.13.1.2 Host Computer*

This is the computer which holds all the Web pages. They have giga bytes of hard-disk storage, considerable Random Access Memory (RAM) and a high speed processor. It runs special Web server software that reads requests sent from various client computers. The host computer also retrieves and sends an appropriate information to the client.

#### *8.13.1.3 Internet Service Provider (ISP)*

I had mentioned about ISP in the last chapter. It is the agency which acts as a media for providing the Internet access.

#### *8.13.14 Communication Network*

The message from client computer is converted to signals and transferred through telephone lines. These then reach the host computer. So to reach the signals fast you have to have very fast network. In India this is done by VSNL. In fact, ISP has a stack of modems that accepts multiple incoming calls simultaneously. Your connection is complete when it reaches the host computer.

### 8.13.2 Running a Browser

The first page that you see on the screen of the browser on the screen is the home page of that browser. So in case of Netscape Navigator you will see Netcentre while in the case of Internet Explorer you would see msn.com. These software can be launched as you would launch any other software in a Windows environment. This can be done from the Start button, Its icon on the desktop or even from Quick Launcher on the Taskbar. Once launched you would see their initial page on the screen. Here I am showing the opening page of Internet Explorer.

### 8.13.3 Working of Internet Explorer

As you would see from the Internet Explorer screen, there are various bars, having various buttons. Let us see what all them mean.

| | |
|---|---|
| Title Bar | It displays the title of the current Web page. |
| Menu Bar | It gives access to all the features of the Explorer. |
| Buttons | The Internet toolbar contains some graphically styled buttons. They provide convenient shortcuts that enable you to navigate through the Web. |
| Link Menu | This menu selects several links to Microsoft related sites. |
| Go Button | After typing the URL, click on this button to display the Web page. |
| Scroll Bars | These bars help to move or scroll the screen up or down. |
| Status Bar | This bar displays information relating to the activity that is being currently carried out. |

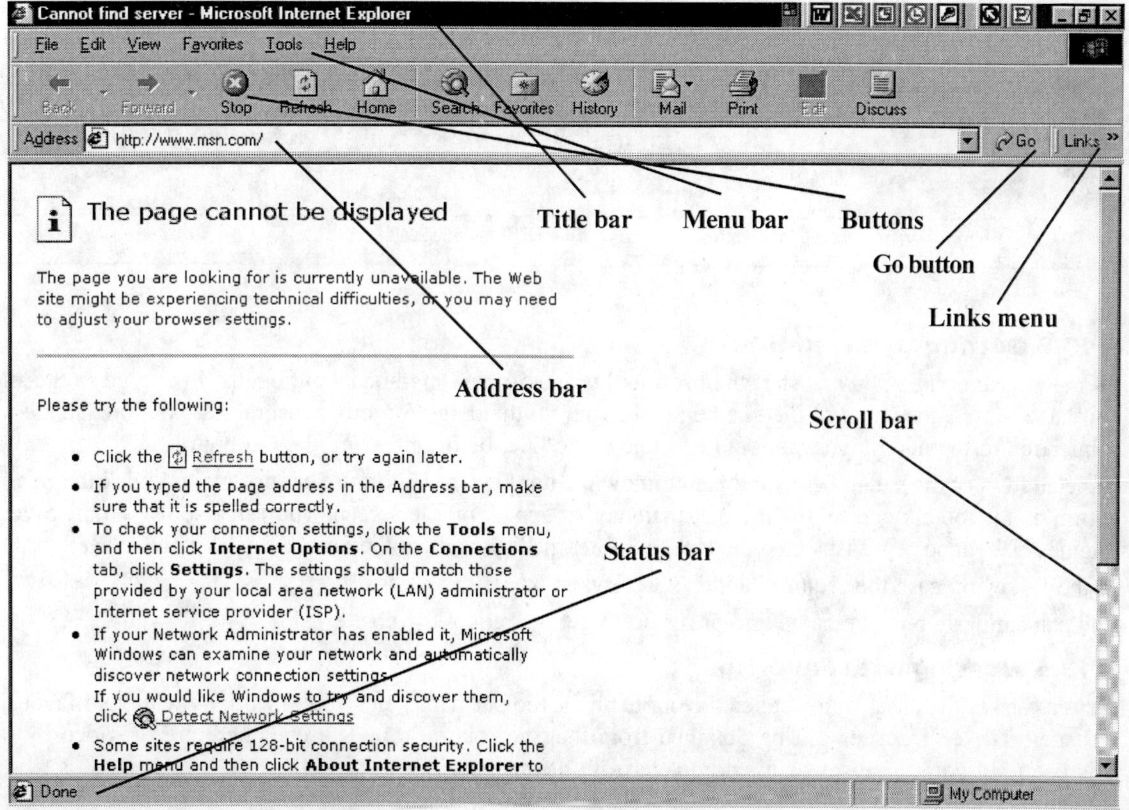

**Address Bar** The URLs of various Web sites are typed on this bar.

### 8.13.4 Toolbar Buttons

As you can see there are various buttons on the toolbar of Internet Explorer. Let me explain what each one of them stands for.

**Back** It displays a page in the list of previously viewed pages.

**Forward** It displays a page in the list next to viewed pages.

**Stop** It stops downloading the current page.

**Refresh** It downloads the current page again, ensuring that the latest version of the Web page is displayed.

**Home** It displays the home page.

**Search** It displays or hides the Search Explorer bar, which provieds access to Internet search engines.

**Favorites** It displays or hides the Favorites Explorer bar, which provides access to your favorite sites.

**History** It displays or hides the History Explorer bar, that provides access to sites you may have visited recently.

**Full Screen** It switches to or from full screen view, which provides maximum viewing space for Internet Explorer's document area.

**Mail** It launches your mail or newsreader program, by default Outlook Express, and lets you send links and pages to others via e-mail.

**Print** It prints the current page, if your printer is online.

### 8.13.5 Getting to a Web Site

As mentioned earlier, you can start the browser by one of the 3 methods mentioned. Now to go to the site, you have to type the name of the site complete with all the dots. You must ensure that you have made the connection to the net via your modem and telephone line, before pressing the Go button.

If the address of the site to be visited is not known, enter keyword/s in the Search Box and click the Search button on the toolbar and follow the instructions that appear on the screen. You can also use on the Search Engines like Yahoo, AltaVista, Google, HotBot. Enter the keywords in the Search Box and click Search or Go.

In the following case the required address was typed to get the website.

You can similarly type the name and press Go to get the required website.

### 8.13.6 Working with Favorites

As you can see there is a button called Favourite on the toolbar. This helps you in working with your favourite websites. These favourites can be obtained from the Start button too. The ones here are provided by the Microsoft but you can always add and delete from them.

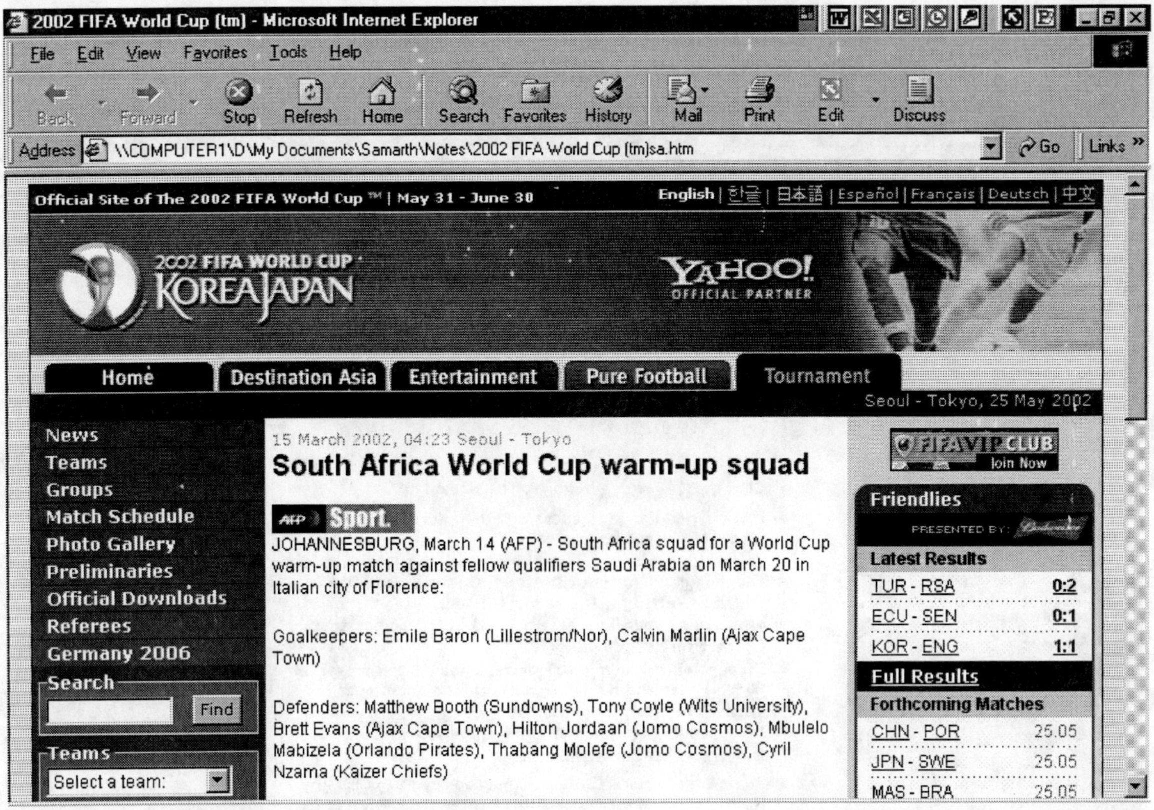

2002 FIFA World Cup (tm) - Microsoft Internet Explorer
File Edit View Favorites Tools Help
Back Forward Stop Refresh Home Search Favorites History Mail Print Edit Discuss
Address \\COMPUTER1\D\My Documents\Samarth\Notes\2002 FIFA World Cup (tm)sa.htm
Go Links
Official Site of The 2002 FIFA World Cup ™ | May 31 - June 30
English | 한글 | 日本語 | Español | Français | Deutsch | 中文
2002 FIFA WORLD CUP KOREA JAPAN
YAHOO! OFFICIAL PARTNER
Home Destination Asia Entertainment Pure Football Tournament
Seoul - Tokyo, 25 May 2002
News
Teams
Groups
Match Schedule
Photo Gallery
Preliminaries
Official Downloads
Referees
Germany 2006
Search
Find
Teams
Select a team:
15 March 2002, 04:23 Seoul - Tokyo
South Africa World Cup warm-up squad
AFP Sport
JOHANNESBURG, March 14 (AFP) - South Africa squad for a World Cup warm-up match against fellow qualifiers Saudi Arabia on March 20 in Italian city of Florence:
Goalkeepers: Emile Baron (Lillestrom/Nor), Calvin Marlin (Ajax Cape Town)
Defenders: Matthew Booth (Sundowns), Tony Coyle (Wits University), Brett Evans (Ajax Cape Town), Hilton Jordaan (Jomo Cosmos), Mbulelo Mabizela (Orlando Pirates), Thabang Molefe (Jomo Cosmos), Cyril Nzama (Kaizer Chiefs)
FIFAVIP CLUB Join Now
Friendlies
PRESENTED BY:
Latest Results
TUR - RSA 0:2
ECU - SEN 0:1
KOR - ENG 1:1
Full Results
Forthcoming Matches
CHN - POR 25.05
JPN - SWE 25.05
MAS - BRA 25.05

### *8.13.6.1 Adding an item to Favorites*

The Add To Favorites command allows you to create a favorite page listing for the page you are currently viewing. Do the following to add.

1. Click the Favorites menu and choose Add to Favorites. Or click Add to Favorites on the Favorites Explorer bar. The Add Favorite dialog box appears.

Add Favorite
Internet Explorer will add this page to your Favorites list.
OK
Make available offline
Customize...
Cancel
Name:
es--CWINDOWSSYSTEMSHDOCLC.DLL-dnserror.htm
Create in >>

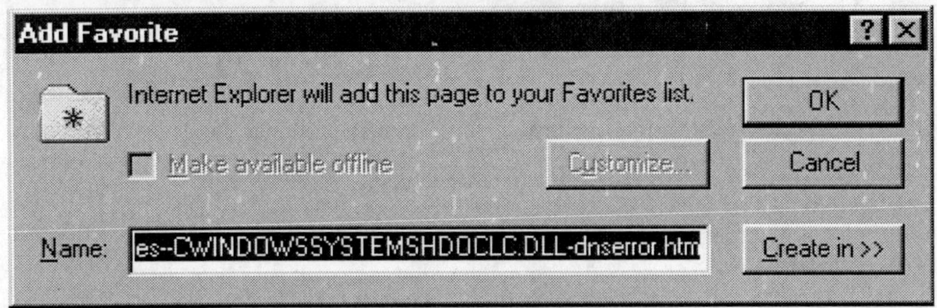

2. In the Name text box, make changes you want to the name of the page.
3. In the create In box select the location of the favorite page.
4. Click the Ok button. This creates a favorite page listing for the current page.

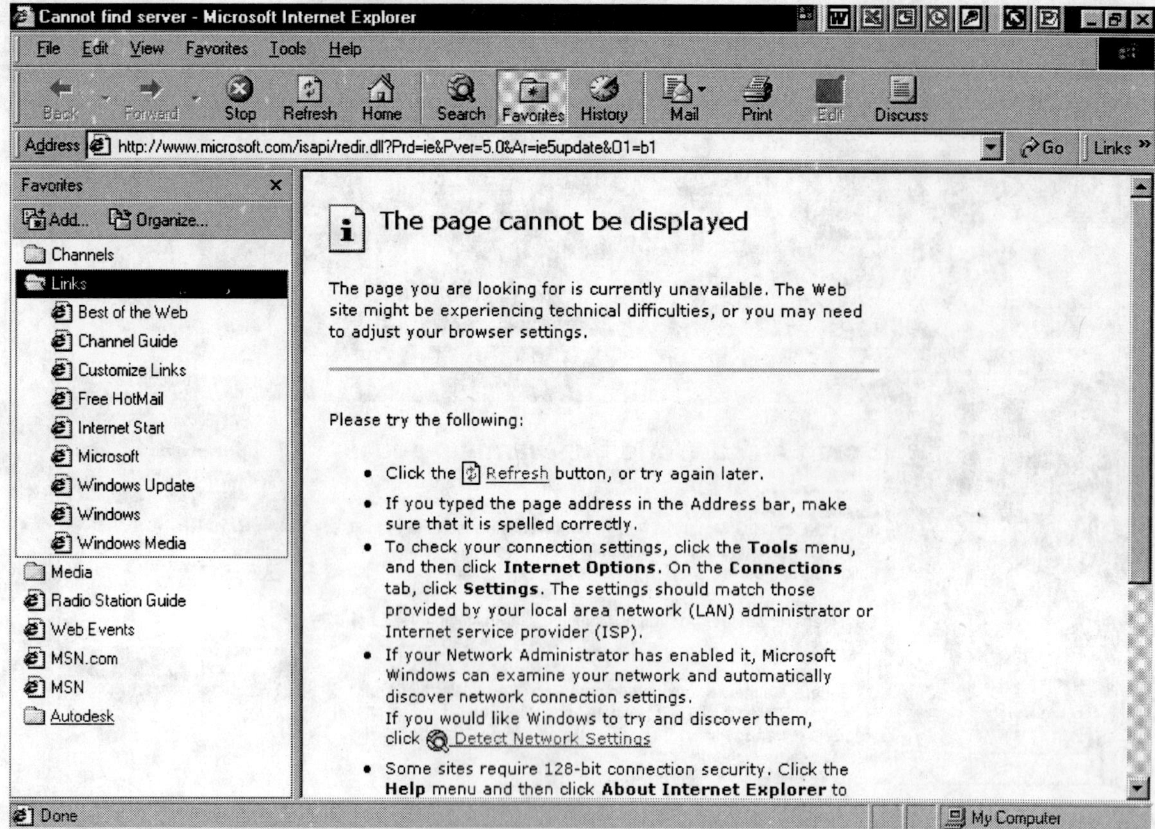


#### *8.13.6.2 Using Search Button*

The search button here is an easy access to various search engines. To use the search feature, use the Search button. To use the search feature do this.

1. To choose a search engine click the customize button in the window.
2. Choose the desired category for your search.
3. Click in the text box in the Search Explorer bar, and type the words or topics you are trying to find.
4. Click the Search button.
5. The results of your query appear in the bottom of the Search Explorer bar.
6. Click one of the result links, and the page appears in Internet Explorer's document area.

On the similar lines you have History.

### 8.13.7 Working with History

Well, you must have guessed it. It keeps the history of the sites which you had visited during the last working time. The various options are:

3 weeks ago

Last week and

Today

All these would give you the list of various sites which you has visited during the last time you had worked with the browser.

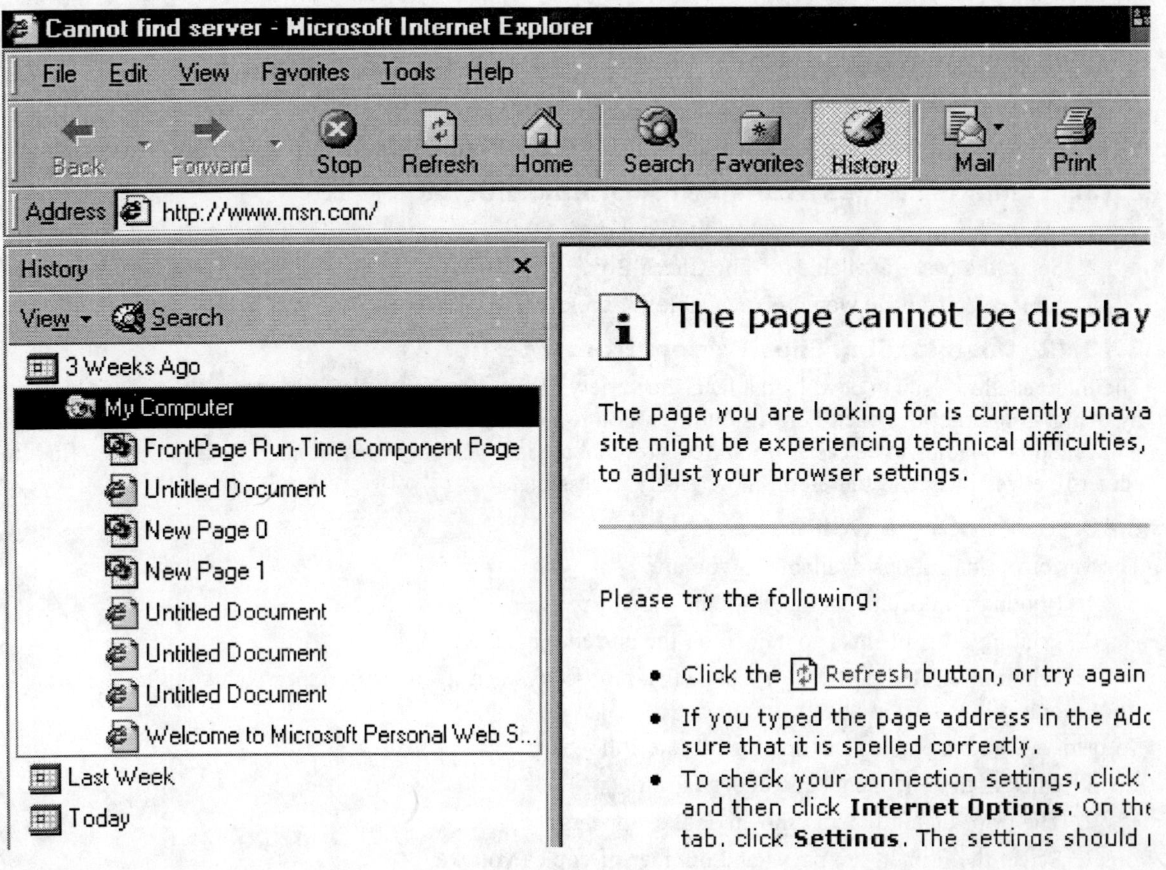


Ok now that you have got the site which you wanted on the screen. The next step would be to work on it. Let us do it.

### 8.13.8 Copying Data

For this follow the following steps:

1. Open the site from where you have to copy the data.
2. Select the data to be copied
3. Click the Edit menu
4. Click at Copy.
5. Minimize the software.
6. Open the software/document where you want to paste.
7. Paste the required data.

### 8.13.9 Saving Pictures from a Web Page

1. Open the site which has the required picture.
2. Right-click on the picture to be saved.
3. Choose the Save As option to save the picture.
4. Your picture would be saved on the clipboard and you can paste it any other software/document.

### 8.13.10 Saving a Page or Picture without opening

1. Right-click the link for the item to be saved.
2. Choose the Save Target As option to save the picture.
3. Your picture would be saved on the clipboard and you can paste it any other software/document.

### 8.13.11 Making pages available for Off-line viewing

1. On the Favorites menu, click Add to Favorites.
2. Select the Make available off-line Check Box.
3. Your selected page would be available for the off-line viewing.

### 8.13.12 Downloading Files/Folders from Internet:

The Internet allows you to download a fantastic variety of files/programs. You can access the needed material by using an Internet Browser. For this purpose, point to a link that is connected to a file on a Web site. You will find downloading to be easier from Web sites that are in your time zone. At night, you may often find the sites to be less busy and therefore, more easily accessible.

### 8.13.13 Printing a web Page

The various print options available to you are:

1. Printing all documents linked to the current page.
2. Printing a list of links contained on the current page.
3. Printing selected portions of a page that has been constructed using frames. This option is available only if the current page has frames.

To print a Web page using the options, do the following:

1. Click at the File menu, and choose Print.
2. The print dialog box, as shown above, appears.
3. Select the printer, the pages and number of copies you want.
4. Click Ok to start printing.

#### *8.13.13.1 Options of the Print dialog box*

| | |
|---|---|
| As laid out on screen | It prints the entire page as it appears on the screen |
| Only the selected frame | It prints one selected frame. This option requires you to select a few words in the area you want to print, prior to printing |
| All frames individually | It prints each frame on a separate page |
| Print All Linked documents | This option generates a printout of every document linked to the current page |
| Print Table of Links | This option produces a short printout listing all the URLs mentioned in the document |

### 8.13.14 Keyboard Shortcuts for Working in Internet Explorer

| | |
|---|---|
| Enter | It activates the selected link |
| Shift + F10 | It displays the context menu for the current link |
| Tab | It selects the next link |
| Ctrl + Tab | Cycled between frames |
| Shift + Tab | It selects the previous link |
| Alt + right arrow | It moves to the next page |
| Alt + left arrow | It returns to the previous page |

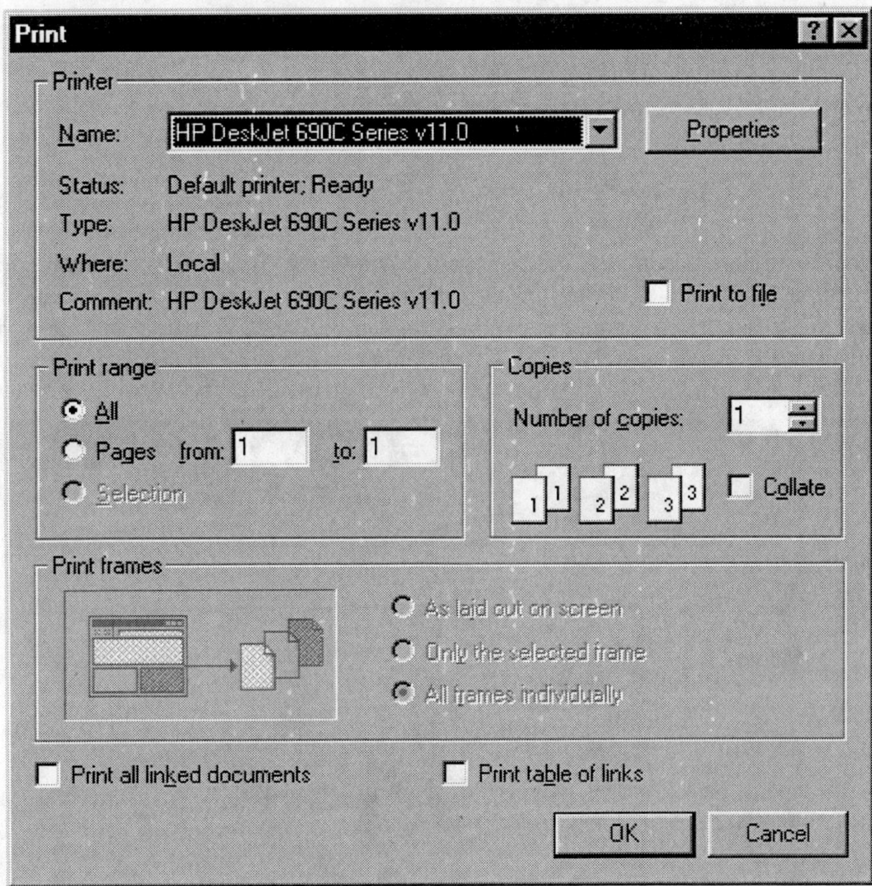


| | |
|---|---|
| F5 | It refreshes display of the current page |
| Esc | It stops display of the current page |
| Ctrl + N | It opens a new window |
| Ctrl + O | It opens a document |
| Ctrl + P | It prints the current page |
| Ctrl + S | It saves the current page as a file |

## 8.14 HTTP

It is a method of preparing and publishing text, ideally suited to the computer, in which readers can choose their own paths through the material. To prepare hypertext, you first divide the information into small, manageable units, such as single pages of text. These units are called nodes. You then embed hyperlinks in the text. When the reader clicks on a hyperlink, the hypertext software displays a different node. The process of navigating among the nodes linked in this way is called browsing. A collection of nodes that are interconnected by hyperlinks is called a web. The World Wide Web is a hypertext system on a global scale.

## 8.15 Publishing Tools

There are a number of Web Publishing Tools developed by various corporations. Some of the more popular ones are:

- Netscape Navigator Gold
- Macromedia's Backstage Desktop Studio
- Other Web Publishing Tools such as HotDog, HoTMetal and WebEdit.

Let us see read more about them.

### 8.15.1 Netscape Navigator Gold

Netscape gold offers a visual editing environment that closely approximates that of a Web page and at the same time adopts many of the concepts used by word processors and document publishing tools. Netscape Gold generates true HTML code, but during the editing phase, this code is hidden form the user by the graphical interface. When creating complex Web pages, you will need to understand the principles behind the HTML language and its various constructs. Using Templates and the Page Wizard, Netscape has reduced the amount of work you need to do when designing a Web page.

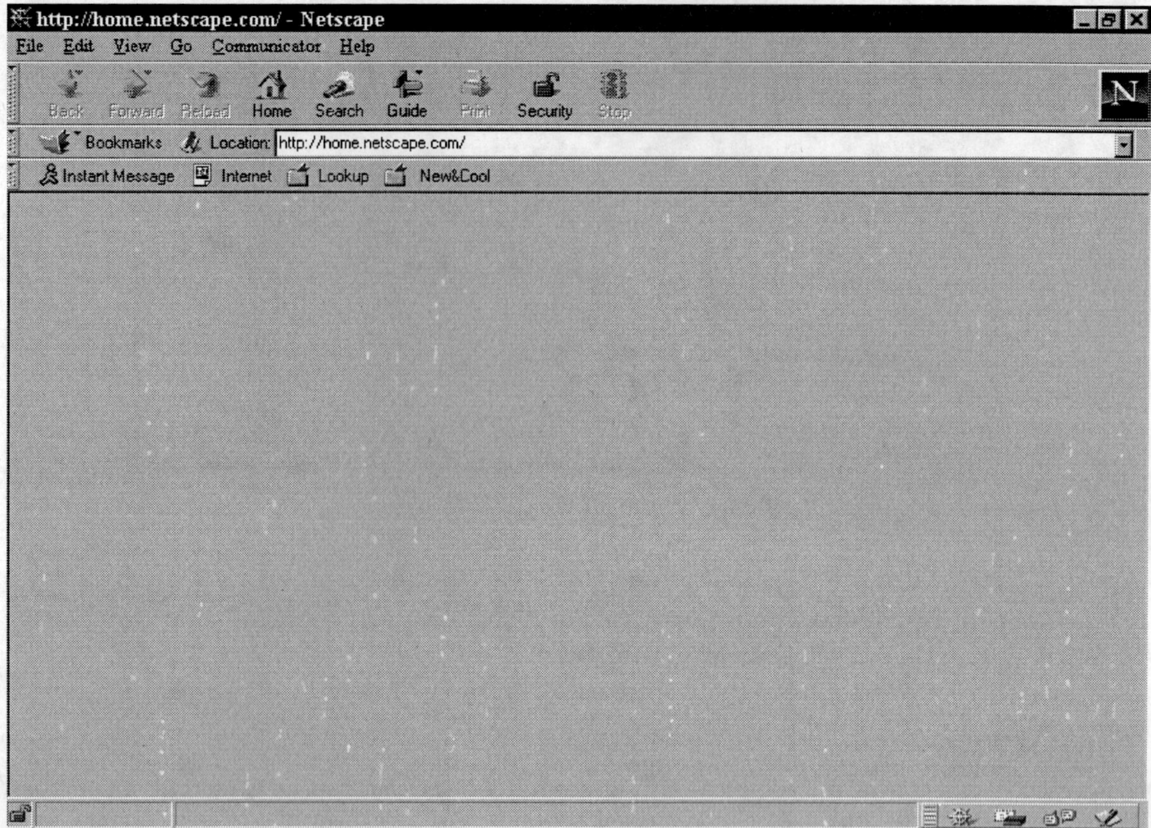


### 8.15.2 Macromedia's Backstage Desktop Studio

It consists of a suite of tools to assemble and manage an end-to-end Web site. The advantage of Macromedia is its excellence in multimedia Web authoring. By combining that experience in imaginary with the simplicity of a point-and-click, drag-and-drop, WYSIWYG strategy for the implementation tools, Macromedia has one of the best tools for designing Web pages. Macromedia's Backstage Desktop Studio is one of the new generation of tools that combine dynamic Web page authoring facilities with Web site management features.

### 8.15.3 Other Web Publishing Tools

There is a wide array of other Web publishing tools. Many of these tools offer value for low price and even some of them are free to download. Some of them are:

#### *8.15.3.1 GoLive 4.0*

Adobe GoLive 4.0 boasts drag and drop authoring features that will have you building your own site in no time. Although Adobe was one of the first big software developers to release a drag and drop Web authoring packages in the shape of PageMill, it did not offer a real contender until the release of GoLive 4.0 The GoLive incorporates cutting edge features.

#### *8.15.3.2 HotDog and HotDot Pro*

HotDog supports HTML, Netscape extension to HTML and Internet Explorer extensions to HTML. When you have multiple documents open in the editor, you can switch between them quickly using tabs at the bottom of the editor window. HotDot has friendly interfaces. HotDog lets you preview your pages without having to save the page. Other features included an advanced correction system that automatically replaces text and file paths when you publish your pages.

HotDot is designed for beginners and experts alike. You will know this immediately when you start HotDot. In addition to being able to insert many common tags into a page directly from the toolbar, hotdog has a dialog box for adding tags. Creating forms with HotDot is easy-just click the Forms icon on the toolbar and HotDog displays a form builder. The form builder provides a friendly interface for selecting the type of element you want to add to a form. HotDot has other friendly tools for managing links, building tables and creating frames. Wit HotDogpro, not only can you customize the toolbar, you can select the icons and labels for toolbar buttons as well. Another nice feature of HotDog Pro is the ability to define your own tags or tag sets that can be accessed via the menus.

#### *8.15.3.3 HoTMetal and HoTMetal Pro*

HoTMetal is an editor from SoftQuad Incorporated (www.sq.com). There are two editions of HoTMetal. HoTMetal is available free! What is even better is that SoftQuad has made a serious commitment to continue to develop and improve this freeware editor.

HoTMetal Pro supports features that put it in the same league as Microsoft FrontPage and macromedia Backsgage. Still, SoftQuad has the market experience to back its offerings with solid support and continual upgrades. Versions of this editor are available for Windows, Macintosh, Power Macintosh and UNIX. HoTMetal pro 3 is an advanced authoring system that supports the most current HTML specification and extensions. HoTMetal Pro supports HTML, Java, ActiveX, objects, scripts and even Shockware. HoTMetal Pro follows an integrated WYSIWYG and tag marker approach.

#### *8.15.3.4 HoTMetal Pro*

A feature you will want to check out is the multiple browser preview with which you can preview your page in any browser at the tough of a button. This feature is great if you want to test your page in several browsers. Other features include automatic conversion of other document formats to HTML. All you have to do is open a MS Word, WordPerfect or AmiPro document in HoTMetal. The best feature of HoTMetal. Pro is the template system.

HoTMetal pro's templates are as advanced as they come. You will find hundreds of templates with which you instantly can create pages, ready-made tables, frames, Java applets, scripts and Shockwave animation. Another feature of HoTMetal Pro is the Frames Editor, which is one of the most advanced you will find anywhere. Creating a frame-enhanced page is done completely with an easy-to-use graphical interface. As you define frames, you can also define the document sources for the frames by dragging and dropping Web pages into your frames.

HoTMetal pro comes with a built-in graphics editor called MetalWorks. Whenever you want to manipulate an image, all you need to do is right-click on the image to display a pop-up menu with which you can define image attributes, create transparent images and build image maps. HoTMetal pro supports both server-side and client-side image maps. Building an image map from an existing image is handled through a dialog box called MetalWorks Maps. Using this dialog box, you can create very precise image maps by enlarging or shrinking the image to suite your needs. Before you can define hot spots on the map, you must select a shape for the hot spot. Hot spots are circular, rectangular or polygonal.

#### *8.15.3.5 WebEdit and WebEdit Pro*

Both editions of WebEdit include toolbar, shortcut keys and a spell checker. Where the editions differ is in the automation routines for creating advanced HTML elements such as forms and frames. The professional edition has many wizards to guide you through the creation process and the basic edition has only a few. Both editions of WebEdit fully support HTML, Netscape extensions to HTML and Internet Explorer extensions to HTML. With WebEdit, you can have multiple documents open at one time. Although WebEdit does not use a Window or Document menu with which you may be familiar to access open documents, it does provide access to the documents using quick tabs.

#### *8.15.3.6 Dreamweaver*

In the space of two short years Macromedia Dreamweaver has become the standard Web authoring tool for creative designers. Now in its fourth version, the package is still in a position to take advantage of future developments on the Web. In the Industry, e-business and e-commerce have become buzzwords and Dreamweaver acknowledge this with Roundtrip Coded data import. The program can be customized for specific projects so that team members and clients alike can use the same package in the development cycle.

Dreamweaver also prepares us for the next wave of Web development with a core built around XML, the extendible scripting language expected to go mainstream as browser support comes on-line. Dreamweaver lets you keep one eye on the future without forgetting what is important now.

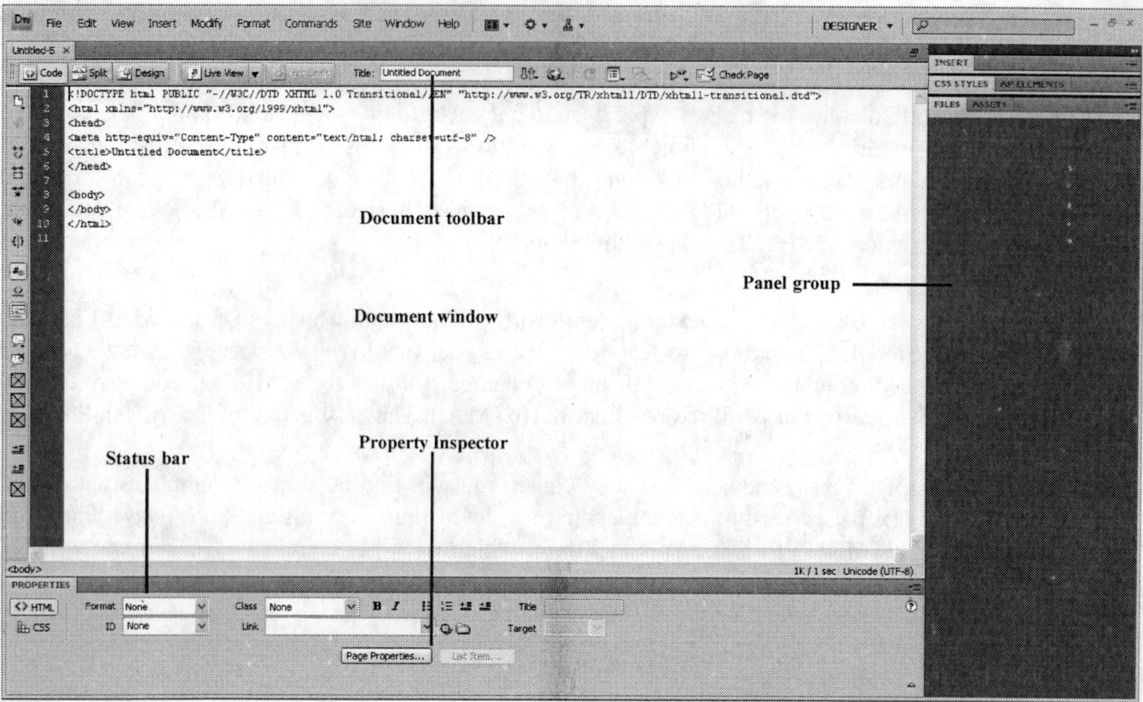

## Let us Revise

1. A web site has to be created and hosted first.
2. You have to pay for registering a domain name and hosting the site.
3. An ISP would help you in doing this.
4. Service provider should give you the required services.
5. There are sites like Yahoo! Store which offer turnkey solutions.
6. There are a variety of Web-hosting companies, in terms of size, services offered, and price.
7. You can create a web site using your own computer too.
8. HTTP it is a connection less protocol.
9. There are two kinds of protocols for the processed transactions on the Internet: stateless and stateful protocols.
10. You have to plan your web site very carefully.
11. You must plan in advance what your site is going to have.
12. Your site should hold the interest of the viewer.
13. Important information which your site should contain are: Home page; Company information; Product description; Online ordering and Response.
14. You can attract viewers using various colours.
15. You can use graphics too in your site.
16. The type of mistakes which you can make in your web site are : Bad Spelling; Being Pushy; Big File Size; Choice of Fonts; Excessive Scroll; Frames; Hidden Navigation Icons; Incompatibility; Overload; Poor Directions; Poor Quality Photos; Poor Targeting; Shifting Styles and Too Much Information.
17. You can use Yahoo! to search a person.
18. You can check with InterNIC for availability of name.
19. Various details you have to fill up for registering your name on InterNIC.
20. There are a number of Web Publishing Tools developed by various corporations.

## Multiple Choice Questions

1. The site for turnkey web site management is :
   (a) Yahoo! store (b) NASA (c) Internet
2. Commonly used site for name registration is:
   (a) Yahoo! (b) InterNIC (c) Indiatimes
3. You can have graphics on your web site :
   (a) Yes (b) No
4. You can create a web site from your computer too:
   (a) True (b) False
5. In order to establish a site, following should be considered:
   (a) Provide new information regularly.
   (b) Let your visitors register for e-mail notification of changes to the site.
   (c) Both of the above
6. ISP stands for :
   (a) Indian Service Provider (b) Internet Service Prover (c) Internet Service Provider

7. Home page is the :
   (a) first page of the site (b) page created at home (c) page having picture of home
8. You cannot find the e-mail address of a person using Yahoo! search:
   (a) True (b) False
9. GoLive is a :
   (a) Web site (b) Browser (c) Web publishing tool
10. Cost of registering your domain name is Rs.:
   (a) 2000 (b) 1000 (c) 3000

## True/False Questions

1. You have to pay for registering a domain name and hosting the site.
2. There are sites like Yahoo! Store which offer turnkey solutions.
3. You cannot create a web site using your own computer too.
4. HTTP it is a connection less protocol.
5. Various details you have to fill up for registering your name on InterNIC.
6. You do not have to plan your web site very carefully.
7. You must plan in advance what your site is going to have.
8. Your site should hold the interest of the viewer.
9. You cannot attract viewers using various colours.
10. You can use graphics too in your site.
11. You can use Yahoo! to search a person.

## Match Columns

Match the matter in Column A with the matter in Column B.

| Column A | Column B |
|---|---|
| A. SGML | 1. Internet Service Provider |
| B. Yahoo! | 2. Software to search on web |
| C. Home Page | 3. Common Gateaway Interface |
| D. ISP | 4. Web site development program |
| E. Front Page | 5. World Wide Web |
| F. Search Engine | 6. Other computer on the network |
| G CGI | 7. Your computer on the network |
| H. WWW | 8. First page of the web site |
| I. Client Computer | 9. Standard Generalized Markup Language |
| J. Host Computer | 10. Popular Web Browser |

## Fill in the Blanks with Appropriate Words

| | | | |
|---|---|---|---|
| a. InterNIC | b. graphics | c. Yahoo! | d. Web Publishing Tools |
| e. Home Page | f. Yahoo! Store | g. HTTP | h. domain name |
| i. hosted | l. Web-hosting | | |

1. There are sites like __________ which offer turnkey solutions.
2. There are a variety of ___________ companies, in terms of size, services offered, and price.
3. __________ it is a connection less protocol.
4. Important information which your site should contain are: ____________; Company information; Product description; Online ordering and Response.
5. You can use ________ too in your site.
6. You can use ________ to search a person.
7. You can check with ________ for availability of name.
8. There are a number of _____________ developed by various corporations.
9. A web site has to be created and _______ first.
10. You have to pay for registering a ________ and hosting the site.

## Descriptive Type Questions

1. How would you sign with ISP?
2. What sort of services can be provided by ISP?
3. Who provides turnkey solutions?
4. What sort of technical support is provided by ISP?
5. What are the various document standards?
6. What steps would you take to plan your site?
7. Describe the various steps taken while developing a web site.
8. Describe the various contents which your web site should have.
9. Which software are available for developing web site on small scale?
10. What precautions you have to take while developing the web site?
11. How would you find a person's e-mail using Yahoo!?
12. How would you find out that your domain name is unique?
13. Describe the process of registering with InterNic.
14. Which are the various publishing tools?
13. Describe the following terms:

| | |
|---|---|
| Dreamweaver | WebEdit |
| HotMetal Pro | HotDog Pro |
| GoLive | FrontPage |
| Visual Page | Graphics Files |
| Layout of the Web site | Stateless Protocol |
| Stateful Protocol | Speed of search |

## Answers to Objective Type Questions

*Multiple Choice Questions*

| | | | |
|---|---|---|---|
| 1. a | 2. b | 3. a | 4. a |
| 5. c | 6. c | 7. a | 8. a |
| 9. b | 10. b | | |

***True False Questions***

| | | | |
|---|---|---|---|
| 1. T | 2. T | 3. F | 4. T |
| 5. T | 6. F | 7. T | 8. T |
| 9. F | 10. T | 11. T | |

***Matching Columns***

| | | | |
|---|---|---|---|
| A. 9 | B. 10 | C. 8 | D. 1 |
| E. 4 | F. 2 | G. 3 | H. 5 |
| I. 6 | J. 7 | | |

***Fill in the Blanks***

| | | | |
|---|---|---|---|
| 1. f | 2. l | 3. g | 4. e |
| 5. b | 6. c | 7. a | 8. d |
| 9. i | 10. h | | |

# HTML Programming Basics 9

## 9.1 Introduction to HTML

HTML stands for Hypertext Markup Language. This is text oriented language used for writing programs to create web sites. There is no need for compiling or doing anything else as you would do in any other programming language. However, there are few things which you have to take care of as you do in your text related documents.

You can have Headings, Paragraphs, Bulleted text, etc. You can even have tables too. However, there is no fix page layout as such. HTML does not support it. You can have the text in Bold, Italics, etc. But, each one of the above set of text, has to be tagged accordingly, e.g., Heading, for the text to be taken as headings. In fact Markup means this only. But, remember the file has to be text and not a word processing document. A simple ASCII text file.

As said earlier, HTML is used to create web sites. Since we now know that the text files are created using HTML but how are these so-called text files going to be used. These text files are used with programs called HTML browsers, take these HTML files and create web sites/

## 9.2 HTML browsers

As said above a browser is used to create web document. It is important that your computer has more than one browser in it. It is important since it lets you view the document through more than one browser. It gives your document more versatility and makes you sure that your document would run all the browsers.

The two most popular browsers are Netscape Communicator (used to be called Navigator) and Microsoft Internet Explorer. Both are quite popular and can be both used in your computer.

### 9.2.1 Netscape Communicator

More web designer use this software than any other. It is also called Netscape. Developed by some of the same engineers who created popular software called Mosaic. It offers more nonstandard features that make its enhanced pages much more attractive to the eye.

### 9.2.2 Microsoft Internet Explorer

Anything with Microsoft tag is bound to create hype. It is fast becoming popular. It is no doubt a viable competitor Netscape.

See here how the HTML file called Index looks like as a text document in WordPad and how it and how it looks in Netscape Communicator and Microsoft Internet Explorer.

## 9.3 Different versions of HTML

While the original HTML standard was developed by CERN, new versions are hashed out through a series of online meetings open to anyone on the Internet. Then they are analyzed, discussed, decided, and published by the W3 Consortium, led by the Laboratory for Computer Science at the Massachusetts Institute of Technology (MIT) and INRIA, a French technology group, in collaboration with CERN.

The W3C has been particularly successful with HTML 4, the current version, and the one that this book describes, which incorporates many of the previously proprietary extensions into a shared standard. In this book, you will learn both standard HTML as well as the extensions developed by Netscape and Microsoft that have made these browsers so popular.

### 9.3.1 DHTML

It is actually a combination of technologies to create dynamic content on Web pages. It draws on HTML 4, Cascading Style Sheets, and usually JavaScript. These elements are supposed to work together following the rules of the Document Object Model (DOM), to change the content of a page even after it has been loaded into the browser.

### 9.3.2 XML

HTML forms part of a large more powerful mark-up language called SGML. In an effort to harness the power of SGML without losing the simplicity of HTML, the W3C has developed Extensible Markup Language, or XML, that can be used to create your own mark-up languages, specifically suited to your topic.

Now we take a look at the various terms used while writing HTML.

## 9.4 HTML tags

These are commands written between less than (<) and greater than (>) signs, also known as angle brackets, that indicate how the browser should display the text. There are opening and closing versions for many (but not all) tags, and the affected text is contained within the two tags. Both the opening and closing tags use the same command word but the closing tag carries an initial extra forward slash symbol /.

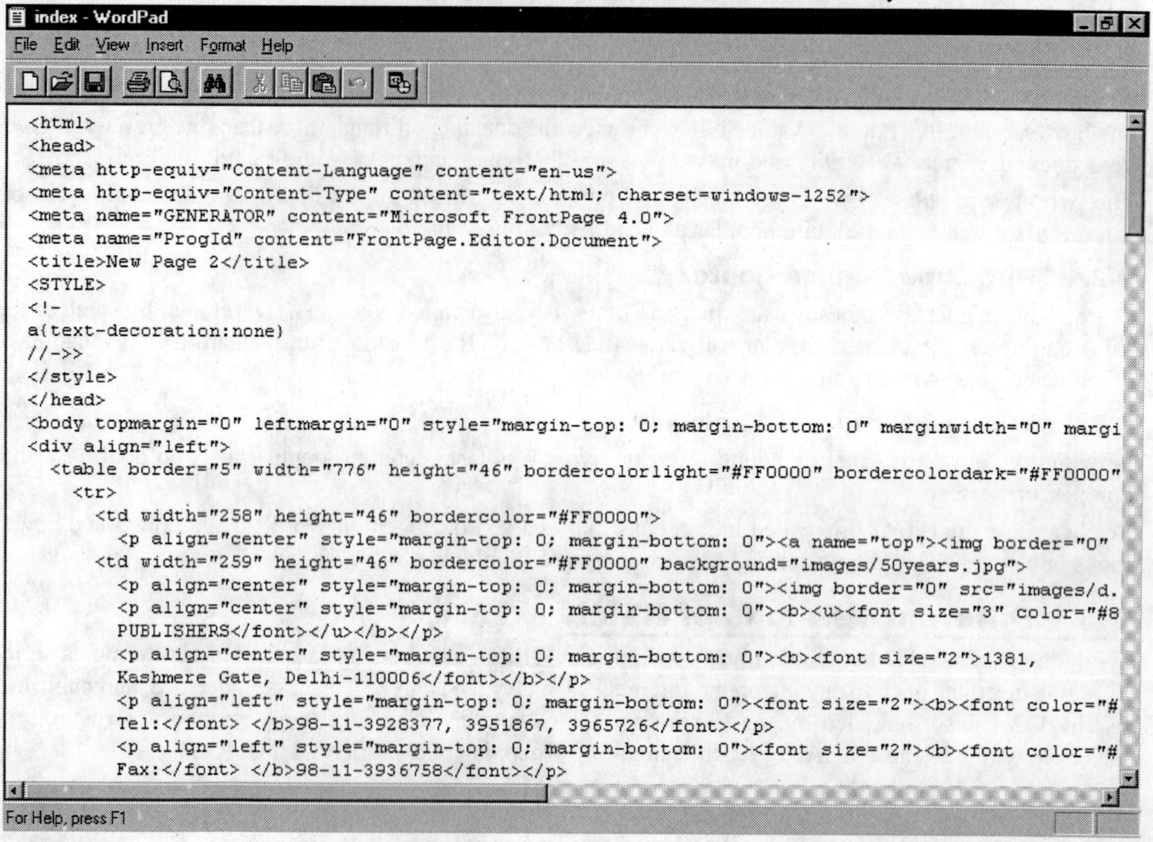

index - WordPad

File Edit View Insert Format Help

```
<html>
<head>
<meta http-equiv="Content-Language" content="en-us">
<meta http-equiv="Content-Type" content="text/html; charset=windows-1252">
<meta name="GENERATOR" content="Microsoft FrontPage 4.0">
<meta name="ProgId" content="FrontPage.Editor.Document">
<title>New Page 2</title>
<STYLE>
<!-
a{text-decoration:none}
//->>
</style>
</head>
<body topmargin="0" leftmargin="0" style="margin-top: 0; margin-bottom: 0" marginwidth="0" margi
<div align="left">
  <table border="5" width="776" height="46" bordercolorlight="#FF0000" bordercolordark="#FF0000"
    <tr>
      <td width="258" height="46" bordercolor="#FF0000">
        <p align="center" style="margin-top: 0; margin-bottom: 0"><a name="top"><img border="0"
      <td width="259" height="46" bordercolor="#FF0000" background="images/50years.jpg">
        <p align="center" style="margin-top: 0; margin-bottom: 0"><img border="0" src="images/d.
        <p align="center" style="margin-top: 0; margin-bottom: 0"><b><u><font size="3" color="#8
        PUBLISHERS</font></u></b></p>
        <p align="center" style="margin-top: 0; margin-bottom: 0"><b><font size="2">1381,
        Kashmere Gate, Delhi-110006</font></b></p>
        <p align="left" style="margin-top: 0; margin-bottom: 0"><font size="2"><b><font color="#
        Tel:</font> </b>98-11-3928377, 3951867, 3965726</font></p>
        <p align="left" style="margin-top: 0; margin-bottom: 0"><font size="2"><b><font color="#
        Fax:</font> </b>98-11-3936758</font></p>
```

For Help, press F1

New Page 2 - Netscape
File Edit View Go Communicator Help
Back Forward Reload Home Search Guide Print Security Stop
Bookmarks Location: file:///C|/My Documents/My Webs/devra/DEVRA/index.html
Search Instant Message Members WebMail Connections BizJournal SmartUpdate Mktplace RealPlayer
Devra Books
EDUCATIONAL PUBLISHERS
1381, Kashmere Gate, Delhi-110006
Tel: 98-11-3928377, 3951867, 3965726
Fax: 98-11-3936758
Mail: devra@vsnl.com
1950-2000 50 YEARS OF EDUCATIONAL EXELLENCE
Buy Books
Place your order for our publications. Click Here
New Arrivals
New Page 2 - Microsoft Internet Explorer provided by Startec Internet Services - [Worki
File Edit View Favorites Tools Help
Back Forward Stop Refresh Home Search Favorites History Mail Print Edit Discuss
Address C:\My Documents\My Webs\devra\DEVRA\index.html
Go
Devra Books
EDUCATIONAL PUBLISHERS
1381, Kashmere Gate, Delhi-110006
Tel: 98-11-3928377, 3951867, 3965726
Fax: 98-11-3936758
Mail: devra@vsnl.com
1950-2000 50 YEARS OF EDUCATIONAL EXELLENCE
Buy Books
Place your order for our publications. Click Here
New Arrivals
Guest Book
Comments, Suggestions & Queries.
Our Publications
Catalogue of our various publications
Reviews
Done
My Computer

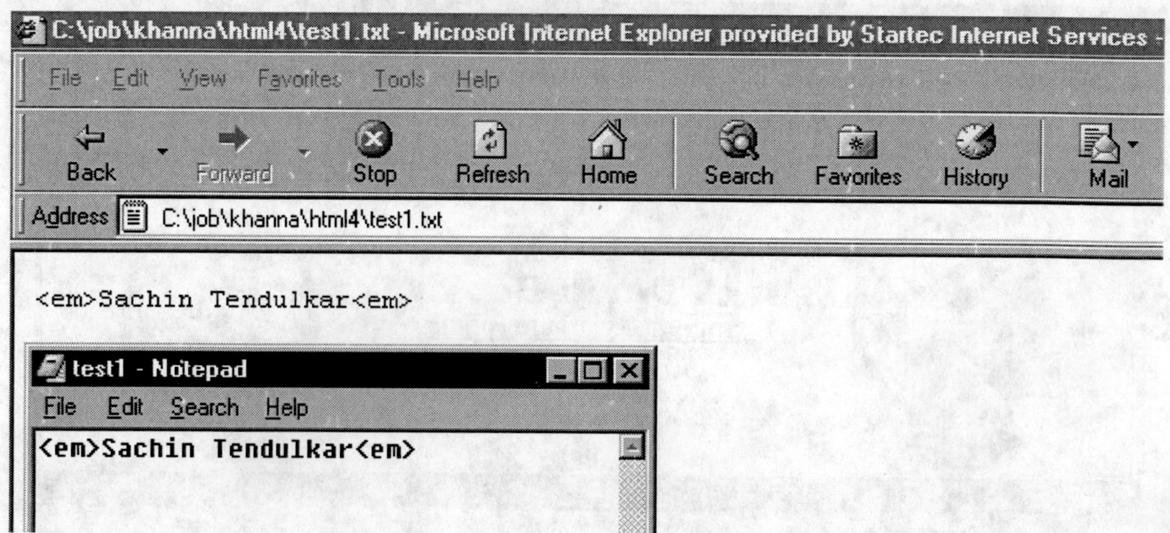


### 9.4.1 Attributes

Some tags have special attributes that offer a variety of options for the contained text. The attribute is entered between two symbols, less than and greater than. Often, you use a series of attributes in a single tag. Simply write one after the other—in any order—with a space between each one.

```
<TABLE BORDER>
```

### 9.4.2 Nesting tags

In some cases, you may want to modify your page contents with more than one tag. For example, you may want to add italic formatting to a word inside a header. There are two things to keep in mind here.

First, not all tags can contain all other kinds of tags. As a general rule, those tags that affect entire paragraphs can contain tags that affect individual words or letters (inline), but not vice versa. Second, order is everything. Whenever you use a closing tag it should correspond to the last unclosed opening tag. In other words, first A then B, then /B, and then /A.

```
<H1>Sachin<EM>Tendulkar</EM></H1>
```

### 9.4.3 Quotation marks

Mostly all values should be enclosed in straight quotation marks " " (NOT curly ones “ ”, note the difference). However, you can omit the quote marks if the value only contains letters (A-Z, a-z), digits (0-9), a hyphen (-), or period (.).

### 9.4.4 Spacing

The best part of spacing is that HTML browsers will ignore any extra spaces that exist between the tags in your HTML document. So you can make use of this and add spaces and returns to help view the elements in your HTML document more clearly while you are writing and designing your page. Also you would not be able to count returns or spaces to format your document. A return at the end of a paragraph in your HTML document will not appear in the browsed page, instead, use a P tag to begin each paragraph. You cannot repeat several P tags to add spaces between paragraphs. The extra tags are simply ignored. How do you control spacing then? Style sheets (you will read about them little later), let you specify with absolute precision just how much space should go between elements in your Web page. In addition, Netscape has developed some tags for the same purpose.

```
index - WordPad
File Edit View Insert Format Help
          <tr>
               <td width="569" colspan="7" bgcolor="#000000">
<p align="justify"><blink><font size="4" color="#00FF00"><b><u>Established in
1950, Students' Book Store, Kashmere Gate, Celebrates its Golden Jubilee this
year. Devra Books, the publishing wing of the Students' Books Store is since
dedicated to provide the best and quality study material to cater the needs of
the students community.</u></b></font>
</blink>
             </td>
          </tr>
            . . .
```

### 9.4.5 Special symbols

Besides the usual ASCII set of characters, HTML supports other characters too. The standard ASCII set characters can be used as it is and will be displayed as it is in the browser.

There are four symbols that have special meanings in HTML documents. These are the greater than (>), less than (<), straight double quotation marks ("), and the ampersand (&). If you simply type them in your HTML document, the browser may attempt to interpret them. To show the symbols themselves, use a name or number code.

Look at the following example, where <BR> has resulted in giving a line break.

### 9.4.6 Tags with Automatic Line Breaks

Block-level tags generally include automatic, logical line breaks. For example, you don't need to use a new paragraph tag after a header, since a header automatically includes a line break. In fact, you only need to insert a new paragraph tag if you're using the tag to apply styles. Some common block-level tags are P, H1, BR, UL, and TABLE. Inline tags that affect only begin on a new line. Some common inline tags are EM, B, and IMG.

#### *9.4.6.1 Values*

Attributes can have values. In some cases, you must pick a value from small group if choices. For example, the CLEAR attribute for the BR tag can take values of left, right, or all. Other attributes are more strict about the type of values they accept. For example, the HSPACE attribute of the IMG tag will accept only integers as its value, and the SRC attribute of the IMG tag will only accept URLs for its value.

## 9.5 Document Overview

HTML stands for Hypertext Markup Language. This is text oriented language used for writing programs to create web sites. There is no need for compiling or doing anything else as you would do in any other programming language. However, there are few things which you have to take care of as you do in your text related documents. You can have Headings, Paragraphs, Bulleted text, etc. You can even have tables too. However, there is no fix page layout as such. HTML does not support it. You can have the text in Bold, Italics, etc. But, each one of the above set of text, has to be tagged accordingly, e.g., Heading, for the text to be taken as headings. In fact Markup means this only. But, remember the file has to be text and not a word processing document. A simple ASCII text file.

As said earlier, HTML is used to create web sites. Since we now know that the text files are created using HTML but how are these so-called text files going to be used. These text files are used with programs called HTML browsers, take these HTML files and create web sites.

Follow the following steps to create a new web page:

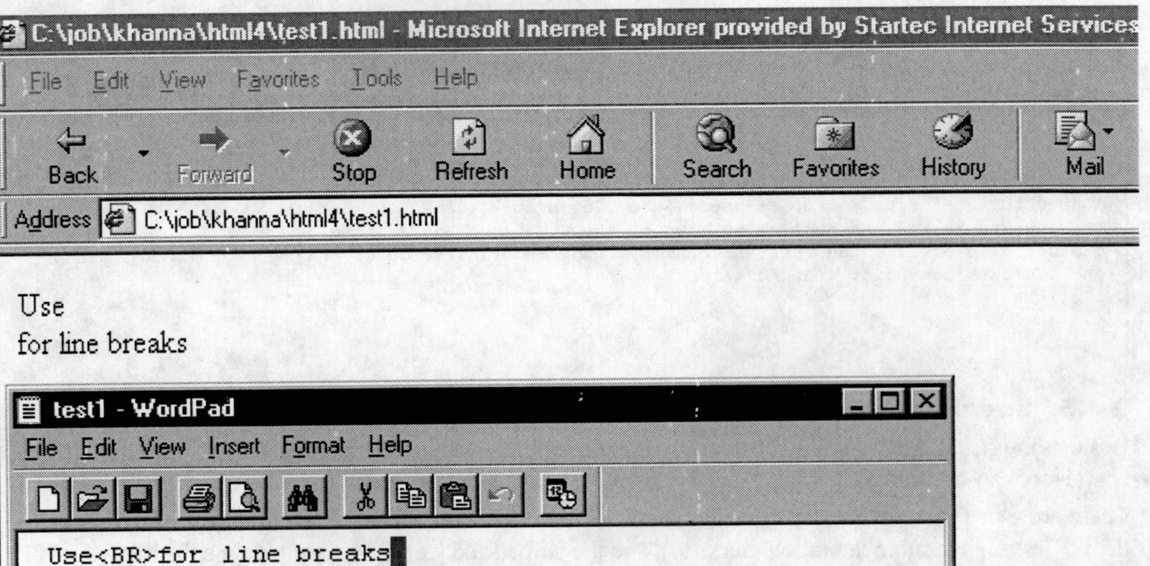


1. Open a text editor or word processor.
2. Choose file> New to create a new, blank document.
3. Type the following text to create the HTML content as shown next:
   Use<BR>for line breaks
4. Choose File>Save As.
5. In the dialog box that appears, choose Text Document for the type.
6. Give the document the .htm or .html extension.
7. Choose the folder in which to save the Web page.
8. Click Save.

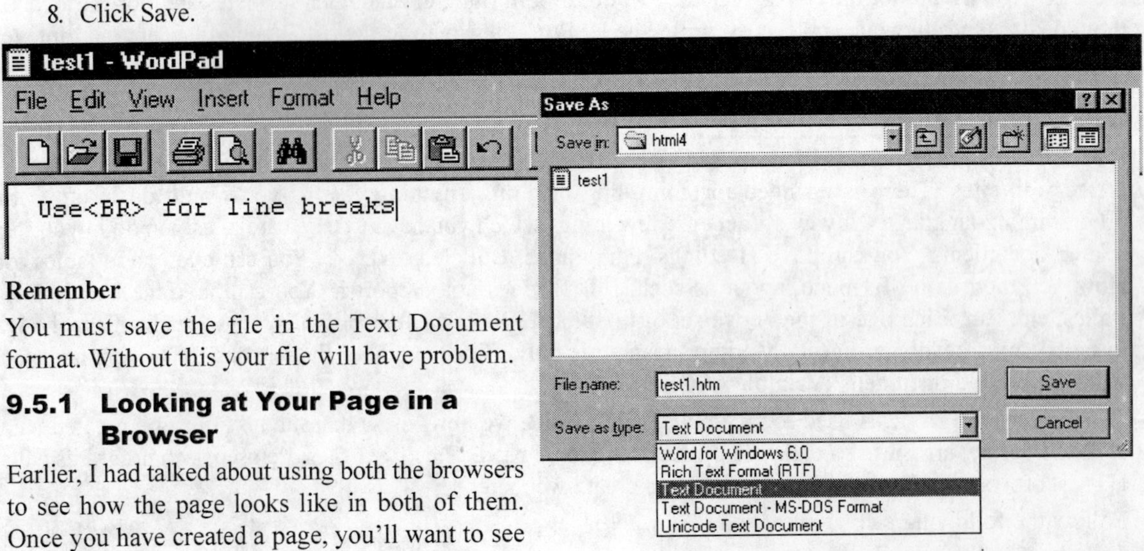


**Remember**

You must save the file in the Text Document format. Without this your file will have problem.

### 9.5.1 Looking at Your Page in a Browser

Earlier, I had talked about using both the browsers to see how the page looks like in both of them. Once you have created a page, you'll want to see how it looks like in a browser. In fact, since you do not know which browser the actual user will be using, it's a good idea to look at the page in several browsers.

Follow the following steps to look at your page in a browser:

1. Open your browser software (Netscape Communicator, Microsoft Internet Explorer, etc.)
2. Choose File > Open, Open File, or Open Page (just not Open Location), depending on the browser.
3. In the dialog box that appears find the Web page that you want as it will appear when you actually publish it on the server.

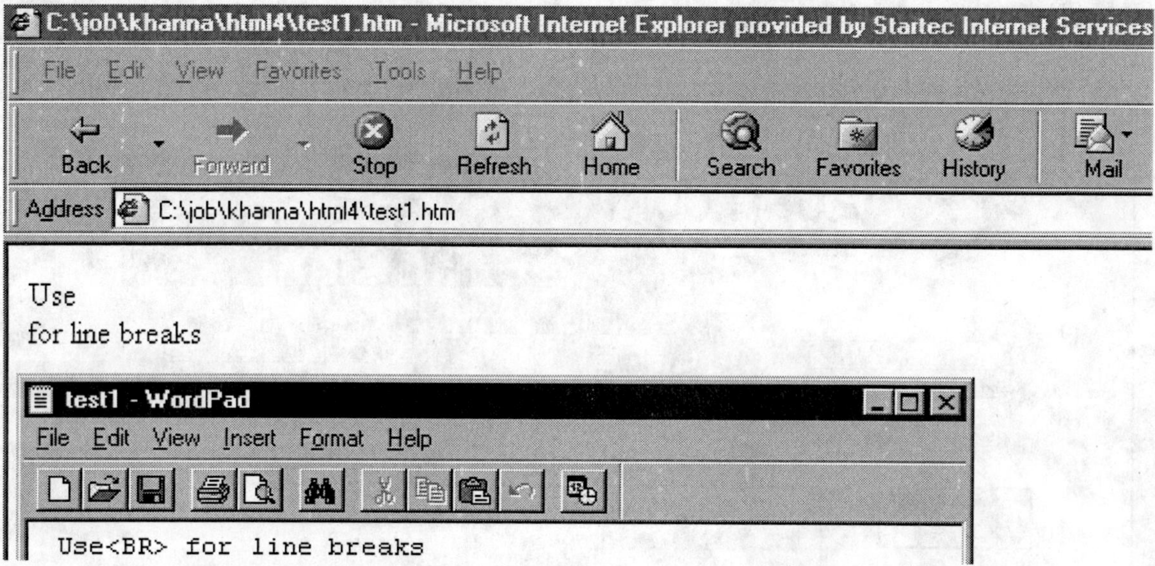


**Remember**

If your Web pages does not appear in the Open dialog box, make sure that you have saved it as Text Only and given it the .htm or html extension.

You don't have to close the document in the text editor before you view it with a browser. This makes editing much faster. You can switch to the editor, make your changes, and then back to the browser and click Reload to view the changes.

It is not necessary to publish your pages on the sever before you view them. Publishing them on the server does not change them in any way (it only moves them to a new location).

### 9.5.2 Home Page Designating

Home page is the page which is shown on the screen, when the site is opened. The most common home page name is index.html but this varies from server to server.

#### *9.5.2.1 To designate one page as the home page:*

1. Create the home page as described above.
2. Name the file index.html (or whatever the default home page name is for your server).
3. Place the home page in the principal directory that contains your Web site.

**Remember**

Your home page should have links to all the other information available at your Web site. Your home page should be a table of contents to your site, not just the first page.

If you want your users to be able to reach the other pages in your site, make your home page clean, neat, and fast.

See the home page of Naukri.com which is self explanatory.

### 9.5.3 Starting your Web page

When you want to see your page in the browser, the browser needs information right away about the kind of document it is, and how it should be displayed. You should begin every Web page with the !DOCTYPE and HTML tags.

Follow the following steps to start your Web page:

1. Type <!DOCTYPE HTML PUBLIC "-// W3C//DTD HTML at the top of your Web page, as shown on the next page.
2. Type the version of HTML you're using, in this case 4.0. If you are using lots of fonts and colours, use the word Transitional with 4.0. If the pages have lots of frames, use HTML 4.0 Frameset.
3. Type //EN"> <HTML>.
4. Now your text file is ready. Save it under a name.
5. Start your browser and open this particular file.
6. See that there is a blank web page since you have not given any substance to your page. This is what we will do in the next step.

**Remember**

While you can get away without either the !DOCTYPE or HTML tags, you should always include both to ensure that your page is correctly recognized, regardless of the browser used.

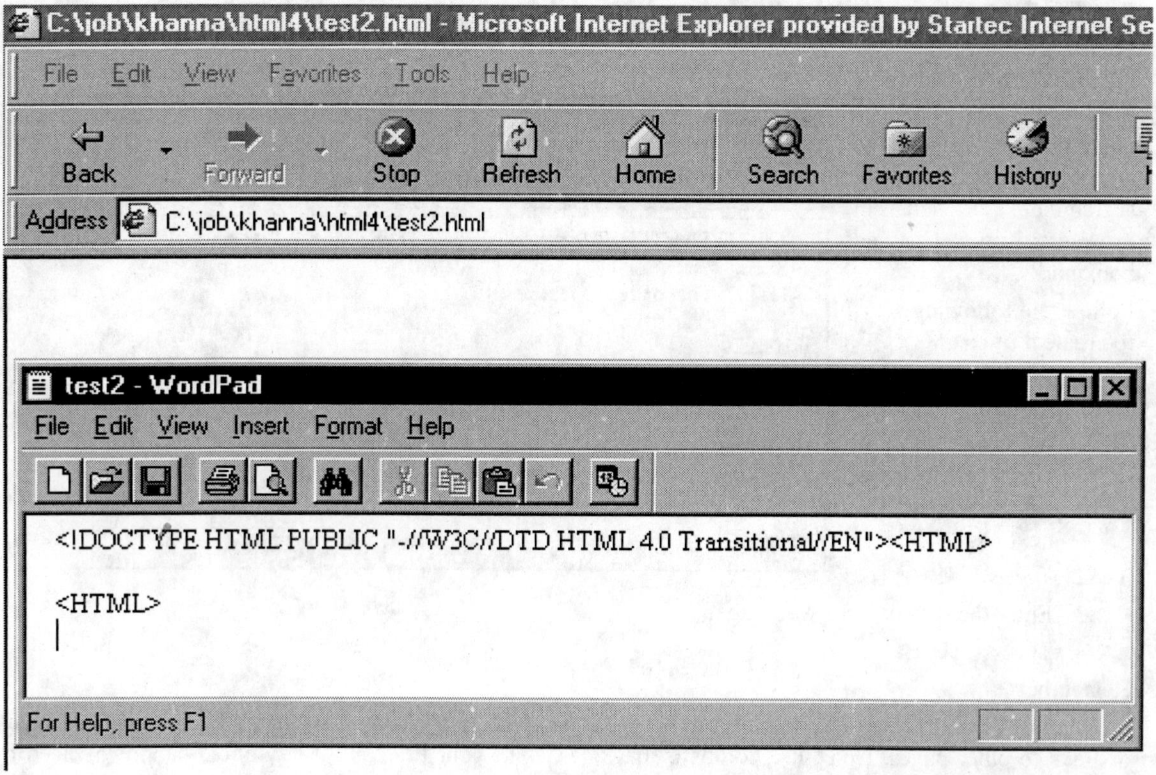

C:\job\khanna\html4\test2.html - Microsoft Internet Explorer provided by Startec Internet Se
File Edit View Favorites Tools Help
Back Forward Stop Refresh Home Search Favorites History
Address C:\job\khanna\html4\test2.html
test2 - WordPad
File Edit View Insert Format Help
<!DOCTYPE HTML PUBLIC "-//W3C//DTD HTML 4.0 Transitional//EN"><HTML>
<HTML>
For Help, press F1

Create a template with the !DOCTYPE and HTML tags already typed in as a starting point for all your pages.

## 9.6 Header Elements

Nothing is complete without a head and a body. Look at yourself and you know what I am talking about. Similarly in HTML too we have Head and Body as the two main sections. The Head section provides information about the URL of your Web page as well as its relationship with the other pages at your site. The only element in the HEAD section that is visible to the user is the title of the Web page. The BODY of your HTML document contains the bulk of your Web page, including all the text, graphics, and formatting.

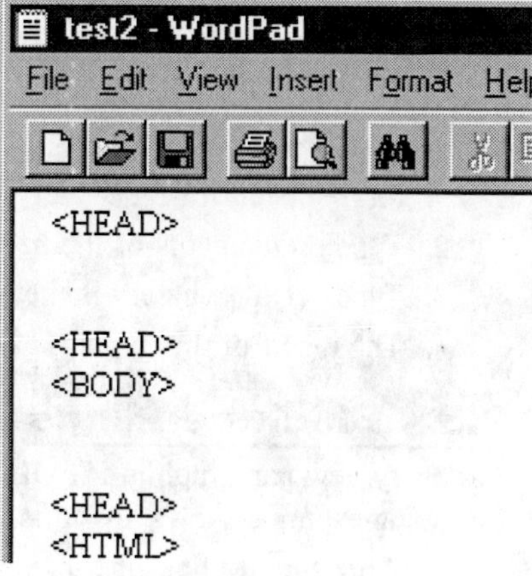

test2 - WordPad
File Edit View Insert Format Help
<HEAD>
<HEAD>
<BODY>
<HEAD>
<HTML>

Follow the following steps to create the Head section:

1. Directly after the initial !DOCTYPE and HTML type <HEAD>.
2. Create the HEAD section, including the TITLE.
3. Type </HEAD>.

Follow the following steps to create the BODY:

1. After the final </HEAD> tag and before anything else, type <BODY>.
2. Create the contents of your Web page.
3. Type </BODY>.

### 9.6.1 Creating a Title

Each page must have a title. A title should be short and descriptive. In some browsers, the title appears in the title bar of the window; in others, the title is centered at the top of the screen. The title is used in search indexes as well as in browsers' history lists and bookmarks.

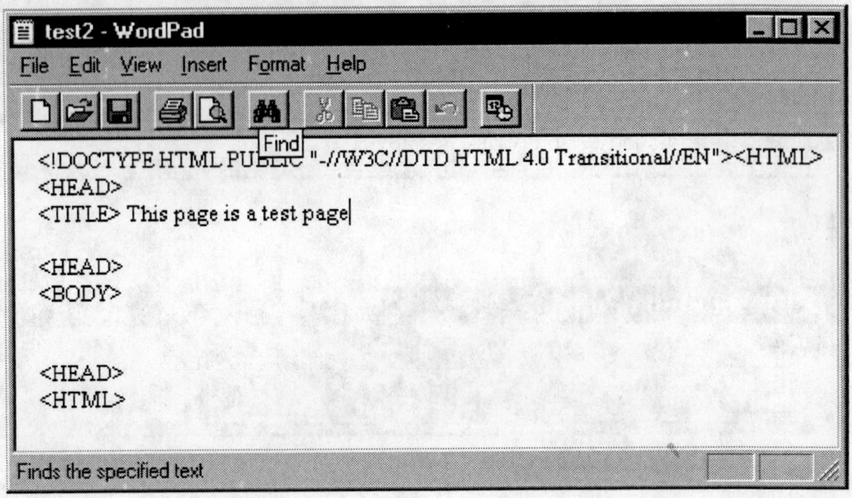

Follow the following steps to create a title:

1. Place the cursor between the opening and closing HEAD tags, as shown on the next page.
2. Type <TITLE>.
3. Enter the title of your web page.
4. Type </TITLE>.

```
test2 - WordPad
File  Edit  View  Insert  Format  Help
Find
<!DOCTYPE HTML PUBLIC "-//W3C//DTD HTML 4.0 Transitional//EN"><HTML>
<HEAD>
<TITLE> This page is a test page

<HEAD>
<BODY>


<HEAD>
<HTML>
Finds the specified text
```

**Remember**

There must be only one TITLE tag in each HTML document. A title cannot contain any formatting, images, or links to other pages. Don't use colons or backslashes in your titles. These symbols cannot be used by some operating systems for file names. It's good idea to use a common element to begin each page's title. For example, you could begin each page with My Page: followed by the specific area described on that page.

## 9.7 Section headings

Various type of headings can be placed in the text. Maximum of 6 headings are allowed. But, you can use only 3 at a time. Each one of the heading is numbered from 1 onward. Obviously you cannot repeat the numbers.

Let us try to create a heading.

1. In the BODY section of your HTML document, type (Hn where n is a number from 1 to 6, depending on the level of header that you want to create). Here I have used it as H1.
2. Type the contents of the header, in this case I have typed it as "Information Technology Class X.
3. Type </Hn> where n is the same number used in step 1, in this case H1.
4. The result of this typing and result in browser are both shown on the next page.

## 9.8 Block headings

For every new paragraph in HTML you must use the p tag, as was mentioned in the earlier paragraph. The following example shows how it is done.

1. After the heading line, press Enter to reach the next line in Word Pad.
2. Type <p> to start the new paragaph.
3. Type the text which you want to put in the paragraph. I have typed here KHANNA PUBLISHING PVT. LTD.

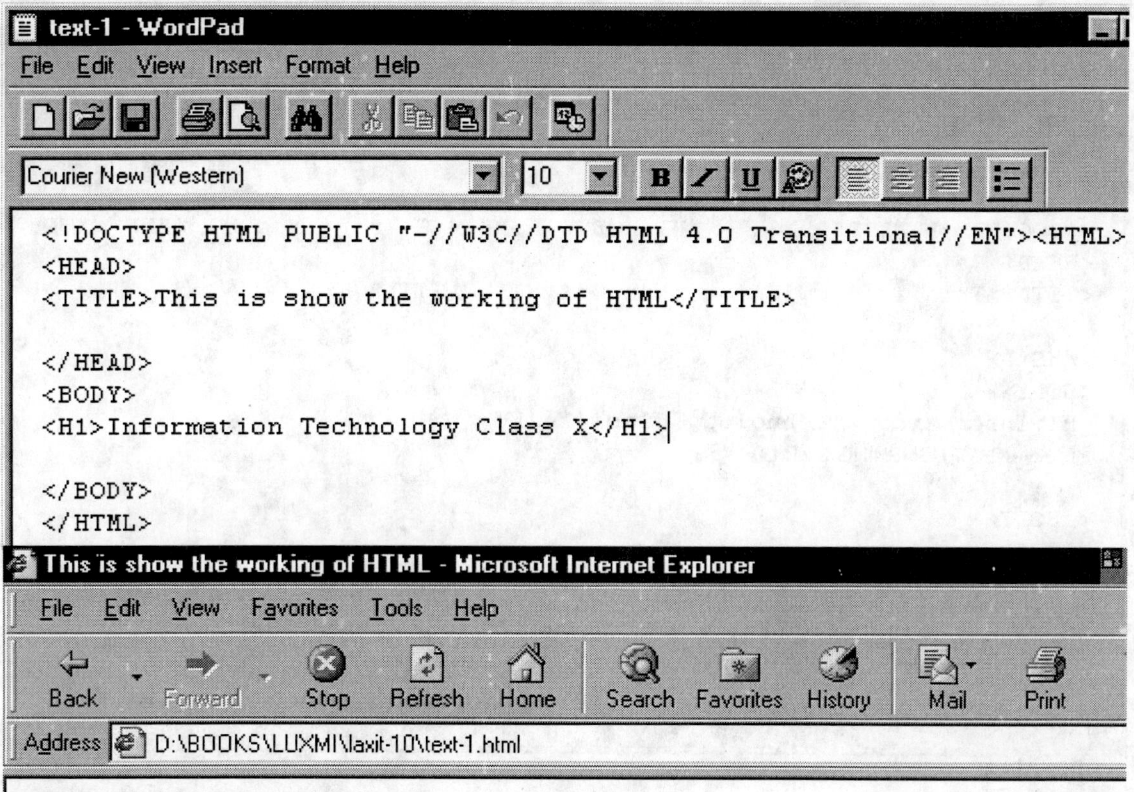


4. Close the paragraph by using the tag </p>.
5. The text in Word Pad and its effect in the browser are shown on the next page.

## 9.9 Lists

HTML support 3 type of lists: Unordered lists, Ordered lists and Definition lists. Ordered lists are numbered in some fashion, while Unordered lists are bulleted. Definition lists consist of a term followed by its definition. Both ordered and unordered lists require start and end tags as well as the use of a special element to indicate where each list item begins (the <LI> tag). Unordered lists can be preceded by one of several bullet styles: a closed circle, an open circle, or a square.

The tags for an unordered list are <UL> and </UL>. Ordered lists can be preceded by Arabic numerals, uppercase or lowercase Roman numerals, or uppercase or lowercase alphanumeric characters. The tags for an ordered list are <OL> and </OL>. Definition lists require a start tag (<DL>) and end tag (</DL>) and two special elements: one for definition terms (the <DT> tag) and one for definitions (the <DD>) tag.

In addition to these three types of lists, HTML also allows two other types of lists that are much less commonly used: Directory lists (which use the <DIR> tag) and Menu lists (the <MENU> tag). However, these two types of lists are not very popular.

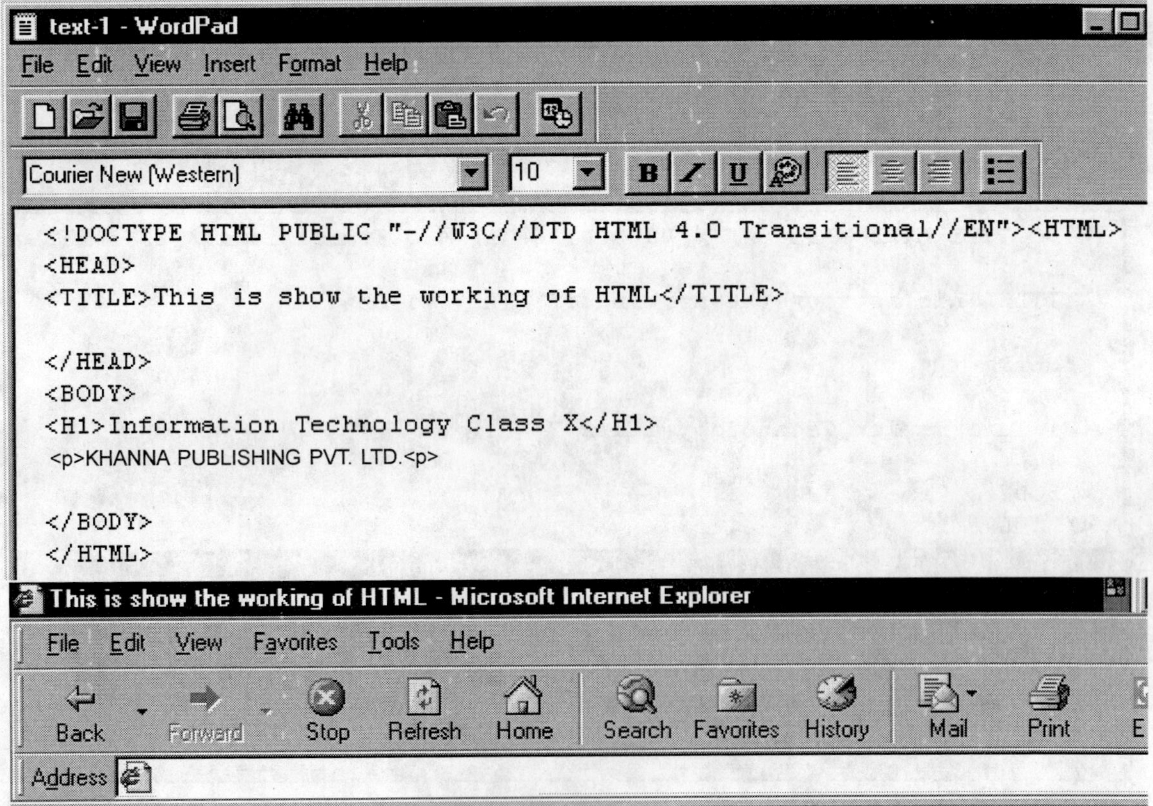


### 9.9.1 Unordered Lists

As said earlier, this list uses the <UL> and </UL> tags. The only element that can be contained inside the <UL> and </UL> tags is a list item, signified with the list item element. The list item element uses the <LI> tag (and optionally the </LI> tag) and contains the actual content of your lists. Both <UL> and <LI> have the same set of attributes:

```
TYPE="CIRCLE"
TYPE="DISC"
TYPE="SQUARE"
```

The CIRCLE attribute value is used for a hollow bullet, the DISC type creates a solid bullet, and the SQUARE value renderes a solid block. The default appearance for a list is with a disc. You can use an optional </LI> end tag at the end of each list item, however, the </UL> end tag is always required at the end of the unordered list.

Even though both the <UL> tag and the <LI> tag can take the TYPE attribute, it's much more common to use the attribute with the <UL> tag so that the entire list takes on the appearance you desire. For example, here is some HTML that generates two separate lists:

```
<TITLE>Menu Card</TITLE>
<BODY>
<p><Breakfast>
<UL>
<LI>Eggs
<LI>Milk
<LI>Apples
<LI>Coffee
</UL>
<p>Dinner
<UL TYPE="SQUARE">
<LI>Soup
<LI>Salad
<LI TYPE="CIRCLE"> Chicken
<LI TYPE="DISC">Rice
<LI TYPE="CIRCLE">Dessert
</UL>
```

See the result of this in the browser next.

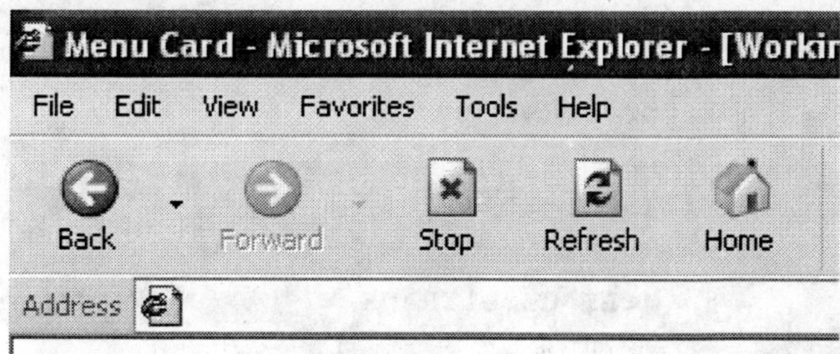


One important aspect of lists is that you can nest one list inside another to create a sublist. The default appearance of the sublists will vary from the main list, with the first sublist using circle bullets and the next nested list, using squares. For example:

```
<UL>
<LI>Microsoft
    <UL>
    <LI>Windows
    <LI>Office
        <UL>
        <LI>Microsoft Word
        <LI>Microsoft Excel
        </UL>
    <LI>Internet Explorer
    </UL>
<LI>Adobe
    <UL>
    <LI>PageMaker
        <UL>
        <LI>Version 7.0
        </UL>
```

```
        </UL>

    <LI>CorelDRAW
        <UL>
        <LI>CorelDRAW 11
            <UL>
            <LI>CorelTRACE
            </UL>
        </UL>
    </UL>
```

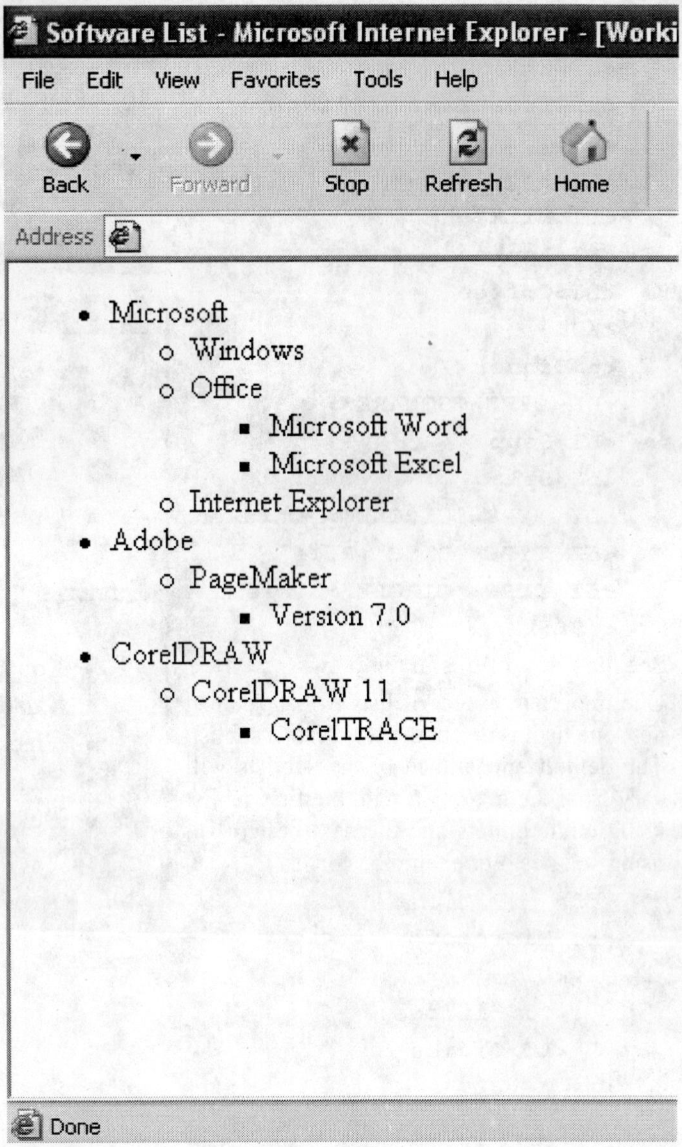

The list would be displayed with the sublists indented beneath the main list, much like we have shown in the source code for readability. There are a total of seven lists here. Each <UL> tag begins a new list. The main list (Microsoft, Adobe, and CorelDRAW) has six sublists - two per bulleted point. The above figure shows the same.

### 9.9.2 Creating Ordered Lists

The ordered list element's <OL> and </OL> tags are used to create ordered lists. Like unordered lists, ordered list must contain list item elements (with the <LI> tag) to contain your list's text. In fact, ordered lists are identical in behaviour to unordered lists, except they use numbers instead of bullets and you can use an attribute to start numbering at a number other than one.

Here are the attributes you can use with the <OL> tag:

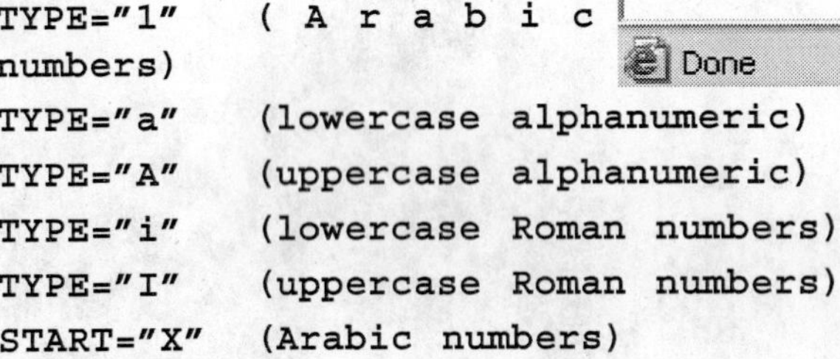

```
TYPE="1"    (Arabic numbers)
TYPE="a"    (lowercase alphanumeric)
TYPE="A"    (uppercase alphanumeric)
TYPE="i"    (lowercase Roman numbers)
TYPE="I"    (uppercase Roman numbers)
START="X"   (Arabic numbers)
```

The Type attribute allows you to specify the numbering system you want to use. Arabic numbers are the default. In addition, when you are using ordered lists, the <LI> tag can use the VALUE attribute to make a particular list item have a certain number.

The value attribute is shown here:

```
<OL>
```

```
<LI>Milk
<LI>Bread
<LI>Ham
<LI VALUE="10">Coffee
<LI>Fruit
</OL>
```

In a browser the order of this list would appear as follows:

1. Milk
2. Bread
3. Ham
10. Dark Chocolate
11. Fruit

### 9.9.3 Definition Lists

The definition list element uses the <DL> start tag and the </DL> end tag to create a definition list. This list is rendered without bullets. The <DT> tag is used for definition terms (that is, the name or title of the item you are defining). The <DD> tag is used for the definitions themselves. For example,

```
<DL>
<DT>Microsoft Excel
<DD>A spreadsheet program
<DT>Microsoft Word
<DD>A word processing program
</DL>
```

Software List - Microsoft Internet Explorer - [W
File Edit View Favorites Tools Help
Back Forward Stop Refresh Home
Address

Microsoft Excel
A spreadsheet program
Microsoft Word
A word processing program

Here is how this would look in the browser.

### 9.9.4 Using Directory and Menu Lists

There are two other types of lists defined in HTML: Directory lists and Menus. However, these two types of lists are rarely used, and Navigator and Internet Explorer treat them identically to the way they treat unordered lists.

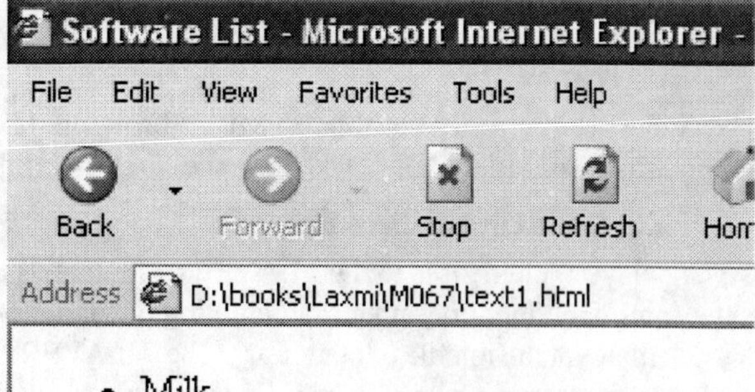


The directory list element is signified by the <DIR> and </DIR> tags. This element was intended to be used for directory lists of short items (some sources recommend 20 or fewer characters so they can be listed in columns 24 characters wide). Here is a quick example of a directory list:

```
<DIR>
<LI>Item 1
<LI>Item 2
<LI>Item 3
```

```
</DIR>
```

Similarly the <MENU> and </MENU> tags make up the menu element, which is used for the menu lists. Menus can appear with different spacing results in different browsers, but Navigator and Internet Explorer don't display menu lists any differently than unordered lists. Here is a quick sample menu:

```
<MENU>
<LI>Milk
<LI>Butter
<LI>Bread
</MENU>
```

For both directory and menu lists, the only item that should be contained is a list-item element (the <LI> tag).

## 9.10 Inline elements

Inline elements can be explained in the following manner.

### 9.10.1 Formatting Inline Text

You can use the <DIV> element to select and apply styles to a block of text, but in those cases where you don't have a well – delineated block of text to work with, you can use the <SPAN> element to select and apply styles. to clarify – you usually use <SPAN> to apply styles inline, for example, in the middle of a sentence. For blocks of text use <DIV> for words or sentences use <SPAN>

In this example, I'm applying a style to a section of text using <SPAN>, turning that text red:

```
<HTML>
    <HEAD>
        <TITLE>
            Using the &lt;SPAN&gt; tag
        </TITLE>
    </HEAD>
    </BODY>
        <H2>
            Is my face <SPAN CLASS="redface" STYLE="color: red">red</
SPAN>?
        </H2>
    </BODY>
</HTML
```

You can see the results of this HTML in browser. The word "red" appears in red and rest of text in black. Though it would look all black since the book is in black and white.

### 9.10.2 Creating Inline Layers

The <Ilayer> element is to the <LAYER> element as the <SPAN> tag is to the <DIV> element. It has much the same function, but rather than creating a stand alone HTML structure, the <ILAYER> is supposed to be used inline (in the middle of other text). The <ILAYER> element lets you create layers inline, as in this example, where I'm creating a new layer inline to move some text up a little higher on the page:

```
<HTML>
<HEAD>
```

```
<TITLE>Working with layer</TITLE>
</HEAD>
<BODY>
   <H1 ALIGN="CENTER">
      Working With Inline Layers
   </h1>
   <BR>
   <H1>
      This text includes some that
      <ILAYER NAME="LAYER1" LEFT = 5 TOP = 15>
      <I>pops up</I><ILAYER>
      a little.
   </H1>
</BODY>
</HTML>
```

You can see the results of this HTML in browser. I have positioned this layer using the Top and Left attributes to push some text up a little.

### 9.10.3 Creating Inline Or Floating Frames

Internet Explorer supports inline frames, also called floating frames. Inline frames can appear wherever you want them, including in the middle of the page. All you have to do is specify the height and width of the frame and the HTML page to load into it and you're set. Inline frames are supported with the <IFRAME> element, which in many ways is Internet Explorer's answer to Netscape Navigator's <LAYER> element. You can use inline frames to display a number of pages in one and if you turn the borders off the result can be much like using the <LAYER> element.

Here's an example showing how to create two inline frames:

```
<HTML>
   <HEAD>
      <TITLE>
         Inline Frames!
      </TITLE>
   </HEAD>
<BODY BGCOLOR="BLACK">
   <CENTER>
      <BR>
      <BR>
      <IFRAME WIDTH = 50% HEIGHT = 25% NAME = frame1
         SRC="frame1.htm">
      </IFRAME>
      <BR>
      <BR>
   </CENTER>
```

```
    </BODY>
</HTML>
```

You can see the results in the browser. Note that it's up to the browser to place these frames, much like other elements, such as images.

### 9.10.4 Creating Inline Video

You can also include videos in your Web pages. One way to do this in Internet Explorer is with the <IMG> element, if you include the DYNSRC attribute. Here, I'm adding a Charlie Chaplin movie to a Web page:

```
<HTML>
    <HEAD>
        <TITLE>
            Video With the &lt;IMG&gt: Element
        </TITLE>
    </HEAD>
    <BODY>
        <CENTER>
            <H1>
                    Video With the &lt; IMG&gt; Element
            </H1>
            <BR>
            <BR>
            <IMG DYNCSRC="chaplin.avi" ALIGN="Top">
            <BR>
            <BR>
        </CENTER>
    </BODY>
</HTML>
```

The results of this HTML can also be seen in the browser. As you can see, the short movie is playing.

## 9.11 Images

HTML supports all kind of graphic images. They can be logos or photographs. Graphics once inserted are displayed on the site page. Follow the following steps to insert an image on a page:

1. Place the cursor where you want the image to appear.
2. Type <IMG SRC=" image.ext" where image.ext indicates the location of the image file on the server.
3. In the example I have typed this after the <HEAD> line. Since I would be using GLOBE.JPG in the text, I have used its location.
4. If desired, type BRODER = n, where n is the thickness of the border in pixels. I have not used any.
5. Type the final >.
6. See the result, how it looks in the browser on the next page. Also note the text how it is typed in the word pad.

**Remember**

You can add graphics with extensions like, GIF, JPEG, PNG, or any other kind of images that the browser recognizes. Don't expect your visitors to he site to wait for more than 30 seconds to load and view your page.

So get the smaller images, create miniatures of large images and let visitors choose to view the larger images only if desired.

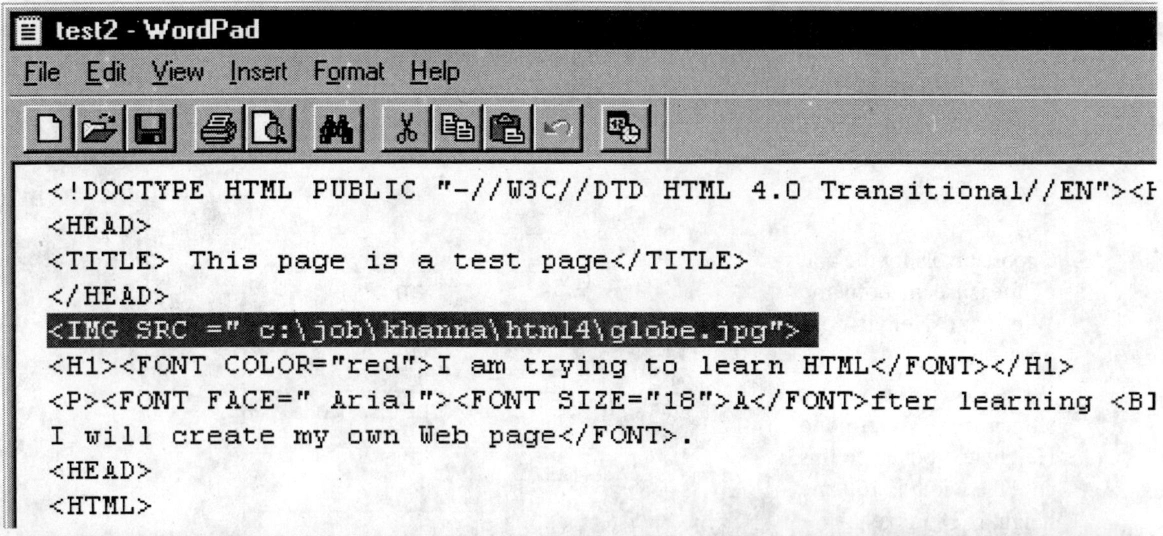


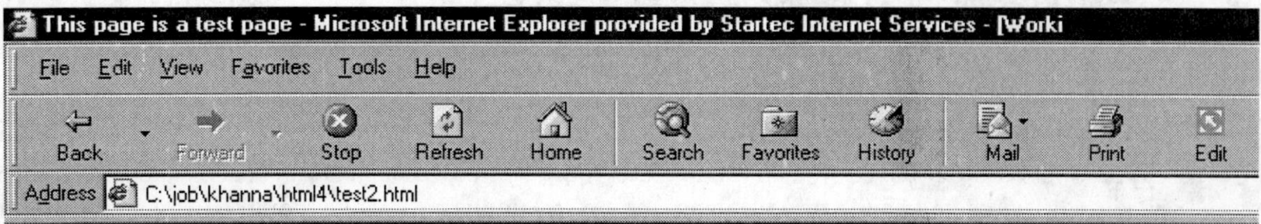

# I am trying to learn HTML

After learning **HTML**, I will create my own Web page.

### 9.11.1 Specifying Size for Fast Viewing

As mentioned above your image should be small so that it can be loaded fast. If you specify the image's dimensions, the browser can fill in the text around the image as the image loads, so that your visitors can read the page without having to wait for the images. Follow the following steps to specify the size of your image:

1. Open the image in Photoshop, or other image editing program.
2. Choose Image > Image Size.
3. Choose pixels for the unit of measure in both the Width and Height pop-up menus.
4. Write down the values shown in the Width and Height text boxes. In this case the width is 150 and height is 185 pixels.
5. In your HTML document where you wish the image to appear, type <IMG SRC = " image.location", where image.location is the location of the image on the server. This is done as was done in the previous case.

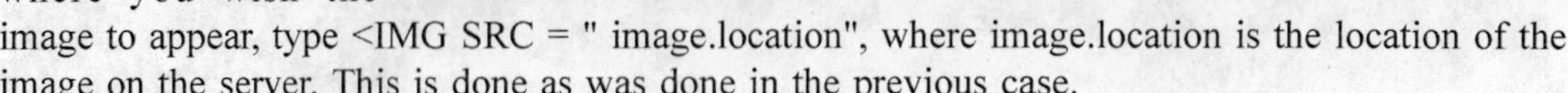

6. Type WIDTH=x HEIGHT=y, using the values you jotted down in step 4 to specify the values for x and y (the width and height of your image) in pixels. In this case width would be 150 and height to be 185.
7. Add other image attributes as described and then type the final >.
8. See how the figure looks like on the next page. I have deliberately used width as 100 and height as

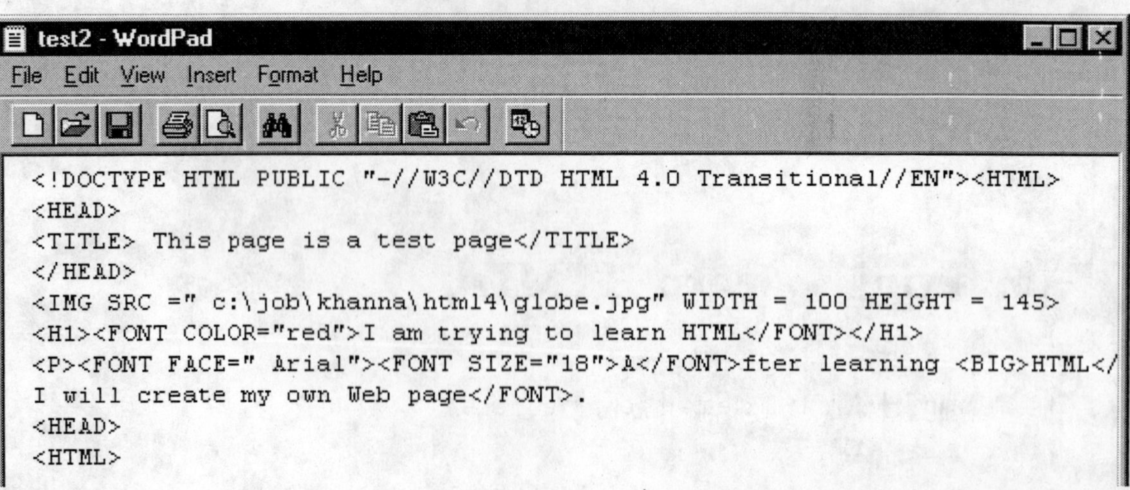



```
<!DOCTYPE HTML PUBLIC "-//W3C//DTD HTML 4.0 Transitional//EN"><HTML>
<HEAD>
<TITLE> This page is a test page</TITLE>
</HEAD>
<IMG SRC =" c:\job\khanna\html4\globe.jpg" WIDTH = 100 HEIGHT = 145>
<H1><FONT COLOR="red">I am trying to learn HTML</FONT></H1>
<P><FONT FACE=" Arial"><FONT SIZE="18">A</FONT>fter learning <BIG>HTML</
I will create my own Web page</FONT>.
<HEAD>
<HTML>
```

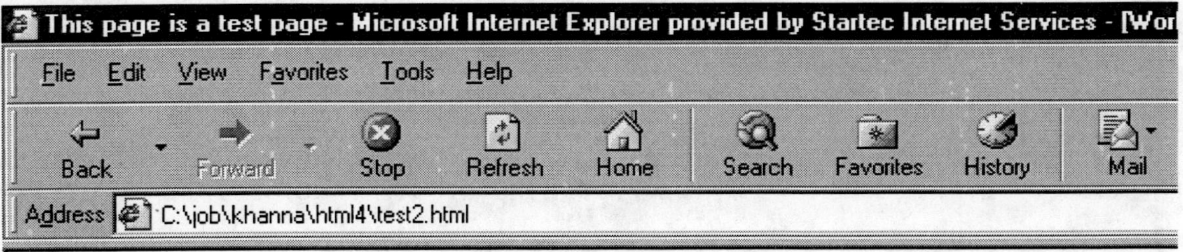

145, since if I had used the same options, you would not have noticed the difference in the picture. Text is also given there.

### 9.11.2 Wrapping Text around Images

It is not that you would always have the image covering the full width of the screen. You can use the ALIGN attribute (with the left and right variables only) to wrap text around an image.

1. Type <IMG SRC = "image.location" as was done earlier.
2. Either type ALIGN=left to align the image to the left of the screen while the text flows to the right or type ALIGN= right to align the image to the right edge of the screen while the text flows on the left side of the image.
3. Add other image attributes, as described in other parts of this chapter, if desired.
4. Type the final >.
5. See the result in the browser, as shown on the next page alongwith the HTML text .

In this case I have used the option of aligning the image to the left and let the text flow on the right.

**Remember**

When you choose ALIGN=right, it's the image that goes to the right (while the text goes to the left). When you choose ALIGN=left, again the image will be on the left side with the text flowing around the right side.

### 9.11.3 Wrapping Text between Two Images

1. Type <IMG SRC=" right.image" ALIGN=right> where right.image indicates the location of the image that should appear on the right side of the screen. In this case I would be using the above Globe.JPG on the right.
2. Type the text that should flow around the first image.

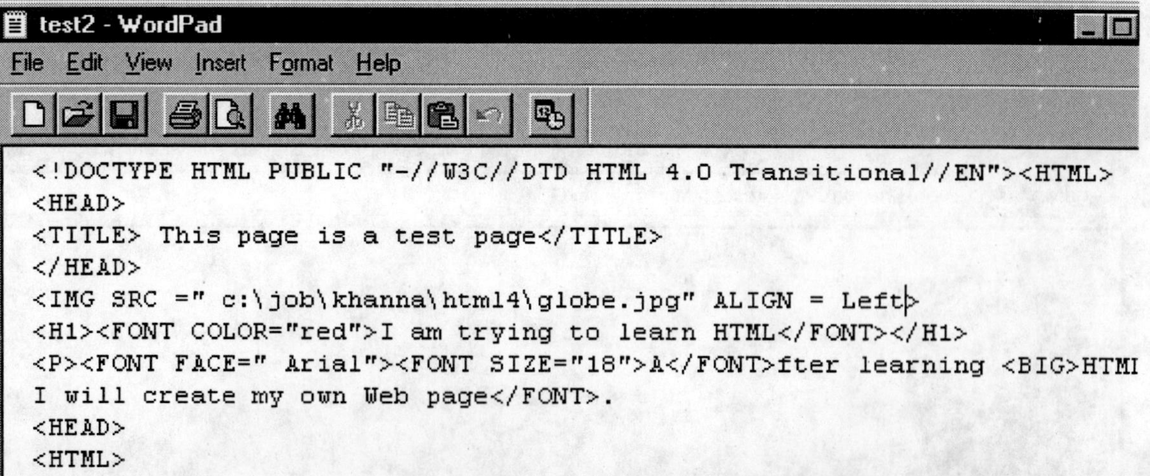

3. Type <IMG SRC=" left.image". ALIGN=left> where left.image indicates the location of the image that should appear on the left side of the screen. In this case I am using another picture of the same globe.
4. If desired, type <P> to begin a new paragraph. that will be aligned with the image placed in step 3.
5. Type the text that should flow around the second image.
6. See the result as it appears in the browser, below. Text is also shown.

**Remember**

Each image will continue to push the text to on side until it either encounters a break or until there is no more text.

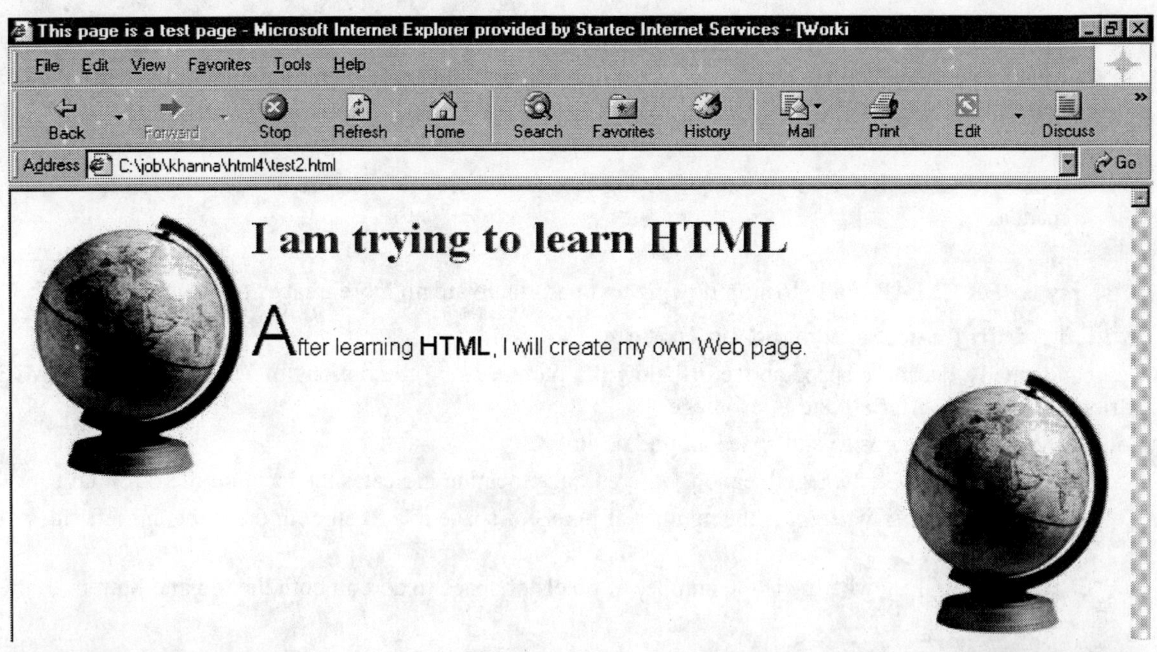


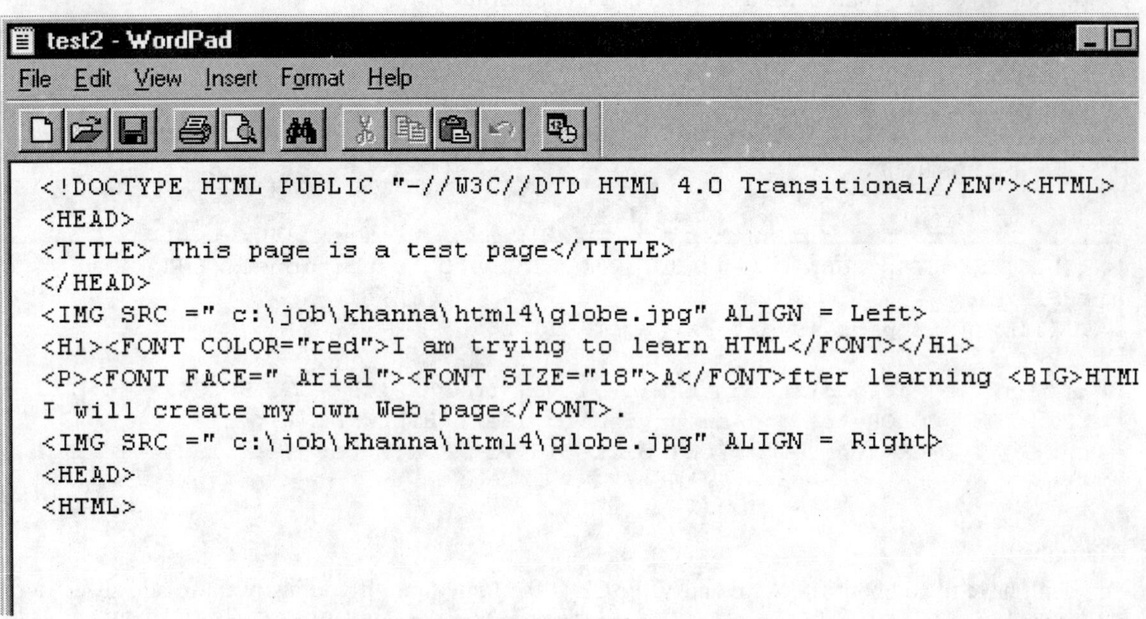


### 9.11.4 Stopping Text Wrap

A wrapped image affects all the text that follows it, unless you insert a special line break. The CLEAR attribute added to the regular BR tag indicates that the text should not begin until the specified margin is clear (that is, at the end of the image or images).

Follow the following steps to stop the text from wrapping:

1. Create your image and the text, as was done before.

2. Place the cursor where you want to stop wrapping text to the side of the image.
3. Either type <BR CLEAR= left> to stop flowing text until there are no more images aligned to the left margin.

   Or

   type <BR CLEAR = right> to stop flowing text until there are no more images aligned to the right margin.

   Or

   type <BR CLEAR = all> to stop flowing text until there are no more images on either margin.

### 9.11.5 Adding Space around an Image

You can actually put more space above or below the picture using the options of VSPACE and HSPACE attributes to add a buffer around your image.

Follow the following steps to add space around an image:

1. Type <IMG SRC =" image.location" where image.location indicates the location of your image.
2. Type HSPACE=x where x is the number of pixels of space to add on both the right and left sides of the image.
3. Type VSPACE=y where y is the number of pixels of space to add on both the top and bottom of the image.
4. Add other image attributes as desired and type the final >.

See, on the next page, how the spaced out image of the globe would look after giving the instructions as shown below.

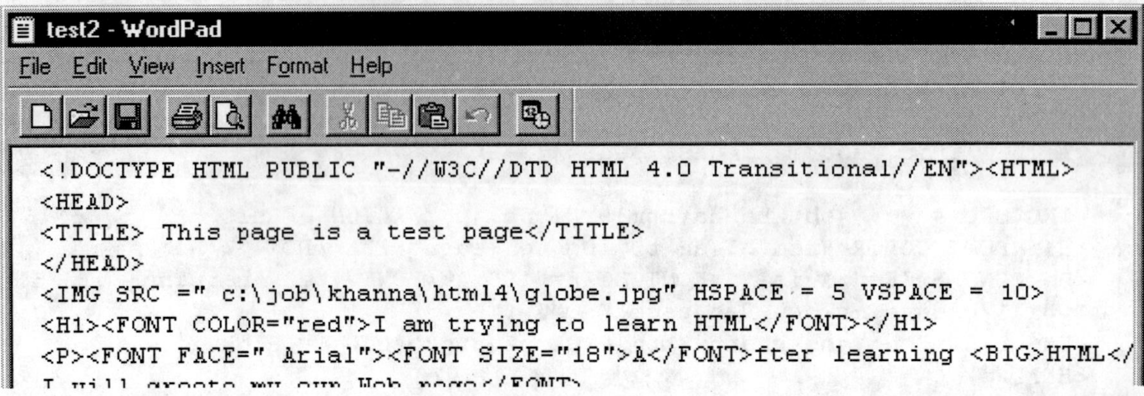


**Remember**

You don't have to add both HSPACE and VSPACE at the same time. If you just want to add space to one side of the image, use Photoshop to add blank space to that side, and skip HSPACE and VSPACE altogether. Microsoft Internet Explorer leaves 4 pixels to the right of the image, by default.

### 9.11.6 Scaling an image

Supposing you want to change the size of an image, you can do it by just specifying a new height and width in pixels. This way you can have large images on your page without long loading times.

Follow the following steps to scale an image:

1. Type <IMG SRC =" image.location where image.location is the location of the image.

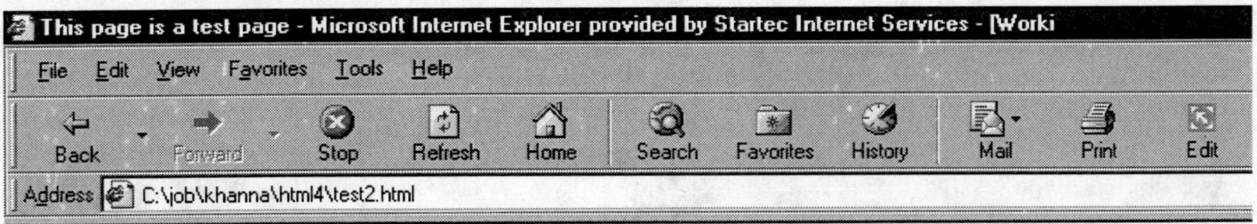

2. Type WIDTH=x HEIGHT=y where x and y are the desired width and height, respectively, in pixels, of your image.
3. Add any other image attributes as discussed earlier and then type the final >.

**Remember**

Do not increase the size of the image too much, it will take more time to load and will make the image messy. Don't use the WIDTH and HEIGHT extensions to reduce the image size. Instead, created a smaller image. It will load faster and look better..

### 9.11.7 Aligning Images

We had earlier wrapped the image to the left and right of the text. Now we will make use of the ALIGN attributes for aligning images with text. You can align an image in various ways to a single line in a paragraph. Follow the following steps to align an image with text:

1. Type <IMG SRC=" image.location" where image.location indicates the location of the image.
2. Type ALIGN= direction where direction is one of the attributes: texttop, top, middle, absmiddle, bottom, or absbottom.
3. Add other attributes as desired and then type the final >.
4. Type the text with which you wish to align the image.

In my example, I have taken the same globe and positioned it at various places with respect the text. See how it looks next. HTML text is shown on the next page.

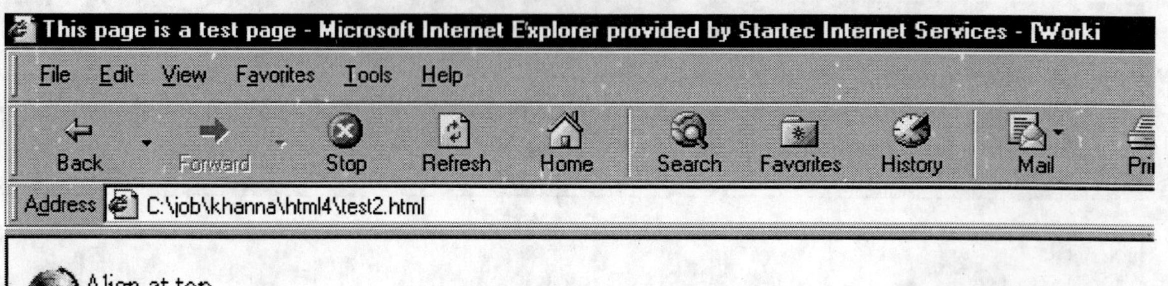


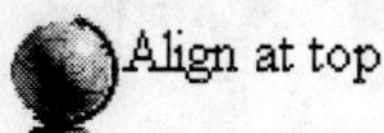


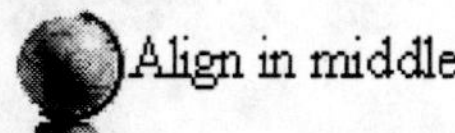


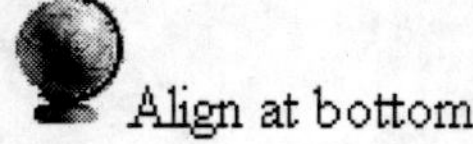


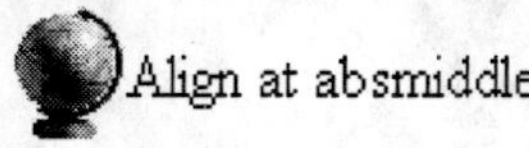


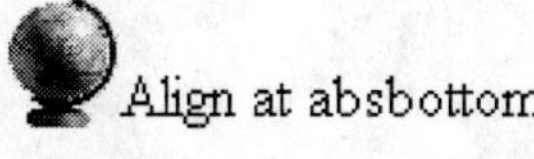


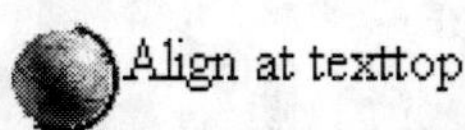


# I am trying to learn HTML

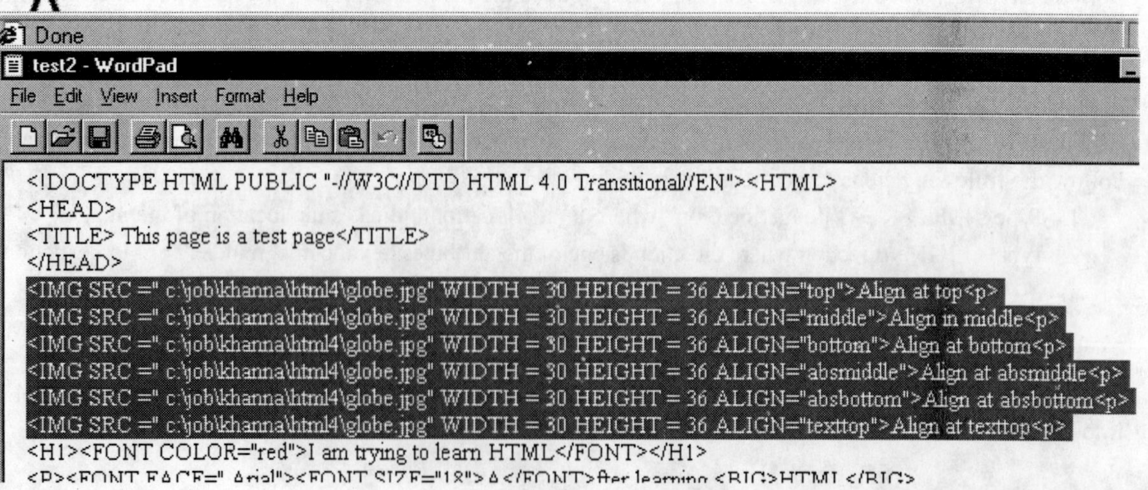


```
<!DOCTYPE HTML PUBLIC "-//W3C//DTD HTML 4.0 Transitional//EN"><HTML>
<HEAD>
<TITLE> This page is a test page</TITLE>
</HEAD>
<IMG SRC =" c:\job\khanna\html4\globe.jpg" WIDTH = 30 HEIGHT = 36 ALIGN="top">Align at top<p>
<IMG SRC =" c:\job\khanna\html4\globe.jpg" WIDTH = 30 HEIGHT = 36 ALIGN="middle">Align in middle<p>
<IMG SRC =" c:\job\khanna\html4\globe.jpg" WIDTH = 30 HEIGHT = 36 ALIGN="bottom">Align at bottom<p>
<IMG SRC =" c:\job\khanna\html4\globe.jpg" WIDTH = 30 HEIGHT = 36 ALIGN="absmiddle">Align at absmiddle<p>
<IMG SRC =" c:\job\khanna\html4\globe.jpg" WIDTH = 30 HEIGHT = 36 ALIGN="absbottom">Align at absbottom<p>
<IMG SRC =" c:\job\khanna\html4\globe.jpg" WIDTH = 30 HEIGHT = 36 ALIGN="texttop">Align at texttop<p>
<H1><FONT COLOR="red">I am trying to learn HTML</FONT></H1>
<P><FONT FACE=" Arial"><FONT SIZE="18">A</FONT>fter learning <BIG>HTML</BIG>
```

**Remember**

You may not align an image and wrap text around it at the same time. Internet Explorer has trouble with aligning more than one image on a line. The results are erratic. In addition, it treats texttop as top, absmiddle as middle and absbottom as Bottom.

### 9.11.8 Using a Banner

Banner is what you place at the top of the web site. It is reflected on all the pages of your site.

Follow the following steps to place a banner at the top of each page:

1. Create an image that measures approximately 450 x 100 pixels, as shown below. You can make it narrower and shorter, but you shouldn't make it much wider, otherwise it won't fit easily on most screens.
2. After converting it to indexed color, using the smallest bits/pixels ratio you can stand, save it as a GIF image.
3. Use this exact same image at the top of each of your Web pages, by typing <IMG SRC=" image.name">, where image.name is the location on the server of the banner.

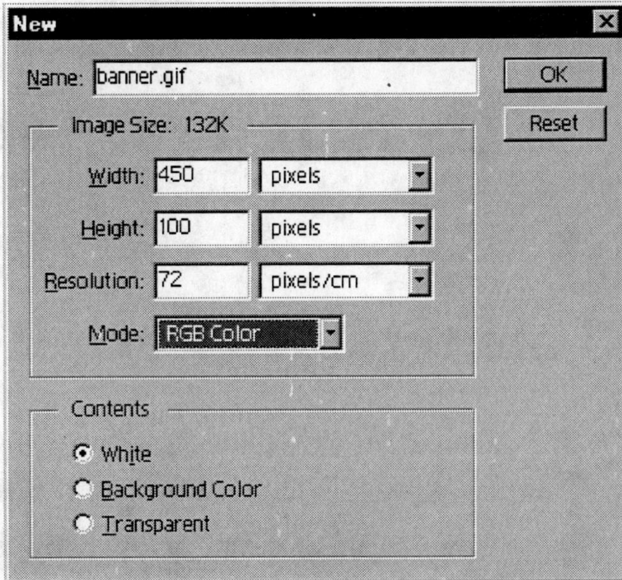


### 9.11.9 Adding Horizontal Rules

This graphic element is completely supported by the majority of the browsers is the horizontal rule. There are several attributes you can use to jazz up horizontal rules. Follow the following steps to insert a horizontal rule:

1. Type <HR where you want the rule to appear. The text that follows will appear in a new paragraph below the new line.
2. If desired, type SIZE=n, where n is the rule's height in pixels.
3. If desired, type WIDTH=w, where w is the width of the rule in pixels, or as a percentage of the document's width.
4. If desired, type ALIGN=direction, where direction refers to the way a rule should be aligned on the page; either left, right or center.
5. If desired, type NOSHADE to create a solid bar, with no shading.
6. Type the final > to complete the horizontal rule definition.

### 9.11.10 Using Alternate Text

It is possible that your browser may not support images at all. Or even if it does it is so slow that you wish that the graphics was not there at all. For this you can create a text that will appear even if the image, for whatever reason, does not.

Follow the following steps to offer alternate text when images don't appears:

1. Place the cursor where you want the image (or alternate text) to appear.
2. Type <IMG SRC = "image.ext", where image.ext is the location of the image.
3. Type ALT =".

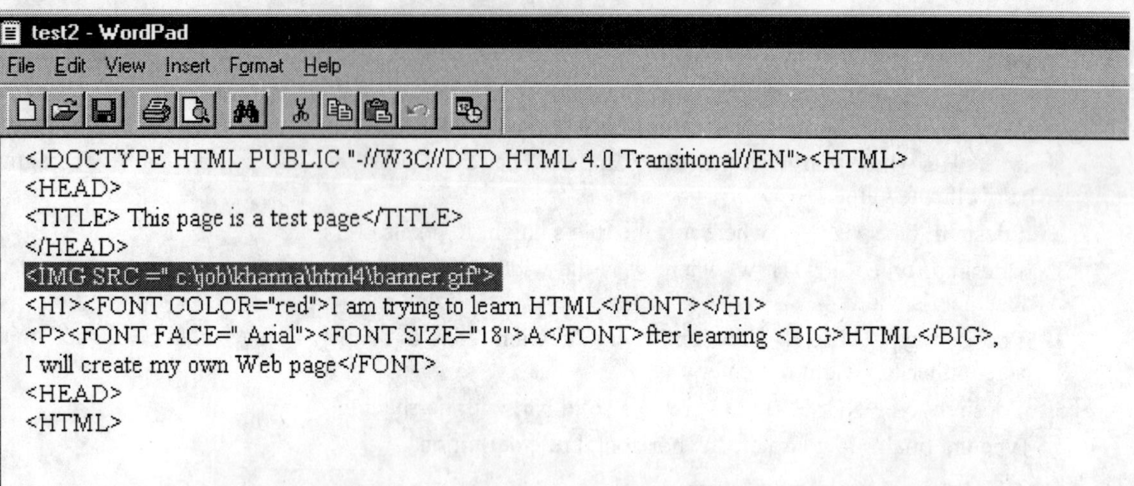


```
<!DOCTYPE HTML PUBLIC "-//W3C//DTD HTML 4.0 Transitional//EN"><HTML>
<HEAD>
<TITLE> This page is a test page</TITLE>
</HEAD>
<IMG SRC =" c:\job\khanna\html4\banner.gif">
<H1><FONT COLOR="red">I am trying to learn HTML</FONT></H1>
<P><FONT FACE=" Arial"><FONT SIZE="18">A</FONT>fter learning <BIG>HTML</BIG>,
I will create my own Web page</FONT>.
<HEAD>
<HTML>
```

4. Type the text that should appear if, for some reason, the image itself does not.
5. Type ">.

### 9.11.11 Linking to External Images

Linking allows you to link instead of actually copying the image. This is done specially in the cases where the image is of a very large size. You can create an icon of the image and place it in your page.

Follow the following steps to link a small icon to your larger image:

1. Place the cursor in your HTML text where you wish the icon to be placed.

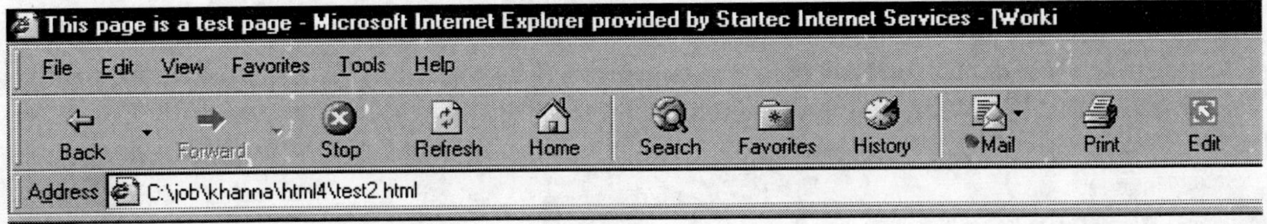


**This is put on top of page**

---

**I am trying to learn HTML**

After learning **HTML**, I will create my own Web page.

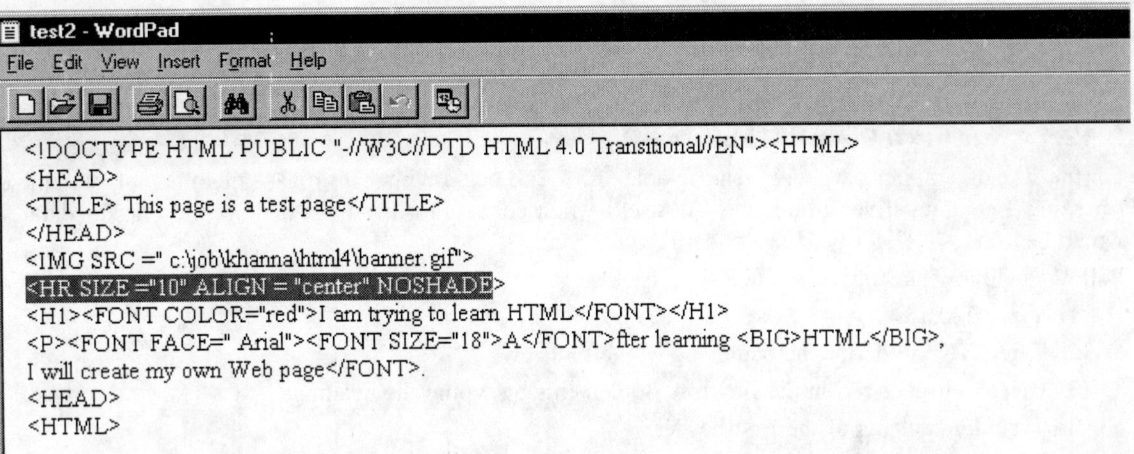


```
<!DOCTYPE HTML PUBLIC "-//W3C//DTD HTML 4.0 Transitional//EN"><HTML>
<HEAD>
<TITLE> This page is a test page</TITLE>
</HEAD>
<IMG SRC =" c:\job\khanna\html4\banner.gif">
<HR SIZE ="10" ALIGN = "center" NOSHADE>
<H1><FONT COLOR="red">I am trying to learn HTML</FONT></H1>
<P><FONT FACE=" Arial"><FONT SIZE="18">A</FONT>fter learning <BIG>HTML</BIG>,
I will create my own Web page</FONT>.
<HEAD>
<HTML>
```

2. Type <A HREF + image.location"> where image.location is the location of the full sized image on your screen.
3. Type <IMG SRC =" icon.location", where icon.location is the location of your icon.
4. If desired, type ALT =" alternate text" where alternate text is the text that should appear if, for some reason, the icon does not.
5. Type the final > of the icon definition.
6. Type </A> to complete the link to the full sized image.

### 9.11.12 Using Low Resolution Images

You can have reference to both high and low resolution versions of your image so that the low resolution image loads quickly and keeps the visitor's interest while the high resolution version impresses your visitors, once it loads in.

Follow the following steps to use a low resolution version of an image:

1. Create a low resolution version of your image using Photoshop or any other image editing program.
2. Place the cursor where you want the full resolution image to appear.
3. Type <IMG SRC = "image.gif", where image.gif is the location on the server of the high resolution image.
4. Type LOWSRC = "imagelow.gif", where imagelow.gif is the location on the server of the low resolution image.
5. Type HEIGHT=x WIDTH=y, where x and y are the height and width in pixels, respectively of the original image. If you do not specify these values, browsers use the size of the low resolution image for both images.
6. If desired, type ALT="substitute text", where substitute text is the text that will appear if the visitor can't view images with their browser.
7. Type the final >.

## 9.12 Working with Tables

As we all know Tables are a way of representing the data in the tabular form which not only is attractive to look at but it also easy to understand when read by the user. Though you can create tables in HTML but the method somehow is not very easy and the result much below the standard of most of the word processing and desk top publishing software.

The tables are divided into horizontal rows and vertical columns. It is this beauty of dividing the page section which gives the page a decent look.

Let us see what we can do with the tables in HTML.

### 9.12.1 Creating a Simple Table

For the sake of simplicity we will create a table of 2 x 2 to begin with. This means that the table will have 2 rows and 2 columns. Even in this we will use the first column for headings and second one for data. We would be using <TH> for headings and <TD> for data.

Follow the following steps to create a simple table:

1. Type <TABLE>.
2. Type <TR> to define the beginning of the first row.
3. Create a header cell in the first row of elements by typing the headings.
4. Type the contents of the first header.
5. Create a regular cell after the header.
6. Type the contents of the regular cell.
7. Repeat steps 2-6 for each row.
8. To finish the table, type </TABLE>.

It may not have been very clear unless you look at it practically. For this we will go back to our old example and create a table in it. Here I am using the marks received by the student in various subjects. Look at the text which has been typed in the HTML and its result in the browser.

**Remember**

If you want you can close each cell with </TH> or </TD>. Close each row with a </TR>. But, these tags are all optional.

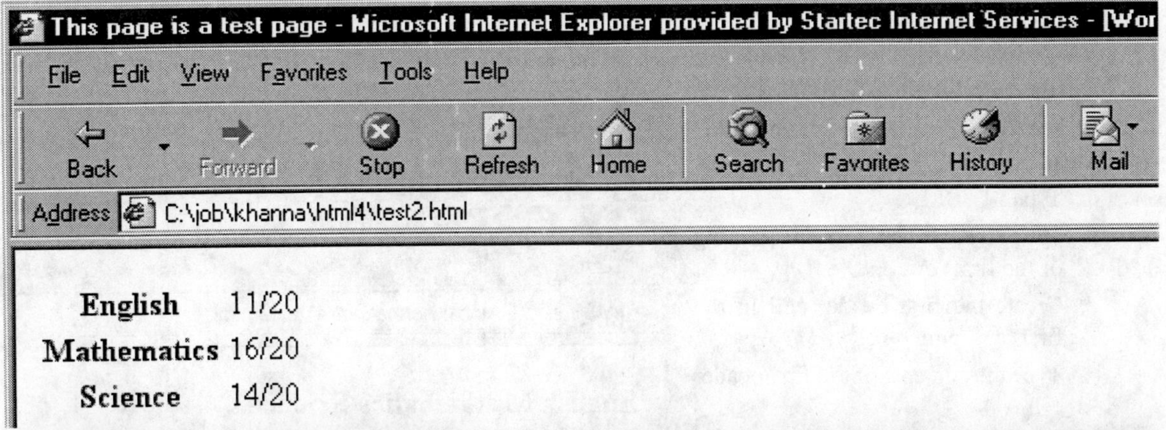


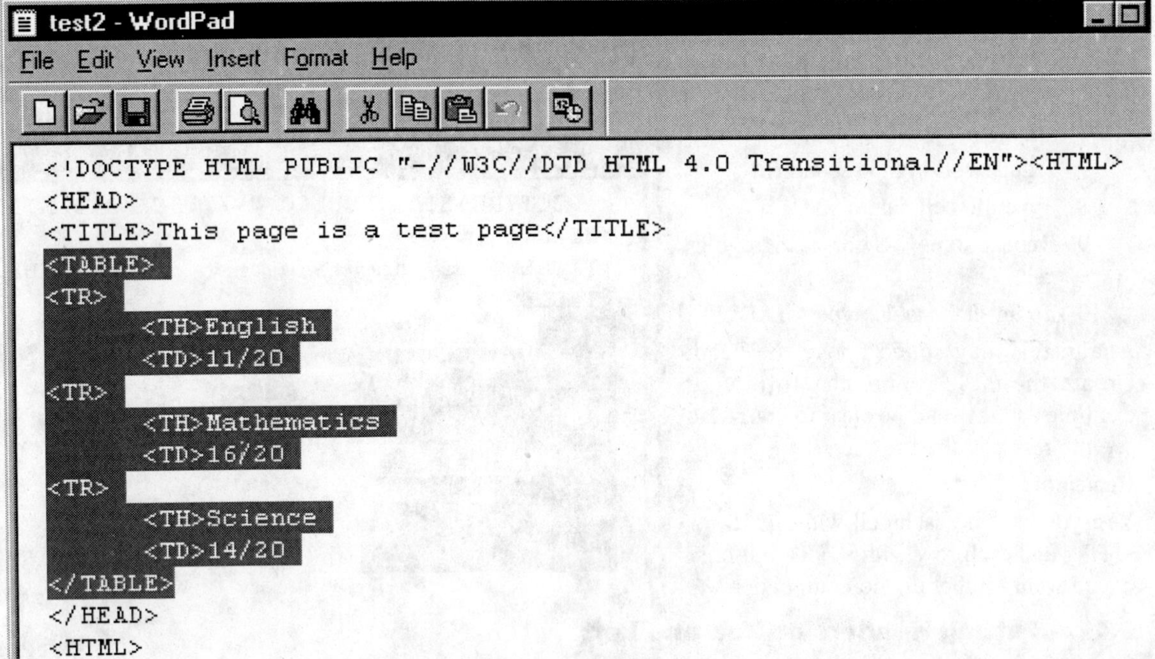


### 9.12.2 Changing a Table's Width and Height

The table created in the above example looks okay but is somewhat crumbersome. So let us increase its height and width to make it more readable. For this we will use the WIDTH and HEIGHT attributes to resize the whole table.

Follow the following steps to change a table's size:

Within the initial TABLE tag, type WIDTH=x HEIGHT =y, where *x* and y are either absolute values in pixels for the height and width of the table.

**Remember**

If the table is too small for the data, the browser will just ignore you. WIDTH is a standard of HTML 4, HEIGHT is not. However, the major browsers recognize both attributes. If the table is narrower than the window, you can center it by adding ALIGN=center to the TABLE tag.

### 9.12.3 Putting Headers

Earlier in our example we had put the headings on the left hand side of the marks. Let us now put them on the top and call them headers.

Follow the following steps to create a table with header:

1. Type <TABLE>.
2. Type <TR> to define the beginning of the first row.
3. Create the first header cell in the first by typing <TH>.
4. Type the contents of the first header cell.
5. Repeat steps 3-4 for each header cell.
6. Type <TR> to begin the second row.
7. Type <TD> to define the first regular cell in the second row.
8. Type the cell data.
9. Repeat steps 7-8 for each regular cell.
10. To finish the table, type </TABLE>.

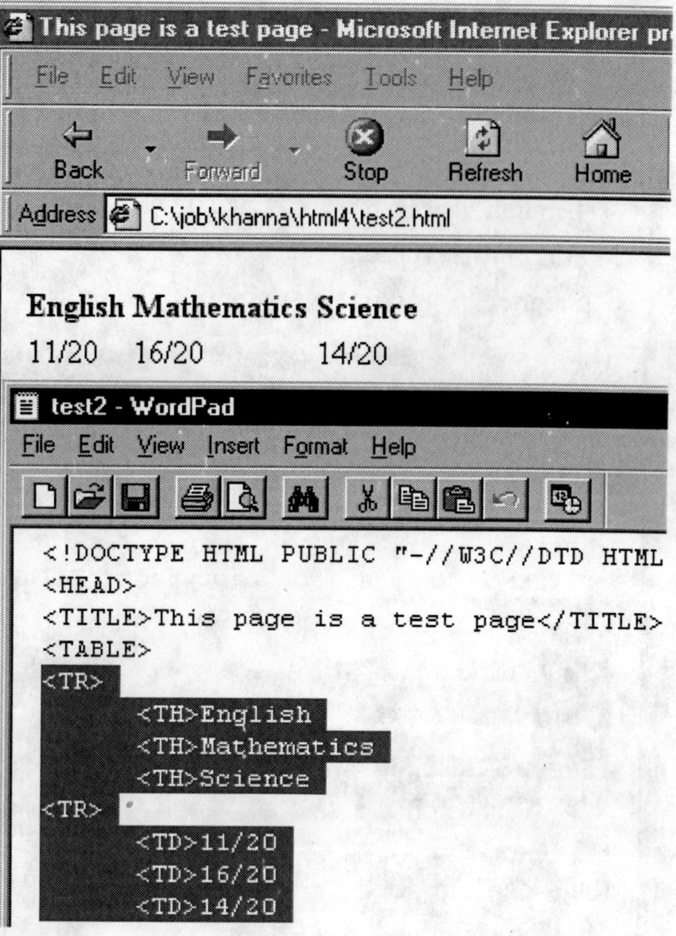


Again, this may sound above the head. Create the table seeing the following example and it would be clear to you. Also see the result in the browser.

**Remember**

Yes, you can end each cell with </TH> or </TD> and each row with </TR> but only if you want to, there is no compulsion.

### 9.12.4 Putting Headers on Top and Left

First we put the headings on the left and then we put them on the top. Let us now put them on both sides, i.e., both left and top.

Follow the following steps to create a table with header cells on top and down the left side:

1. Type <TABLE>.
2. Type <TR> to define the beginning of the first row.
3. Create the empty cell in the top left corner by typing <TD><BR>
4. Create a header cell by typing **<TH>cell contents** where cell contents is the data of the cell.
5. Repeat step 4 for each header cell in the first row.
6. Type <TR> to begin the second row.
7. To define the first header on the left side, type **<TH>cell contents**, where cell contents is the data of the cell.

8. To create a regular cell after the header cell in the second row, type **<TD>cell contents**, where cell contents is the data that the cell should contain.
9. Repeat step 8 for each remaining regular cell in the row.
10. Repeat steps 6-9 for each remaining row.
11. To finish the table, type </TABLE>.

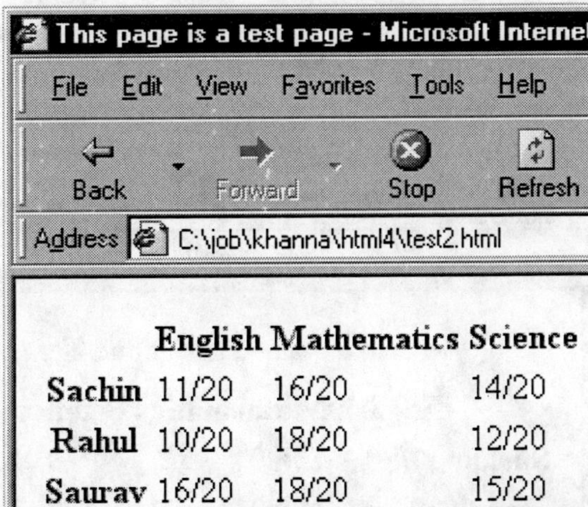


I know it is very difficult to understand this without the example. Follow the example given on the next page and then try to follow these steps to understand it better. Also don't forget to see the result in the browser.

### 9.12.5 Adding a caption

We have created a table but have not named it. For this we need a tag called CAPTION which lets us attach a descriptive title to our table.

Follow the following steps to create a caption

1. Directly after the initial <TABLE> tag, but not inside any row or cell tags, type <CAPTION.
2. If desired, type ALIGN=direction, where direction is either top, bottom, left, or right.
3. Type the final >.
4. Type the caption for the table which is taken as the heading of the table.
5. End with typing </CAPTION>.

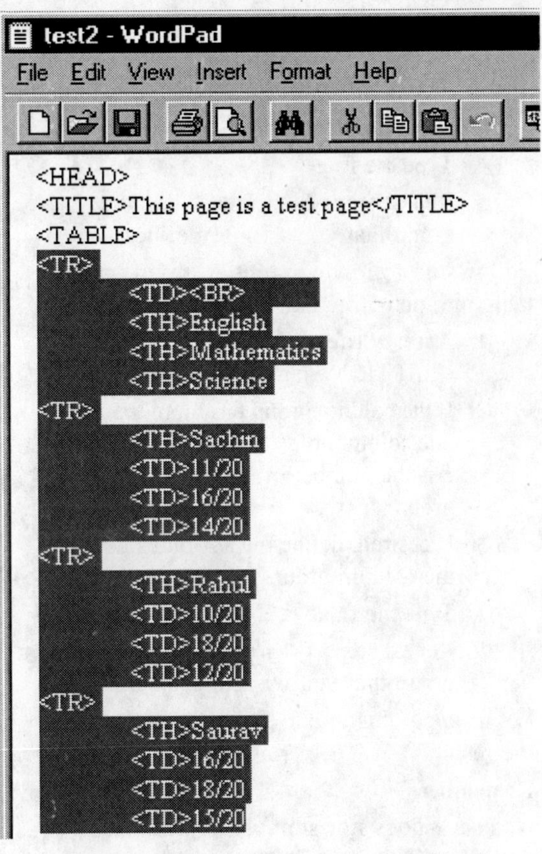


Let us put one in our example and see the result shown below. The HTML text is shown on the next page.

**Remember**

There is no way to place the caption at the bottom left or bottom right. Netscape only supports the top and bottom values for ALIGN and not right or left.

### 9.12.6 Dividing Table into Columns

In HTML you work with two kinds of column groups: Structural and Non-structural. In the case of structural you can control where to put dividing lines, or rules, etc. In the second you can't. However, both allow you to apply formatting to an entire column (or groups of columns) of cells all at once.

Follow the following steps to divide a table into structural column groups:

1. After the <TABLE> and <CAPTION> tags, type <COLGROUP. You will read about <CAPTION>, a little later.
2. If the column group has more than one column, type SPAN=n, where *n* is the number of columns in the group.

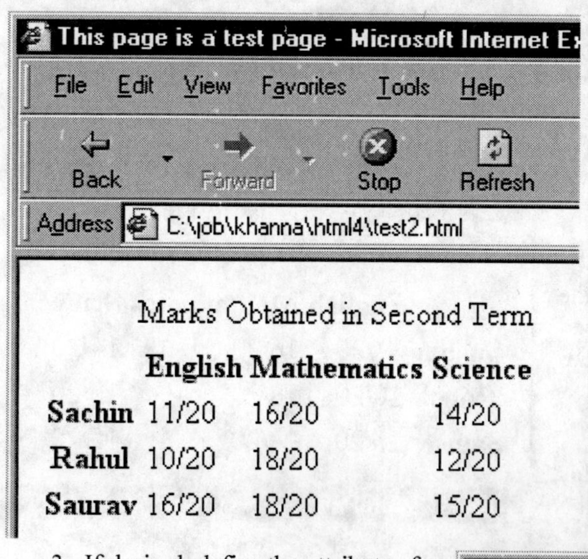


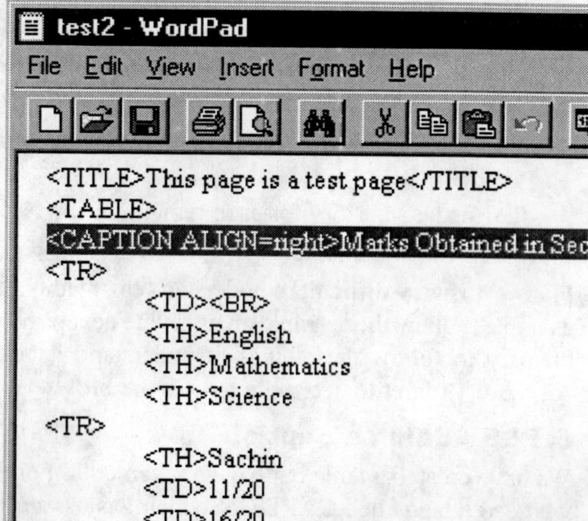


3. If desired, define the attributes for the column group.
4. Type the final >.
5. Repeat steps 1-4 for each column group that you wish to define.

Follow the following steps to divide a table into non-structural column groups:

1. After the <TABLE> and <CAPTION> tags, type <COL.
2. If the column group has more than one column, type SPAN=n, where *n* is the number of columns in the group.
3. If desired, define the attributes for the column group.
4. Type the final >.
5. Repeat steps 1-4 for each column group that you wish to define.

Let us apply this to our example and see the result.

**Remember**

Netscape does not support any one of these. Use COLGROUP when you want to determine where dividing lines (rules) should go. Use COL for everything but deciding where dividing lines go. If the column group contains only one column, you don't need to use the SPAN attribute. Its default is 1.

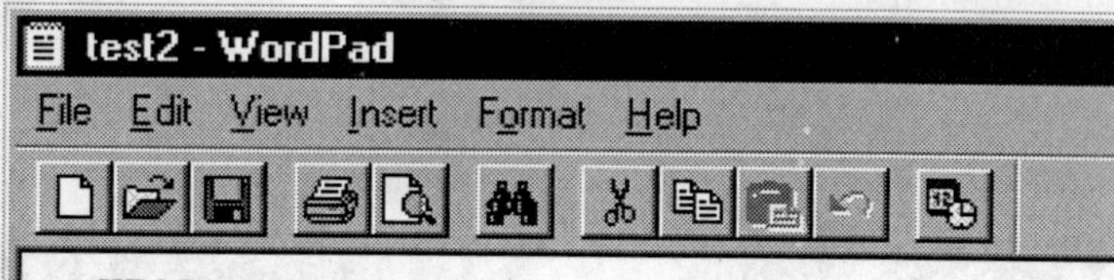

## 9.13 Working with Forms

Forms are used to get information from the visitors of your site. There are two basic parts of a form: the structure or shell, that consists of fields, labels, and buttons that the visitor sees on a page and hopefully fills out, and the processing script that takes that information and converts it into a format that you can read or tally.

For constructing a form's shell you can create text boxes, special password boxes, radio buttons, check boxes, drop-down menus, larger text areas, and even clickable images. You will give each element a name that will serve as a label to identify the data once it is processed. Processing the data from a form is a bit more complicated. Before I go any further let me tell you something about the CGI script first.

### 9.13.1 CGI Script

CGI, which stands for Common Gateway Interface, is simply a standardized way for sending information between the server and the script. So, to resume, a CGI script is a program (usually written in a programming language called Perl) that communicates with the server in a standard (CGI-like) way. Each element on your form will have a name and a value associated with it. The name identifies the data that is being sent. It might be something like visitor-name. The value is the data; and can either come from you, the Web page designer, or from the visitor who types it in a field.

When a visitor clicks the submit button or an active image, the name-value pair of each form element is sent to the server. The CGI script takes all the name-value pairs and separates them out into something a real human can read and understand.

There are two ways to send information to the server: GET and POST.

The GET method appends the name-value pairs to the end of the URL. This information is then passed to the QUERY_STRING variable. The CGI script must then breaks down the QUERY_STRING environment variable to analyze the incoming data. The principal disadvantage of the GET method is that the amount of data you can retrieve is limited. Its chief advantage is that you can create a link that accesses a CGI script.

The POST method sends a data file with the name-value pairs to the server's standard input, together with the Content Type and the Content Length in bytes. The CGI script then takes the data from standard input and analyzes it. The principal advantage of this method is that it has no size limit.

If you want to make a link to a CGI script, use GET. If you're worried that the data will be truncated, use POST. The most important thing is that the CGI script that you use knows how to parse information gathered with the method that you choose.

### 9.13.2 Security

You must know that GGI scripts can leave your server wide open to invaders. That's one reason many ISPs do not allow their users to use CGI scripts. If your ISP does allow you to run CGI-scripts, you should still read up on security issues. If your ISP okays your use of CGI scripts, your next step is to get your hands on one. If you are a programmer, you can write your own. If not, you can find scripts on the Web and adapt them for your own use.

Perl is the most common language used for CGI scripts, partly because it's easily ported from one platform to another, partly because it's great for massaging data into understandable information. You can use other programming languages, like C++, Visual Basic, or even AppleScript to create CGI scripts. One extra nice thing about Perl programmers is that they like to share. You can find tons of ready-to-use CGI scripts written in Perl all over the Web.

### 9.13.3 Getting a Script

Whether you've written your own script or are using someone else's, you'll have to do a couple of things to get it ready for use with your form.

If you're using a Perl script that you've downloaded from someone else, you'll have to open it up and see what variables and path names it uses. You will have to change these to reflect your particular situation.

The next step is to copy the script to the server, generally with an FTP program like Fetch or WS-FTP. Some servers require that all CGI scripts be located in the cgi-bin directory. Others provide a personal cgi-bin directory for each user. Still others let you store CGI scripts wherever you want, as long as you add a particular extension to them for identification. You'll have to ask your ISP. If your page is on a Unix server, you will have to use chmod to make the CGI script accessible and executable.

So you've got your CGI script on your server, ready to go. The only thing left is to add it to your form, so lets do it.

### 9.13.4 Creating a form

Form has 3 important parts:

FORM tag, which includes the URL of the CGI script that will process the form;

Form elements, like fields and menus;

Submit button, which sends the data to the CGI script on the server.

Follow the following steps to create a form:

1. Type <FORM.
2. Type METHOD=method, where method is either GET or POST.
3. Type ACTION="script.url"> where script.url is the location on the server of the CGI script that will run when the form is submitted.
4. Create the form's contents.
5. Type </FORM> to complete the form.

Let us use this information to create a form and fill the information as shown in the HTML text shown below and see it in the browser.

**Remember**

In order for your visitor to send you the information on the form, you'll need either a submit button (if your form contains fields, buttons, and other elements that your visitors will fill in) or an active image. You can use tables to layout your form elements more precisely.

### 9.13.5 Creating menus

Creating menus for your visitors makes it easy for them to enter information or provide criteria for a search. Follow the following steps to create menus:

1. In the FORM area of your HTML document, type the introductory text for your menu, like heading of the menu etc.
2. Type <SELECT.
3. Type NAME="name", where name will identify the data collected from the menu when it is sent to the server.
4. Type SIZE="n", where n represents the number of options that should be initially visible in the menu.
5. If desired, type MULTIPLE to allow your visitor to select more than one menu option.
6. Type >
7. Type <OPTION.
8. Type SELECTED if you want the option to be selected by default.
9. Type VALUE="value", where value specifies the data that will be sent to the server when the option is selected.

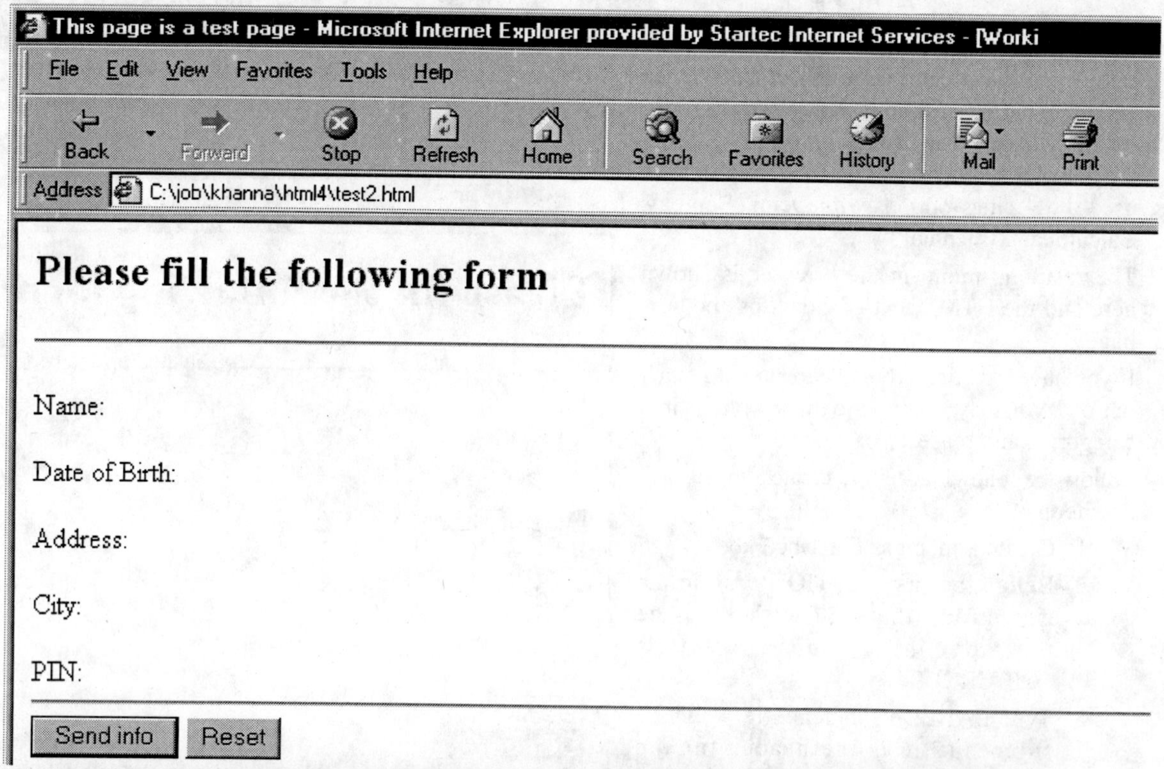

This page is a test page - Microsoft Internet Explorer provided by Startec Internet Services - [Worki

File Edit View Favorites Tools Help

Back Forward Stop Refresh Home Search Favorites History Mail Print

Address C:\job\khanna\html4\test2.html

## Please fill the following form

Name:

Date of Birth:

Address:

City:

PIN:

Send info Reset

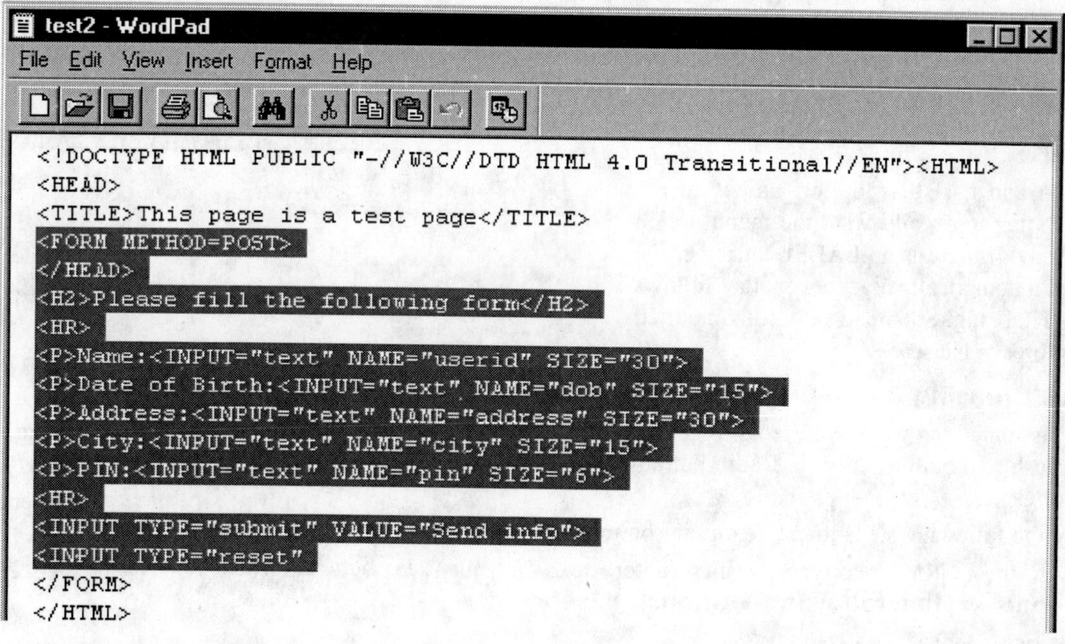
test2 - WordPad

File Edit View Insert Format Help

```
<!DOCTYPE HTML PUBLIC "-//W3C//DTD HTML 4.0 Transitional//EN"><HTML>
<HEAD>
<TITLE>This page is a test page</TITLE>
<FORM METHOD=POST>
</HEAD>
<H2>Please fill the following form</H2>
<HR>
<P>Name:<INPUT="text" NAME="userid" SIZE="30">
<P>Date of Birth:<INPUT="text" NAME="dob" SIZE="15">
<P>Address:<INPUT="text" NAME="address" SIZE="30">
<P>City:<INPUT="text" NAME="city" SIZE="15">
<P>PIN:<INPUT="text" NAME="pin" SIZE="6">
<HR>
<INPUT TYPE="submit" VALUE="Send info">
<INPUT TYPE="reset"
</FORM>
</HTML>
```

10. Type >.
11. Type the option name as you wish it to appear in the menu.

12. Repeat steps 7-11 for each option.
13. Type </SELECT>

Let us use this menu option in our form made earlier. What we will do is to add various cities for the visitor to the site to choose from. From the text of the HTML, you will notice that I have used the 4 cities options with Delhi, Bombay, Calcutta and Chennai.

The resultant menu in the browser is shown here and the HTML text is shown on the next page.

If you have a particularly large menu with many options, you may want to group the options into categories and place them in submenus.

Follow the following steps to create a menu with submenus:

1. Create a menu as described above.
2. Before the first <OPTION> tag in the first group that you wish to place together in a submenu, type <OPTGROUP.
3. Type LABEL="submenutitle">, where submenutitle is the header for the submenu.
4. After the last <OPTION> tag in the group, type </OPTGROUP>.
5. Repeat steps 2-4 for each submenu.

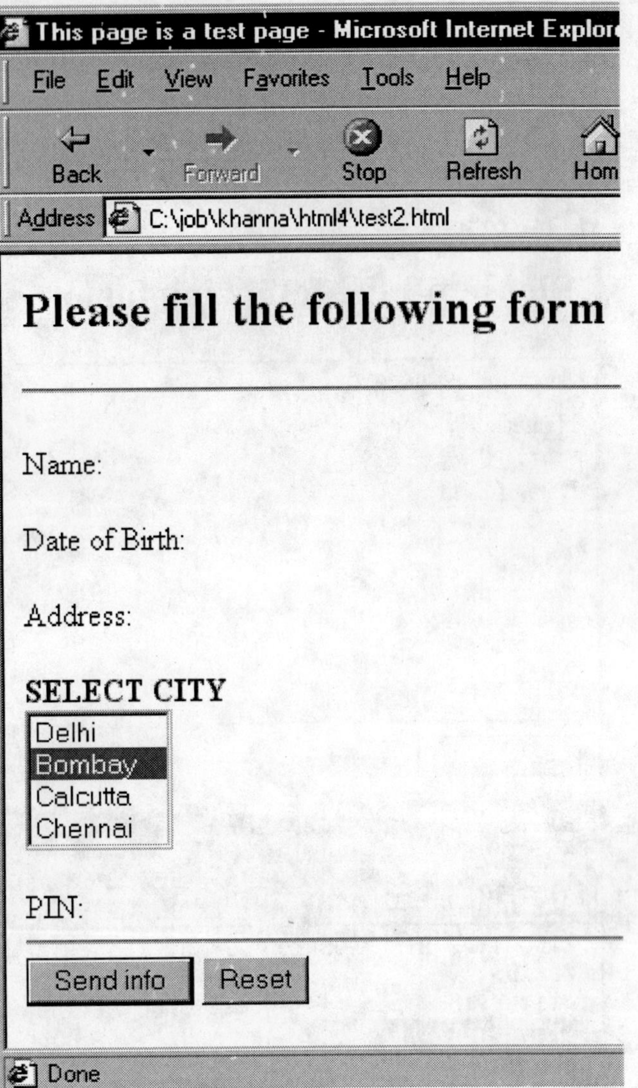


**Remember**

You can add LABEL="option_name" to the OPTION tag to specify what the menu option should say. If there is no LABEL attribute, the browser automatically uses the text that follows the OPTION tag. Submenus are not supported by Explorer or Netscape.

### 9.13.6 Creating Radio Buttons

Button is something which you press to get result as you do on most of the push button machines. You can never push two buttons at once. Radio buttons on forms work the same way, except you would not get a Pepsi or Coke.

Follow the following steps to create a radio button:

1. In the FORM area, type the introductory text for your radio buttons, which may be like **Select one of the following options**.
2. Type <INPUT TYPE="radio".
3. Type NAME="radioset", where radioset identifies each radio button in a particular set. Only one radio button in a set can be checked by a visitor.

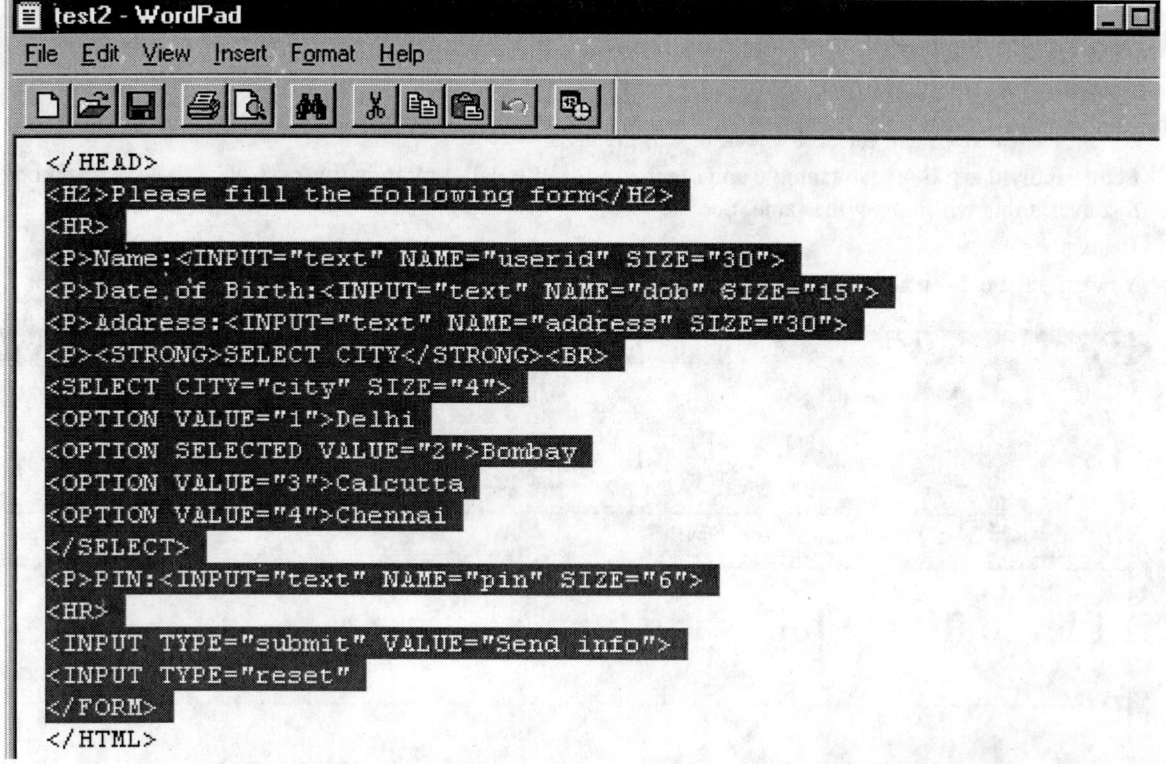


```
</HEAD>
<H2>Please fill the following form</H2>
<HR>
<P>Name:<INPUT="text" NAME="userid" SIZE="30">
<P>Date of Birth:<INPUT="text" NAME="dob" SIZE="15">
<P>Address:<INPUT="text" NAME="address" SIZE="30">
<P><STRONG>SELECT CITY</STRONG><BR>
<SELECT CITY="city" SIZE="4">
<OPTION VALUE="1">Delhi
<OPTION SELECTED VALUE="2">Bombay
<OPTION VALUE="3">Calcutta
<OPTION VALUE="4">Chennai
</SELECT>
<P>PIN:<INPUT="text" NAME="pin" SIZE="6">
<HR>
<INPUT TYPE="submit" VALUE="Send info">
<INPUT TYPE="reset"
</FORM>
</HTML>
```

4. You must define a value for each radio button. Type VALUE="data", where data is the text that will be sent to the server if the radio button is pressed or checked.
5. If desired, type PRESSED to make the radio button active by default when the page is opened.
6. Type the final >.
7. Type the text that identifies the radio button to the visitor.
8. Repeat steps 2-7 far each radio button in the set.

In the above example, instead of having the cities under the menu option, we can have them on the radio buttons. This is what has been used as can be seen in the HTML text shown on the next page. The effect of this in the browser can be seen below.

### 9.13.7 Creating Check Boxes

The main difference between a check box and a radio button is that while radio buttons can accept only one answer per set, a visitor can check as many check boxes in a set as they like. Like radio buttons, check boxes are linked by the value of the NAME attribute.

Follow the following steps to create check boxes:

1. In the FORM area of your HTML document, type the introductory text like **Select one or more of the following** for your check boxes.
2. Type <INPUT TYPE="checkbox". where checkbox is a single word.
3. Type NAME="title", where title is the word that identifies all of the check boxes in a particular set.
4. Type VALUE= "value" to define a value for each check box. The value will be sent to the server if the check box is checked.

5. Type CHECKED to make the check box checked by default when the page is opened. You (or the visitor) may check as many check boxes as desired.
6. Type > to complete the check box.
7. Type the text that identifies the check box to the user.
8. Repeat steps 2-7 for each check box in the set.

Let us apply this too on our example and see the result. Instead of radio in this case we will have checkbox, rest everything will remain the same. See the result on the next page and the HTML text also.

**Remember**

You can create a separate keyboard shortcut for each check box in a set.

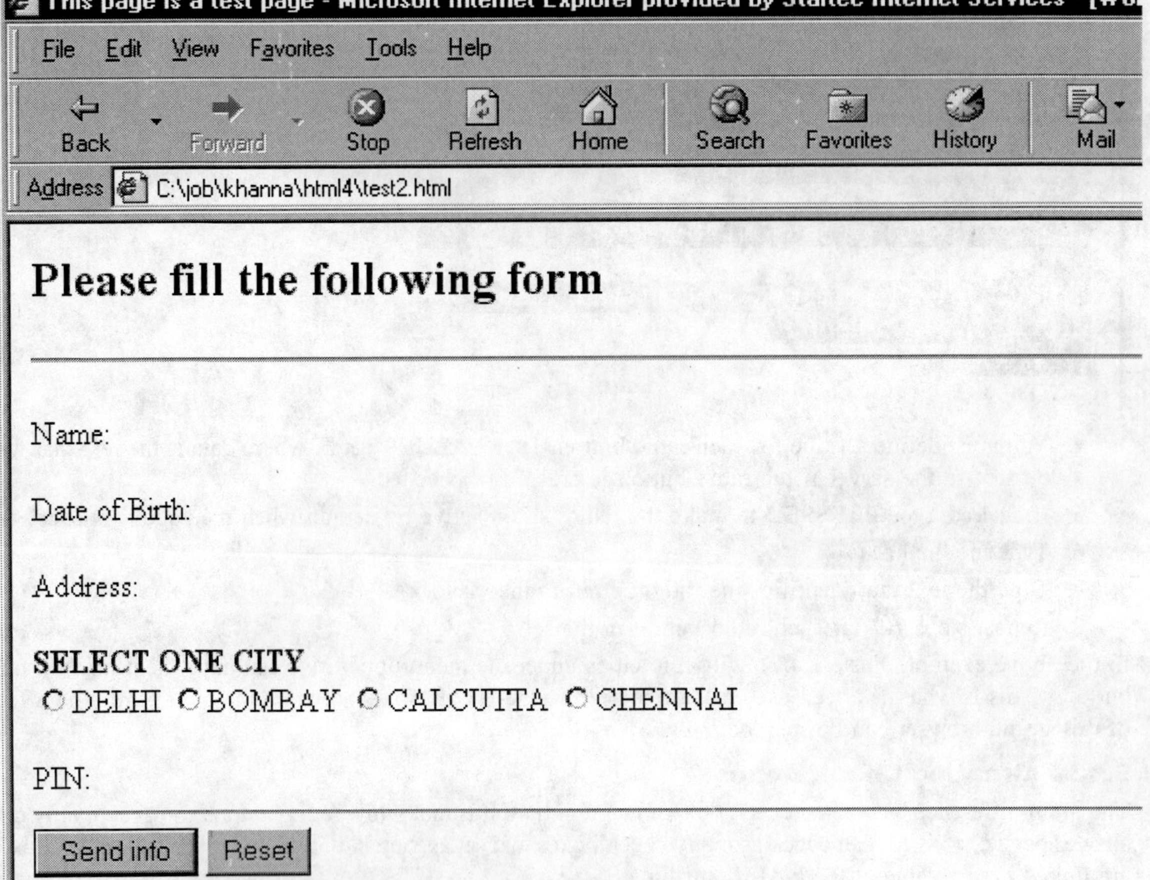


### 9.13.8 Creating Text Boxes

Text boxes are like forms only where you provide a box for the visitor to fill in the data like name, address, etc.

Follow the following steps to create a text box:

1. Inside the FORM area of your HTML document, type the title of the text box.
2. Type <INPUT TYPE="text".

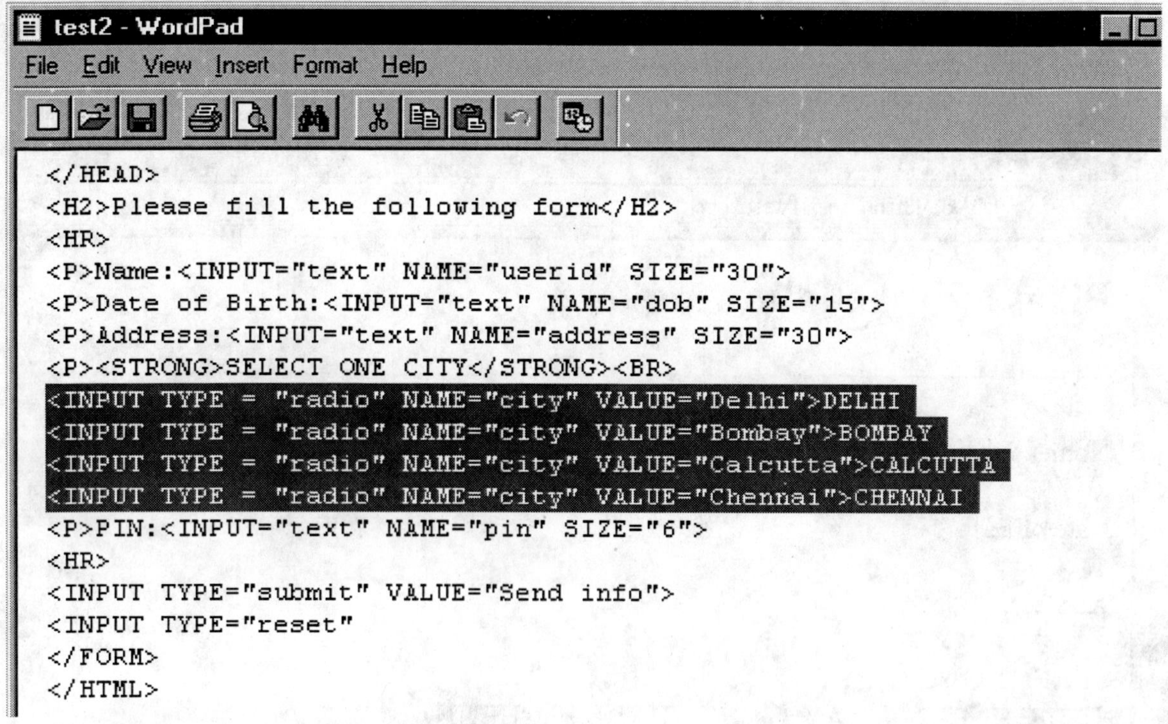

```
</HEAD>
<H2>Please fill the following form</H2>
<HR>
<P>Name:<INPUT="text" NAME="userid" SIZE="30">
<P>Date of Birth:<INPUT="text" NAME="dob" SIZE="15">
<P>Address:<INPUT="text" NAME="address" SIZE="30">
<P><STRONG>SELECT ONE CITY</STRONG><BR>
<INPUT TYPE = "radio" NAME="city" VALUE="Delhi">DELHI
<INPUT TYPE = "radio" NAME="city" VALUE="Bombay">BOMBAY
<INPUT TYPE = "radio" NAME="city" VALUE="Calcutta">CALCUTTA
<INPUT TYPE = "radio" NAME="city" VALUE="Chennai">CHENNAI
<P>PIN:<INPUT="text" NAME="pin" SIZE="6">
<HR>
<INPUT TYPE="submit" VALUE="Send info">
<INPUT TYPE="reset"
</FORM>
</HTML>
```

3. Type NAME="title", where title is the word that identifies the data entered in the text box when it is collected by the server.
4. If desired, define the size of the box on your form by typing SIZE="n", replacing n with the desired width of the box, measured in characters.
5. If you want you can even set the maximum number of characters that can be entered in the box by typing MAXLENGTH="n", where n is the desired maximum length in characters.
6. Finish the text box by typing a final >.

In the same example, now replace each option with INPUT TYPE to have the text boxes to be filled in by the visitor to the site. See the required HTML text below and its effect in the browser on the next page.

**Remember**

The default value for the SIZE attribute is 20. Visitors can add more text than fits in the text box, up to the value defined for MAXLENGTH.

### 9.13.9 Creating Larger Text Areas

Sometimes you have to give visitor a lot of room for typing in the information. Text areas may be as large as your page, and will expand as needed if the person enters more text than can fit in the display area.

Follow the following steps to create larger text areas:

1. In the FORM area of your HTML document, type the introductory text for your text area, if desired.
2. Type <TEXTAREA.
3. Type NAME="name" where name is the variable name you give to your text area. The name identifies the data when it is collected by the server.
4. If desired, type ROWS="n", where n is the height of the text area in rows. The default value is 4.

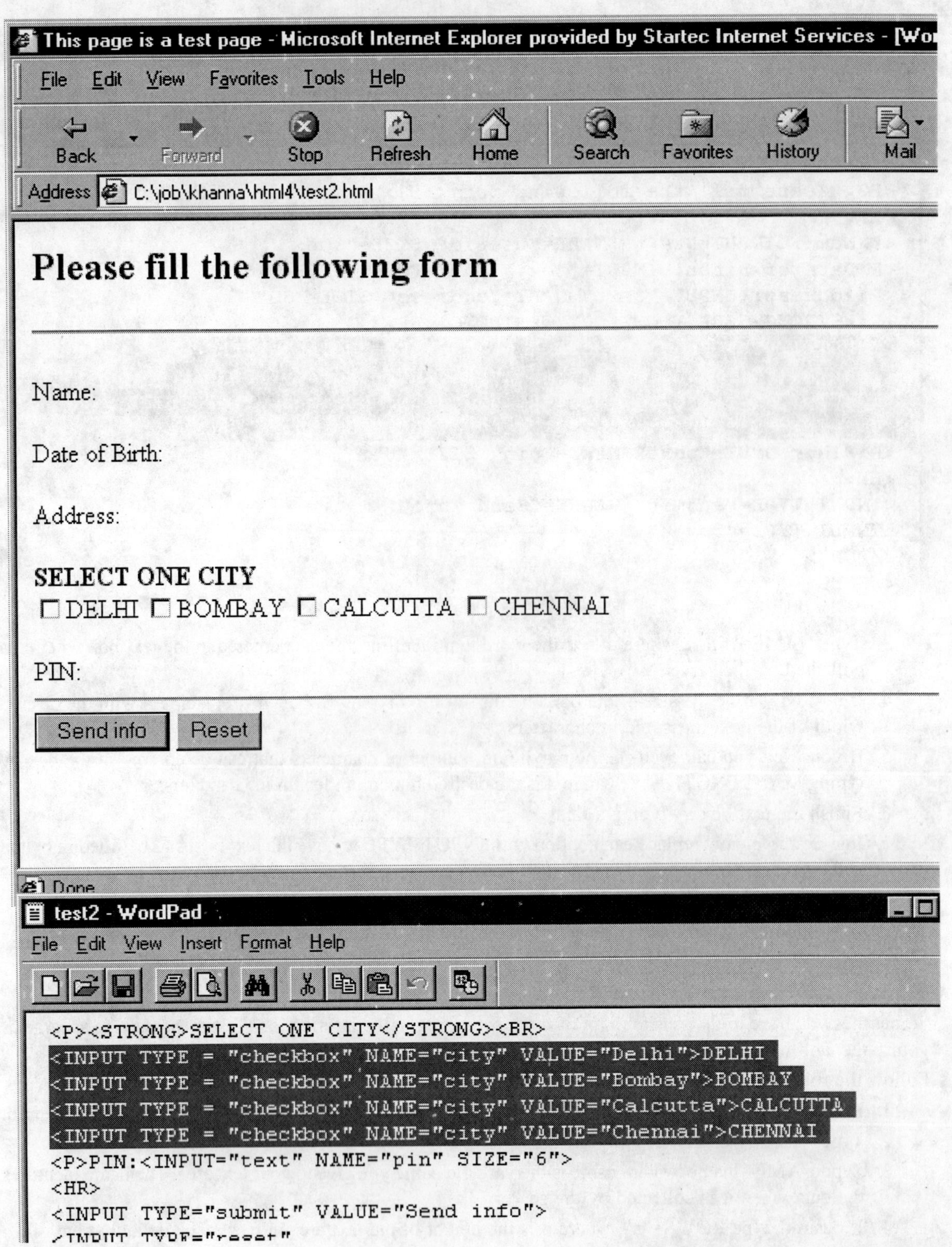

This page is a test page - Microsoft Internet Explorer provided by Startec Internet Services - [Wo
File Edit View Favorites Tools Help
Back Forward Stop Refresh Home Search Favorites History Mail
Address C:\job\khanna\html4\test2.html
Please fill the following form
Name:
Date of Birth:
Address:
SELECT ONE CITY
DELHI BOMBAY CALCUTTA CHENNAI
PIN:
Send info
Reset
Done
test2 - WordPad
File Edit View Insert Format Help
<P><STRONG>SELECT ONE CITY</STRONG><BR>
<INPUT TYPE = "checkbox" NAME="city" VALUE="Delhi">DELHI
<INPUT TYPE = "checkbox" NAME="city" VALUE="Bombay">BOMBAY
<INPUT TYPE = "checkbox" NAME="city" VALUE="Calcutta">CALCUTTA
<INPUT TYPE = "checkbox" NAME="city" VALUE="Chennai">CHENNAI
<P>PIN:<INPUT="text" NAME="pin" SIZE="6">
<HR>
<INPUT TYPE="submit" VALUE="Send info">
<INPUT TYPE="reset"

5. If desired, type COLS="n", where n is the width of the text area in characters. The default value is 40.
6. If desired, type WRAP so that when the visitor types the lines are automatically wrapped within the margins.
7. Type >.
8. Type the default text, if any, for the text area. You may not add any HTML coding here.
9. Type </TEXTAREA> to complete the text area.

Since the area for address is very small in our example, so we will create a larger text area block for the visitor to type out his address accordingly. I have used the area of 4 rows and 60 cols for filling in the data. See the HTML text below and resultant browser result on the next page.

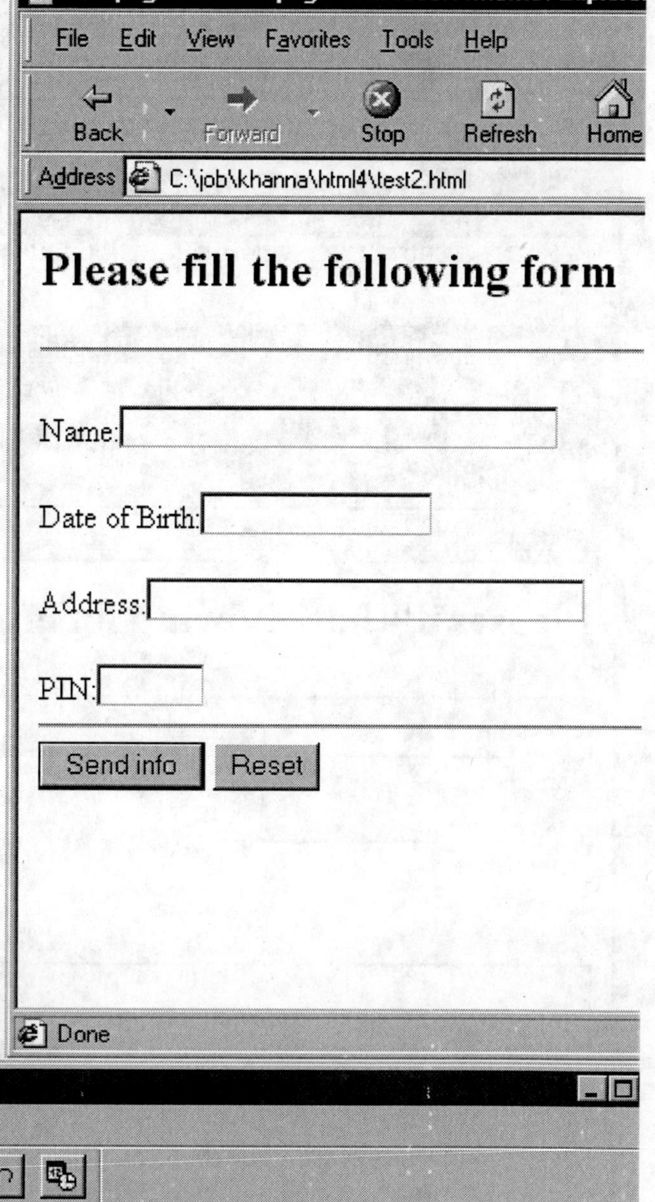


**Remember**

Visitors can enter up to 32,700 characters in a text area. Scroll bars will appear when necessary. Explorer automatically wraps text even without the nonstandard WRAP.

### 9.13.10 Creating Password Boxes

A password box is similar to a text box, but when the visitor types in it, the letters are hidden by bullets or asterisks.

Follow the following steps to create password entry boxes:

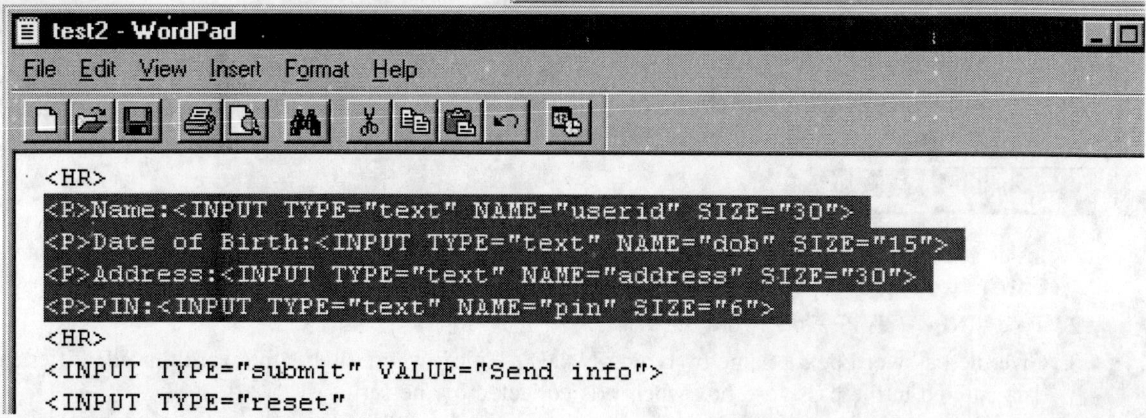

test2 - WordPad
File Edit View Insert Format Help
<P>Date of Birth:<INPUT TYPE="text" NAME="dob" SIZE="15">
<P>Address
<BR><TEXTAREA NAME="address" ROWS="4" COLS="60">
You can type here your answer....</TEXTAREA>
<P>PIN:<INPUT TYPE="text" NAME="pin" SIZE="6">
<HR>

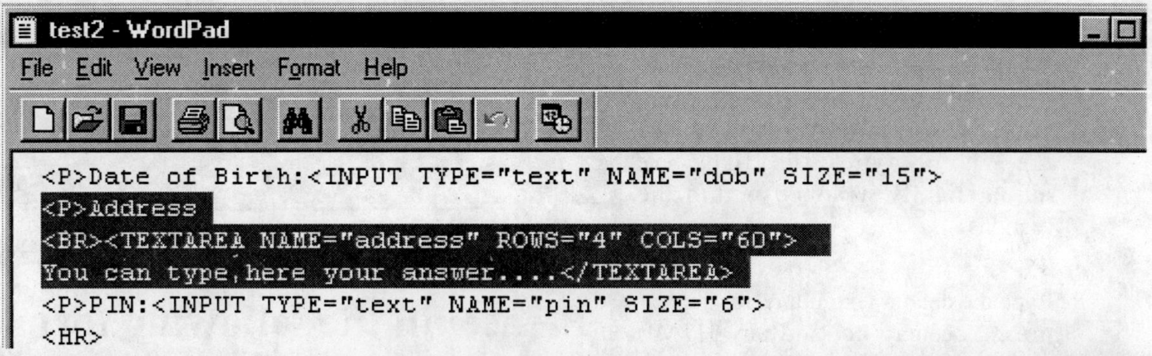

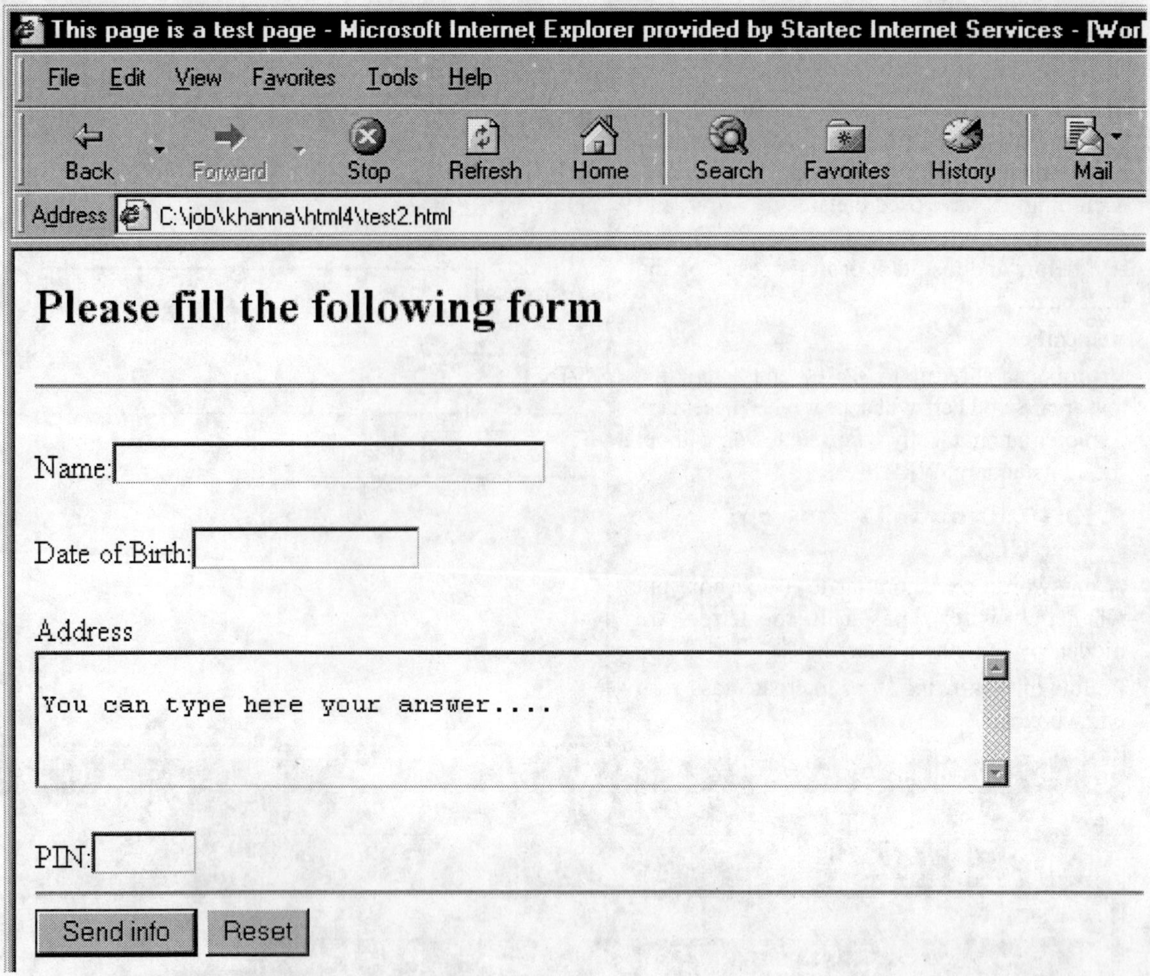

This page is a test page - Microsoft Internet Explorer provided by Startec Internet Services - [Wor
File Edit View Favorites Tools Help
Back
Forward
Stop
Refresh
Home
Search
Favorites
History
Mail
Address C:\job\khanna\html4\test2.html
Please fill the following form
Name:
Date of Birth:
Address
You can type here your answer....
PIN:
Send info
Reset

1. Inside the FORM area of your HTML document, type the title of the password box, for example, **Enter password**.
2. Type <INPUT TYPE="password".
3. Give the password box a name by typing NAME="title", where title is the word that identifies the data entered in the password box when it is collected by the server.

4. If desired, define the size of the box on your form by typing SIZE="n", replacing n with the desired width of the box, measured in characters.
5. If desired, define the maximum number of characters that can be entered in the box by typing MAXLENGTH="n", replacing n with the desired value.
6. Finish the text box by typing a final >.

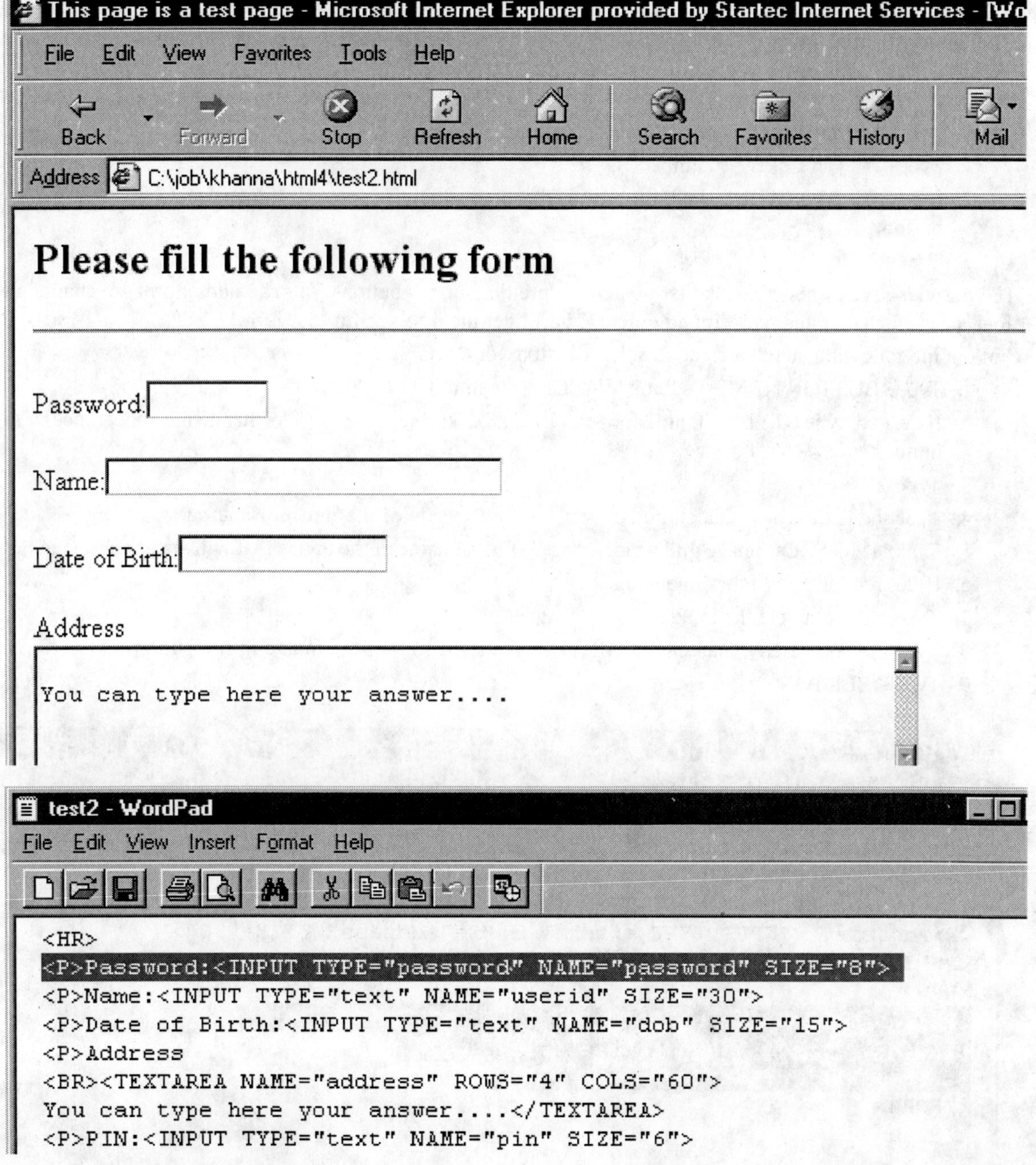


```
<HR>
<P>Password:<INPUT TYPE="password" NAME="password" SIZE="8">
<P>Name:<INPUT TYPE="text" NAME="userid" SIZE="30">
<P>Date of Birth:<INPUT TYPE="text" NAME="dob" SIZE="15">
<P>Address
<BR><TEXTAREA NAME="address" ROWS="4" COLS="60">
You can type here your answer....</TEXTAREA>
<P>PIN:<INPUT TYPE="text" NAME="pin" SIZE="6">
```

We would also like to put a password in our form. So just add password in the form before the name. See how the HTML text would change, as shown on the next page. The resultant effect as seen in the browser is shown below.

**Remember**

Since the data is not encrypted when the information is sent to the server, moderately experienced crackers can discover the password without much trouble.

### 9.13.11 Submit Button

This button is used to send the information to the server by the visitor. You can create a submit button simply without an image or style information, or you can use HTML tags to make a button so gorgeous that your visitors won't be able to resist pressing it.

Follow the following steps to create a submit button:

1. Type <INPUT TYPE="submit".
2. If desired, type VALUE="submit message" where submit message is the text that will appear in the button.
3. Type the final >.

HTML adds several new tags that let you create prettier submit buttons You can add an image, change the font, or even change the background colour. That'll get them to submit that form!

Follow the following steps to create a submit button with an image

1. Type <BUTTON NAME="submit" VALUE="submit" TYPE="submit".
2. If desired, type STYLE="font: 24pt Arial Black; background: yellow" to change the appearance of the button text.
3. Type >
4. Type the text, if any, that should appear on the left side of the image in the button.
5. Type <IMG SRC="image.gif" where image.gif is the name of the image that will appear on the button.
6. If desired, add any other image attributes.
7. Type > to complete the image.
8. Type the text, if any, that should appear on the right side of the image in the button
9. Type </BUTTON>

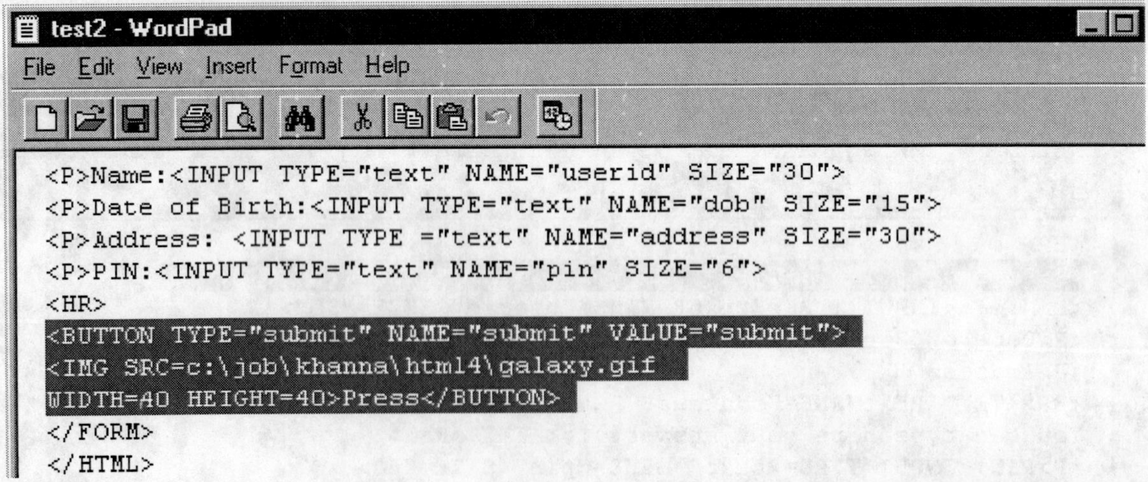

Let us put a button in our form too. I have used here the galaxy.gif for the image of the button and have asked visitor to press it to submit. See the text of the HTML and the its resultant effect in the browser below.

**Remember**

You can use the BUTTON tag to create a submit button without an image. Only Microsoft Internet Explorer supports the BUTTON tag.

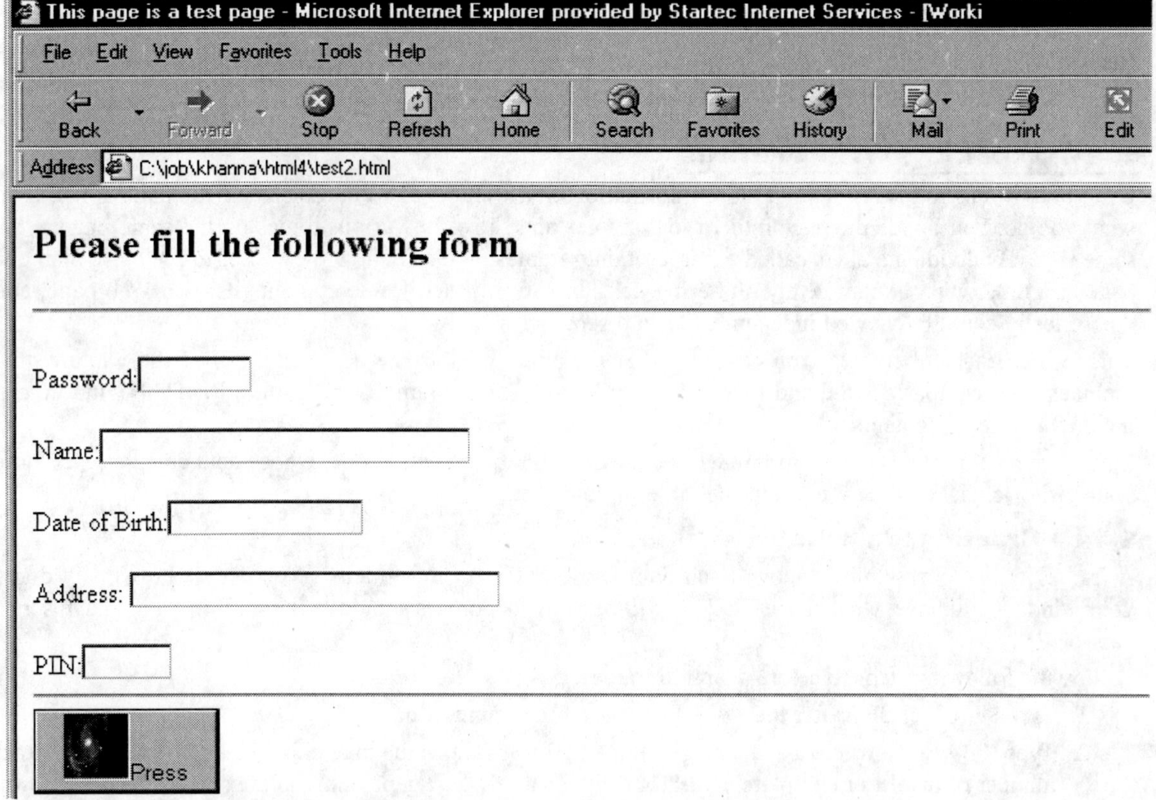


### 9.13.12 Resetting the Form

While filling up the form, it is very likely that the visitor may make a mistake which can of spelling, or second thought. You can give your visitors a reset button so that they can start over with a fresh form.

Follow the following steps to add a reset button:

1. Type <INPUT TYPE="reset".
2. If desired type VALUE= "reset message" where reset message is the text that appears in the button. The default reset message is Reset.
3. Type >.

With HTML 4 (and Explorer for the time being), you can add images, font choices, and even a background color to your reset button.

Follow the following steps to create a reset button with an image:

1. Type <BUTTON NAME="reset" VALUE="reset: TYPE="reset".
2. If desired, type STYLE="font: 24pt ArialBlack; background:yellow" to change the appearance of the button text.

3. Type >.
4. Type the text, if any, that should appear on the left side of the image in the button.
5. Type <IMG SRC="image.gif", where image.gifis the name of the image that will appear on the button.
6. If desired, add any other image attributes.
7. Type > to complete the image.
8. Type the text, if any, that should appear on the right side of the image in the button.
9. Type </BUTTON>.

**Remember**

You can also use the BUTTON tag to create a reset button without an image.

## 9.14 Working with Frames

Everybody wants to give more and more information on a web page. Well, the size of the page is fixed. So what you do. You divide the page into various frames and show the various topics on the same page at the same time. By dividing a page, called a frameset, into frames, you can allow the visitor to see more than one page at a time, without completely cluttering up their screen. Each frame contains its own Web page, and theoretically could be viewed independently in a separate window.

This is the beauty of frames. You can have a stationary banner frame across the top of the window that includes your company name and logo. Meanwhile, a dynamic frame on the left side of the window can include a table of contents.

Finally, the main frame of the window will be devoted to the contents frame, whose data changes each time your visitor clicks on a new topic in the table of contents.

### 9.14.1 Creating Frameset

A frameset is a door within window. Each door shows different information. You decide how many doors your window will have, what size each door will be, how its borders should look and if it should have scroll bars or not.

Follow the following steps to create a simple frameset:

1. Type <FRAMESET after the </HEAD> tag on the frameset page.
2. Type ROWS= "a where a is the height of the first row. The value may either be a percentage, an exact number of pixels, or completely variable with an asterisk: * depending on the size of the other rows.
3. Type, b where b is the height of the second row, again expressed as a %, an absolute value in pixels, or a variable with an asterisk *.
4. Repeat step 3 for each additional row.
5. Type "> to complete the row definition.
6. Type <FRAME to assign a URL and other attributes to the top row/pane.
7. Type NAME="name" where name is a word that identifies this particular frame's use, like banner; index, or contents.
8. Type SRC="content.html"> where content.html is the URL for the page that will be initially displayed in this frame when the visitor first navigates to this frameset.
9. Repeat steps 6-8 for each row you defined in steps 2-4.
10. Type </FRAMESET> to complete the frameset and the construction of your "window".
11. Create the pages that will be displayed initially in the frames, that is, those referenced by the SRC tag in step 8. This is the "landscape" behind the window.

In the example shown here, I have divided the page into 2 rows of 50 each. The above one has the information from the file called TEST1.HTML and the second one has the picture directly from the source. See both the HTML text and the its result in the browser next.

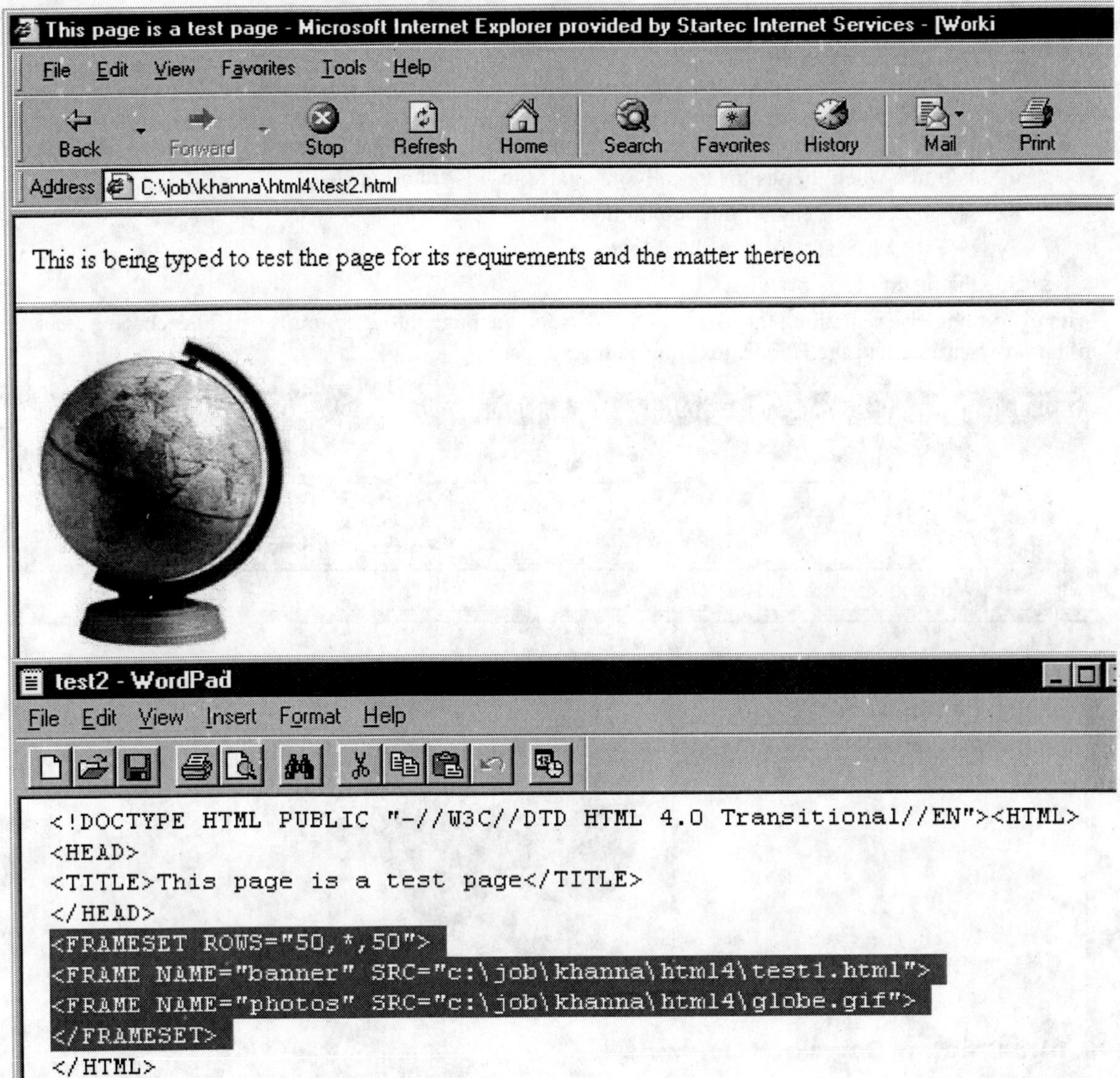


**Remember**

Asterisk (*) is used to allocate to a frame whatever leftover space there is available in the window. If the first two frames occupy 40 and 60 pixels respectively, and the window size is 250 pixels, the frame with the asterisk will occupy 150 pixels. You can use more than one asterisk at a time. The remaining space will be divided equally among the frames marked with an asterisk. The BODY tag is not used at all in frameset pages.

### 9.14.2 Creating Columns

You can divide the page into columns too instead of rows.

Follow the following steps to create frames in columns:

1. Type <FRAMESET after the </HEAD> tag in the frameset page.
2. Type COLS="a,b"> where a and b represent the width of the corresponding columns as percentage, number of pixels or variable.
3. Type <FRAME to define the leftmost frame/column.
4. Type NAME="name" where name is a word that identifies this particular frame's use, like banner, index, or contents.
5. Type SRC="content.html"> where content.html is the URL of the page that you want to be displayed in this frame when the visitor initially navigates to this frameset.
6. Repeat steps 3-5 for each frame/ column.
7. Type </FRAMESET> to close the frame.
8. See the result in the browser.

With everything else remaining the same, I have divided the page into 2 columns of 100 each. See the result in the browser here and the HTML text on the next page.

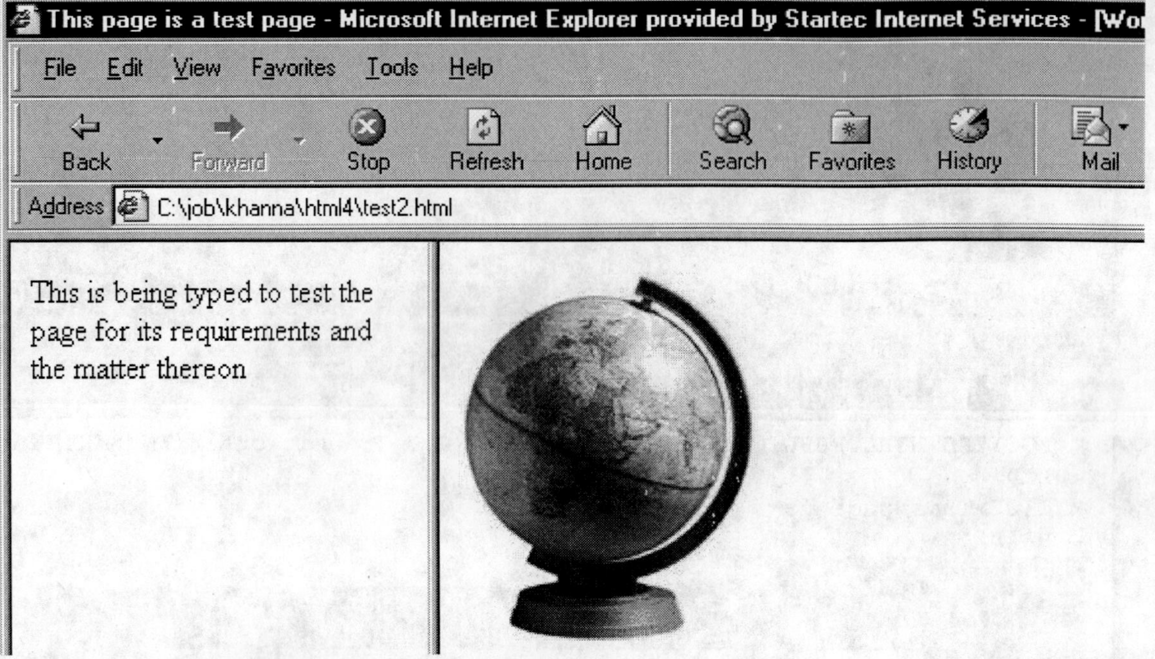


### 9.14.3 Creating Rows and Columns

So far I have talked about Rows and Columns. There maybe a time when you have to divide the page into both rows and columns. You can create both rows and columns in the same frameset to accommodate different kinds of information.

Follow the following steps to create a frameset with both rows and columns:

1. Type <FRAMESET to begin.
2. Type ROWS ="a, b" where a and b (and any others) represent the height of the corresponding rows.
3. Type COLS="x, y" where x and y (and any others) represent the width of the corresponding columns.
4. Type >.

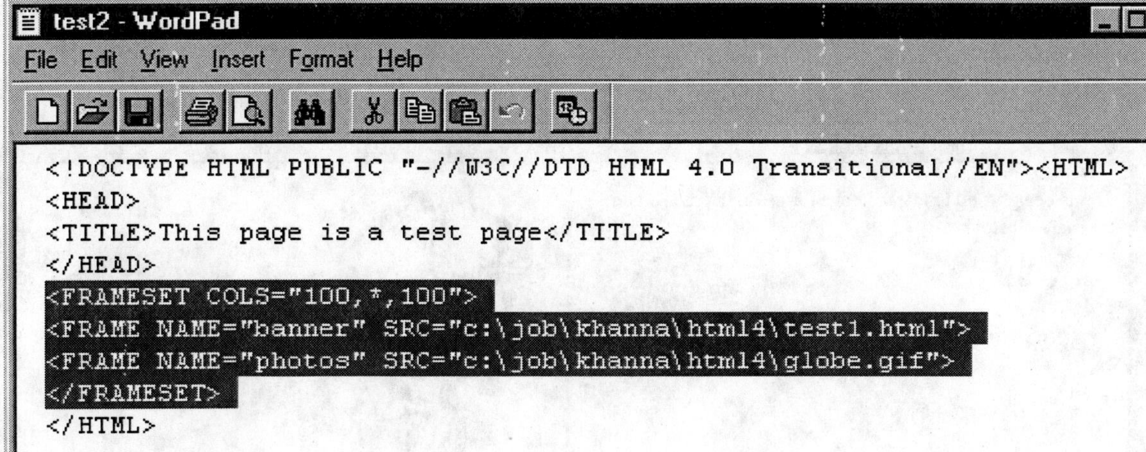


```
<!DOCTYPE HTML PUBLIC "-//W3C//DTD HTML 4.0 Transitional//EN"><HTML>
<HEAD>
<TITLE>This page is a test page</TITLE>
</HEAD>
<FRAMESET COLS="100,*,100">
<FRAME NAME="banner" SRC="c:\job\khanna\html4\test1.html">
<FRAME NAME="photos" SRC="c:\job\khanna\html4\globe.gif">
</FRAMESET>
</HTML>
```

5. Define the first frame in the first row by typing <FRAME NAME="name" SRC="initialurl.html">.
6. Define the rest of the frames in the first row from left to right.
7. Repeat steps 4 and 5 for each row, from top to bottom.
8. Type </FRAMESET > to complete the frameset.

In the same example I have now used 2 rows and 2 columns. The first and fourth frame contains the same text from the file called TEST1.HTML. The second frame contains picture from GOLOBE.GIF and the 3rd one contains picture from the file called BALL.GIF. See the result in the browser and the HTML text.

**Remember**

Defining rows and columns in this way limits you to the same number of frames in each row or column.

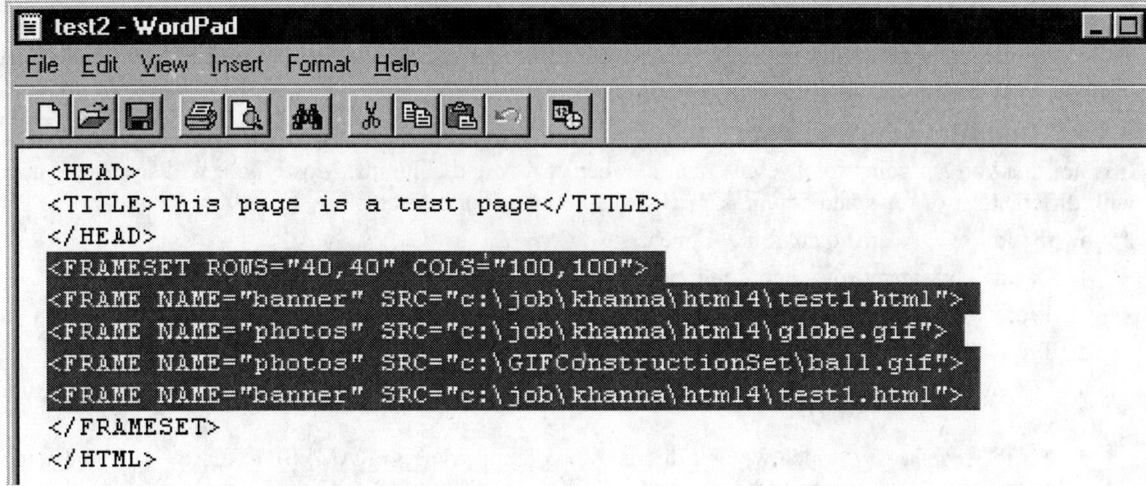


```
<HEAD>
<TITLE>This page is a test page</TITLE>
</HEAD>
<FRAMESET ROWS="40,40" COLS="100,100">
<FRAME NAME="banner" SRC="c:\job\khanna\html4\test1.html">
<FRAME NAME="photos" SRC="c:\job\khanna\html4\globe.gif">
<FRAME NAME="photos" SRC="c:\GIFConstructionSet\ball.gif">
<FRAME NAME="banner" SRC="c:\job\khanna\html4\test1.html">
</FRAMESET>
</HTML>
```

### 9.14.4 Adjusting Frame's Margins

By default, both Netscape and Explorer display a frame's contents with a margin of 8 pixels on each side. You can adjust the margin so that there is more space, or, if you prefer, so that the frame's contents begin in the top left corner.

Follow the following steps to adjust a frame's margins:

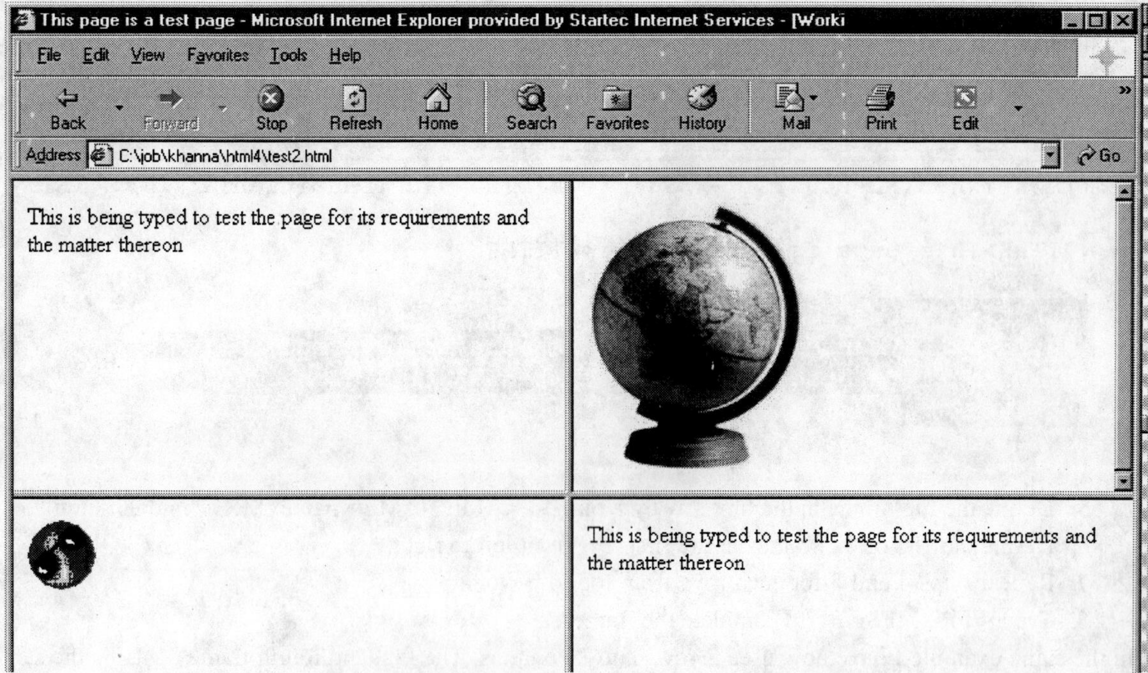


1. In the desired FRAME tag, before the final > , type MARGINWIDTH=w where w is the desired amount of space, in pixels, between the left and right edges of the frame and the frame's contents.
2. Type MARGINHEIGHT =h where h is the desired amount of space, in pixels, between the top and bottom edges of the frame and the frame's contents.

**Remember**

The margin is transparent and thus always appears to be the same color as the background of the page displayed in the frame.

### 9.14.5 Combining Framesets

It is not that you are going to have an equal number of row and columns. Mostly you will see a web page with different set of rows and columns. Let us see how these are created.

Follow the following steps to combine framesets:

1. Decide how many rows and columns you need on your page.
2. Type <FRAMESET to begin.
3. Type ROWS="a, b"> where a and b represent the height of the corresponding rows.
4. For a row with just a single frame, type <FRAME NAME="name" SRC="contents.html"> in the usual way.
5. For the second row, which we will divide into columns, type <FRAMESET COLS="a, b"> where a and b represent the width of each column in the row.
6. Type <FRAME NAME="name" SRC="contents.html"> where name is the reference for the frame and contents.html is the page that will be initially shown in that frame.
7. Repeat step 6 for each frame in the column.
8. When you have finished defining the frames/columns in the divided row, type </FRAMESET>.

9. Continue defining each row individually. For a row with just one frame (i.e., just one column), just use a FRAME tag. For rows divided into multiple columns, repeat steps 5-8.
10. Type </FRAMESET> to complete the outer frameset.

Now see what I have done in my example. I have divided the page into 2 rows first and then divided the intermediate section into 2 columns and each one of them has a picture, i.e., a globe and a ball. The last one of the row again contains the text which is there in the first row too. See the result here in the browser. Also note the HTML text which is shown on the next page.

**Remember**

There is no rule that you have to assign rows first. You can have columns first. The only thing to watch is that each frameset have opening and closing <FRAMESET> tags, and that each frameset is contained completely with no overlapping. It is important to stress that not every row need be divided into columns. For rows with a single frame, i.e., that span the entire window from left to right, just use a FRAME tag. For

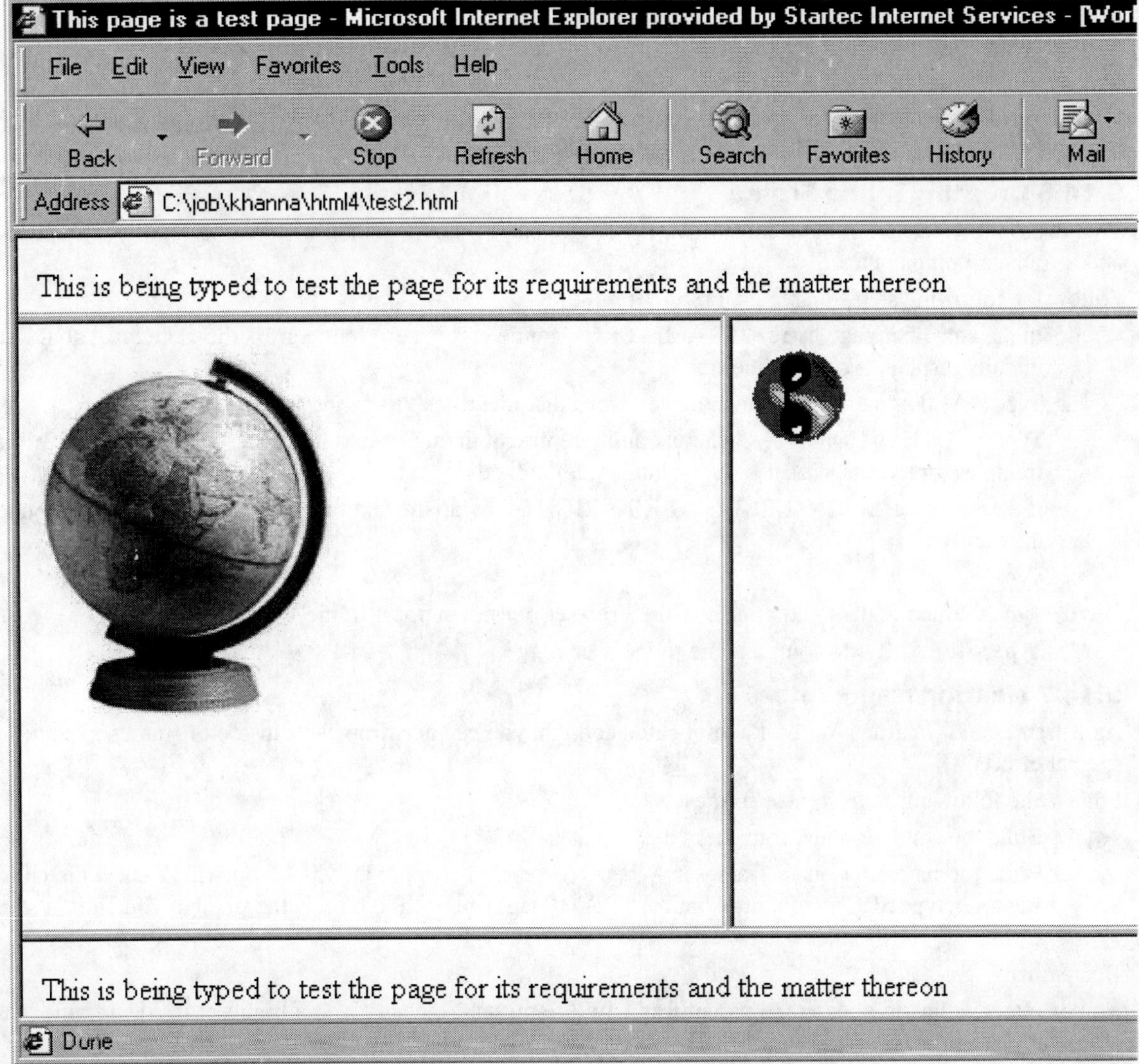

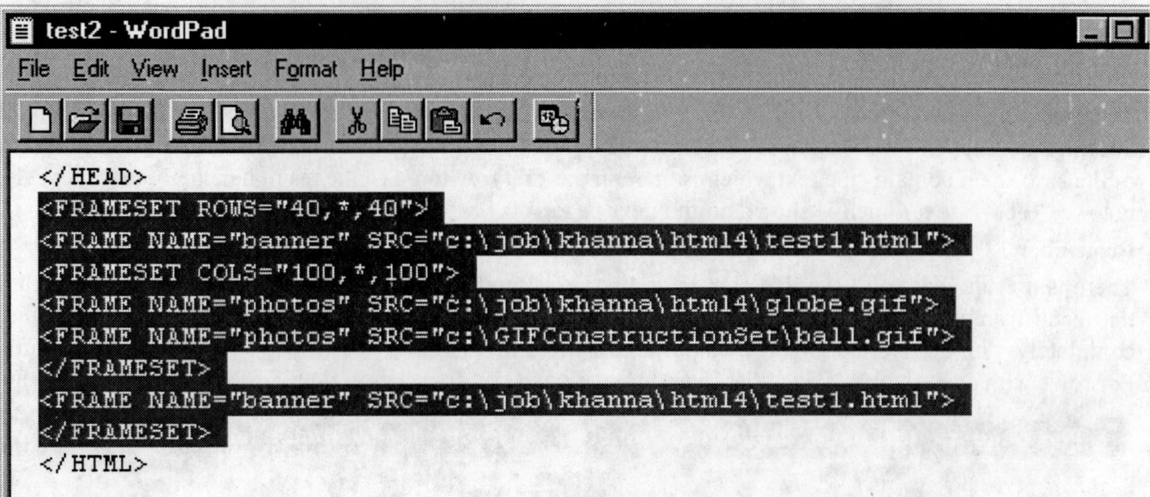


```
</HEAD>
<FRAMESET ROWS="40,*,40">
<FRAME NAME="banner" SRC="c:\job\khanna\html4\test1.html">
<FRAMESET COLS="100,*,100">
<FRAME NAME="photos" SRC="c:\job\khanna\html4\globe.gif">
<FRAME NAME="photos" SRC="c:\GIFConstructionSet\ball.gif">
</FRAMESET>
<FRAME NAME="banner" SRC="c:\job\khanna\html4\test1.html">
</FRAMESET>
</HTML>
```

rows divided into columns, use an inner frameset. If you want to create the same number of frames in each row and each column, you don't need to combine multiple framesets.

### 9.14.6 Creating Inline Frame

This is used to create an inline frame which is nothing but a frame which allows you to mix text, graphics, and a frame all on one page.

Follow the following steps to create an inline frame:

1. In the container page, type <IFRAME, SRC="frame.url", where frame.url is the page that should be initially displayed in the inline frame.
2. Type NAME="name", where name is a word that identifies this inline frame's use.
3. Type WIDTH=x HEIGHT=y where x and y represent the width and height respectively of the inline frame as a percentage or as an absolute value in pixels.
4. If desired, type ALIGN=LEFT or ALIGN=RIGHT to wrap the text that comes after the frame around the frame.
5. Type >.
6. Type the text that should appear if the browser doesn't support inline frames.
7. Type </IFRAME> to complete the inline frame.

### 9.14.7 Nesting framesets

As if frames and framesets weren't complicated enough, you can nest framesets inside of frames to achieve special effects.

Follow the following steps to nest framesets:

1. Build the child, or inner, frameset.
2. Build the parent, or outer, frameset. When you reach the frame in which you wish to nest the child frameset, type SRC="child.html" in the FRAME tag, where child.html is the file that you built in step 1.

**Remember**

You can target a link to open in the parent frame of a frameset. You can't nest a frameset inside a frame that is in that same frameset.

### 9.14.8 Keeping Visitors from Resizing Frames

It is possible that visitor might change the size of the browser window, so to avoid this you may use this command. However, you can also choose whether to let the visitor resize individual frames.

Follow the following steps to keep visitors from resizing your frames:

1. Type NORESIZE in the FRAME tag for the desired frame.

**Remember**

Netscape displays resizable frames with a small hash mark in the middle of the border. The mark disappears if you've used the NORESIZE attribute. If you use very small pixel values for your frames and the visitor views the frameset page in a very large window, the width of the frames will probably not be quite as you wished. The entire frameset is always stretched to fill the window. If you set the border width to 0 with the BORDER tag, visitors who view the page in Netscape won't be able to resize the frames at all. The borders will remain flexible in Internet Explorer, since Explorer doesn't recognize the BORDER tag.

### 9.14.9 Targeting Links to Particular Frames

The initial contents of a given frame is specified in the frameset page with the SRC tag. However, you can have other pages appear in that same frame. The trick is to add a pointer, called a target, to the links to those pages. The target says, "open this link in frame xyz".

Follow the following steps to target a link to a particular frame:

1. Make sure the target frame has a name.
2. On the page where the link should appear, type <A HREF="page.html" where page.html is the file that should be displayed in the target frame.
3. Type TARGET="name" where name is the reference given to the target frame within the FRAME tag.
4. Add any other attributes as desired to the link and then type the final >.

### 9.14.10 Changing the Default Target

Coming back to links if a frame contains a link, the link will open up in that same frame, by default, unless you change the target earlier. You can change the default target for all of the links on a page by using the BASE tag,

Follow the following steps to change the default target:

1. In the HEAD section of the page that contains the links, type <BASE,
2. Type TARGET="name", where name is the word that identifies the frame or window in which you want the links to appear, by default,
3. Type > to complete the BASE tag,

**Remember**

You can override the target specified in the BASE tag by choosing a target in the link itself.

## Let us Revise

1. HTML is the language of Internet.
2. HTML tags are written within the less than (<) and greater than (>) signs.
3. Mostly all values should be enclosed in straight quotation marks.
4. There is no restriction on the number of spaces given by you.
5. HTML supports most of the special characters.
6. Any word processor can be used for creating a text file for HTML.
7. You can see your text in a browser.
8. Your text should have the html or htm extension.
9. The first line of the text defines the HTML.
10. Main body of the text is divided between <BODY> and </BODY>.
11. Headings in the text are divided between <HEAD> and </HEAD>.
12. You can have as many as 6 headings in the text.
13. You can have graphics too in your HTML files.
14. The tag for using graphics is IMG SRC.
15. You can change the weight and height of the image in HTML.
16. You can align your text with respect to the image.
17. You can add lines of various widths in your text.
18. You can wrap the text in between two images.
19. HTML support 3 type of lists: Unordered lists, Ordered lists and Definition lists.
20. Unordered lists can be preceded by one of several bullet styles: a closed circle, an open circle, or a square.
21. Ordered lists can be preceded by Arabic numerals, uppercase or lowercase Roman numerals, or uppercase or lowercase alphanumeric characters.
22. Definition lists require a start tag (<DL>) and end tage (</DL>) and two special elements: one for definition terms (the <DT> tag) and one for definitions (the <DD>) tag.
23. There are two other types of lists defined in HTML: Directory lists and Menus.
24. To create a table you use the tag <TABLE>.
25. You use COLGROUP to divide table in columns.
26. Horizontal rows are set using the tag <TR>.
27. Table headers are created using <TH>.
28. You can add a border too to the table.
29. You can add a background image to the table.
30. Using ALIGN you can align the text in the cells.
31. A form is used to get the feedback from the visitors to the site.
32. You can create a form using the tag <FORM>.
33. You can give various options using the tag <OPTION>.
34. Values can also be given to the Options.
35. Check boxes allow the visitor to click in them.
36. Text boxes are used to allow visitor to write text.
37. Large text can be left using the tag TEXTAREA.

38. Submit button can also be set by using the INPUT tag.
39. You can divide your web page into various frames so that you can add more information using these frames.
40. A frameset is a door within window. Each door shows different information.
41. You can divide the page into columns instead of rows.
42. You can create both rows and columns in the same frameset to accommodate different kinds of information.
43. It is not that you are going to have an equal number of row and columns. Mostly you will see a web page with different set of rows and columns.

## Multiple Choice Questions

1. Full form of HTML is:
   (a) Hyper Text Markup Language
   (b) Hyper Text Monitor Language
   (c) Hyper Type Markup Language
2. HTML tags must be written within :
   (a) () (b) [] (c) <>
3. Values in HTML are provided within :
   (a) Question mark (b) Quotation marks (c) Left and right brackets
4. Your text file should have the extension :
   (a) html (b) htm (c) any of the 2 above
5. HTML definition is given in the text in :
   (a) Last line (b) Not given (c) First line
6. What character is used to end the tag :
   (a) / (b) ? (c) !
7. Tag for using graphic is IMG followed by :
   (a) SRC (b) RCS (c) CRS
8. For giving a line in the page, we which tag:
   (a) Line (b) HR (c) SR
9. For giving space around the image we use:
   (a) VSPACE (b) HSPACE (c) Both
10. For creating a table, you would use the tag:
    (a) <TABLE> (b) <CREATE> (c) <TAB>
11. Table can be divided into cols and :
    (a) semi colons (b) rows (c) cells
12. Horizontal rows are created by using :
    (a) <TH> (b) <TR> (c) <CR>
13. You can put header to a table using the tag:
    (a) <TH> (b) <TR> (c) <CR>
14. A form is used for :
    (a) filling data (b) getting information (c) displaying data

15. Tag used for creating menu is :
    (a) OPTION (b) TYPE (c) MENU
16. Radio buttons are so called because :
    (a) They look like radio buttons
    (b) They were created by radio
    (c) You have to switch on radio for using them
17. Form is used for :
    (a) Giving information to the visitors
    (b) Getting information from the visitors
    (c) To display graphics
18. TEXTAREA is used to :
    (a) Providing text to the visitors
    (b) Providing information to the visitors
    (c) Provide space for visitor to fill up
19. You can divide the page into rows and :
    (a) Columns (b) Tables (c) Frames

## True/False Questions

1. Mostly all values should be enclosed in straight quotation marks.
2. Any word processor can be used for creating a text file for HTML.
3. The first line of the text defines the HTML.
4. You can have as many as 8 headings in the text.
5. You can change the weight and height of the image in HTML.
6. You cannot wrap the text in between two images.
7. Ordered lists can be preceded by Arabic numerals, uppercase or lowercase Roman numerals, or uppercase or lowercase alphanumeric characters.
8. To create a table you use the tag <TABLE>.
9. Table headers are created using <TE>.
10. Using ALIGN you can align the text in the cells.
11. You can give various options using the tag <OPTION>.
12. Text boxes are not used to allow visitor to write text.
13. You can divide your web page into various frames so that you can add more information using these frames.
14. You can create both rows and columns in the same frameset to accommodate different kinds of information.

## Match Columns

Match the matter in Column A with the matter in Column B.

| Column A | Column B |
|---|---|
| A. DHTML | 1. Dividing page into parts |
| B. XML | 2. Button on Form to register |
| C. <p> | 3. List of various options |

D. Form
E. Frameset
F. Radio Button
G Submit Button
H. Check Box
I. Menu list
J. Columns

4. Dynamic HyperText Markup Language
5. Boxes with option checked
6. eXtensive Markup Language
7. Tags for paragraph
8. Website divided into various frames
9. A form for user to fill and submit
10. Button on the site in the form of radio button

## Fill in the Blanks with Appropriate Words

| | | | | | | | |
|---|---|---|---|---|---|---|---|
| a. | Check boxes | b. | image | c. | <TR> | d. | columns |
| e. | Menus | f. | HTML | g. | html or htm | h. | <FORM> |
| i. | INPUT | l. | <HEAD>, </HEAD> | m. | IMG SRC | n. | Unordered |
| o. | lines | p. | special characters | | | | |

1. _______ tags are written within the less than (<) and greater than (>) signs.
2. HTML supports most of the ___________.
3. Your text should have the ____________ extension.
4. Headings in the text are divided between _____ and ______.
5. The tag for using graphics is ________.
6. You can add ________ of various widths in your text.
7. ___________ lists can be preceded by one of several bullet styles: a closed circle, an open circle, or a square.
8. There are two other types of lists defined in HTML: Directory lists and ________.
9. Horizontal rows are set using the tag ______.
10. You can add a background ______ to the table.
11. You can create a form using the tag ______.
12. _________ allow the visitor to click in them.
13. Submit button can also be set by using the ________ tag.
14. You can divide the page into _______ instead of rows.

## Descriptive Type Questions

1. What is HTML used for?
2. How are HTML tags written?
3. How are the values given in HTML?
4. How is the text typed for HTML?
5. How would you start and end the body of the text?
6. How many headings you can have in a page?
7. What all goes in the first line of HTML text? Explain them.
8. Describe the process of inserting graphics.
9. How would you create a banner?
10. How would you add a horizontal line?

11. How would you wrap text around the image?
12. How would you set margins for the page?
13. Describe how would you create tables in HTML?
14. How would you divide the table in various cols?
15. How would you put background colour to the table?
16. What do you understand by Unordered list?
17. How would you create a Ordered list?
18. What do you understand by Directory and Menu lists?
19. Describe the process of dividing the table into columns?
20. How would you give headers to the table columns?
21. What is a Form?
22. How is a Form created?
23. How would you create menus?
24. What are radio buttons?
25. What do you understand by Frameset?
26. How would you combine various framesets?
27. How would you give space between framesets?
28. How would you nest various framesets?

## Answers to Objective Type Questions

### *Multiple Choice Questions*

| | | | |
|---|---|---|---|
| 1. a | 2. c | 3. b | 4. c |
| 5. c | 6. a | 7. a | 8. b |
| 9. c | 10. a | 11. b | 12. b |
| 13. a | 14. b | 15. c | 16. a |
| 17. b | 18. b | 19. a | |

### *True False Questions*

| | | | |
|---|---|---|---|
| 1. T | 2. T | 3. T | 4. F |
| 5. T | 6. F | 7. T | 8. T |
| 9. F | 10. T | 11. T | 12. F |
| 13. T | 14. T | | |

### *Matching Columns*

| | | | |
|---|---|---|---|
| A. 4 | B. 6 | C. 7 | D. 9 |
| E. 8 | F. 10 | G. 2 | H. 5 |
| I. 3 | J. 1 | | |

### *Fill in the Blanks*

| | | | |
|---|---|---|---|
| 1. f | 2. p | 3. g | 4. l |
| 5. m | 6. o | 7. n | 8. e |
| 9. c | 10. b | 11. h | 12. a |
| 13. i | 14. d | | |

# Interactivity Tools 10

## 10.1 ASP

An Active Server Page is a standard HTML file that is extended with additional features. Like a standard HTML file, an Active Server Page contains HTML tags that can be interpreted and displayed by a Web browser. Anything you could normally place an HTML file – Java applets, blinking text, client-wide scripts, client-side ActiveX controls – you can place in an Active Server Page. However, an Active Server Page has three important features that make it unique.

- An Active Server Page can contain server-side scripts. By including server-side scripts in an Active Server Page, you can create Web pages with dynamic content. To take an extremely simply example, you can create a Web page that displays different messages at different times of the day.
- An Active Server Page provides several built-in objects. By using the built-in objects accessible in an Active Server Page, you can make your scripts much more powerful. Among other things, these objects enable you to both retrieve information form and send information to browsers. For example, by using the Request object, you can retrieve the information that a user has posted in an HTML form and respond to that information within a script.
- An Active Server Page can be extended with additional components. Active Server Pages comes bundled with several standard, server-side ActiveX components. These components enable you to do such things as work with databases, send email and access the file system.

These standard ActiveX components are very useful. However, you're not limited only to these components. You can buy third-party components or create additional ActiveX components of your own. There's no limit to how you can extend Active Server Pages.

These three features define an Active Server Page. An Active Server Page is a standard HTML page that has been extended with server-side scripts, objects and components. By using Active Server Pages, you can create Web sites with dynamic content. The best way to understand how Active Server Pages work is by contrasting the process of retrieving an Active Server Page with the process of accessing a normal HTML page. The process of serving an HTML page can be broken into the following steps:

1. A user enters the Internet address of an HTML file into the address bar of a Web browser and presses Enter to request a Web page (for example, http://www.aspsite.com/hello.htm).
2. The browser sends a request for the Web page to a Web server such as Internet Information Server (IIS).
3. The Web server receives the request and recognizes that the request is for an HTML file because the requested file has the extension .htm or .html.
4. The Web server retrievers the proper HTML file from disk or memory and sends the file back to the browser.
5. The HTML file is interpreted by the user's Web browser and the result are displayed in the browser window.

Of course, this process is often more complicated (for example, the contents of forms are posted and query strings are passed). But, in broad strokes, these steps outline the moment-to-moment activity of a typical Web server. A server receives requests for particular files and responds by sending the correct file, retrieving it from the hard drive or memory.

Although IIS can be used to server static HTML pages. Active Server Pages enable IIS to serve dynamic content as well. Using Active Server Pages, you can create pages with new content in response to user requests. The Web server itself becomes active in the process of creating the Web page.

It's important to understand how this process of serving an Active Server Page contrasts with the normal process of serving an HTML page, so we'll break it into steps:

1. A user enters the Internet address of an Active Server Page file into the address bar of a Web browser and presses Enter to request an Active Server Page (for example, http://www.aspsite.com/hello.asp).
2. The browser sends a request for the Active Server Page to IIS.
3. The Web server receives the request and recognizes that the request is for an Active Server Page file because the requested file has the extension .asp.
4. The Web server retrieves the proper Active Server Page file from disk or memory.
5. The Web server sends the file to a special program named ASP.dll.
6. The Active Server Page file is processed from top to bottom and any commands it encounters are executed. The result of this process is a standard HTMl file.
7. The HTML file is sent back to the browser.
8. The HTML file is interpreted by the user's Web browser and the results are displayed in the browser window.

From the perspective of the Web server, an Active Server Page is very different from a normal HTML page. A normal HTML file is sent without processing to the browser. All the commands in an Active Server Page, on the other hand, must first be executed to create an HTML page. This allows an Active Server Page to contain dynamic content.

From the perspective of the browser, on the other hand, an Active Server Page is almost exactly the same as a normal HTML page. The only difference is that an Active Server Page typically must end with the extension .asp rather than .htm or .html. When a request is made for an Active Server Page, the browser receives a normal HTML page. This enables an active Server Page to be compatible with all browsers.

### 10.1.1 Integrating Objects and Components into Active Server Pages

An Active Server Page is primarily a scripting environment. This book assumes that you will be creating Active Server Page scripts with Microsoft's VBScript. However, you can use other scripting languages with Active Server Pages such as Jscript and PerlScript as well. Any scripting language that has a scripting engine compatible with the ActiveX scripting standard can be used in an Active Server Page.

The easiest way to add a script to an Active Server Page is by using the script delimiters <% and %>. Any text enclosed within these delimiters will be processed as a script. Here's is an example:

```
<HTML>
<HEAD><TITLE>ASP Script</TITLE></HEAD>
<BODY>
This is a
<% For i=1 to 10 %>
very,
<% NEXT %>
```

```
very long sentence.
</BODY>
</HTML>
```

When this Active Server Page is displayed by a Web browser, the following sentence is displayed:

**This is a very, very, very, very, very, very, very, very, very, very, very long sentence.**

The script creates 11 copies of the word very by using a VBScript FOR…Next loop.

By default, an Active Server Page assumes you'll be using VBScript as your primary scripting language. This means that you don't need to do anything beyond using the <% and %> script delimiters to use this language. However, there are three ways to explicitly specify a language for use in an Active Server Page.

First, you can use the Internet Service Manager to specify a particular scripting language as the default language for all your Active Server Pages. To do this, perform the following steps:

1. Launch the Internet Server Manager from the Microsoft Internet Information Server program group on the Start menu.
2. Right-click the name of your Web site. If you haven't changed the default configuration, the name of this Web site will be default Web Site.
3. Choose Properties to open you Web site's property sheet.
4. Click the Home Directory tab.
5. Click the Configuration button. (To do this, you must have an existing application. If you don't, create one now by clicking Create.)
6. In the Application Configuration dialog box, click the App Options tab.
7. In the Default ASP Language text box, enter the name of the scripting language that you want to use as your primary scripting language; for example, enter VBScript or script.

After you have specified a particular scripting language as the default scripting language, you can use it in your Active Server Pages simply by using the delimiters <% and %>. If you plan to use Jscript for the majority of your Active Server Pages, for example, you should configure this language as your default language.

You can also specify the primary scripting language for a particular page. To do this, place the Language directive as the very first line in your Active Server Page file, as shown in this example:

```
<%@ Language=Jscript %>
<HTML>
<HEAD><TITLE>ASP Script</TITLE></HEAD>
<BODY>
This is a
<% for i=1;I<11;I++) { %>
very,
<% } %>
very long sentence.
</BODY>
</HTML>
```

The directive in the first line of this script indicates that all the scripts contained in the file should be executed as scripts created with Jscript, rather than some other scripting language. When you use this directive, be sure to include a space between the @ character and the keyword Language. Furthermore, it's very important that this directive appear before my other commands in your Active Server Page file (otherwise you'll get an error).

A third alternative exists for including scripts in your Active Server Pages. You can use Microsoft's extended <SCRIPT> HTML tag, as in this example:

```
<HTML>
<HEAD><TITLE>ASP Script</TITLE></HEAD>
<BODY>
<SCRIPT LANGUAGE="Jscript" RUNAT="server">
function sayhello()
{
response.write("Hello!")
}
</SCRIPT>
<%
sayhello()
%>
</BODY>
</HTML>
```

Here, the <SCRIPT> tags contain a Jscript function. The Language attribute of the <SCRIPT> tag specifies which scripting language to use. The Run at attribute indicates that the script should be executed on the server rather than on the client (the browser).

The function named sayhello() is defined in the first script. The second script, marked with the usual <% and %> tags, is where the Jscript function is actually called. This Active Server Page prints the text Hello! To the screen.

If you have created client-side Jscript or VBScript scripts, you should be familiar with the <SCRIPT> tag. Microsoft's extended <SCRIPT> tag can be used to specify either client-side or server-side scripts. If you neglected to include the RUNAT="server" attribute in the preceding example, the script would be treated as a client-side script. In this case, the server would ignore the script and the browser would attempt to execute the script. (It would fail miserably because the script isn't a valid client-side script).

Why would you ever want to use the <SCRIPT> tag rather than the <% and %> script delimiters? Normally, you wouldn't use the <SCRIPT> tag. However, there are two significant differences between these two ways of specifying a script.

First, scripts that are contained in the <SCRIPT> tag are executed immediately, no matter where they appear in an Active Server Page. For example, consider the following page:

```
<HTML>
<HEAD><TITLE>ASP Script</TITLE></HEAD>
<BODY>
This is the first sentence.
<SCRIPT LANGUAGE="Jscript" RUNAT="server">
response.write("this is the second sentence.")
</SCRIPT>
</BODY>
```

```
</HTML>
```

Looking the script, you might be tempted to believe that the sentence This is the first sentence and the sentence "This is the second sentence" are printed to the screen in that order. However, when the Active Server Page is displayed in a browser, the order of the two sentence is actually reversed (or worse, nothing is displayed, because an invalid HTML page is generated).

Why does this happen? Whatever is contained in the <SCRIPT> tag is executed before anything else in a page. If you sue the View Source command on your Web browser, you'll see the following results from the preceding Active Server Page:

```
This is the second sentence,<HTML>
<HEAD><TITLE>ASP Script</TITLE></HEAD>
<BODY>
This is the first sentence.
</BODY>
</HTML>
```

This behavior of the <SCRIPT> tag has two implications. First, you can place scripts contained in a <SCRIPT> tag anywhere you want in an Active Server page. Second, the <SCRIPT> tag, for most purpose, is restricted to containing functions or procedures. The output of any script that's not contained in a function or procedure is displayed immediately and results in an invalid HTML page.

The <SCRIPT> tag has one main advantage over the <% and %> script delimiters. Using the <SCRIPT> tag, you can mix multiple scripting languages within a single Active Server Page. Consider the following example:

```
<%@ Language=Jscript %>
<HTML>
<HEAD><TITLE>ASP Script</TITLE></HEAD>
<BODY>
<SCRIPT LANGUAGE="Jscript" RUNAT="server">
function sayhello()
{
response.write("Hello!")
}
</SCRIPT>
<%
for i=1 to 10
sayhello()
NEXT
%>
</BODY>
</HTML>
```

This script prints Hello! 10 times in a row. But notice how it does this. The script contained in the <% and %> delimiters is a Visual Basic script. However, this script calls a Jscript function. The Jscript function is defined within the <SCRIPT> tag. When you want to use one scripting language as your primary scripting language, but you need to call a function from another language, you can use this method. This is useful when one language has particular functions or methods that another language lacks.

To summarize, there are three methods of including a script in an Active Server Page:

- Specify a scripting language for all your Active Server Page by using the Intenret Service Manager to specify a default language.
- Specify a scripting language for a single page by using the Active Server Page directive <%@ Language="scripting language" %>.
- Mix multiple scripting language in a single Active Server Page by using the extended <SCRIPT> tag.

Before ending this section, one final Active Server Pages directive should be discussed.

By using the Active Server Pages' output directive, you can display the value of an expression. Here's an example:

```
<HTML>
<HEAD><TITLE>ASP Example</TITLE></HEAD>
<BODY>
At the tone, the time will be: <%=TIME%>
</BODY>
</HTML>
```

You use the delimiters <%= and %> to print the value of a variable, method or function. In the preceding example, the output directive is used to output the value of the VBScript TIME function.

There's another way to accomplish the same thing. Consider the following example:

```
<HTML>
<HEAD><TITLE>ASP Example</TITLE></HEAD>
<BODY>
At the tone, the time will be: <% Response.Write(TIME) %>
</BODY>
</HTML>
```

In this example, the value of the VBScript TIME function is outputted by using the Active Server Pages Response object. The Write() method of the Response object output the value of expressions to the screen. When should you use the Response.Write() method rather than the <%= and %> output directive? It really doesn't matter. Active Server Pager internally represent the output directive as a Response.write() method call in any case. The two methods of outputting the values of expressions are completely interchangeable. Nevertheless, there are situations in which one method of outputting the values of expressions is more convenient than the other. For example, when you need to output the value of an expression within a script, the Response.Write() method is often easier to use. On the other hand, when you want to output the value of an expression within a section of HTML code, the <%= and %> directive is often easier to use. The following illustrates both approaches:

```
<HTML>
<HEAD><TITLE>ASP Example</TITLE></HEAD>
<BODY>
<%
for i=1 to 10
myvar=myvar&"very,"
Response.Write(I&":&myvar&"<BR>)
NEXT
```

```
%>
<HR>
This is a <%=myvar%> long sentence.
</BODY>
</HTML>
```

In this example, the Response.Write() method is used within the loop to display the value of the variable named myvar as it increases in size. The <%=and %> output directive is embedded within normal HTML code. The output directive is used to display the value of myvar.

### 10.1.2 Understanding Objects and Components

Active Server Pages include several built-in objects and installable ActiveX components. These objects and components can be used to extend the power of your Active Server Pages scripts. What are the objects and components?

An object is something that typically has methods, properties or collections. An object's methods determine the things you can do with the object. An object's properties can be read or set to specify the state of the object. An object's collections constitute different sets of key and value pairs related to the object.

To take an everyday example, the book Tom Sawyer is an example of an object. The object has certain methods that determine the things you can do with it. For example, you can read the book, use it as a doorstep or even, if you're feeling particularly malicious, tear it into shreds. The object has certain properties. For example, it has a certain number of pages and a particular author. Finally, it has a collection of key and value pairs. Each page number (the key) has a corresponding page of text (the value).

An ActiveX component is similar to an Active Server Page built-in object. However, when you are using Active Server Pages, there is one important difference between a component and an object. An instance of a component must be explicitly created before it can be used.

### 10.1.3 Active Server Pages Objects

Active Server Pages include several built-in objects. These objects enable you to extend the power of your scripts. For example, by using these objects, you can gain access to browser requests and control how the server responds to these requests. The built-in objects also provide you with control over user sessions and Web-server applications.

You have already been introduced to one example of a built-in object- the Response object. You can use the Response object to send output to a browser. However, the Response object also has several other important properties, collections and methods.

The following chapter explain in detail how to use each of the built-in objects. The following list provides a quick overview of each of the built-in objects:

- The Application object – The Application object is used to store and retrieve information that can be shared among all users of an application. For example, you can use the Application object to pass information between users of your Web site.
- The Request object – The Request object can be used to access all information sent in a request from a browser to your server. You can use the Request object to retrieve the information that a user has entered into an HTML form.
- The Response object – The Response object is used to send information back to a browser. You can use the response object to send output from your scripts to a browser.
- The Server object – The Server object enables you to use various utility functions on the server. For example, you can use the Server object to control the length of time a script executes before it times out. You can also use the Server object to create instances of other objects.

- The Session object – The Session object can be used to store and retrieve information about particular user sessions. You can use the Session object to store information that persists over the course of a visit by a user to your Web site.
- The ObjectContext object – The ObjetContext object is used to control Active Server Pages transactions. The transactions are managed by the Microsoft Transaction Server (MTS).

### 10.1.4 Active Server Pages Components

Like the built-in objects discussed in the preceding section. Active Server Pages components can be used to extend the power of your scripts. Components differ from the built in objects because they're typically used for more specialized tasks. The following list provides a brief overview of some of the components bundled with Active Server Pages:

- The Ad Rotator component – The Ad Rotator component is used to display banner advertisements on the Web pages of a Web site. You can use this component to specify how frequently different banner advertisements should be displayed.
- The Browser Capabilities component – The Browser Capabilities component can be used to display different HTML content, according to the capabilities of different browsers. For example, you can use this component to display Web pages with frames only to frames-compliant browsers.
- The Content Linking component – using the Content Linking component, you can link together several HTML pages so that they can be navigated easily. For example, you can use this component to display the pages of an online book.
- The Counters components – The Counters components can be used to keep track of the number of visitors to your Web site. You can use the Counters components to add a hit counter to a Web page.
- The Content Rotator component – The Content Rotator component enables you to rotate through HTML content on a page. For example, you can use the component to randomly display different announcements on the home page of your Web site.
- The Page Counter component – The Page Counter component is exactly like the Counter component, in that it can be used to track the number of visitors and to add a hit counter to particular Web page.
- The Permission Checker component – The Permission Checker component can be used to display links to Web pages only to those users who have permission to see them. You can use this component to create Web pages that can be viewed only by the administrators of a Web site.
- The Collaboration Data Objects – The Collaboration Data Objects (CDO) enable you to send and retrieve email from within your Active Server Pages. You can use these objects to send email to new user after the user registers at your Web site.
- The ActiveX Data Objects – The ActiveX Data Objects (ADO) enable you to retrieve and store data in a database such as Microsoft SQL Server. These objects are extremely important.

### 10.1.5 Using Components in Active Server Pages

Before you can use a component, you must first create an instance of it. Although you can automatically access the properties, collections and methods of the built-in objects on every page, before you can use a component, you must create an instance of the component with a particular scope. In the following three sections, you will learn how to create an instance of a component with page, session and application scope.

### 10.1.6 Creating a Component with Page Scope

In most cases, you'll create an instance of a component with page scope. A component with page scope is created on a single page and dies when processing on the page ends. You can use a component with page scope only on the page where it is explicitly created. To create an instance of a component with page scope, you can use either the Server.CreateObject() method or the HTML <OBJECT> tag.

Here's an example of how you can use the CreateObject method to create an instance of the Dictionary object with page scope:

```
<%
Set MyDict=Server.CreteObject("Scripting.Dictionary")
MyDict.Add "CA", "California"
MyDict.Add "MA", "Massachusetts"
MyDict.Add "MI", "Missouri"
%>
My dictionary has <%=MyDict.Count %> entries.
<BR>
The first entry in my dictionary is <%=Mydict.Item("CA")%>
```

When this script is executed, an instance of the Dictionary object is created. Next, three key and value pairs are added to the dictionary. Finally, two properties of the dictionary are displayed.

The first statement in this example uses the Server.CreateObject method to create an instance of an object with page scope. In this example, an instance of the Dictionary object is assigned to a variable named MyDict.

After an instance of an object has been created, its methods can be called. In this example, the Add method of the Dictionary object is called to add entries to the dictionary. The first Add method call is used to add the key and value pair CA and California.

After an instance of an object has been created, you can also access its properties. In this example, the Count property of the Dictionary object is read to determine the number of entries in the dictionary. The Item property is also read to return the value of a particular key.

Finally, when you're finished using an instance of an object, you can destroy it. An object created by the preceding method will automatically be destroyed after the server finished processing the Active Server Page. Therefore, there's usually no reason to explicitly destroy an object. However, you can destroy the MyDict object explicitly by assigning MyDict to a new value or by setting the variable to the value Nothing like this:

```
<% Set Mydict=Nothing %>
```

This example illustrates the most typical method of creating and using ActiveX components in Active Server Pages. You create an instance of an object by calling the Server.CreateObject() method. After you create a new object, you can call its methods and read and set its properties.

There exists a second method for creating object with page scope. Instead of using the CreateObject method, you can create an instance of an object with the Microsoft Extended HTML <OBJECT> tag. Here is an example:

```
<OBJECT RUNAT="Server" ID="MyBrow"
PROGID="Music.BrowserType"></OBJECT>
```

Because the preceding code is not a script, you should not add it to an Active Server Page within the <% and %> script delimiters. The <OBJECT> tag is an HTML tag and it should appear within the normal HTML content of your page.

This example shows how to use three properties of the HTML <OBJECT> tag. The Id attribute provides the component with a unique identifier (a name), so you can refer to it in your Active Server Pages scripts. The PROGID is used to specify the component's registered name. This is the name the server uses to identify the component when it creates an instance of it. It's the same name you would pass to the Server.CreateObject() method.

When would you use the <OBJECT> tag, instead of the CreateObject method, to create an instance of an object? The one advantage of the <OBJECT> tag is that it does not create an instance of an object until a property or method of the object is actually called. If an Active Server Page contains object that might never be called, you should use the <OBJECT> tag to save some memory.

Microsoft recommends that you create the majority of your components with page scope. By creating components with page scope, you place less of a burden on the Web server. A page scope component releases any memory and other resources it requires when the processing of the page comes to an end.

### 10.1.7 Creating Components with Session Scope

Instead of creating components that are accessible only within a single Active Server Page, you can create components that are accessible on multiple Active Server Pages. One way to do this is to create a component with session scope. A component with session scope is available to a single visitor to your Web site on every page that the visitor requests. An instance of the component is created for each visitor. The component instance does not leave memory until the visitor leaves.

Two methods are available for creating components with session scope. One method assigns a component to a session variable by using the Server.CreateObject() method, as in the following example:

```
<%
Set Session("MyBrow")=Server.CreateObject("MSWC.BrowserType")
%>
```

This script assigns an instance of the Browser Capabilities component to the session variable named MyBrow. You can place this script within any Active Server Page or the Global.asa file. Normally, it makes sense to create the object instance in the Session_OnStart subroutine of the Global.asa file because you need to create the instance only once for each visitor.

After you have created a component with session scope, you can use its properties and methods by referring to the session variable that contains the components. For example, the following script displays the value of the Frames property of the Browser Capabilities component created with the previous script:

```
<%
if session("MyBrow").Frames = True then
   response.write "your browser supports frames!"
end if
%>
```

This method of creating a component with session scope has a significant disadvantages. The Server.CreateObject() method immediately creates an instance of a component. Even if the instance of the component is never used, it still drains resources form the server. Because a new instance of a session object is created for each visitor, this can be a significant drain.

Fortunately, there's a second way to create a component with session scope. You can create a component by using he Microsoft HTML <OBJECT> tag, like this:

```
<OBJECT RUNAT="Server" SCOPR="Session" ID"MyBrow"
PROGID="MSWC.BrowserType"></OBJECT>
```

When you crate an instance of a component with session scope with the </OBJECT> tag, you should create the instance within the Global.asa file. Create the object instance outside the Application_OnStart, Application_OnEnd, Session_OnStart and Session_OnEnd subroutines.

This example uses four properties of the, OBJECT> tag. The Scope attribute indicates that the component created should have session scope. The ID attribute provides the component with a unique identifier (a name), so you can refer to it in your Active Server Pages scripts. The PROGID is used to specify the component's registered name. This is the name the server uses to identify the component when it creates an instance of it. It's the same name you would pass to the Server.CreateObject() method.

When you create an instance of a component with the HTML <OBJECT> tag, you can access any of its methods and properties just as if the object were a built-in Active Server Page object. For example, the following script displays a property of the Browser Capabilities component.

```
<%
If MyBrow.Frames = True then
   Response.write "your browser supports frames!"
End if
%>
```

When a component is created with session scope in either of the two ways just described, any of its methods, collections or properties are available on any page that a particular user requests. However, a particular instance of the component must be created for each user. A component with session scope is created relative to a particular user session.

### 10.1.8 Creating Components with Application Scope

When you create an instance of a component with application scope, you treat it as if it were a built-in object. After it is created, any methods, collections or properties of the component can be accessed by any user on any page. The component remains available until the server shuts down, the Global.asa file is modified or the application is unloaded.

You can create a component with application scope by using methods similar to those used to create a component with session scope. First, you can create a component with application scope by using the Server.CreateObject() method. Look at this example:

```
<%
Set Application("AdRot")=Server.CreateObject("MSWC.AdRotator")
%>
```

Here, an instance of the Ad Rotator component is assigned to an application variable. You could create a component in this way within any of your Active Server Pages. However, normally, you create an instance of an object with application scope only once within the Application_OnStart event of the Global.asa file. The object then becomes available to all users of your Web site.

After an instance of the Ad Rotator component has been created with application scope, you can use its properties on any Active Server Page. For example, the following script calls the Ad Rotator's getAdvertisement property to display a banner advertisement:

```
<%=Application( "adRot" ).getAdvertisement( "schedule.txt")%>
```

You can also create a component with application scope by using the Microsoft HTML <OBJECT> tag, like this:

```
<OBJECT RUNAT="Server" SCOPE="Application" ID="AdRot"
PROGID="MSWC.AdRotator"></OBJECT>
```

When you create an instance of a component with application scope with the <OBJECT> tag, you can only create the instance within the Global.asa file. Create the object instance outside the Application_OnStart, Application_InEnd, Session_OnStart and Session_OnEnd subroutines.

In this example, four properties of the <OBJECT> tag are used. The SCOPE attribute indicates that the component should have application rather than session scope. The ID attribute provides a name for the component. The PROGID attribute enables the server to identify the component.

After creating an instance of an application object in the Global.asa file with the <OBJECT> tag, you can use the component in exactly the same way as you use an Active Server Page built-in object. You can call any of the object's methods and properties on any page without creating another instance of it.

### 10.1.9 Troubleshooting Active Server Pages

Before you can use Active Server Pages, make sure that it is properly installed on your system. If you installed Internet Information Server while installing Window NT Server, Active Server Pages might not be installed. Active Server Pages is included with IIS versions 3.0 and above (the current version is version 4.0 and version 5.0 will be released with Windows 2000). To download the latest version of Active Server Pages, visit the Internet Information Server section of the Microsoft Web site as http://www.microsoft.com/iis.

After Active Server Pages is installed, you must configure IIS to use Active Server Pages. Configure at least one directory in your Web site with permission to execute an Active Server Pages file. Follow these steps:

1. Launch the Internet Service Manager from the Microsoft Internet Information Server program group on the Start menu.
2. In the left pane of the Internet Service Manager, negative to your default Web site. (If you haven't changed anything, the Web site will be named Default Web Site)
3. Choose the directory in your Web site where you want to store your Active Server Pages files by navigating to it in the Internet Service Manager.
4. Right-click the name of this directory and choose Properties.
5. Click the tab labeled Directory or Visual Directory (depending on the type of directory).
6. In the Permission section, choose either Script or Execute.

Now that you have created a directory with permissions to execute your Active Server Pages, you must store all Active Server Pages in this directory in order to use them. If the directory is a physical directory, you can simply store your pages in the directory with this name. If the directory is a virtual directory, you must determine the physical path to this directory on your hard drive. You can determine the physical path of a virtual directory by looking at the same tabbed dialog box where you just configured the permissions.

To load an Active Server Page into a browser that's located on the same machine as IIS, use the address bar of your Web browser. For example, if the Active Server Page is located in the root directory of your Web site, you can load the page by typing http://localhost/mypoage.asp into the address bar of your Web browser. This will load the Active Server Page named mypage.asp.

### 10.1.10 Testing Your Configuration

You can test whether Active Server Page is configured properly on your system by creating a simple Active Server Page. If you can display this page successfully in your Web browser, you know that everything is set up properly. To create an active Server Page, you can use any text editor. For example, you can use Notepad, which is included as an accessory with Windows NT Server. Start Notepad (or your favorite text editor) and enter the following text:

```
<HTML>
<HEAD><TITLE>ASP Page</TITLE></HEAD>
<BODY>
<%
Response.Write("Hello World")
%>
</BODY>
</HTML>
```

Save the Active Server Pages file as test.asp make sure that your text editor doesn't append an extra .txt extension to the filename. Also, make sure that you save the file in a directory with executive or Script permission.

Now, launch your favorite Web browser in order to display your new Active Server Page. If you saved your Active server Page in the root directory of your Web site, you can load the page by typing http://localhost/test.asp. If you saved the Active Server Page in a subdirectory of this root directory, include the full path by entering an address such as http://localhost/mysubdir/test/asp. If you saved the page in a virtual directory, include the name of the virtual directory in the address. For example, in your virtual directory is named myvirtualdir, you should type http://localhost/myvirtualdir/test.asp.

If everything works, the Active Server Page should be displayed. The text Hello World! Should appear in your Web browser's window.

### 10.1.11 Variables

Variables are used to store information. This example demonstrates how to create a variable, assign a value to it and insert the variable value into a text.

```
<html>
<body>
<%
Dim name
Name="Bachchan"
Response.write("My name is:" & name)
%>
</body>
</html>
```

#### *10.1.11.1 Lifetime of Variables*

A variable declared outside a procedure, could be accessed and changed by any script in the ASP page where it is declared. A variable declared inside a procedure, is created and destroyed every time the procedure is executed. No scripts outside that specific procedure can access or change that variable. To make a variable accessible in several ASP pages, declare session variables or application variables.

#### *10.1.11.2 Session Variables*

Session variables stores information about one single user and are available to all pages in one application. Common information stored in session variables is username and userid. To create a session variable, store it in an Session Object.

#### *10.1.11.3 Application Variables*

Application variables are also available to all pages in one application. Application variables are used to hold information about all users in a specific application. To create an application variable, store it in an Application Object.

## 10.2 VB Script

We have seen how to say hello to the world in many different ways using HTML. Now let us say the same thing using Visual Basic Script, or sometimes called VB Script. Here, when you load the Web page, the script will run and pop up a dialog box telling us Hello. You will notice a big difference between this example and the one used in HTML and XML. HTML is primarily utilized for text output, whereas Visual Basic Script is utilized for programming behind the scenes.

Here is the actual example:

```
<HTML>
<title>Beginning to learn Visual Basic Script</title>
<h1><Font size=3 Colour=maroon>
<b><i>Hello World Visual Basic Script></I></b></font></h1>
<hr>
<Body Language="vbScript" onLoad=StartSub>
<SCRIPT LANGUAGE="VBSript">
'StartSub is our sub routine that is first loaded
Sub StartSub
   ' The MsgBox function with the first
   ' argument as "Hello World!" to define the message
   MsgBox "Hello World!"
End Sub
</SCRIPT>
<br>This is to test VB Script</br>
</BODY>
</HTML>
```

This will give you on screen the message, as shown on the next page.

### 10.2.1 Adding VB Script code to HTML

It was easy to see that we can use both HTML and VBScript for Web pages. But, can we use them together. Let's see that. In the above example we make some changes to include both HTML and VBScript codes. The resultant text now becomes:

```
<HTML>
<title>Beginning to Learn Visual Basic Script</title>
<h1><font size=6 colour=blue>
<b><i>Hello World Visual Basic Script</I></b></font></h1>
<hr>
<INPUT TYPE=BUTTON VALUE="Click Here!" NAME="Hello">
<SCRIPT LANGUAGE="VBScript">
'This subroutine is run when the button is selected
Sub Hello_OnClick
   ' Msgbox function with three parameters. The first is the
   ' message, the second indicates what buttons to show and
   ' the last is the title of the msgbox
   MsgBox "Hello World!", 0, "HTML and VBScript combined"
End Sub
</SCRIPT>
</BODY>
</HTML>
```

The HTML section begins with the usual <SCRIPT></SCRIPT> tags. The key is defining a way for our code to run whenever the button is clicked. The button has an OnClick event so that if we define the event in our script, the specified code will run.

In this example, the Hello_OnClick subroutine in the script will be run whenever the button is clicked. And in this case, we have a message box for our "Hello World!" message. An event is run whenever an event takes place in the browser. Thus, in our example, the click of a button fires off the OnClick event.

### 10.2.2 Adding a Script to Your Documents

You have seen small examples tags. The first tag will indicate the script language and the end tag will end the scripting section. Following is an example:

```
<SCRIPT LANGUAGE="VBScript">
<!–
...
...
...
–>
</SCRIPT>
```

You need to specify the language, since Microsoft Internet Explorer Version 3.0 can support other scripting languages such as JavaScript. If you are deploying your HTML pages on the Internet for anyone to see, there is a good chance that someone who is using a browser that does not support Visual Basic Script may venture across your Web page. The HTML comment tags, <!—and —> placed as shown, will prevent these browsers from displaying the script code.

Where you place script code in a page can be at your discretion. You can even break the script code up into different sections of the document. Most likely though, it will be easier to keep all your code together in one section of your HTML document.

You can attach Visual Basic Script code to your document in order ways, though keeping your code together in one section is generally recommended. One way of add short sections of code (inline) is in the tag defining an HTML element. For example, the following HTML input button has an OnClick even that shows a message box:

```
<INPUT NAME="A button" TYPE=BUTTON
   VALUE="A Button" OnClick='MsgBox "I was clicked!"'>
```

You can place the Visual Basic Script code right in the declaration of the input element. The event name, in this case OnClick, is followed by the Visual Basic Script code in single quotes. In our example, we will call the MsgBox function. Multiple Visual Basic Script statements can be included as long as they are separated with colons (:).

You can also write a <SCRIPT> tag so that it applies only to a particular event for a specific HTML input element. In the following example, we have the same code for the AButton HTML button defined.

```
<INPUT NAME="AButton" TYPE=BUTTON VALUE="A Button">
<SCRIPT LANGUAGE="VBScript" EVENT="OnClick" FOR="AButton">
<!–
   MsgBox "I was clicked!"
–>
</SCRIPT>
```

In this case, the sample script will just be run whenever the AButton is clicked by the user. Notice that in the script definition we have defined which event we want the script to run FOR, in this case the OnClick event for the button.

### 10.2.3 Data Types of Visual Basic

One of the first things to understand about using variables in Visual Basic Script is how long the life of a variable is. Just because you may be wrong with variable Monica in one section of your code does not mean the value of Monica is available in another area of your code. You can think of this like a corporation. A global corporation will be accessed all over the world, whereas a local corporation will be accessed only in its home country, state, or city.

There are really three types of data to consider when working in a program. The first is called a **Local** variable, the second is a **Global** variable and the third is **Persistent** Data. Generally, we refer to a variable's scope to determine whether it is global or local. A variable can either be in scope, which means it is accessible or out of scope which means it is not.

### 10.2.4 Global Variables

Let's take a look at a simple Global variable example.

```
<!–Start the Script –>
<SCRIPT LANGUAGE=:VBScript">
Dim OurGlobal
StartSub
Sub StartSub
….OurGlobal = 5
….CheckGlobal
….MsgBox OurGlobal
End Sub
Sub CheckGlobal
….MsgBox OurGlobal
….OurGlobal = 10
End Sub
</SCRIPT>
```

### 10.2.5 Local Variables

Now let's take a look at utilizing Local variables in script code.

```
<!–Start the Script –>
<SCRIPT LANGUAGE=:VBScript">
StartSub
Sub StartSub
….Dim StartLocal
….StartLocal = 10
….DemoSub
….MsgBox StartLocaL
…MsgBox DemoLocaL
….DemoSub
End Sub
```

```
Sub DemoSub
....Dim DemoLocaL
....MsgBox "Demo Local = " & DemoLocaL
....DemoLocaL = 30
....MsgBox "StartLocaL = " & StartLocal
End Sub
</SCRIPT>
```

In this example, our startup routine is StartSub, the set of code that will be run first when the browser starts the script. It initializes the StartLocaL variable to 10. We then run DemoSub. In DemoSub, we have another Local variable, DemoLocaL. To ensure that DemoLocal is empty, we display the value. We then set its value to 30. We also display the value of StartLocal. Since DemoSub has no reference to StartLocal, the value is empty. We then return to StartSub and this displays both the value of StartLocal and DemoLocal. Since Startsub has not yet finished, StartLocal is still 10 and of course DemoLocal is empty because StartSub has no access to its value. Finally, we run DemoSub again. Now, you might think the value of DemoLocal is still 30. But, our first running of DemoSub has finished; that means that the instance of DemoLocal we had then is no longer around. Thus, we are starting with a newly initialized value of DemoLocal and it will be empty initially. Again, try this code in the browser and play around with it.

### 10.2.6 Strings in Script

All variables contain variant data. Variants in their basic form contain either numeric data or strings (alpha, numeric and special characters). Strings are very important in working with data. For example, if you want someone to enter his or her name and address information, the data will be stored in a string. But, if you want the user to enter his or her weight, then that will be stored in numeric subtype.

The first thing to point out about working with strings in Visual Basic Script is that they are always surrounded by double quotes (for example, "Hello"). The following is an example of how to set a variable to a string:

```
Dim strTest
strTest = "This is a String in Quotes!"
```

In this example, the variable strTest is set to contain the string: This is a String in Quotes! You will always need to ensure that you utilize the double quotes or Visual Basic Script will politely inform you that you have an error. Visual Basic Script provides a wide range of functions for working with strings. These include, but are not limited to Left, Right, Mid and Trim. Let's take a look at a few quick and simple example of working with strings to help get some basic string manipulation ideas down. Let's first look at basic string concatenation (or addition) using the & operator. To get started, let's review a visual example.

Now, let's look at a Visual Basic Script example that builds on our above graphical example. The following code will build the string "HelloWorld".

```
Dim strTest1
Dim strTest2
Dim strTest3
strTest1 = "Hello"
strTest2 = "World"
strTest3 = strTest1 & strTest2
```

You can think of the & symbol as acting like addition and in reality it concatenates (combines) two strings. Note that the new value is "HelloWorld" with no space between Hello and World. Taking from our visual example, the following example will build the string with a space.

```
Dim strTest1
Dim strTest2
Dim strTest3
strTest1 = "Hello"
strTest2 = "World"
strTest3 = strTest1 & " " & strTest2
```

In this case, we don't have a variable that defines the space; we simply place a literal string of "" into our string concatenation equation. The result is that strTest3 has "Hello World" with a space dividing the two words.

Simply adding strings together is not all we can do. We have access to powerful string manipulation functions including Left, Right and Instr for parsing strings. Let's set up an example of splitting off the extension of a filename. In our example, the filename will be "very wonderful.htm". In order to strip off the two parts surrounding the "-", we will have to find the location of the "-" in this string. Knowing where this character is located will help us determine where the filename ends and the extension begins. Fortunately, we have many built-in utilities to help us tear this string apart.

```
Dim intPos
Dim strFileName
Dim strLeft
Dim StrRight
StrFileName = " very wonderful.htm"
intpos = Instr(1, strFileName, ".")
```

Instr first wants to know where in the string we would like to start searching. In this case we will start in position 1. It then wants to know what string we are going to look in which in this case, is the filename stored in strFileName. Last we have to tell it what string to search for, which is ".". In this case intPos will have a value of 15, which is the location of the ".". Now let's get all of the characters to the left of the period using the Left function:

```
strLeft = Left(strFileName, intPos - 1)
```

This will return the string "very wonderful". We know the "-" is at position 15, so if we get the left 14 characters of the string, we will have "very wonderful". Now, let's get the extension of the filename:

```
strRight = Right(strFileName, Len(StrFileName) - intPos)
```

In order to do this, we have to utilize one more string function, Len. This will return the length of the filename, which is 18. So, if we get the right of characters of the string for a length of 3, we will have "htm". Since the "-" is at 15 and the length is 18, we can subtract the "-" position from the length to get the extension (18-15).

Visual Basic Script is rich in string manipulation tools; this has always been one of the strengths of the Visual Basic language.

Let's first take a look at the use of the ASC and Char functions in the ConvertAsc_ChrDemo subroutine of the code. Every character in a string has a corresponding value of 65. The ASC function will return the ASCII value of a character and the CHR function will convert as ASCII value into a character (string) representation. The first set of code in the subroutine converts integer 65 into a string, A.

```
....' Get the character representation
....' For ASCII 65
....strWork = chr(65)
```

The next set of code then converts the capital A back into a value of 65.

```
.....' Retrieve the ASCII value for the
.....' the character
...... intWork = asc(strWork)
```

The second subroutine, PaperStringDemo, demonstrates parsing or taking apart, a string using a wide variety of functions. Let's review how a couple of these work. First, the mid function us utilized as follows:

```
......' Set out working string
.......strWork = -ABCDEFGHIJKL"
.......' Get the Mid
......StriTemp = Mid(strWork,1,3)
```

The Mid function is a powerful string parser. It allows you to select which part of a string you would like to work with. In the above code example, we will get the section of the "ABCDEFGHIJKL" starting with visualize some of the Mid, Left, Right, and Inter functions.

### 10.2.7 Numbers in Script

Let's move on to working with numbers. As mentioned in the last session, all variables are of a variant data type, which means they can contain any subtype whether it be a string, number or date. Often, you will want to work with just variables that are numeric. So, if you are building a Web page to help to work with just variables that are numeric. So, if you are building a Web page to help millionaires track their money, you would want a long data type. If you are a science wizard calculating the nth root of the pie in the sky of the earth, you would want to use the double data type.

Of course when working with numeric data, there is not just one numeric subtype. In fact there are several, including Boolean, Byte, Integer, Long, Single and Double.

Using these numeric data types comes down to how precisely you need to define your number. If it is a simple yes or no, then using a Double would be a little bit of an overkill. Likewise, if you are doing scientific work, an Integer or even a Long will most likely not cut it. But, fortunately, Visual Basic Script will handle adjusting the data subtype for your.

Visual Basic Script also provides a wide range of functions for working with numbers. These functions loosely fall into three categories:

Standard Operators

Logical Operators and

Math Functions.

Standard Operators consists of those familiar math operations such as *, -, *, / and =. But this also includes some operators that may not be as familiar and obvious. For example, the integer division operator, \ is similar to the division operator, /, but performs a little different function. Let's look at the following example:

```
Dim intVar1
Dim intVar2
intVar1 = 17
intVar2 = intVar1 / 3
intVar3 = intVar1 \ 3
```

With normal division, intVar2 will have a value of 5.66667(17/3). With integer division, intVar3 will have a value of 5. If you only need an integer after a division operation and want the remainder to be discarded, the \ integer division operator is a valuable tool. Another function to utilize when working with division remainders is the Mod function. Mod performs modules arithmetic on two numbers with return the remainder after the division of the two numbers. Let's look at another example:

```
Dim intVar1
Dim intVar2
intVar1 = 17
intVar2 = intVar1 mod 3
```

In this case, intVar2 will have a value of 2 (3 goes into 175 times with 2 left over) which is the remainder of the division. Logical operators perform logical with operations on two variables. Let's look at a simple example of performing a logical AND operation.

```
Dim intVar1
intVar1 = 1 & 0
intVar1 = 1 & 1
intVar1 = 0 & 0
```

In the first case, intVar1 is going to return 0. In the second, the return value is 1. In the last case, the return value is 0. The logical AND of two values will only be true if both values are 1 or TRUE. The OR operator combines the values differently as outlined as follows:

```
Dim intVar1
intVar1 = 1 & 0
intVar1 = 1 & 1
intVar1 = 0 & 0
```

In the first and second case, 1 will be returned; in the last, 0 will be returned.

There are four sections to the script: Standard Operators, then Logical Operators followed by Match Functions and the last section showing several miscellaneous functions. Let's take a look at two of these miscellaneous functions: Int and Fix. The code for following with these is as follows:

```
...... Dim varWork
......' Set the initial value
......varWork = -57.98
......' Show the integer of the value
......document.write "Int(varWork) = " & Int(varWork) & "<br>"
......' show the 'fix' of the value which
.......' Will round down
......document.write "Fix(varWork) = " & Fix(varWork) & "<br>"
```

The Int and Fix functions return the Integer portion of a number. But, if a number is negative, Int returns the first negative integer less than or equal to the number. Fix returns the first negative integer greater than or equal to the number. Review the other code examples to see the effect of the different operators and functions. Most of these will be as familiar as your high school math. Some will only be useful if you are a heavy duty math person.

### 10.2.8 Dates and Time in Script

This session is good for single people to review since we will use Visual Basic Script to show you how to get a date and make time to be with that date. Visual Basic Script provides a variable subtype of Date that can be utilized for working with both dates and time. If you need to work with dates or time in your Visual Basic Script pages, you will be glad this date type is built into the language. There are many powerful built-in functions for manipulating both. Let's first look at how we can retrieve the current date and time using the Date, Time, and Now function:

```
Dim dtVar1
Dim dtVar2
Dim dtVar3
dtVar1 = Date
dtVar2 = Time
dtVar3 = Now
```

The dtVar1 variable will contain the current system date in the format of "1/1/96". The dtVar2 variable will contain the current system time in the format of "10:37:30 PM". Finally, the dtVar3 variable will contain both the current system data and time in the format of "5/10/96 to 10:37:30 PM".

The following table briefly overview the Date functions provided in Visual Basic Script

| *Function* | *Description* |
|---|---|
| Date | Returns the current system date |
| Time | Returns a Variant of subtype Date indicating the current system time. |
| DateSerial | Returns a Variant of subtype Date for a specified year, month and day. |
| DateValue | Returns a Variant of subtype Date. |
| Day | Returns a whole number between 1 and 31, inclusive, representing the day of the month. |
| Month | Returns a whole number between 1 and 12, inclusive, representing the month of the year. |
| Weekday | Returns a whole number representing the day of the week. |
| Year | Returns a whole number representing the year. |
| Hour | Returns a whole number between 0 and 23, inclusive, representing the hour of the day. |
| Minute | Returns a whole number between 0 and 59, inclusive, representing the minute of the hour. |
| Second | Returns a whole number between 0 and 59 inclusive representing the second of the minute. |
| Now | Returns the current date and time according to the setting of your computer's system date and time. |
| TimeSerial | Returns a Variant of subtype Date containing the time for a specific hour, minute and second. |
| TimeValue | Returns a Variant of subtype Date containing the time. |

Fortunately, Visual Basic Script provides solid, built-in functionality for working with dates and times. These functions are easy and straightforward to use.

### 10.2.9 Arrays in Script

So far we have been working with variables known as scalars. Scalar variables only allow you to assign a single value to the variable. Many times, however, you will want to easily track many values at one time. Let's say you have a Web page that, depending on a class number, shows all of the students in the class. And, this Web page will allow you to enter the grade for each student. There are several challenges to making this happen. First, each class might have a different number of students. Second, it would be very unwieldy to try to declare and work with enough variables to define each student and grade. Just imagine having variables intStudent1 through intStudent50 to try to do this.

Fortunately, there is a special type of variable in Visual Basic Script called an Array that allows you to easily work with large amounts of data in a convenient fashion. Dimensioning an Array variable is very easy, as follows:

```
Dim arrVar(5)
```

The array arrVar has a single dimension with six elements. Note that there are six elements and not five because the first element of the array starts at zero, not one. Let's look at an example defining an array of students from our class example.

```
<SCRIPT LANGUAGE="VBSript">
Dim arrStudents(50)
arrStudents(0)  =  "Akash Chopra"
arrStudents(1)  =  "Virendra Sehwag"
arrStudents(2)  =  "Rahul Dravid"
arrStudents(3)  =  "V V S Laxman"
arrStudents(4)  =  "Saurav Ganguly"
arrStudents(5)  =  "Parthiv Patel"
</SCRIPT>
```

In this example, we have an array of students, arrStudents(50) that has 51 elements. We have defined the first six elements to have the student's names by using a numerical index into the array. Note that the remaining elements remain empty. To access the value of an element in the array, simply use the index as follows:

```
strTestVar  =  arrStudents(1)
```

In this case strTestVar will be equal to Johny Anderson. Arrays can also have two dimensions. Let's implement the ability to also store the students' grades along with their names as follows:

```
dim   arrStudents(50,1)
......arrStudents(0,0)  =  "Akash Chopra"
......arrStudents(0,1)  = 5

.....arrStudents(1,0)  =  "Virendra Sehwag"
.....arrStudents(1,1)  =  15

....arrStudents(2,0)  =  "Rahul Dravid"
....arrStudents(2,1)  =  25
```

In this example, our arrStudents variable has two dimensions. The best way to think of two-dimensional arrays is as a table with columns and rows. You can have multidimensional arrays for working with all kinds of data relationship.

You may have noticed that in our examples with arrStudent, we have dimensioned 51 elements but are only using a few of these. Let's look at another way to dimension and work with array size.

```
<SCRIPT LANGUAGE="VBScript">
Dim   arrStudents()
Dim intNumsStudents
IntNumStudents  =  GetNumbersStudents
ReDim arrStudents(intNumStudents)
...
```

```
...
...
intNumStudents = GetNumberStudents
ReDim Preserve arrStudents(intNumStudents)
</SCRIPT>
```

You can also declare an array whose size changes at any time your script is running. This is called a dynamic array. The array is initially declared locally within a procedure or globally using the Dim statements as with any other array. The difference is that no size or number of dimensions is placed inside the parentheses. To use a dynamic array, you must subsequently use ReDim to determine the number of dimensions and the size of each. In the above example, ReDim to determine the number of dimensions and the size of each. In the above example, ReDim sets the initial size of the dynamic array to the value returned from a function called GetNumberStudents. Now let's say that later we need to check again how many students there are in a class, in case some have been added or deleted. A subsequent ReDim statement resizes the array to the new number of students, but uses the Preserve keyboard to preserve the contents of the array. Without the Preserve keyword, all data in the array would have been erased.

The topic of our code example for this session is working with several of the array functions provided in Visual Basic Script. Utilizing these functions will help you in your endeavors with arrays. Arrays are powerful tools for dealing with large amounts of data. Remember that an array's elements can be of any data subtype and allow you to mix and match what type of data you will be working with, as in our student name and grade example.

### 10.2.11 Getting the Message Across

With new tools provided in Visual Basic Script, a whole new set if opportunities is available for communicating directly with your users. Now that we have the ability to manipulate HTML buttons, the windows status bar and so on, the information displayed in these items can be dynamically controlled.

For example, from Visual Basic Script can change the caption of an HTML button with a simple statement, as follows:

```
button.Value = "new value"
```

Simply by setting a new value for the button control, we have new options, for making our controls state dependent. An example would be playing a game. While the game is stopped, the button value could be Play. While the game is in play, the button value could be stop. Thus, this one HTML button can now be used for different purposes.

Another example of available options is the ability to set the status bar text of the Internet Explorer browser by referencing the status property of the Window object. We can set this status based on user actions in our Web document.

When the button is clicked on, the code reference the caption value of the label control and its caption is updated to display the new text, "Updated!". The following code demonstrates the changes in the button values using visual Basic Script.

```
Sub Button1_OnClick()
......Click1Count = Click1Count + 1
......Button1.Value = "Clicked " & Click1Count & " times"
End Sub
```

In this example, there is a global counter that is incremented each time the button is clicked. We then display the new button value by concatenating the "Clicked" text with the counter value and then the "times" text. Each button will reflect the number of times each was clicked.

Finally, the browser status bar is set by clicking on the other three buttons using the following code:

```
Sub Status1_OnClick()
…..SetStatus "You clicked the first status button"
End Sub
Sub SetStatus(Status)
…..window.status = status
End Sub
```

A general subroutine, SetStatus is provided to set the window status value based on the Status argument. Each click event for the buttons calls this subroutine and passes in the text to be displayed. Remember that the browser also uses the status bar based on various events the user may initiate on the Web page.

## 10.3 Java Script

Like many other programming languages JavaScript is a programming language, which is mainly used with Web Pages. This language is very useful when providing interactivity to a Web page. There are lots of JavaScript programs available over the net which can be copied and made use by making alterations desired by you. A JavaScript is a program which is included on an HTML page. On the HTML page you enclose the JavaScript program within <SCRIPT> and end it up with </SCRIPT>. When you run it with a browser, it knows that this is a program written under JavaScript it runs it to give you the result instead of just giving the text of the script. The <SCRIPT> tag is most often found within the <HEAD> section of the HTML page, though you can, if you wish, have scripts under the <BODY> section.

### 10.3.1 What you can do with JavaScript?

There are lots of thing which you can do with JavaScript to enhance your Web page besides making it more interactive. It allows you to have Web pages users feedback by providing buttons on the Web page.

You can create forms which the users of the Web page can fill to provide you with the information needed by you. You can even do calculations on these forms using CGI. It also allows you to create new windows, display alert boxes and messages on the Web pages.

### 10.3.2 JAVA and JavaScript

Let me make it very clear once and for all, JAVA and JavaScript have only name in common and nothing else. They are poles apart. JAVA is basically a programming language which is enhancement of C++ having a distinctive feature of being able to run on various machines and operating systems like Windows NT, Mac OS or even Unix.

### 10.3.3 JavaScript as Object Oriented Language

An object is some kind of a thing. A computer, a mouse, etc., are all objects. To JavaScript they are all objects it deals with in Web browsers such as windows, forms and elements of the form such as buttons and check boxes.

### 10.3.4 Events

Events are actions that the user performs while visiting your page. Submitting a form and moving a mouse over an image are two examples of events. JavaScript deals with events with commands called event handlers. There are as many as 12 JavaScript event handlers, as listed below. An action by the user on the page triggers an event handler in your script.

#### *10.3.4.1 Event Handlers*

| ***Event*** | ***What it handles*** |
|---|---|
| onAbort | The user aborted loading the page |

| | |
|---|---|
| onBlur | The user left the object |
| onChange | The user changed the object |
| onClick | The user clicked on an object |
| onError | The script encountered an error |
| onFocus | The user made an object active |
| onLoad | The object finished loading |
| onMouseOver | The cursor moved over an object |
| onMouseOut | The cursor moved off an object |
| onSelect | The user selected the contents of an object |
| onSubmit | The user submitted a form |
| onUnload | The user left the window |

### 10.3.5 Writing first JavaScript program

For creating the text file, you can use any of the text program, I am using here Notepad. As you can see I have created a new file for this.

As you would notice that I have given the name of the file as New1 with html extension and run it under Netscape to get the result as shown on the next page.

So you how you have been able to run your first JavaScript program and see the result too. Let me now tell what has gone into it.

| | |
|---|---|
| <SCRIPT> | This is the opening script tag which tells the browser to expect JavaScipt instead of HTML. |
| document.write | This is your first line of the program for execution which has been taken up by the browser in the document window and shown the result. |
| "Learning JavaScript" | I have given this, you could have given anything else of your choice. |
| </SCRIPT> | This shows the end of the JavaScript program. |

Rest of the commands are from HTML, I would not explain them here, since I presume that you must be knowing them.

### 10.3.6 Putting Comments

As you would have done in any other program which you would have written, you need to put comments in the programs. Each programming language allows you to do the same. Some of them give you the option of REM or /* or any other similar command.

JavaScript also gives you the option in the form of /*. So anything written after this is not executed till it comes across another command as */ which breaks the comment option and starts executing the further lines.

In the above example, you will see that I have put "This is a comment line and is not to be executed" within the scope of /* and */.

The result is not required to be shown because it will remain the same despite these lines.

### 10.3.7 Using Quotes

As you have seen in the above example, I have used quotes for displaying the text. What would happen if I have to display the quotes themselves?

Let me explain this with the help of another example. The text of the program is shown here and the output of it is given on the next page.

If you are still not clear about the various quotes, have a look at the table given below and everything would be clear to you.

| *Character* | *Meaning* |
|---|---|
| \' | single quote |
| \" | double quote |
| \\ | backslash |
| \n | new line |
| \r | carriage return |
| \f | form feed |
| \t | horizontal tab |
| \b | backspace |

### 10.3.8 Using Alert

You can alert the user about anything by using the alert symbol. You can create an alert window that will pop up and give the user the vitally important information that they need to know about your page.

All you need to do is to put the following line in your text and the following alert symbol will appear on the page.

```
alert("This is Learning JavaScript")
```

### 10.3.9 Functions

These can be called as many times as needed during the running of the script. For example, let us say that you have gotten some information that a user typed into a form and you have saved it using JavaScript. If you need to use that information again and again, you could repeat the same code over and over in your script. It is then better to write that code once as a function, then call the function whenever you need it.

A function consists of the word function followed by the function name. There are always parentheses after the function name, followed by an opening brace.

The statements that make up the function go on the following lines, then the function is closed by another brace.

Here is how a function looks like:

```
function saySomething() {
    alert("Whatever you want to say")
}
```

Notice that the line with alert is indented. That makes it easier to read your code. All of the statements between the first brace and the last one are part of the function.

Let us see this with a live example. On the next page, you would see a JavaScript program which has been written to have 3 buttons each one of them having a new text underneath it. This text can be displayed by clicking at the corresponding button.

The text displayed by the various buttons is also shown.

Next we will use the conversion functions to find out the values of various variables. Most common among them is the eval function which is used to evaluate the value.

### 10.3.10 eval Function

This can be used to convert a string expression to a numeric value. Supposing we have to find out the value of the string 5 + 6 = . You can use this function to find out the value as 11. Not only this you can use the various mathematical operations too in this. Let us find out the value of following expressions using JavaScript.

5 * 6

6 / 5

I have used these examples on the next page to find out the values, see the text and the result on the next page which have been given as 30 and 1.2 respectively. Now since we are going to use all these mathematical expressions, we must know what sort of precedence they follow.

***10.3.10.1 Order of precedence***

parentheses, function call, or array subscript

!, ~, -, ++, –, typeof, new, void, delete

*, /, %

+, –

<<, >>, >>>

<, <=, >, >=

= =, !=, = = =, != =

&

^

|

&&

||

?:

=, +=, –=, /=, %=, <<=, >>=, &=, ^=, |=

The comma (,) operator

Now keeping this in mind, you can go ahead and perform the mathematical and other functions in JavaScript.

## 10.4 Java

First we had C and then we had C++ and now we have Java. These computer languages can be called so having the hierarchy like this. Much of the characters of Java are inherited from these two languages. From C, Java derives its syntax. Many of Java's object-oriented features are influenced by C++. In fact, several of Java's defining characteristics come from—or are responses to—its predecessors. Moreover, the creation of Java was deeply rooted in the process of refinement and adaptation that has been occurring in computer programming languages for the past three decades.

### 10.4.1 History of Java

In 1991, while working at Sun Microsystems, James Gosling, Patrick Naughton, Chris Warth, Ed Frank, and Mike Sheridan conceived Java. It took them 18 months to develop the first working version of the software language. This was initially called "Oak" but was renamed "Java" in 1995. Between the initial implementation of Oak in 1992 and the public announcement of Java in 1995, many more people contributed to the design and evolution of the language. Bill Joy, Arthur van Hoff, Jonathan Payne, Frank Yellin, and Tim Lindholm were the key players.

When Java was developed, no body thought of it for a platform like Internet. Instead, the primary motivation was the need for a platform-independent language that could be used to create software to be embedded in various consumer electronic devices, such as microwave ovens and remote controls. As you can probably guess, many different types of CPUs are used as controllers. The trouble with C and C++ (and most other languages) is that they are designed to be compiled for a specific target. Although it is possible to compile a C++ program for just about any type of CPU, to do so requires a full C ++ compiler targeted for that CPU.

The problem is that compilers are expensive and time-consuming to create. An easier—and more cost—efficient-solution was needed. In an attempt to find such a solution, work began on a portable, platform-independent language that could be used to produce code that would run on a variety of CPUs under differing environments. This effort ultimately led to the creation of Java. Around the same time that the details of Java were being worked out, a second, and ultimately more important, factor was emerging that would play a crucial role in the future of Java. This second force was, of course, the World Wide Web. Had the Web not taken shape at about the same time that Java was being implemented, Java might have remained a useful but obscure language for programming consumer electronics.

However, with the emergence of the World Wide Web, Java was propelled to the forefront of computer language design, because the Web, too, demanded portable programs. Most programmers learn early in their careers that portable programs are as elusive as they are desirable. While the quest for a way to create efficient, portable (platform-independent) programs is nearly as old as the discipline of programming itself, it had taken a back seat to other, more pressing problems.

Further, because much of the computer world had divided itself into the three competing camps of Intel, Macintosh and UNIX, most programmers stayed within their fortified boundaries, and the urgent need for portable code was reduced. However, with the advent of the Internet and the Web, the old problem of portability returned with a vengeance. After all, the Internet consists of a diverse, distributed universe populated with many types of computers, operating systems, and CPUs. Even though many types of platforms are attached to the Internet, users would like them all to be able to run the same program.

What was once an irritating but low-priority problem had become a high-profile necessity. During 1993, it became obvious to members of the Java design team that the problems of portability frequently encountered when creating code for embedded controllers are also found when attempting to create code for the Internet. In fact, the same problem that Java was initially designed to solve on a small scale could also be applied to the Internet on a large scale. This realization caused the focus of Java to switch from consumer electronics to Internet programming. So, while the desire for an architecture-neutral programming language provided the initial spark, the Internet ultimately led to Java's large-scale success.

Java, as said before, derives much of its character from C and C++. This is so because, the Java designers knew that using the familiar syntax of C and echoing the object-oriented features of C++ would make their language appealing to the legions of experienced C/C++ programmers. In addition to the surface similarities, Java shares some of the other attributes that helped make C and C++ successful.

*Firsty,* Java was designed, tested, and refined by real, working programmers. It is a language grounded in the needs and experiences of the people who devised it. Thus, Java is also a programmer's language.

*Secondly,* Java is cohesive and logically consistent.

*Thirdly,* except for those constraints imposed by the Internet environment, Java gives you, the programmer, full control. If you program well, your programs reflect it. If you program poorly, your programs reflect that, too.

Putting differently, Java is not a language with training wheels. It is a language for professional programmers. Because of the similarities between Java and C++, it is tempting to think of Java as simply the "Internet version of C++." However, to do so would be a large mistake. Java has significant practical and philosophical differences. While it is true that Java was influenced by C++, it is not an enhanced version of C++. For example, Java is neither upwardly nor downwardly compatible with C++. Of course, the similarities with C++ are significant, and if you are a C++ programmer, then you will feel right at home with Java. One other point: Java was not designed to replace C++. Java was designed to solve a certain set of problems. C++ was designed to solve a different set of problems. Both will coexist for many years to come.

The environmental change that prompted Java was the need for platform-independent programs destined for distribution on the Internet. However, Java also embodies changes in the way that people approach the writing of programs. Specifically, Java enhances and refines the object-oriented paradigm used by C++. Thus, Java is not a language that exists in isolation. Rather, it is the current instance of an ongoing process begun many years ago. This fact alone is enough to ensure Java a place in computer language history. Java is to Internet programming what C was to systems programming: a revolutionary force that will change the world.

### 10.4.2 Java as Internet Language?

As mentioned earlier, Java programming is the key factor of Internet programming. This is so because Internet helped catapult Java to the forefront of programming, and Java, in turn, has had a profound effect on the Internet. The reason for this is quite simple: Java expands the universe of objects that can move about freely in cyberspace. In a network, two very broad categories of objects are transmitted between the server and your personal computer: passive information and dynamic, active programs. For example, when you read your e-mail, you are viewing passive data.

Even when you download a program, the program's code is still only passive data until you execute it. However, a second type of object can be transmitted to your computer: a dynamic, self-executing program. Such a program is an active agent on the client computer, yet is initiated by the server. For example, a program might be provided by the server to display properly the data that the server is sending. As desirable as dynamic, networked programs are, they also present serious problems in the areas of security and portability. Prior to Java, cyberspace was effectively closed to half the entities that now live there. Java addresses those concerns and, by doing so, has opened the door to an exciting new form of program: the applet.

### 10.4.3 Keywords of Java

As in any other software or programming language, it is very important to understand the keywords first and then jump on to using it. Although the fundamental forces that necessitated the invention of Java are portability and security, other factors also played an important role in moulding the final form of the language. The key considerations were summed up by the Java team in the following list of keywords:

#### *10.4.3.1 Simple*

As the computer programming has grown over the years the language itself has taken care of most of the aspects leaving programmer with less and less work. I remember, in way back in 1970s, we used to languages like AutoCoder, FORTRAN, etc, which would need a real complicated programming. As we grew, the computer languages not only became easier to code but simple to use. So keeping the tradition going Java is also simple to use.

Assuming that you have some programming experience, you will not find Java hard to master. If you already understand the basic concepts of object-oriented programming, learning Java will be even easier. Best of all, if you are an experienced C++ programmer, moving to Java will require very little effort. Because Java inherits the C/C++ syntax and many of the object-oriented features of C++, most programmers have very little trouble learning Java. Also, some of the more confusing concepts from C++ are either left out of Java or implemented in a cleaner, more approachable manner. Besides its similarities with C/C++, Java has another attribute that makes it easy to learn: it makes an effort not to have surprising features. In Java, there are a small number of clearly defined ways to accomplish a given task.

#### *10.4.3.2 Object-Oriented*

Java was never designed to be source-code compatible with any other language. This allowed the Java team the freedom to design with a blank slate. One outcome of this was a clean, usable, pragmatic approach to objects. Borrowing liberally from many seminal object-software environments of the last few decades, Java manages to strike a balance between the purist's "everything is an object" paradigm and the pragmatist's "stay out of my way" model. The object model in Java is simple and easy to extend, while simple types, such as integers, are kept as high-performance nonobjects.

#### *10.4.3.3 Security*

This one factor is probably the important factor why Java is more popular with the Internet. As you are aware, every time you download a normal program, you are risking a viral infection. Prior to Java, most users did not download executable programs frequently, and those who did scanned them for viruses prior to execution. Even so, most users still worried about the possibility of infecting their systems with a virus. In addition to viruses, another type of malicious program exists that must be guarded against. This type of program can gather private information, such as credit card numbers, bank account balances, and passwords, by searching the contents of your computer's local file system.

Java answers both of these concerns by providing a firewall between a networked application and your computer. When you use a Java-compatible Web browser, you can safely download Java applets without fear of viral infection or malicious intent. Java achieves this protection by confining a Java program to the Java execution environment and not allowing it access to other parts of the computer. The ability to download applets with confidence that no harm will be done and that no security will be breached is considered by many to be the single most important aspect of Java.

#### *10.4.3.4 Portable*

Many types of computers and operating systems are in use throughout the world—and many are connected to the Internet. For programs to be dynamically downloaded to all the various types of platforms connected to the Internet, some means of generating portable executable code is needed. The same mechanism that helps ensure security also helps create portability.

#### *10.4.3.5 Robust*

As mentioned earlier, Java is platform free and works on most of the platforms. To make it so makes extraordinary demands on a program, because the program must execute reliably in a variety of systems. Thus, the ability to create robust programs was given a high priority in the design of Java. To gain reliability, Java restricts you in a few key areas, to force you to find your mistakes early in program development. At the same time; Java frees you from having to worry about many of the most common causes of programming errors. Because Java is a strictly typed language, it checks your code at compile time. However, it also checks your code at run time. In fact, many hard-to-track-down bugs that often turn up in hard-to-reproduce run-time situations are simply impossible to create in Java. Knowing that what you have written will behave in a predictable way under diverse conditions is a key feature of Java.

To better understand how Java is robust, consider two of the main reasons for program failure: memory management mistakes and mishandled exceptional conditions (that is, run-time errors). Memory management can be a difficult, tedious task in traditional programming environments. For example, in C/C++, the programmer must manually allocate and free all dynamic memory. This sometimes leads to problems, because programmers will either forget to free memory that has been previously allocated or, worse, try to free some memory that another part of their code is still using. Java virtually eliminates these problems by managing memory allocation and deallocation for you. In fact, deallocation is completely automatic, because Java provides garbage collection for unused objects.

Exceptional conditions in traditional environments often arise in situations such as “division by zero” or “file not found,” and they must be managed with clumsy and hard-to-read constructs. Java helps in this area by providing object-oriented exception handling. In a well-written Java program, all run-time errors can—and should—be managed by your program.

#### *10.4.3.6 Multithreaded*

Java was designed to meet the real-world requirement of creating interactive, networked programs. To accomplish this, Java supports multithreaded programming, which allows you to write programs that do many things simultaneously. The Java run-time system comes with an elegant yet sophisticated solution for multiprocess synchronization that enables you to construct smoothly running interactive systems. Java's easy-to-use approach to multithreading allows you to think about the specific behaviour of your program, not the multitasking subsystem.

*10.4.3.7 Architecture-Neutral*

One of the main problems facing programmers is that no guarantee exists that if you write a program today, it will run tomorrow-even on the same machine. Remember what happened to programs written in 70s to 90s which would not run in 2000, leading to a massive Y2K problem. Operating system upgrades, processor upgrades, and changes in core system resources can all combine to make a program malfunction. The Java designers made several hard decisions in the Java language and the Java Virtual Machine in an attempt to alter this situation. Their goal was "write once; run anywhere, any time, forever." To a great extent, this goal has been accomplished.

*10.4.38 Interpreted and High Performance*

As described earlier, Java enables the creation of cross-platform programs by compiling into an intermediate representation called Java bytecode. This code can be interpreted on any system that provides a Java Virtual Machine. Most previous attempts at cross-platform solutions have done so at the expense of performance. Other interpreted systems, such as BASIC, Tcl, and PERL, suffer from almost insurmountable performance deficits. Java, however, was designed to perform well on very low-power CPUs. As explained earlier, while it is true that Java was engineered for interpretation the Java bytecode was carefully designed so that it would be easy to translate directly into native machine code for very high performance by using a just-in-time compiler; Java run-time systems that provide this feature lose none of the benefits of the platform-independent code. "High-performance cross-platform" is no longer an oxymoron.

*10.4.3.9 Distributed*

Java is designed for the distributed environment of the Internet, because it handles TCP /IP protocols. Infact, accessing a resource using a URL is not much different from accessing a file. The original version of Java (Oak) included features for intra-address-space messaging. This allowed objects on two different computers to execute procedures remotely. Java has recently revived these interfaces in a package called Remote Method Invocation (RMI). This feature brings an unparalleled level of abstraction to client/server programming.

*10.4.3.10 Dynamic*

Java programs carry with them substantial amounts of run-time type information that is used to verify and resolve accesses to objects at run time. This makes it possible to dynamically link code in a safe and expedient manner. This is crucial to the robustness of the applet environment, in which small fragments of bytecode may be dynamically updated on a running system.

## 10.5 Front Page

FrontPage provides complete tools for creating, publishing and managing your World Wide Web sites. Over the years Web has become a necessity for the all users of the computers. Earlier, only those people who had quite a good knowledge of computer programming (HTML programming language) could design a Web page. With FrontPage , **HTML** knowledge is no longer required. FrontPage carries out the programming for you in the background, allowing you to concentrate on the other features in your Web pages such as design, feel and functionality. The program is easy to learn and contains simple controls as well as advanced tools to create Web pages.

### 10.5.1 Starting Microsoft FrontPage

You can start Microsoft FrontPage by one of the following methods:

*10.5.1.1 Using the Start Menu*

1. Click on Start button. The start menu will appear.

2. Click at **Programs**.
3. Click on **Microsoft Office** and then **FrontPage** .

*10.5.1.2 Using Shortcut*

You can use this feature if the icon of the software has been created and is put on the desktop.

1. First, locate the **Microsoft FrontPage** shortcut icon.
2. When you find it, position the mouse over the icon and click it to open the software.

Using any of the above options you will start the software and get the opening screen, which is shown next.

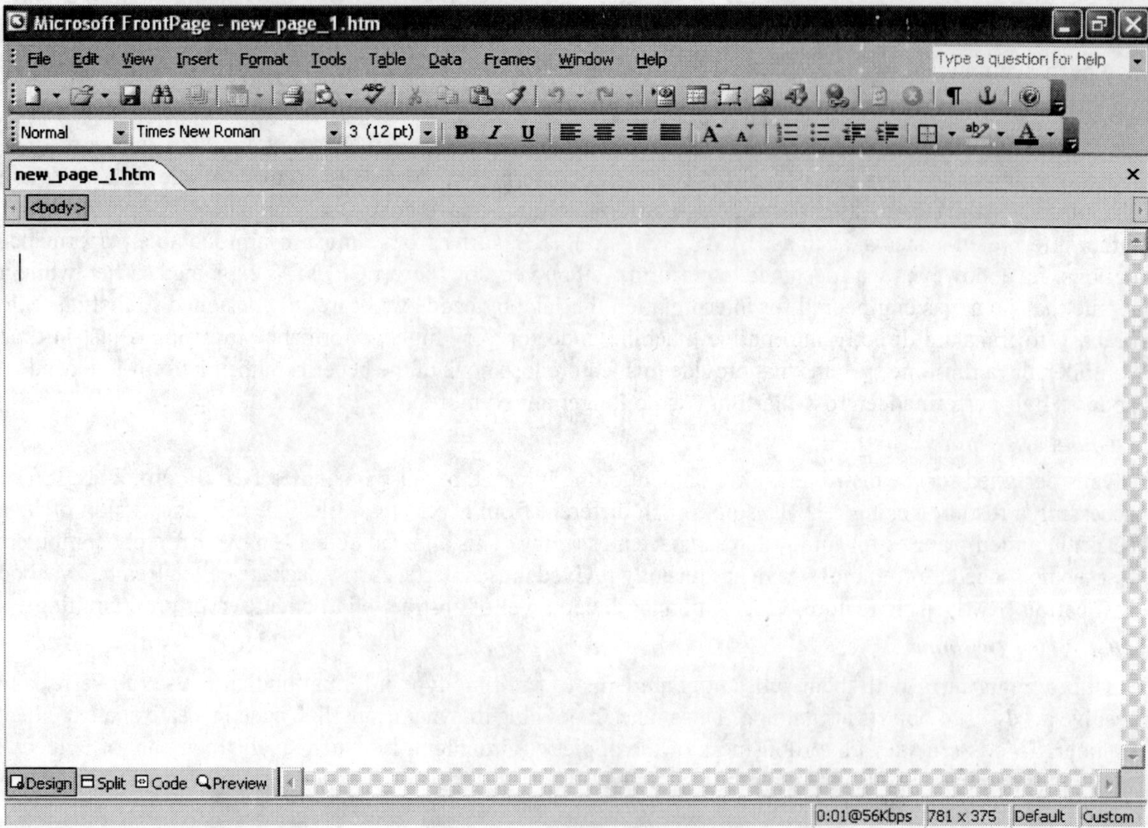


## 10.5.2 FrontPage Window

Whichever way you choose to work, you will be working on the FrontPage Window, contents of which are shown on the next page. The description here is shown alphabetically for easy tracing.

## 10.5.3 Using Wizards

FrontPage provides you a complete sit back type of Wizard which allows you to just sit back and allow FrontPage to create the Web Page for you. Only thing that you have to do is to answer few of the queries of the software.

FrontPage has two type of wizard; one which creates the **whole site** and the one which creates a **single page**.

## 10.5.4 Creating a Web Page using Wizard

You can create a Web Page in Microsoft FrontPage by the following method:

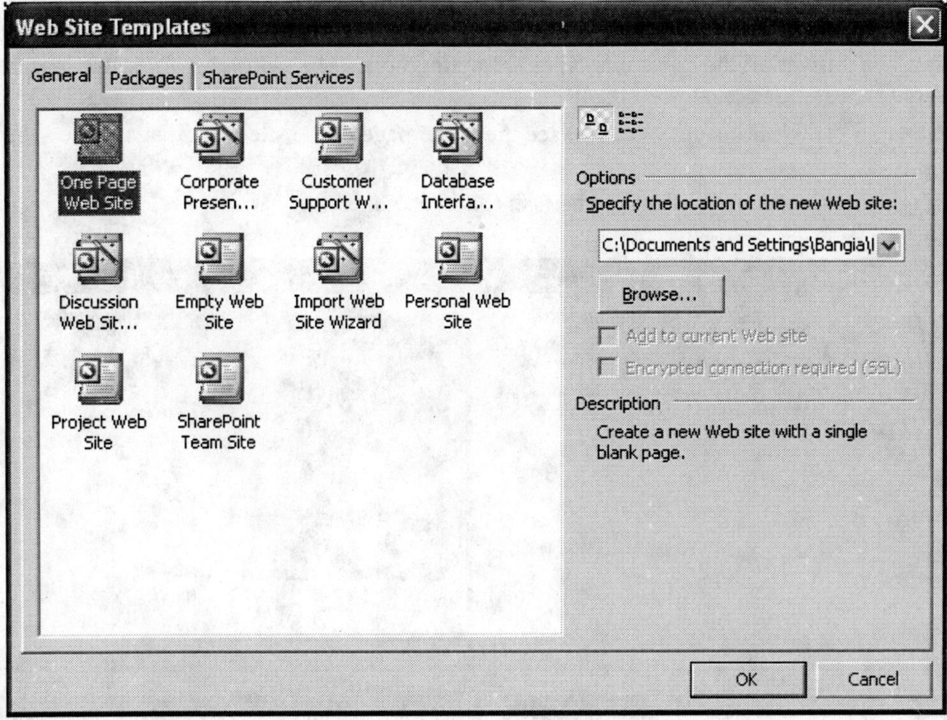


1. Click on **New** from the File menu.
2. Click at **One Page Web Site** from the Task Pane.
3. A new dialog box will appear, as shown on the next page.
4. Let us choose to create a **Corporate Presence Wizard** which is one of the options here. This wizard guides you through the process of developing a professional Web.
5. Click at the icon of the Wizard to start it.
6. It has numerous features that make it easier to establish a company's Web.
7. When you select this wizard, you will have to fill information in a series of 13 different dialog boxes, as shown on the following pages.
8. Fill up the data known to you.
9. To be able to fill the data in the dialog boxes, we suggest you keep the following information ready with you:
   - The products or services that will be promoted on the Web.
   - Whether feedback is required from the visitors or not.
   - Whether the feedback is to be saved, if yes, how.
   - Whether the Web needs to have its own search engine.
   - The company's information to be displayed on the Web page.
   - All the relevant company information like e-mail address, etc. and the Web related inquiries.
10. In case of any doubt leave the box as it is, since you can always come back to old box by pressing Back.

11. The Corporate Wizard includes a lot of explanatory text that describes what it is capable of creating.
12. After you answer all the questions on all 13 dialog boxes, the Corporate Presence Wizard is finally ready to create the actual Web itself.
13. Following the wizard pages, you will see the home page of the site and a page named Press Release 1.
14. Using this information you can create a similar web page.

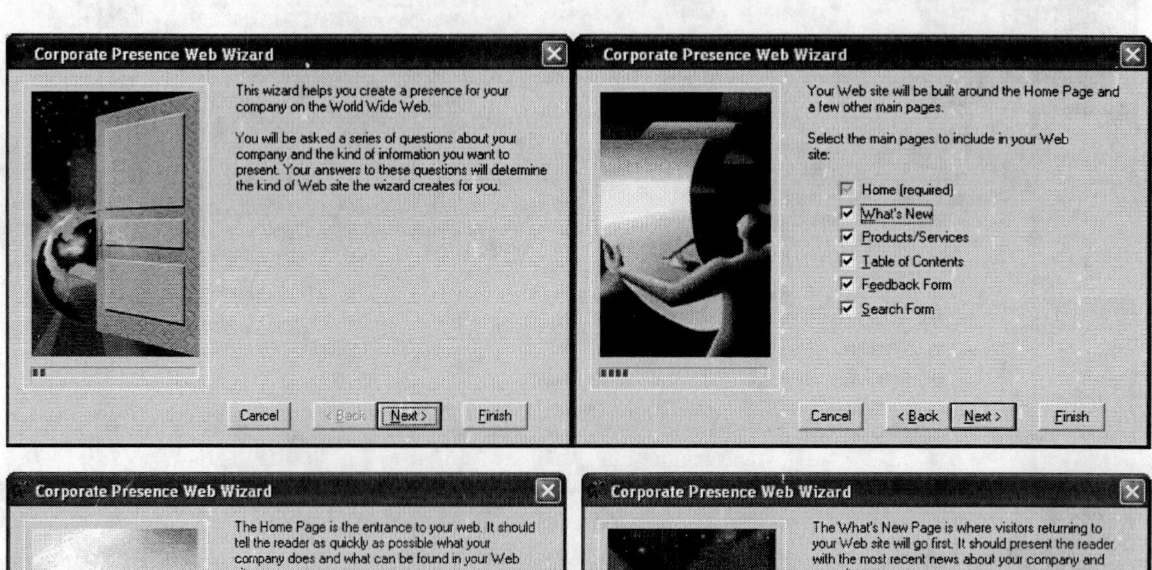


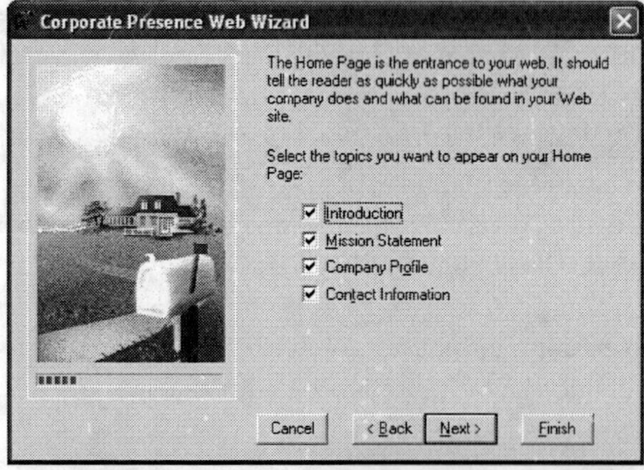


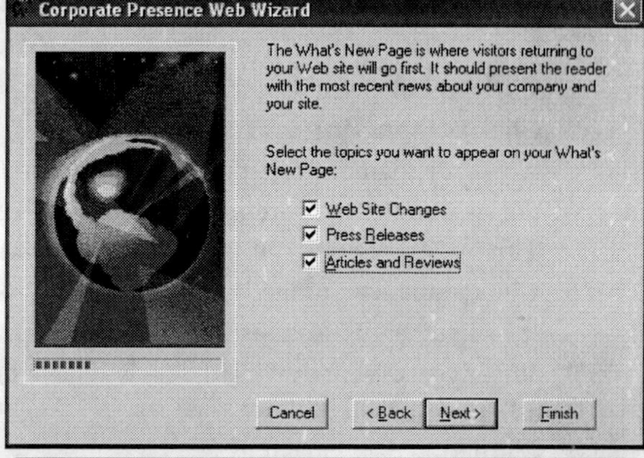


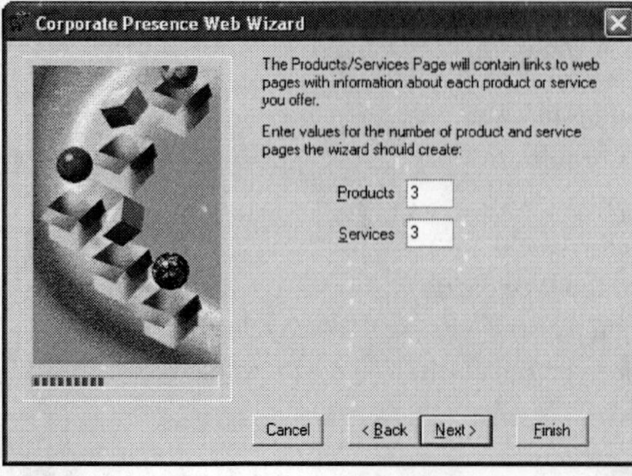


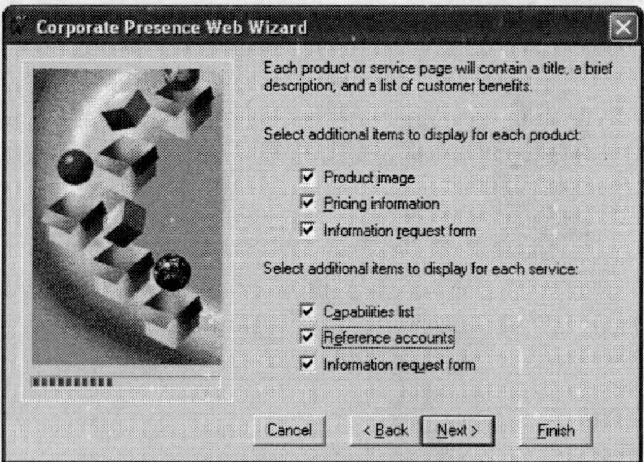

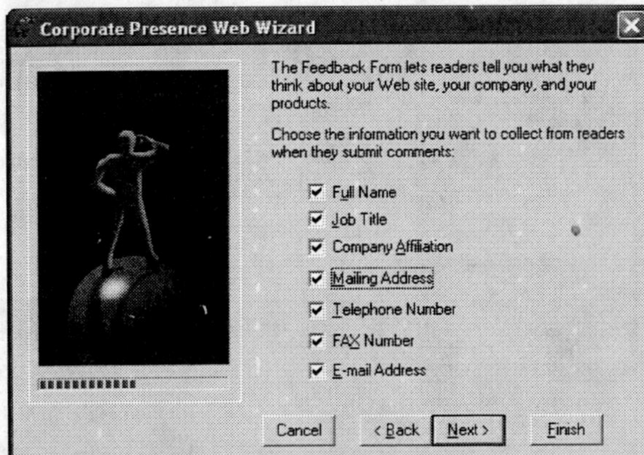
Corporate Presence Web Wizard
The Feedback Form lets readers tell you what they think about your Web site, your company, and your products.
Choose the information you want to collect from readers when they submit comments:
Full Name
Job Title
Company Affiliation
Mailing Address
Telephone Number
FAX Number
E-mail Address
Cancel
< Back
Next >
Finish

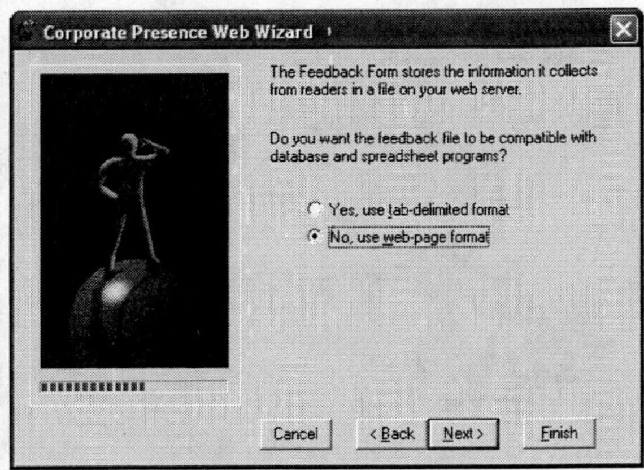
Corporate Presence Web Wizard
The Feedback Form stores the information it collects from readers in a file on your web server.
Do you want the feedback file to be compatible with database and spreadsheet programs?
Yes, use tab-delimited format
No, use web-page format
Cancel
< Back
Next >
Finish

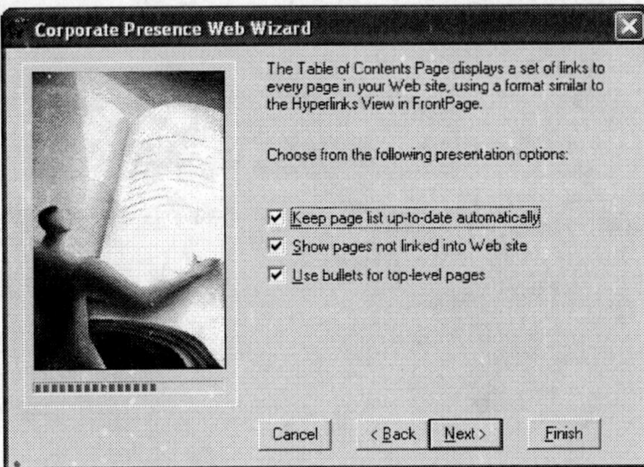
Corporate Presence Web Wizard
The Table of Contents Page displays a set of links to every page in your Web site, using a format similar to the Hyperlinks View in FrontPage.
Choose from the following presentation options:
Keep page list up-to-date automatically
Show pages not linked into Web site
Use bullets for top-level pages
Cancel
< Back
Next >
Finish

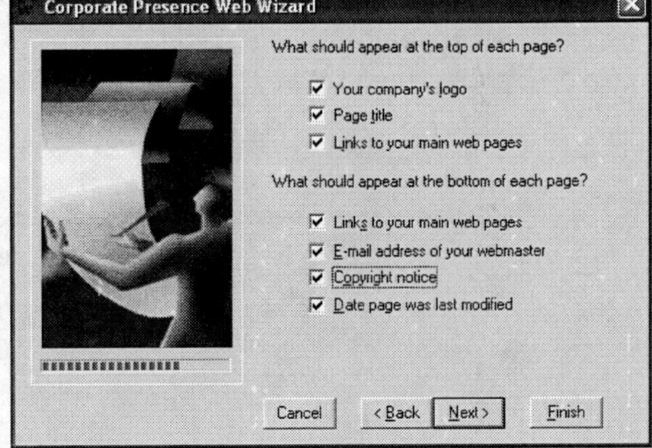
Corporate Presence Web Wizard
What should appear at the top of each page?
Your company's logo
Page title
Links to your main web pages
What should appear at the bottom of each page?
Links to your main web pages
E-mail address of your webmaster
Copyright notice
Date page was last modified
Cancel
< Back
Next >
Finish

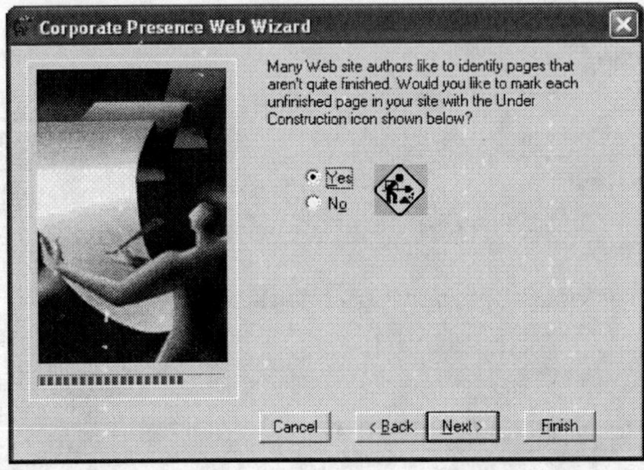
Corporate Presence Web Wizard
Many Web site authors like to identify pages that aren't quite finished. Would you like to mark each unfinished page in your site with the Under Construction icon shown below?
Yes
No
Cancel
< Back
Next >
Finish

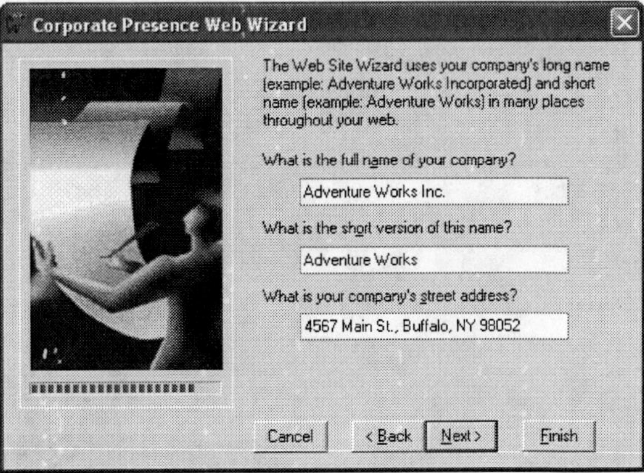
Corporate Presence Web Wizard
The Web Site Wizard uses your company's long name (example: Adventure Works Incorporated) and short name (example: Adventure Works) in many places throughout your web.
What is the full name of your company?
Adventure Works Inc.
What is the short version of this name?
Adventure Works
What is your company's street address?
4567 Main St., Buffalo, NY 98052
Cancel
< Back
Next >
Finish

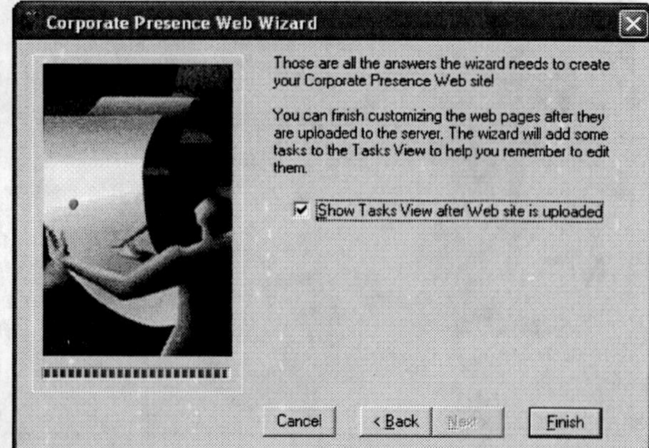


### 10.5.5 Creating a Web Page using Template

FrontPage provides ready to use **templates**. There are as many as 48 different templates, we are sure at least one of them would suit your style of Web page. Before you can create a page in FrontPage , you must create a Web that will contain that page.

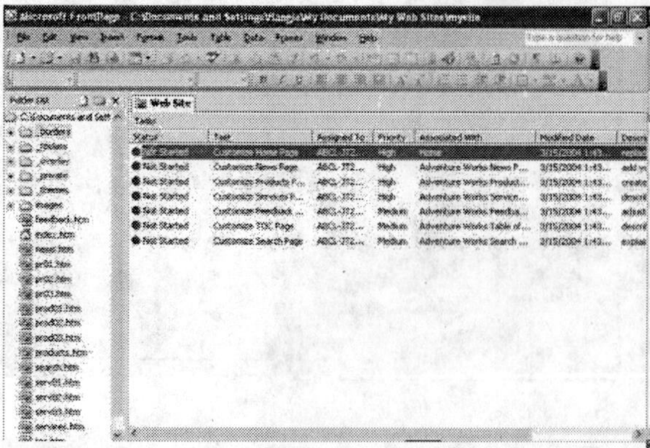

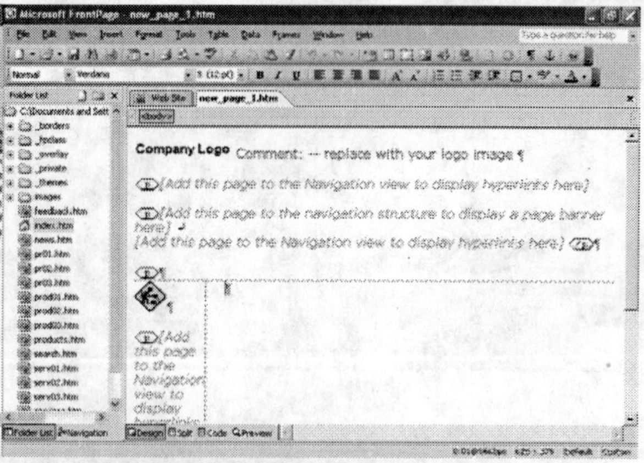

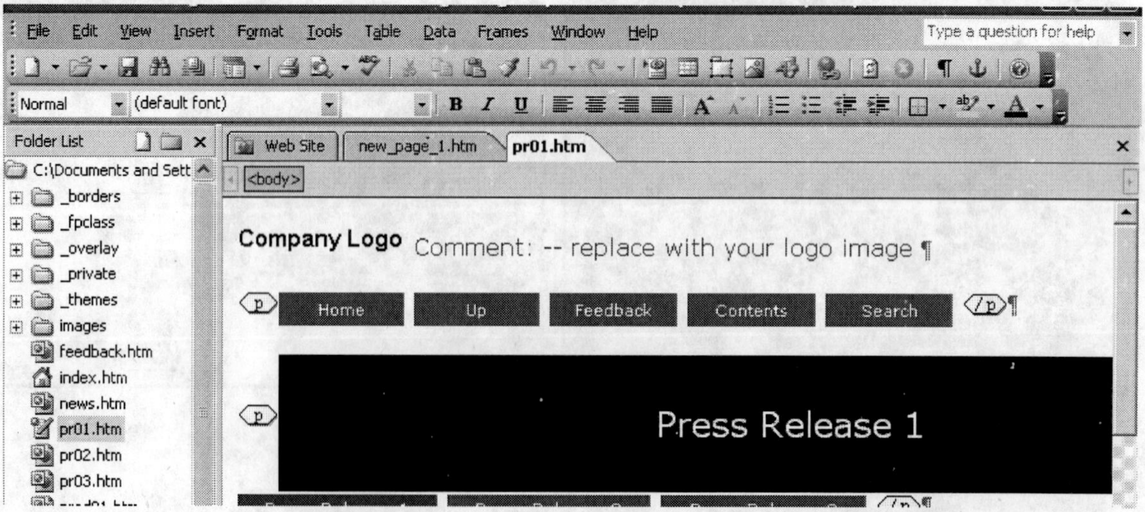

### 10.5.6 Selecting a Web Template

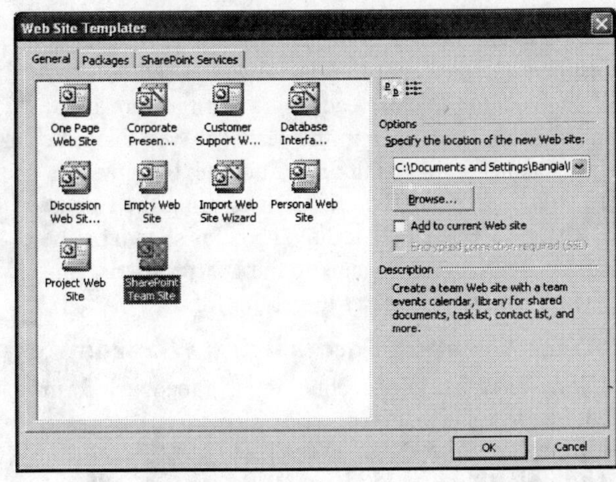


1. Click on **New** from the File menu.
2. Click at **Web** from the submenu.
3. A new dialog box will appear, as shown on the next page.
4. You can choose here one of the following:

   **One Page Web**
   **Corporate Presence Wizard**
   **Customer Support Web Site**
   **Database Interface Wizard**
   **Discussion Web Site Wizard**
   **Empty Web Site**
   **Import Web Site Wizard**
   **Personal Web Site**
   **Project Web Site**
   **Share Point Team Site**
5. You will have to inform the location of the Web page in the hard disk too.
6. Choose **Personal Web Site** from here.
7. You will get your personal web page with details shown on the next page.
8. A **navigation view** of the same page will look like the one shown on the next page (bottom).
9. As can be seen there are 4 main pages on this:

- A main page called Home page for all the information which can be obtained by clicking at aboutme.htm
- A page to describe your interests by clicking at interest.htm.
- You can get feedback in the form of a form, about which you will learn in the next chapter, using feedback.htm.
- A page to display your photos by clicking at photo.htm.
- A page to list your favourite Web sites by clicking at favorite.htm.

Click at **index.htm** to get the main page of this Web.

This page contains a timestamp component immediately after the text "This page last updated on" and before

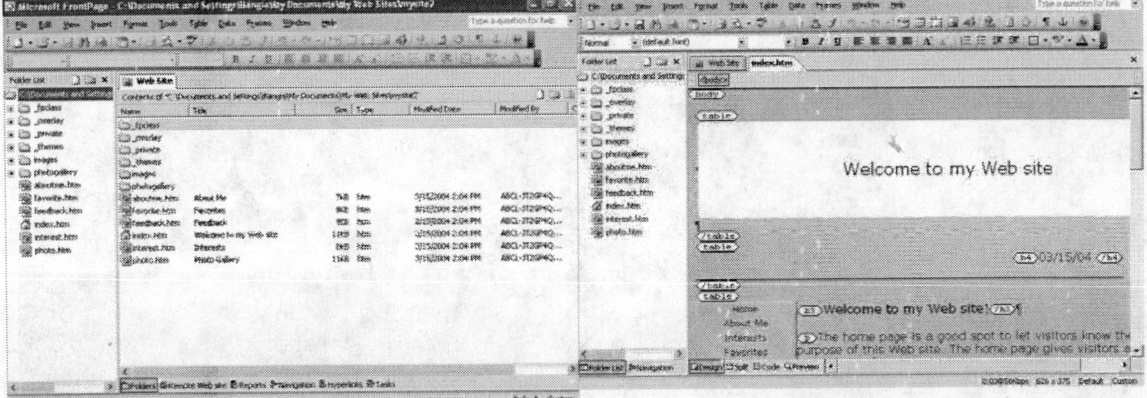

the period at the end of the sentence. The timestamp displays the date that the page was last edited, and changes automatically each time changes are made to the page. Each page in the personal Web template has a banner at the top. It can be both text or graphics. To change it, **double click** it to bring the **Page Banner Properties** dialog box, as shown on the next page. Now come back to the **Page view** and click at **favorite.htm** to get the figure.

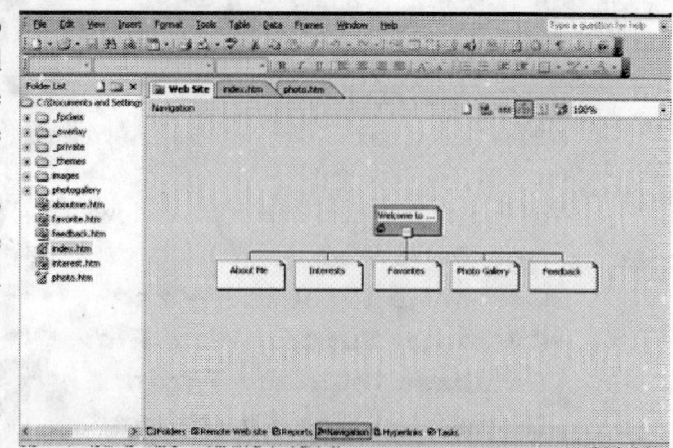


### 10.5.7 Creating Forms using Wizards

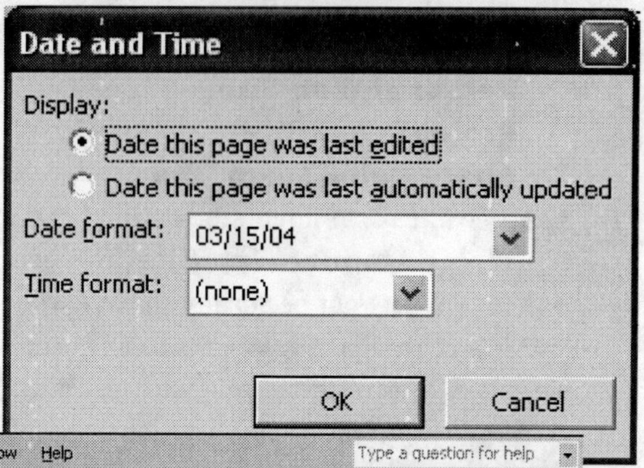

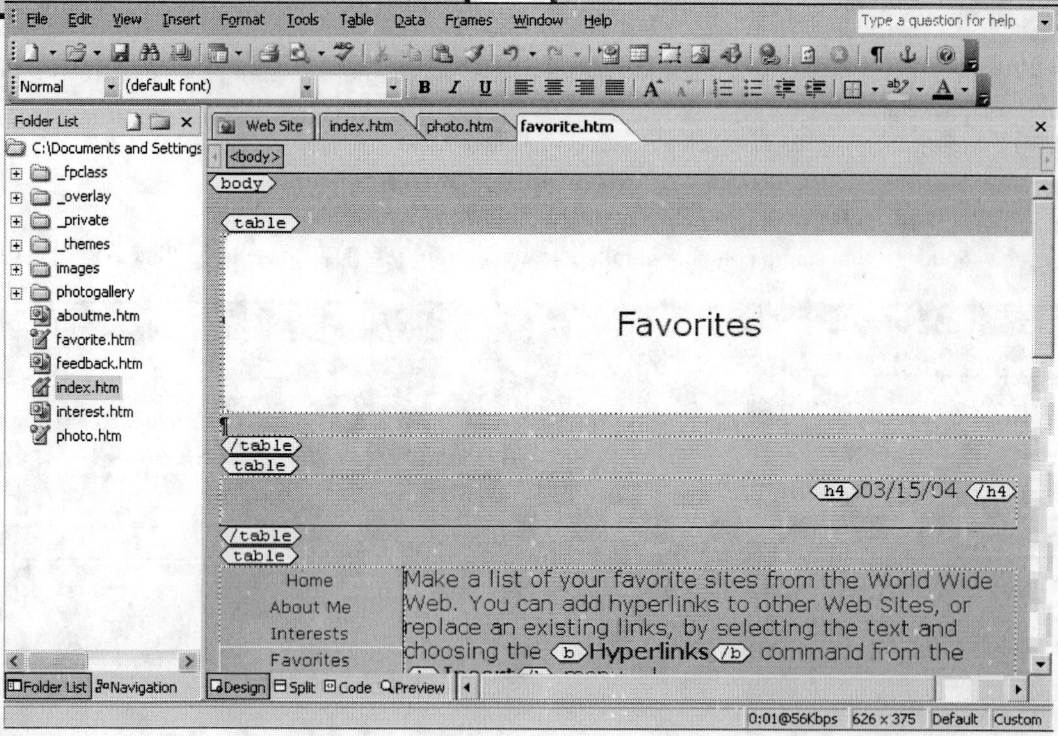

A form in Web related technology is a feedback form which you ask users of your site to fill up as a feedback effort. This helps in keeping track of the visitors to your site.

FrontPage allows you to create a **Form** in a wizzy by using the wizard called **FormWizard**. It asks you a series of questions which in turn you want to ask those who are visiting your site. Forms can be used for user surveys, visitor feedbacks, polls, questionnaires, tests and many other things where you want a feedback from the users.

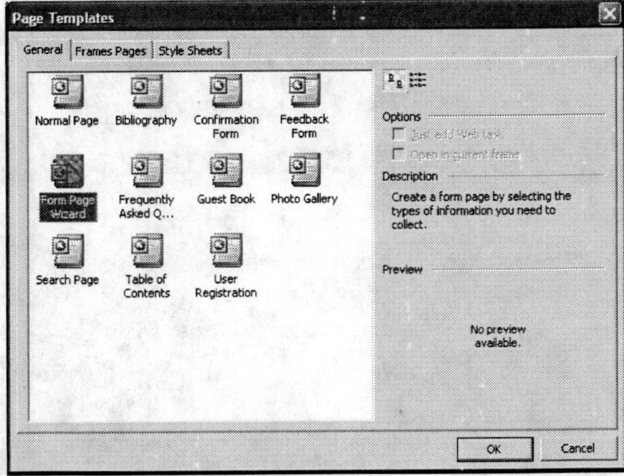


You have also to define where to store the information that you receive in the form of Forms.

Once you go through the various screens of the Wizard, shown on the next few pages, you will realize the type of questions which are asked by the Wizard and you can get ready with the answers before doing it on your own computer.

Once the wizard has created the form, it will be shown to you, as shown later.

It is not that the forms can be created by the wizards only. You can do it manually too. For this read the next para.

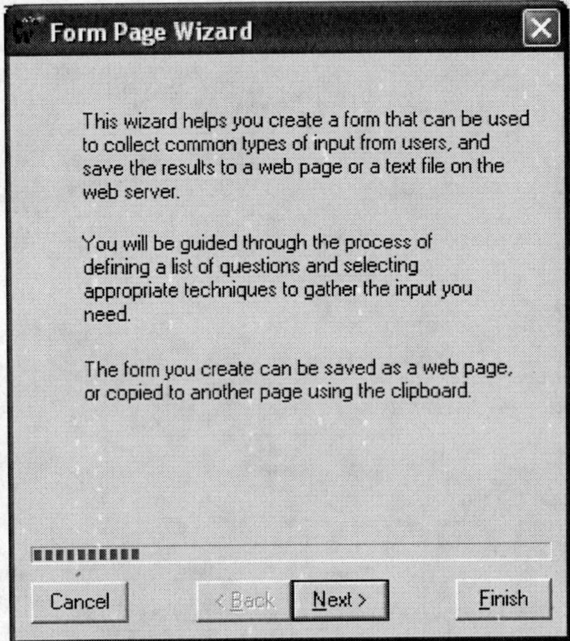


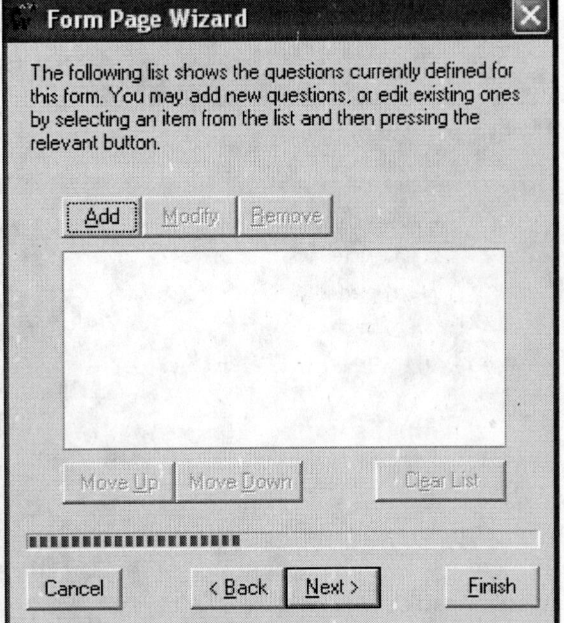


### 10.5.8 Creating forms

Earlier we had created a form using the Form Wizard. Here we will do the same but without the help of the wizard.

If you choose **Form** from the **Insert** menu, you will see the following items on the submenu:

- Form
- Textbox

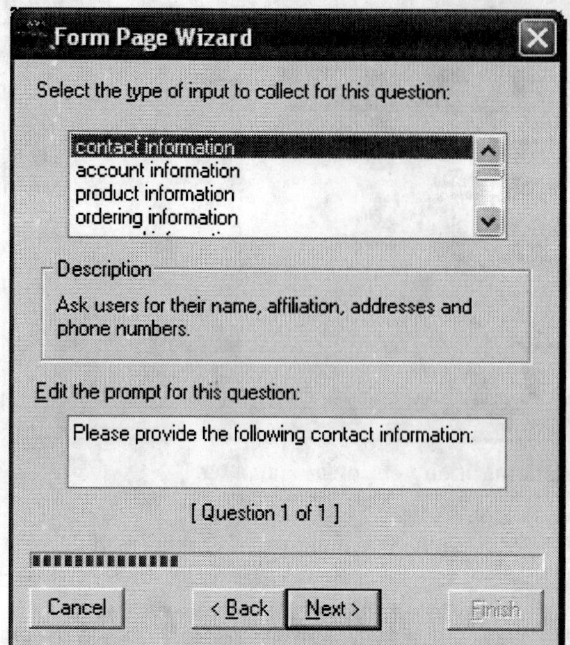


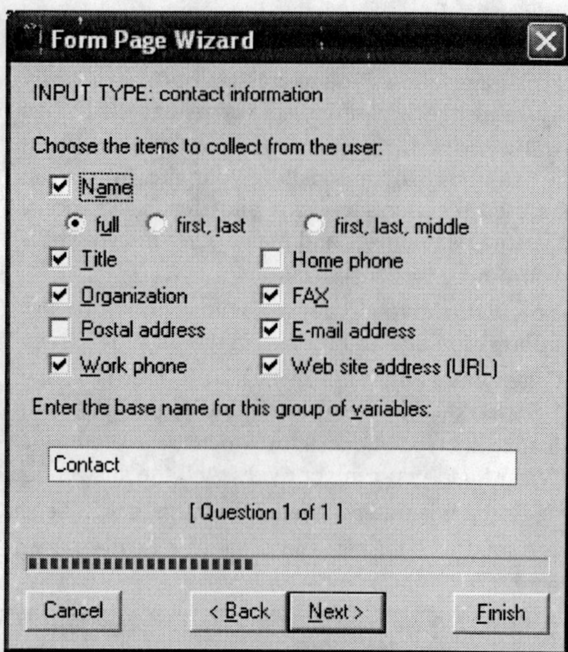


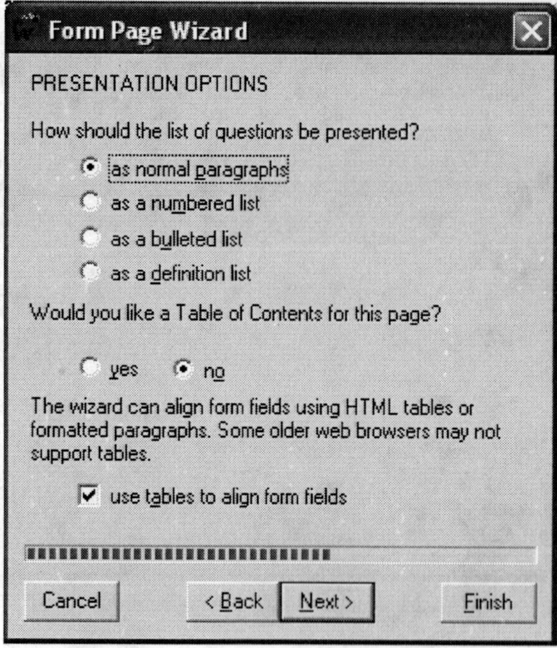


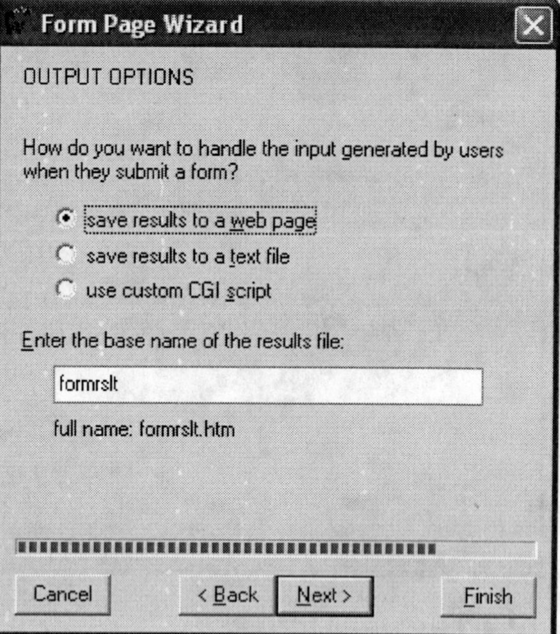


- Text Area
- File Upload
- Checkbox
- Option Button
- Group Box

- Drop-Down Box
- Push Button
- Advanced Button
- Picture
- Label

When you select **Form** from the **Insert** menu and **Form** submenu, you are given two buttons on the Web page, as shown on the next page. They are:

**Submit** It is used for transmitting the information collected on the form.

**Reset** It is used for clearing out all answers on a form and starting it all over again.

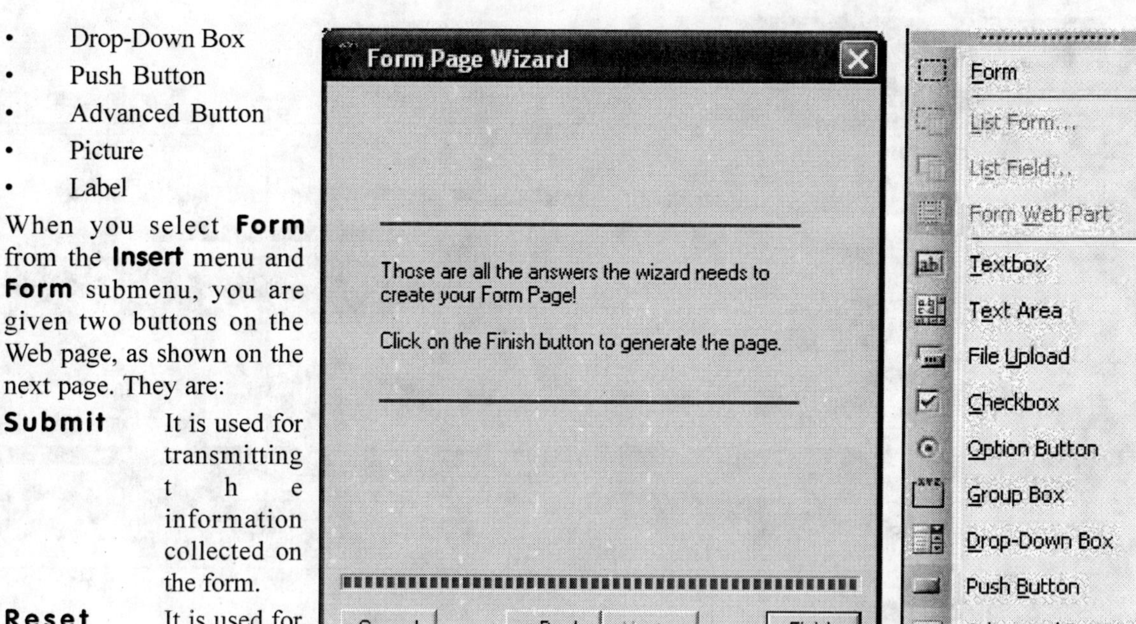


### 10.5.9 Adding Text boxes

You can add either a single line text box or an unlimited number of lines if you use **Scrolling** text boxes. The choice is yours, which one to use. In the text box you can add text. By default FrontPage sets the boxes according to the place available at its own will.

However, if you feel like changing its size, etc., you can change it by **double clicking** at the text box to get the dialog box where you can change the dimensions of the box. If you want to change the style of the name, you click at style to get the above dialog box and change one of the above mentioned 5 parameters. If you click at **validation**. The dialog box then received will let you validate the fields specially numeric ones.

### 10.5.10 Option button

A radio button is an element which has two possible values. You can give the value to the option button, as was done in the case of text boxes, by double clicking to get the dialog box and then giving the value and name to the radio button. The opion button properties box is shown here, while the option button in its position is shown on the next page.

### 10.5.11 Adding Check Box

It is very similar to radio button having two values mainly ON or OFF. You can define your own and give the name and value as was given in the case of Radio button.

The check box properties dialog box is shown here.

### 10.5.12 Adding Drop-Down Box

These are similar to radio buttons. Here you have a full menu with various options to choose from, as you see in your **FrontPage File** menu. In the drop-down menu properties dialog box received by double-clicking at the drop-down menu button, the following options are seen.

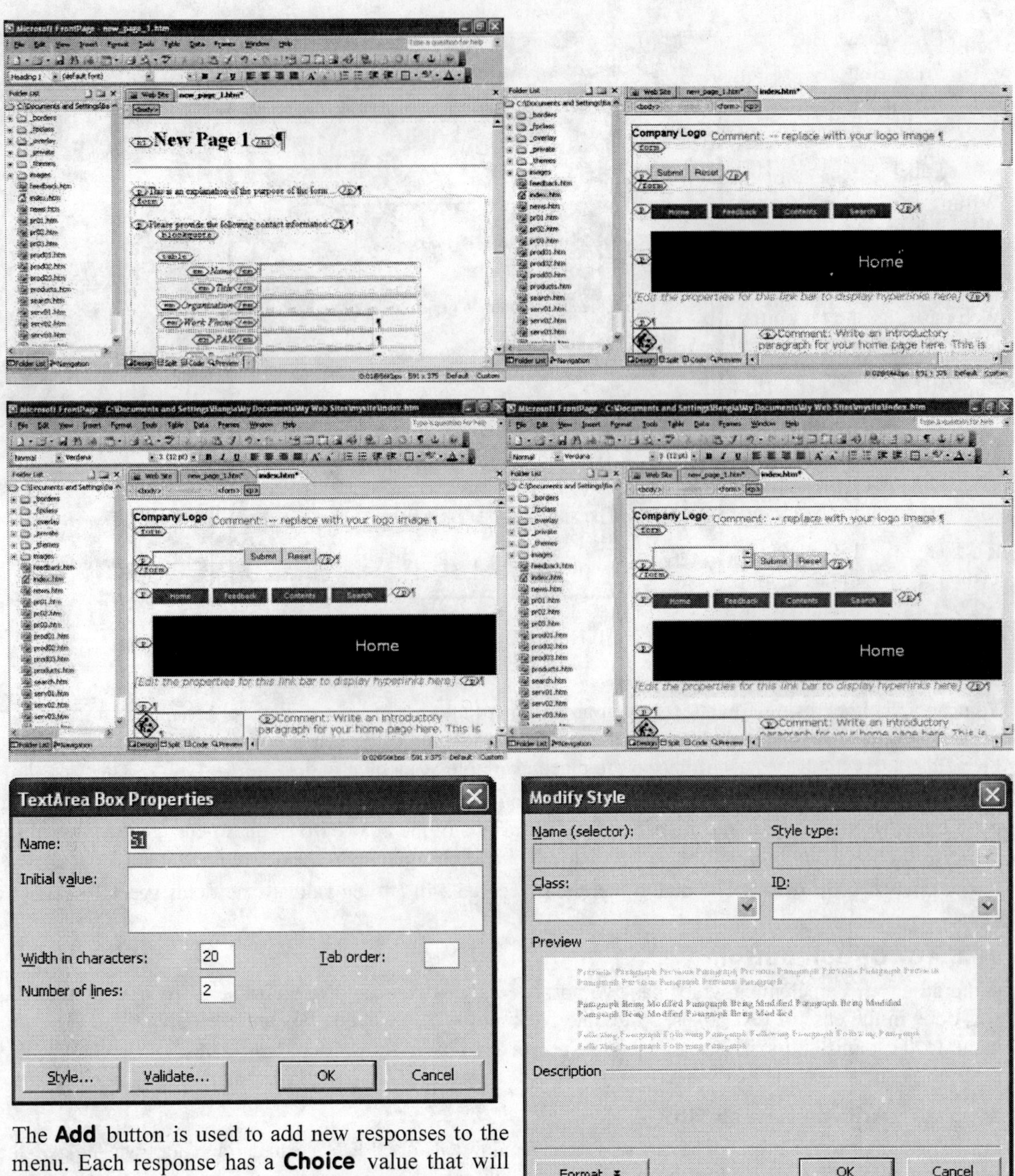


The **Add** button is used to add new responses to the menu. Each response has a **Choice** value that will appear on the menu, and the **Selected** value is transmitted with the form unless you specify an alternative.

### 10.5.13 Adding Pushbuttons and Pictures

Pushbuttons are like any other buttons but they can be associated with hyperlinks, so you can add them to a form as links to other pages. For example, you can use it as a Help button.

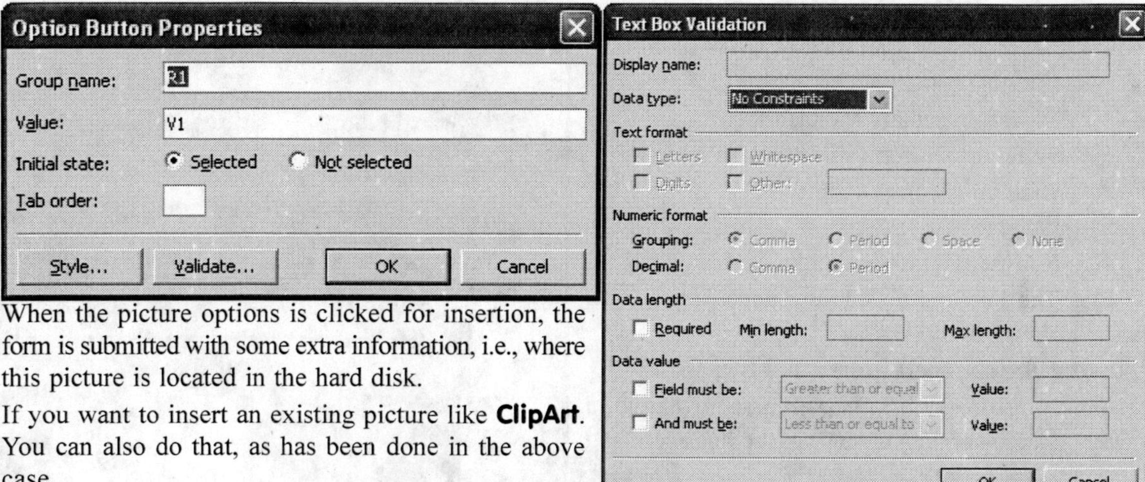


When the picture options is clicked for insertion, the form is submitted with some extra information, i.e., where this picture is located in the hard disk.

If you want to insert an existing picture like **ClipArt**. You can also do that, as has been done in the above case.

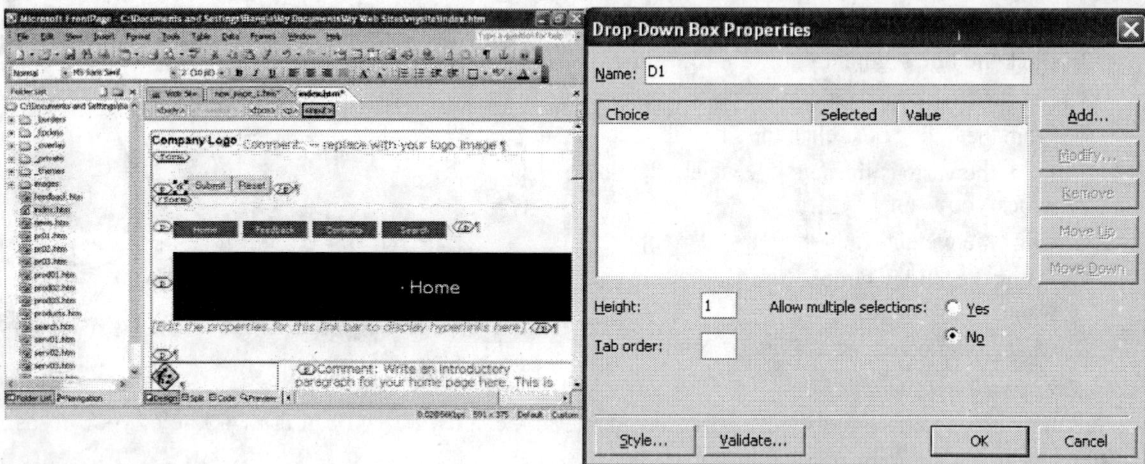


## 10.6 Flash

Flash is the most popular program for creating animations not only for Windows based programs but for Internet too. Lots of web sites are using Flash tools to create animations to enhance the looks of the site.

### 10.6.1 Drawing Various Objects in Flash

Using the various drawing tools you can draw the various objects on the screen.

### 10.6.2 Drawing Lines

Line tool allows you to draw various lines on the screen.

Follow the following steps to draw line.

1. Click at line tool.
2. Move the mouse pointer over the Stage area until the pointer changes from Arrow to Plus.
3. Drag to draw a line of your desired length.
4. Release the mouse button.
5. The line appears as required by you.

*10.6.2.1 Drawing Free Form Line*

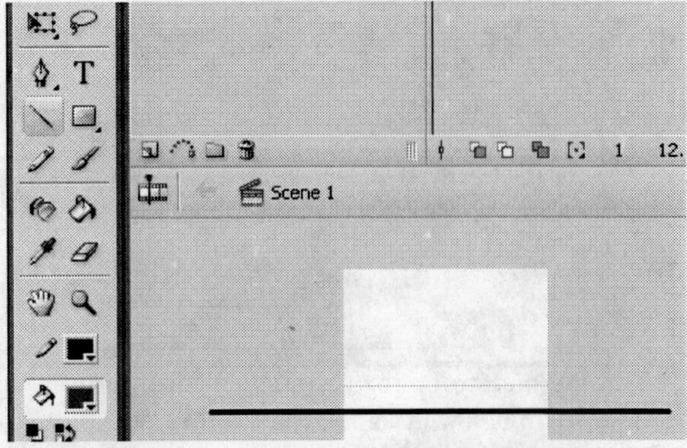


Follow the following steps to draw a free form line.

1. Click at pencil tool.
2. Click at Pencil mode tool.
3. Select the freeform line from the options.
4. Drag your cursor on the Stage to draw the line.
5. Release the mouse button.
6. The line appears to your specifications, as shown here.

*10.6.2.2 Formatting the line*

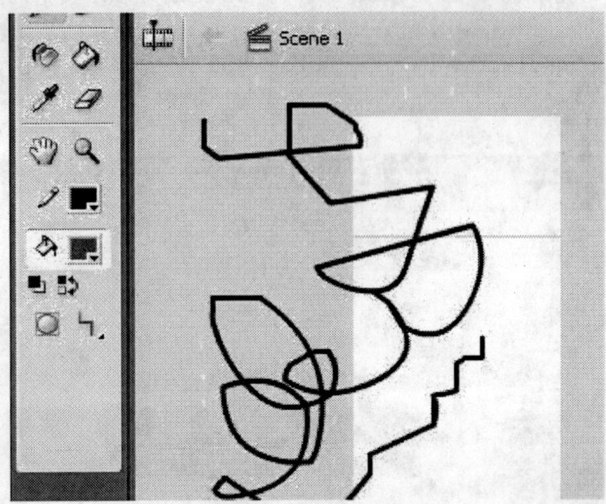


Using the various readymade formats available in Flash you can change the shape of the line according to your needs.

Follow the following steps to format the line.

1. Click at Arrow tool.
2. Click the line segment you want to format.
3. Get the Properties dialog box on the screen.
4. From the dialog box, click the line sub-menu.
5. From the various lines visible, select the one which you want.
6. Click the weight of the line, a slider appears.
7. From the slider choose the thickness you want.
8. Change the colour of the line if needed.

*10.6.2.3 Drawing a Custom Line*

Using the various readymade styles of lines available in the software you can draw a line of your needs.

Follow the following steps to create a line.

1. Click at Pencil or Line tool.
2. Click Windows menu.
3. Click Properties.
4. Click at Custom.
5. The stroke dialog box appears.
6. Click at the thickness of the line you want.
7. Click at Type of line you want.

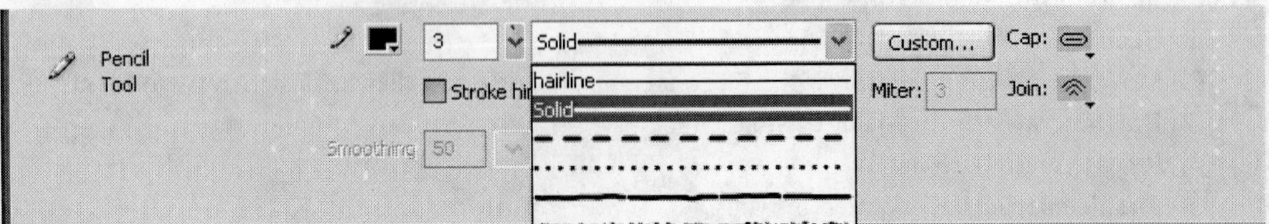

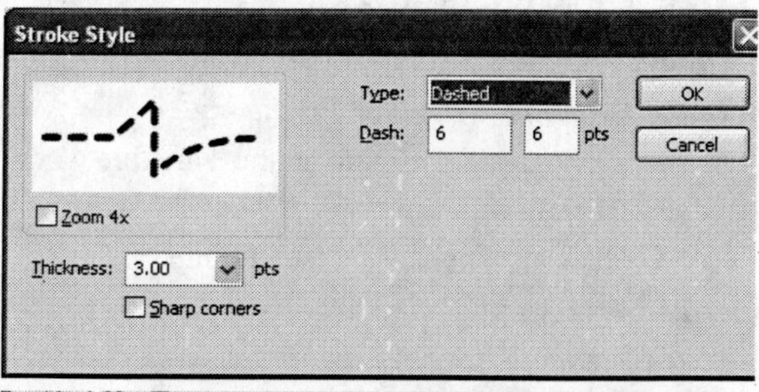


8. With each type you get the option, like in this case of Dashed, you get the Dash spacing, which has been defined as 6.
9. If you want you can make the corners sharp.
10. Click Ok.
11. Draw your custom line on Stage.
12. The line appears as per your needs, as shown here.

*10.6.2.4 Drawing Curves with the Pen Tool*

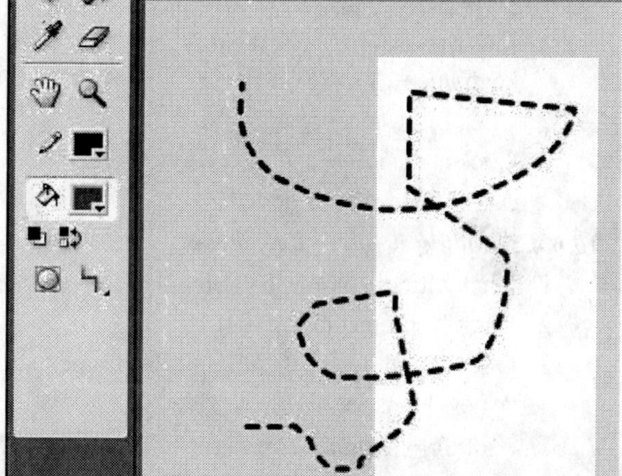

Using the pen tool too you can draw curves.

Follow the following steps to create curves.

1. Click at Pen tool.
2. Move the cursor pointer over the Stage area until the pointer changes from Arrow to Pen
3. Begin dragging to start the curve.
4. A curve bar appears.
5. You can rotate the curve bar by dragging tool to achieve the bend and line length you want for the curve.
6. Start dragging and release the mouse button when you have drawn the curve you want.
7. You can add more curves to an existing curved line as long as the Pen tool is still active. Simply drag another line segment.
8. Flash automatically attaches the second line segment to the first curved line.

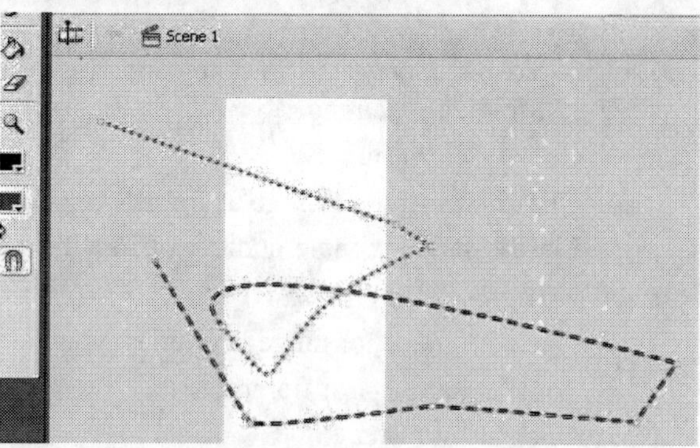


*10.6.2.5 Working with Animation*

Animation involves lots of steps. An animation in fact is running the various scenes together. So for running an animation, you must know how many scenes are there, how much time each has to take, and so. In this chapter, you will read about all this.

### 10.6.3 Setting Speed and Dimensions of the Document

Follow the following steps to set the properties of the movie.

1. Click at Modify.
2. Click Document.
3. The Document Properties dialog box appears.
4. Type the number of frames per second you want the movie to play in the Frame Rate text box.
5. Type a width value in the Width text box.
6. Type a height value in the Height text box.
7. Click Ok.
8. The new dimensions are adjusted.

## 10.6.4 Adding Frames

Follow the following steps to set frames for the movie.

### *10.6.4.1 Adding A Regular Frame*

1. Click an empty frame on the Timeline where you want to insert a new frame.
2. Click Insert menu.
3. Click at Timeline and then Frame.
4. A new frame is added.

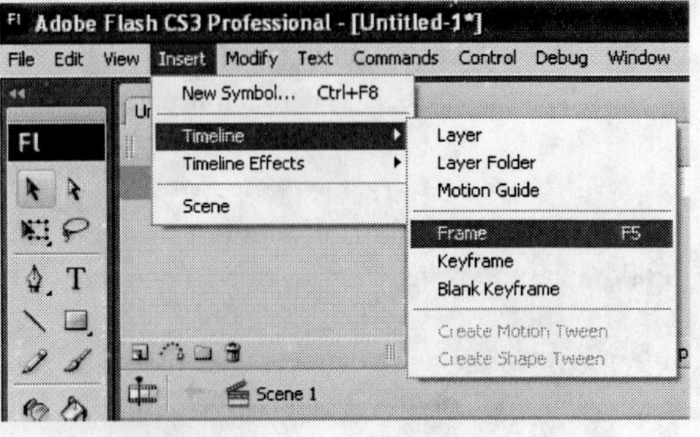


### *10.6.4.2 Adding A Keyframe*

1. Click an empty frame or a regular frame on the timeline where you want to place a new keyframe.
2. Click Insert menu.
3. Click at Timeline and then Keyframe.
4. A new keyframe is added.

### *10.6.4.3 Adding A Blank Keyframe*

1. Click a frame on the Timeline where you want to insert a blank keyframe.
2. Click Insert menu.
3. Click Timeline and then Blank Keyframe.
4. A new blank keyframe is added.

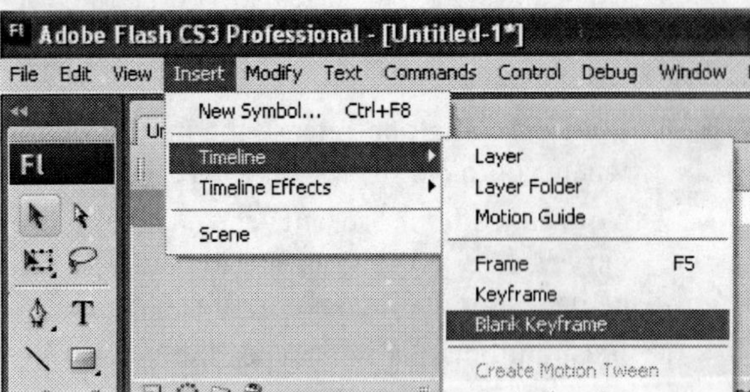


### *10.6.4.4 Adding Multiple Frames*

1. Select two or more frames by clicking them.
2. To select multiple frames, click the first frame in the range, press the Shift key and click the last frame in the range.
3. Click Insert menu.
4. Click Frame to insert regular frames, or click Blank Keyframe to make the new frames all keyframes.
5. Flash inserts the same number of new frames and lengthens the movie.

### *10.6.4.5 Deleting A Keyframe*

1. Click the frame, or range of frames, you want to delete.
2. To delete a range of frames, select the range first.
3. Click Insert menu.
4. Click Remove Frames.
5. The required frame/frames are deleted.

### *10.6.4.6 Removing Keyframe Status*

1. To convert a keyframe to a regular frame, first click on the keyframe you want to change.
2. Click Insert menu.
3. Click Clear Keyframes.
4. The required frame/frames are converted.

## 10.6.5 Creating Animation Frame by Frame

Follow the following steps to create a movie frame by frame.

*10.6.5.1 Add Content to the First Frame*

1. Click the first frame in the layer you want to frame.
2. Place the object you want to animate or just insert an image from the clipart.
3. Click the next frame in the Timeline.
4. Add a keyframe. Flash inserts a keyframe that duplicates the previous frame's contents.
5. Change the object slightly. I have changed it to $90^0$ to the right, as can be seen below.
6. Repeat the steps 4 and 5. This time the image will turn face down, as shown on next page.
7. Now again repeat the same steps, making the figure turn to $270^0$ so that now it faces to the left, as shown on next page.
8. This way you can change the angle to a smaller degree and make more frames if you want to have real fun.
9. Click at first keyframe in the layer and press Enter.
10. You animation will be shown on the screen.

*10.6.5.2 Onion-skinning an Animation*

1. Click a frame.
2. Click Onion icon at the bottom of the Flash Timeline.
3. Flash displays dimmed images from the surrounding frames and places onion-skin markers at the top of the Timeline.
4. To turn off onion-skinning, you can click the onion icon again.

*10.6.5.3 Onion-skinning Outlines*

1. Click a frame.
2. Click Onion skin outline icon at the bottom of the Flash Timeline.
3. Flash displays outlines of the images from the surrounding frames and places onion-skin markers at the top of the Timeline.
4. To make the content of the onion-skin frames editable, click onion-skin outline marker.

*10.6.5.4 Changing the Marker Display*

1. To change how the onion-skin markers appear on the Timeline, click at Modify Onion Markers icon.
2. The Modify menu appears with options for changing the marker display.
3. Click the marker setting you want to apply.

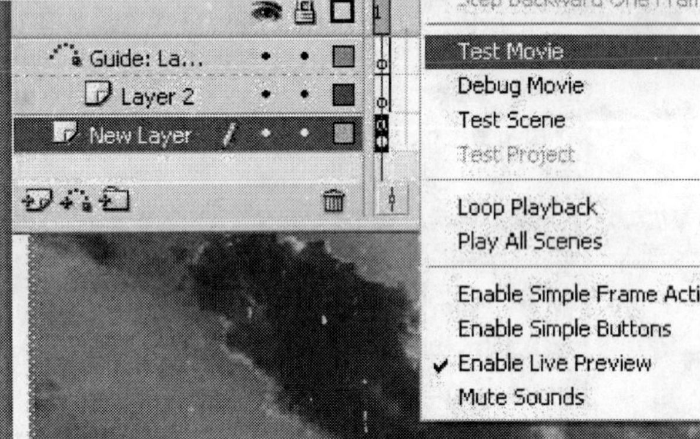


#### *10.6.5.5 Previewing Your Animation*

1. Click Control menu.
2. Click Test Movie.
3. Flash exports your movie to the Flash Player and plays the animation.

#### *10.6.5.6 Adjusting the Animation Speed*

1. Click the keyframe you want to add frames to.
2. Click Insert menu.
3. Click Frame. Flash adds a frame after the keyframe.
4. Because adding just one regular frame is not always enough, repeat steps 2 and 3 above to add a few more frames to the sequence.
5. To test the animation, click the first frame in the Timeline and press Enter.

### 10.6.6 Creating Buttons

After adding sound, let us now add buttons to the various operations of the animation. In this chapter, you will read more about these buttons.

*10.6.6.1 Creating a Button Symbol*

This can be done by following the following steps.

*10.6.6.2 Create a New Symbol*

Follow the following steps to create a new symbol.

1. Click at Insert menu.
2. Click New Symbol.
3. The Symbol Properties dialog box appears.
4. Type a name for the new button.
5. Click the Button behaviour type.
6. Click Ok.
7. The button's Timeline opens a symbol-edit mode with four frames. You can now create each frame's button state.

*10.6.6.3 Create the Up State*

Follow the following steps to create a up state.

1. By default, Flash selects the Up frame and inserts a keyframe.
2. Create a new object to be used as the button or place an existing object on the stage.

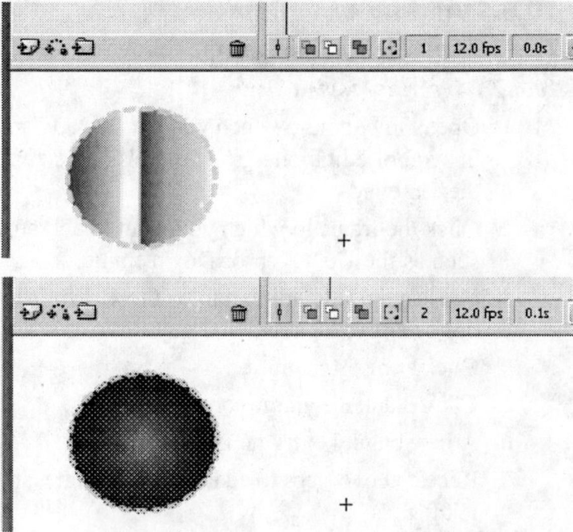

*10.6.6.4 Create the Over State*

Follow the following steps to create a over state.

1. Press F6 to insert a keyframe into the frame.
2. Click the Over frame.
3. Flash duplicates the object you placed in the Up keyframe.
4. You can make minor changes to the object.
5. Here I have changed the colour of the circle to Blue from Red.

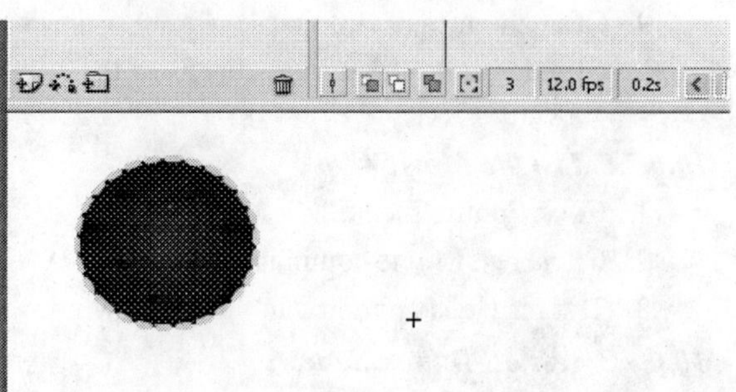

*10.6.6.5 Create the Down State*

Follow the following steps to create a down state.

1. Press F6 to insert a keyframe into the frame.
2. Click the Down frame.
3. Flash duplicates the object you placed in the Over keyframe.
4. You can make minor changes to the object.

*10.6.6.6 Create the Hit State*

Follow the following steps to create a hit state.

1. Click the Hit frame.
2. Press F6 to insert a keyframe into the frame.
3. Flash inserts a keyframe that duplicates the Down frame object
4. Users do not see the object contained in the Hit frame.

*10.6.6.7 Place the Button on the Stage*

Follow the following steps to place the button on the stage.

1. Click the Scene name to return to the movie edit mode.
2. Click Library Info dialog box by clicking its icon.
3. Click and drag the button from the Library and place it on the Stage.

*10.6.6.8 Previewing the Button*

Follow the following steps to preview the button created by you.

1. In the symbol-edit mode (you can call it by pressing Ctrl + E), click the button's Up frame.
2. Press Enter.
3. Flash plays through the 4 button frames.

## 10.6.7 Adding an Animation

This can be done by following the following steps.

*10.6.7.1 Insert a Movie Clip*

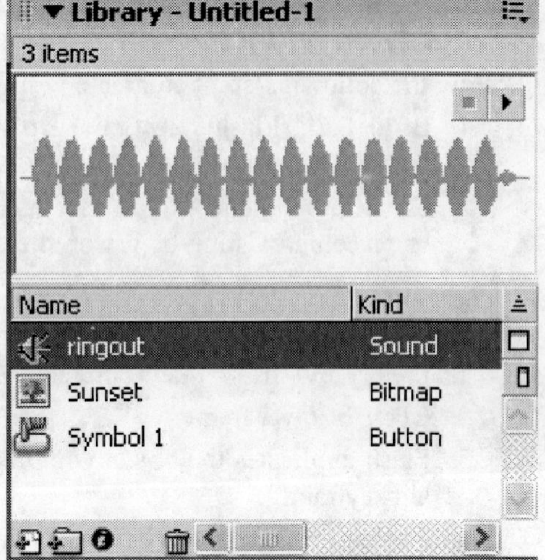


1. Open the button to which you want to add an animation in symbol-edit mode. The button's name appears above the Timeline.
2. Click the frame to which you want to add an animation, such as the Up, Over, or Down frame.
3. You cannot add animation to the Hit frame, since it is not seen by the user.
4. Click at Insert menu.
5. Click Blank Keyframe command.
6. A new blank keyframe is inserted.
7. Repeat above steps to add blank keyframes in Down and Hit frames.
8. Click Library icon to open the Library dialog box.
9. Click the movie clip that you want to insert.
10. Clip and drag the movie clip from the Library window and place it on the Stage where the button appears.

*10.6.7.2 Test the Movie Clip*

1. Click Control menu.
2. Click Test Movie command.
3. The movie is animated in the Flash window.

*10.6.7.3 Test All Button States*

1. Click the Up frame to select it.
2. Press Enter.
3. On the Stage, Flash plays through the 4 button frames including the animation effect.

## 10.6.8 Assigning a Button Action

This can be done by following the following steps.

*10.6.8.1 Add an Action to a Button*

1. Click the button to switch to symbol-edit mode.

2. Click Show Action tool on the toolbar.
3. The Object Actions dialog box appears on the screen.
4. From the Object Actions Toolbox list, click Basic Actions.
5. Search through the list of actions and locate the one you want to apply.

6. Click and drag the action from the list and drop it in the Actions list box.
7. You can double-click the action name to immediately place it in the Actions list box.
8. Flash adds the necessary action components to the Actions list.
9. To see the Actions list in full size, you can click Arrow button.
10. Depending on the action you choose, additional parameters might appear at the bottom of the Object Actions dialog box.
11. You can change the parameter settings, if required.
12. Click Actions Button icon to close the Object actions box when finished.

***10.6.8.2 Testing a Button Action***

1. Click Control menu.
2. Click Enable Simple Buttons.
3. You can now move the pointer over the button and click to see the associated action.

## Let us Revise

1. An Active Server Page is a standard HTML file that is extended with additional features.
2. An Active Server Page can contain server-side scripts.
3. An Active Server Page provides several built-in objects.
4. An Active Server Page can be extended with additional components.
5. All the commands in an Active Server Page, must first be executed to create an HTML page. This allows an Active Server Page to contain dynamic content.
6. An Active Server Page is primarily a scripting environment.
7. By default, an Active Server Page assumes you'll be using VBScript as your primary scripting language.
8. You can also specify the primary scripting language for a particular page.
9. This behavior of the <SCRIPT> tag has two implications. First, you can place scripts contained in a <SCRIPT> tag anywhere you want in an Active Server page. Second, the <SCRIPT> tag, for most purpose, is restricted to containing functions or procedures.
10. Active Server Pages include several built-in objects and installable ActiveX components.
11. Active Server Pages include several built-in objects.
12. The Application object is used to store and retrieve information that can be shared among all users of an application.
13. The Request object can be used to access all information sent in a request from a browser to your server.
14. The Response object is used to send information back to a browser.
15. The Server object enables you to use various utility functions on the server.

16. The Session object can be used to store and retrieve information about particular user sessions.
17. The ObjetContext object is used to control Active Server Pages transactions.
18. The Ad Rotator component is used to display banner advertisements on the Web pages of a Web site.
19. The Browser Capabilities component can be used to display different HTML content, according to the capabilities of different browsers.
20. Using the Content Linking component, you can link together several HTML pages so that they can be navigated easily.
21. JavaScript is a programming language.
22. JAVA and JavaScript have only name in common and nothing else.
23. Events are actions that the user performs while visiting your page.
24. A string value is a word or words enclosed in quotes.
25. There are various assignment operators in use in JavaScript.
26. For JavaScript you can create text in any word processor.
27. JavaScript gives the option of wiriting comments in the form of /*.
28. You can alert the user about anything by using the alert symbol.
29. There are always parentheses after the function name, followed by an opening brace.
30. Many of Java's object-oriented features are influenced by C++.
31. Java is object oriented programming language.
32. Java answers both of these concerns by providing a firewall between a networked application and your computer.
33. Java enables the creation of cross-platform programs by compiling into an intermediate representation called Java bytecode.
34. FrontPage by Microsoft, has a suite of three sets of tools that help you to develop and administer local and remote Web sites.
35. VBScript has been derived from the Visual Basic language.

## Multiple Choice Questions

1. This operator's syntax consists of an expression + expression :
   **(a) Addition** (b) Sum (c) Expression
2. This statement is used to shift control to a new procedure :
   (a) Control **(b) Shift** (c) Call
3. To add 2 strings you can use :
   (a) Add **(b) Concatation** (c) Two
4. Use this function to return a date with a time interval :
   (a) DateAdd (b) Return **(c) Date**
5. Use this statement to declare variables :
   **(a) DIM** (b) Declare (c) Variable
6. Use this function to calculate an expression and deliver the result :
   **(a) Calc** (b) Result (c) Eval
7. Use this function to return a value using a currency symbol as up on your system :
   (a) Currency **(b) FormatCurrency** (c) Symbol

8. Use this function to return a string that shows the hexadecimal value of a number :

(a) Hex (b) **String** (c) Value

9. Use this function to show a dialog box containing a message specified in the code:

(a) Message (b) Box (c) **MsgBox**

10. Use this statement when you want to create public variables and designate storage :

**(a) Private** (b) Public (c) Designate

11. Buffer is cleared by :

**(a) Clear method** (b) Clean method (c) Buffer method

12. The method which allows you to add text to the Web Server Log for a specific request is called.

(a) AddToLog **(b) AppendToLog** (c) Log

13. This property contains the number of bytes that are in the parameter portion of an Active Server Page call:

(a) Bytes (b) Total **(c) TotalBytes**

14. JAVA and JavaScript are same:

(a) TRUE **(b) FALSE**

15. Events are :

(a) Buttons (b) Icons **(c) Actions**

16. For assigning values to variables, you use :

(a) Functions (b) Assignments **(c) Variables**

17. JavaScript version mentioned in this chapter is :

**(a) 1.4** (b) 1.3 (c) 1.5

18. Tag for JavaScript is :

(a) <SCRIPT> **(b) <JAVASCRIPT>** (c) <JAVA>

19. In function, a function name has to be preceeded by :

(a) > (b) word FUNCTION **(c) <**

20. JAVA programming is similar to :

(a) COBOL **(b) C++** (b) BASIC

21. Front Page has been developed by :

(a) IBM (b) Sun **(c) Microsoft**

22. Line tool is used for :

**(a) Drawing line** (b) Drawing rectangle (c) Drawing circle

23. To choose the thickness of the line, you adjust :

**(a) pen** (b) slider (c) arrow

24. Gradient tool is used to fill :

(a) figures (b) text **(c) colours**

25. A keyframe is a part of the :

**(a) animation** (b) keys (c) drawing

## True/False Questions

1. An Active Server Page can contain server-side scripts.

2. All the commands in an Active Server Page, must first be executed to create an HTML page. This allows an Active Server Page to contain dynamic content.
3. **You cannot specify** the primary scripting language for a particular page.
4. Active Server Pages include several built-in objects.
5. **The Response object** is not used to send information back to a browser.
6. The ObjetContext object is used to control Active Server Pages transactions.
7. Using the Content Linking component, you can link together several HTML pages so that they can be navigated easily.
8. Events are actions that the user performs while visiting your page.
9. **For JavaScript you** cannot create text in any word processor.
10. There are always parentheses after the function name, followed by an opening brace.
11. Java answers both of these concerns by providing a firewall between a networked application and your computer.
12. VBScript has been derived from the Visual Basic language.

## Match Columns

Match the matter in Column A with the matter in Column B.

| Column A | Column B |
|---|---|
| A. Application object | 1. HTML format with additional features D |
| B. JavaScript | 2. Programming language for Internet F |
| C. Server object | 3. Programming language E |
| D. Active Server Pages | 4. A program to generate animation G |
| E. C++ | 5. A program to create web sites H |
| F. Java | 6. Allows you to utility functions C |
| G Flash | 7. Programming language of Web B |
| H. Front Page | 8. Used to store and retrieve information A |

## Fill in the Blanks with Appropriate Words

| | | | |
|---|---|---|---|
| a. string | b. Ad Rotator | c. C++ | d. /* |
| e. Application object | f. Java bytecode | g. <SCRIPT> | h. JavaScript |
| i. Server object | j. built-in | k. Active Server Page | |

1. An Active Server Page provides several ________ objects.
2. An ______________ is primarily a scripting environment.
3. This behavior of the _________ tag has two implications. First, you can place scripts contained in a <SCRIPT> tag anywhere you want in an Active Server page. Second, the <SCRIPT> tag, for most purpose, is restricted to containing functions or procedures.
4. The _______________ is used to store and retrieve information that can be shared among all users of an application.
5. The _____________ enables you to use various utility functions on the server.
6. The ___________ component is used to display banner advertisements on the Web pages of a Web site.

7. __________ is a programming language.
8. A ________ value is a word or words enclosed in quotes.
9. JavaScript gives the option of writing comments in the form of _____.
10. Many of Java's object-oriented features are influenced by _______.
11. Java enables the creation of cross-platform programs by compiling into an intermediate representation called _______________.

### Descriptive Type Questions

1. What is ASP?
2. How do Active Server Pages work?
3. What are Objects and Components?
4. How would you create components using Session Scope?
5. How would you test your configuration?
6. What are variables?
7. What are procedures?
8. What are ASP forms?
9. How would you declare variables?
10. Describe the variable naming convention.
11. What is Implicit Declaration?
12. What is Explicit Declaration?
13. What are Object Hierarchies?
14. What are various type of Collections?
15. Describe the various types of Response methods.
16. What are ASP Applications?
17. What are Server Objects?
18. What is JAVAScript?
19. Describe the various words reserved by JAVA.
20. How would you write a program in JavaScript?
21. How would you put comments in JavaScript?
22. How would you put quotes in JavaScript?
23. How are functions used in JavaScript?
24. When was Java developed?
25. Describe the various keywords of Java.
26. How is FrontPage used as Interactivity tool?
27. Write shortnotes on :

    JavaScript Events　　JavaScript Operators

    JavaScript Assignments　　JavaScript Comparisons
28. How would you draw with various lines?
29. How would you customize a line?
30. How would you draw curves with the Pen tool?

31. How would you draw an oval shape?
32. How would you draw a rectangle shape?
33. How is brush tool used?
34. How is paint bucket tool used?
35. How would you set speed and dimensions of a movie?
36. How would you add various frames?
37. Describe the process of creating an animation frame by frame.
38. How would you select frames?
39. How would you modify frame properties?
40. How would you move, copy, select a frame?
41. How would you create a button?
42. What are shape changing buttons?
43. Describe the various states.
44. How would you assign an animation to a button?
45. How would you insert a movie clip?
46. How would you test a button action?

## Answers to Objective Type Questions

***Multiple Choice Questions***

| | | | |
|---|---|---|---|
| 1. a | 2. b | 3. b | 4. c |
| 5. a | 6. a | 7. b | 8. b |
| 9. c | 10. a | 11. a | 12. b |
| 13. c | 14. b | 15. c | 16. c |
| 17. a | 18. b | 19. c | 20. b |
| 21. c | 22. a | 23. a | 24. c |
| 25. a | | | |

***True False Questions***

| | | | |
|---|---|---|---|
| 1. T | 2. T | 3. F | 4. T |
| 5. F | 6. T | 7. F | 8. T |
| 9. F | 10. T | 11. T | 12. T |

***Matching Columns***

| | | | |
|---|---|---|---|
| A. 8 | B. 7 | C. 6 | D. 1 |
| E. 3 | F. 2 | G. 4 | H. 5 |

***Fill in the Blanks***

| | | | |
|---|---|---|---|
| 1. j | 2. k | 3. g | 4. e |
| 5. i | 6. b | 7. h | 8. a |
| 9. d | 10. c | 11. f | |

# Internet Security Management Concepts 11

## 11.1 Overview of Internet Security

Internet is always threathened by the following :

### 11.1.1 Data Interception

The observation of user data during a communication by an unauthorized user.

### 11.1.2 Denial of Service

The prevention or interruption of a communication or the delay of time critical operations.

### 11.1.3 Identify Interception

The identify of one or more of the users involved in a communication is observed for misuse.

### 11.1.4 Manipulation

The replacement, insertion, deletion or disordering of user data during a communication by an unauthorized user.

### 11.1.5 Mis-routing

The mis-routing of a communication path intended for one user to another.

### 11.1.6 Pretending

The pretence by a user to be a different user in order to gain access to information or to acquire additional priviledges.

### 11.1.7 Rejection

The denial by a user of having participated in part or all of a communication.

### 11.1.8 Reply

The recording and subsequent replay of a communication at some later date.

### 1.1.9 Traffic analysis

The observation of information about a communication between users (e.g. absence/presence, frequency, direction, sequence, etc.)

## 11.2 Firewalls

It is among the very popular concept of stopping your web site from potential dangers. It works on both internal computer network and LAN. Every corporate network connected to it is vulnerable to attack.A company's network can be harmed in the following manner.

- They could steal or damage important data.
- Damage individual computer or the entire network.

- Use the corporate computer's resources or use the corporate network and resources as a way of posing as a corporate employee.

Well, Firewall is the solution for above problems. The firewalls stop crackers, hackers or others on the Internet from gaining access to the corporate network and causing damage.

### 11.2.1 Advantages of Firewall

The main benefits of using a firewall are:

- Protection from Atacks
- Unauthorized Access
- Security
- Misuse
- Enforcement

### 11.2.2 Types of Firewalls

Firewalls are one of the following two types:

#### *11.2.2.1 Packet filtering*

It inspects each IP packet flowing through it. Using the specific fields in the IP datagram header, the firewall decides whether to allow the packet to reach the protected site or reject the packet.The TCP/UDP ports are used by the application services like FTP, TELNET, HTTP etc. to communicate on the network. Since the packet filtering firewall can also scan the TCP/UDP port numbers, it can permit or deny a specific service from reaching a spot.

#### *11.2.2.2 The Application Gateway*

Here, the remote host or network can interact only with the proxy service. The proxy service hides the internal host and service. If the proxy service authenticates the remote host/user or the network, it then creates a session between the application gateway and the internal host. It then allows the bytes from the authenticated connection to flow to the shot over this session. The application gateway logs the entire communication.

### 11.2.3 Properties of a Good Firewall System

You should check for the following properties in a Firewall system before adapting it.

- The firewall should be able to support the design policy of the network used.
- The firewall should be flexible.
- The firewall should contain advanced authentication measures.
- The firewall should employ filtering techniques to permit or to dent services.
- The firewall should use proxy services for FTP and TELNET.
- The firewall should accommodate public access to the sites.
- The firewall should contain mechanisms for logging traffic and suspicious activity and should contain mechanisms for log reduction so that logs are readable and understandable.
- If the firewall requires an operating system such as Unix, a secured version of the operating system should be part of the firewall.

### 11.2.4 Firewall Architectures

Firewall uses a variety of architectures to manage access control. These are:

#### *11.2.4.1 Packet-Filtering Firewalls*

This type of firewalls examine all the packets it sees, then forwards them or drops them based on predefined rules. This rudimentary firewall provides only basic protection. Packet-filtering firewalls are restrictive since network managers can only define a few parameters.

#### *11.2.4.2 Proxy Firewalls*

This type of firewall acts as an intermediary of user requests, setting up a second connection to the desired resource either at the application layer (an application proxy) or at the session or transport layer (a circuit relay). Proxy firewalls tend to take a performance hit since it relies on application layers and are restrictive when it comes to allowing or denying evolving or new types of applications.

#### *11.2.4.3 Stageful Inspection Firewalls*

This is the new generation of firewall technology patented by Check Point Software technologies. Stageful Inspection provides full application-layer awareness without requiring a separate proxy for every service to be secured. This results in multiple benefits to customers including excellent performance, reliability and the services quickly and easily.

Stageful inspection architecture is unique in that it understands the state of any communication through the firewall machine, including packet, connection and application information. Packet filters do not track application or connection state. Application proxies rack only application state, not packet or connection satate which intorudce some vulnerabilities.

## 11.3 Internet Security Management Concepts

In Internet, as you know that we are basically connecting our computer system to other computer systems. There is every likelyhood that while doing this, some unauthorized person can also get into this and access our data. Manipulating security becomes more important when we use internet as a commercial transaction. We need to make sure that messages are private and financial transactions are secure. Methods of Internet security are described below:

### 11.3.1 Authentication

It is the process of determining the identify of a user who is attempting to access a system. Also for security purpose, the verification of the identify of a person or process is necessary. Thus, it is the verification of a user's claim of identify by passwords, personal challenge, response calculations or random password generator.

#### *11.3.1.1 Authentication Methods*

There are two primary models for token based user authentication systems:

- **One-time Password Systems**: The user token displays a "current password" which the user enters in any context that would require a conventional password. The server system can calculate the password on demand and verify the authentication request.
- **Challenge/Reponse Systems**: The user first receives a challenge generated by the authentication server. The challenge is then copied by the user into his token. The token then calculates and display a response which depends on the challenge. The user then copies this response back into the application prompting for authentication information.

The server system calculates the expected response and compares with the response submitted by the user. However, since challenges are generated at random by the server, attacks associated with replaying authentication information are not an issue for well designed system. As a result, the server does not need to retain information regarding which "passwords" have been used.

Some of the Authentication Methods are given in the following subsections.

#### *11.3.1.2 Passwords*

Passwords are the most common form of computer security. Some networks require multiple levels of passwords to gain access to various servers or databases.

#### *11.3.1.3 Callback*

Callback is a security feature that works like this. A user dials into a communications server and enters a user name and password. The communications server then hangs up the modem connection, searches its database to authentication the user and then calls the user back at a pre-defined number.

#### *11.3.1.4 Packet Filters*

Packet filters allow network administrators to limit a user's access to specific services on the network. For example, a user may be allowed to send electronic mail but not copy data files from the network.

#### *11.3.1.5 Authentication Severs*

They can be set up in variety of ways, depending upon the security scheme of the network they are serving. The basic process for authenticating a user includes the following steps: A user dials into a network through a communications server or Network Access Server (NAS). The NAS forwards the user identification and password to the Authentication Server. Then the Authentication server validate the user and provides access privileges to the network.

#### *11.3.1.6 RADIUS (Remote Authentication Dial-up User Service)*

RADIUS is a system of distributed security that solves the problems associated with meeting the security requirements of remote computing. The solution eliminates the need for special hardware and provides access to a variety of state-of-the-art security solutions. Distributed security separates users authentication data. And authorization from the communications process and creates a single central location for user authentication data. RADIUS is freely available distributed security system developed by Lucent Technologies. RADIUS provides an open and scalable client-server security system.

### 11.3.2 Authorization

Authorization is the process of determining how an authenticated user is permitted to use specific resources. An authorization mechanism automatically enforces a management policy automatically enforces a management policy regarding resource object use. For example, in a computer system, resources typically include data files, operator commands, transaction I/O devices and program processes.

The specific rules for authorizing access to data objects usually enforce confidentiality and integrity by either granting or denying access to read, modify or create data records and by controlling the creation or deletion of data objects. While authentication control who can access network resources, authorization says what they can do once they have access to the resources. Authorization grants privileges to processes and users. Authorization lets a security administrator control parts of a network, for example, directories and files on servers.

### 11.3.3 Auditing and Accountability

Auditing is the process of data collection and analysis that allows administrator and others, such as IT auditors, to verity that the users and authorization rules are producing the intended results are defined in a company's business and security policy. Individual accountability for attempts to violate the intended policy depends on monitoring relevant security events, which initiates the auditing feedback reporting loop.

The monitoring process can be implemented as a continuous automatic function, as a periodic check or as an occasional verification that proper procedures are being followed. The auditing information may be used by security administrators, internal audit personnel, external auditors, government regulatory officials and in legal proceedings. The auditing and individual accountability monitoring functions also apply to documenting the activities of security administrators and auditors to ensure that they are not abusing their authorized capabilities.

To effectively analyze the security of a network and to respond to security incidents, procedures should be established for collecting network activity data. Collecting data is called accounting or auditing. For networks with strict security policies, audit data should include all attempts to achieve authentication and authorization by any person. It is especially important to log "anonymous" or "guest" access to public servers. The data should also log all attempts by users to change their access rights. The collected data should include user and host names for login and logout attempts and previous and new access rights for a change of access rights. Each entry in the audit log should be time stamped

## 11.3.4 Information Privacy

Privacy means the concept in which user's data such as stored files, e-mail, etc. are not be seen by any other person without the main user's permission. Inotehr words, it is private communication accomplished when the sernder and intended receiver can read the message. In this section, important points related to privacy such as E-mail privacy are described.

### *11.3.4.1 E-Mail Privacy*

When you send an e-mail, the message is broken into several packers and each packet is sent through the Intenret. Number of packets are dpends on the length of the message. Each packet which is sent over the Internet has Internet address of the sender nad recipient's address. Packets of the single message may take different routes to reach the destination.

Before reachinghte destination, messages pass through different systems. This means the content of the message and the address of the sender and receiver are examined by all the systems through which each packet is routed. So, in the absence of cods and protection, e-mail could be very public. Most o fhte system administrators adopt a code under which they will not examine someone's e-mail.

### *11.3.4.2 ElectronicCommunication Privacy Act*

Electronic Communication Privacy act passed on 1986 for the privacy of e-mail. It prohibits anyone to access-e-mail messages withoug sender's permission. It also prohibits individual's private message accessed by government officer without legal permission. This act allows system administrator to examine e-mail message only when it is necessary for any operation or the security of the system.

### *11.3.4.3 Encryption*

When you send a message to someone, the message is transmitted in the same form you have typed it, whether it is illegal for someone to read it or not. One way to avoid this, use encryption (in which message is sent to the receiver in some secret code) the message can't be read unless the code and the method of encryption is know to reader. This code is called key. The reader must know the key to decode the message for reading.

## 11.4 Copyright issues

There is a tremendous number of files, documents and images available on the Internet. They can be viewed, saves in a file, print and passed on to others. We can create copy of any information which we can find on the Internet only when it is legal for doing so. The right to copy or duplicate materials can be granted only by the owner of the information. This is called the copyright. Many documents or fiels on the Internet contain a statement that shows the doucemnt is copyrighted.

## 11.5 Asymmetric Cryptosystems

RSA is an algorithm for public-key cryptography. It was the first algorithm known to be suitable for signing as well as encryption, and one of the first great advances in public key cryptography. RSA is widely used in electronic commerce protocols, and is believed to be secure given sufficiently long keys and the use of up-to-date implementations.

### 11.5.1 History

The algorithm was publicly described in 1977 by Ron Rivest, Adi Shamir and Leonard Adleman at MIT; the letters RSA are the initials of their surnames. Apocryphally it was invented at a Passover Seder in Schenectady, N.Y.

Clifford Cocks, a British mathematician working for the UK intelligence agency GCHQ, described an equivalent system in an internal document in 1973, but given the relatively expensive computers needed to implement it at the time, it was mostly considered a curiosity and, as far as is publicly known, was never deployed. His discovery, however, was not revealed until 1997 due to its top-secret classification, and Rivest, Shamir, and Adleman devised RSA independently of Cocks' work.

MIT was granted US patent 4405829 for a "Cryptographic communications system and method" that used the algorithm in 1983. The patent expired on 21 September 2000. Since a paper describing the algorithm had been published in August 1977, prior to the December 1977 filing date of the patent application, regulations in much of the rest of the world precluded patents elsewhere and only the US patent was granted. Had Cocks' work been publicly known, a patent in the US would not have been possible either.

### 11.5.2 Security

The security of the RSA cryptosystem is based on two mathematical problems: the problem of factoring large numbers and the RSA problem. Full decryption of an RSA ciphertext is thought to be infeasible on the assumption that both of these problems are hard, i.e., no efficient algorithm exists for solving them.

The RSA problem is defined as the task of taking eth roots modulo a composite n: recovering a value m such that c=me mod n, where (e, n) is an RSA public key and c is an RSA ciphertext. Currently the most promising approach to solving the RSA problem is to factor the modulus n. With the ability to recover prime factors, an attacker can compute the secret exponent d from a public key (e, n), then decrypt c using the standard procedure. To accomplish this, an attacker factors n into p and q, and computes (p-1)(q-1) which allows the determination of d from e. No polynomial-time method for factoring large integers on a classical computer has yet been found, but it has not been proven that none exists.

As of 2005, the largest number factored by a general-purpose factoring algorithm was 663 bits long, using a state-of-the-art distributed implementation. RSA keys are typically 1024–2048 bits long. Some experts believe that 1024-bit keys may become breakable in the near term (though this is disputed); few see any way that 4096-bit keys could be broken in the foreseeable future.

Therefore, it is generally presumed that RSA is secure if n is sufficiently large. If n is 256 bits or shorter, it can be factored in a few hours on a personal computer, using software already freely available. If n is 512 bits or shorter, it can be factored by several hundred computers as of 1999. A theoretical hardware device named TWIRL and described by Shamir and Tromer in 2003 called into question the security of 1024 bit keys. It is currently recommended that n be at least 2048 bits long.

In 1994, Peter Shor published Shor's algorithm, showing that a quantum computer could in principle perform the factorization in polynomial time. However, quantum computation is still in the early stages of development and may never prove to be practical.

### 11.5.3 Practical considerations

#### *11.5.3.1 Key generation*

Finding the large primes p and q is usually done by testing random numbers of the right size with probabilistic primality tests which quickly eliminate virtually all non-primes. p and q should not be 'too close', lest the Fermat factorization for n be successful, if p-q, for instance is less than 2n1/4 (which for even small 1024-bit values of n is 3x1077) solving for p and q is ultra-trivial. Furthermore, if either p-1 or q-1 has only small prime factors, n can be factored quickly by Pollard's p-1 algorithm, and these values of p or q should, therefore, be discarded as well.

One should not employ a prime search method which gives any information whatsoever about the primes to the attacker. In particular, a good random number generator for the start value needs to be employed.

These are not the same criteria; a number may have been chosen by a random process (ie, no pattern in the results), but if it is predictable in any manner (or even partially predictable), the method used will result in loss of security. For example, the random number table published by the Rand Corp in the 1950s might very well be truly random, but it has been published and thus can serve an attacker as well. If the attacker can guess half of the digits of p or q, he can quickly compute the other half (shown by Coppersmith in 1997).

It is important that the secret key d be large enough. Michael J. Wiener showed in 1990 that if p is between q and 2q (which is quite typical) and d < n1/4/3, then d can be computed efficiently from n and e. There is no known attack against small public exponents such as e=3, provided that proper padding is used. However, when no padding is used or when the padding is improperly implemented then small public exponents have a greater risk of leading to an attack, such as for example the unpadded plaintext vulnerability listed above. 65537 is a commonly used value for e.

This value can be regarded as a compromise between avoiding potential small exponent attacks and still allowing efficient encryptions (or signature verification). The NIST draft FIPS PUB 186-3 (March 2006) does not allow public exponents e smaller than 65537, but does not state a reason for this restriction.

#### *11.5.3.2 Speed*

RSA is much slower than DES and other symmetric cryptosystems. In practice, Bob typically encrypts a secret message with a symmetric algorithm, encrypts the (comparatively short) symmetric key with RSA, and transmits both the RSA-encrypted symmetric key and the symmetrically-encrypted message to Alice.

This procedure raises additional security issues. For instance, it is of utmost importance to use a strong random number generator for the symmetric key, because otherwise Eve (an eavesdropper wanting to see what was sent) could bypass RSA by guessing the symmetric key.

#### *11.5.3.3 Key distribution*

As with all ciphers, how RSA public keys are distributed is important to security. Key distribution must be secured against a man-in-the-middle attack. Suppose Eve has some way to give Bob arbitrary keys and make him believe they belong to Alice. Suppose further that Eve can intercept transmissions between Alice and Bob. Eve sends Bob her own public key, which Bob believes to be Alice's. Eve can then intercept any ciphertext sent by Bob, decrypt it with her own secret key, keep a copy of the message, encrypt the message with Alice's public key, and send the new ciphertext to Alice. In principle, neither Alice nor Bob would be able to detect Eve's presence. Defenses against such attacks are often based on digital certificates or other components of a public key infrastructure.

#### *11.5.3.4 Timing attacks*

Kocher described a new attack on RSA in 1995: if the attacker Eve knows Alice's hardware in sufficient detail and is able to measure the decryption times for several known ciphertexts, she can deduce the decryption key d quickly. This attack can also be applied against the RSA signature scheme. In 2003, Boneh and Brumley demonstrated a more practical attack capable of recovering RSA factorizations over a network connection (e.g., from a Secure Socket Layer (SSL)-enabled webserver). This attack takes advantage of information leaked by the Chinese remainder theorem optimization used by many RSA implementations.

One way to thwart these attacks is to ensure that the decryption operation takes a constant amount of time for every ciphertext. However, this approach can significantly reduce performance. Instead, most RSA implementations use an alternate technique known as cryptographic blinding. RSA blinding makes use of the multiplicative property of RSA. Instead of computing cd mod n, Alice first chooses a secret random value r and computes (rec)d mod n. The result of this computation is r m mod n and so the effect of r can be removed by multiplying by its inverse. A new value of r is chosen for each ciphertext. With blinding applied, the decryption time is no longer correlated to the value of the input ciphertext and so the timing attack fails.

### *11.5.3.5 Adaptive chosen ciphertext attacks*

In 1998, Daniel Bleichenbacher described the first practical adaptive chosen ciphertext attack, against RSA-encrypted messages using the PKCS #1 v1 padding scheme (a padding scheme randomizes and adds structure to an RSA-encrypted message, so it is possible to determine whether a decrypted message is valid.) Due to flaws with the PKCS #1 scheme, Bleichenbacher was able to mount a practical attack against RSA implementations of the Secure Socket Layer protocol, and to recover session keys. As a result of this work, cryptographers now recommend the use of provably secure padding schemes such as Optimal Asymmetric Encryption Padding, and RSA Laboratories has released new versions of PKCS #1 that are not vulnerable to these attacks.

### *11.5.3.6 Branch Prediction Analysis (BPA) attacks*

Many processors use a Branch predictor to determine whether a conditional branch in the instruction flow of a program is likely to be taken or not. Usually these processors also implement Simultaneous multithreading (SMT). Branch Prediction Analysis attacks use a spy process to discover (statistically) the private key when processed with these processors.

Simple Branch Prediction Analysis (SBPA) claims to improve BPA in a non-statistical way. In their paper, "On the Power of Simple Branch Prediction Analysis", the authors of SBPA (Onur Aciicmez, Cetin Kaya Koc and Jean-Pierre Seifert) claim to have discovered 508 out of 512 bits of an RSA key in 10 iterations.

## Let us Revise

1. Internet is always threathened by various outside forces.
2. Firewall is among the most common use of stopping your web site from potential dangers.
3. Among the various advantages of Firewall are that it does not allow misuse of the system.
4. A good firewall system should be able to handle all type of problems.
5. Firewall uses various type of architectures.
6. Authentication is a process of determining the identify of a user.
7. The popular authentication process is providing password.
8. Auditing can also detect the error in the system.
9. Privacy means the concept in which user's data such as stored files, e-mail, etc. are not be seen by any other person without the main user's permission.
10. Encyption is a method in which you send the coded message.

## Multiple Choice Questions

1. Firewall is :

   (a) a wall made of fire (b) a security measure (c) a wall

2. A code provided without which the access is not allowed is called :

   (a) Code (b) Password

## True/False Questions

1. Firewall is among the most common use of stopping your web site from potential dangers.
2. A good firewall system may not be able to handle all type of problems.
3. Authentication is a process of determining the identify of a user.
4. Auditing cannot detect the error in the system.
5. Encyption is a method in which you send the coded message.

## Match Columns

Match the matter in Column A with the matter in Column B.

| Column A | Column B |
|---|---|
| A. SMT | 1. Simple Branch Prediction Analysis |
| B. RADIUS | 2. Secure Socket Layer |
| C. Firewall | 3. Method to send coded message |
| D. SSL | 4. Simultaneous Multithreading |
| E. Encryption | 5. A software to protect from threats |
| F. SBPA | 6. Remote Authentication Dial-up User Service |

## Fill in the Blanks with Appropriate Words

a. password  b. permission  c. Firewall  d. architectures
e. outside forces

1. Internet is always threathened by various _______________.
2. Among the various advantages of ___________ are that it does not allow misuse of the system.
3. Firewall uses various type of __________.
4. The popular authentication process is providing _________.
5. Privacy means the concept in which user's data such as stored files, e-mail, etc. are not be seen by any other person without the main user's ___________.

## Descriptive Type Questions

1. Describe the various type of threats on the system.
2. What is firewall?
3. Describe the various type of firewalls.
4. What you should look for in a good firewall system?
5. What sort of architure are used in Firewall?
6. Which various methods of authentications are used?
7. How would Auditing help in tracing the violation of rules?
8. What do you understand by Information Privacy?

## Answers to Objective Type Questions

*Multiple Choice Questions*

1. b
2. b

*True False Questions*

1. T
2. F
3. T
4. F
5. T

*Matching Columns*

A. 4
B. 6
C. 5
D. 2
E. 3
F. 1

*Fill in the Blanks*

1. e
2. c
3. d
4. a
5. b

# Glossary

# G

**24 x 7** A reference to something that is open 24 hours a day, seven days a week.

**Access Provider** Company that sells Internet connection. Known as Internet Service Providers too.

**ActiveX** A Microsoft technology that facilitates information sharing among applications. It is primarily used for developing interactive applications and Web content.

**Address** A Network address. It has two forms; numbers and alphanumeric.

**Affiliate** An organization or individual whom you have formed a formal or informal agreement with to either sell or receive products, services, content, traffic, etc.

**Animated GIF** A graphical interchange format (image) that appears to move or change as a result of multiple layered images.

**Anonymous FTP** A FTP (File Transfer Protocol) session in which a user connects to a remote host, by using a username as anonymous. The user's identity is not validated in such cases.

**ANSI** Computers use several methods for deciding how to put information on the screen and how the keyboard interacts with the screen.

**Archive** The name given to a historical or old files, which are normally compressed using a compression technique.

**Applet** A computer program written in Java. Applets are similar to applications, but they don't run as stand-alones. Instead, applets conform to a set of conventions that let them run within a Java-compatible browser.

**APRANet** A predecessor of the Internet where the methodology and software on which the Internet is based were tested. No longer in existence.

**Article** A message or file that is part of the Usenet newsgroup.

**ASCII** American Standard Code for Information Interchange. This is de-facto worldwide standard for the code numbers used by computers to represent all upper and lowercase English letters, numbers, punctuation, etc.

**Attachment** A file delivered as part of an e-mail message.

**Backbone** A high speed network that connects several powerful computers. In the U.S., the backbone of the Internet is often considered to be the NSFNet, a government funded link between a handful of supercomputer sites across the country.

**Backoffice** All of the functions in a company that occure behind the scenes away from public such as accounting, service work, warehousing, and management.

**Bandwidth** A measure of the amount of data that can flow thru a network channel at a given point of time.

**Banner Ad** The long thin ads usually located at the top and bottom of web pages.

**Baud** The speed at which modems transfer data. One baud is roughly equal to one bit per second. It takes eight bits to make up one character.

**BBS** Bulletin Board System. A computerised meeting and announcement system that allows people to carry on discussions, upload and download files and make announcements.

**Binary File** A file containing information such as a program, compressed archive, an image or a document, etc. The contents of the file generally can't be displayed or printed without using some program.

**Bit** A binary digit. A single digit number represented in base-2. In other words, there are two digits either one or zero.

**Bookmark** A list of links to URLs on the Internet maintained within a web browser.

**Bounce** When e-mail is underliverable, it is sent back to the sender and is said to have bounced back.

**BPS** Bits per second. Same as baud.

**Browser** A client program (software) that is used to view resources on the Internet, particularly Web pages.

**Byte** A set of bits that represent a single character. Generally there are 8 bits in a byte.

**Buzz** A term used to describe conversations and general discussions about a particular company or technology.

**CERN** Conseil europeenee pour la Recherche Nucleaire, the European Laboratory for Particle Physics in Geneva, Switzerland, where in the 1980s a team of pioneering engineers led by Tim Berners-Lee developed the World Wide Web technology.

**CGI** Short for Common Gateway Interface, software that allows communication between a web server — for example code that processes interactive forms or which searches databases on the server for information requested by a user.

**Chat Room** An online place for people to post and read electronic messages.

**Click-through** The term that describes when a visitor to a Web site uses a link to access another Web site.

**Client** A software program or Internet service that works on your behalf to retrieve information from a server located on the network.

**Cookie** A file stored on your hard disk and used to identify your computer or your preferences to a remote computer. Cookies are frequently used to identify visitors to web sites.

**Command line** On character based computer systems, such as UNIX, DOS, etc. Also called the system prompt, where commands are entered.

**Communications software** A program that controls the modem and establishes connectivity with another computer.

**Compression** An algorithm or scheme used to compress or shrink a file. A file in the compressed form must be uncompressed before it can be used.

**Content** The collective name for the text, pictures, sound, data, or other information presented by a web site.

**Convergence** The movement of various types of software toward common standards.

**Crack** To break a program's security, integrity or registration system or fake a user's ID.

**Crash** When a program or operating system fails to respond or causes other program to malfunction.

**Cross niching** Finding commonality between two or more subdivisions of the customers in a market after they have been divided into niches.

**Cyberspace** Word used to describe a whole range of information resources available through computer networks.

**Cybersquatting** The act of trying to divert customers from a Web site by using a similar name and identical look as another site or the act of obtaining and holding domain names for resale.

**DDN** Defence Data Network, a portion of the Internet, which connects U.S Military Bases, and contractors, used for non-secure communications. .

**Dial-up access** Access to the Internet through a telephone line and a modem.

**Direct connection** A connection, such as SLIP or PPP, whereby our computer becomes a live part of the Internet.

**Data mining** Locating, reviewing, and analyzing stored operational information to assist in decision making.

**Direct connection** A connection, such as SLIP or PPP, whereby our computer becomes a live part of the Internet.

**Distributed computing** The technical architecture where the network clients, as opposed to central processing and storage areas, perform some or all application processing or information storage.

**DNS** Domain Name System, a distributed database system for translating computer names.

**DNS Server** A server that works as the directory for the DNS system.

**Domain** The smaller network making up the Internet, and having many computers or even smaller networks within it, is called a domain. The domain may represent either a type of organisation or a geographical location.

**Domain Name** An addressing scheme assigns names and numbers to identify the computers on the Internet.

**Download** Copying a file from a host system to your computer. In other words, transferring a file from a remote computer to your computer.

**e-bank** An online bank that provides regular bank services over the Internet.

**e-commerce** Business conducted exclusively through an electronic format.

**E-Mail** Electronic mail, a basic Internet service for sending or receiving messages electronically over a computer network.

**EDI** (Electronic Data Interchange) The transmission of electronic data in a specific EDI format or series of EDI standards.

**EFT** (Electronic Fund Transfer) An electronic transfer of information that equates to moving funds from one financial institutions to another.

**Emoticons** A combination of keyboard characters using which facial expressions such as a smile or a frown are represented.

**Encryption** A procedure of jumbling data by using a mathematical function. A decryption technique is required to use this data.

**ERP** (Enterprise Resource Planning) A model for building software in which all the operation processes that impact resource management use integrated software.

**FAQ** Frequently Asked Questions. A list containing the questions and their answers on a specific topic.

**File** anything stored on a computer, such as a program, image or document.

**Firewall** Software intended to prevent unauthorized access to a computer network.

**Flame** An E-Mail message or article in a Usenet newsgroup that is meant to insult someone or provoke controversy.

**Followup** A message responding to a previous posting, which will appear in the newsgroup following the original posting.

**Freeware** Software that is available on the Internet for free.

**FTP** File Transfer Protocol. A specific set of protocols used by computers connected over the Internet to transfer files.

**FTP Archive** A collection of files available on the Internet by using anonymous FTP.

**FYI** A common abbreviation in mail and news, meaning for your information.

**Gateway** A hardware or software set up that enables translation between two different protocols.

**GIF** Graphic Interchange Format. It is used for storing photoquality graphic images. Now commonly used on the WWW.

**Gigabyte** A measurement of electronic file size equalling roughly one billion bytes.

**GUI** Graphical User Interface. Uses icons and images in addition to text to represent information.

**Hacker** A person who enjoys stretching hardware and software to their limits, seeing just what they can get their computers to do.

**Handshake** The process of two modems connecting with each other and establishing common parameters such as speed, error-correction and data compression.

**Header** A portion of an e-mail message containing information such as the address of the sender, address of the recipient and when the message was sent.

**History List** A list of Internet sites, services and resources that have accessed through a Web browser.

**Hit** A visit to a Web site by a Web surfer.

**Home Page** The first screen or page of a site on the WWW.

**Host** A computer on the Internet containing and providing access to various resources and services.

**HTML** Hyper Text Markup Language. The computer language used for creating documents on the WWW.

**HTTP** Hyper Text Transport Protocol. The protocol used to transfer information over the WWW.

**Hyperlink** A reference or link which; when clicked, will automatically transfer an Internet user to another page or site on the Internet.

**Hypertext** Electronic text in a format that provides instant access, via links, to other hypertext within a document or in another document.

**IETF** Internet Engineering Task Force. A committee that reviews and supports Internet protocol proposals.

**i-center** An online customer service center that mayor may not allow interaction with humans via video, sound, or electronic messages.

**i-commerce** Business conducted through an electronic format on the Internet.

**Integrated systems** The concept of having software that communicates and operates as one seamless unit.

**Interest group** An interest group focuses on a single topic for group discussion and sharing information by e-mail or over the usenet.

**InterNIC** Internet Network Information Center. A controlling body that administers and registers domain names and IP address.

**Internet** In its most general sense, an internet is a large computer network made up of a number of smaller networks. When capitalized, it refers to the physical network that makes up the Web and makes global e-mail possible.

**IP** (Internet Protocol) Address Internet Protocol address is the numeric address used to located physical or virtual computers or sites on the Internet.

**IP Address** The Internet Protocol address of a computer connected to the Internet usually represented by dots and decimal notations.

**IPO** (Initial Public Offering) The first public offering of a stock.

**IRC** Internet Relay Chat. A communication method, which people from anywhere in the world communicate with each other over the Internet. The IRC provides a multichannel, multi-user, keyboard based conferencing system.

**ISDN** Integrated Services Digital Network. A method for faster dial-up data transfer on standard phone lines.

**ISP** Internet Services Provider. A company or organisation providing Internet access.

**JAVA** An object-oriented programming language developed by Sun Microsystems. It is used to create applets or programs which can be attached to Web documents. An applet can be included in an HTML page, much as an image can be included. When you use a Java-capable browser to view a page containing a Java applet, the applet's code is transferred to your system and executed by the browser.

**JPG or JPEG** Short for Joint Photographic Experts Group, a type of graphic file format suitable for use in Web documents.

**Kbps** A thousand bits per second.

**Keys** Alphanumeric codes that are used in encryption to ensure that other computers on the network cannot read encrypted information without the keys.

**Killer app** The concept identified by Larry Downes & Chunka Mui in their book Killer App as "a new good or service that establishes an entirely new category and, by being first, dominates it, returning several hundred percent return on initial investment."

**Kill file** a newsreader file into which we can enter keywords and e-mail addresses to stop unwanted articles.

**Kilobyte** One kilobyte is equal to 1024 bytes.

**LAN** Local Area Network. A computer network with certain limitations like networking within same building or campus.

**Leased line** A dedicated line providing a permanent connection between two computers.

**Link** Also known as a hyperlink, a link is an address embedded in a Web document. The browser transfers to that address when the link is clicked.

**Linux** A free, Unix-like operating system for computers created by Linus Torvalds.

**Login** The process of connecting to a host computer or public access site.

**Logistics** Shipping and distribution functions in an organization. Sometimes used to define a role that manages all the company's resources.

**Log off** Disconnect from a host system.

**Log on** Same as login.

**Lurking** Listening to or reading a newsgroup's discussion without participating in the on-going chats.

**Lynx** A text based browser software used for accessing information on the WWW.

**Megabyte** A measurement of electronic file size equalling one million bytes.

**Message body** The text part of the e-mail message.

**Micropayment** A very small payment that is accumulated and paid once a specified threshold is attained. Usually used or traffic or click-throughs.

**Modem** A computer peripheral that connects a computer to a data transmission line similar to a telephone line. It converts between analog and digital signals.

**MIME** Multipurpose Internet Mail Extensions. Extensions to standard e-mail programs making it easy to send, receive, and include non-text files.

**Multimedia** Term used for any content that combines text, sound, graphics, and/or video.

**Netiquette** A set of common-sense guidelines or etiquette recommended over the Internet.

**Network** A communications system that links two or more computers together so that they can share resources.

**Neural Network** The storage and retrieval of data by systems that have the capability of making changes to their methodologies through the use of statistical and mathematical algorithms.

**Newbie** Somebody new to the Internet.

**Newsgroups** Groups or forums on the Usenet in which users can share information, idea, tips, and opinions on a particular subject. Newsgroups are organized by topics that number in the thousands.

**Node** Any single computer connected to a network.

**NSF** National Science Foundation. Funds the NSFNet, a high-speed network that once formed the backbone of the Internet in the U.S.

**Offline** When your computer is not connected to a host computer system or the Internet, you are offline.

**Online** When your computer is connected to another computer, bulletin-board system or public access site.

**Packet** A bundle of data. Data on the Internet is broken into small pieces called packet.

**Packet Switching** The method used to move data around on the Internet. In packet switching, all data being transmitted out of a computer is broken up into packets, each packet has the address of the sender and the recipient.

**Page** An individual frame of content on the World Wide Web, defined by a single HTML file and referenced by a single URL.

**Password** A code used to get access to a locked system. A good password must contain letters and numbers which are not easy to guess.

**PC** Acronym for a personal computer.

**Platform** The hardware and system software that are the basic foundation of a computer system.

**Plug-in** A software component or module that extends the capability of web browsers. Plug-ins enable the display of rich content as audio, video, and animation.

**POP** Post Office Protocol. Refers to the way e-mail software gets mail from a mail server.

**Pop-up Windows** Windows, other than the main browser window, that open when you open a Web site.

**Port** 1) A place where information goes into or out of a computer, or both, e.g., serial port where modem is connected. 2) On the Internet, port is often mentioned as number that is part of a URL appearing after colon right after the domain name.

**Post** To compose a message and then send it out electronically as in e-mail or Newsgroup messages for others to see.

**PPP** Point-to-point protocol. It allows a computer to establish a TCP/IP connection using a regular telephone line and a modem.

**Prompt** See command line.

**Protocol** A set of rules or procedures for exchanging information between networks or computer systems.

**Push technology** The delivery of content to usrs periodically as opposed to when the user requests it. Primarily used to deliver time-sensitive information like stock market quotes, news, or sports scores.

**Real-time systems** Information systems that instantaneously process a transaction and all associated information about the trnasaction.

**Relational database** A structured table of data, where data in records are keyed or related to data records in another table of tables.

**Rich media** Online advertising that has some form of functionality that allows the user to obtain objects, such as video of sound, or interact with the ad by providing information, choosing information, etc.

**Router** A special purpose device (hardware) that handles the connection between two or more networks. Routers look at the destination addresses of the packets passing through them and decide which route to send them on.

**Routing** The process of finding a path to a destination host. Routing is generally used for Point-to-Point serial connections running TCP/IP.

**Scrip or Script Language** A programming shortcut that gives non-technical users a way to create richer content on their computers and gives programmers a quick way to create simple applications.

**Search Engine** A software application or service used to locate files on an intranet or the Web. Generally accessed with browsers, a few of the most common web search engines include Excite, Yahoo!, WebCrawler, Infoseek, and Lycos, but new search engines are added constantly.

**Server** A computer that provides access to the Internet.

**Service Provider** An organisation that provides access to the Internet.

**Shareware** Software that is made available on a limited time trail basis.

**Signature** An optional portion of an e-mail message consisting of information about the sender such as full name, address, telephone number, etc.

**Site** A collection of related web pages, residing on the same server and interconnected by hotlinks.

**SLIP** Serial Line Internet Protocol. Used to connect computers to the Internet over a TCP/IP account.

**SMTP** Simple Mail Transfer Protocol. The Internet standard protocol used to transport e-mail from one computer system to another.

**Spam** A message that is unnecessarily posted to multiple newsgroups with the purpose of annoying others.

**SSL** (Secure Socket Layer) A security measure in which encryption is used to make a secure connection between a Web server and a client so that others cannot see the transfer of information.

**Streaming** The sending of a repeated stream of packets from a server to another computer connected to the same network or Internet. Usually used for sound or video broadcasts.

**Steamed Audio** Sound files captured in an audio file or transmitted over the Internet in real time. A plug-in to a web browser decompresses and plays the data as it is transferred to your computer over the Web.

**String** A set of alpha-numeric characters used as input to calculations or searches.

**Subscribe** Selecting a particular newsgroup so that it appears in your personal list of newsgroups.

**Supply chain** The entire process of accepting a customer order through to the delivery of the product to the customer inclusive of supply procurement and production of the product.

**Surf** Slang for "to browse on the Internet". Can refer to browsing aimlessly, rather than seeking out specific content.

**Sysop** A system operator. The administrator or manger of a host computer or server.

**Tags** The formatting codes used to create HTML documents.

**TCP** Transmission Control Protocol.

**TCP/IP** Transmission Control Protocol/Internet Protocol.

**Technology template** A series of standards that the corporation has decided will be the long-term technological environment of the organization.

**Telecommuting** Wroking away from an office and using a PC to communicate with the organization.

**Telnet** A terminal emulation program used for logging on to other computers, especially large, mainframe computers such as those containing the on-line catalogues of libraries. When you use Telnet to log on to a library's computerised catalogue, you are gaining access to the files that constitute the library's records.

**Text File** A file that contains text only characters in a plain human readable format.

**Thin client** A client computer on a network that has limited peripheral devices and storage.

**Thread** A thread is a collection of all the articles, which were posted in a reply or as a follow-up to a given article.

**Time out** A time out is what happened when two computers are talking and one computer for any reason fails to respond. The other computer will keep on trying for a certain amount of time, but will eventually give up.

**Traffic** Visits to a Web site.

**UNIX** A computer operating system. UNIX is designed to be used by many people at the same time (it is multi-user) and has TCP/IP built in.

**Unsubscribe** Deselecting a particular newsgroup.

**Upload** To transfer a file from your computer to your home directory on the host system.

**URL** Uniform Resource Locator, an address on the World Wide Web.

**Username** Same as login name. A unique name which is assigned to each user on a given host computer.

**Usenet** A system of electronic bulletin boards on which readers can share information, ideas, tips, and opinions. Nowadays usually referred to as Newsgroups.

**UUCP** Unix to Unix copy. A facility for copying files between UNIX systems.

**UUencode** A method of encoding binary files into text so that they may be attached to mail or posted to Usenet. They have to be UUdecoded to convert them back. The better mail and news programs do this automatically.

**Virtual employees** Employees who work offsite or away from their organization.

**VRML** Short for Virtual Reality Modelling Language, a set of codes used for writing the files for three-dimensional, virtual reality programs.

**VT100** A terminal emulation protocol. A specific type of terminal, most commonly used with Internet services.

**WAN** Wide Area Networks. Any network that covers an area larger than single building or campus.

**Warez** Software, usually pirated.

**Web authoring** Designing and publishing Web pages using HTML.

**Web Browser** A program used for browsing or viewing the resources available on the World Wide Web.

**Web page** A series of HTML or XML files that can be viewed by using a browser Webcast. A webcast is the streaming of electronic data between a server and a client computer.

**Wizard** Computer based help that guides you through the steps necessary to complete a task.

**WWW** Word Wide Web or the Web.

**XML** (Extensible Markup Language) The next generation of standard Internet presentation language created by a worldwide consortium.

**Zine** An online magazine.

**Zip** PC file compression format that creates files with the extension .zip using PKZip or WinZip software. Commonly used to reduce file size for transfer or storage on floppy disks.

# Index

# Sample Paper - 1 S1

## Part A

**Answer all questions, each of them carries one mark**

**Multiple Choice Questions**

1. Internet is network of :
   (a) Networks (b) Humans (c) Workers
2. e-commerce is another name for doing _______ on Internet.
   (a) logging (b) business (c) research
3. A topology is:
   (a) Arrangement of networking
   (b) A way of cheating
   (c) A way to connect to the Internet
4. To get information from the users you use :
   (a) Tables (b) Queries (c) Forms
5. You can print a web page on the screen:
   (a) Yes (b) No
6. For replying you use which button :
   (a) REPLY (b) SEND (c) RE
7. Prompt for ftp commands is:
   (a) fpt> (b) f> (c) ft>
8. To start telnet, you type command followed by name of the :
   (a) remote host (b) remote server (c) nothing
9. You can set Usernet in your computer using:
   (a) Windows (b) Paintbrush (c) Outlook Express
10. Graphic representations in messages on the Internet are called :
    (a) Icons (b) Smileys (c) Graphs
11. You can create a web site from your computer too:
    (a) True (b) False
12. GoLive is a :
    (a) Web site (b) Browser (c) Web publishing tool

13. Your text file should have the extension :
(a) html (b) htm (c) any of the 2 above
14. Superscript _______ the character.
(a) lowers (b) raises
15. For setting margins for the page, we give space on the left and :
(a) Right (b) Top (c) Bottom
16. You can put header to a table using the tag :
(a) <TH> (b) <TR> (c) <CR>
17. JAVA and JavaScript are same:
(a) TRUE (b) FALSE
18. In function, a function name has to be preceeded by :
(a) > (b) word FUNCTION (c) <

## Part B

**Answer all questions, each of them carries one mark**

### True False Questions

1. Internet is not a commercial information service.
2. The network NSFnet was later renamed as Internet.
3. FTP servers store files that you can transfer to or from your computer if you have an FTP client.
4. Every computer system on the Internet has both a domain name and the domain address.
5. You can use application package such as Word to access the Web server
6. Indexing is the process of a document representation by assigning content descriptions or terms to the document.
7. A Web browser is also referred to as a Web client.
8. All incoming e-mail messages are to be stored in the Outbox folder.
9. E-mail messages are usually addressed and delivered to only one or two people.
10. Binary command in FTP changes the mode to binary from ASCII.
11. The most common terminal emulation on Telnet is the VT100.
12. WWW is older than Usenet.
13. Unix has Daemon program that is usually invisible to the user, providing important system services.
14. In Web site designing you should make the title catchy, descriptive and accurate.
15. HTML files are text files only.
16. Tags are used to define the structure of a HTML document.
17. An applet is a small Java program that can be embedded in another application.
18. RMF is a new audio format which allows you to interact with music in many ways.
19. The pretence by a user to be different user in order to gain access to information or to acquire additional privileges is a threat to Internet security.

## Part C

**Answer all questions, each of them carries one mark**

**Matching Questions**

| | | | |
|---|---|---|---|
| A. | Internet | 1. | Uniform Resource Locator |
| B. | Terminal emulation | 2. | Search engine |
| C. | WHOIS* | 3. | Prohibit anyone to cause damage |
| D. | <BR> | 4. | Internet Explorer |
| E. | URL | 5. | Rich Music Format |
| F. | Yahoo! | 6. | Network of networks |
| G. | Firewall | 7. | Feed a line |
| H. | Bookmarks | 8. | Displays all information about everyone |
| I. | RMF | 9. | VT 100 |
| J. | Browser | 10. | Favorites |

## Part D

**Answer all questions, each of them carries one mark**

**Fill in the Blanks with Appropriate Words**

| | | |
|---|---|---|
| (a) ISP | (b) Unzip | (c) LAN |
| (d) browser | (e) HTML | (f) proxy server |
| (g) Inbox | (h) messages | (i) All frames |
| (j) Telephone line | (k) Usenet | (l) tag, attribute |
| (m) mIRC | (n) Video conferencing | (o) Delete name |
| (p) Java | | |

1. The Internet is most often used for the exchange of ________ and information.
2. Connecting to the Internet requires four things: PC, modem, __________ and Internet software.
3. __________ networking solution is suitable for networking in a building.
4. For a small Web site, one needs to buy space from _________.
5. _________ codes are written specially for display in browser applications designed for the World Wide Web.
6. ___________ option prints each frame on a separate page, individually.
7. To read incoming mail choose ____________.
8. Once you have compressed file, you will need to ______ or decompress it to get to the setup file and install the program.
9. _________ deletes the file name on the FTP server.
10. __________ is comprised of discussion groups like the forums on CompuServe or the messages areas on America Online.
11. Client software for IRC is ____________.
12. With the help of _________ you can see the Web pages as stored on the Web server.

13. ________ is a server which performs an action for another computer.
14. Two major elements of HTML are ________ and __________.
15. __________ is a simple and object oriented language.
16. In ______________, we can talk and see someone live on our computer screen.

## Part E

### Answer any 10 questions, each of them carries five marks

### Descriptive Type Questions

1. What is Internet?
2. What are TCP/IP protocols?
3. What is World Wide Web?
4. What is a Search Engine?
5. What are Favorites?
6. Which are the different folders in Outlook Express?
7. How would you create your own signature?
8. What steps would you take for accessing an Anonymous FTP?
9. Which are the basic commands of FTP?
10. What is the concept of Telnet?
11. What is the difference between Usenet and Internet?
12. Define the commands which are always available?
13. What is a NetMeeting? How is it used?
14. What sort of technical support is provided by ISP?
15. Which software are available for developing web site on small scale?
16. Which are the various publishing tools?
17. How is the text typed for HTML?
18. Describe the process of making characters Bold and Italics.
19. What all goes in the first line of HTML text? Explain them.
20. How would you set margins for the page?
21. How would you divide the table in various cols?
22. How would you align text in cells?
23. What are check boxes? How are they created?
24. Describe the various words reserved by JAVA.
25. When was Java developed?

## Part F

### Answers to Objective Type Questions

***Multiple Choice Questions***

| | | | | | | | |
|---|---|---|---|---|---|---|---|
| A.1. | a | A.2. | b | A.3. | a | A.4. | c |
| A.5. | a | A.6. | c | A.7. | a | A.8. | b |
| A.9. | a | A.10 | b | A.11 | c | A.12 | c |
| A.13 | b | A.14. | a | A.15. | a | A.16 | b |
| A.17. | b | | | | | | |

***True/False Questions***

| | | | | | | | |
|---|---|---|---|---|---|---|---|
| B.1. | F | B.2. | T | B.3. | T | B.4 | T |
| B.5. | F | B.6. | T | B.7. | F | B.8 | F |
| B.9. | F | B.10. | T | B.11. | T | B.12. | F |
| B.13. | T | B.14. | T | B.15. | T | B.16. | T |
| B.17. | T | B.18. | T | B.19. | T | | |

***Matchin Questions***

| | | | | | | | |
|---|---|---|---|---|---|---|---|
| C.A. | 6 | C.B. | 9 | C.C. | 8 | C.D. | 7 |
| C.E. | 1 | C.F. | 2 | C.G. | 3 | C.H. | 10 |
| C.I. | 5 | C.J. | 4 | | | | |

***Fill in the Blanks***

| | | | | | | | |
|---|---|---|---|---|---|---|---|
| D.1. | h | D.2. | j | D.3. | c | D.4. | a |
| D.5. | e | D.6. | i | D.7. | g | D.8. | b |
| D.9. | o | D.10. | k | D.11. | m | D.12. | d |
| D.13. | f | D.14. | l | D.15. | p | D.16. | n |

## This page left blank for rough work

# Sample Paper - 2

# S2

## Part A

**Answer all questions, each of them carries one mark**

**Multiple Choice Questions**

1. Initially Internet was used for:
   (a) Medicine (b) Military Intelligence (c) Communications
2. The first page that you see on the web site is called :
   (a) First page (b) Home page (c) Web page
3. The browser is which is available free:
   (a) Internet Explorer (b) Netscape Navigator (c) Lynx
4. Browser is :
   (a) Hardware (b) Software (c) Computer
5. In India, the main networking service provider is :
   (a) BSNL (b) VSNL (c) MTNL
6. For deleting a message you use Ctrl + :
   (a) D (b) Del (c) Esc
7. For downloading files you can use the commands get and :
   (a) use (b) mget (c) down
8. Usenet is a collection of:
   (a) discussion groups (b) networks (c) users
9. The main parts of an article of the newsgroup are, Header, Body and :
   (a) Signature (b) Text (c) Footer
10. You cannot send a message using NetMeeting:
    (a) True (b) False
11. In order to establish a site, following should be considered:
    (a) Provide new information regularly.
    (b) Let your visitors register for e-mail notification of changes to the site.
    (c) Both of the above
12. Cost of registering your domain name is Rs.:
    (a) 2000 (b) 1000 (c) 3000

13. HTML definition is given in the text in :
   (a) Last line (b) Not given (c) First line
14. Subscript ________ the character.
   (a) lowers (b) raises
15. For indenting we use the tag :
   (a) Tag (b) Space (c) SPACER
16. A form is used for :
   (a) filling data (b) getting information (c) displaying data
17. Events are :
   (a) Buttons (b) Icons (c) Actions
18. JAVA programming is similar to :
   (a) COBOL (b) C++ (b) BASIC

## Part B

### Answer all questions, each of them carries one mark

### True False Questions

1. Any computer on the Internet can be comnnected to any other computer using telephone line.
2. Hiring leased lines is cheaper than a dial-up connection on the Internet
3. The domain name with an extension .com describes a company or commercial organization.
4. WWW is a large-scale implementation of client-server architecture.
5. The problem with directories, which store knowledge is that classification is labour-intensive activity, and there are more publishers than classifiers on the Web.
6. The Back and Forward buttons cannot be used to visit only pages from the same website.
7. The e-mail component of Internet Explorer is called Outlook Express.
8. The FTP client that comes with Windows NT is a graphic based client.
9. The literal command sends a literal string to the remote FTP host.
10. Usenet and Internet are the same thing.
11. One advantage of IRC is that people can get to know each other without the bias that often occurs when people meet each other in person.
12. A method to decrease the download time is to use a cable modem or take ISDN connection.
13. Netscape Messagener is the e-mail client packaged with Netscape Communicator 4.0.
14. <HR> tag draws lines and horizontal rules.
15. The first way to break text into paragraph is to use <p>.
16. Java is not suitable for Internet.
17. The UDP protocol does not keep resending packets if they are misplaced or other problems occur in the TCP.
18. Protection from services which are inherently more prone to attacks is one of the benefits of using a firewall.

## Part C

**Answer all questions, each of them carries one mark**

### Matching Questions

| | | | |
|---|---|---|---|
| A. | History | 1. | Home page |
| B. | ISP | 2. | Stateless protocol |
| C. | AOL | 3. | Internet language |
| D. | Outbox | 4. | Active Server Pages |
| E. | Java | 5. | Internet Service Provider |
| F. | Lynx | 6. | Secret code |
| G | ASP | 7. | Pages visited last time |
| H. | Encyption | 8. | Americal online |
| I. | HTTP | 9. | Mail sent out |
| J. | First page on WWW | 10. | Text mode browser |

## Part D

**Answer all questions, each of them carries one mark**

### Fill in the Blanks with Appropriate Words

| | | | | | |
|---|---|---|---|---|---|
| (a) | Internet | (b) | anonymous | (c) | Secure |
| (d) | Bus | (e) | smileys | (f) | downloading |
| (g) | <BR> | (h) | web site | (i) | HTML |
| (j) | Hypertext | (k) | tags | (l) | Internet Explorer |
| (m) | ASCII base | (n) | Browser | (o) | Bcc |
| (p) | news server | | | | |

1. The central structure that connects elements of a network is known as the ______.
2. Netscape Navigator Web browser software is a ________ software.
3. _________ topology shares a single channel on which all station can receive and transmit.
4. __________ is a non-linear text.
5. ________ also incorporates elements that are not complaint with the generally accepted HTML standard.
6. In any good communication system, the message should be safe and _______. It should reach to the person for whom it is meant.
7. ________ is called Blind Carbon Copy.
8. Many web browsers can access _________ FTP site.
9. Telnet is an ______ service.
10. Articles posted on the newsgroup are distributed over the internet by ___________.
11. _________ is a method to personalize the written message.
12. A Web page is generally a single _________ document, which includes text, graphics, sound and hypertext links.
13. IITML tag for creating a line break is _________.
14. HTML commands surrounded by < and > are called _________.

15. A program written in Java that's presented on a Web page and runs automatically when a page is called ___________.

16. VRML is _______ language for creating 3D interfaces with the WWW.

## Part E

**Answer any 10 questions, each of them carries five marks**

### Descriptive Type Questions

1. How was Internet developed?
2. What is Ethernet?
3. What are the basic features of World Wide Web?
4. Write short notes on the following:

   | | |
   |---|---|
   | Yahoo! | Lycos |
   | WebCrawler | Excite |
   | HyperText | Searching Criterion |

5. What is Search button used for?
6. Which type of messages you have in Outlook Express?
7. Describe the process of attaching a file to your message.
8. How are files and directories stored in FTP?
9. Which commands are used for connecting to FTP?
10. How would you start Telnet?
11. Who runs Usenet?
12. Define the commands which are available when you access an article.
13. Describe the following terms:

   | | |
   |---|---|
   | Approved | Control |
   | Date | Distribution |
   | Expires | Followup-To |
   | From | Keywords |
   | Lines | Message-ID |
   | Newsgroups | NNTP-Posting Host |
   | Organisation | Path |
   | References | Reply-To |
   | Sender | Subject |
   | Summary | Xref |
   | Internet Relay Chat | |

14. What are the various document standards?
15. What precautions you have to take while developing the web site?
16. Describe the following terms:

   | | |
   |---|---|
   | Dreamweaver | WebEdit |

| | |
|---|---|
| HotMetal Pro | HotDog Pro |
| GoLive | FrontPage |
| Visual Page | Graphics Files |
| Layout of the Web site | Stateless Protocol |
| Stateful Protocol | Speed of search |

17. How would you start and end the body of the text?
18. How can characters by superscripted and subscripted?
19. Describe the process of inserting graphics.
20. Describe the method of giving space between paras?
21. How would you put background colour to the table?
22. Describe the process of putting a common heading for various cells.
23. What is a text box? How is it created?
24. How would you write a program in JavaScript?
25. Describe the various keywords of Java.

## Part F

### Answers to Objective Type Questions

***Multiple Choice Questions***

| | | | | | | | |
|---|---|---|---|---|---|---|---|
| A.1. | a | A.2. | b | A.3. | a | A.4. | c |
| A.5. | a | A.6. | c | A.7. | a | A.8. | b |
| A.9. | a | A.10 | b | A.11 | c | A.12 | c |
| A.13 | b | A.14. | a | A.15. | a | A.16 | b |
| A.17. | b | | | | | | |

***True/False Questions***

| | | | | | | | |
|---|---|---|---|---|---|---|---|
| B.1. | F | B.2. | T | B.3. | T | B.4 | T |
| B.5. | F | B.6. | T | B.7. | F | B.8 | F |
| B.9. | F | B.10. | T | B.11. | T | B.12. | F |
| B.13. | T | B.14. | T | B.15. | T | B.16. | T |
| B.17. | T | B.18. | T | B.19. | T | | |

***Matchin Questions***

| | | | | | | | |
|---|---|---|---|---|---|---|---|
| C.A. | 6 | C.B. | 9 | C.C. | 8 | C.D. | 7 |
| C.E. | 1 | C.F. | 2 | C.G | 3 | C.H. | 10 |
| C.I. | 5 | C.J. | 4 | | | | |

***Fill in the Blanks***

| | | | | | | | |
|---|---|---|---|---|---|---|---|
| D.1. | h | D.2. | j | D.3. | c | D.4. | a |
| D.5. | e | D.6. | i | D.7. | g | D.8. | b |
| D.9. | o | D.10. | k | D.11. | m | D.12. | d |
| D.13. | f | D.14. | l | D.15. | p | D.16. | n |

**This page left blank for rough work**

# Sample Paper - 3

# S3

## Part A

**Answer all questions, each of them carries one mark**

**Multiple Choice Questions**

1. What is not needed for running Internet:
   (a) Modem (b) Telephone Line (c) Printer
2. A browser allows you to search and log :
   (a) web sites (b) hard disk (c) modem
3. Which of the following is not a search engine:
   (a) Yahoo! (b) Internet Explorer (c) Lycos
4. Search button helps you in accessing :
   (a) Search engines (b) Hard Disk (c) Directories
5. Commonly used program for e-mail is:
   (a) Outlook Express (b) Internet Explorer (c) Microsoft Windows
6. ftp is the short form of :
   (a) File Transfer Protocol (b) File Transfer Program (c) File Transfer Public
7. For displaying the current status of the job, you can use the command:
   (a) Status (b) Current (c) Job
8. Usernet is run by:
   (a) NASA (b) the users (c) USA
9. q command is used for:
   (a) quiting the program (b) returning to previous level (c) putting in queue
10. The site for turnkey web site management is :
    (a) Yahoo! store (b) NASA (c) Internet
11. ISP stands for :
    (a) Indian Service Provider (b) Internet Service Prover (c) Internet Service Provider
12. Full form of HTML is:
    (a) Hyper Text Markup Language
    (b) Hyper Text Monitor Language
    (c) Hyper Type Markup Language

13. What character is used to end the tag :
   (a) /   (b) ?   (c) !
14. Tag for using graphic is IMG followed by :
   (a) SRC   (b) RCS   (c) CRS
15. For creating a table, you would use the tag :
   (a) <TABLE>   (b) <CREATE>   (c) <TAB>
16. Tag used for creating menu is :
   (a) OPTION   (b) TYPE   (c) MENU
17. For assigning values to variables, you use :
   (a) Functions   (b) Assignments   (c) Variables
18. Front Page has been developed by :
   (a) IBM   (b) Sun   (c) Microsoft

## Part B

### Answer all questions, each of them carries one mark

### True False Questions

1. Internet is a single, but very large network of networks of computers.
2. In a workgroup, user accounts are defined locally on the machine that holds the resource. In a domain, user accounts are defined locally on the machine that holds the resourse.
3. PPP is a network protocol to send network traffic along parallel lines.
4. HTTP is used for create home pages for the world wide web.
5. If you get lost on the Internet while browing WWW, the easiest method is to press Home button.
6. Multi-keyword queiries take a longer time to produce results in a search engine than single words queries.
7. Netscape Messager is the e-mail client packaged with Netscape Communicator 4.0.
8. When typing a URL for an FTP server into a Web browser, the transfer protocol is FTP.
9. If you want to send files to a site (where you have permission to upload), simply drag a file into the browser window and click No to upload it.
10. Usenet has no central governing body.
11. The Web pages of your Web site cannot be connected by hyperlinks.
12. Using an image map, you can create a graphic image with multiple hot spots.
13. HTML does not allow a Web page to include an image.
14. The <BODY> tag is assumed by the browser after the HEAD section, if you have omitted it in the HTML page.
15. VBScript lets the user interact with a Web page rather than simply view it.
16. There is no need to decalare a function in Java Script.
17. Videoconferencing is the technology that lets you use your computer to have live video conferences across the Internet.
18. The TCP/UDP ports are used by the application services like FTP, TELNET, HTTP, etc., to communicate on the network.

## Part C

**Answer all questions, each of them carries one mark**

### Matching Questions

| | |
|---|---|
| A. Append | 1. Viewing pages on Internet |
| B. TCP/IP network | 2. Language used for describing the structure of a Web page |
| C. Usenet | 3. Searching topic on Internet |
| D. Internet Explorer | 4. Application gateway |
| E. E-mail | 5. Upload a file to an existing file |
| F. HTML | 6. Networking card |
| G Web browser | 7. Web browser |
| H. Ethernet | 8. ARPANET |
| I. Robust security | 9. Newsgroup |
| J. Search button | 10. Internet service |

## Part D

**Answer all questions, each of them carries one mark**

### Fill in the Blanks with Appropriate Words

| | | |
|---|---|---|
| (a) taskbar | (b) Internet | (c) HTTP |
| (d) domain | (e) <p> | (f) Read news |
| (g) <TITLE> | (h) dialup | (i) Mosiac |
| (j) password | (k) Function | (l) Remote procedure call |
| (m) text mode | (n) Address book | (o) an e-mail client |
| (p) Hyperlinks | | |

1. In ________ connection, you can connect your computer to an ISP server, with the help of modem.
2. On the Internet ____________ is similar to a telephone.
3. ________ is a collection of sites that are related in some sense.
4. ________ is a non-persistent, stateless protocol.
5. ________ was the first widely available graphical browser for Web users.
6. PCs connected with ________ can also be used for education, entertainment, etc.
7. Messenger allows you to store e-mail addresses in its ___________.
8. ________ was used for plain ASCII text.
9. Telnet client software can be started by clicking ________ on the task bar and then choose run.
10. Click on the Mail button on the Internet Explorer toolbar and choose _________ button to access usenet.
11. If someone asks for your _________, do not be tempted to give it.
12. The pages of your Web site are connected by _________.

13. The most commonly used Head feature is HTML is the ______ tag.
14. _________ tag is used to show a Web browser what text in your document constitutes a paragraph.
15. The basic building block of a script in Java Script is the ________.
16. Packet Filtering firewalls do not handle _________.

## Part E

**Answer any 10 questions, each of them carries five marks**

### Descriptive Type Questions

1. What all you need for running Internet?
2. What is Local Area Networks?
3. Describe the various popular web browsers.
4. What is a browser?
5. Write short notes on the following:
   Client Computer
   Host Computer
   Internet Service Provider
6. Describe the process of replying to a message.
7. What is ftp?
8. What do you understand by Path?
9. What are the different options of Directory command?
10. What is the use of Ctrl+] command?
11. How would you setup Usenet in your computer?
12. What is Chat?
13. How would you sign with ISP?
14. What steps would you take to plan your site?
15. How would you find a person's e-mail using Yahoo!?
16. What is HTML used for?
17. How many headings you can have in a page?
18. Describe the process of making text coloured.
19. How would you create a banner?
20. How would you give indent in a para?
21. Can you have a border for your table, if yes, how?
22. How would you create a form?
23. How would you create a larger text box?
24. How would you put comments in JavaScript?
25. How is FrontPage used as Interactivity tool?

## Part F

### Answers to Objective Type Questions

***Multiple Choice Questions***

| | | | | | | | |
|---|---|---|---|---|---|---|---|
| A.1. | c | A.2. | c | A.3. | b | A.4. | a |
| A.5. | a | A.6. | a | A.7. | a | A.8. | b |
| A.9. | a | A.10 | a | A.11 | c | A.12 | a |
| A.13 | a | A.14. | a | A.15. | a | A.16 | c |
| A.17. | b | A.18 | c | | | | |

***True/False Questions***

| | | | | | | | |
|---|---|---|---|---|---|---|---|
| B.1. | T | B.2. | T | B.3. | T | B.4 | T |
| B.5. | T | B.6. | T | B.7. | T | B.8 | T |
| B.9. | F | B.10. | T | B.11. | F | B.12. | T |
| B.13. | F | B.14. | F | B.15. | T | B.16. | T |
| B.17. | T | B.18. | T | | | | |

***Matchin Questions***

| | | | | | | | |
|---|---|---|---|---|---|---|---|
| C.A. | 5 | C.B. | 8 | C.C. | 9 | C.D. | 7 |
| C.E. | 10 | C.F. | 2 | C.G | 1 | C.H. | 6 |
| C.I. | 4 | C.J. | 3 | | | | |

***Fill in the Blanks***

| | | | | | | | |
|---|---|---|---|---|---|---|---|
| D.1. | h | D.2. | o | D.3. | d | D.4. | c |
| D.5. | i | D.6. | b | D.7. | n | D.8. | m |
| D.9. | a | D.10. | f | D.11. | j | D.12. | p |
| D.13. | g | D.14. | e | D.15. | k | D.16. | l |

## This page left blank for rough work

# Sample Paper - 4

S4

## Part A

### Answer all questions, each of them carries one mark

### Multiple Choice Questions

1. e-mail is part of the Internet usage:

   (a) Yes (b) No

2. HTML language is used for:

   (a) Creating web site (b) Running CD (c) Displaying Windows

3. A URL is like a :

   (a) Name (b) Vegetable (c) Food

4. History shows the sites visited, Today, Last Week and :

   (a) 1 week ago (b) 2 week ago (c) 3 week ago

5. You half finished messages are stored in:

   (a) Inbox (b) Outbox (c) Drafts

6. Other than your computer, the other computer is called:

   (a) HOST (b) REMOTE HOST (c) OTHER HOST

7. Telnet is:

   (a) Telephone which connect to net

   (b) A service for connecting to net

   (c) Network service provider

8. Each USERNET site is however run by:

   (a) Administrator (b) NASA (c) User

9. PgDn is used for:

   (a) displaying the current page

   (b) displaying the previous page

   (c) going to next page

10. Commonly used site for name registration is:

    (a) Yahoo! (b) InterNIC (c) Indiatimes

11. Home page is the :

    (a) first page of the site (b) page created at home (c) page having picture of home

12. HTML tags must be written within :
    (a) ()   (b) []   (c) <>
13. A new paragraph can be started using :
    (a) Enter   (b) r   (c) p
14. For giving a line in the page, we which tag :
    (a) Line   (b) HR   (c) SR
15. Table can be divided into cols and :
    (a) semi colons   (b) rows   (c) cells
16. Radio buttons are so called because :
    (a) They look like radio buttons
    (b) They were created by radio
    (c) You have to switch on radio for using them
17. JavaScript version mentioned in this book is :
    (a) 1.4   (b) 1.3   (c) 1.5

## Part B

**Answer all questions, each of them carries one mark**

### True False Questions

1. E-mail address are case-sensitive.
2. The TCP/IP protocol family includes IP and TCP.
3. Hypertext enables you to read and navigate text and visual information in a nonlinear way based on what you want to know next.
4. Lycos contains about 66 million pages in its data bases.
5. The act of exploring Web is known as surfing.
6. The shortcut menu changes with the context.
7. Mail-header is offset from mail body by a line of asterisks.
8. When logging into an FTP set as anonymous, always enter your real password.
9. Telnet is commonly used for such tasks as remotely configuring routers or running applications on different hosts on the network.
10. Threads are ongoing conversations that are grouped by topics.
11. You should include a lot of fancy graphics and sound clippings on your Web site so that it takes lot of time for the visitor to access it.
12. The power of hypertext is its simplicity and transparency.
13. A URL does not tell a browser which composer to connect.
14. Elements allowed within the <HTML> tag are the <HEAD> and <TITLE> elements.
15. Java is a language developed by Sun Microsystem.
16. You can participate in virtual worlds and join in "virtual chat" sessions on the Internet.
17. It is necessary to compress the Real Audio clip.
18. Password is the method of authentication.

## Part C

### Answer all questions, each of them carries one mark

#### Matching Questions

| | | | |
|---|---|---|---|
| A. | Inbox | 1. | Plain text |
| B. | <HR> | 2. | Macromedia |
| C. | Tree topology | 3. | Hyperlinks |
| D. | VBScript | 4. | Netmeeting |
| E. | FTP | 5. | Horizontal ruler |
| F. | Chat | 6. | Topology like a tree |
| G | GoLive | 7. | Derivative of Visual Basic language |
| H. | Web navigation element | 8. | Adobe |
| I. | Dreamweaver | 9. | File transfer protocol |
| J. | ASCII text | 10. | Incoming mail collector |

## Part D

### Answer all questions, each of them carries one mark

#### Fill in the Blanks with Appropriate Words

| | | | | | |
|---|---|---|---|---|---|
| (a) | HTML tags | (b) | Outlook Express | (c) | document |
| (d) | IRC networks | (e) | <UL> | (f) | Web site |
| (g) | WWW | (h) | ftp protocol | (i) | PPP |
| (j) | flexible | (k) | faster | (l) | Web page |
| (m) | Telnet | (n) | HTTP | (o) | tremendous |
| (p) | Browser | | | | |

1. Web pages are the documents that use ________.
2. Faster connection will be possible on the Internet with the help of ________ modem.
3. ________ is a serial protocol.
4. An Internet server may not be a part of the ________.
5. Internet Explorer is the default ________ in newly installed Windows system.
6. The e-mail component of Internet Explorer is called ________.
7. One problem with downloading files over the Internet is that some files so large it takes ________ time to down load them.
8. The ________ is used to access files by FTP.
9. ________ provides a convenient way to access your e-mail server from anywhere in the world.
10. The backbone of IRC is ________.
11. A progam that runs on a Web server to process forms is called ________.
12. Web pages formatting command is called ________.

13. The _______ tag is used for bulleted, unordered list.
14. The first HTML tags are the ______ tags.
15. VBScript language can be embedded in ________.
16. A good Firewall system should be ___________.

## Part E

### Answer any 10 questions, each of them carries five marks

### Descriptive Type Questions

1. Write short notes on the following:

   Information Retrieval — Internet and e-mail
   Newsgroups (Usenet) — Accessing People
   Telnet — Chat
   FTP (File Transfer Protocol) — Anonymous FTP
   e-commerce — Employment Generation
   Medicare — Shopping Online
   Entertainment — World Wide Web (WWW)
   Educational Opportunities on the Net
2. What is a domain name? What does it consist of?
3. What is the use of a Web server?
4. Define the various items on the Internet Explorer screen.
5. What is e-mail?
6. How would you forward a message?
7. What is Anonymous FTP?
8. How would you start the FTP program?
9. Describe the various setting commands of FTP.
10. Describe the following commands:

    Open — Close
11. Define the format of a newgroup article.
12. Describe the processing of registering for Internet Chat.
13. What sort of services can be provided by ISP?
14. Describe the various steps taken while developing a web site.
15. How would you find out that your domain name is unique?
16. How are HTML tags written?
17. How are BIG and SMALL used?
18. What tags would you use for making the text underlined?
19. How would you add a horizontal line?
20. How would you set background colour of the page?

21. What tags are used for Table heads and Table rows?
22. How would you create menu like options?
23. What role does Submit and Reset buttons play?
24. How would you put quotes in JavaScript?
25. Write shortnotes on :

| | |
|---|---|
| JavaScript Events | JavaScript Operators |
| JavaScript Assignments | JavaScript Comparisons |

# Part F

## Answers to Objective Type Questions

***Multiple Choice Questions***

| | | | | | | | |
|---|---|---|---|---|---|---|---|
| A.1. | a | A.2. | a | A.3. | a | A.4. | c |
| A.5. | c | A.6. | b | A.7. | b | A.8. | a |
| A.9. | c | A.10 | b | A.11 | a | A.12 | c |
| A.13 | c | A.14. | b | A.15. | b | A.16 | a |
| A.17. | b | | | | | | |

***True/False Questions***

| | | | | | | | |
|---|---|---|---|---|---|---|---|
| B.1. | T | B.2. | T | B.3. | T | B.4 | T |
| B.5. | T | B.6. | T | B.7. | T | B.8 | T |
| B.9. | T | B.10. | T | B.11. | F | B.12. | T |
| B.13. | F | B.14. | F | B.15. | T | B.16. | T |
| B.17. | T | B.18. | T | | | | |

***Matchin Questions***

| | | | | | | | |
|---|---|---|---|---|---|---|---|
| C.A. | 10 | C.B. | 5 | C.C. | 6 | C.D. | 7 |
| C.E. | 9 | C.F. | 4 | C.G | 8 | C.H. | 3 |
| C.I. | 2 | C.J. | 1 | | | | |

***Fill in the Blanks***

| | | | | | | | |
|---|---|---|---|---|---|---|---|
| D.1. | n | D.2. | k | D.3. | i | D.4. | g |
| D.5. | g | D.6. | p | D.7. | b | D.8. | h |
| D.9. | m | D.10. | d | D.11. | f | D.12. | a |
| D.13. | e | D.14. | c | D.15. | l | D.16. | j |

**This page left blank for rough work**

# Sample Paper - 5

# S5

## Part A

**Answer all questions, each of them carries one mark**

**Multiple Choice Questions**

1. Using Internet you can chat with other users :
   (a) Yes (b) No
2. Which of the following, domain name does not have?
   (a) Country (b) Computer Id (c) Serial number
3. Web server is a :
   (a) Hardware (b) Software (c) Both
4. You cannot copy an image from the web site :
   (a) Yes (b) No
5. For sending and receiving messages you click at:
   (a) Send/Receive button (b) Send button (c) Receive button
6. The main directory of UNIX is _____ directory:
   (a) Main (b) New (c) Root
7. In Telnet, the client computer is called:
   (a) LOCAL (b) NODE (c) REMOTE
8. Usernet category can be identified by:
   (a) Full name (b) Middle name (c) First name
9. You cannot chat using Internet.
   (a) Yes (b) No
10. You can have graphics on your web site :
    (a) Yes (b) No
11. You cannot find the e-mail address of a person using Yahoo! search:
    (a) True (b) False
12. Values in HTML are provided within :
    (a) Question marks (b) Quotation marks (c) Left and right brackets
13. For making the characters bold, you use the tag :
    (a) <B> (b) <L> (c) <D>

14. For giving space around the image we use :

(a) VSPACE (b) HSPACE (c) Both

15. Horizontal rows are created by using :

(a) <TH> (b) <TR> (c) <CR>

16. Submit button is so called because :

(a) It allows visitors to submit his response to the web site

(b) It submits all the information to the visitor's hard disk.

(c) You have to submit its printout to the web site

17. Tag for JavaScript is :

(a) <SCRIPT> (b) <JAVASCRIPT> (c) <JAVA>

## Part B

### Answer all questions, each of them carries one mark

### True False Questions

1. A set of rules is known as protocol.
2. The RFCs core topics are Internet and the TCP/IP protocol suites.
3. All the Web servers on the Internet are collectively referred to as the World Wide Web.
4. The two parts of an e-mail address are separated by @ symbol.
5. You use Mosiac to access a Web server.
6. To organise your bookmarks, place menu into sections, separators.
7. Recipient's log-in name must form a part of his e-mail address.
8. The append command tells FTP to transfer the local file and append it to the end of remote file.
9. You cannot establish Telnet sessions over the phone.
10. All conversations on the IRC are in English.
11. Your ISP does not play any role when you want to transfer the files to a Web server.
12. In HTTP, by identifying the type of object in a header field, the client receiving the object can handle it appropriately.
13. The contents of a single file of hypertext is called a Web page.
14. The <ADDRESS> tag is similar to italics or emphasis.
15. JavaScript has no facilities for communicating between the Web browser and the HTTP server.
16. Some of the extensions of sound files are .doc and .exe.
17. VRML files can be very large.

## Part C

**Answer all questions, each of them carries one mark**

### Matching Questions

| | | | |
|---|---|---|---|
| A. | PPP | 1. | Excite |
| B. | <TITLE> | 2. | Telecommunication network |
| C. | Hotspots | 3. | Manners over Internet |
| D. | Front Page | 4. | Internet Relay Chat |
| E | Search tool | 5. | Same as close |
| F. | IRC | 6. | Web publishing |
| G | Disconnect | 7. | Microsoft |
| H. | Telnet | 8. | Point to Point Protocol |
| I. | Authoring tools | 9. | Beginning of a title |
| J. | Netiquette | 10. | Hyperlinks |

## Part D

**Answer all questions, each of them carries one mark**

### Fill in the Blanks with Appropriate Words

| | | | | | |
|---|---|---|---|---|---|
| (a) | end of a line | (b) | Web forms | (c) | HTML server |
| (d) | packet switching | (e) | Stateful protocol | (f) | Protocol |
| (g) | Internet Protocol | (h) | virus | (i) | head, body |
| (j) | Hyperlinks | (k) | Web server | (l) | Use Datagram Protocol |
| (m) | Authorization | (n) | instant messaging | (o) | Routing |
| (p) | Start, Run | | | | |

1. A __________ is a powerful computer that acts as a shared storage resource on the Internet.
2. _________ means rules for exchange of message between two or more hosts.
3. In order to transfer messages in a computer network, we use the techniques called _________.
4. A ____________ is a host that is connected to two or more physical networks simultaneously and is configured to switch packets between them.
5. _______ gives you the ability to upload or post information in to a Web site.
6. The process of directing a message to the recipient's host is called ___________.
7. The principle source of entry for computer ________ is downloading of files on the Internet.
8. ASCII is the common standard for text, but one feature is not standard, how the _________ of text is represented.
9. Telnet software can be started by clicking ________ on the task bar and then choosing _______.
10. In _________ chatting you can chat privately.
11. Each Web page created is stored in a separate file and ________.

12. __________ kept state information even after a transaction has been processed.

13. Full form of IP is ______.

14. HTML document has two parts a _____ and a ________.

15. UDP stand for __________.

16. ________ is the process of test whether an authorized use is permitted to use resources or not.

## Part E

**Answer any 10 questions, each of them carries five marks**

**Descriptive Type Questions**

1. What is a Protocol?
2. Write short notes on the following:

   Point to Point Protocol
   File Transfer Protocol
   Terminal Emulation Protocol
   Trnamission Control Protocol
   Internet Protocol
   Network News Transport Protocol
   SLIP
   PPP
   Host
   Media
   Nodes
   Server
   Workstation
   FDDI
   Wide Area Networks
   Metropolitan Area Networks
   Bridges
   Routers
   Gateways
   Public Networks
   Private Networks
   Bus Topology
   Ring Topology
   Star Topology
   Mesh Topology
   Hybrid Topology
   Leased Lines
   Shell Account
3. What is a URL?
4. Describe the various buttons on Toolbar.
5. How would create your own e-mail account?
6. How would you create your own stationery?
7. How can you use browser Anonymouse FTP?
8. Describe the alternative method of starting FTP.
9. What is Telnet?
10. What is Usenet?
11. How can you post your article in the newsgroup?
12. Describe the various types of smileys.
13. Who provides turnkey solutions?
14. Describe the various contents which your web site should have.